KANT AND THE LIMITS OF AUTONOMY

KANT AND THE LIMITS OF AUTONOMY

SUSAN MELD SHELL

HARVARD UNIVERSITY PRESS
Cambridge, Massachusetts, and London, England
2009

Copyright © 2009 by the President and Fellows of Harvard College
All rights reserved
Printed in the United States of America

Library of Congress Cataloging-in-Publication Data

Shell, Susan Meld
Kant and the limits of autonomy / Susan Meld Shell.
  p. cm.
Includes bibliographical references and index.
ISBN 978-0-674-03333-7
1. Kant, Immanuel, 1724–1804. 2. Autonomy (Philosophy) I. Title.
B2798.S515 2009
193—dc22   2008041251

Contents

Acknowledgments   *vii*

Introduction: Taking Autonomy Seriously   *1*

I GETTING THERE

1. "Carazan's Dream": Kant's Early Theory of Freedom   *17*

2. Kant's Archimedean Moment: *Remarks in "Observations Concerning the Feeling of the Beautiful and the Sublime"*   *39*

3. Rousseau, Count Verri, and the "True Economy of Human Nature": *Lectures on Anthropology*, 1772–1781   *85*

4. The "Paradox" of Autonomy   *122*

II COMPLICATIONS ON ARRIVAL

Introduction to Part II: Late Kant, 1789–1798   *163*

5. Moral Hesitation in *Religion within the Boundaries of Bare Reason*   *186*

6. Kant's "True Politics": *Völkerrecht* in *Toward Perpetual Peace* and *The Metaphysics of Morals*   *212*

7. Kant as Educator: *The Conflict of the Faculties*, Part One   *248*

8 Archimedes Revisited: Honor and History in *The Conflict of the Faculties*, Part Two 277

9 Kant's Jewish Problem 306

Concluding Remarks: The Limits of Autonomy 335

Notes 345

Index 423

Acknowledgments

Conversation with many friends and colleagues has enriched my understanding of Kantian autonomy in countless ways. Among the most notable are Karl Ameriks, Alan Arkush, Nasser Behnegar, Christopher Bruell, Robert Faulkner, Peter Fenves, Christopher Kelly, Marc Plattner, Richard Velkley, and John Zammito. I also owe a debt of gratitude to many present and former students at Boston College, with a special nod to Andrew Bove, Aleksander Chance, Robert Clewis, Corey Dyck, Michael Ehrmantraut, Michael Grenke, Louis Hunt, Benjamin Lorch, Charles Robinson, and Phillip Wodzinski. Research for this book was conducted with the generous support of the American Council of Learned Societies, The Earhart Foundation, The National Endowment for the Humanities, and the College of Arts and Sciences of Boston College. I am additionally grateful to Howard Williams, Thomas Pangle, Albert Denker, the late Delba Winthrop, Harvey Mansfield, Steven Smith, Jack Rakove, Michael Gillespie, Fred Baumann, and Alix Cohen for the opportunity to deliver earlier versions of these chapters before lively and discerning audiences. I am particularly indebted in this regard to João Espada and the Institute of Political Studies at the Catholic University of Portugal, whose annual summer conferences on issues of politics has served for many years as an inspiring model of enlightened trans-Atlantic discourse.

Earlier versions of Chapters 3, 5, 6, and 7 appeared as "Kant and the 'True Economy of Human Nature': Rousseau, Count Verri, and the Problem of Happiness," in *Essays on Kant's Anthropology*, ed. Brian Jacobs and Patrick Kain (Cambridge: Cambridge University Press, 2003); "Faith and Freedom Within the Boundaries of Bare Reason," in *Freedom and the Human Person*, ed. Richard Velkley (Washington D. C.: Catholic University of America Press, 2007); "Kant on Just War and Unjust Enemies: Reflections on a Pleonasm," *Kantian Review* 10: 2005; and "Kant as Educator: Reason and Religion in *The Conflict of the Faculties: Part One*," in *Kant's Legacy: Essays in Honor of Lewis White Beck*, ed. Predrag Cicovacki (Rochester: University of Rochester Press, 2001). Chapter 9 was first published in the *Journal of Hebraic Political Studies* (Winter 2007, vol. 2: no. 1). This material is included here with the kind permission of the publishers.

Thanks are also due to Jiyoon Im, Kimberly Stewart, and David Levy for help with the preparation of the final manuscript, to Shirley Gee for her consummate aid on many fronts, and to my editors at Harvard University Press.

My largest debt of gratitude is to my husband, to whom this book is dedicated.

Except where noted, references to Kant cite the volume and page of the *Akademie* edition (*Kants gesammelte Schriften*, herausgegeben von der Deutschen [formerly Königlichen Preussischen] Akademie der Wissenschaften, 29 vols. [Berlin: Walter de Gruyter, 1902]). References to the *Critique of Pure Reason* instead cite the standard A and B pagination of the first and second editions.

KANT AND THE LIMITS OF AUTONOMY

Introduction: Taking Autonomy Seriously

In today's liberal world the term "autonomy" both describes a fact—the ability to choose (with more or less deliberation)—and suggests a right—the right to exercise that ability without external interference, either by overt force or by lack of truthful information. Autonomy, so understood, is both a quality that a self must minimally possess to be a self at all and one that all (adult) selves are presumed to insist on or deserve.

This double meaning was nicely captured by U.S. Supreme Court Justice Anthony Kennedy when he stated, in a recent landmark case, that "liberty presumes an autonomy of self that includes freedom of thought, belief, expression, and certain intimate conduct" (*Lawrence v. Texas* [02–102], 538 U.S. 558 [2003]). In overturning the Texas antisodomy law, the court reached beyond the "right to privacy" to "autonomy of self" as a fundamental legal and moral principle. Freedom so construed goes beyond (either further or deeper than) the traditional liberal understanding of civil liberty. Certainly it is nothing that the framers of the Constitution had explicitly in mind; the liberties enumerated in the Bill of Rights do not mention sexual conduct. And yet, in the view of the Court, those enumerated liberties point to, and would ultimately make no sense without, a self that is also free in this most intimate respect. Far from being outlandish, the fundamental right to conduct one's sexual life as one pleases is, in the current view of the Court, among the most obvious of individual rights. Freedom in areas of sexual conduct is not an extension of other, more basic freedoms, but an articulation of what lies at their core.

What, then, is this "autonomy of self" that civil liberty, in the words of Justice Kennedy, "presumes"? Most informed discussions of autonomy draw upon Kantian sources, whether explicitly or implicitly. One could say that Kant put individual "autonomy" on the map. Prior to Kant, the term "autonomy" referred almost exclusively to political independence. After Kant, autonomy is also, and even mainly, individual freedom with a positive, morally charged meaning.

1. Autonomy: Kant's "Precarious Standpoint"

I undertook the following study in the hope that a fuller engagement with Kant's own understanding of autonomy—both how he came to it and what, over time, he saw to be its complications—can add something useful to contemporary liberal discourse. Kantian autonomy ennobles liberal concepts of freedom and equality by grounding them in an objective moral principle—a principle that is deemed to be accessible to all ordinary human beings on the basis of reason alone and that does not depend on a particular religious dispensation or the blind acceptance of authority. For Kant, autonomy is not just a synonym for the capacity to choose, whether simple or deliberative. It is what the word literally implies: the imposition of a law on one's own authority and out of one's own (rational) resources.

To be sure, the image of a healthy soul as "self-governing" is very ancient. And Kant's concept of autonomy surely draws, in part, upon ancient sources, especially Stoicism. Kantian "autonomy" is, in a way, a version of what the Stoics called "self-rule."[1] But Kantian autonomy differs from classical notions of rational self-rule in at least two decisive respects. *First*, Kant's "rule of reason" is oriented, first and foremost, not by theoretical knowledge of the end or ends by which a human life is properly ordered and/or a related "law of nature" (as with the Stoics), but by immediate, practical awareness of a moral "law" that sets certain necessary limits (and related goals) to free action.[2] Kantian reason takes its fundamental bearings from the voice of conscience, albeit understood in a peculiar way. *Second*, respect for such moral constraints is not motivated by independent knowledge of their *goodness* (as with the Stoics)—a knowledge that might require special study or a particularly gifted intellectual endowment—but is instead *sui generis*. The moral law, as Kant famously states, is its own sufficient incentive. In short, Kantian autonomy presumes that all normal human beings ought and can act rightly just because it is right and that their capacity to do so is ultimately grounded in their freedom. Kantian autonomy, unlike Stoic autarky, puts human freedom, rather than nature (and our knowledge thereof), front and center.

Autonomy so conceived gives human beings, in their capacity as co-legislators of the law, unconditional worth or dignity. But our knowledge of that worth is itself conditional on our recognition of the law as immediately and unconditionally binding—i.e., on our sense of moral duty as an expression of what Kant calls "practical necessity." (Human) freedom may be the *ratio essendi* of the law—the reason or ground without which it would not exist—but law, and the sense of duty through which we recognize it, is the *ratio cognoscendi* of freedom.

The "binding" or obligating side of Kantian autonomy is sometimes given short shrift in contemporary Kant studies. It can be tempting to reduce autonomy and its demands to an expression of our own considered, culturally derived understanding of "who we are." It is easy to forget the paradox inherent in Kant's original claim that the law binds us unconditionally, precisely on the basis of our own freedom and hence without primary regard for any good other than the law itself.[3]

And yet the two sides of autonomy—both its origin in human freedom and its generation of a motivating, unconditional "ought"—must be held together if the full power and paradox of Kant's practical thought is to be adequately grasped. If this paradox is not admitted, we are unlikely to understand the struggle that from Kant's own point of view human morality entails and hence the power that it calls forth. Kant's peculiar answer to the ancient questions—What is right? and Why act rightly?—places us in a "precarious standpoint" [*mißlichen Standpunkt*], as he puts it, that "should be steady" [*fast*] [4: 425–426] but becomes so "in deed" only through the hard-won victory of reason over itself. Reason as lawgiver determines the will immediately. But reason in its ordinary, instrumental use (or what Kant sometimes calls "vernünfteln") is not easily won over. The moral law commands unconditionally, and still we seek a *reason* to obey it—a reason, that is to say, looking to some further good beyond the law itself. Acting justly may be rational (as Plato's Glaucon wished Socrates to prove), but this fact does not move us as it ought, and as it would, were it based on the sort of knowledge that Glaucon demands and that Kant specifically rules out. In sum: The foundation of Kant's system in the "principle of autonomy" goes against the grain of [human] reason itself (as he admits)—both in that ordinary practical use which seeks to bring about the greatest future good at least expense, and in a higher use that confuses reason with an empty aspiration toward transcendence.

The demand that we do right just because it is right is both obvious, for anyone of normal ethical development, and, at the same time, deeply perplexing, as Socrates' interchange with Glaucon at the beginning of the *Republic* shows.[4] Classical thought ultimately claimed to find a path beyond ordinary morality (and its perplexities) to the higher vantage point of theoretical knowledge. Such knowledge either vindicates or questions the goodness of moral virtue proper but in either case claims to transcend it. On the other hand, the biblical ideal of righteousness frankly admits the insufficiency of human reason to fully understand the rightness of God's command—hence our need to trust in superhuman aid. Kant unites elements from each approach: He insists both on the sufficiency of human reason as a guide to human conduct and on the insufficiency of human reason to comprehend the goodness of the law through its own theoretical insight. Kantian autonomy combines the majesty of law—a majesty formerly associated with the authority of God—with the idea of reason as a judge to which every claimant to authority, including God himself, must first submit. Kant, in short, admits that morality has a mysterious core—a core that cannot be made fully intelligible—while continuing to insist on the sovereignty of human reason.

Kant's singular harmonization, through the idea of freedom universalized, of the unconditional demands of duty and the authority of human reason has obvious advantages for a morally robust liberalism. At the same time, it poses a peculiar set of difficulties. The critical settlement that gives rise to the supremacy of an autonomous reason makes reason a faculty, in the first instance, of self-legislation rather than of knowledge. Accordingly, a human being who would be guided by reason must, in the last analysis, take his or her bearings solely by the "form" of law rather than the "matter" or "end." Reason ultimately proceeds on the basis of a formal declaration of independence from all external sources of authority, rather than on the basis of the real or apparent goodness of some aim or purpose. We must find our way by virtue of our sheer determination to be free—without either theoretical knowledge of the reality of freedom or the consolations for human ignorance furnished by traditional religious faith.[5]

The following chapters are informed, then, by this guiding thought: Kant's practical philosophy cannot be entered into with full seriousness, or adequately pondered as a potential resource for liberal politics today, without due recognition of the difficulty, as Kant sees it, of reason's victory over itself and hence the limits of autonomy as Kant himself perceived them.

Some of these chapters originated as efforts to work out a consistent reading of a text, often in response to a specific textual puzzle. Gradually I came to see that most of these puzzles were related to what Kant comes to call his "paradox of method" and thus to the paradox and limits of autonomy as such.[6]

Kantian autonomy has lately come under attack for its alleged failure to do justice to the "other." The chapters that follow do not evade these charges. Among the limits of Kantian autonomy, as I will argue, is a distinct premium on persevering effort as the primary currency of human worthiness. Kant's temptation to associate that quality with Europeans as a biological race and Christianity as a religious institution was not (as I conclude) a necessary one. Still, its presence is sufficiently disturbing to deserve attention. Both the peculiar strengths and the peculiar limitations of Kantian liberalism may well derive from the same initiating paradox.

2. Rawls and Autonomy

The thought of John Rawls casts an especially long shadow over the contemporary understanding of autonomy. A brief consideration of his views may shed additional light on current thought and bring out both the distinct strengths—and potential weaknesses—of autonomy as Kant conceived it.

Rawls, who is both a professed (albeit modified) Kantian and perhaps the most influential liberal thinker of our time, invokes "autonomy" in at least three different senses.[7]

"Rational autonomy" describes the narrow (or "economic") rationality of parties in the original position, a "decision procedure" designed to assure the emergence of basic social rules under conditions of "fairness." Those conditions dictate that parties choose such rules under a "veil of ignorance" that deprives them of specific knowledge of their own future life chances and "comprehensive theories of the good." "Rational autonomy" is thus Rawls's term for the abstract capacity for weighing preferences that is typically assumed by economic theory.

"Full political autonomy" characterizes members of society who live by principles of justice that would be chosen by such parties. Such members are "reasonable" as well as "rational."

Finally, "moral autonomy" (or "full autonomy" simply) is an ideal held within one or another comprehensive theory of the good (such as those of Kant or Mill). Autonomous agents in the third sense will also be autonomous agents in the other two, though the reverse does not apply.

Rawls's published lectures on Kant's moral theory contain a particularly thoughtful treatment of the Kantian ideal of moral autonomy, an ideal that

Rawls evidently found personally attractive. His general deviations from the strict letter of Kant's argument are thus especially revealing. These deviations are threefold and affect the overall structure of the theory that Rawls advances in his own name. First, unlike Kant, Rawls has little truck with notions of desert and merit understood as primary moral phenomena.[8] As he famously states in *A Theory of Justice*, all particular personal qualities—including even the "willingness to make an effort"—are to be construed as "arbitrary from a moral point of view."[9] Second, for Rawls, self-esteem is a primary good largely derived from the opinion of others, rather than, as with Kant, an internally derived consequence of virtue.[10] Third, the ultimate aim of moral action is not the "highest good" (or virtue plus the happiness that the virtuous deserve), but the institution of a society based (in Rawls's words) on "self-supporting rules of justice." Thus Rawls's version of Kant (unlike Kant himself) has no use for practical postulates concerning the existence of God and personal immortality, which Kant invokes to secure the possibility of that highest moral end (the "highest good").[11] For Rawls's Kant, no more is needed to supply the hope for a life of moral purpose than a vaguely progressive view of history—a view based mainly on secular sources and assumptions.[12] Both in Rawls's "political philosophy" and in the "Kantian" moral ideal that he seems personally to prefer, Rawls systematically excludes Kant's emphasis on desert as a primary moral phenomenon *and* his related insistence on the moral necessity of religion of some kind.

The ultimate source of these deviations becomes clearer if one considers Rawls's distinction between the rational and the reasonable, which he puts forward as equivalent in a "restricted sense" to the Kantian distinction between hypothetical and categorical imperatives.[13] Many things are rational (in a calculative or "economic" sense) without being reasonable. What makes something reasonable is its adherence to the condition that one make no claims on one's own behalf that express a demand for more consideration than one is willing to grant others. Although something like Kant's notion of "equal dignity" lies at the basis of Rawls's understanding of the "reasonable," he does not follow Kant in trying to ground it in a transcendental principle, applicable to all rational beings; instead, he appeals to a certain shared (liberal) intuition about what is "fair."

Embedded in that "intuition" as to what is reasonable or fair is the presumption that no comprehensive theory of the good is able to establish its own superiority on the basis of reason alone. Rawls's skepticism on this point exceeds that of classic liberal thinkers (such as Locke and Kant) who continued to insist on the universal validity of their own liberal principles. Rawls, by way of contrast, implicitly adopts the more radically skeptical view that no universal standpoint, theoretical or practical, can, in the last analysis, be rationally defended. That is the ultimate reason for his claim that no comprehensive theory of the good may ever justly be imposed on others.[14]

In *A Theory of Justice* Rawls responds to this difficulty by attempting to construct a system of justice in which individuals are taught to adopt a comprehensive theory of the good in which liberal principles of justice are valued for their own sake. Such a system of justice—though not, strictly speaking, "true"—can, as Rawls then believed, at least be "self-sustaining." In *Political Liberalism* he abandons that attempt. His "liberalism" is now "political" in the sense of resting, not on "metaphysical" truth, but instead upon what individuals can "reasonably" be expected to accept given conditions of "pluralism" where there is widespread disagreement over comprehensive theories of the good. Political liberalism takes its bearings not only from the requirements of justice as earlier defined and as *A Theory of Justice* had tried to show could be self-sustaining, but also from certain facts on the ground that make that early attempt appear unreasonable.

A wag might say that "political liberalism" is what happens when Great Society hopes are mugged by the "identity politics" of the 1970s and 1980s or (less contentiously) when some liberals who wish to remake the world discover that they cannot practically or in good conscience force others to adopt their vision of a life well lived. ("Reasonable," one could say, does not just mean "fair"; as with Hobbes, it also connotes a willingness to be "realistic.")

The resulting understanding of "autonomy" continues to enjoy a certain Kantian glow; unlike its strictly Kantian counterpart, however, it now includes a variety of "reasonable" comprehensive theories of the good, both individual and collective. Autonomy, so understood, is no longer adherence to a law that is both self-given and universally binding.[15] It means, rather, living in the light of an ideal that makes room for the ideals of others. Its goal is not the highest good, in Kant's specific sense of happiness commensurate with virtue, but mutual coexistence under conditions of "reasonable pluralism." A similar "live and let live" attitude applies when Rawls elucidates Kant's own comprehensive theory of the good. In Rawls's preferred version of Kant, there is no primary, universal standard of desert in terms of which someone (either myself or others) might be judged worthy of reward or penalty.[16]

If one finds oneself dissatisfied with such a non-binding (and hence fundamentally unlawlike) version of autonomy, Kant's own understanding of autonomy may well seem newly attractive, both as a subject for careful study and as an object of possible retrieval. To properly assess that possibility, one must be willing to take seriously his own conceptions of duty and desert (as in "virtue equals worthiness to be happy") as primary moral phenomena. Such conceptions furnish a crucial point of juncture between the idea of freedom on the one hand and that of binding obligation on the other. The reluctance of Rawls (and many other contemporary scholars) to give this fact due weight does liberalism no service.

3. Kant and the Limits of Autonomy: General Outline

This book does not aim to be a comprehensive study of Kantian autonomy and the arguments that might be marshaled in support of or against it. It is rather an attempt to think through with Kant both the early quandaries that helped give rise to the idea and the challenges—both theoretical and practical—that it was later forced to address. At the same time, the purpose of this study is not merely antiquarian. By focusing attention on Kant's less-familiar early and late writings, I hope to bring out some of the deeper implications of Kantian autonomy (and the moral and political stance accompanying it) that are given relatively short shrift in some more-familiar works of the 1780s, implications that have ongoing theoretical and practical relevance. Part I examines in detail the myriad considerations that brought Kant to adopt autonomy as an ultimate standpoint—a standpoint, as it were, without foundations external to itself; Part II takes up the shifting circumstances and new insights that led him to define it ever more narrowly. A vital common thread throughout is Kant's novel philosophic use of human history—at first to shore up confidence in the plausibility of morality's demands and later, when the principle of autonomy appears to put such doubts definitively to rest, to help overcome the moral "hesitation" that persists in spite of it.

a. Part I: Early and Mature Writings [1755–1787]

Kant's mature concept of autonomy was a long time coming. Only with the *Groundlaying of the Metaphysics of Morals* [1784], which is devoted to "establishing [*festsetzen*] autonomy of the will" as "the supreme principle of morality" [4: 392, 440] does the term first appear in print—three years after publication of the first edition of the *Critique of Pure Reason*. But Kant was already deeply concerned with related issues as early as the mid-1750s—well before his reading of Rousseau and the proto-critical "revolution" in Kant's thinking that it prompted.[17] The works examined in Part I reflect successive stages in Kant's understanding of the relation between freedom and law, from his earliest published considerations on the topic to the concept of autonomy in its final form. Attention to these rarely considered works makes more fully evident, as I hope to show, certain crucial cosmological, anthropological, and moral difficulties over which Kant labored during the two decades in which he was also at work on a "critique of human reason." These projects were not unrelated. It was only by solving a series of problems concerning the relation between law and freedom (problems to which autonomy ultimately provided a definitive answer) that he found his way to overcoming the final theoretical barrier to a "critique of pure reason." In sum: Without his discovery of a way to understand the possibility of reason's sovereignty over itself (a path charted with particular clarity in the *Lectures on Anthropology*), there would have been no final breakthrough to the critical philosophy.

Kant's reading of Pietro Verri in 1777 (a topic that has largely been ignored in the literature)[18] had a pronounced effect, both on his expectations of anthropology and on his emerging understanding of reason itself. Verri, an avowed follower of John Locke, established to Kant's satisfaction that a preponderance of pain over pleasure is a necessary condition of organic life, which strives to alter its state only when so prompted by discomfort. Henceforth, Kant conceives of "life" as essentially divided, at least where human consciousness is concerned, between its animal and spiritual expression. Freedom (and the spiritual life accompanying it) is no longer something we intuit directly, but only by virtue of the observable rules and laws by which reason itself proceeds. Life is directed, not by its "end," but either by animalistic "impulse" or, contrarily, by the sheer power of reason to lay down a law or principle. The latter alternative provides, in turn, not only the basis for Kant's theory of autonomy in its final form, but also the long-sought formula for a theoretical determination on reason's part of its own "limits."

Many of the works treated in Part I (e.g., the *Remarks* and the *Lectures on Anthropology*) were not intended for publication. This has obvious disadvantages for the interpreter; in the case of such texts, it is often hard to know both whether Kant actually held the positions advanced there, and in what ways, if any, he might have been willing to make them known publicly (meaning, in some cases, beyond the classroom). But these drawbacks for the interpretor are partly offset by the greater freedom here afforded Kant to experiment with what are arguably his most searching arguments without fear of public damage to himself or others.

The lengthy intellectual journey traced in Part I is of more than scholarly interest for two reasons. First, its difficulties serve, by Kant's later critical lights, as a model for the challenges of moral education generally. Second, the struggles of an individual as intelligent and single-minded as Kant is almost bound to touch instructively upon universal human quandaries. Such quandaries include, but are not limited to, the conflict between freedom (e.g., the freedom we attribute to those whom we blame or punish) and necessity (or our recognition of certain features of the world as beyond our power to change); and the perplexity surrounding our notions of moral sacrifice, which we typically find admirable but hard to justify on the basis of reason alone.

The main stages of this journey are roughly as follows:

1. 1755–1760: *Universal Natural History and Theory of the Heavens; New Elucidation* (Chapter 1). Kant here adapts the Wollfian-Liebnizian understanding of freedom as "internal determination" in light of the moral and religious critiques of Knudsen and Crusius. The upshot is a novel reconciliation of freedom and natural determinacy that gives special emphasis to "effort" or its lack as the basis of moral merit and demerit.
2. 1763–1768: *Observations on the Feeling of the Beautiful and the Sublime; Remarks in "Observations on the Feeling of the Beautiful and Sublime; Dreams of a Spirit-Seer"* (Chapters 1 and 2). *Remarks* is a difficult text to interpret. Nevertheless, when read carefully, it presents a remarkably consistent and mature understanding of the human problem as Kant then conceived it, a problem that lies, above all, in the tension between freedom and law. Although *Remarks* anticipates many of Kant's later anthropological and moral views, two peculiarities not carried forward into the 1770s bear mentioning: an oscillating, rather than progressive, model of history, and pronounced pessimism as to the possibility of anything other than a purely negative role for metaphysical inquiry.
3. 1769–1776: *Dissertation of 1770: On the Forms of the Sensible and Intelligible World; Lectures on Anthropology* (*Collins/Parow* [1772] through *Menschenkunde* [1781]). The lectures considered in Chapter 3, most of which have only recently become generally available to scholars, contain rich material for understanding Kant's emerging views during the crucial "silent" decade preceding completion of the *Critique of Pure Reason* in 1781. Following on the heels of his *Inaugural Dissertation* of 1770, *Lectures* reflects both Kant's newfound confidence in the possibility of a pos-

itive role for metaphysics and his initial, empirically based experiments along such lines. In earlier lectures, he deems freedom to be both empirically accessible, through an immediate feeling for "life," and susceptible to conceptual ("lawful") elaboration.[19] In later lectures he abandons this attempt in favor of a new conception of rational "sovereignty" that anticipates his final formulation of the principle of autonomy.

4. 1784–1787: *Groundlaying of the Metaphysics of Morals; Critique of Practical Reason* (Chapter 4). Kant's initial metaphorical presentation of the sovereignty of reason in the *Critique of Pure Reason* leaves unresolved the question of whether the idea of lawful freedom suffices in itself to determine the will. That question is settled in the *Groundlaying*, which presents, for the first time, "autonomy" as the fundamental principle of morality and hence of all uses of reason. In defending that principle against the sophistry of human reason, it permits the status of religion to remain unsettled. Kant returns to the problem in the *Critique of Practical Reason*, in the context of growing religious reaction. Here the issue calling for "critique" is no longer the synthetic *a priori* use of practical reason (now established directly through the "facticity" of the moral law) but the ambiguity that surrounds our concept of the good.

b. Part II: Late Kant, 1788–1798

Part II picks up the trail in the late 1780s, following a period of growing professional and personal success on Kant's part earlier in the decade. Throughout the earlier period, Kant enjoyed exceptionally good relations with Prussian authorities, both religious and secular. Frederick the Great's official censor, Baron von Zedlitz, to whom Kant dedicated the first edition of the *Critique of Pure Reason*, was a personal friend. And Frederick himself, if not in all ways an ideal monarch, was from Kant's perspective at the time an especially advantageous ruler, for reasons that he spells out in *What Is Enlightenment?* [1784]. Frederick's famous "Argue as much as you like, only obey!" seemed a workable formula for historical progress, allowing for the possibility of political and moral reform "from below" by ensuring civil order from above. That such an order was motivated by honor and self-interest on the ruler's part, rather than moral duty (a point also stressed in the *Idea for a Universal History* [1784]), constituted no necessary impediment to a progressive interpretation of history, so long as one could suppose ongoing freedom to publish. Frederick the Great's manner of governing, which Kant was happy to call "republican in spirit," made that presupposition seem not reasonable.[20]

The relatively serene political conditions that characterized the early 1780s, along with the untroubled assumptions about political and moral progress that they tended to support, collapsed under the weight of two sudden and dramatic events: the ascension to the throne of Frederick William II in 1786 and the French Revolution of 1789. This double change in fortune was more than personal. Under Frederick the Great, Kant had seen fit to declare that an "age of enlightenment" had arrived. The reign of Frederick William II challenged that claim almost from the start.[21] Intellectually and morally weak, the new monarch soon fell under the influence of Johann Christoph Wöllner, a member of the Rosicrucian Order and a forceful opponent of enlightened religious attitudes of the sort Kant favored. By 1788 Wöllner had replaced von Zedlitz—the liberal-minded minister of state to whom Kant had dedicated the first edition of *Critique of Pure Reason*—and was also named minister of ecclesiastical affairs. In July the Prussian government issued an Edict of Religion, followed in December of that year by an Edict of Censorship. The first edict sharply rebuked Protestant ministers for taking liberties with orthodoxy "under the much abused banner of Enlightenment." The second furnished legal means for suppressing all non-orthodox writings.[22]

In 1789 the French Revolution intervened with greater geographic distance, but equal drama, in Kant's intellectual and personal life. Contemporary reports testify to his personal excitement over events in France, which struck him as betokening, in the words of one report, "the glory of the world." In a late writing, Kant would cite such disinterested enthusiasm, rather than the Revolution itself (along with the Terror that followed), as the "event" on which hope in moral progress should be pegged.[23]

As the chapters of Part II will argue, Kant is less concerned with bringing about a "kingdom of heaven on earth" (though that remains a hazily distant goal) than with motivating individual action in the here and now. It is thus misleading to imply, as do some recent commentaries, that "Kant does not think [one] can achieve [the] inner revolution toward goodness entirely on [one's] own," but only with the help of others.[24] It is true that the *thought* of our collective struggle (and its always-endangered success) is, on Kant's account, morally empowering. It would be going too far, however, to suggest that our personal effort to improve depends, for him, upon the historical transformation of society, not only because we are obligated *now* to make ourselves better human beings, but also because the precariousness of human progress is itself—as Kant indicates again and again—a necessary condition of our freedom, a freedom that belongs to us, first and foremost, as individuals. From the late 1780s onward, Kant's primary focus of practical pedagogical concern shifts from "syncretism," or the confusion of autonomous and heteronymous motives, to an "inner duplicity" that trades upon doubts as to one's own moral adequacy. Kant's later practical works aim mainly at assuaging such doubts—rather than at the establishment of some future utopian scheme. In sum: Kant's progressive hopes are chastened by a focus on the needs of the present and a related sobriety and "realism" that has been widely ignored. My own hope is that a better grasp of what Kant himself intended can enrich contemporary liberal discourse, not least in international relations, where his thought is frequently identified with a naïve cosmopolitanism.

Kant's increasingly delicate political situation (especially prior to the death of Frederick William II in 1797), combined with a growing, internally driven emphasis on "inner honesty," placed extraordinary demands on his skills as an author—skills that have, generally speaking, been insufficiently recognized. The complicated unfolding of his argument and accompanying tonal shifts place unique burdens on the reader—burdens different, but no less pressing, than those imposed by the writings to be considered in Part I. The payoff in extending to these works the special interpretive care that they require is, as I hope to show, at least twofold: on the one hand, a clearer and more internally consistent reading of Kant's practical philosophy as a whole than is otherwise possible, and on the other hand, a deeper understanding of what it means to take autonomy seriously as the ultimate foundation for moral and political life. At the very least, such attention should destroy any lingering impression that Kant is a naïve optimist "from Venus."

The major works considered in Part II are as follows:

Chapter 5: *Religion within the Boundaries of Bare Reason* [1792]
Chapter 6: *Toward Perpetual Peace* [1795], *The Metaphysics of Morals:* Part One ("Doctrine of Right") [1797]
Chapter 7: *The Conflict of the Faculties,* Part One ("On the Conflict between the Theological and Philosophic Faculties") [1797]
Chapter 8: *The Conflict of the Faculties,* Part Two ("On the Conflict between the Legal and Philosophic Faculties") [1797]
Chapter 9: *Critique of Judgment, Religion, The Conflict of the Faculties*

The historical context of Kant's thought—once virtually ignored by English-speaking critics—has been the subject of new and growing interest in recent years.[25] The present work differs in its explicit disavowal of the "historicist" assumption that guides many of these studies. "Historicism" assumes that philosophic arguments are embedded in their times in a way that prevents them from addressing "permanent" human questions. In my view, the historicism that pervades contemporary histories of philosophy is not unconnected to the weakness of most defenses of liberalism today, both in and outside the academy. Whatever the intellectual merits of academic liberalism, it is rarely willing to defend the core principles of liberalism as simply true. The defense of liberalism is "political, not metaphysical." But there is a limit to how far an appeal to "consensus"—even, and especially one that is "overlapping"—can go, once the historical culture that supports it has been shaken or otherwise deeply challenged (e.g., by a newly resurgent Islam).

The present study takes its bearings from the contrary view that some human beings may indeed see beyond the limits of their time. Appreciation of the historical context and internal development of a philosopher's thought is important, on this understanding, not to disabuse today's audience of a false sense of timelessness (or facilitate removal of what no longer belongs to today's "overlapping consensus") but to better grasp the meaning of what is put to us. In urging that Kant's late writings be read with special sensitivity to their political context, then, I do not seek to "relativize" their claims. The aim of these chapters is not to free the Kantian bits we like from their less-attractive metaphysical and religious supports but to better understand the arguments that led Kant to develop and deploy the principle of autonomy as he did.[26]

In attending to Kant's language more closely than is common, I have attempted to follow his own indications as to the manner of philosophic writing, especially when it assumes a morally educative purpose.[27] And in attending to Kant's own shifting situation, especially in the late writings, I have tried to address his own suggestions as to the situated character of moral action.[28] Few have appreciated better than Kant the possibilities, both hopeful and catastrophic, harbored by "enlightenment" in the modern sense. The following study, then, is both an intellectual biography and an extended meditation on the challenges faced by modern liberalism. It aims to offer a better understanding not only of Kant's thinking as a whole but also of the peculiar difficulties of our present situation—difficulties Kant both warned of and, in some ways, heightened.

I

GETTING THERE

1

"Carazan's Dream": Kant's Early Theory of Freedom

1. Freedom in the *New Elucidation*

Kant's earliest writings are rarely examined for their moral and anthropological content;[1] focused attention on these works, however, reveals a consistent set of philosophic and "historical" inquiries, reaching back into the 1740s and early 1750s, that bear importantly on his emerging understanding of the condition of man as a free and embodied rational being.

Kant's earliest thematic treatment of human freedom appears in the *New Elucidation of the First Principles of Metaphysical Cognition* [1755].[2] The *New Elucidation* is, on the face of things, an exercise in metaphysical cosmology. Leibniz had famously insisted that substances are "windowless monads" that represent the universe from their own unique point of view. Substances, on this account, do not interact, well-founded appearances to the contrary. They are related to one another, or constitute a "world," only "ideally" or in the mind of God who created them so that their inward states would harmonize.

Pietist philosophers such as Christian August Crusius and Martin Knudsen, Kant's own teacher, argued in reply that interaction among substances is "real." In making this argument (the so-called theory of "physical influx"), Knudsen called upon the authority of Newton, of whom he was an early German champion.[3] The deeper worries of Crusius and Knudsen concerned the moral and religious implications of a world in which real action does not occur. In what way, given such a world, would duties to perform this or that act make sense? Similar concerns led Crusius to deny the (Leibnizian) principle of sufficient reason. To preserve the possibility of human freedom, he argued that human action is undetermined by any antecedent cause—a view that Kant refers to as "indifferentism." Crusius also insisted that the forces of the soul cannot be reduced to a single "vis representiva" (as the Wolffians claimed). Rather, the human soul has two separate faculties, one cognitive, the other bound up with willing.

The struggle between the Wolffians and the Pietists occupied a prominent place in German universities in the early half of the eighteenth century, culminating in the infamous expulsion of Wolff from the University of Halle on the grounds (alleged by his enemies) that his teachings would produce disobedient subjects—a claim that Frederick William I evidently found compelling.[4]

The New Elucidation stakes out a novel position that combines elements of each approach. On the one hand, Kant preserves the principle of sufficient reason in a somewhat altered form (which Kant calls "the principle of determinate reason"). On the other hand, he defends human freedom on the basis of an argument missing in Leibniz (or Christian Wolff, his German expositor and popularizer). The key to this reconciliation is a concept of the "world" as a "real" whole—a concept already introduced in Kant's earliest publication, *On the True Estimation of Living Forces* [1749]. Kant claims (following Crusius) that the world is made up of substances that "really" interact—i.e., change or determine one another's accidental states, rather than consisting of isolated monads as Leibniz argued. But he does so on the novel ground that isolated monads would be incapable of undergoing change, and hence incapable of activity of a sort that even Leibniz grants.

Change, on the view here expounded, is a function of the mutual dependence of substances. Interaction does not imply a literal "flowing" of reality from one substance to another (as the term "physical influx" seems to imply); rather it describes a condition of coexistence in which the state of each substance is "determined" by the others, and conversely. Reciprocal determination—not an absurdly contrived "influxus"—makes worldly connection "real" rather than merely "ideal"—as it seems to be for Leibniz. And this is so despite the fact that such connection would be impossible without a "ground" in God. Because each substance contains only the grounds of its own determinations, the existence of one substance cannot by itself determine anything in another. If there is to be worldly connection, then, there must be a ground that allows this real nexus to come about. God, the "common source" of substances, is the only being who can provide the basis (necessary if there is to be a world at all) of worldly interaction. The manifest changes in consciousness that we undergo (when one representation is succeeded by another) bear witness, for their part, to our real-worldly condition.[5] By virtue of that condition, our soul both affects and is affected by other worldly substances.[6] And since bodies are also substances, embodiment seems to be a necessary condition of worldly consciousness. Finally (to complete the summary) the existence of time and space is conditional upon the worldly connection of substances. God (along with any isolated substances he may choose to create) is not a member of the world and thus exists outside of time and space.

It may seem difficult to regard the distinction between Kant's understanding of a world and that of Leibniz as a genuine difference, given that both claim that God is the necessary ground of worldly connection. But Kant's insistence on real interaction understood as interdependence has this important consequence: Whereas for Leibniz, the difference between God's representation of the world and our own is one of infinite degree, for Kant it is absolute. For Leibniz, a monad's representation of the world is infinitely less clear and distinct than that enjoyed by God but otherwise not qualitatively different. For Kant, by way of contrast, time and space set a qualitative barrier between divine cognition of the universe and our own. Time and space exist only for members of a world, whose representation of the world thus differs essentially, and not merely as a matter of degree, from God's grounding idea, an idea that "immediately" contains all possible determinations of the substances that comprise it. (Kant is already primed to recognize the basic primary cognitive distinction—later elaborated in the *Inaugural Dissertation* of 1770—between the sensible [with its forms of time and space] and the intelligible.)[7] We will soon have reason to return to this consideration, which already sets Kant's cosmology apart from that of Wolf and Leibniz despite some superficial similarities.

Despite Kant's endorsement of Crusius's claim that substances really interact, human freedom might well still seem to be impossible, given Kant's accompanying insistence on the (Leibnizian) principle of determining reason.[8] Kant, however, maintains that this principle is indeed compatible with human freedom. He advances two arguments on freedom's behalf. One of these is loosely Leibnizian; the other is, at least in part, peculiarly his own.

According to the *first* argument, human action is free because it is determined by an "inner principle" rather than driven (as with animals) by external stimuli [1: 404]. Whereas animals respond automatically to passive representation of these stimuli, free beings determine themselves to act (or act "from an inner principle") in accordance with what their understanding "represents as best." It is not indeterminacy (as Crusius claims), but determination through "motives of the understanding," that distinguishes free actions from their unfree counterparts, which are determined by the "blind" forces of nature. Freedom, in short, does not imply an absence of determination but determination that happens through an inner spiritual principle.

Kant's *second* argument addresses itself specifically to the issue of human culpability—a possibility that the first argument appears to slight. What is best, to a perfect understanding, is the contemplation of creation itself.[9] In the case of God (and created beings whose rational power is readily dominant), the will is moved by notions of what is good that easily outweigh all lesser attractions. In the case of man, by way of contrast, the will confronts two "equally attractive" motives. When men act evilly, they are determined by a flawed inner principle that inclines the will toward the lower motive, corresponding to a false representation of what is best.

Kant gives two arguments as to why we are culpable for such an inclination. On the one hand, the fact that this inner principle, although "antecedently determined," consists in doing as one likes marks it as imputably one's own. His first argument is similar to ones put forward by Wolff and Leibniz: To act freely "is to act in conscious conformity with one's desire," and this the sinner manifestly does. No one is "dragged by the neck" when he "drinks, games and makes sacrifices to Venus" [1: 401]. In short, the fact that men have evil natures does not exonerate them from blame, inasmuch as it reflects what they "most inwardly" desire, i.e., deem best.

But Kant does not leave matters here—i.e., with a view of human spontaneity that he will later famously dub "the freedom of a turnspit." God, on the above account, might seem blameworthy in allowing human evil-doers to exist at all. Against this charge to God's account, Kant advances two defenses of God's justice: the greater good that the existence of such evils makes possible (an argument that recalls Leibniz's own theodicy) and (here Kant charts new territory) the remedies for evil that God himself provides:

> The infinite goodness of God strives toward the greatest possible perfection of created things and toward the happiness of the spiritual world [*mundus spiritualis*]. With the same infinite striving to reveal Himself, God addressed Himself to creating not only a more perfect sequence of events, which was later destined to spring from the order of grounds, but also, and with a view

to ensuring that no good, even those of a lesser degree, should be missing, and that the totality of things . . . should embrace everything from the highest to the lowest degree of perfection possible for finite things, *even including, so to speak, nothing itself,* God also allowed things to creep into his scheme which, in spite of the admixture of many evils, would yield something which was good and which the wisdom of God would elicit from them in order to embellish with infinite variety the manifestation of His divine glory. *It was perfectly consistent with the wisdom, power and goodness of God that this whole should include the history of the human race; dismal* [lugubris] *as that history is, it would contain, even in the turmoil of evils, numberless testimonies of the divine goodness.* [1: 404; emphasis added][10]

Humanity's "dismal history" is necessary if Creation is to yield its full plenitude of good. This does not mean, however, that God intends that history. Rather:

It was the good upon which His eyes were focused: He knew that, once the balance of grounds had been drawn up, the good would nonetheless remain. He knew that the elimination of this good, along with the wretched tares, would not be worthy of His supreme wisdom. For the rest, mortals commit sins voluntarily and as a result of an inmost state of mind, for the chain of antecedent grounds does not hurry them along or sweep them away against their will; it attracts them. . . . Nor, for this reason, may one suppose that the divine power abhors the sins the less on the grounds that, having admitted them, God has in a way given His approval to them. *For the real end which the Divine Artist had in view was to compensate for the evils, which had been permitted and which were to be remedied by strenuous effort. . . . By thus pruning away the branches which yield an abundant harvest of evils, and, in so far as it is compatible with human freedom, eliminating them, He has in this way shown Himself to be someone who hates all wickedness, but also to be someone who loves the perfections that can nonetheless be extracted from this source.*
[1: 404–405; emphasis added]

In sum: In addition to the (Leibnizian) excuse of the greater good, God, in Kant's novel view, is exonerated by the remedial pains he takes to produce the greatest possible perfection from the evil he necessarily allows. He does so by striving to elicit, both by warnings and encouragements and by otherwise "supplying the means," man's own "strenuous effort" to overcome the sensual distractions that entangle him. Man, as Kant sees matters, is pulled in two directions: toward a lower goal whose goodness is evident to the senses, and toward a higher one whose goodness he perceives only fleetingly and by dint of a burdensome expenditure of intellectual effort. God "compensates" for evil, so to speak, by extracting from it all the goodness it can yield consistent with man's freedom. Man's own strenuous effort furnishes the remedy, one is almost tempted to say, that justifies Creation.

Kant's early theodicy rests, then, on an incipient moral anthropology—an interpretation of man's "dismal history" as a divine "pruning" that is intended to extract most from least. Pushed to its limit, that transformative engine, fueled by the labor of human reason, verges on turning nothing into something, and thus allows Creation in its plenitude to include even, "so to speak, nothing itself."

The anthropological and moral implications of this historical schema are developed more fully in Part Three of Kant's *Universal Natural History and Theory of the Heavens,* which will be considered in greater detail below. For the present it is enough to note the following: "Strenuous effort" is the price that man (and man alone) must pay to fulfill the Divine purpose. And that effort is concerned, above all, with a turning of attention from bodily goods (drinking, gaming, and making sacrifices to Venus) to the goods proffered by the understanding. If, as Kant here insists, the ultimate purpose of Creation is the happiness of the spirit world, a happiness that consists in contemplating the goodness of the whole, man (alone among created beings [with the possible exception of the Martians]) must work to make himself worthy of that perfection [1: 366]. Man alone must earn his spiritual spurs. His location in the universe, midway between "wisdom and unreason" [1: 365], connects him to a bodily machine that is too gross to make such contemplation effortless, and too fine to exonerate him for his failure to resist the opposing blandishments of sensual pleasure. The same cosmic predicament that makes human history "dismal" also makes man uniquely responsible for his own success or failure to achieve the end for which he was created. Virtue, meaning, above all, a willingness to labor, is already Kant's moral watchword. But virtue is here in the service not of the categorical imperative but of cosmic contemplation, the draw of which cannot move our will without energetic effort on our part to resist the "equally powerful" pull of sensual pleasure.

Indeed, the very illusion of "indifference" or indeterminacy of will that *The New Elucidation* means to refute arises from this predicament, which makes us "feel ourselves to be the authors" of our own representations:

> The natural force of desire, inherent in the human mind, directs itself not only towards objects but also towards the various representations which are to be found in the understanding. Accordingly, in so far as we feel ourselves

> to be the authors [*sentimus auctores esse*] of the representations which contain the motives for choice in a given case, so that we are eminently able either to focus our attention on them, or to suspend our attention, or turn it in another direction, and are consequently conscious of being able not only to strive toward the objects in conformity with our desire but also to interchange the reasons themselves in a variety of ways and as we please—insofar as all this is the case we can scarcely refrain from supposing that the addressing of our will in a given direction is not governed by any law nor subject to any fixed determination. [1: 403; translation slightly altered]

The power to focus our attention upon an object, suspend it, or turn it in another direction gives rise to the illusion that our will is not governed by a law or otherwise determined. Kant counters this illusion with a practical experiment:

> Suppose [assuming the presence of this illusion] that we make an effort to arrive at a correct understanding of the fact that the inclination of the attention towards a combination of representations is in this direction rather than a different one. Since grounds attract us in a certain direction, we shall, in order at least to test our freedom, turn our attention in the opposite direction, and thus make it preponderant so that the desire *is directed thus and not otherwise*. In this way, we shall easily persuade ourselves that determining grounds must certainly be present.
> [1: 403; translation slightly altered]

By making the effort to put freedom to the test, one "easily convinces oneself" that the will is moved by a directing ground or reason—in this case, the desire to thus put freedom to the test. The theory of indifference is thus internally refuted by an experiment directed by the will upon itself. Freedom and rational determination go hand in hand; but it is not yet determination by a law of one's own will (i.e., autonomy). Still, freedom already finds its touchstone in our feeling of control over our own mental forces, a feeling of being able to direct attention to and from representations that attract us. That such direction demands effort, if only in the end to make one's goal easier to attain, indicates the peculiar intellectual weakness to which human freedom ultimately testifies. God, who has the total "account" of good and evil in view, inclines his will with infallible certainty in the direction of the good. And higher created beings are drawn toward this greater good willy-nilly. Man, by way of contrast, is called upon to expend his finite force toward an end whose preponderant goodness is not fully evident to him and that the "natural force of desire" fails to register definitively.

We will have reason to return to this human peculiarity, which makes us (alone) responsible for our own failure or success "to achieve the end for which we were created." For now it is enough to note the importance Kant already places on power over attention as a central vehicle of human freedom—a power his later *Anthropology* will associate with "freedom of the capacity for thought" [*Freiheit des Denkensvermögens*] and "the self-control of the mind" [*Eigenmacht des Gemüths*], or as he also puts it, *animus sui compos* [7: 131]. Whereas Leibniz and Wolff trace all the powers of the soul to a single representative activity they call attention [*attentio*], Kant, even at this early stage of his thinking, follows Crusius in dividing the powers of the soul between intellect and will. To attend to a representation is as much an act of will as it is of intellect. And yet, unlike the more orthodox Crusius, for whom freedom of the will implies its indeterminacy, Kant attempts to unite freedom with the Leibnizian/Wolffian principle that everything has its reason—a principle necessary, as it seems, for any comprehensive science of nature.

2. Freedom in the *Universal Natural History and Theory of the Heavens*

Kant's *Universal Natural History*—a work completed around the same time— is an attempt at just such a comprehensive science, a science that adheres to the principle of determining reason without denying either the existence of a creative God or the possibility of human freedom. Its full title reflects the scope of Kant's ambition: *Universal Natural History and Theory of the Heavens: or Essay on the Constitution and Mechanical Origin of the World Structure Treated according to Newtonian Principles.*[11]

The key to Kant's "theory of the heavens" is a model that replaces the "clinemen" of Epicurus and Lucretius—the chance "swerving" that, according to these ancient authors, deflected the primal atoms from their initial downward fall—by the law-governed, "Newtonian" forces of attraction and repulsion. According to Kant's Newtonian revision of Lucretius, the initial dispersal of the primal atoms of matter gives rise, by virtue of these laws, to a process of galactic and planetary formation around a common "sinking point" or gravitational center.

The main, and only reliably "certain" aspect of Kant's exercise, on his own account, is an argument for what is now called "intelligent design": By showing that the universe could only have arisen from a matter whose intrinsically law-like character betrays its immaterial source in the mind (and will) of an intelligent creator, Kant hopes to defeat the derivation of "reason from unreason," and thereby reconcile a comprehensive natural science with Christianity.

As in the *New Elucidation,* Kant is concerned not only with cosmology but also with its moral and religious implications. Thus, in addition to a providing a physical cosmogony on Newtonian lines (a task, one would think, already large enough), the *Universal Natural History* advances what Kant calls a "most plausible" theory as to the relation between matter and spirit (or intelligence) generally.[12] This relation proves to have important epistemological and moral consequences. Man's earthly status places him in the middle of the cosmic scale, connected to a bodily machine that is too dense to let him contemplate the universe with ease (as with the effortlessly contemplative Saturnians) and too rare to excuse him from the effort (as with the guiltlessly sensual Mercurians) [1: 360–365].

This brings us to Kant's (rarely considered) interplanetary pneumotology, which he presents "poetically," and yet in all apparent seriousness. Its professed purpose is to add weight to Kant's more general effort to replace Lucretian chance with a lawful general providence, and thereby forestall the installation of "Lucretius in the midst of Christendom." Kant here argues, on the basis largely of "analogy," for the plausibility of a double universe, its physical system furnishing the platform for a spirit world—the community of intelligent substances, that is to say, viewed from God's own vantage point.

If even the physical universe, beholden to mechanical laws, betrays an intelligent author, whose aims it serves, a path is opened toward a consideration of the purposes of the intelligent creatures who inhabit it. If, *ex hypothesi,* it is inconsistent with God's nature as "most real being" to leave "shut up" (as in a storehouse) any force that might be actively expended—if everything that can be is, or will be in the future—then nature is a complete plenitude. The purpose of intelligent nature is to contemplate this beautiful perfection (or the harmony of manifoldness and unity), a task to which Kant's own work is itself devoted. That task is, however, an encumbered one. Peculiarly burdened as we are, that temporal-spatial effort must at some point fall short. At such moments, abysmal in their implications for ordinary understanding, arise opportunities for sublime feelings of transcendence—intimations of participation in an eternal spirit world that communicates with God without temporal-spatial mediation. Such "upward swings" [*emporschwingen*] (or invitations thereto) arise throughout Kant's essay, mainly where efforts to imagine an infinite series overreach our capacity and collapse upon themselves. The vision "the starry heavens on a clear night" [1: 367] (a phrase later echoed in a famous passage from Kant's *Critique of Practical Reason*) is "sublime," by virtue of the fact that it provides an opportunity for transcendence that arises precisely from the failure of the mind to progress in a straight linear path toward actualization, *per impossibile*, of the infinite. At some point, that cannot be determined in advance, the mind balks at its own demands and either lazily gives up or "nobly" rises to or from the challenge. As increasingly emerges, the task of Kant's essay is not "theoretical" in the usual narrow sense; "theory" is indissolubly linked, at this early stage of Kant's thinking, with a moral and spiritual goal of extraordinary high ambition for any human being, let alone a provincial private tutor in his early thirties.

Even at this relatively early stage in his career, Kant is primed to admit the limits of theoretical reason. He already appreciates, that is to say, the need for (as well as of the dangers of) poetic "supplement," if the "noblest" human demands are to be met. Haller, whom Kant calls "sublimest" of the German *Dichter* (and who is also a successful scientist in his own right), rather than Lucretius, is Kant's professed "philosophic poet," if not actually his model.

The *Universal Natural History* thus betrays goals that are as much moral and poetic as they are cosmological and scientific. Kant's general strategy, as appears more and more evidently as the work progresses, is to invite ever more catastrophic failures of representation (arising from a straining of our combining power to its utmost), failures that provide a more than compensating pleasure to (and only to) the spiritually deserving.

Such moments begin with Kant's attention to a series of systematic centerpoints (of the solar system, the galaxy, and, ultimately, the universe) into which matter would abysmally collapse without an offsetting material repulsive force (and/or an initial dispersion) that transforms a *Senkungspunkt* into a supporting "Unterstutzungspunkt" or pivot. Order progresses outward from these controlling gravitational centers, until world systems, having run their eon long course, collapse back into chaos. The ensuing circle within a circle—one defined by the border between chaos and order, the other by the border between order and chaos—expands infinitely outward, only to be repeated by another, similar wave, as order (for reasons "similar to those present at the beginning") arises once again from chaos. Constant progress and constant repetition of the same are thereby formulaically combined in a way that at once stimulates and stymies the imagination.

In all of this, it is as much the chaos that concerns Kant as the "phoenix-like" order to which it is supposed to give rise. Nature exhibits its "inexhaustible richness" through an infinite "wastefulness" [*Verschwendung;* cf. *verschwinden* = "vanish"] that, though terrible for us (who must also someday pay the "tribute" of "vanity/idleness" [*Eitelkeit*]—i.e., "vanish"), "costs it nothing." Acceptance of the necessary laws of an economy of true abundance should allow us to regard the ensuing upheavals [*Umstürzungen*] with a kind of delight [*Wohlgefallen*] [1: 319]. And yet regard for nature's "phoenix" would merely "sink" our spirit in "astonishment," were it not offset by a consideration of eternity, especially our own:

> Unsatisfied with so great an object whose transitoriness cannot sufficiently satisfy the soul, it wishes to know more closely the being, the greatness of whose understanding is the source of light that spreads itself out over collective nature, so to speak, as from its center [*Mittelpunkt*]. [1: 321]

Only in relation to such a center "so to speak," is the soul, uplifted [*erhoben*] into a state of restfulness [*Ruhestand*], finally to be satisfied "sufficiently":

> O happy, when/if among the tumult of the elements and the rubble of nature, it is always set on a height from which it can see the ravages, brought about by the frailty/downfalling character [*Hinfälligkeit*] of things, so to speak, rush by beneath its feet! Such a happiness, which reason dare not even once be bold enough to wish for, revelation teaches us to hope for with conviction. When, then, the fetters that keep us bound to the vanity of creatures falls away in the moment determined/destined for the transformation of our being, then the immortal spirit, freed from dependence on finite things, will find the enjoyment of true happiness in community with the eternal being. [1: 322]

Given these spiritual aims, Kant finds it especially important to distinguish his approach from the apparently similar claims of one Thomas Wright, who identifies the material center of the universe with its paternally divine source and apex [1: 329]. For Kant, such confusion of matter and spirit is particularly pernicious. Kantian "transcendence" is stimulated, not by direct representation of the material universe, but by the ever-renewed perception of the inadequacy of one's attempt to do so, and by the "divine idea" evoked by that perception.[13]

There are other reasons, however, for Kant to permit himself here a certain poetic license to exceed the limits of the material universe. Of the happiness for which reason (which needs the resistance of matter to "keep it in track") cannot be bold enough "even to wish," imagination may furnish a "foretaste." The wish for such a foretaste furnishes one reason for Kant's lengthy "appendix" ("Part Three: of the inhabitants of the stars").

The explicit purpose of this addition to the main body of Kant's text is to overcome that which (alone), he says, makes his "universal theory of the heavens" less than "fully satisfying" [1: 345–346]. The harmony between the material order and the purposes of intelligent life—a harmony required to maximize the "beauty" of the whole by uniting material and purposive causation in a single formula—would itself call into question the adequacy of Newton's laws to the task proposed were there not available a plausible principle of coordination linking material and spiritual development. This attempted reconciliation of the material and the spiritual takes the form of a kind of interplanetary bestiary, with man serving as the "general foundation and reference point."

Drawing on an earlier insight as to the dependence of a creature's representation of the world on its own worldly embodiment, Kant posits a direct, fixed relation between a mind's aptness in combining its impressions, the density of the matter through which it receives them, and the distance of that matter from the sun (or comparable sinking point and source of heat and life). However infinite the distance between the force of thinking and the motion of matter, however little may otherwise be known concerning life on other cosmic spheres, and however much our "inner nature" remains for us an "unexplored problem," man's relation to the matter with which he is conjoined is clear enough: Thinking is a difficult [or "heavy" {*schwerig*}] task that most people shirk or otherwise avoid. Although the faculties required to satisfy our material needs develop soon enough, the higher ability to think—a faculty that "ought to dominate"—develops late or never. Most men are content to "suck fluid, propagate their kind, and die," without achieving the (contemplative) purpose for which they were created. Man would thus be the most despicable of creatures, were he not "lifted up" [*erhübe*] by hope in a future life, in which all the faculties enclosed in him will develop in their entirety [1: 355–356].

Man is in this regard a prisoner of his own earthly location, whose middling status condemns him to a bodily machine too dense to make thinking easy and too rarified to provide the excuse enjoyed by lesser rational beings, who lack the mental strength to overcome the distractions of the senses:

> [Given] the crudeness of the matter in which [man's] spiritual part is sunk, the inflexibility [*Unbiegsamkeit*] of the fibers and the inertia [*Trägheit*] and immovability of the fluids which should obey [his] stirrings, the nerves and liquids of his brain deliver only crude and unclear concepts. And because he lacks sufficient force to set, in the interior of his thinking capacity, counter-

weighing representations against the enticements of sensible impressions, he is torn away by passions. . . . The exertions [*Bemühungen*] of reason to rise [*sich erheben*] against this, and to drive away this confusion with the light of the force of judgment, are like flashes of sunlight whose cheerfulness is unceasingly [*unablässig*] interrupted and darkened by thick clouds.
[1: 356–357]

Confusion and depravity, however, are not the only wages of earthly life: Death, too, comes sooner to bodily machines that are made from denser matter. The vessels of our bodies, thickening internally, eventually cut off the fluids that they are meant to carry. The grosser the machine, the sooner life completes its self-terminating circuit [1: 362–363].

Spiritual beings elevated to a level further from the sun will live longer, judge more easily and aptly, and master the distractions of the senses with less effort or temptation. As for the "saturnians" who inhabit the spheres furthest from the center:

What advances in knowledge would [they] . . . not achieve! What beautiful consequences would this enlightening of their insight not have on their moral makeup! The insights of understanding, when they possess the appropriate degree of perfection and clarity, have much more lively charms [*Reizungen*] than do sensual allurements, and have the capacity to master them victoriously, and trod them under foot [*unter den Fuß zu treten*]. How masterfully would not God himself, who paints himself in all creatures, paint himself in these thinking natures, which, like a sea unmoved by the storm of the passions, restfully accepted and reflected back God's image! [1: 360]

Even the "need for time" may be "relative," so that what for lower beings is only a moment for higher beings constitutes many centuries [1: 361].

Nature is at once the site of our progressive advance (supposing our palingenetic ascent, in future lives, to ever finer planets) and the source of our fatality. Kant's God communicates a universal harmony to beings placed further from the sun—creatures who calmly receive, in the silence of their passions, what earthly beings can only struggle toward. "Sin," on this account, is literally a function of geography, without this fact relieving us of responsibility for our own failure to achieve our purpose, and the (early) death that naturally accompanies our inertial lack of effort [1: 353].

Kant's project is thus shown to have a distinctly pedagogical as well as moral aim.[14] His scientifically "plausible" account of the formation of the cosmic system makes our own struggle to combine sensations easier, lessening the weight that makes thinking so laborious for us. Such an exhibition of the beauty of the whole (which is as manifest "in the lowest of its members as in the highest/most sublime [*erhabnern*]" [1: 365]) strengthens our ability to "offset" the distracting counterweight of sensual allurement.

Significantly, reason here need not go it alone. Having remained "true," thus far, to the "leading strings" [*Leitfaden*] of physical relationship which make conjecture worthy of rational belief, Kant permits himself—grounded plausibility and arbitrary fiction having "no clear boundary" [*Grenze*]—a final digression [*Ausschweifung*] into the "field of fantasy," which allows him to identify man's cosmological position with a capacity for sin that is ours alone or— "sorry comfort"[15]—shared with our nearest cosmic neighbors [1: 366].

Unlike the "entertaining (as in "*belustigen*") images Kant earlier dismissed, these are "permissible" and "decent," albeit "uncertain" and hence no suitable "ground" for hope [1: 367]. Still, Kant goes on immediately to predict that, after vanity or idleness [*Eitelkeit*] has extracted its share from human nature:

> The immortal spirit will swing itself upward with a quick swing over all that is finite, and set forth its existence in a new relation to the whole of nature, originating in a closer connection to the highest being. Henceforth, this uplifted [*erhöhte*] nature, which has the source of happiness in itself, will no longer dissipate itself among outer objects, seeking repose [*Beruhigung*] in them. The entire *Inbegriff* of creation, which has a necessary harmony with the delight [*Wohlgefallen*] of the highest being, must also have it with its own pleasure, and will not move it otherwise than with ever-enduring satisfaction. [1: 367]

What, then, distinguishes these speculations from the enjoyable images Kant earlier dismisses as contemptible diversions? What differentiates such poeticizing philosophy from an "idle dream"?

The proof, it seems, lies in the pudding—i.e., in the peculiar feeling of sublimity to which such speculations give rise. "In fact" [*In der That*]:

> If/when one has filled one's mind [*Gemüth*] with the foregoing considerations, the vision [*Anblick*] of a starry heaven on a clear night gives an enjoyment [*Vergnügens*] only felt [*empfinden*] by noble souls. In the universal stillness [*Stille*] of nature and the quiet [*Ruhe*] of the senses, the hidden knowledge capacity [*verborgene Erkenntißvermögen*] of the immortal spirit speaks an ineffable [*unnennbare*] language, and gives undeveloped concepts that allow themselves to be felt but not described. If there are, among the thinking creatures of this planet, base [*niederträchtige*] beings who, inatten-

tive to all the charms with which a so great object can seduce them, are in a state [*Stande*] of fastening themselves into servitude of vanity [*Dienstbarkeit der Eitelkeit*]—how unhappy/unfortunate is this sphere, that it was able to educate [*erziehen*] such miserable creatures! But how happy/fortunate it is, on the other hand, that to it/them, among conditions in all ways worthy of acceptance, a way is opened up to it/them to reach a happiness and height which is lifted up [*erhaben ist*] infinitely far over the preferments [*Vorzüge*] that the most entirely advantageous arrangements of nature can achieve on all world bodies! [1: 367–368]

Kant maintains a studied ambiguity here as to whether the "way" in question is the orthodox revelation of Scripture (which redeems the many), or the education opened up by Kant's own work. Is it God's word or is it Kant's own philosophic poetry (which makes room for revelation within the boundaries of a comprehensive natural science without requiring it) that invites the human spirit to swing itself upward? Kant had earlier distinguished Wright's "arbitrary" and "enthusiastic" representations from his own "plausible conjectures." Contrary to Wright's fanatical *Begeisterungen,* which placed God in the center of the material universe, divinity, says Kant, is "everywhere present in the infinity of the whole world-space": "[*allenthalben*] where there are natures capable of swinging themselves above [*sich . . . empor zu schwingen*] the dependency of creatures, God is to be found equally near" [1: 329]. (As Kant will put it in the *Inaugural Dissertation of 1770,* God's presence in the world is "virtual" rather than "actual.") In the feeling of sublimity so understood, Kant finds, or posits, another sort of *Unterstutzungspunkt.*

In contrast to the vanity [*Eitelkeit*] that characterizes both a hyper-spiritualism and a hyper-materialism (the former "lazy," and the latter "futile"), Kant claims to have discovered "new lands" on the basis of a dangerous journey undertaken on small speculation [*Vermuthung*] [1: 221]. His willingness to expose his work before the tribunal of the sternest "orthodox aereopagus" bears witness, moreover, to Kant's probity and courage [1: 222]. And yet, given the above-stated ambiguity concerning the "way" at issue, has Kant overcome the obstacles before him, as he "boldly claim[s]"? Has he genuinely dispelled the "monstrous cloud" that he associates with orthodox religious objections to his project?[16]

Scattered passages suggest that Kant was less than fully satisfied with his own efforts. It might seem that in a project like his "one can give freer reign to fantasy than would a painter in depicting the plants and animals of undiscovered lands" [1: 351]. Is not Kant just such a painter, begging the indulgence of his audience less on the basis of truth than of their pleasure? Or is the peculiar pleasure of the sublime its own self-authenticating "trade-mark"?

Indeed, Kant seems to grant that his argument here is an at least partial failure. "We do not," he says, "want to allow to the boldness of our conjectures, to which (as he admits) we have perhaps permitted too much, to slip the leash to the point of arbitrary fictions." However confidently Kant may describe our external relations, man's "inward constitution" remains an "unexplored problem" [*unerforschtes Problema*]; we do not yet know what man rightly is or might one day become [1: 355, 366]. And an important element of the mystery would seem to lie with human evil itself. As Kant puts it in the *New Elucidation*, man's "voluntary inclination toward what is base" is the crucial "pivot" [*cardo*] on which turns his exclusion from the happiness of the spirit world [*mundus spiritualis*]:

> If, as happens with machines, intelligent beings were to comport themselves passively . . . I should not deny that blame for all things could be shifted to God as Architect of the machine. But those things that happen through the will of beings endowed with understanding and the spontaneous power itself of self-determination obviously issue . . . from conscious desires and a choice of one of the alternatives. . . . Hence, no matter how much the state of things prior to the free acts has been constituted by some ground . . . futurition is determined by grounds that are constituted in such a way that voluntary inclination toward the base serves as the pivot. [1: 404; translation altered]

This pivot is the source of human failure. And our inability to grasp it nonmechanically (or from God's vantage point) culminates in Kant's final complaint, at the conclusion of the *Universal Natural History*, that we know neither what man is nor what he might become. The "substance" of our soul (or spirit), it is true, is necessarily imperishable (as Kant here maintains). But anticipation of a future without the body evokes images of changelessness that seems a kind of living death. Our only recourse is belief either in 1) our embodied rebirth in another, intellectually and morally more favorable, cosmic location (e.g., Saturn) or 2) participation in a "spirit world" with which God communicates directly. Hope in such future rests in turn either upon belief in revelation or upon an aesthetic intimation supplied by our own feeling for the cosmological sublime.

Kant's work closes by appealing to such an intimation, provoked by the cosmological "considerations" to which his essay as a whole has been devoted

[1: 367–368]. His reference here to an "unspeakable" spiritual language, elicited, in noble souls, by "the sight of the starry heavens on a clear night," calls to mind his later famous juxtaposition of "the starry heavens above us" and "the moral law within us." But in the *Universal Natural History* nobility is associated with contemplation (and an accompanying virtuous resistance to the attractions of sensual pleasure), not, as in the later passage, with obedience to the moral law.

Kant's early metaphysical claims as to the status of the world as a "real" whole, the impossibility of change in isolated substances, the necessity of God as a ground of real worldly connection that we cannot ourselves fully comprehend, the freedom of the soul, and the purpose of creation yield a strikingly ambitious and coherent teaching regarding man and his place in the universe—i.e., an incipient "anthropology" and "metaphysics of morals." To be sure, grave difficulties remain, beginning with Kant's admission that the inner constitution of man is still an "unexplored problem." Additionally, Kant's final recourse in the *Universal Natural History* to a poetic rhetoric intended to evoke feelings of the sublime suggests a failure on the part of "theory" Kant seems unlikely to have found wholly satisfying. The goal of theory—comprehension of the "whole"—necessarily founders, on Kant's early account, upon a worldly status on which time, and hence self-consciousness as we presently know it, also depends. Human "perfection" thus remains an inherently paradoxical goal. Contemplation of the universe, the "purpose for which we were created," is attractive only to the very few, and even to them, only after monumental struggles of self-overcoming, and in the face of a clear knowledge that the goal in question cannot be fully achieved, given the present conditions of human life. The only available solution to this dilemma is hope—either in a future advance of knowledge through rebirth on planets at a more favorable distance from the sun, or in a wholly spiritual participation in the "divine schema of creation."[17] In promising to supply a "foretaste" of such spiritual community, Kant's cosmological speculations continue to evoke—in language if not meaning—the Pietist hymns of Kant's own childhood.

3. Kant's Anthropological Revolution

Both those metaphysical claims, and that incipient anthropological and moral teaching, undergo a radical change beginning in the early 1760s. These changes bear especially on Kant's judgment as to the status of his own activity as a scientist and researcher. Whereas he had earlier linked human "nobility" with the few capable of theoretical speculation, he now (and henceforth) associates it with the practical transformation of human life, and, in particular, with "establishing the (equal) rights of man." How might one account for this extraordinary intellectual and moral transformation?

a. Reading Rousseau

A number of scholars whose views I broadly share regard Rousseau, above all, as the decisive intellectual influence and provocation.[18] Hume may have "awakened" Kant from his dogmatic slumber (as he puts it in a well-known passage of the *Prolegomena*) but Rousseau "set [him] upright" [20: 44]. The singular importance of Rousseau is considered in detail and, in some novel ways, in the chapters that follow. For the more limited purposes of this chapter, it will be helpful to sketch out the major changes in intellectual orientation that characterize Kant's thought between the early 1760s until the late 1770s, the period just prior to his completion of the *Critique of Pure Reason*.

These are the years in which Kant was most preoccupied with anthropology as a specific subject. Indeed, an early (and unusually becoming) portrait, painted in 1764, shows him holding a volume with the word "Anthropology" clearly discernable on its spine.[19] This was also the period in which he published his most successful non-academic work, *Observations on the Feeling of the Beautiful and the Sublime*, which went through several printings in his lifetime. Shortly afterward, he began teaching a course on anthropology as a companion to one on "physical geography," an academic topic that Kant introduced to Germany almost single-handedly. Kant's course on anthropology remained highly popular throughout the period under discussion and continued through the so-called silent decade in which Kant hardly published, and the little that went to press—a review of Moscoti's Rousseau-inspired work on human anatomy, two essays on the concept of race, and two brief endorsements of a Rousseau-inspired local school—were all anthropological in theme and focus.

This explicitly anthropological focus is partly explained by new doubts on Kant's part as to the character of human perfection. Man's natural "purpose" cannot be known directly (as works like the *Universal Natural History* had assumed). This is so not only because all such claims are theoretically suspect but also, as Rousseau's first *Discourse* persuasively shows, because they are likely to arise from a misguided and misguiding *amour propre*. Rousseau's "state of nature," rightly understood, promises a solution by suggesting "fixed points" toward which man, caught up in the "flux" of things, can reliably direct his efforts; rightly understood, the "state of nature" furnishes a model of ordered freedom that elicits human aspiration while confining it within the limits of necessity, both physical and moral.

Kant's elaboration of this criterion is facilitated by his discovery of the concept of "real opposition" and an accompanying clarification, in his mind, of the principle of worldly connection more generally. This new conception of real opposition, which is expounded in detail in the *Essay on Negative Quantities* [1763], is likely to have been prompted by Hume's critique of the idea of causal necessity, which Kant probably first read sometime in the late 1750s. (A German edition of Hume's *Inquiry* appeared in 1755.)[20] As Eric Watkins has suggestively argued, Hume's argument posed a special difficulty for Kant's earlier understanding of worldly connection, the necessitating character of which Kant had not yet been able adequately to explain. Clearly, the relation between members of a common world could not be a *logically* necessary one, given Kant's definition of substance as something "self-subsistent" and hence capable, in principle, of existing in isolation. But referring that connection to the divine "understanding" and its "schema" was a virtual admission of the inadequacy of the human mind to fully understand the worldly principle to which it itself is subject. Kant's rethinking of the issue led him to identify real interaction more closely with the Newtonian principle of the conservation of matter. The "zero" produced by logical opposition is a simple contradiction; the "zero" constituted by real opposition, on the contrary, is not only consistent with existence but (if Newton's law is to be credited) one of its defining physical conditions.

But if that principle makes the formal ground of the world newly accessible to human reason, it does so at a price. The enhanced clarity, but diminished reach, of Kant's new principle of worldly connection undercuts the ambitiously synthetic project he had attempted in the *Universal Natural History*. The mutual cancellation to zero of opposing homogeneous forces postulated by Kant's new principle leaves no obvious room for final causation or for freedom (as had the appeal to a divine schema). The physical world that it describes necessarily excludes these and other spiritual matters with which his earlier cosmology had boldly dealt. The relation between body and soul can no longer be regarded as essentially the same as worldly interaction generally.[21]

Though it falls short of providing the ambitiously comprehensive cosmological principle Kant had earlier sought, the concept of real opposition is useful, as Kant now insists, in other humanly significant ways. In ethics, for example, it helps clarify certain commonsense intuitions about the nature of moral evil. Henceforth, Kant will describe evil, not as a mere lack of goodness (as he does in the *Optimism* essay of 1759), but as having a negative "reality" of its own. On this view, moral evil is a state of moral indebtedness, not just a lack of moral capital. Moral evil, that is to say, stands to moral goodness as (minus A) relates to (A), rather than as (zero) relates to (A).

The notion of real opposition also lends new significance to the mind's ability to turn its attention, or "abstract," from the representations of sensibility, a power whose importance the *Universal Natural History* and *New Elucidation* had already emphasized. Human cognition, as Kant newly sees, requires a "real power" to "turn away" from what is given—an activity demanding an expenditure of effort that gives enhanced "living" evidence of human freedom.

Perhaps most importantly, Kant's new understanding of the principle of worldly connection permits him to construct a *moral* version of the intelligible world (or world of spirits) on the analogy of the physical world. The world of spirits cannot be known theoretically, as Kant now definitively concludes. (He will later permit republication of the *Universal Natural History* only if the "extravagant" account of the world of spirits is omitted.) Still, something morally useful can be done with the notion. Just as certain physical principles (like that reflected in Newton's law of motion) establish conditions of "real possibility" within the physical world, so certain ethical principles establish conditions of "real possibility" within the moral one. Such a morally constructed world is "intelligible," as we shall see, in the precise sense of abstracting from the sensible determinations that ordinarily shape our experience. The intelligible world, morally construed, is not an object of theoretical knowledge; but it is also not an arbitrary fiction, since it is anchored in a felt "obligation" or "moral necessity" that is consistent both with man's natural limits and with a formal rule of ordered freedom.

b. "Carazan's Dream"

A footnote on the "terrifying sublime" in *Observations on the Feeling of the Beautiful and the Sublime* bears striking literary witness to this transformation. Kant cites the story of one Carazan, a rich (Persian?) merchant who has "closed his heart" to others. As Carazan reports:

> One evening, while I was drawing up my accounts and going over my profits . . . I was overcome by sleep. . . . The angel of death overcame me like a whirlwind and struck me before I could utter a terrified scream. I was struck dumb as I feared that my die was caste for eternity, and that all the good I had done could not be augmented nor all the bad taken away. I was led before him who dwells in the third heaven. The sight that flamed before me spoke thus: "Carazan, your divine service is rejected. You have closed your heart to love of man and held onto your treasure with an iron hand. You have lived only for yourself and thus you shall live for eternity alone and cut off from all community with the whole of creation." At this moment I was grasped by an unseen power and thrown through the shimmering edifices of creation. I had already left uncountable worlds behind me. As I approached the outermost boundaries of nature, I observed that the shadows of limitless emptiness stretched into the depths that sank before me. A fearsome realm of eternal quiet, loneliness and darkness! Inexpressible terror befell me at this moment. I gradually lost sight of the last stars and finally the last glimmering appearance of light in the outermost darkness. The death angel of despair grew with every moment, just as my distance from that last inhabited world increased. I considered with unbearable anguish of the heart that if ten thousand times a thousand years went by . . . I would still hurl forward into the immeasurable abyss of darkness without help or hope of return.— In this state of stupor I stretched out my hands toward real objects with such impetuosity that I thereby awoke. And now I have learned to esteem human beings highly. For in that horrifying isolation [*Einöde*] I would prefer to all the treasures of Golconda even the lowliest of those whom in my proud fortune I drove from my door. [2: 209–210n][22]

The terrifying thought of one's utter solitude—negatively presented as a total absence of sensation [*Betäubung*]—brings home the virtual identity, for subjective human purposes, of "worldless" self-sufficiency as a kind of living death. We cannot imagine ourselves worldless without canceling in thought the possibility of inward changes of state and with it self-consciousness as we now know it. Bereft of outer relations, the unity of the I is an empty shell. And yet imagining that emptiness gives rise to feelings of transcendence that are not altogether unpleasant. In the *Universal Natural History* Kant interpreted such feelings as the intimation of our participation in a contemplative world of spirits, elevated above the fray of time and space. Here, those feelings have an altogether different intellectual and moral valence. Carazan, the proud miser, "awakens" with a new yearning to "connect" with his fellow human beings, the lowliest of whom now seems infinitely precious. Moral community, based on a feeling for the dignity of all human beings, beckons where unwarranted pride had failed. In sum: The tale of Carazan translates hope for the future (or for imaginable participation in a wholly spiritual community) from the metaphysical to the moral plane; we are on the threshold of the "revolution" in Kant's thinking that would finally lead him to the principle of autonomy as we now know it.[23]

2

Kant's Archimedean Moment:
Remarks in "Observations Concerning the Feeling of the Beautiful and the Sublime"

Beginning in the early 1760s, Kant's early cosmological claims undergo a radical change. This alternation bears not only on his understanding of human freedom and its implications for natural science, but also on his judgment as to the status of his own theoretical activity. Whereas he had heretofore identified human "nobility" with the acquisition of knowledge, he now (and henceforth) links it with the practical improvement of human life, and, in particular, with "establishing the rights of man." How explain this extraordinary transformation?

Hume may have "awakened" Kant from his dogmatic slumber but Rousseau, as earlier noted, "set [him] upright" in a way decisive for his subsequent intellectual career [20: 44]. The singular importance of Rousseau is taken up at length, and in some unexpected ways, in this and the following chapter.

The tale of Carazan, as we have seen, translates hope for future (or imaginable) participation in spiritual community from the metaphysical to the moral plane, bringing Kant to the threshold of re-conceiving the intelligible world as a "perfect republic" in which, as he will later put it, moral forces of "attraction" and "repulsion" stand in dynamic balance. That moral recuperation of the noumenal world is thematic in both the *Remarks in "Observations on the Feeling of the Beautiful and the Sublime"* and in the nearly contemporaneous *Dreams of a Spirit-Seer*. It also furnishes much of the intellectual framework for the *Dissertation* of 1770 and his longer-term project of specifying the limits of human reason. As Kant puts it in *Dreams:*

> Questions concerning spiritual nature, freedom, . . . and the like initially set all the forces of the understanding in motion, and . . . through their excellence draw a person into the rivalry [*Wetteifer*] of speculation. . . . But if this inquiry should turn into philosophy that judges over its own procedure, and does not only know objects by themselves but in their relation to human understanding, . . . its boundaries will contract in size and its marking-stones will be laid, never more allowing inquiry to digress beyond its own proper circle. [2: 369][1]

Kant's new theoretical modesty does not lead him to abandon teleological reasoning in every respect. Living beings display a capacity for orderly growth and self-maintenance manifestly lacking in inanimate bodies.[2] Accordingly, he invests his study of anthropology with certain key hypotheses as to the purposiveness of all organic life. Applying this assumption to human history, Kant claims to find a natural principle of "return," a principle that limits how far social depravity can go before prompting a countermovement of recovery.

Kant's stated goal, in notes written in the mid-1760s, is to accelerate this natural correction, a goal he sets forth in explicitly "Archimedean" terms: He will set his fulcrum upon the "state of nature" in order to "move the emotions" of human beings. Human perfection, as we will see below, lies neither in the rude simplicity of savage nature nor in the virtue of the ancient citizen but in the "moment of return" to it. In thus leveraging the laws of nature on behalf of freedom, the instigator of such a moment both confronts and overcomes the "terror" felt by uncorrupted savages before the prospect of subjection to another will—i.e., freedom without law.

For all its potential interest, *Remarks* is among the most neglected of Kant's early writings.[3] Given its manifest peculiarities, this neglect is not entirely surprising. The text that has come to be known as the *Remarks* consists of handwritten comments inserted into Kant's own copy of his *Observations on the Feeling of the Beautiful and the Sublime* [1764], the first of his works intended for the general reading public. Why Kant chose to write such extensive and substantive comments into his own copy of the *Observations* is a matter of some speculation. Kant's hand-written remarks do not obviously form a continuous argument; they are rich in allusion, sometimes fragmentary, and often elusive as to tone and meaning. One does not always know in whose voice Kant is speaking or on which sources he draws.[4] The notes do not seem to have been made with revision of the *Observations* directly in mind. Few of the notes bear directly on contiguous passages in the printed text. Indeed, the *Ob-*

servations was subsequently reprinted, essentially unchanged, several times during Kant's lifetime.

What cannot be doubted is the deeply searching character of these notes, which sketch out or otherwise anticipate essential elements of Kant's mature theoretical and practical philosophy. Not least noteworthy is the extraordinarily personal character of many passages, written by an author who famously avoided the first person in most of his writings and greatly distrusted psychological introspection as a general mode of inquiry. Nowhere is that personal character more evident than in a frequently cited confessional note:

> I myself am by inclination an inquirer. I feel in its entirety a thirst for knowledge and yearning restlessness to advance along this way along with satisfaction with each forward step. There was a time when I thought that this alone could constitute the honor of mankind, and I scorned the masses, who know nothing. *Rousseau* set me upright. [I] This blinding preference [*Vorzug*] vanishes. I learn to honor human beings, and I would find myself far more useless than the common worker if I did not believe that this consideration could bestow value to all others, to establish the rights of mankind. [20: 44][5]

As the above passage suggests, the *Remarks* reflects a turning point in Kant's life, in which earlier scientific pursuits and metaphysical preoccupations assume a new political and moral direction. "After Rousseau" [20: 44], the "blinding" opinion that such preoccupations and pursuits could constitute "the honor of mankind" vanishes. In its place, Kant evinces a determination to order his lifework henceforth around the goal of "establishing the rights of mankind." Later in the *Remarks* he will speak of a "decision," absent which virtue is impossible. And much later in his philosophic career, he will refer to a decisive act of will, rarely undertaken before the age of forty (the age at which *Remarks* was written), in which human character first manifests itself. Whatever weight one gives to this passage—and scholars differ on its significance—it seems to reflect a mind gripped by questions in which life and thinking intersect, and in which Kant's career, understanding that term in its original sense, seems to find its organizing principle. To put matters simply: Through reading Rousseau, Kant appears to discover his own true calling or vocation, described not as a rectification by God, but as a self-rectification or "setting upright" that lets him assume his proper "place" within the physical and moral universe.

The *Remarks* not only enables us to better understand the bearing of Kant's "Rousseauist turn" on his later writings; it also opens a window on the crucial thinking that surrounds it. Whatever the limitations inherent in attempting to interpret such a text, its content is sufficiently important and revealing to merit close attention.

Most scholars agree the *Remarks* were written several years after Kant's first exposure to Rousseau's thought, and—in particular—to the three works to which, taken together, Rousseau [himself] attributed a distinct "unity" of argument: *Emile*, the *Discourse on the Origins of Inequality*, and the *Discourse on the Arts and Sciences*. A fourth work, *The Social Contract*, which Kant also read at this time, expands on themes presented in *Emile* in an abbreviated form. The *Remarks*, then, marks not so much the initial impact of Rousseau, already evident in works such as the *Observations* and the *Essay on Negative Quantities* [1763], as deepened meditations provoked by protracted rereading and rumination. As Kant himself insists: "Having taste is an inconvenience for the understanding. I must keep reading Rousseau until the beauty of the expression does not at all unsettle me; then I can take him up with my reason from the very beginning" [20: 30].

More provocatively for would-be interpreters, Kant's notes register his struggle to make sense of Rousseau's famous paradoxes, which alternately delight, irritate, and ultimately (or so it seems) enlighten him:

> The first impression felt by an <intelligent> reader <who does not read> the works of Mr. *J. J. Rousseau* <out of mere vanity or in order to pass time>, is that he finds there a [great] rare mental perspicacity, a noble élan of genius, and a sensitive soul, and this perhaps in the highest degree that a writer has ever possessed all of them together [indeed scarcely ever], regardless of the period or people he comes from. [The next judgment that arises is concerns the] The impression that follows next is astonishment before strange and paradoxical opinions which conflict so strongly with what is generally admitted that one is inclined to suppose that the author only wanted to show, [through his] by virtue of his extraordinary talents, [wanted to demonstrate <only show> to elicit wonder] [the] the [show the power of an enchanting wit and through a] magical power of his eloquence and [to create a strange man]to pose as the [the] odd one [by that he] who, by [the] a novelty that captivates <without one's knowing it>, distinguishes himself from his rivals through his wit. The third thought, which one arrives at with difficulty because it occurs only rarely. [20: 43]

The elusive breaking off leaves readers in the dark as to what "rare thought" Rousseau finally precipitated in Kant. But the remainder of the *Remarks* leaves solid clues as to where reading Rousseau led him. Briefly, the encounter seems to have stimulated at least five interrelated sets of reflections: on aesthetic and moral feeling and their connection with civilized happiness and unhappiness; on relations between men and women; on social and political community; on the foundation of morality and religion; and on the role of philosophy in working out the "limits of reason" and the "determination of man" [20: 181].[6]

Throughout the *Remarks* Kant takes his central bearings from the "state of nature" understood in a peculiar sense. The state of nature for Kant (following Rousseau) is not, principally, an historical condition, though it may also be this, but a hypothetical construction, resting on certain grounding insights or assumptions as to the goodness of nature and the freedom of man.[7] On the basis of that construction, which bears certain affinities with Newton's methodological presupposition of a frictionless universe, the "deeply hidden" laws that regulate the shifting shapes of human experience reveal themselves.

Although an early passage speaks only of a "flux" without fixed banks, Kant comes to make out a distinct order of nature that assigns to man a place consistent with his freedom, and, ultimately, with his happiness, if not always with his wishes. According to the laws that mark that order, excesses provide their own antidote and principle of recovery. A flooding river, as he later remarks, makes new banks as it recedes.

After Rousseau, "providence is justified" for Kant—not in the Leibnizian sense of affirming God's creation as the "best world possible"—but in a way, rather, that leaves something, and perhaps the decisive thing, to us. The self-corrective character of human events turns, as we shall see, on our ability and willingness to "return to nature."

In gauging the impact of Rousseau, and for purposes of arriving at a better understanding of the *Remarks* more generally, two earlier works are especially illuminating: the *Universal Natural History and Theory of the Heavens* [1756], which Kant completed at the age of thirty-six, shortly before his initial reading of Rousseau, and *Observations on the Feeling of the Beautiful and the Sublime* [1764], which he completed shortly afterward.

As we saw in Chapter 1, the explicit and implicit goal of Kant's *Universal Natural History* is as much moral (and aesthetic) as it is scientific. Recognition of that earlier work's practical aims and failures enables one to better understand the larger significance of the famous confessional note quoted above. Rousseau set Kant "upright"—not least—by teaching him to orient his activity in relation to the human condition and its limits. "The correct knowledge of the constitution of the universe in accordance with Newton is perhaps the most beautiful product of inquisitive human reason." Still, despite such beauty, and as with "sublime considerations about the heaven of the blessed," it is "unnatural" to lose oneself beyond the circle that heaven has fixed for us [20: 120]. Instead: "the most important matter for man is to know how to occupy his place in creation properly, and to understand correctly what he must be in order to be a man." Or again:

> I can climb from here to the planet *Jupiter* just as little as I can demand to have the qualities that are appropriate only for that planet. He who is wise in some other place in creation is a fool in the place where he lives.
>
> I do not at all have the ambition to want to be a seraph; my pride is only that I am a man. [20: 47]

Kant no longer sees physical cosmogony as the main avenue of his ambition. Newly instructed by Rousseau, he will direct his energies, instead, toward determining "the condition that best suits" us inhabitants of earth (the planet that revolves "200 solar widths from the sun").

And yet the question of what "best suits" human beings proves "difficult to decide":

> <whether> it <lies or> does not lie in nature, i.e., nature has not given us an impulse in this sense; rather, the impulses are artificial; none of these infirmities is innate; rather, they developed by accident. The other proposition is easier: it does not accord with nature, i.e., this is in conflict with what actually lies in nature. Rousseau often proceeds according to the first proposition, and because human nature has now acquired such a desolate form, natural foundations become dubitable and unknowable. [20: 48]

The above passage registers Kant's growing insight into how Rousseau's anthropological insights are best deployed. One can take the more difficult route, on which "Rousseau often proceeds," of trying to discover directly what "lies in" nature; or one can take the easier one of seeking what "accords" with nature. The first route is difficult because it is hard to determine what constitutes man's original endowment, owing to the artificial shapes that presently disguise it. As Rousseau himself observes at the beginning of the *Second Discourse*, humanity has acquired so "desolate" a form as to make its primitive outline almost irrecoverable.

1. *Observations on the Feeling of the Beautiful and the Sublime* [1764]

Observations can plausibly be read as an experiment along the provisionally "Rousseauist" lines that seeks what "lies in" (rather than what "accords with") nature. As such, *Observations* provides clues both to what Kant found unsatisfying in Rousseau on a first and second reading, and to the "rare" thought that Kant claimed to uncover on further reflection. In *Observations* Kant seems still to believe—naïvely, in retrospect—that nature is directly accessible through observation of the varieties of human taste.

That Kant claims in *Observations* to speak "more as an observer than a philosopher" [2: 207] already places him in an ambiguous position *vis-à-vis* his earlier claims as to the supreme value of speculative science. On the one hand, the essay's expressed goals are largely practical and civic: to improve aesthetic taste and help cultivate morality (or a "feeling for the beauty and the dignity of human nature" [2: 217]) in the society around him. He does not address an elite group of actual and potential "scientists," but the general literate public, male and female (or every potential "young world citizen" [2: 256]). At the same time, in treating "finer feeling" and its peculiarly "universal" pleasures, Kant specifically abstracts from the "even finer feeling" that he reserves to the few capable of genuine scientific inquiry [2: 208]. Distancing himself from his earlier position without necessarily wholly abandoning it, Kant stands somewhere between his earlier celebration of the poet-scientist and his decisive elevation, in the *Remarks,* of practical over theoretical aims. In short, *Observations* appears to mark the transition from Kant's earliest opinion of Rousseau, based on a first (and second) reading, to the final, more stable and considered view elaborated in the *Remarks*.

Kant's *Observations* presents the beautiful and the sublime as distinct, yet mutually dependent qualities that together reconcile the simplicity of nature with the refinement of the civilized. Each alone is lacking: Sublimity without beauty oversteps the bounds of nature and becomes "adventurous" or, at worst, "grotesque" (as with medieval knights and monks, respectively), while beauty without sublimity lacks seriousness and is merely pretty [2: 213–214]. "Crude" nature, on the other hand, is not necessarily beautiful even in this lesser way.

Finer feeling of a moral sort also involves a combination of beauty and sublimity. Among moral qualities, "true virtue alone is sublime" [2: 215]. Qualities like tenderheartedness are beautiful, inasmuch as they indicate "kindly participation in the fate of other people." Yet, tenderheartedness is also weak and sometimes blind—for example, when a tenderhearted person neglects duty out of pity for the less deserving [2: 216]. Only when benevolence is extended to the entire human race and becomes a "principle" to which one's affection is subordinated does moral disposition becomes genuinely virtuous:

> When universal affection toward the human race has become a principle in you, to which you always subordinate your actions, then love toward one who is needy still remains, only it has now been set, from a higher standpoint, in true relation to your entire [*gesammte*] duty. Universal affection is a ground of sympathy [*Theilnehmung*] for the ill he suffers, but also of the justice whose prescripts must forestall this action. [2: 216]

The feeling that accompanies virtue thus incorporates beauty as well:

> True virtue can only be grafted onto principles, such that the more general they are, the more sublime and noble they become. These principles are not speculative rules, but rather consciousness of a feeling that lives in every human breast and stretches much further than upon the particular grounds of sympathy and complaisance. I believe that I would grasp it all together [*fasse alles zusammen*] if I were to say it to be the **feeling of the beauty and the dignity of human nature**. The first is a ground of universal affection, the second of universal respect, and if this feeling should attain the greatest perfection in a human heart, this human being would, to be sure, love and esteem himself, but only insofar as he is one of all those over whom this broadened and noble feeling extends itself. Only if one were to subordinate one's own inclination to one so enlarged could our kindly [*gütige*] drives be used proportionately and bring about the noble bearing [*Anstand*] that is the beauty of virtue. [2: 217]

In thus combining beauty and dignity, moral feeling of the most genuine sort resembles aesthetic feeling at its height. The *distinction* between aesthetic and moral feeling remains crucial, however. Aesthetic feeling is a specific kind of "subjective" pleasure while virtue, and its accompanying "feeling of the beauty and dignity of human nature," registers the *subordination* of one's individual desire for pleasure to the claims of "universal affection" and an accompanying sense of justice.

Insofar as aesthetic taste is motivated by subjective feeling, while moral virtue subordinates subjective feeling to something universal, the aesthetic and the moral remain incommensurate. And yet each involves a capacity to transcend nature at its crudest without leaving nature as such behind. That finer feeling, broadly accessible to all cultivated men and women, now supplements the pleasures of the speculative intellect, which the *Universal Natural History* had presented as the sole means (other than through revelation) by which human beings can overcome the pull of animal desire (or a life devoted to "sucking fluid, propagating one's kind and dying" [1: 356]). Kant, in other words, no longer rests human dignity solely in the ability and willingness of some to undertake the arduous task of speculative inquiry.

But Kant is also not yet ready to make "establishing the rights of mankind" central to his understanding of what alone makes philosophic inquiry worthy of esteem.[8] Instead, *Observations* marks out an alternative position, in which human "dignity" is universally but unevenly distributed.

According to Kant's present account, a feeling for the "beauty and dignity of human nature" can be evoked "aesthetically" by a representation of the "fittingness" of a variety of human qualities. The portrayal of sublime virtue, beautiful tenderheartedness and complaisance, love of honor—even crude desire—all play a role in arousing this feeling, to which Kant's own "sketch" means, in its own way, to contribute [2: 227].

That virtue proper needs, or is aided by, these supplementary impulses makes the beauty and dignity of human nature all the more manifest [2: 234]. Drives like tenderheartedness bring about "beautiful actions" that would otherwise be stifled "by crude self-interest," and are "ennobled" by their "kinship" with the genuinely virtuous. And even crude self-interest contributes to the common good, albeit without intending it. Finally, "love of honor," which is "universally" but "unevenly" distributed, promotes a "hidden incentive" to judge one's actions from the standpoint of a universal spectator. By showing how these qualities all contribute to virtue's own universal end, Kant's proffered "portrait of the human race" exhibits the "beauty and dignity of moral nature," and thus arouses an aesthetic "feeling" similar in its way to moral virtue proper [2: 227]. In sum: *Observations* seems directed toward the beginnings of something like an "aesthetic education of the human race."

That "the most powerful impulses all derive from sexual desire" makes the latter especially significant to such a task. The "complementary drives," which "move some to beautiful actions even without principles" and give "greater impulse" and "impetus" to principles [2: 227] themselves, depend on finer feelings that derive from, or are "interwoven" with, sexual attraction [2: 234, 254]. The relation of the sexes is thus crucial, on Kant's present account, "for all education and instruction" and, indeed, as he puts it, for "all attempts at moral perfection" [2: 228].

Sections Three and Four of Kant's *Observations* are largely devoted to an elaboration of this striking claim. Section Three, "On the Difference between the sublime and the beautiful in the conter-relation [*Gegenverhältniß*] of the sexes," discusses how sexual love both contributes to, and obstructs, the moral perfection of men and women.

Kant's presentation is freighted, however, with a series of unresolved tensions between the claims of finer feeling and those of sexual inclination or impulse. On the one hand, we are told that sexual impulse is the source of all finer feeling between the sexes, and especially of the feminine beauty uniquely equipped to refine the feeling of men [2: 235]. On the other, we are told that finer feeling of the sort Kant has in mind and sexual impulse mustn't come "too near" each other [2: 237]. On the one hand, finer feeling depends on modesty and a related "secrecy" or "veiling" of the sexual act itself [2: 228, 234]. On the other, the most perfect relation requires that each sex esteem the other at his or her true value. Finally, the extraordinary and barely veiled candor with which Kant sketches out his own erotic ideal, and thus reveals his own deepest and most intimate feelings, is offset by the ironic suggestion that the woman to whom his (frustrated) longings are addressed is a refinement that overleaps the possibility of physical fulfillment, and in doing so destroys what Kant calls nature's "great intention." The woman in whom beauty and dignity most perfectly unite, and who might, as such, be thought most likely to stimulate, at least in men, moral feeling for the beauty and dignity of human nature, is herself, as Kant ultimately hints, in all likelihood an unnatural delusion [2: 238–239].

These tensions suggest that Kant was himself not yet fully clear as to the relation between sexual desire and moral perfection. He is not quite willing to follow Rousseau's reductively materialist hint in *Emile* that virtue is merely a refinement of sexual desire—a peculiar "distillation," to use Rousseau's own metaphor, of the animal "spirits" that accompany puberty. But Kant does go so far as to grant that the "finest" and "liveliest" of human inclinations are "engrafted" onto or draw life from this "most powerful" natural impulse. And, like Rousseau, he presents feminine "modesty" or "shame" as the mediating link between sexual desire and the development of virtue [2: 234–235].

Woman's modesty serves both to contain male desire and to increase it by preventing the "indifference" or "disgust" that too much "familiarity" would bring about. Refusal on a woman's part is thus an intrinsically ambiguous signal. A man cannot know whether a woman who refuses him is nobly transcending her own desire, or (ignobly) trying to stimulate his lust. There is, indeed, a further possibility linked to women's capacity for "finer feeling" of an aesthetic sort. A woman can simply find a man ugly or repulsive on aesthetic grounds. The most "sublime" women, it is true, will respond to men's character rather than their faces [2: 241]. But those whose "beauty" tends toward "charm" rather than "sublimity" will respond to, as they express, an attractiveness whose "moral" quality is "adoptive" rather than primary.

Kant's preferred version of feminine beauty is moral, rather than just pretty, and sublime, rather than just charming. Such beauty "seizes hold" of a man's inclination and esteem, arousing feeling on his part that is tender, respectful, and constant [2: 236]. It is, however, unclear, as we have seen, whether such women actually exist. And, as Kant immediately notes, qualities that make women's beauty *seem* sublime are easily feigned (e.g., by painting on a pale face).

Hence, the subject to which Kant's observations "naturally" lead [2: 238]— the difficulty of steering between coarseness of taste, that goes out to all women, and overrefinement, that "actually goes out to none"—is personally, as well as generally, pertinent. In the case of overrefinement, Kant says, one occupies oneself:

> with an object that enamored inclination creates in thought and decorates with all the noble and beautiful properties that nature seldom unites in one human being, and still more seldom leads to him who might be able to esteem them and who might perhaps be worthy of such a possession. [2: 239]

If finer feeling does not tap the root of natural (sexual) desire, it tends to break free of nature entirely, as with the "monkish" virtue that Kant associates with the false sublime. If sexual taste becomes too refined, it "misses nature's aim" and becomes similarly "sterile." And yet if sexual desire remains too crude, it fails to provide nourishment for those impulses that make virtue most effective in accomplishing its ends. Finally, if sexual taste remains at the level of the merely aesthetic (i.e., fails to "speak to the heart"), it reduces all too easily to vanity, or a concern for mere appearance.

Kant therefore advises "noble souls" to "refine feeling" to the utmost so far as it concerns themselves but to "maintain their taste in its simplicity" insofar as it concerns "what they . . . expect from others"—"if only," as he pointedly adds, he "saw how this were possible to achieve" [2: 239]. In short, Kant seeks, but has not yet found, a route to moral self-perfection that avoids the illusions of love or demanding more of women than can reasonably or naturally be expected.

Thus, in the end, the position staked out in *Observations,* for all the evident charm of Kant's own writing, is strikingly inconclusive. Sexual inclination, Kant insists, could serve to ennoble the male sex if women's "moral qualities" were more seasonably developed. She would then better recognize men's noble qualities, and in so doing reveal her own sublimity, for it is in treasuring men's noble qualities (despite the "grotesqueness" of their faces) that the sublimity of woman's soul uniquely shows itself [2: 241]. Such a woman (expert in the *human science* that, according to Kant, is woman's special province) would not only look beyond the physical defects of a man[9] to the noble qualities that shine through,[10] but herself supplement and complete them. Such a woman would, moreover, be uniquely teachable by a man of similarly elevated spirit and demeanor. As we are, however, reminded, "nature seldom unites all noble and beautiful qualities in one human being," and "even more seldom brings that human being to one who would be worthy of them."

This inconclusiveness is all the more significant, given the hopes with which his essay closes, hopes that apply especially to Europe's historical pre-eminence. Europe's superiority to the other continents lies, above all, in its appreciation for the moral side of female beauty and the unity of nature and ideal aspiration that this appreciation uniquely facilitates:

> The **European** alone has discovered the secret of embellishing the sensual charm of a mighty inclination with so many flowers and interweaving it with so much that is moral that he has not merely very much elevated its agreeableness as such but has also made it very decent. [2: 254]

The "decorating" and "interweaving" that both veil and elevate the charms of sexual desire recall Rousseau's own comparison of civil law to chains garlanded by flowers. Aesthetic culture of the sort Kant has in mind would substitute for civil rigors imperfectly disguised the sweeter charms of a natural desire made decorous through a mysterious process of "engraftment."

Section Four, on "national characters, in so far as they depend upon the distinct feeling of the sublime and beautiful," elaborates upon this central mystery. Only by virtue of a certain moral idealization of feminine beauty does Europe rise above the common human plane, in which beauty is no more than an object of sexual commerce. Only by virtue of this special taste is humanity rescued from a natural exchange in which man (and woman especially) is only a commodity.

Peoples of the non-European continents are distinguished from their European counterparts by two pertinent qualities: a lack of feeling for the morally beautiful, and the subjection of women.[11] (A single exception among the American savages is more than canceled by the labor with which their women are burdened [2: 255].) Though feeling for the sublime flourishes in Asia and America, only Europe mixes sublimity with beauty, and is thus fully open to the taste that Kant associates with moral feeling in its truest form.

As for the varied finer tastes of Europe, Germany emerges from Kant's discussion as a nation of peculiarly mixed status, be it owing to its "brilliant" and "splendid" sublimity, or to its central position, hedged between the sublimity of England and the beauty of France: the German, who has a special feeling for the sublime and beautiful "in combination," "happily" avoids the defects of excess strength on either side [2: 243–244, 248].

Where overheated and trifling Frenchmen esteem women too little, and cold, under-socialized Englishmen esteem women excessively, the German's cool and methodical approach to love [2: 248] lets him occupy his head with reflection on human appearances.[12] Where Frenchmen need more morally developed women if they are ever to improve, the sexually more matter-of-fact Germans need to develop their aptitude for spectatorship, above all, through elimination of linguistic awkwardness and stiffness that impedes the beautiful simplicity of their "way of writing [*Schreibart*]" [2: 249]. It is not difficult to see Kant's *Observations,* often praised as an early masterpiece of modern German style, as a conscious step in that direction.

As for the originality associated with the human genius (in which Germans have been heretofore deficient), a glance at history, according to Kant, reveals a taste for the sublime and beautiful arising in republican Greece and Rome, degenerating into splendor and then false shimmer under the Caesars, only to give way to a barbarian taste in which loftiness of spirit took the perverted form, in art, religion, and scholarship alike, of grotesquerie, adventurousness, and idleness. More recently, however, the human genius has happily lifted itself anew "from an almost complete destruction through a kind of palingenesis, so that we now see bloom forth [*aufblühen*] the correct [*richtigen*] taste of the beautiful and noble, as much in the arts and sciences as with regard to morals [*Sitten*]" [2: 256].

And yet the "problem" of education, as Kant finally admits, remains a secret "yet to be uncovered." If that problem is not solved, modern European "fineness" of feeling threatens to remain as "idle" as the brooding monkishness that it replaces. In that case, the history of taste would be nothing more than a "Proteus of ever changing shapes" [2: 255], i.e., it would lead nowhere.

In sum: Kant's appeal to "nature" in the *Observations* is, in the last analysis, abortive. Nature cannot serve directly as a standard of moral and aesthetic perfection for the very reason the *Remarks* later acknowledges: the deceptive shape of modern human beings. Nature cannot simply be identified with what delights or moves us, for our taste and feelings may be corrupted. And even nature, under civilized conditions, can give rise to "fantastic longings" that fail to correspond to anything real.

The difficulties that cloud the otherwise "charming" and "instructive" *Observations* serve to throw into relief the achievement of the *Remarks*. Newly resigned to the inaccessibility of human nature through the simple observation of current taste, Kant now turns to a hypothetical construction that he calls (following Rousseau) the "state of nature." This state can be defined as any condition in which free but dependent beings (like us) can coexist harmoniously—any condition, in the words of Rousseau, in which men can be good for themselves without ceasing to be good for others. This "state of freedom," as Kant also calls it, furnishes a new *Unterstützungspunkt*—an "Archimedean" point "neither outside the world nor in it"—from which to "move the emotions" of men. The "state of nature" is intended less as an historical depiction of our original situation than as the schema of a moral world in which human aspirations toward transcendence can express themselves effectually.

2. Reconstructing the Argument of *Remarks*

In a work as fragmentary and exploratory as *Remarks*, uncovering a single and consistent argument is especially difficult. Still, it is possible to reconstruct an internally consistent set of claims in keeping with the overall text. For purposes of attempting such a reconstruction, three passages are especially helpful. In the first, Kant states in stark terms—which recall the "melancholy" Heraclitus—the general problem posed by our condition:

> Everything passes by us in a flux, and the changing taste and shapes of man make the entire game [*Spiel*] uncertain and deceptive. Where will I find fixed [*feste*] points of nature that man can never disturb and that could give him marking signs concerning the bank on which he has to hold himself? [20: 46]

In echoing Heraclitus, Kant also indicates his dissatisfaction with his own earlier efforts. Without a coherent solution to the problem of education, the philosopher is reduced, as the *Observations* concluded, to mere observation of the "changing tastes" that go on around us, an ultimately trivial exercise that gives us no genuine purchase on the world. The solution here sketched lies in finding, in the face of such a flux, targets toward which to aim. Accordingly, Kant, like a seafarer with his astrolabe, seeks "fixed points of nature" by which to ascertain that shore.

> If <there> is some science which man [actually] needs [necessary for man], it is [the] the one that teaches him to occupy <or hold> <properly> the due place which was designated for him in creation and from which he can learn what [he] one must be in order to be a man. Supposing that he had become acquainted with [deceitful] deceptive allurements [over or] above and below him which, unnoticed, took him [out] out of his <proper> place, then this teaching will lead him back to the state of man once again [and], and, however small and imperfect he may find himself, he will [nonetheless] nonetheless be very good for the position that was designated for him because he [is neither more nor less than] will be <precisely> what he should be. [20: 45]

Given the constant tendency of events to dislodge us from this place, rediscovering it and remaining there requires, it seems, both knowledge and a distinct act of will.

Kant's past error (of which the *Universal Natural History* and *Observations* are in different ways guilty) lay in taking either (low) desire or (high) aspiration at face value.

> The error that consists in saying [one does not know any], "this is universal for us, so it follows that it is general everywhere" is easy for the intelligent to avoid. But the following judgments are even more pseudo-apparent: nature gave us the chance to have pleasure, so why not make use of it?; we have the aptitude for the sciences, so nature calls us to engage in their research; we feel in us a [moral] voice that says, "this is noble and right. It is a duty to act thus."
> [20: 39]

One cannot derive nature's standard directly from appearances: the corruption of human nature is such as to make current desires and aspirations a highly misleading guide. In their place, Kant proposes an anthropological version of the original Copernican hypothesis that, with the help of Newton, made the physical cosmic order newly visible.

a. Justifying Providence: Kant's First "Copernican Revolution"

As the physical illusion that the sun revolves around the earth gives rise to the false theory of Ptolemy, the moral illusion that the universe is made to suit our current inclinations makes "everything seem backward to us." We complain of a divine government that does not conform to our "futile wishes," instead of taking our unhappiness for a sign that they are out of step with nature's order.

> Newton was the first to view order and regularity bound up with great simplicity; before him, only disorder and poorly-arranged diversity were to be found, whereas, since then, comets travel in geometrical trajectories.
> Rousseau was the first to discover, beneath the diversity of humanly acquired shapes, their deeply hidden nature and the secret law whose observation justifies Providence. Before him, the objection of King Alphonso [way of Na] and Manes was still valid. After Newton and Rousseau, God is justified and the doctrine of Pope is henceforth true. [20: 58][13]

Providence should not be expected to agree with men who leave the order of nature:

> Providence is to be praised above all in that it is very much in harmony with the current condition of men; namely, their futile wishes do not correspond to the divine direction, they suffer on account of their follies, and nothing will harmonize with the man who steps outside of the order of nature. Consider the needs of animals and plants: Providence agrees with them. It would be very backwards if the divine government had to change the order of things according to the illusion of men insofar as the latter changes. It is also just as natural that, insofar as man leaves this order behind, everything must seem backward to him on account of his degenerate inclinations. [20: 56]

The major effect of this appearance of perversity is a "false" theology, at once credulous and crude, that encourages an attitude of slavish submissiveness:

> From this illusion, a type of theology arises as a phantom of the brain belonging to luxury (for this is always [fuller] weak and superstitious) and also as a certain shrewdness or prudence that, through one's submission, weaves the Highest into one's affairs and projects. [20: 57]

King Alphonso and Manes (i.e., Manicheus) had famously complained that the Ptolemaic universe was too ill-constructed to shed much glory on its maker. Kant finds, through Rousseau, a law whose "observation" justifies providence and thus completes the task begun by Newton's observation of the physical laws of motion. In "justifying providence," Kant's new science corrects a false theodicy that, as we shall see, poses a particularly grave obstacle to human happiness.

Newton's constructive methods serve here as an especially useful model. Beginning, like Rousseau, with the dual insight or assumption that man is free and nature good, Kant is led (beyond Rousseau) to the discovery of a moral principle of "return," comparable to Newton's law of motion (For every action, there is an equal and opposite reaction). Like a cresting river that creates new banks as it recedes, "evils cannot be brought to their highest point without the balance swinging back to the other side" [20: 107]. Neither virtue nor corruption can increase indefinitely in human nature [20: 105]; likewise, "the corruption of one is the generation of another" [20: 137].

Discovery of such a law yields the prospect of making conscious and deliberate use of it. More optimistic than Rousseau as to the self-regulating possibilities of collective human nature, Kant claims an Archimedean point from which the laws of nature and those of freedom can be made to work in tandem. If Rousseau's "starting point" is "to move the best talents through love" [20: 50], Kant sets his fulcrum, instead, in the state of (natural) freedom: To the question—"whether, to move my or other *emotions* [Affecten], I should take a fulcrum point outside the world or within it"—he answers: "I find [that point] in the state of nature, that is, of freedom" [20: 56].

If nature is good and man free, than a state of ordered freedom must make up man's original endowment. Kant's state of nature is best understood not as an historical description of man's earliest condition (though it is may also be that), but as an intellectual construction based on the premise that freedom in harmony with itself is naturally possible. Like Newton's frictionless universe in which "for every action, there is an equal and opposite reaction," Kant's state of nature depicts a condition in which the social forces of attraction and repulsion stand in perfect equilibrium.

b. Freedom and the State of Nature

Kant's state of nature takes several forms. The simple version (the "original" state of nature) is a state of ordered freedom (or freedom in harmony with itself), assuming the development of only those capacities necessary for human life at its most primitive.

The state of nature so understood yields two formal "touchstones" or criteria on the basis of which the "naturalness" of current human practices and institutions can be judged, however much the "changing tastes" of men may have drifted from their original form:

> Two touchstones of the difference between the natural and the unnatural: 1) whether it is appropriate to what one cannot change; 2) whether it could be common to all human beings or only a few, with oppression of the rest.
>
> [20: 35]

The first of these "touchstones" asks whether the practice in question suits what cannot be changed; the second asks whether it can be common to all, or whether, rather, its enjoyment by a few would injure the rest. The first, in short, looks to necessity, or the limits of what is physically possible; while the second calls for justice understood as a certain rule of equality. Together, these two criteria reveal whether or not a given practice "accords with" nature, i.e., is consistent with the possibility of ordered freedom under human conditions of dependence in its various forms. As the state of nature constitutes an Archimedean point, within the flux of human affairs, that neither man nor nature can dislodge, so Kant's two touchstones indicate the place along the shore toward which man, submitted to that flux, should aim.

Withal, Kant assumes two fundamentally different sorts of human powers. First, man, as a "dependent" being, has passive needs along with the accompanying desires and pleasures necessary to move him to provide for them. Second, man, as a free being, possesses "active" force that issues forth spontaneously. Such active force, as we shall see, is double-edged. Especially in its more developed forms, it allows man to "poeticize" and otherwise take pleasure in the active exercise of freedom. Among these pleasures is the peculiar joy and self-esteem that accompanies awareness of one's status as a "free ground of the good." For a free, uncorrupted being, to so act has a higher worth than any secondary good that might arise from it. On the other hand, man's freedom allows him to deviate from the simple order of nature, both by leading him to want more than nature readily provides and by bringing him into potential conflict with the wills of others. Man's unhappiness is thus a function of his freedom wrongly used and misdirected.

A remarkable passage bearing the title "on freedom" explains the relation between freedom and the peculiar misery to which human beings are uniquely susceptible. The greatest terror for a human being who has not been "corrupted" is the prospect of submission to another will:

> Man depends on many <external> things [partly for satisfaction], whatever condition he finds himself in. . . . He depends at all times on certain things through his needs and on other things through his greed, and because he is <indeed> the administrator of nature but not its master, he must <prefer to>

Kant's Archimedean Moment

> [to send often in the yoke of necessity, and submit to the order of nature and conform himself to its laws, if it] conform himself to the constraint that nature imposes because he does not find that nature always wants to conform to his desires. What is far harder <and unnatural> than this yoke of necessity is the [dependency] submission of one man to the will of another. There is no misfortune more terrible, for him who would be [is] used to freedom <and who would have enjoyed the good that freedom brings> than [oneself under] to see oneself delivered over to a creature of his own species who could force him (to abandon his own will) to do whatever he wants. [20: 91]

What accounts for the singular horror of dependence on another will? Kant's answer is twofold.

First, the ills of nature are regular and law-like, allowing us to decide either to expend our force against them, or, if necessary, to endure them as the lesser evil. The ills arising from dependence on another will are, by contrast, unpredictable:

> All other [natural evils follow laws] natural evils are still submitted to certain laws that man becomes acquainted with in order later to choose how far one yields to them or desires to submit oneself to them. The heat of the burning sun, the raw wind, and the movements of the waters always allow man to imagine something that would protect him from these things . . . [20: 92]

If, one has once been "free" in this way:

> nothing can open up to me a more atrocious prospect of sorrow and despair than that in the future my condition should not depend on my own will but on the will of another. [I imagine only the extreme cold] It is extremely cold today: I can go out or stay at home, as it pleases me; but the will of another does not determine what is most agreeable to me <but>, this time, <to him>. I want to sleep, so he awakens me. I want to relax or play, so he makes me work. The wind that rages outside forces me to flee into a cave, but, here or elsewhere, it finally leaves me in peace; yet my lord visits me and, because the cause of my unhappiness has reason, he is far more capable of tormenting me than are all the elements. I even presuppose that he is good: what assures me that he will not change his mind? The movements of matter do obey a certain determinate rule, but the stubbornness of man has no rule. [20: 92–93]

But dependence holds a terror deeper than that arising from external danger:

> In submission [also some], there is not only a dangerous exterior element but [some] yet a certain ugliness and a contradiction that at the same time

> indicates its illegitimacy. An animal is not yet a complete being because it is not conscious of itself and, if its impulses and inclinations do, or do not, meet resistance on the part of another, it certainly feels it as an evil, but the evil has at every moment disappeared for him and he does not know of his own existence. But assume that, in the same way, man himself does not need a soul, and [through a] has no will of his own, and that the soul of another moves my members—this is absurd and backwards: even in our constitution, we scorn every man who is in submission to a high degree.... Instead of freedom seeming to elevate me above the beast, it puts me even more below it because I can be constrained better. [20: 93]

The human advantage of self-consciousness implies a capacity to choose between resisting pain or submitting to it as the "lesser evil" (i.e., exercise what Kant will much later call an "economy of reason"). As in Rousseau's *Emile*, freedom and the acceptance of necessity (in the form of certain natural laws of action and reaction) do not stand in opposition. My freedom is challenged not by natural necessity but by the "stubborn" indeterminacy of other wills—an unpredictability that makes my own will indeterminate in turn. To have in prospect the direction of one's actions by another will is thus to be unable to think of oneself as a determinate or "complete" being.

But how do we know that such a preference for freedom so understood over all other, merely passive satisfactions, is not itself the product of a corrupted imagination? The answer presumably lies in its meeting the two tests earlier described: to so value freedom does not contradict what can't be changed (and thus lies within the limits of the physically possible) and it can be acted on without oppressing others (and thus lies within the limits of the morally possible).

On the first point: For ordered freedom to exist under primitive conditions, individuals must there be able to satisfy their own basic needs and reproduce without oppressing or exploiting others. Kant calls this primitive capacity "natural sufficiency [*Gnugsamkeit*]" and the accompanying limitation of desire to what can be readily procured "natural simplicity [*Einfalt*]." Moreover, for such conditions to obtain for any length of time, men must not only have been relatively self-sufficient but also have actively desired to remain so. Ordered freedom under primitive conditions thus requires that man be naturally equipped with sufficiency, simplicity, and a desire for freedom capable of resisting the allure of passive pleasure.

On the second point: Primitive men could express a preference for freedom over all other, merely passive, pleasures without denying others like expression.

This conclusion follows both from the ability of men, under primitive conditions, to disperse almost without limit, and from the lack of incentive, given the general simplicity of taste under such conditions, to take a woman belonging to another man (women constituting, in Kant's view, the most primitive form of property).

c. Civilization: Discontents and Remedies

Civilized man goes wrong in two directions. We seek unnecessary pleasures that undermine our capacity for passive satisfaction; and we pursue false ideals that exhaust our active powers in ineffectual longing. These twin vices of luxury and moral illusion can be traced to the same source: the expansion of desire by imagination or a faculty for invention [*erdichten*]. This power to invent is, as we have seen, deeply ambiguous in its implications for human happiness and perfection; on the one hand, it ennobles feeling by enabling us to respond not just passively, to what we sense, but actively, to what we ourselves create. In so doing, imagination renders taste "spiritual" and "ideal" ([20: 117]; see also [20: 18]), but it also liberates desire from the constraints of natural simplicity. As men become less simple in their tastes, they become less and less able to satisfy even their necessary wants. The strong are increasingly led to exploit the weak, and the weak have an increasing incentive to submit. Additionally, as men become more and more focused on general means to satisfy their ever more expansive desires, they are ever more tempted to take means for final ends—e.g., the miser who pursues money or the courtier who pursues outward honor for its own sake.

In sum: Civilized life has a corrupting effect on both the passive and the active powers of the human soul. It increases our passive desires beyond the point of natural sufficiency; it thus makes us more physically dependent, and in so doing leads us either to wish to exploit others or to be willing to submit to them. At the same time, civilization weakens, through vanity, laziness and ignorance, those active powers of the soul in which our freedom is immediately expressed.

Kant's solution to the dilemma of civilization lies in using the "state of nature" as a device for generating ideals that address our longings while confining them within the limits of the physically and morally possible.

1. WISE SIMPLICITY. Kant's first ideal, "wise simplicity," seeks to restore, under civilized conditions, the sufficiency and simplicity of taste that enabled

primitive man to be "content with little." The man of wise simplicity is capable (unlike the savage man) of "ideal feeling" and its accompanying pleasures; but he is also able (unlike the luxurious man) to "dispense with" these pleasures when they conflict with his true "needs." Such self-restraint can thus be thought of as an exercise in prudence, undertaken with a view to maximizing one's total satisfaction. The man of wise simplicity permits himself those ideal pleasures that are consistent with his power to physically satisfy himself more generally. By recognizing and accepting these necessary limits, the wise are able to cultivate their active powers and their accompanying pleasures without compromising their own natural sufficiency. Unlike the ignorantly simple, the wise are armed against temptation and thus enjoy the added satisfaction of knowing that their sufficiency is secure. Wise simplicity, to be sure, requires strength of soul (or "virtue" of a kind)—i.e., a certain self-control and the ongoing vigilance needed to sustain it.

The man of wise simplicity, so understood, has what Kant calls a "sensitive [*gefühlvolle*] soul at rest" [20:3]. By "sensitive" Kant here has in mind not only passive sense but also a feeling fully expressive of the active powers of the soul. By "rest" he means the serenity of mind that accompanies the knowledge that one is ready for whatever fortune may present, i.e., that one's natural "sufficiency," or power to satisfy desires consistent with one's unchangeable needs, remains intact.

II. VIRTUE. But "tranquility" of soul is evidently not enough. Kant wonders, in one late passage, whether the doctrine of wise simplicity might not suffice to ground morality in general:

> The question arises whether all of morality could be derived through the soul at rest, meaning, of course, in the natural man. Amusements and debaucheries are against peace. The sexual inclination finds peace only in marriage. Offending others disquiets oneself. *Emotions* in general disquiet. It is too bad that no other man profits from this *morality*. <Besides the fact that it is already a great virtue not to do evil.> [20: 154]

Though it does no harm, serenity of soul falls short of requiring that we actively contribute as much as we might to a good beyond our own. More seems demanded of us. How can we be sure that this demand does not constitute a "moral illusion," or the taking of "a possible moral perfection for a real one"? [20: 173] Consider the moral expectation that one take immediate interest in the good of others. Is this expectation warranted? Or might there be an alternative understanding of moral sacrifice that yields a more "realistic" human standard?

In attempting such an alternative understanding, Kant begins from the observed fact that we take special, positive pleasure in the sheer exercise of free activity:

> We take pleasure in certain perfections of ours, but much more so when we ourselves are the cause. And this pleasure is the greatest when we are the freely acting cause. [20: 144]

This pleasure makes it possible to "override" our concern with passive satisfaction whenever it comes into conflict with free activity as such.

> The capacity to recognize something like perfection in others does not mean that we ourselves feel pleasure from it. But if we do have the feeling of having pleasure here, we will also be inclined to desire it and to use our powers for it. The question is therefore to know if we immediately feel pleasure at the good of others or if, in fact, the immediate desire in the possible exertion of our powers consists in promoting it. Both cases are possible, but which is real? Experiment/experience teaches that, in the simple condition, a human being considers the happiness of others with indifference; but if he promoted it, it would please him infinitely more. Other people's trouble is ordinarily just as indifferent; but if I cause the trouble, it hurts me. It is the same if someone else caused it. In what concerns the sympathetic instincts of compassion and favor, we have good reason to believe that only great efforts to remedy the troubles of others—born of the approval that the soul gives itself—produce these sentiments.
>
> The feeling of pleasure and displeasure concerns either that with which we are passive, or it concerns ourselves as an active *principle,* through freedom, of good and evil. The latter is the moral feeling. Past physical evil [hurts] delights us, but past moral evil saddens us, and the type of joy about the good that happens to us is altogether different from that about what we do. [20: 144]

Of two possible accounts of moral feeling—immediate sympathy with the pleasure and pain of others, or pleasure in our own active promotion of the good—only the latter is consistent with natural simplicity and hence "real." Sympathy, for its part, is "artificial" except under "rare" conditions.

Understanding moral feeling as an expression of the supreme value of freedom helps explain our sense of a morally good will as good "immediately," and apart from any further good it may accomplish, either for the agent or for others whom he seeks to help:

> Because the greatest inner perfection, and all perfection that arises from it, consists in the subordination of the whole of the faculties and receptivities to the free power of choice, the feeling for the *goodness* of the free will must immediately be completely different from, and also greater than, all the good consequences that can be *actualized* through it. [20: 145]

The morally good will is thus fully "praiseworthy" whether or not it realizes its object because in either case what ultimately matters is subordination of all else to the "free power of choice." Anticipating his later characterization of good will in the *Groundlaying* as the only thing "that could be held good without limitation" that "it is possible to think," Kant writes:

> The entire conditioned goodness of an action depends on either a possible condition (as it is for problematic questions) or on an actual condition (as it is for rules of prudence: everyone wants to be reasonable). However, in mediated or conditioned goodness, willing *per se* is not good so long as the necessary strength and right circumstances of time and place are missing. The will is good insofar as it is efficacious; but one can also consider this goodness insofar as it depends on the will alone. Strength may be lacking; the will, however, is still praiseworthy. With regard to great deeds, it is enough only to have willed them. Insofar as it is left undetermined whether or not the will is efficacious, this absolute perfection is called moral. [20: 148]

Kant's understanding of good will as unconditionally good, combined with his earlier discussion of the overriding value of (ordered) freedom, yields the following new definition of moral perfection:

> The will is perfect insofar as it is, according to the laws of freedom, the greatest ground of the good in general. Moral feeling is the feeling for this perfection of the will. [20: 136]

Or, alternatively:

> To *subordinate* everything to free will [*Willkühr*] is the greatest perfection. And the perfection of the free will, as cause of possibility, is far greater than all other causes of the good, even if they brought forth its actuality [*Wirklichkeit*]. [20: 144]

Unlike the "unnatural" and "unreal" expectation that men immediately sympathize with the feelings of others, Kant's new standard of moral perfection builds on rules that govern primitive man, albeit unwittingly, inasmuch as he prefers death to slavery and refrains from taking what belongs to others. Accordingly, the most perfect will is that which maximizes a general good that includes as its *sine qua non* the harmonious general exercise of freedom itself. Such a standard is appropriate to human conditions of dependence, because the delight we take in our own free activity outweighs passive satisfaction without denying the necessity of our concern for it.

Promotion of the greatest good consistent with laws of freedom thus sets a formal limit to the moral goodness of a will under (human) conditions of dependence. An effort to bring about the "greatest good" will place universal freedom ahead of all other, lesser goods however much they may otherwise contribute to human satisfaction. We are morally required to sacrifice our (passive) happiness only when it comes at the expense of freedom, whether our own or someone else's. The laws of freedom trump the necessities that flow from man's natural condition of dependence.

The duty thus to sacrifice constitutes what Kant calls a "moral need":

> The *duties of beneficence* can never in themselves bring it about that one dispense with one's own needs, but the *duties of obligation*, because they are moral needs, can indeed [do so]. [20: 128]

"Moral necessity" so understood transforms the principle that implicitly regulates the original state of nature (maximize the good, consistent with the laws of freedom!) into an explicit obligation. The maximum that can be morally demanded is exceeded, according to this rule, whenever man is asked to sacrifice his freedom for the merely passive happiness of others.

The "feeling of justice" expressed by this demand imparts a sense of moral certitude comparable to the logical certitude secured by science. The "natural obligation" that arises from this rule has a measure that is easy to determine:

> Obligation that is <natural toward men> has a determinate measure; the duty to love does not. The former consists in nothing more happening than what I myself induced another to want, and in giving him only what is his. Consequently everything according to such an action is equal. (Sympathy is excepted from this.) [20: 157]

Duties of benevolence or sympathy, by way of contrast, come into play only when one has more forces than he requires to satisfy his needs while others remain needy. In this case, moral feeling, or a feeling for "the perfection of the will," prompts us to use our additional strength on their behalf. Kant's definition of moral perfection thus yields a general criterion for recognizing genuine duties of benevolence: Such duties are "true," rather than "chimerical" or "idle," whenever the additional force expended increases the "general good"—a good of which universal freedom is the *sine qua non*.

> We have sentiments that are self-interested and those that are for the common interest. The former are older than the latter, which first arise with the sexual inclination. Man has needs, but also mastery over them. Man in the state of nature is more capable of sentiments that are for the common interest as well as active; man in the state of luxury has imaginary needs and is self-interested. One takes part more in the misfortune of others, above all in the injustice they suffer, than in their well-being. The sympathetic sentiment [*theilnehmende Empfindung*] is true when it is equal to the forces of the common interest, otherwise it is chimerical. It is general in an indeterminate way insofar as it is directed toward anyone I can help; it is true in a determinate way when directed to help anyone who suffers. The latter is chimerical. Goodheartedness arises from the *cultivation* of the moral, but inactive, sentiments and is a moral illusion. [20: 172–173]

Natural man, who has greater forces than he needs, "is more capable" than luxurious man of active sentiments "for the common interest" though he has fewer occasions to express them. And civilized man, who has more forces still, will be yet more perfect to the extent that his additional desires remain "dispensable"— as with the man of wise simplicity.

Together, duties of obligation and benevolence define a moral standard capable of guiding the will with due appreciation for both man's condition of dependence and his (spiritual) need to regard himself as a free being. Unlike the fantastic goals induced by luxurious and artificial tastes (e.g., "goddesses" of love), Kant's new standard makes room for "sacrifice" [20: 3] without overstepping the necessary limits that are imposed by our condition of dependency. In so doing, Kant avoids what he identifies as the twin pitfalls of crudeness and moral illusion—i.e., of a morality "that affirms only self-interest" and one that "wants loud disinterestedness" [20: 173].

In sum: The *Remarks* advances two "natural" standards of perfection, each with its own crude and civilized versions. The first ideal—simplicity—arises either directly from impulse (the simplicity of "ignorance") or from impulse guided by the rule of prudence (the simplicity of "wisdom"). The second, higher ideal—moral perfection of the will—applies the extra force at the disposal of a naturally or wisely sufficient human being in a way that maximizes the general good consistent with the laws of freedom. The order that informs the state of nature at its crudest gives formal guidance to the higher state of freedom that applies when men's faculties are more fully developed. Moral feeling can thus be thought of as a feeling for the presence in us of a "general will" directed (like the sexual drive that is its physical counterpart [20: 168]) to the perfection of the whole. To feel oneself to be in sympathy or "consensus" with that general will is to feel oneself to be a free cause or greatest possible ground of the general good—i.e., to achieve moral "perfection" of the will to the extent that it is humanly possible.

There arises, however, this difficulty. Duties of benevolence, though real, are never determinate, because in the case of duties of this kind (unlike those of "justice"), we cannot know for sure which acts contribute most to the "general good." Whether I best maximize the good, consistent with laws of freedom, by helping this or that particular unfortunate remains a guess. No freedom-robbing act of injustice, by way of contrast, can ever be the object of a good will, whatever other goods that act might bring about.

Moral perfection is directed, then, toward the actualization of an ideal that is only partly specified. Just as the sexual drive naturally contributes to the physical perfection of the species without sexually driven individuals necessarily intending such a good, so moral feeling contributes to the general good without morally motivated individuals necessarily having it in mind:

> Providence has certainly given us . . . moral feeling for sake of the perfection of the whole, yet in such a way that it is not thought of wholesale [*in der Grösse*], just as we have the sexual drive toward reproduction without [having] to *intend* it. [20: 168]

The good will is the will that feels itself to be in harmony or "consensus" with providence so understood. The moral order by which the good will takes its bearings is the order that would prevail if laws of freedom were universally obeyed, men's passive desires were limited to their needs, and all surplus force devoted to the perfection of the whole.

What can reason tell us about the concrete content of such a will? In a late series of passages, Kant suggests a formula for moral order based on an analogy with the laws of Newton:

> The drive for honor is grounded on the drive toward equality and the drive toward unity. They are, as it were, two forces that move the animal world. The instinct toward unity is either unity in judgments and thoughts, or also in inclinations. The former leads to logical perfection, the latter to moral perfection.

> The single natural, necessary good of a human being in relation to the will of others is equality (freedom), and *with respect* to the whole, unity. *Analogy.* Repulsion [*Zurückstoßung*], through which a body fills its own space just as another fills its own. Attraction [*Anziehung*], through which all parts combine into one. . . .
>
> The natural instincts for active benevolence toward others consist in love towards the fair sex [*das Geschlecht*] and towards children. Kindness towards other human beings lies merely in equality and unity.
>
> There is unity in the *sovereign* state but not equality. Equality combined with unity constitutes the perfect *republic*. [20: 165–166]

The forces of attraction and repulsion that inform the physical universe supply models for constructing an analogous moral whole, in which repulsion (or the drive for equality) and attraction (or the drive for unity) stand in a similarly conceivable dynamic balance exemplified in the idea of what Kant calls the "perfect republic." Without unity, the drive for equality would result, presumably, in an infinite dispersion, as human beings strove to avoid domination and submission. The sovereign state (or absolute monarchy) provides a counterforce that binds men together into a unity without granting their equality as citizens. Without the compensating mutual "repulsion," the drive toward unity results in sovereignty without equality and an "active benevolence" that is appropriate only toward one's natural dependents (i.e., women and children). The perfect republic is thus an idea, or invention of reason, that escapes the charge of artifice by remaining true to nature, albeit in a peculiarly expanded sense that builds on an analogy with the structure of the known physical world.

The idea of the republic suits Kant's purpose in a deeper way by suggesting a solution to the unstable dynamic that arises from the tension between sexual desire (or the force of "attraction") and the (male) love of freedom (or the force of "repulsion"). Men fight, first and foremost, over and for the sake of women. The war of all against all therefore finds a satisfying conclusion in a regime that recognizes the formal equality of all while elevating adult men to a civic status from which women and children are excluded [20: 21, 50, 74, 98, 103].

III. SEXUAL MODESTY. Kant's resolution of the tension between sexual desire and the love of freedom goes together with a newly chastened understanding of feminine perfection and the sort of love that women can properly be expected to inspire in men. All feminine beauty, he now insists, is rooted in sexual attraction, a fact that he acknowledges with an edge of warning:

> Voluptuous love is the reason for the sexual inclination. That is why, when this is not presupposed, all the beautiful and the sublime in this type of love is only a phantom of the brain. The husband must be a man by day and night. This remark also serves as a warning about tender and respectful love between the sexes, for the latter often degenerates into an outbreak of voluptuousness. [20: 76]

The husband must be "a man" by night as well as day if he is to have his wife's respect. Woman's greater sexual capacity, and accompanying inability to transcend her sexual desires without unhappiness, is a fact of life that wise men will acknowledge among themselves, if not openly discuss in mixed company.

Republican civic life (rather than the ideal woman sketched in *Observations*) now serves as the model of the sublime and beautiful united:

> In all that concerns the sensation of the beautiful or the sublime, the best we can do is to let ourselves be guided by the model of the ancients: in sculpture, architecture, poetry and eloquence, in ancient morals, and in the ancient political constitution. The ancients were closer to nature; we have much frivolous or luxurious or servile corruption between us and nature. Our age is the *century* of beautiful trifles and *bagatelles*, or of sublime *chimeras*. [20: 71]

Kant traces inequality of honor among men to the primitive relation of the sexes and the competition among men to which those relations necessarily give rise. Under the simplest conditions, the combined effect of male and female nature is domestic unity in isolation:

> The man who has a woman is *complete*, separates himself from his parents, and, in the state of nature, is alone. He is so disinclined to associate with others that he even fears the approach of another. Thus the state of war
> *Hobbes* [20:74].

The "complete" human being is not only self-aware but also a member of a sexually differentiated couple. Women are thus the original form of property, a status to which their own sexual and maternal needs incline them to willingly submit. Man, in turn, "has a natural need to acquire a wife [*Frau*]." This desire breeds a concern for equal honor on the part of men: To keep a wife a man "needs the opinion not of superiority, but of equality, with other men." That opinion "comes easily," and yet proves fragile. The drive for honor soon exceeds equality, "in part because freedom is more assured," in part because the man "begins to prefer one woman to another and so that she also prefer him" [20: 163]. Still, the drive for unequal honor is kept in check, under primitive conditions, by isolation and an accompanying crudeness of sensibility. Man, as Kant says, "must already be civilized if he is to choose a wife in accordance with taste" [20: 29].

Under luxurious conditions, by way of contrast, taste develops to the utmost. Unnecessary pleasures become indispensable, and unequal honor, the desire for which initially arises as a means to sexual pleasure, becomes desired for its own sake. The civilized drive for honor will be "true" where it remains governed by a love of freedom, as in Sparta. In luxurious countries, on the other hand, "where freedom is lost":

> the honor of artificial need becomes more and more necessary. At the same time, the honor of illusion arises mostly with respect to sexuality, to which, at last, that honor which is a means to pleasure is sacrificed. [20: 163–164]

The Spartan drive for honor remains benign because it is linked to the maintenance of "freedom" rather than with "artificial need." In luxurious countries, on the other hand, women's natural ability to make men think women "better and more pleasant than they are" [20: 64] encourages pursuit of an illusory honor to which pleasure itself is ultimately sacrificed. Men make "goddesses" of their love—or merely pretend to, making fools, in turn, of women.

Kant's recapitulation here of the Rousseauist critique of solon society and other features of contemporary courtly and aristocratic life lays special stress on the susceptibilities of the male imagination [20: 68–75]. Kant attributes the tendency of men to "divinize" women to a secret shame in sacrificing freedom to their own sexual desire and the female will that governs it:

> Because the sexually aroused man chooses the woman as his ruler, he imagines her very marvelous, for one does not submit to a miserable goddess; conversely, the woman wants to rule. *Spectator:* sea-kitten [*Meerkätchen*]. *Applied* to the hidden mystery of all tender inclination toward the fair sex.
> [20: 131][14]

Addison's *Spectator* had likened the then-fashionable woman's bustle to an Egyptian temple erected to house a "little black monkey." Kant extends the comparison to cover the entire "mystery of all tender inclination" toward the female sex. Without dwelling on Kant's striking choice of image, one can say this much: Sexual and religious illusion both arise, on his account, from a common tendency toward idol worship, or the confusion of material and spiritual objects of attraction.

Rather than allow male disillusionment to run its unhappy course, Kant proposes a prophylactic bath of sexual disillusion, combined with a new feminine ideal that is both more realistic and more favorable to human freedom. The man instructed by Kant's science will recognize that woman's greater sexual desire is necessary to the order of the whole. Were they not originally so endowed, women living in the crudest conditions would have been subject to rape (as Lucretius, for his part, assumes), and the original state of nature would not be a state of freedom. And were women not naturally endowed with a capacity and desire to deceive, their greater desire, uncloaked by modesty, would render them unattractive to men.

The knowing will adapt their expectations to this necessity. The perfect woman, newly and rightly understood, uses her natural endowments to maintain a home, to care for others, and to flatter men. A wise man will not see the ordinary qualities of women as weaknesses but as providentially supportive of an orderly domestic life. He will appreciate their aptness at household economy. He will see courage in their loyalty, prudence in their coyness, and magnanimity in their flattery, especially when it masks their own inevitable physical frustration.

In sum: By frankly acknowledging women's needs, Kant's new domestic ideal counters the false expectations of female virtue with which *Observations* had flirted. Like the ideal of wise simplicity, that of perfected domesticity freely reinstates the natural limits that would automatically obtain under primitive conditions. By making these limits a matter of deliberate choice, civilized domesticity (like wise simplicity) "perfects" an orderly condition that originally obtained without anyone needing to intend it.

Women can be "consoled" for their frustration through satisfaction of their vanity. Put less abrasively: Virtue is for men what outer honor is for women; insofar as women's desire for honor exceeds their physical desire, they can make men more chaste than women are themselves. Woman can thus be regarded as a kind of "whetstone," who sharpens the edge of virtue without herself possessing it. "*Frangere vix cotis* [the sharpening of the side suffices] [20: 109], prompting the development of what Kant calls the "helpful instinct of chastity [*Keuschheit*]," an instinct through (or along with) which he would "plant human beings" [20: 108].

Those who want to make a "friendship out of marriage" unreasonably and unjustly demand a "self-overcoming" of which women are incapable:

> There are far more men who have cause to praise the magnanimity of women who do not exercise the right which nature gives them to satisfy her reasonable [*billige*] claims on her husband, perhaps through other men, than there are men who could complain. With many enervated men there also arises a

ridiculous or chimerical marriage project [*Eheproject*], according to which they want to make a friendship out of marriage and demand from the wife great virtues for self-overcoming of those stirrings which are reasonable and cannot be quieted. [20: 109]

Woman is "not so very virtuous that she is capable of making men virtuous." Still, she is "the greatest means of chastity in men, for an inconstant man is not made more chaste by anything other than love for a girl" [20: 109].

Women's coldness, rightly understood, becomes an "excellence" that calls forth the virtue of men by giving it an "object":

if the woman herself were virtuous, the exercise of masculine virtue [toward] would not have any object, for she would then be able to do without it.
[20: 109]

Perhaps, Kant muses, "this is a hidden cause of why we are always so attached to woman, whether we like it or not."

What, then, is chastity, for Kant? It does not imply a "lack of amorous passion," which would represent an imperfection, but consists either in "mediated modesty [*Schamhaftigkeit*]" or in "a concern to scorn one's sexual properties" arising from a "general concept of honor." The latter involves, in turn, either a "simple concern not to attract ignominy" or, insofar as it is "tied to sincerity," "a tender susceptibility to an inner self-reproach." When Kant calls chastity "the best preserver of virtue," he seems to have this peculiar susceptibility to self-reproach in mind [20: 96].

Chastity, then, is a kind of inner honor, concerned less with the opinion of others than with an inner appreciation of the tension between sexual desire and a self-esteem rooted in self-mastery. Kant turns this tension to related use when he urges that we imagine rulers and others whom we are overly inclined to venerate engaging in marital intercourse—a prime reason, he suggests, for the Church's insistence on priestly celibacy [20: 138]. That tension, as we have seen, arises from men's need to find a higher purpose for their sexual properties than brute satisfaction, an end they properly find debasing, prompting them to falsely divinize the woman who attracts them. The tension can be resolved, within marriage (if at all) through men's enlightened dedication of their sexual properties to purposes that transcend brute satisfaction without succumbing to romantic mystification—purposes such as procreation, the promotion of wifely fidelity and "respect," and men's own mental and moral hygiene—in sum, serenity of soul in its many facets.

IV. RELIGION. The human tendency to falsely idealize the object of a desire of which one is secretly ashamed also supports religious illusion, with respect not only to priests but also to religious faith more generally. The "theology of fantasy" encourages the belief that we can bend the natural order to our own individual purposes through prayer and other acts of flattering submissiveness to God. This attitude of "sly subjection" draws strength from the illusion that the natural order is out of joint in a way that calls for God's direct interference to set things right. Kant's new theodicy, by way of contrast, shows that man's present suffering is a sign of nature's goodness:

> Providence is to be praised above all in that it very well agrees with human beings in their current condition; namely, their inane wishes do not correspond to the direction [*Direktion*], they suffer on account of their follies and nothing harmonizes with human beings who step out of the order of nature. We see the needs of animals and plants; providence provides for them. It would be quite perverse if divine governance were to change according to the illusions of humanity as though it altered the order of things. It is thus even natural that so far as he departs from it in accordance with his degenerate inclinations, everything must appear perverse to him.
>
> Out of this illusion arises a kind of theology as a fantasy [*Hirngespinst*] of luxury (because this is always [more completely] soft and superstitious) and also as a certain slyness or prudence from subjection which introduces the Highest into one's affairs and projects. [20: 57]

By "changing positions"—i.e., by adopting the standpoint of a "general will" that intends the greatest good—one dispels the "pre-Copernican" illusion that places our own individual concerns at the center of things. When one adopts such a standpoint, the appearance of disorder vanishes, revealing a natural principle of "return" that prevents corruption from advancing beyond a certain point:

> The highest peak of fashionable taste is <when young men early on> acquire distasteful boldness and the young women lay aside their reserved demureness.... In such a society, a rational man looks like a dolt or a pedant, a modest and demure woman like a common landlady.... Reason and domestic virtue are old, rusted monuments of taste to be preserved for remembrance. Only here one again finds a standstill and regress, as one does with every evil which one can never bring to the highest point without having the balance swing back to the other side. [20: 107]

Religion rightly understood, and the theology that properly accompanies it, will thus have two branches: one negative, aimed at combating morally perverse opinions about God; the other positive, aimed at enhancing moral feeling (e.g., by conceiving it, hypothetically, as the effect of a general will in which God too cooperates). Religious opinion of some kind, it seems, is natural to man, giving rise to the following typology: primitive religion (or the false and "morally useless" religion of savages), "civilized" religion of an "artificial" sort, and "natural" religion (or the religion discoverable by reason). False religion encourages the "sly humility" described above. Primitive religion is false, without serious moral consequence. Civilized religion of an "artificial" sort performs the in some ways useful role of encouraging civil obedience without, however, genuinely "improving" men. That improvement requires what Kant calls "natural" religion, or civilized religion that finds its "touchstone" in "natural morality" [20: 19]. Piety properly understood is thus a "part" of virtue [20: 23].

In what specific ways might religion serve genuine moral interests? As we have seen, Kant is critical of longings for an imaginary perfection that deflect us from our proper circle and the common duties to which it gives rise:

> A heart broadened by sensibility disposes itself to longing and in the end becomes worn-out in the presence of the sensations of all the things of life; that is why it longs for something that is outside the circle of this life, and, as true as this devotion may be in itself, it is also still fantastic with respect to most men, for they are themselves chimerical and show their love and sincerity only with respect to God, and are cold with respect to one person and false with respect to another. This comes about because one can deceive oneself more easily in considering the former than in considering the latter. [20: 22]

Man is not capable, absent supernatural help, of perfect disinterestedness or "moral purity." One must thus accept human beings as they are:

> Because one can form a concept of higher moral qualities—sacrifice for the common good, constant devotion, fulfillment of matrimonial aims without voluptuousness, and immediate inclination for the sciences without honor—one imagines that all this is appropriate to the state of a human being, and finds the condition that one sees corrupt. But such desires are fantastic and develop out of exactly the same sources as does general corruption. Even the lack of these will no longer be considered blameworthy with respect to human beings, if the rest of what is corrupted is improved. [20: 22]

Kant now gives short shrift to the "broadened heart," to which his *Observations* had appealed. The primary purpose of religion is mainly negative—i.e., dispelling the illusions that support civil oppression.

It is true that in an early passage Kant speaks of the peculiar "moral beauty" of "sacrifice and self-denial":

> Common duties do not require as a motive hope in another life, but greater [ones do]. Sacrifice and self-denial do indeed have an inner beauty, but our feeling of pleasure over this can never in itself be so strong as to outweigh the vexation of the hardship, where one is not aided by the representation of a future state in which such moral beauty lasts, and of the happiness that increases due to one finding oneself even more capable of such actions. [20: 12]

Representation of a future life in which such sacrifice endures and happiness is thereby increased is supposed to make sacrifice easier in the present. It is unclear, however, to whom the happiness in question belongs. If it is my own future happiness that Kant has in mind, it is hard to see how moral beauty, here identified with "sacrifice," can be maintained. If that happiness is not my own, it is hard to see why its increase should make my present sacrifice any easier. In sum, Kant here attempts to objectify the goal of virtuous willing without being able, quite, to describe that goal coherently.

In any event, luxurious conditions give rise to excessive obstacles to moral feeling, obstacles that only a more mercenary religion can overcome:

> It must be asked how far inner moral reasons [*Gründe*] can bring a human being. [It] They will perhaps bring him to the point where, in the state of freedom, he is good without facing any great temptations; but if the injustice of others or the constraint of illusion do violence to him, then this inner morality is not sufficiently strong. He must have *religion* and embolden himself through the promise of rewards in a future life; human nature is not capable of an immediate moral purity. But if purity is supernaturally effected in him, then the future rewards no longer have the quality of motives. [20: 28]

Under luxurious conditions, injustice and illusion prevent "inner moral reasons" from moving men as they otherwise would. In such times, certain "restraints" upon the promulgation of a purely natural religion become difficult to avoid [20: 31]. But these same restraints encourage the very vices that make them necessary:

> When men subordinate *morality* to religion (which is possible and necessary only with oppressed masses), they thereby become hostile, hypocritical, and calumniating; if they subordinate religion to *morality*, however, they are benevolent, have goodwill, and are just. [20: 153]

Kant's dilemma is thus the following. Corrupted men need more than natural religion, which presupposes a degree of moral virtue. But artificial religion, which supports the "illusion" of inequality as well as other sources of disorder, makes such virtue difficult to come by.

If a merely natural religion, rooted in "natural morality," will not do (until men are rescued from "corruption"), natural religion with an appropriate positive or dogmatic supplement may help start things moving in the right direction. Such positive theology does not rest on "speculation," which is "uncertain" and "dangerous," but on moral "faith"—a faith that takes "supernatural" as well as "natural" forms:

> Natural theology, natural religion. A supernatural theology may nevertheless be united with a natural religion. Those who believe Christian [religion] theology in this way have nevertheless only a natural religion, insofar as morality is natural. The Christian religion is supernatural with respect to doctrine and to the strength needed to practice it. . . . The knowledge of God is either *speculative*—and this is uncertain and subject to dangerous errors—or moral, through faith, and this knowledge does not think of any quality in God other than those that aim at morality. This faith is natural or supernatural;. . . . /   [20: 57]

Although Kant does not here resolve the precise relation between natural and supernatural faith, this much is clear: Here and elsewhere in the *Remarks* Kant leaves room for the possibility, in individual cases, of moral strength beyond the ordinary limits of human nature (which is incapable of "moral purity" without supernatural help), strength, or "virtue" that can be understood as a kind of special supernatural gift. Natural faith, by way of contrast, mainly consists in conceiving as connected to the will of God the moral feeling to which conscience independently testifies.

The positive theology arising from that faith, be it natural or supernatural, contains statements like the following:

> The best reason to create is that it is good. It must follow that, because God found himself to be good, with his might and great knowledge, he also found good everything that can thereby be *actualised.* Secondly, it must follow that he also feels content about everything that is likewise good, yet feels the most contentment with what aims at the greatest good. The first is good as a consequence, the second as a principle.   [20: 33]

> The ground for the *divine legislative power* is not to be found in goodness because the motive would then be the thankfulness (*subjective* moral ground, type

of feeling) and thus not strict duty. The ground of *legislative power* presupposes inequality and makes [the] a man lose a degree of freedom with respect to another. This can come about only when he himself sacrifices his own will to the will of another; if he does this for all his actions, he makes a *slave* out of himself. A will that is submitted to that of another is [is] imperfect [because the] and contradictory because man is endowed with *spontaneity;* if it is submitted to the will of another man (even if he himself can already choose well), it is detestable and disdainful; but if it is submitted to the will of God, it is natural. One must not, in obedience to another man, carry out those actions that one could already do from inner motives, and he who requires obedience where inner motives would have brought about everything creates *slaves*. [20: 65–66]

We belong, as it were, to the divine things; we exist through God and by reason of his will [the]. There can be many things in conformity with the will of God that would not at all be good with respect to their inner motives, e.g., putting his son to death. Now, the *goodness* of obedience rests on that. My will is, according to its proper destiny, always submitted to the will of God; thus it is most in harmony with itself when it is in harmony with the divine will, and it is impossible that [the] it be bad to be in conformity with the will of God. [20: 68]

One must not consider savages without religion in such a way that they are placed beneath us who have religion. For he who does what God wills him to do—through the incentives that he has put in his heart—obeys God without knowing his existence. He who recognizes God but is brought to such actions only through the naturally good *morality* has theology, or, if he honors God on account of his morality, this is only a morality whose object was broadened. Christians can just as little become blessed, if their faith is not a living one, as those who have no revelation; with the former, however, something more has happened than what naturally comes about. [20: 104]

Insofar as something depends merely on one's will, it can never contradict itself (objectively). The divine will would contradict itself if it willed men to contradict their own will. The will of men would contradict itself by willing something that their general will would abhor. [20: 161]

The general tenor of these remarks is something like the following: Moral feeling, and the "general will" to which it testifies, can be thought of as the will of God acting in us through the "incentives" he places in our heart. God prefers, as more like Himself, that which actively wills the good to that which only passively brings it about. Hence, he prefers a good produced through human freedom to one arising passively or slavishly. Human obedience to God's will is not slavish, inasmuch as 1) God is our true superior; 2) in so doing we confirm, rather than deny, our equality with other human beings; 3) obedience to God's will so understood is equivalent to the freest act of which a human being is capable.

Kant here restores to Rousseau's concept of a "general will" something of its original theological meaning. Malebranche had sought to distinguish natural events, which arise from God's "general will," from miracles, which arise from his "particular will." Leibniz had replied that God, even when he produces miracles, never acts from a "particular will" but only from some "general truth or will." Kant combines that theological usage with Rousseau's own moralized conception of the general will as one in which particular wills balance one another out in favor of the general good. Kant's concept of supernatural power as one consistent with the general will does not commit him to belief in "miracles" in the usual sense, but only to the possibility of a kind of moral "blessedness," or "living" spirit, that exceeds ordinary human strength. (In so doing, Kant is able to reconcile the divine voluntarism favored by Crusius with Leibniz's insistence on a divine order accessible to human reason.)

In sum: Kant treatment of religion is both negative (or zetetic) and positive (or dogmatic). First and foremost, it seeks to dispel the "religious illusion" that we can control God through our own immoral acts—above all, a slavish submission that places other, lesser goods ahead of that of (equal) freedom. That illusion is abetted by the appearance, in corrupt times, of worldly disorder, an appearance that is made worse by the pretensions of a vain metaphysics. Kant's negative "destruction" of religious illusion is thus accompanied by a positive, or dogmatic theology—a new "science" of religion—rooted not in "speculation" but in what he calls "natural" moral faith, i.e., a faith based in "natural morality." Significantly, Kant leaves open the possibility of "supernatural faith" (or faith in supernatural assistance), albeit only insofar as it is morally of use.

Kant associates his teaching concerning moral blessedness with "authentic" Christianity as conveyed by St. Paul:

> The legislative power [*gesetzgebende Gewalt*] of God is grounded for the first human beings on property [*Eigenthum*]. The human being was recently placed in the world; all trees belonged to God and he forbade man one of them.
>
> This *idea* came to an end. The legislative power of God over the Jewish people is grounded upon the social contract. God wanted to lead them out of Egypt and give them a different land if they obeyed him. Consequently, when they had kings God retained his over-lordship and they were only

satraps and vassals. In the New Testament this ground came to an end. The general ground of the legislative authority [*Gewalt*] is presupposed but obligation rests merely on a benevolence [*Gütigkeit*] that does not want to employ severity. In authentic Christianity this is entirely cancelled in the legislator and the father is introduced.

<*Then he was not a God of human beings but of the Jews.>

Paul judges that the law only fosters reluctance, for the law causes one to do unwillingly what is ordered, and so it is, too. Thus he sees the law abolished through Christ and sees merely grace, namely, a ground for loving God straight from the heart, which is not possible according to nature and through which actions are brought toward *morality* and not *theocratic politics*.
[20: 90]

As Christian is to Jew, so is authentic moral faith to an inauthentic theocratic politics. Kant's supernatural theology becomes identifiably Christian through its contrast with Judaism understood as an exclusionary creed bereft both of sincerity and of universal moral content—an understanding that persists in Kant's later and more famous religious writings. Lacking as they do "the idea of equality," Jews deceive others with impunity:

All truthfulness [*Warhaftigkeit*] presupposes an idea of equality. Therefore, the Jews, who in their opinion have no duties toward others, lie and deceive others without any bite of conscience. *haereticis non est fides* [in heretics there is no faith]. [20: 158]

Kant's moral transfiguration of orthodox Christianity thus turns on tracing sin to the same "illusion" of inequality that is mainly responsible, as we have seen, for both man's moral and political corruption and his previous intellectual failures.

d. Kant's Archimedean Moment

The primary purpose of theoretical science, as we have seen, is not the accumulation of new facts but the destruction of false beliefs, especially those arising from human vanity. "Metaphysics," as Kant already puts it, "is the science of the limits of human reason" [20: 181]. On this understanding, sincerity, or the intention to be truthful to oneself and others, is more important than knowledge, which is often useless if not harmful:

In itself, truth [*Wahrheit*] has no value: it does not matter whether an opinion concerning the inhabitation of many worlds is true or false. One must

> not confuse truth with truthfulness [*Wahrhaftigkeit*]. Only the way [*Art*] in which one arrives at truth has a determinate value, for that which here leads to error can also do so in practical things. [20: 175]

It hardly matters whether there is life on Jupiter or not. What matters is the way or method by which one arrives at truth, and this mainly for its practical effect.

Science, then, is neither necessary nor natural, but useful only to the extent that it helps relieve the evils that it brings about. Just as:

> The loss of freedom and the exclusive authority of a ruler is a great misfortune, yet just as well does it become an orderly system; indeed, there is actually more order, though less happiness, than in free states. Softness in morals, idleness, and vanity bring forth the sciences. These lend new decoration to the whole, deter much evil and if they are raised to a certain height, ameliorate the evil which they themselves have brought about. [20: 42–43]

Though itself a product of decadence, science, "once it has been raised to a certain height," corrects the ills that it itself has caused, in keeping with the aforementioned principle of "return" [20: 107].

Two of "the greatest" of those evils are as these: first, "that [science] takes away so much time that the moral education of youth is neglected"; and, second, that "science so habituates minds to the sweetness of *speculation* that good actions are not done" [20: 43]. Science, rightly understood, addresses both by emphasizing the overriding importance of moral education, the futility of most human speculation, and the inadequacy of even the most refined hedonism as a sole standard of the good life.

Beginning with the first: In placing science in the service of moral and civic education, Kant dedicates his own life to the improvement of others (who are formally his equals). Such "sacrifice" can be morally accommodated only by the prospect of instructing others in sufficient numbers:

> It is unnatural that a man spends most of his life teaching a child how he should himself live one day. That is why courtly private tutors such as *Jean Jacques* are artificial. In a state of simplicity, a child receives only a few services; as soon as he has some strength, he does the small, useful activities of an adult, such as occurs with the peasant or the artisan, and gradually he learns how to do the rest.
>
> It is nevertheless fitting that a man spends his life teaching so many children how to live that the sacrifice of his own life is not regretted. Schools are thus necessary. But for schools to be possible, one must extend/propagate

> [*ziehen*] *Emile.* It would have been desirable if Rousseau had shown how schools could come about here.
> Preachers in the countryside could begin to do this with their own children and with their neighbors' children. [20: 29]

The sacrifice of Kant's life to educating others is justified, by his own newly elaborated standard, only if the good thereby achieved outweighs his own uncommon sacrifice. "Schools are therefore necessary." And country preachers could begin to carry out this task. Kant here anticipates, in a few elliptical remarks, the civic-pedagogic strategy he will describe almost thirty years later in *The Conflict of the Faculties*. By teaching country preachers to subordinate religion to natural morality, Kant can reach the masses and thereby undertake the "sacrifice" of his own life without rational regret.

As for the second evil caused by science—a taste for "sweetness of speculation" that keeps men from doing good—here, too, science itself ultimately provides a remedy, by establishing the limits of reason and with them the futility of most human speculation. The purpose of science is not pleasure but discovery of the truth, especially about man:

> If pleasure taken from the sciences were the motive, it would not matter whether it were true or false. The ignorant and the precociously prudent [would] have an advantage here over the intelligent and cautious. The final end is to find out the destiny/determination of man. [20: 175]

If pleasure were the motive of science, the ignorantly arrogant (who believe that they know more than they do) would be better off than those with genuine knowledge.

Sheer love of truth, however, is also insufficient to explain an inclination for science, an inclination that is both unnatural and often painful in its disappointment of our wishes. Hence, "an immediate inclination" for the sciences, "without honor," is "an illusory ideal" [20: 22]. Science is a peculiar expression of the love of honor. Such honor "without illusion" Kant calls "pride" or "dignity," and attributes to a (true) opinion of "important accomplishments" that is not accompanied by disdain for others. But there is a thin line between such admirable pride, consistent with the rule of equality, and the arrogance of the "petit maitre" whom Kant cheerfully despises:

> Inner honor. Self-esteem. External honor as a means of assuring oneself of the former. Thus a man of honor, *honestas*. External honor as a means is true, as end, an illusion. The former is either for self-preservation, equality, or

> preservation of the kind, and is directed toward advantage. Desire for honor (immediate) is directed either toward the opinion of important accomplishments (*patriotism*) and is called ambition [*Ehrgeitz*] or to trifles and is called vanity. The consciousness of honor that one believes oneself to possess—and indeed without measuring oneself by others—is called pride [*Stoltz*]. Dignity. *Gallantry* is either that of pride or of vanity. The former is that of a *petit maitre*, the latter of a fop. The proud man who despises others is arrogant. If he wants to indicate this through splendor, he is haughty. The arrogant man who lets his contempt be seen is conceited. [20: 130]

Science right understood is motivated, or at least "spurred," by a love of honor whose "inward" character is secured by the recognition of equality that necessarily accompanies it. Kant's Rousseau-inspired philosopher enjoys the pride of "important accomplishment" without succumbing to a morally and intellectually corrupting arrogance. Only "through Rousseau" and the revolution he inspires in Kant can "even the philosopher"—upright, learned, and "without help from religion"—be brought to regard himself as no better than the common man [20: 176] and metaphysics become "the science of human limits." That revolution in standpoint sets us right, above all, by dispelling "moral illusion," which consists in taking a moral perfection that it is possible to imagine (the so-called ideals of luxury) for a real one [20: 172]. Just as gravity compels us to remain on earth even though we can "see other worlds in the distance," nature compels us to remain human beings, even though we can imagine "the perfections of spirits above us" [20: 153].

Brought back to earth in this way, reason can apply itself to the task of human self-improvement, where it can at last play the positive role of constructing new ideals in keeping with nature. Now is a particularly auspicious moment for such a project of "return," owing to the civil freedoms that are uniquely possible in such corrupt times as the present. Accordingly, Kant urges the unabridged freedom of the press, despite any apparent short-term harm to public morals:

> One must not forbid any book now; that is the only means [the damage] so that they annihilate themselves. We have now arrived at the point of return. Rivers, if one lets them overflow, form their banks themselves. The dam that we raise up against them only serves to render their destructions incessant. Because the authors of useless things can excuse themselves by the injustice of others. [20: 105]

Men are also made "unequal" by "the opinion of inequality" [20: 176]. So long as monarchs permit scholars like Kant to publicize their thoughts, subjects can be brought to regard themselves as citizens and republican order gradually restored.

But with the prospect of a return to civic order comes a new difficulty: If science is a product of decadence, what role will it have once civic health has been recovered?

> Rousseau's education is the only means of giving back prosperity to civil society. For, since luxury grows more and more, from which arise misery, oppression, contempt of the social classes and war, the laws cannot set anything straight, as is the case in Sweden. Through this, all governments will become more orderly and war more rare. It would be necessary to institute *censors*. But where would the first ones come from? [20: 175]

The question is not only "who will educate the educators?" but also "what will happen to the very 'science' that makes a return to virtue possible?" Without freedom to "think and speak" science will presumably disappear. If science is "nothing necessary"—if it lacks intrinsic worth and has value only as a remedy—then its disappearance in healthy times should not concern us (assuming an ongoing supply of "censors").

Kant, however, does not easily renounce the intrinsic merit of his own activity. Thus his claim, in perhaps the strangest and most arresting passage in the entire text, that the "most perfect state" for a human being does not lie in free civic life but in the moment of "return" to it.

> Man in his perfection is not in the state of [simplicity also not in] moderation nor in the state of luxury, but in the return from the latter to the former. Strange condition of human nature! This most perfect state stands on a hair-tip. The state of [nature can] simple and original nature does not last long; the state of restored nature is more lasting but never as innocent. [20: 153]

The "most perfect state," which rests upon a "hair-tip," lies neither in the primitive nor the more enduring "state of nature" but in the moment of "return" from luxury to civic moderation. The most perfect human being is not the virtuous citizen, it seems, but he who, poised on that hair-tip, wields the fulcrum that brings civic virtue back.

This suggestion furnishes an answer to the question earlier left hanging: How give the idea of human moral perfection determinate content? Kant refers elsewhere in *Remarks* to a kind of "sympathy" that is rare without being artificial; and he elsewhere argues that benevolence, which lacks the obvious "determinate measure" of justice, is warranted nevertheless whenever those who are satisfied with little expend what they can spare on those weaker than themselves. But how far may one push oneself in this regard without diminishing rather than enhancing the general good, and thus oneself succumbing to the "moral illusion" of taking an imaginary perfection for a real one? Kant suggests, as we have seen, that teaching the young on a sufficiently large scale (literally, "wholesale") might provide the necessary assurance to the teacher that a life thus "sacrificed" need not be regretted. We can now add the following precision. To attempt to educate the greatest possible number in a "Rousseauian" manner is to exercise precisely the art or science of "return" that is currently at issue. To thus act, Archimedes-like, as a free cause, or ground, of the greatest good would be to experience one's own free activity to the utmost, within the limits of our human condition. For it is ultimately not the effect of one's resolve but the resolve itself that matters. Absent that resolve, virtue, in a corrupt state like ours, is impossible [20: 151]. And with it, ultimate success may be unnecessary. *With regard to great deeds, it is enough only to have willed them* [20: 148].

Human perfection finds its formal definition in a formula that minimizes human need while maximizing human benevolence. The natural human being, Kant says, is "more perfect" insofar as he can "do without," and more morally perfect insofar as he "retains strength to promote the needs and happiness of others," and thus enjoys the feeling of a will "that does good outside itself" [20: 146]. Given the vexed relation between freedom and sexual desire, the most perfect human being might well choose (like Kant) to express his sympathetic impulse by "propagating," or "plant[ing] human beings," pedagogically rather than sexually [20: 108]. In any case, in choosing this vocation he will live life to the maximum permitted by his fate or fortune: "to live long and little, or to live short and much, to live much in enjoyment or in action. Both in the greatest proportion is the best" [20: 168].

3. Conclusion

The *Remarks* expresses a peculiar understanding of history as oscillating (rather than as progressive, as in Kant's later work), punctuated by moments of recovery resembling the far-most boundaries of a river that periodically overruns its banks. Both those banks and those boundaries—the extremes of human order and corruption—are the outcome of competing human forces of repulsion and attraction. Under human conditions of dependence, these moral forces are expressed, in the first instance, in the tension between sexual desire and the love of freedom, and in the (false) idealizations to which that tension gives rise. By replacing the sexual force of attraction with a civic one, Kant's republican idea supplies a stable model of perfection in keeping with "the order of nature." This conception of a perfect civic world is one that earthly politics can only approximate (given, among other things, the human need to reproduce sexually), and finds its purest application in theology, which projects that conception into the afterlife: "there is a most perfect (moral) world according to the order of nature, and it is about this world that we ask as about one that is supernatural" [20: 16]. By dint of such a world, Kant hopes to "move human emotion" in a manner favorable to a return of civic flourishing.

Such an Archimedean project calls to mind the moment of terror Kant describes in his long remark on freedom. The occasion of that terror was the recognition of lawless freedom in another and the thought thereby prompted of one's own cancellation as a "complete" or free and active being. In subjecting freedom to itself, Kant's pivot of "return" answers to that moment. The *Remarks* anticipates, in this regard, his later treatment of juridical community as the recognitive struggle that drives human history, an argument that will be appropriated, albeit in different ways, by both Fichte and Hegel. At the same time, Kant leaves open the possibility that such inter-worldly force might itself be supernaturally aided. Not to "need" religion may well be the surest sign of "grace" authentically conceived.

In sum: The *Remarks* sets out a remarkably coherent set of reflections on the human condition broadly understood and on what might be done to improve our present situation in a manner that is both in keeping with the laws of nature and favorable to human freedom. They anticipate such features of Kant's later thought as the essentially negative role of speculative metaphysics and the fundamentally practical character of reason and its idea. Kant's reflections on morality, religion, and politics often approach in their very wording his later and more famous published writings on these topics. But the *Remarks* also falls short of, or is lacking, key insights. On the theoretical plane: There is nothing yet to suggest that the limits of human reason prevent us from knowing reality as such, or the thing-in-itself. Kant's discovery of the "ideality" of space and time, and with it, the merely phenomenal character of human experience, lies in the future. On the practical plane: The "categorical imperative" may exist *in nuce;* that it arises solely from the free activity of reason *and* that reason suffices to enjoin us to obey it (as the principle of autonomy will later insist) is not yet clear. The pinnacle of human perfection remains identified with the

Archimedean efforts of the philosopher-tutor, who sets his fulcrum in the "state of nature" in order to "move emotions."

Such motion is vexed, however, by the following difficulty: If successful, it would destroy the conditions that make it both possible and necessary. Kant's philosopher-tutor installs a state of lawful freedom that does not include him personally. The Rousseauian tension between perfection of the many and perfection of the few remains unresolved. Kant's solution to this unsettling problem would come only after a decade-long experiment in anthropology.

3

Rousseau, Count Verri, and the "True Economy of Human Nature"

Lectures on Anthropology, 1772–1781

1. Kant's "Silent Decade"

Chapter 2 traced the initial "revolution" in Kant's thought that was provoked by his reading of Rousseau. This chapter takes up the story approximately eight years later and focuses mainly on lectures on anthropology [*Vorlesungen über Anthropologie*] of the 1770s and early 1780s, many of which were recently published for the first time.[1]

The decade immediately preceding the appearance of the *Critique of Pure Reason* in 1781 has long been a puzzle to scholars. After two decades of energetic and ambitious authorship, and at what might well be thought the height of his intellectual powers, Kant published nothing for ten years other than a brief review of a work on anatomy by Moscoti [1771][2] and a short *Essay on the Various Races of Men* [1775]. That these publications elaborate or revisit themes explored in the *Lectures on Anthropology* suggests that during this crucial period anthropological concerns were close to the center of Kant's thinking. The earlier lectures express a new confidence on Kant's part as to the possibility of a metaphysical psychology ultimately rooted in the feeling of "life." As we shall see, that attempt gives way, in later lectures, to a conception of rational "sovereignty" that anticipates in crucial ways his final formulation of the principle of autonomy.

Remarks had left unresolved several important moral-anthropological problems. Unable to know man's perfection directly, on the basis of theoretical reasoning, we can distinguish true ideals from false ones, according to the *Remarks*, only by subjecting them to the double test of physical and moral necessity. Physical necessity speaks to what is in man's primitive or inborn physical power (or to what "can't be changed"); moral necessity looks to what is just according to the law of equality. Moral necessity demands a sacrifice of self-interest whenever our desire for happiness conflicts with another's freedom. Physical necessity forces moral longing to remain within the limits of what is naturally possible. Kant's "state of freedom" attempts to keep both requirements in focus. But that effort does not fully succeed. Primitive man has few needs and can do much for others without sacrificing his own needs. Under civilized conditions, on the other hand, order may require the sacrifice of one's own physical needs to support the "rights" (or moral needs) of others. Is such a demand in keeping with man's natural powers? If not, that ideal fails the only test available for distinguishing goals justifiable by reason from those of a luxuriating imagination. But a morality that demands no sacrifice at all seems debasingly beneath human self-expectation. How protect from the charge of wishful thinking the human aspiration to transcend nature in its crudest form? Kant's simple answer, in *Remarks,* is a return to the social conditions (especially pertaining to relations between the sexes) that support the virtues of the republican citizen. But the most perfect human being, who most fully reconciles freedom and law, is not the citizen but the philosopher *cum* social engineer who makes a return to civic virtue possible. The philosopher, who stands in a kind of Lucretian "intermundia," is less a member of the "moral world" then its Lucretian god.

2. The *Inaugural Dissertation of 1770*

Kant's lectures on anthropology address these difficulties following a "great light" that dawned around 1769 and whose early fruits appear in the *Inaugural Dissertation of 1770* [*On the Form and Principles of the Sensible and the Intelligible World*].[3] The gist of that discovery (which may have been encouraged by his reading of Leibniz's *New Essays*), was a new insight into the irreducibility of spatial relations to purely conceptual analysis. Hereafter Kant treats intellect (or understanding) and sensibility as separate and distinct sources of knowledge, each with its own *a priori,* world-informing principle. In the case of sensibility, the relevant world-form is space and time. In the case of understanding, it is the concept of a reciprocal community of substances.

The intelligible world, so understood, gives new, albeit qualified, metaphysical heft to the *mundus spiritualis* that *Dreams* had opted to treat in purely moral terms. Kant the theoretical metaphysician is once again in business. Pure intelligible concepts, as Kant now sees matters, have two primary uses: on the one hand, and negatively: to keep what is "sensitively conceived" distinct from *noumena;* on the other hand, and dogmatically: to make available *exempla* of noumenal perfection as first principles for judgment. In the case of theory, that *exemplum* is God; in the case of practice, it is moral perfection. Moral philosophy, "insofar as it furnishes the first principles of judgment," is thus only cognized "by the pure understanding"; and Epicurus is "very rightly blamed" for reducing its criteria to the feeling of pleasure and pain [2: 396].[4]

These *exempla* can be understood as ideals or "maxima." The human mind arrives at these ideals by subtracting from a given property the hindrance that limits its quantity. Moral perfection, for example, is virtue minus the resistance of the senses that ordinarily burdens or inhibits it. And theoretical perfection (or God) is intellect minus the dependence on bodily sensation that characterizes human experience. To be sure, Kant is less than clear as to the precise cognitive status of these *exempla:* The desired apodeictic proof of God's existence is not forthcoming [2: 409].[5] In the absence of such proof, which would establish a necessary connection between the *exemplum* and its object, we seem thrown back upon the skeptical position sketched in *Dreams*—a position that left no role for metaphysics other than a practical one [2: 373].

But Kant is not content to let matters rest where they had in *Dreams*. His *Dissertation* ends with a "scholium" that by his own admission verges on the "mystical":

> If even a small step beyond the limits of apodeictic certainty which befits metaphysics were permitted, it would seem worthwhile to investigate certain matters concerning not merely the laws but also the causes of sensitive intuition, which may be known through the *understanding* alone. For, indeed, the human mind is only affected by external things, and the world is only exposed to its view, lying open before it to infinity, in so far as the mind itself, together with all other things, is sustained by the same infinite force of one being. [2: 409]

Space and time, on this suggestion, are the "phenomenal co-presence" and "phenomenal eternity," respectively, of a "general cause" that is "inwardly present to" and "sustaining of" all things. And the human mind, by mediating between sensibility and understanding, is a point of worldly intersection that registers that virtual and sustaining presence. Still, as Kant hastens to add, it seems "more advisable" to avoid such "mystical investigations," keeping close, instead, "to the shore of the cognitions granted to us by the middling [*mediocritatum*] character of our understanding" [2: 409–410]. Might such cognitions grant further insight into the general cause whose "infinite force" eludes pure understanding?

The early anthropology lectures can profitably be understood as an extended experiment along such lines, exploring—from a standpoint closer to the shores of human mediocrity—the "mystical" suggestion of Kant's scholium. The focus of these investigations is a concept of "life" already broached in the *Remarks* and *Dreams*[6] and now given new teleological thrust: All living beings, as Kant now puts it, are destined to mature. One immediate result is replacement of the "oscillating" view of history featured in *Remarks* with the familiarly progressive one generally associated with Kant's thought. As we will see, Kant's reliance on the concept of life, and a related metaphysical (but nonetheless "empirical") psychology, reaches its peak in the Friedländer lectures of 1775, prior to his reading of Pietro Verri's *Del piacere e del dolore*,[7] which appeared in German in 1777.[8] After that reading (and his related discovery of what he calls "the true economy of human nature") Kant denies what he had maintained in earlier lectures: namely, that the presence of the "soul as substance" can be intuited directly. Freedom is not known directly, through an intuition of spiritual life (and with it, by a certain "mystical" extension, God). Instead, it must be inferred from the (observable) rules and principles by which reason itself proceeds. This crucial insight, as I will argue below, provides the long-sought formula for a theoretical determination on reason's part of its own "limits."[9] That formula anticipates, in turn, Kant's notion of autonomy in its final form.

3. Anthropology Lectures prior to 1777

Kant offered a course on anthropology forty-eight times during his long career as a university teacher—a number exceeded only by his course on logic. Generally, he taught anthropology and ethics in adjoining semesters to first-year students. The anthropology lectures resituate Kant's pedagogical project—broadly Rousseauian in character and tentatively sketched in the *Remarks*—within the general framework provided the *Inaugural Dissertation of 1770*. That framework supplies the metaphysical background for a new concept of "life" as point of juncture between the sensible and intelligible worlds.

a. Kant's Incipient Science of "Life"

Kant's empirical psychology during the early and mid-1770s distinguishes *three* primary faculties of soul—knowledge, desire, and feeling.[10] Life is the capacity to be moved by feeling[11] [cf. 6: 211]. Owing to that power, living beings are self-sustaining unities rather than lifeless heaps of matter. Living beings are "determined" to activity by their awareness (via pleasure) of what promotes their life and by their awareness, via pain, of what retards it [28: 246–247]. Where animals are only aware of momentary pains and pleasures, man, as a rational being, also has a feeling for his life as a "whole." This feeling goes together with the freedom to resist momentary pains and pleasures for the sake of the whole. For example, we can accept a partial hindrance to life (e.g., the pain of strenuous labor) in order to promote it in the long run. And we can give up a partial promotion of life (e.g., the pleasure associated with narcotic stimulants) for the sake of general health. Happiness and misery imply a judgment as to the value of existence as a whole. Thus animals can feel pleasure and pain, but cannot be happy or miserable [see, for example, 25: 27, 35, 369].[12]

Our feelings of pleasure and pain are not exhausted by those arising from our bodily receptivity. Feeling for what is aesthetically pleasing and displeasing testifies to a community of taste among individuals who share the same active powers of shaping what is received through sensibility. And feelings of moral approbation and disapprobation testify to a spiritual community (or free activity in harmony with itself) that transcends the sensible conditions of organic life entirely.

To the extent that man can make such harmony his end, he possesses what Kant here calls "spiritual" life. What hinders our whole life insofar as we are animals or members of society may promote it insofar as we are spiritual beings, as when we risk bodily harm or give up social pleasures for an important moral end. (To be sure, much turns on the status of such "spiritual" incentives, which Kant already treats as problematic, both theoretically and practically.)

Freedom is the capacity to be motivated by an active feeling for the unity of life, or spirit. Animals, by way of contrast, are motivated solely by external stimulation and the passive feelings to which it gives rise. The soul's experientially based knowledge of itself as spiritual substance establishes its membership in the (an) intelligible world—i.e., in a real community of substances that the idea of God's "virtual presence," according to the *Dissertation*, can alone make comprehensible. To be a member of that world is thus to be open to

God's (living) presence, an openness that by Kant's own admission verges on the mystical.

Such intimations, to be sure, must not be pressed too far. Although we know the soul as substance to be indestructible (according to Kant's current view), we cannot be sure on the basis of consciousness alone that the soul survives its separation from the body (or corporeal death) as a thinking being or "personality." Though the soul's "living force" is indestructible, we cannot readily foresee the "state" or "condition" of our soul after we die. We thus lack the knowledge that human beings (as Kant puts it in the mid-1770s) "most crave."

b. Collins *and* Parow *[1772–1773]: "Thinking Without the Body"*

Collins introduces anthropology as a practical empirical science devoted to distinguishing what is "natural" to man from what is artificial or habitual [25: 8]. This Rousseau-inspired question is, however, given a peculiarly metaphysical (and moral) focus: By observing what is characteristically human in all times and places, one considers "the mind in isolation from the body" and can thereby hope to learn "whether the influence of the body is necessary for thinking." Anthropology thus promises to provide the "surest ground of proof" as to "the immortality of the soul." Kant's professed disinterest in the mind-body question at this time is thus easily misunderstood. Although he writes to Marcus Herz that his new course on anthropology omits "entirely the subtle ... and eternally futile inquiries as to the manner in which the bodily organs are connected with thought,"[13] Kant is by no means uninterested in the question of our future state (or whether thinking is possible "without the body"). The main source of this interest is not theoretical but practical and moral: If it is possible to think (and thus be conscious of ourselves) without a body, then it is possible to anticipate a future in which we are conscious of existing without bodily impediment. Any rational estimation for the value of one's life as a whole, on this assumption, will be relatively indifferent to the passive pains and pleasures that now accompany the human condition, provided that one has done nothing to make oneself "unworthy" of enjoying a better one. In sum: If the proof in question succeeds, moral motivation can be explained with the tools furnished by a general science of life. Kant takes his initial bearings from the word "I"; in that "little word":

> there is not merely an intuition of self, but also of the simplicity of *our self;* for it is the most perfect singularity. The word expresses, further, my sub-

stantiality, for I distinguish the I, as a final subject, that cannot be predicated of anything else, and *the* self is the subject of all predicates. The little word also expresses a rational substance, for it expresses my conscious making of myself an object of my thoughts. There also lies in it personality. Every man, every creature, that can make itself an object of its thoughts cannot regard itself as a portion of the world filling up the emptiness of creation, but as a member of creation, and as both a center of it and its end. . . . In the word "I" one finds the concept of freedom, the consciousness of self-activity; for the I is no external thing. We see through analysis of the I . . . nothing but an immediate intuition of our self. [25: 10]

"I" expresses an immediate intuition of the self as a "most perfect singularity." But it also implies an ability to reflect: to turn away from immediate sense impression and thus "make oneself an object of one's thoughts." The reflecting "I" is free in the specific sense of having conscious control over the object of its thoughts—of being able to attend to something or abstract from it at will. In so doing, the "I" seems capable of making itself an "object" apart from any sensible sensation, and thus of being self-aware without the passive receptivity associated with the possession of a body.[14]

Morally, the reflecting "I" has "immediate value" to itself (once again, apart from any sensible representation associated with its bodily condition). It necessarily regards itself not as a mere portion of the universe, filling up its emptiness, but as "a center" of the universe and "its end." At the same time, man "esteems himself more when he is active than when he is passive" [25: 11, 29]. He also holds himself (and others) accountable (for failure, presumably, to be as "active" as one might be) and thus has "personality."

On the basis of the soul's threefold nature (passive, active, and capable of preferring the active to the passive), Kant distinguishes three "standpoints" from which we can "observe ourselves" or "feel our life"—1) as passive or affected by bodily impressions (=*anima*), 2) as self-active (=*mens, Geist*), and 3) as both active and passive (=*animus*, mind [*Gemüth*]) [25: 16, 247]. These three ways of feeling life are accompanied by three kinds of pleasure [*Lust*]: what pleases in sensation (=*anima*) is "agreeable"; what pleases in concepts (=*mens, Geist*) is "good"; what pleases according to laws of appearance (=*animus, Gemüth*) is "beautiful" [25: 175, 167].[15] Spirit [*Geist*] is pure activity, or what Kant sometimes calls the "principle of life." *Anima* is the self in its passive capacity. And *Gemüth* or "heart" [*Hertz*] is the self's "constitution," i.e., the "inner source of inclinations" that we can "master but not change" [25: 248].

A soul with a heart strong enough to give up "unnecessary pleasures" has the power to be contented, or to find the totality of its state "worth wishing for." Such a soul will enjoy unnecessary pleasures when it can but not miss them when it can't. And it will maintain a calculated equanimity that renders it immune to both gaity (or inordinate pleasure) and dejection (or inordinate sadness). A strong soul does not let momentary pains and pleasures (which do not affect the value of life as a whole) "reach the mind" or "disturb its mental rest." Thus those who estimate the value of pain and pleasure correctly[16] are generally pleased with life. One who "rightly estimates the value of things" through "a voluntary application of his reason" possesses the "sovereign power over fortune" that money falsely promises the miser [25: 371, 397]. For persons of virtue and of stout heart, the value of existence will always be greater than zero and thus "worth wishing for." Even the harshest deprivation need not rob one of happiness, so long as one maintains "composure" through meditation on (this) life's brevity and insignificance and through exact compliance with the precepts of morality [25: 170, 369–370].[17]

"The Stoic rule of not letting oneself be *overpowered* by inclinations" is thus "the true rule of wisdom." The difficulty lies in applying it. Stoics "speak well only theoretically, without showing the means by which their *rules* can be made effective" [25: 38–39]. To preach moral rules to a person overcome by passion is as "useless" as to "prescribe rules of happiness to a galley slave" [25: 38]. The idea of an afterlife in comparison with which the pains and pleasures of our present life are insignificant may help sustain composure, but it is ineffective in those who lack it. Still, as the example of the galley slave suggests, we all have some inkling, whether "composed" or not, as to the superiority of spiritual pleasure over pleasures of a lesser kind. Freedom is desirable both as a means to passive pleasure and as a pleasure in its own right, the loss of which no passive pleasure can compensate for. Even those who find themselves in the most miserable of conditions "would not be willing to be made happy according to the opinion of another." We feel life only through our own activity [25: 254]; and though we like to remain passive, we prefer unhappiness to giving over our power of choice to others—a preference that Kant attributes to a certain "love of activity above all else" [25: 256].

In sum: Awareness of our own freedom, as expressed, above all, in our unwillingness to renounce our independence for the sake of satisfying our passive inclinations, bears witness to the overriding value of free activity as such. To fully register that value in one's estimate of pain and pleasure is to undergo a "palengensis," or "rebirth" of the soul. How such definitive subservience of *anima* to spirit can be achieved, however, remains a mystery, given that motion (as both *Dreams* and the *Dissertation* maintained) pertains only to the sensible world. "Good and evil properly belong not to feeling but to understanding." Accordingly, there are many who "teach virtue unremittingly and yet are indifferent to it personally." Similarly, though everyone esteems virtue, few enjoy it [25: 397]. Indeed, the very concept of "spiritual motion" (or spirit active in the sensible world) represents a "contradiction in thinking." For a human being even to *think* spiritual motion is to commit the fallacy of "contradiction *in adjecto*" [25: 397–398].[18]

The inconceivability of spiritual motion poses a distinct problem for one engaged (like Kant) in moral education:

> Here arises the question: how can we bring about the so-called feeling of pleasure and aversion [concerning that which is morally good or evil]? It is hard to have insight into the ground of this, for it is very certain that there can be no spiritual movement [*geistige Regung*]. [25: 398]

How, then, is the idea of moral perfection to be made effective in the world?

Kant here turns by way of answer to a mysterious sentiment ("analogous to taste") through which moral goodness moves us and the force of spirit makes its presence felt we know not how [25: 398, 403, 411, 412]. Leaning on that analogy, *Collins* and *Parow* look principally to the aesthetic realm (or to the "culture of taste"), both as a model for ethical instruction and as the best preparation for the political and moral transformation of society more generally.

Aesthetic pleasure is especially associated here with *animus*, which joins the active and passive aspects of the soul.[19] Like the purely sensual contentment that follows a large meal, aesthetic feeling lets us to "feel our life *in toto*" [25: 388–389]. Unlike physical satiety, however, it does so in a way that calls upon the higher, or more active mental faculties, yielding a pleasure that is both "ideal" and valid universally.

Judgments of taste and beauty please by freely activating our powers of mind, setting its powers "in play," in "harmony" with "ideas" developed [*gebildet*] either by rules of reason or by rules of sensibility [25: 27, 379, 384]. The cultivated man chooses what "universally pleases" and regards things "from a universal standpoint" [25: 191]. Taste, which eases the harshness of morality's command, is "the analog of perfection." It is "in intuition what morals [*Sittlichkeit*] is in reason" and "a constant culture" and "preparation" of virtue [25: 195].

Kant, to be sure, is less than clear about the character of human perfection, owing to a certain indeterminacy surrounding the idea of happiness. The representation of an intellectual composition is called an "idea," which one makes oneself "in thinking the maximum of a concept"; when it comes to happiness, however, "this can happen in various ways." Thus the competing Stoic and Epicurean "ideas of human perfection" arise from different ways of thinking about happiness. In one case, equanimity is maximized, in the other, pleasure [25: 98]. Kant's preferred ideal of human perfection is obviously the Stoic one; but in matters pedagogical at least he cannot yet see his way clear of the Epicurean alternative.

Hence the great importance of "human taste," whose "school" is social intercourse [*Umgang*], in which men learn to please women [25: 201, 394]: "tender love" consists not in great "affect," but in "fineness of judgment," on the part of men, concerning everything that the beloved might find agreeable [25: 423]. The resulting elevation of sensibility (which turns on granting women more than they deserve) both refines and universalizes judgment, and thus prepares the way for virtue proper. National character can thus easily be judged on the basis of a nation's taste, which revolves mainly around its treatment of women [25: 398–399]. Turkey, where women "dance alone," is without taste, as, for the most part, is the rest of Asia, which substitutes sense for reason rather than making sense reason's servant [25: 401–402].

In sum: The taste and beauty that are promoted by mixed society play a predominating role in moral education, much as it had a decade earlier in *Observations on the Feeling of the Beautiful and the Sublime*. Gone are the sourer notes on women sounded in the *Remarks*. Through social intercourse with cultivated women, young men abandon or transform raw sexual desire (which treats the beloved object as a "thing") and instead seek what pleases others. An aesthetic culture based on social intercourse between the sexes supports virtue in Kant's current view rather than destroying it. Hence (for reasons drawn mainly from Rousseau's *Emile*),[20] the manifold weaknesses of women should be excused. To be sure, without the opinion of men, women "would be nothing" (or, alternatively, "the lowest creatures in the world" [25: 462]),[21] and yet women are proud and demand men's tribute. The amazing thing is that men are so glad to see this pride and prickliness in those whom they love. This double fissure [*Zweispalt*] of nature in regard to the sexes is "very important"; and knowledge concerning it has "the most considerable uses" in social *intercourse*, marriage, and education [25: 238]. Not surprisingly, then, both *Collins* and *Parow* end with an extended treatment of the relation of the sexes.

c. Friedländer *[1775–1776]: Life as a Determinate Sum*

The lecture series of winter semester 1775–1776 (*Friedländer*) introduces the concept of "pragmatic" anthropology, as a branch of "knowledge of the world" or, alternatively, "knowledge of all relations." Whereas theoretical learning is especially associated with "understanding" and consists in knowing what is required for certain ends, pragmatic learning is associated with "judgment" and "making all skill [*Geschichlichkeit*] serve one" [25: 469]. This new pragmatic perspective is accompanied by a newly unified approach to problems that Kant's early lectures had left unresolved.

Although Kant is no less confident in the ability of anthropology to yield true knowledge of human nature—i.e., of those constant properties that do not vary with time and place—he no longer holds out the promise (as in *Collins*) of "the best possible proof" as to the immortality of the soul (or its capacity to "think without the body") [cf. 25: 8].[22] No less than *Collins/Parow*, however, *Friedländer* is centrally concerned with moral education. "The reason why moral ... discourse, which is so full of admonitions ... has so little *effect* is lack of knowledge of man." Thus, "morals must be combined with knowledge of human beings" [25: 472; cf. 25: 7]. Accordingly, Kant takes expanded anthropological interest in matters of "race" and "history," including a "world history" or "history of humanity" (as he also puts it) of a sort that "no one has yet written" [25: 471].[23] History replaces the afterlife as prime locus of human transformation.

In keeping with these other changes, Kant no longer associates mind [*animus; Gemüth*] (as distinguished from *mens* and *anima*) primarily with the aesthetic. "Mind" designates both the way the soul is affected by things and its capacity to reflect and to relate things to itself (hence its peculiar affinity with pragmatic knowledge of the world, with its similar emphasis on "knowledge of relations") [25: 474–475]. The conflict between intelligence (or "personality") and animality is now firmly seated in the mind, which registers both our dependence on the body and our capacity to master it [25: 476].[24]

Despite the dual character of human life, we *feel* it, as Kant here insists, as a single sum. Pain is the "feeling of a hindrance in a place of life," pleasure a feeling of its partial furtherance. If in feeling "the entire sum of life" from which pain "subtracts" enjoyment outweighs pain, we gladly go on living; if pain "so outweighs the sum of life" that we are no longer able to feel "life's enjoyment," we prefer to die [25: 559].

Feeling can be brought to its highest pitch by a representation of life at its maximum—i.e., without any hindrance. *Collins/Parow* conceived this hindrance as mainly physical: maximum freedom was equivalent to "thinking without the body." In *Friedländer*, by way of contrast, the hindrance in question is one that freedom poses to itself when it is "lawless." Lawless freedom, in other words, is a "hindrance to itself" (a phrase that will famously appear in Kant's much later *Metaphysics of Morals* [6: 230–232]). Although freedom is "the greatest life of man" through which he exercises his activity "without hindrance," freedom, and hence life, is hindered when freedom is not subject to the compulsion of a rule. Accordingly, intellectual pleasure is nothing other than consciousness "of the lawful use of freedom" [25: 560].[25]

Kant's new understanding of intellectual pleasure as consciousness of lawful unity has an important implication for the problem of happiness as earlier sketched. Because all our pleasures "aim at" or "relate themselves" to lawful unity, they may now be regarded, "whatever their source," as "alike in kind" [25: 561]. Although "the *objects* of our enjoyments are different in kind [*nicht gleichartig*]," the *enjoyments themselves*" can be added up to form a "sum" that constitutes "total well-being" [*gantze Wohlbefinden*] [emphasis added].[26] Composure, or equanimity, is now defined as "consciousness of a magnitude/quantity [*Größe*] of well-being that outweighs all external circumstances" [25: 561]. Equanimity involves a "self-feeling" analogous to the "self-feeling" of a "completely healthy body." Just as the pleasurable feeling in a healthy body of its own life force is not diminished by incidental pains whose causes do not sap that force, so the pleasurable feeling, in a healthy soul, of the very source of life, is not diminished by bodily pain, even when its causes are life threatening:

> Health of soul and body is ... the maximum sum [*größte Summe*] of pleasure and enjoyment, a greatest sum of pleasure one always feels even when there are pains. The basis of this lies in the human being himself. He who has such strength of mind as to feel the whole sum [*ganze Summe*] of pleasure and enjoyment ... neither gladdens himself over enjoyment, nor grieves himself over pain. ... Well-being must thus be a determinate sum [*bestimmte Summe*] that I feel in myself, one that can neither be extraordinarily enlarged through supplements of pleasure, nor extraordinarily diminished through disappointments. [25: 561–562]

The "composed and steady" man, in other words, estimates his pleasures and his pains by their relation to the "whole" and "determinate" sum that corresponds to his life principle [25: 571–572].

Physical and moral pleasure, according to the view here expounded, are homogeneous expressions of life activity—a point made even more forcefully in Kant's roughly contemporaneous lectures on metaphysics: *"Whatever harmonizes with freedom agrees with the whole of life. Whatever agrees with the whole of life pleases"* [28: 250]. The result is an assimilation of physical and moral life that verges on vitalism. Spirit no longer "grounds" activity or "uses" life, but is the "activity" of life itself. It is not surprising that unpublished remarks from this period experiment with notions of a "world soul" and other appeals to a single, unified life spirit.[27] *Friedländer* thus represents a high-water mark in Kant's experiment with the view that moral virtue is motivated by a kind of pleasure that is greater than but no different in kind from any other. To be sure, estimation of the pleasure corresponding to the "sum" of life requires "reason" as well as "sense"—raising issues concerning the relation between a sensibly intuited and rationally thought whole that are taken up at length in Kant's contemporary lectures on metaphysics.[28]

But if Kant flirts with vitalism, he does not commit to it. Just as the nature of "feeling" is "hard to determine" [28: 246], the workings of desire are too "subtle" to clarify precisely:

> Desire is pleasure [*Wohlgefallen*] in the *reality* [Wirklichkeit] of the object. Desire cannot be explained exactly [*Genau kann man die Begierden nicht erklären*]; still, insofar as it belongs to anthropology, it is in thinking being what moving force is in the corporeal world. It is a thinking being's active force of determining itself to action. This is something subtle.   [25: 577]

Although Kant no longer speaks of "spiritual movement" as a "contradiction *in adjecto*," the precise nature of the "active force" by which a thinking being "determines itself to action" remains "something subtle." All desire is driven, in Kant's current view, by the "foretaste of future rest"—rest being a "delight that all men seek." Each "thinks first about what he should learn, then about assuming a post, then about marrying, and dying at peace, and this lazy effort to acquire rest makes us industrious." Whereas *Parow* had spoken of an intrinsic pleasure in activity, *Friedländer* insists that we are driven to act by the desire for satisfaction or peace. Peace, however, takes both a passive and an active form. Chronologically speaking, the passive form is primary: Naturally "inert," individuals and states are incited to industry and culture only by conditions external to themselves (such as rivalry with others) [25: 580].

But peace or rest also has a higher, active form: We are also "at rest" when our mind is "composed" [*in Fassung ist*]—that is to say, "under the control of our will" [*unter unserer Willkühr ist*]. Composure is not only compatible with activity but itself demands it. On the one hand, a composed mind can both feel (as when one senses the beauty of a sunlit morning) and desire (as when one is "busy at one's post" or "with some plan"). On the other hand, "it takes much effort and exercise to maintain the mind at rest," which one accomplishes, above all, by "stipulating to oneself [*sich festsetze*] that one act from principles" [25: 588]. To be mentally at rest is to be active in the constant labor of maintaining one's composure.

Such "active" rest involves a pleasure that is intrinsically superior to that which motivates men still under the (partial) sway of animality. The latter work for nature rather than themselves: Affects and passions are nature's way of "straining our powers" until reason is on the scene to carry out its own ends directly [25: 617]. In contrast, the "composed" human being is able to act "effectively" toward some deliberate end consistent with his own principles. The person whose mind is in motion may well serve nature's purposes (e.g., by reproducing) but does not feel his own life as a "determinate sum of pleasure." Only the composed, who feel their lives as a whole, "properly estimate the value of an object in relation to [their] total well-being." The decision of the will to take control transforms a life that has value (or is "justified") from nature's standpoint (whose end is the perfection of the species as a whole) to a life worth living from the standpoint of the individual himself.

Only the composed feel the pleasure of life as a "determinate sum." Hence the paradoxically "repellent" character of an indefinitely extended life (like other "comedies" whose incompleteness we find "irksome") [25: 615, 28, 290]. However great the total, it would never constitute a "*determinate* sum," and hence a "feeling for the unity of life as a whole."

That feeling, which involves subordination of all subsidiary activities to a "rule of understanding," is necessarily associated with concepts. But how concepts can move the will is a question Kant still cannot answer:

> The power [*Vermögen*] to act from principles [*Grundsätzen*] and maxims consists in a man being able to act from concepts [*daß der Mensch nach Begriffen handeln kann*]; concepts must be his incentives [*Triebfeder*]. To be sure, concepts can't be incentives, for what is an object of understanding can't be an object of feeling. But an incentive must be an object of feeling if it is to be able to move us. Nevertheless, although the concepts of good and evil aren't objects of feeling, they can still serve to arouse feeling.... To be sure, one cannot see [*einsehen*] why the concept, e.g., of injustice done to someone

should arouse feeling and how it can move a human being to lend aid, and yet it happens [*aber es geschicht doch*]. [25: 649–650]

The ideal of the composed mind unites the virtue of the Stoic with the pleasure of the Epicurean. But it does not adequately address Kant's original complaint: "the Stoic rule of not letting oneself be *overpowered* by inclinations" is "the true rule of wisdom." The difficulty lies in showing how to make it effective [25: 38–39]. The perfect man may well derive an overriding pleasure from his virtue; but the novice in virtue has nothing to motivate him but the promise of a quantity of pleasure he cannot sensibly anticipate.

How intellectual concepts can move the will remains as mysterious as in *Collins/Parow*. But Kant's response is different. Instead of seeking recourse in a moral sentiment "analogous to taste" (as in *Collins/Parow*), he now looks to knowledge of "what happens" (or, alternatively, to "history" [*Geschichte*]). Although we "cannot comprehend" how the mere "concept" of injustice can "move a human being," "*it happens*" [es geschicht doch; emphasis added] [25: 650]. That the possibility of being "moved by concepts" rests, finally, on our knowledge of "what happens" (or, if one prefers, our knowledge of human "history") puts pragmatic anthropology (or knowledge of all worldly relations) at center stage.

What "happens" to human beings, both individually and collectively, takes its model, in turn, from the developmental process of organic nature. Composure is now described as maturity of mind, i.e., a kind of "ripeness" that falls between the "madness" of youth and the "folly" of old age, or between a need for rules as "go-carts" and descent into dry pedantry [25: 620]. The age appropriate for marriage is the age of mental ripeness generally:[29]

> Middle age [*Mittel Alter*], or the age of manhood, is the age of wisdom [*Klugheit*], in which one can *rightly* estimate the value of things, and at which one can arrive between one's 30th and 40th year.... Judgment concerning the true value of things is found neither in youth nor in old age. Thus the young do not like to let the old make decisions for them about marriage. The old have already forgotten what it is like to be in love. They cannot grasp how one can spoil a fortune for the sake of a pretty face while the young man on his part cannot grasp why he should give up charm for money. There is thus a middle age, in which one knows how rightly to estimate the value of things. For there is a madness of youth and a folly of old age. [25: 620]

The "seasonable development" that allows one to estimate things at their true value (or to take "immediate enjoyment in the good") is a mean between impetuosity and avarice. And yet a certain asymmetry prevails in favor of youth: Whereas youth can be helped by "rules," age suffers from a vice that "reason cannot cure":

> Avarice [*Geitz*] is the only passion that has no end, no object, but concerns itself merely with a means [*Mittel*]. The miser is thus also absurd, because he contradicts himself. He who saves money to be employed hereafter [*hernach*], in order to do something with it, or to pursue another end—such a person is not stingy but rather one who saves without any end at all.... No moralist or priest has ever improved a miser.... Here reason doesn't help because he is in conflict with himself. [25: 618]

That avarice in the old is in keeping with the ends of animal nature does not make it any less contrary to reason: Although "there is a natural [animal] tendency to be parsimonious [*kargen*]," reason "commands opposing this inclination and saving [*sparen*] only with intention [*Absicht*]" [25: 617]. The absurdity of avarice does not lie in saving "without intention" (in the manner of an animal who thus provides, albeit unwittingly, for its own offspring) but in doing so, as it were, intentionally. By pursuing means as if they were a final end, the miser turns reason on its head—leading Kant to call for "philosophical investigations" into how "avarice is possible" [25: 619].

The proper use of rules (neither as go-carts nor in the manner of the pedant) falls to "common healthy understanding." Understanding (in the broad sense, which includes all higher mental faculties) is either "common" or "speculative." The former judges "in concreto," the latter "in abstracto." Common healthy understanding is concerned with judgment "in the particular case," rather than in the abstract; thus speculative understanding, which deals only in the abstract, is never "healthy" [25: 538]. Pedantry, or knowledge without judgment to apply it to the particular case, arises from lack of "exercise in applying all one's knowledge to the world." The specific remedy for pedantry (if not for avarice as such) is thus pragmatic anthropology [*Weltkenntniße* {25: 539}].

Understanding in the broadest sense is the faculty of "bringing representations under the universal rules of knowledge" or, alternatively, the "force of making use of all representations," Thinking is not "representing things," which "happens [*geschiehet*] through sensibility," but the "working over of material that sensibility dispenses." Understanding without sensibility is thus like a "government [*Regierung*] without subjects" or "economizing [*Wirthschaft*] without something over which to exercise economy [*etwas über man wirthschaften kann*]" [25: 537].

Mental immaturity is in some cases the result of a defective nature, in others of poor education. Thus some peoples (e.g., Russians) require external guidance, while others, capable of governing and thinking for themselves, are made "stupid" by unnecessary compulsion, especially the "compulsion of imitation" [25: 547]. Feminine understanding is perpetually immature [*unmündig*], despite the early ripening of women's ability to manage a household. The economizing that young girls perform, as it were, by nature, emerges in men only once they are in a position to know the cost of things "in effort" [25: 542–543].

Reason, narrowly construed, derives rules *a priori*, while understanding, narrowly construed, derives them from experience. To judge experience on the basis of *a priori* rules belongs to reason rather than understanding; thus a minister "only needs understanding to carry out the orders of a king, but needs reason to make the plan itself" [25: 545].

Kant's political example, and the accompanying analogy, is particularly instructive: Reason may be the minister who "makes the plan," but it is not the sovereign. Something more is needed to give those plans authority. Reason, in Kant's current view, is not self-commanding; still it seeks the ground of things. Thus reason ("which will have reasons [*Gruende*]!") makes a person mutinous against unjust compulsion [25: 547]. Rulers wrongly conclude that popular education is dangerous: Subjects should not "quibble" [*vernuenfteln*] with soldiers but obey them. Kant counters that a people unaccustomed to making use of their own reason may be more tractable in the short run (they will not "quibble" with soldiers); in the long run, however, they remain "stiff-necked" and "stupid" [25: 456]. Wise rulers, we are encouraged to conclude, will both foster the development of reason in their subjects and avoid compelling them without reason or unjustly.

Reasoning comes to an end in reasons that have moral necessity—e.g., compulsion recognized as just. Accordingly, "healthy, common reason" supplies knowledge of "how things must be" by virtue of its "idea" or "model" of "how things ought to be disposed" [25: 550–551].[30]

This capacity on healthy common reason's part answers to a specific tendency among the thoughtful toward "misology"—arising from reason's "futile effort" [*vergeblicher Bemühung*]. As Kant goes on to explain:

> It is a property of meditative persons who set about investigating their future determination [*Bestimmung*] and chief end [*Hauptzweck*] that they finally conclude [*die sich zuletzt darinn endigen*] that man has insight into his lack of knowledge [*Unwissenheit*]. Now if the reason of the knowing cannot do

> enough—if it cannot satisfy man in this—so that man cannot look away to the goal/boundary [*Ziel*] and end of all things [*Ende aller Dinge*], then man takes to simplicity, and renounces reason entirely, just as someone becomes a misanthrope out of susceptibility to virtue, that is to say, not because he hates human beings, but because he finds none as he wishes them to be. [25: 553]

The lover of reason, disappointed in his hopes, becomes a hater—above all, where the love concerns "knowledge of the future."

It is not only rulers uninstructed in the true political economy, then, who threaten reason's ripening. Reason itself is prone to *vernünfeln*—i.e., "lifting itself beyond the limits of practical use." Such exercises in futility make reason reasonably hateful to itself [25: 546, 577–578]. Misology arises from the effort of a reasoning person to determine the conditions of his own future life (if any). The "greatest yearning of a human being," according to *Metaphysik 1*, is "not to know the actions of the soul, which we cognize through experience, but to know its future state" [28: 263].

But reason can also "make an idea" of its own "limits" or "determination," and in so doing inhibit reason's tendency toward exertions whose futility reason itself finds hateful. The main business of philosophy is to "lay out" these limits—i.e., to use reason in the manner of an "architect" [*architectonische*] rather than a "technician" [*technische*]:

> The technical use of reason consists only in executing—not in laying out—the plan. To this is related all difference between a *rational artisan* [Vernünftkunstlers] *and one learned in the law* [Gesetzkundigen] *of reason.* The difference here is the same as that between a surgeon and a medical doctor. The latter has the idea, which the former executes. The true meaning of "philosopher" is *"one who is learned in the law* of human reason." The philosopher must lay out the first grounds and have insight into the highest rules and principles of the determination of reason and its limits. [25: 551]

This task, however, cannot be fully carried out:

> We can well have insight about the laws and rules, but to have insight into *the* spirit of the rule and the field of reason's use is something entirely different. Man thus approaches the philosopher the more he meditates [*nachdenkt*] upon the determination of human reason. [25: 551]

It is one thing to grasp the (stiff-necked) letter of the law; it is an altogether different thing to take in its "spirit." Completion of *the* philosophic task—"sketching out" (or, alternatively, "announcing") the laws of human reason on the basis of this latter insight—is one that man "approaches the more he meditates upon the determination of human reason."

The proper object of human meditation [*nachdenken*] is not one's own "future determination" (as the misologist wrongly believes) but the determination of human reason itself. But how is this meditation to be reasonably conducted?

In partial answer, Kant sets forth the following "maxim" of healthy reason: to *adopt only those rules "that permit the greatest possible use of reason" and by which "the use of reason is made easier* [*erleichtert*]" [25: 549; emphasis added]. If reason is a tool for the attainment of our ends, it should be used (like any tool) to gain most with least. The healthy reasoner is a kind of miser of the mind. In ruling out ghost stories and other claims that can't be empirically tested, the "maxim of healthy reason" makes no speculative assertion as to whether ghosts do or do not exist; it rules them out only with a view to maximizing and easing the pursuit of *Gründe* generally [25: 549]. The general economic rule (pursue ends by the easiest possible means) is here applied by reason (which will have *Gründe*) to itself. A healthy use of reason (as distinguished from *vernünfteln*) is one that can be corroborated [*bestätigt*] by experience, absent which test reason expends itself without real effect.

The boundary between metaphysics and anthropology is thus a shaded one. Rational psychology must "borrow from experience" [*Metaphysik 1*, 28: 263, 288].[31] As the academic subject of empirical psychology expands, trips will have to be "*undertaken in order to cognize human beings, as they have been undertaken to become acquainted with plants and animals*" [*Metaphysik 1*, 28: 224, original emphasis]. In sum: Anthropological research directed toward observation of the similarities and differences among human beings of the various sexes, nationalities, and races promises metaphysics the empirical corroboration that it requires if reason is to remain "healthy."

Current evidence in this regard[32] suggests the following: The limits of reason include dependence on certain bodily conditions and a related temperamental balance that experience suggests to be uniquely European.[33] According to the evidence available, nature has denied races originating from other continents the ability to judge from concepts (as opposed to images) and with it any possibility of genuine morality.[34] Where intellectual and moral progress is concerned, physical geography, it seems, is destiny [25: 551]. All peoples who are unable to judge from concepts, but instead "play with images of the intuition of ghosts," are (as Kant here punningly puts it) "tropical" [*tropische*] [25: 552].[35]

Among those who can judge from concepts (i.e., Europeans), full spiritual maturity must strike a balance between the impetuosity of youthful love and the calculated prudence of miserly old age. To one who can be moved by concepts—i.e., who "intuits" the concept of good and evil—good action is easy—as easy as accepting a bride who is both agreeable to one's inclination and advantageous to one's interest [25: 650, 620–621]. Why some lack this intellectual intuition—whether it be a lack of feeling or its overrefinement—is ultimately, Kant grants, beyond human comprehension. Still the would-be teacher is not without recourse. As he goes on to state in a remarkable passage:

> The incentive to act from good principles might well be the idea that were all to act thusly this earth would be a paradise. This motivates me [*treibt mich an*] to contribute to this eventuality, and if it does not happen [*geschicht*] at least this doesn't lie with me. I for my part am still a member of this paradise, which would occur were everyone so. Thus can the concept of the good be an incentive, and this is good character. [25: 650]

Where he had earlier addressed the problem of moral motivation by appealing to visions of eternity (or "thinking without the body"), he now turns to an idea of history expressive of the value of human existence overall, and absent which the development and use of reason would have cost man more than it is worth. The idea of man's joint physical and moral perfection, progressively achieved, is thus made morally effectual in the here and now. The anticipated effect of this idea is twofold: On the one hand, it should stir us to moral action; on the other, it should relieve our concern about the future. The paradise that I anticipate is one that I belong to already. This dual structural effect—both immediate and indefinitely deferred—will remain a crucial element in all subsequent deployments of Kant's historical *Lieblingsidee* in its various versions.

According to Kant's current scheme, historical progress is initially propelled by rivalry and competition stemming from natural inclination [see, e.g., 25: 581–582, 612, 679]. In keeping with the scheme, he now classifies nations mainly by their choice of general means (be it wealth, honor, health, or freedom) to satisfy inclination, rather than by their taste, as formerly [25: 583]. Without this strife, man, being naturally lazy and inert [*träge*], would always have remained so. Man's natural inclination to rest must be disrupted by external hardship: hence the necessity of strife and competition [25: 681]. To be sure, if we could not ascend beyond external compulsion, humanity would "have lost more than it gained" in abandoning the rude state of nature [25: 692]. Civilization will represent a gain for mankind as a whole only when the compulsion it demands is morally internalized. When that happens, an upright man will not only find his life "worth wishing for"; he will enjoy it to the maximum possible extent.

To facilitate that end (which aims to reconcile Stoic and Epicurean ideas of perfection), "the philosopher must make his concepts known," and the student "must develop [*bilden*] his own character." From such beginnings, much, in turn, would follow:

> If teachers and preachers were educated [*gebildet*], if among them concepts of pure morality were master, matters would soon swing upward to the throne, regents would attend school, and the whole would accordingly become educated. [25: 691]

Such considerations make it possible to survey "the entire plan" of human progress, from savagery to the civil condition, up to and including a senate of nations that "finally puts an end to war" [25: 691, 696]. The moral purpose of philosophy, on such an understanding, is not recovery of a state in which philosophy itself is neither possible nor necessary (as in *Remarks*) but to initiate a progressive transformation of humanity and/or inspire us with the thought that paradise on earth is possible.

The idea of history thus finds experiential confirmation in yet another way. Whereas speculation as to our future state as individuals (the knowledge "we most crave") leads only to misology, meditation on the end of history is itself "very agreeable":

> [because one here deals with] an idea that is also possible, even though it may demand thousands of years [to realize]. Nature will always suffice [*zureichen*], until a paradise on earth comes about. Just as nature has always *developed itself* [sich ... *ausgebildet hat*] and still does, and approaches the end for which things are determined, as with the earth's ecliptic which gradually approaches the equator so that sometime in the future day and night will be of equal length all over the earth though it require 140,000 years. In this very way the human species also forms/educates itself, and as many years may fly away before the highest degree of perfection is achieved. [25: 696–697]

Unlike the impossible, and hence idle longings earlier described as "moral wind" [25: 406], the idea of history is one whose possibility is supported by empirical evidence and which thus (uniquely) meets the test of rational health. To be sure, the end of history is an "earthly paradise" that no one presently alive "has any hope of experiencing for himself" [25: 696]. This lack is rectified, however, by a worldly science that reveals a sufficiency on nature's part that extends even to the surface of the earth—whose gradual evening out promises to put an end to "tropicality" [25: 696–697].

The special role of women now lies, above all, in bringing about civil order and refinement "through inclination" rather than compulsion [25: 701, 706]. For this role, civilized woman, despite all her apparent faults, is very aptly equipped—the sister always at home, who in her conversation, politeness, decency, and so on "far surpasses her older brother away at university" [25: 701]. For this women need only a "negative education" that preserves their native wit and playfulness and encourages a sense of (outer) honor: The letters of a housebound sister have more wit and vivacity [*Lebhaftigkeit*] than those of her college-educated brother [25: 705].

Men's and women's specific differences in virtue and vice are expressions of nature's "double end and object"—union, on the one hand, disunion on the other—moving forces necessary to prevent "all sink[ing] into . . . inactivity" [25: 718]. Even the war between the sexes is enlisted in the services of such vitalizing motion:

> Human beings have an inclination to society but also to war; it is *vis activa* and *reactiva*, for otherwise human beings might congeal [*zusammenschmelzen*] into constant union, from which would arise complete inactivity and quiet.[36] Thus in marriage too there is a predisposition to unity and to war. The female aptitude gives occasion to quarrel and war, which serves new unification; and even peace founded after such a war serves to enliven the household, so long as there is no *subjection* but instead complete equality. [25: 719]

In the relation between the sexes as in the relation among nations (as *Toward Perpetual Peace* will warn twenty years later) peace should not be bought at life's expense. Indeed, all of women's apparent imperfections can be traced, in the first instance, to nature's interest in maximizing reproductive vitality [*Lebhaftigkeit*]. Because "receiving is easier than giving," man must be stronger [25: 709].[37]

Boys, who are naturally both stronger and less refined than girls, require for that very reason greater discipline. Accordingly, Kant praises Basedow's school, the *Philanthropin* (the "greatest phenomenon to appear in this century for the improvement of the perfection of humanity" [25: 722–723]), where, in a departure from the strict teaching of Rousseau, young boys are, for example, taught a second language.[38] Youths need more than the purely negative education of Rousseau—that "finer Diogenes, who posited perfection in the simplicity of nature" [25: 724]. The final level of education is respect for the dignity of man in one's own person (or "true love of honor"), only after which one turns (in good Emilian fashion) to ethics and religion:

> *When* must religious education begin? At the point at which the child can see [*einsehen kann*] that there must be an author [*Urheber*]. If a child becomes accustomed to religion earlier, so that he babbles his prayers in mimicry, this has no effect. . . . [39] But if he *learns to see the order in nature and the traces of its author*, then one must say to him that there is an author, and what this author will have—what is his law and will—and then one can influence him to be grateful to God. [25: 728, original emphasis]

Gratitude toward God—precisely on the grounds that nature's purposiveness reveals the traces of His wisdom—does not limit itself to the merely physical order, stressed by Rousseau's tutor,[40] but, and even especially, extends to human affairs.[41] Pragmatic anthropology, so construed, becomes a quasi-religious exercise—a physico-theology that not only yields "agreeable hope" but also exercises the "influence" that helps make up youth's "positive" instruction in morality. That Kant's auditors are of just the age for which, on his account, such instruction is appropriate makes Kant's pragmatic anthropology the natural continuation and completion of the pedagogy that informs Basedow's *Philanthropin*.[42]

In sum: Kant's *Friedländer* lectures represent a high point in his effort to reconcile nature and freedom in terms of a single principle of "life," in which sense and reason, concept and intuition, are united.[43] The goal of humanity, on such a view, is the simultaneous earthly realization of our animal and human perfections, the two natural ends whose historical divergence moves mankind forward. And yet the "peace" we seek threatens to "congeal" into a lifeless heap. All of nature's purported purposiveness would founder on this fact, but for the "double" end nature pursues by virtue of the sexual difference—which Kant here calls "important" and "worthy of philosophy" [25: 707]. No less than in his earlier anthropological writings, sex carries out a crucial role, here providing a needed moment of transition between physical inertia (or rest as the essential feature of dead matter) and spiritual composure (or rest as the proper end of reason). Hence, the special debt of gratitude men owe to women, whose divergent goal keeps human affairs in motion and thus guarantees the ongoing progress and perfection of the species. This gratitude is reflected, perhaps, in Kant's particularly lively and sympathetic depictions of women in these lectures, side by side his usual criticisms.

3. Anthropology Lectures after 1777

The first extant lecture of this period is *Pillau*.

a. Pillau: *Count Verri and the Sovereignty of Reason*

The *Pillau* lectures of 1777–1778 are the first to mention the theories of Pietro Verri, whose essay on pleasure and pain appeared in German in 1777. Here, for the first time, Kant endorses Verri's claim that in life, pain inevitably outweighs pleasure—a thesis that Kant will hereafter consistently maintain.[44] The *Pillau* lectures display other new features related to that change, including 1) New emphasis on the difference between happiness and what he calls "self-satisfaction."[45] 2) A continuation of the trend, already registered in *Friedländer*, that puts greater emphasis on work and a work-related characterization of peoples as a source of human progress. The special advantage of Europe no longer lies, essentially, in its treatment of women but instead in its unique possession of "spirit" and accompanying qualities of inventiveness and industriousness.[46] 3) A new insistence on the difference between the subjective feeling of life's furtherance or hindrance and the objective reality [25: 785–786]. 4) A marked change in tone: Where *Friedländer* is almost contemplative, *Pillau* is all business—the former, inviting meditation on the purposiveness of human nature as a mark of divine authorship, the latter, resting that purposiveness, more precariously and urgently, upon future human effort and discovery.[47] *Pillau* ends, not, as with the *Friedländer* lectures, in a humanized and historicized physico-theology, but in a list of human inventions. These historical "milestones" stretch from the development of agriculture and the division of labor through the discovery of money, the compass, and gunpowder, and culminate in "the thought of Rousseau." Kant continues, by way of explanation:

> [Rousseau] has written a book that has made a great stir, called "On Human Inequality," in which much misanthropy rules but out of benevolence. He shows what is terrible and intolerable in the civil condition and, on the other hand, what is agreeable in the raw condition. But one must not understand this to mean that he preferred the raw condition to every civil condition; instead he shows only that our present civil condition is less in conformity with human nature than was the raw condition we left behind, and if we had no hope of going further he would advise our going back to the state of nature. But he does not maintain, as some believe, that the destiny of man was to live in the forest. . . . Rousseau showed how a civil constitution must be to

achieve the entire *end* of human nature. He showed how youth must be educated. . . . and in which constitution various peoples must step in order to reduce many barbaric wars to friendly conflict. He thus showed, above all, that the seeds of the development of our determination lie in us, and that we need on this account a civil constitution in order to fulfill the ends of nature. But if we remain in the current civil constitution, it would be better to return to the state of savagery. [25: 846–847]

Rousseau remains Kant's guide—indeed, Kant now compares his thought to such epochal human achievements as the discovery of agriculture and the invention of writing. The proof text, however, has changed, from *Emile* to the *Discourse on Inequality*. The accompanying "misanthropy" bespeaks a new and sober resolution. Man is naturally driven forward, not by his anticipation of future rest (as *Friedländer* had equivocally held), but by present pain.

5) Most dramatically: Reason is no longer merely a ministerial "tool" (useful for "drawing up the plans") but itself the "lawgiver." As Kant now emphatically puts it:

A lawgiver [*Gesetzgeber*] uses reason; a teacher of the law [*Gesetzlehrer*] uses understanding; and a judge [*Richter*] uses judgment [25: 774]. . . . *Rule* pertains to a certain preferred end. *Law*, however, determines the end. Because the end is the highest ground of unity, reason is the lawgiver [*die Gesetzgeberin*]. [25: 777]

Reason, in short, furnishes the idea or principle that establishes the "unity" of the whole [25: 777].

It is not only reason's law-giving function that bears noting here, but also the new relation laid down between law and reason's "end." Reason is not "determined" to its primary activity as giver of the law [*Gesetzgeber/geberin*] by some end (such as future rest); instead its law-giving activity is *sui generis*. Reading Verri seems to have liberated Kant from his formerly fixed view that human beings are necessarily moved to act by the representation of an aim or "object" and an accompanying "pleasure" (or other felt register of goodness).

The good will, on that earlier understanding, is "determined" to activity by its object no less than is the will subject to domination by sensible desire. The object of a good will is distinguished, according to Kant's earlier view, by two characteristics: its ideal character (or origination among the higher mental faculties) and its compatibility with membership in an intelligible community. As we shall see, Verri's argument as to the necessary preponderance of pain over pleasure gives rise to an understanding of life that makes it possible to conceive human reason as free in a new and more radical sense. If animal life is always characterized by more pain than pleasure, our natural purpose cannot be happiness. And if we are sensibly "driven" to activity, not by anticipation of future rest=pleasure, but by "ineffable" pains of which we are hardly aware, then the "ground" that underlies the higher movements of the soul may also escape conscious notice.

Kant's early experiments in *Pillau* with this new understanding look to the "form" rather than the "matter" of the will exercising the determining influence. And they now associate the feeling of life with "work" rather than satisfaction and composure:

> Work is that to which one is driven by desire; it prolongs our life, as experience shows, for human beings can only become old by working; for life does not maintain itself by resting [*durch die Ruhe*]. When we have worked a great deal, only this gives us an idea of having lived a long time. [25: 796]

The "end," for its part, no longer motivates the will, but merely lends it focus. The point of life is no longer rest and its accompanying pleasure but work directed into the incalculable/unforeseeable [*unabsehlich*] future.

The extraordinary significance, both theoretical and practical, of Kant's new understanding of the "laws of desire" is hinted at in various unpublished reflections of the late 1770s. By detaching the reality of freedom from direct insight into the soul "as substance," the "true economy of human nature" dissolves the last intellectual hurdle standing in the way of a definitive determination by human reason of its own limits. In theory as in practice, the end or object of reason is secondary to self-legislation. Reason in its theoretical use is now primarily conceived as laying down the conditions of the lawful unity of experience, just as, in its practical use, it lays down the lawful conditions of a possible moral world. Formal lawgiving in each case takes precedence over the idea of totality to which reason's formula gives rise, an idea that is "regulative" for reason rather than "constitutive" of a possible object of experience. As Kant puts it an extended reflection from the late 1770s:

> Lawgiving necessarily has ideas, which can never be fully executed. But they are not nothing or over-reaching [*überschwendliche*] on this account. Transcendental philosophy needs ideas as necessarily as morality does. Plato's hyperbolic uplifting of ideas as original forms are not to be complained of when personified in the highest intelligence. They are the measures of things, which limit one another and do not attain their individual ends, so that no experience is congruent with them. [from *Duisburg 9*, 18: 226–227]

As he goes on to say:

> We can call reason the faculty of ideas. There are sensible ideas and also ideas of pure reason. These are either practical or speculative; the latter are transcendental ideas. These are necessary concepts of reason of which no object can be given in experience.... As necessary concepts of reason they must contain the entire use of understanding, i.e., that use in its totality, and as transcendent concepts this totality must go beyond all sensible intuition. [18: 228]

In practice, too, Kant is emphatic as to the primacy of law-giving over the ideas with which it is inextricably connected. Reason's law-giving is necessarily bound up with "ideas" that "cannot be executed." The reality of freedom is not intuitable, Kant now insists; it lies rather in a transcendental act through which reason binds itself to carry out a task that cannot be completed—an act known only as it were by its effects.

To be sure, the dual character of this self-legislation produces mysteries of its own:

> The only insoluble metaphysical difficulty is this: connecting the highest condition of all practical unity with the condition of speculative unity: that is, freedom with nature or the causality of understanding in regard to appearances. For freedom is the possibility of actions from causes through understanding [*Verstandes-Ursachen*]. The spontaneity of understanding in the series of appearances is the riddle. Absolute necessity is the second riddle, which nature doesn't yield, but only pure understanding. This is the original condition of the possibility of nature. By the first an appearance isn't necessary but contingent under the conditions of appearance. By the second something is unconditionally necessary. [*Reflexion* 5121, 18: 98]

The connection between freedom and the "causality of understanding in regard to appearances" remains elusive:

> Freedom and absolute necessity are the only pure concepts of reason that are objective but unclarifiable. For by reason one understands the self activity to go from the universal to the particular, and to do this *a priori*, hence with necessity simply. Absolute necessity with regard to the determined, and freedom with regard to the determinable. [*Reflexion* 5441, 18: 183]

This much, however, *is* clear to Kant: Though we can have no experience of freedom, the moral law commands us, and this suffices:

> Do we have an experience of being free? (No! For then we would have to be able to experience [say] in the case of all men that they can withstand the

greatest stimulus. On the other hand, the moral law says: you should withstand; it must follow that they can.) [*Reflexion* 5434, 18: 181]

There is a strong analogy, then (however imperfectly clarified), between reason's two world-forming functions, or between "universally made apprehension" and "universally made appetition": "reason lays down conditions of knowledge in general, and of universal validity concerning judgment as to well-being and ill-being" [*Reflexion* 5620, 18: 258].

Kant is at special pains to insist that even in the latter case (or what he here calls "universal appetition"), the "impulsive cause" lies in reason rather than its object or the pleasure that accompanies its realization. As he puts it in a series of reflections:

> The will is a faculty/capacity of acting according to the representation of a rule as law. Faculty [according to] ends. stimuli are pleasures that precede the law. independence from stimulus means law preceding pleasure. (pure will) (freedom is causality of pure reason in the determination of choice.).
> [*Reflexion* 5435, 18: 181]

or again:

> Freedom is the faculty/capacity of being determined through reason alone, and not merely mediately but immediately, thus not through matter but form of law. thus moral.   [*Reflexion* 5436, 18: 181]

Freedom, in other words, is "the faculty of acting according to self-given laws" [*Reflexion* 5439, dating ambiguous, 18: 182].

Though he occasionally flirts with his older opinion, according to which "moral laws do not originate in reason" [*Reflexion* 5445, 18: 184], his more settled view identifies freedom as "the faculty of acting according to self-given laws" [*Reflexion* 5439, dating ambiguous, 18: 182]. Accordingly, moral feeling is so "only by analogy, expressing something [not receptivity] without a name" [*Reflexion* 5448, 18: 185]. Pleasure "either precedes or follows the law." In the latter case "it is respect" [*Reflexion* 5615, 18: 255].

This feeling without a name that Kant comes to call "respect" is the consequence, not the *causa impulsiva*, of rational self-legislation. Contrary to his earlier view, a rational will is not moved by the anticipation of future rest. Perfection is not to be identified with rest, however "actively" conceived:

> Happiness in this world consists in progress; hence it can never be fully achieved. Each moment drives us out of our present condition. Morally perfection as well. Thus the future toward which there should be progress.

> Accordingly, not improvement in dying. Not eternity of condemnation or making blessed but rather the inforeseeability/incalculability [*Unabsehlichkeit*] of progress. [*Reflexion* 5480, 18: 194–195]

Both "happiness," and "moral perfection" now extend into the "incalculability of progress," profoundly altering Kant's concept of an afterlife: Dying no longer offers the ambiguous promise of immediate "improvement" through separation from the body.

The "knowledge of our future state" that constituted the object, in Kant's earlier view, of our "deepest longing" has been firmly set beyond the limits of experience. Eternity is now understood in the manner of a mathematical limit—i.e., as a placeholder toward which perfection may be conceived to proceed indefinitely.[48] In sum: Kant is on the verge of that critical use of sublime images as symbols for ideas for which no representation can be adequate. Ideas are not "representations" at all, but instead, the "imaginary foci" of tasks—in principle endless—that the human mind imposes on itself. In this scheme of things, *Unabsehlichkeit* stands as a token for reason's own transcendence of the merely calculable and representable. In short, Kant's new position opens up a kind of space between the limits of experience and the limits of reason as such: "understanding gives unity to appearances; reason gives it to the rules of understanding" [25: 777]. Reason's "great dignity" lies in its being "highest"—i.e., in being a source of lawful unity that applies to experience only indirectly. The space, as it were, in which reason operates is transcendental, as he will later say, without being transcendent. *Vernünfteln*—i.e., the abuse of reason—no longer lies in using it beyond the limits of experience but using it without principles or regard for "true *ends*" [25: 1039, 1481].

Ideas, in Kant's current understanding, establish the *a priori* possibility of a certain kind of whole. An idea is the intuition of "that in a thing which is possible *a priori* through knowledge." Prudent actions "are possible through concepts derived from experience; virtuous actions, on the other hand, are possible through concepts *a priori*" [25: 777]. Ideas testify to a peculiar sort of *a priori* possibility independent of the conditions that define a possible experience. They thereby validate a task (be virtuous!) whose (complete) execution is impossible in time. That necessary incompleteness should no longer give rise to "irritation" (as in *Friedländer*), because its source can now be seen to lie, properly, in reason itself. In sum, the boundary between a rational idea and a high-flying chimera can now be limned precisely.

What remains unknown is how far man can in this life approach the goal set before us by our own reason. Moral education furnishes some evidence as to the natural disposition that lies "hidden in the soul" but even this is riven by uncertainty.

> The disposition to morality that lies in human nature is discovered through education; but we cannot know whether a much better sort of education might not be invented by which the moral disposition (otherwise hidden away in the soul) might be better revealed. [25: 838]

Despite his earlier encomiums to Rousseau, Kant ends in hopeful anticipation of further discoveries in the field of moral education [25: 847].

b. Menschenkunde [1781–1782]

This new orientation is extended in the *Menschenkunde* lectures of 1781–1782, which reaffirm reason's lawgiving status as that which gives it "its entire dignity" [25: 1039]. Reason is now the late bloom of one capable of "thinking for himself" [25: 1037]. And the *Vernünftler* [*raisonniren*] is one whose reason judges without a proper "concept of the whole" [25: 1041]. To be sure, the *Publicum* should not reason [*raisonniren*] but obey. And yet, as Kant states with even greater emphasis than in *Friedländer*, a people must be free to make mistakes in reasoning lest the species make no further progress [25: 1042].

Philosophy, for its part,

> is the lawgiver of human reason; who must therefore be distinguished from one who is merely an artisan of reason [*Vernunftkünstler*], who applies reason with regard to his own particular end.... But the philosopher shows to what purpose all of this is to be used.... In this way reason is actually [*wirklich*] lawgiving.... Philosophy shows what all these [e.g., mathematics, physics, etc.] have as a final end; it thus furnishes the highest principles and maxims, and in this consists philosophy's true dignity.... The organon of philosophy that should contain the highest principles and limits of our use of reason, is the highest matter [*Stufe*] of reason. [25: 1042–1043]

Philosophy is no longer bent on an unfinished quest for reason's "limits." Progress has moved from the arena of fundamental discovery to that of application to "particular objects" whose working out falls under reason's "guidance" [25: 1043]. Whereas understanding is taken up mainly with the present, reason is taken up with the future, "because this must be completed [*geschlossen*]" [25: 1045].

Menschenkunde also reaffirms Count Verri's claims, which "ground," as Kant now states, a "true economy of human nature" [25: 1073]. The general tone is established early on:

One wonders whether enjoyments can be present alone . . . , and whether we are capable of having one at any time, or whether they must always be preceded by pains, so that enjoyment is merely the cancellation of pain, and not lasting, pain alone being self-sufficient. *Here human life seems to be melancholy* and not to contain anything of value. [25: 1069]

Yet this indeed seems to be the case. Human life, Kant now confidently insists, involves more pain than enjoyment. With Verri's help, Kant is able to resolve the difficulty created by the fact that pleasures are not homogeneous—a consideration that once led him to dispute the Stoic claim, repeated by Maupertuis, that our pains necessarily exceed our pleasures.[49] Life force expresses itself in a certain neutral measure of well-being [*Wohlbefinden*]. Enjoyment is possible only when this force is somehow reduced, so that a hindrance to life can be canceled and life thereby promoted. Thus, enjoyment must follow pain, but not conversely. Because pain is self-sufficient, whereas enjoyment requires contrast, pain can persist indefinitely; man, on the other hand, "cannot stand ever-enduring pleasure" [25: 1070]. Hence, the total sum of pain always outweighs the total sum of enjoyments. We find ourselves "constantly gripped by nameless pains," which we call "restlessness" and "desire"; and the more life force one has, "the more strongly one feels pain" [25: 1075]. As Kant will put it in the *Groundlaying of the Metaphysics of Morals:*

> The value of life for us, if it is assessed merely in terms of *what one enjoys/delights in* [was man genießt] (the natural end of the sum of all inclinations, happiness), is easy to decide. It sinks below zero; for who would enter life anew under the same conditions, or even according to a new, self-projected plan (though in conformity with the course of nature), were it set merely toward delight? [4: 434n][50]

Because of this painful feeling endemic to earthly life, time without an alteration of impressions weighs heavily on us; boredom literally makes time pass more slowly. And since pain makes life longer to us, "it must constitute the true [*recht*] feeling of life." Enjoyment, on the other hand, makes time shorter—another proof that it is not a positive enhancement of life, but merely a negation of life's hindrance [25: 1074].[51]

Enjoyment does not "entice us into the future" but instead encourages us to conserve our forces. (Enjoyment is thus "conservative" in a most literal sense.) Pain, on the other hand, impels us to "propose something new" [25: 1071]:

> A kind of impatience assails men to alleviate their little pains—one sees from this that we seek out an object of enjoyment in advance; without yet

knowing that object, we merely ferret it out as a cure for the unrest that drives and torments us.... If man is constantly occupied, and always making plans, it is not that he is enticed by the prospect of enjoyment; rather, he himself first seeks to acquire it; he is driven to leave behind the condition of pain in order to procure alleviation. [25: 1070]

Even when nothing hurts our body, we are racked by "nameless pains" that compel us to "propose something" [25: 1070–1071]:

> When we direct our eyes to the course of things, we find a drive in us that compels us at each moment to go out of our condition. We are forced [*genöthigt*] to this by a goad [*Stachel*], a driving spring, through which all men (as animals) are set in activity: man is always troubled [*gequält*] in thought.... He ... lives always in a future time, and cannot linger [*verweilen*] in the present.... Man thus finds himself in constant pain, and this is the spur to activity in human nature. [However it may be with creatures on other planets] our lot is so constituted that nothing endures with us but pain.
> [25: 1069–1070]

Kant here definitively abandons the attempt, advanced in *Friedländer*, to understand happiness as a determinate sum of pleasure that enables one to "feel one's life as a whole." Contrary to earlier claims, the notion of our condition as a whole cannot be united with one of maximum pleasure. (Accordingly, Kant no longer praises "fullness of feeling" as "the greatest enjoyment" [25: 794]).[52] Happiness understood (following Lucretius) as the "maximum sum of joys" or "complete satisfaction of all our inclinations" is "a kind of ideal" of which "we can make no concept" [25: 1081]:[53]

> We cannot even a single time represent such a possibility to ourselves of a life entirely composed of delight in pure enjoyments. We can never bring forth a complete whole with which we might be completely satisfied; this is thus an image [*Einbildung*] to which no concept corresponds. [25: 1081]

According to Kant's new economy of human nature, we can represent constant suffering but not constant joy. Pain, not the "foretaste of future delights," has the power to impel us:

> Although Mohammed tried to fill heaven with pure, sensible wantonness, it effected as little as when we promise unnamable joys. Pain effects more forcefully; of it we can make a graspable [*faßlich*] concept—as is already shown by the Mosaic story of creation.... Happiness [*Glück*] is what frees us from pain.... Man cannot represent to himself what an enduring enjoyment would be, in which fear and hope did not interchange. Mohammed said of Paradise

> that it contains a very great supply of food, and very great enjoyment with the female sex, with the so-called beautiful Houris. But human beings are not much enticed by this, and fear of future ill has more effect; for we cannot think to ourselves an idea of unbroken happiness [*Glück*]; our concepts of happiness depend upon an exchange of well-being and pain. [25: 1073–1075][54]

To be sure, happiness can also be understood (in the manner of Zeno the Stoic and Diogenes) as sufficiency.[55] And "one can represent to oneself such happiness," which touches upon "very cheap conditions." The difficulty is that "we cannot see how a merely negative satisfaction can be a motive;" for if we could give up enough to be self-sufficient, "we would lack the motive spring to action." Desire cannot arise from the mere representation of its absence.[56] Hence, though we can represent it, we can find "no true example of such satisfaction" [25: 1081–1082]:[57]

> We can call life happy when it is equipped with all remedies directed against pain; for we have no other concept of happiness [*Glück*]. Satisfaction is when one would persist in the condition *in which one is,* and will dispense with all means of enjoyment. Thus the dispensability of all enjoyments is the condition of well being, in which one is above all remedies against pain; only this is not a condition we find with any human being. [25: 1072]

Either understanding of happiness—as the satisfaction of all inclinations or as "sufficiency," i.e., the cancellation of every need—can provoke idle longing, but not true desire, which presupposes the ability to effectuate its object [25: 1109].[58] Happiness, then, is not the perfection of our nature, as the Stoics, Cynics, and Epicureans differently believed. We are *naturally* impelled by pain to develop our rational talents [25: 1075, cf. 681–682]. And we are *rationally* motivated by "the moral example that man gives himself"—the sole ground of desire consistent with human freedom.

Man is thus led beyond instinctual determination of desire, not just by external obstacles, but by human consciousness itself, which is intrinsically inventive: we seek out objects of enjoyment (as remedies for our pain) even before "we [are in a position to] know the object" [25: 1070]. Although some might think it "ungrateful to creation" to speak so of providence, it is in fact a "wise establishment of human nature" in order to "drive us to activity"—terms that anticipate Kant's famous assertion that we should thank nature for so arranging things that we have nothing for which to thank her [25: 1071].[59]

And yet, Kant adds, "we find that we might be happy, according to our concept of happiness" as panacea. The best remedy for the pain of being alive is work [*Arbeit*]. Work is "compelled occupation" and differs from idle time [*Muße*], in that work involves burdens that one undertakes "for the sake of an end" [25: 1075]:

> One should therefore think that work gives enjoyment only with respect to the end; only, work must give our mind greater rest, and the end cannot promote the enjoyment of man. For the *possession* of enjoyment does not constitute *delight* in it; delight lies, rather, in that which is in prospect. Because work, however, is nothing more than an effort, it can serve thereby to make us ready for the happiness of life, in that work holds back pain; for in work we forget the unnamable griefs that always pursue us.   [25: 1075–1076]

The happiness available through labor, according to Kant's new economy, gives us "more" (but not "total") peace of mind—a remedy for pain consistent (as liquor and opium are not) with ongoing (if not total) pleasure. Work provides "constant relief" from life's discomforts by allowing enjoyment in prospect. Unlike possessed enjoyments, which quickly grow stale, enjoyments in prospect delight us continually through the alleviation they provide, above all, to boredom: Work is "the best way of killing [*vertreiben*] time" [25: 1075], but also makes life at the end seem longer, so that we are the readier to leave it.[60] Enjoyments in foretaste are the most forceful [25: 1087]. Ordinary enjoyments are "discharges" that "spend/squander" the life force, whereas what is disagreeable compresses it [25: 1089]. Sexual enjoyment especially exhausts itself, profligacy in youth spelling a limp old age. Enjoyment from work, on the other hand, is an ever-renewable resource; like ideal enjoyments, it puts one in a position "to produce more of the same" both for oneself and others [25: 1087]. Like ideal enjoyment, and unlike ordinary delight, work nourishes our talents and thus encourages rather than exhausting our life force. By such means, "no tool [*Organ*][61] of our life force is converted [*verwandt*][62]; the life principle remains [*steckt*] in thinking spirit" [25: 1089]. Like money well invested, such improvement through labor is capital [*ein Fonds*] for true enjoyment.[63]

The effort we expend, moreover, allows us to claim credit for developing what nature lays in us; labor and exertion transform something passively received into something actively produced: Man is "determined/destined to become himself the author of his own fitness [*Geschicklichkeit*], and even his benignity, through the development of his inner *Anlagen*" [25: 1195]: Man is fashioned so that the development of his *Anlagen* must be the effect of his own labor [25: 887]. Since character is a matter of free will, Kant now emphasizes, "we see it not as a gift of nature, but as something meritorious":

> We characterize a human being either through that which is a gift of nature and not to be imputed to him, or we can characterize what constitutes him through what is most inward in a human being. The first is called a merit of fortune. The proper character of a human being, however, consists in the relations of a human being through that which properly belongs to him, and is not to be attributed either to nature or to fortune. This character consists in the fundamental *Anlage* of the will to make good use [*bedienen*] of all one's talents and to manage well with one's temperament. Through a good character a man becomes author [*Urheber*] of his own value; he can also substitute for lack of talent through industry [*Fleiß*]and this must originate in character. The foundation for the improvement of all our talents lies in character. One calls it will, and it is the *Anlage* to make use of one's talents for the best ends. It thus depends upon a human being whether he has a character or whether he has a good or bad character. [25: 1174–1175][64]

In short, man is now the "author of his own value." Man, not God, is the one to whom gratitude is due [cf. 25: 728]; "man has himself to thank for his perfection, though the *Anlagen* thereto lies in nature" [25: 877]. The tension between character as natural *Fond* and character as personally earned is mediated by the notion that effort, which is in our power, deserves reward. By actively cultivating our talents we enhance what we are given (like the good servants in the parable of the talents) with interest that is to our credit. But not just any effort will do: to be genuinely our own it must be directed toward an end that flows from rational self-legislation. The cultivation of character is thus, above all, a cultivation of the talent of reason.

But if effort establishes, or at least marks, desert, it also has its drawbacks as a mode of cultivation:

> We make use of wit to pass the time and of reason out of duty. Hence all exercise of reason is a serious occupation for us; but man gladly calls reason away from its post and abandons himself to carefree and agreeable foolishness.... Reason is a human property that man most highly esteems, to be sure, yet doesn't love, and he seeks to escape its compulsion. Reason is too earnest [*ernsthaft*] for man, and very much constrains him.   [25: 1044]

Hence, it seems, the special value of social intercourse as a kind of antidote to labor [25: 896], stimulating activity without compulsion. In taking the side of Home (Lord Kames)[65] here against Rousseau, Kant has in mind the value of such society in furthering human cultivation. For the first time, Kant alludes to Rousseau's "fantastical" suspicion of others—a distrust, Kant says, bordering on madness [25: 1010]. Rousseau's inordinate suspicion of society blinded him, it seems, to the positive value of social intercourse, not only as a vehicle of moral self-improvement [25: 931], but also as an enlivening relief from work too focused and constrained to be consistent with good health [25: 1151]. That such society diminishes satisfaction and equanimity is not too high a price to pay for these advantages [25: 1103–1105]:[66]

The measured praise of Rousseau in *Menschenkunde*—in striking contrast with his near apotheosis in *Pillau*—emphasizes Kant's renewed insistence on man's state of self-division. Rousseau is right to question the compatibility of luxury and human happiness but wrong to think that nature's purpose is our happiness. Both individually, and collectively, nature has so arranged things that we have only ourselves to thank for our perfection. Man's consciousness is "twofold" [25: 862], a claim in keeping with the first *Critique*, with which *Menschenkunde* is (nearly) contemporaneous.[67]

In sum: The "true economy of human nature" supports Kant's newly established, critical outlook by freeing us from the illusion of happiness as a "maximum sum" of enjoyments. Happiness is merely an "ideal of the imagination," an imaginary goal that lacks any rule capable of determinately guiding us toward its progressive realization. As Kant will put it in the *Groundlaying of the Metaphysics of Morals*:

> although every human being wishes to attain [happiness], he can still never say determinately and self-consistently what he really wishes and wills. . . . The cause is that all the elements belonging to the concept of happiness are . . . empirical . . . and that nevertheless the idea of happiness requires an absolute whole, a maximum of well-being in my present and every future condition. [4: 418]

But "it is impossible for a most insightful and most powerful and yet finite being to make here a determinate concept of what he really wills" [4: 419].

Kant's "true economy" is thus consistent with his critical distinction between infinity (in the field of appearances) and totality (as an idea of reason) more generally.[68] Human nature is such "that man will have a unity of the whole, and is not satisfied unless he sees all in a particular connection to an end" [25: 886]. That rational demand for unity, however, is in tension with the twofold nature of human consciousness. Satisfaction is thus best represented, not as a determinate whole but rather as an ongoing task,[69] congruent with philosophy, which shows the relation of all to the final end of human reason [25: 1042–1043].[70]

But the relation of that end to human happiness, which we are naturally driven to pursue, remains unsettled. Kant is less than clear, initially, on whether rational determination of the will applies only to moral judgment (by supplying it with a rational standard) or is also sufficient to motivate us to *act*. In the late 1770s through the period in which he completes the first edition of the *Critique of Pure Reason*, Kant leans toward the former option: Reason immediately lays down a principle for moral judgment, but motivation to act (consistently) upon those judgments requires the supplementary "promises" and "threats" of rational theology and related appeals to happiness and "hope."[71] Only in later works, beginning with the *Groundlaying*, will Kant insist upon the possibility of "pure practical reason" for purposes of action in the world as well as judgment as to right and wrong (i.e., of a purely rational determination of the will). Only with the *Groundlaying*, in other words, does the "principle of autonomy" as such appear. It might well seem, on the basis of that principle, that all positive need for a rational theology (formerly required to support the necessary "promises" and "threats") would end. Events would soon prove that presumption wrong.

4

The "Paradox" of Autonomy

That autonomy is "paradoxical" by Kantian lights is a fact not often noted.[1] Among the many excellent Kant studies that have proliferated in recent years, few dwell upon the specific *resistance* that autonomy's demands, in Kant's view, necessarily provoke in us.[2] That resistance expresses itself, as he sees it, in two separate but related ways: suspicion of the adequacy of the moral law as an incentive of the will and confusion as to the meaning of "the highest good." Kant addresses the first problem in the *Groundlaying of the Metaphysics of Morals;* the second is taken up in the *Critique of Practical Reason*.

1. Autonomy in the *Groundlaying*

The *Groundlaying of the Metaphysics of Morals* is widely regarded as *the* seminal work of modern ethics. At the same time, there is little consensus as to the content or success of its most basic claims. (This is particularly true of Section Three, which is generally dismissed as either hopelessly puzzling or as a patent failure that Kant later came to recognize as such.) Careful attention to the work's stated purpose, as I will try to show, helps bring to light a unified and compelling argument that lays many of these issues to rest; at the same time, it also helps bring out the genuine difficulties that an autonomy-based ethic must confront.

With the *Groundlaying* Kant moves beyond the position staked out in the *Critique of Pure Reason* [1781]. There, reason showed itself to be the adjudicating source of its own theoretical norms. The competing claims over which critical reason there presides are not silenced but merely required (in the name of "fairness" [A 750 = B 778]) to "lower their tone"—that is to say, to abandon their pretension to speak for reason as a whole, rather than (as is actually the case) on behalf of one of reason's several and competing interests [A 744–749 = B 772–777].

The *Critique of Pure Reason* refers the question—"what ought I do"—to a "moral" realm beyond the proper purview of critique [A 805 = B 833]. By the time he writes the *Groundlaying*, Kant has amended this view: Pure *practical* reason, he now insists, must also critically establish the fitness of its claims. Not yet prepared to present a complete "critique of pure practical reason," Kant offers for the present a "laying of the ground" [4: 392]—in which he identifies freedom for the first time as "autonomy" of the will. Although he does not aim thereby to "prove" that pure reason can be practical, this much, he says, can be done, namely:

> to indicate in the imperative itself the renunciation of all interest, in volition from duty, by means of some determination the [moral] imperative contains, as the specific mark distinguishing categorical from hypothetical imperatives; and this is done in . . . the idea of the will of every rational being as a *will giving universal law*. [4: 431–432][3]

With this formula of autonomy, Kant unambiguously asserts for the first time the sufficiency of law as incentive of the will [4: 433; cf. 450].

So much is relatively well known. Less understood is the motive and aim that informs the *Groundlaying*, which is at once more modest and more ambitious than is generally recognized—more modest, because Kant does not try to derive the moral law's validity from our practical (but not moral) presupposition of freedom, as is sometimes urged.[4] Absent the primary orientation implicit in what Kant calls "ordinary moral understanding" (and with it, "common ethical rational cognition"), we would be indifferent to the law's demand. In aiming to "seek out and set fast" the supreme principle of morality, then, the *Groundlaying* does not claim to give us new reason to be moral, but to release us from a moral sophistry that obscures what is "before our eyes."[5] It is true that Kant urges the necessity of presupposing freedom even in the case of *non-moral* action. But this is not (as is sometimes asserted) because he means to "deduce" the moral law from a non-moral premise. Its purpose is, rather, to help overcome the dialectical resistance to its own law to which human reason is generically prone. At the same time, the *Groundlaying* is also more ambitious than is often recognized, aiming not only to establish the limits of human reason but also to indicate (from a point touching on those limits) "something" beyond.

A brief survey of what the *Groundlaying* shares with some of Kant's earlier writings can help bring those aims (and the obstacles that prompt them) into sharper focus. As previous chapters of this study showed, a surprisingly mature version of the claim that good will is the one thing worthy of esteem is already present in the *Remarks*. And rational ideas, understood as adjudicating *a priori* norms, are elaborated upon throughout the 1770s, assuming a final critical form in the A edition of the *Critique of Pure Reason*. What that *Critique* does *not* do is grant moral ideas, and the moral law related to them, sufficiency as an incentive of the human will. As Kant there puts it:

> It is necessary that our whole course of life be subordinated to moral maxims; but it is at the same time impossible for this to happen if reason does not connect with the moral law, which is a mere idea, an effectual cause which determines for such conduct an outcome precisely corresponding to our highest ends. . . . *Thus without a God and a world not now visible but to be hoped for the masterful ideas of morality are, to be sure, objects of emulation and awe but not incentives for resolve and execution, because they do not fulfill the entire end that for every rational being is naturally and necessarily determined a priori through the same pure reason.* [A 813 = B 841; emphasis added]

In the *Critique of Pure Reason* the incentive of a rational will is still dependent on some end: absent belief in the God and afterlife that make this end possible, the moral law is an object of "awe" but not of "execution." In the *Groundlaying*, by way of contrast, the good will is determined by the law's form alone, without reference to any (determining) end.[6] With that new move comes recognition of a related dialectic of *practical* reason, whose burden philosophy itself cannot escape. Philosophy, as we shall see, must overcome its *own* resistance to the idea of autonomy before philosophy can be of (other) moral use.

In what, then, does that moral use consist? A metaphysics of morals [*Metaphysik der Sitten*] is "indispensably necessary," Kant says, not merely from "a motive of speculation," but also because "morals themselves" remain "precarious" [*mißlich*] and "subject to all kinds of corruption" so long as their "guiding thread and highest norm of correct judgment" are lacking [4: 390]. The main purpose of such a moral metaphysics—the "entirely new realm/field [*Feld*]" on which Kant proposes to enter—is thus to secure this highest norm against forces (not yet specified) that make it "waver."

To be sure, Kant is not ready fully to complete that enterprise. The present "groundlaying" of the metaphysics of morals is an anticipatory substitute for the "ground" that can only be furnished, he says, by a complete critique of pure practical reason. Still, the present work, which aims at "the seeking out and establishment [*Aufsuchung und Festsetzung*] of the **highest principle of morality**" is a "separate business" whose delay would itself be morally suspect [4: 492].

In sum: Moral philosophy is not only philosophy *about* morality; philosophy that does not have a moral aim (which includes, first and foremost, overcoming the resistance of human reason to acknowledging its own fundamental principle) is not *moral* philosophy at all [4: 390]. This consideration helps explain Kant's "method" and a related division of the work that many commentators have found puzzling. To anticipate: Section One ("transition from common ethical rational knowledge to philosophic ethical rational knowledge")[7] draws attention to and clarifies the pure principle contained in ordinary rational knowledge of morality. Section Two ("transition from popular moral philosophy [*Popularphilosophie*] to the metaphysics of morals") picks up the thread with a reason that has lost its "innocence," issuing in a "natural dialectic" that exposes it to the sophistry exemplified in *Popularphilosophie*, a powerful intellectual movement of Kant's time.[8] Worldly experience abetted by such sophistry gives rise to doubt that the concept of duty has any object to be encountered in the world. A "metaphysics of morals" responds by showing that such an object is determinately conceivable in moral terms, i.e., as member of an intelligible world made up of rational agents. Section Three ("Final step from the metaphysics of morals to the critique of pure practical reason") uses the concept of such a world to show that proof that autonomy itself is possible (i.e., that pure reason can be practical) is a demand that an adjudicating reason can and should disregard.

a. Section One: "From Common to Philosophic Ethical Rational Knowledge"

The first sentence of Section One conveys *in nuce* what Kant means by "common ethical rational knowledge":

> It is not possible to think of anything in the world, or even outside it, that could be held to be good without limitation except a **good will.** [4: 393]

By "good without limitation [*Einschränkung*]" he has in mind something like the following: One arrives at "ideas" by "subtracting" in thought or "canceling" those limitations that normally apply to our use of *a priori* concepts.⁹ Kant's nearly contemporaneous lectures on *Philosophical Theology* cast instructive light on the importance of such "canceling in thought" to the formation of practical ideas generally. As he there tells us, one arrives at *practical* ideas—e.g., that of "perfect friendship"—by canceling in thought the self-interested motives that ordinarily stop us from giving up everything for the welfare of a friend. By the same token, one forms an idea of "perfect vice" by subtracting in thought any extenuating circumstances (e.g., a deprived childhood) that might limit it. Human reason needs such ideas "of a highest perfection" to "serve as a standard according to which it can make determinations." Such ideas are not mere phantoms of the brain, Kant adds, because we can *use* them to bring things nearer perfection.

Taking the concept of "good will" as an idea of this sort[10] allows one to say the following: Good will is what is left when we cancel in thought those (experiential) conditions that qualify or limit our assessment of something as good = worthy of being chosen. The sum total of all things that make our *condition* worth choosing is called "happiness." What will maximize that total cannot be assessed with certainty. (When to enjoy the moment and when to save for a rainy day is a question that yields no single, determinate answer.) The goodness of things valued in this way varies with "external circumstances"; hence, they cannot be held good "without limitation" or "absolutely."

As to the goodness of happiness as such, two issues come into play. First, we can form no rational idea of happiness [4: 395–396]. If we attempt to remove in thought everything that might limit our happiness, we are left (as we saw in Chapter Three) without anything determinate to think. Hence, happiness (or the goal of maximizing the choice-worthiness of the conditions of existence) is not a practical idea in the specific Kantian sense of constituting a standard, based on reason alone, for determination of the will. Prudent choice in such matters is always, in the final analysis, a gamble.

But there is a further, positive reason why happiness cannot be held "good without limitation": namely, the conditionality of its goodness on something else that *can* be so held. As paragraph one continues:

> Understanding, wit, judgment, and whatever else such *talents* of spirit may be called, or courage [*Muth*], resolution and firmness of purpose as qualities of *temperament*, are undoubtedly good and worth wishing for [*wünchenswert*] from many points of view [*in mancher Absicht*]; but they can also become evil and harmful ... if the will is not good. It is the same with gifts of *fortune*

[Glücksgaben]. . . . Complete well being and satisfaction with one's condition under the name of happiness [*Glückseligkeit*] makes for courage [*Muth*] and hence often arrogance [*Übermuth*] where there is lacking a good will to correct and make generally purposive its influence upon the mind and with it the entire principle of action; not to mention that a rational impartial observer can never take delight [*Wohlgefallen*][11] in the unbroken prosperity of a being that shows no trace of a pure and good will, and so good will seems to constitute the indispensable condition itself of worthiness of being happy [*der Würdigkeit glücklich zu sein*]. [4: 393]

The rational impartial observer takes "delight" in the sight of unbroken prosperity—i.e., approves of it morally—only when the one it befalls shows some trace of having a will that is pure and good.[12] Good will, then, is "the only thing that can be held good without limitation that it is possible to think": in every other case the goodness of the thing in question is both uncertain and/or indeterminate *and* conditional on one being worthy of it.

In sum: It is only by virtue of ordinary moral understanding and its standards that we can hold *anything* good without limitation. What is, as it were, "first for us" is not the idea of a pure and good will, but the ordinary moral judgments that implicitly invoke these standards. We arrive at the idea of will that is good without limitation by canceling in thought everything that ordinarily limits our esteem and hence the moral satisfaction that we take in someone prospering without interruption. The idea of a good will is formed, in other words, when we subtract in thought those defects and blemishes that ordinarily color our everyday moral assessments.

Such an understanding of the phrase "good without limitation" is both consistent with Kant's treatment of practical ideas generally and crucial, as we shall see, to the remaining argument of Section One.[13] At the same time, it gives notions of "desert" a moral primacy that many recent studies of Kant seek to avoid.[14] Granting that primacy forces one to take seriously the claim that persons are fundamentally responsible for their own actions. Transcendental idealism (with its insistence on the noumenal/phenomenal distinction) supports that claim, for many contemporary commentators, at too high a theoretical cost. Better to "naturalize" ethics (and de-emphasize moral desert), the thinking goes, than cling to Kant's own doubtful assertions concerning the timeless acts of noumenal selves.[15] Desert, however (as I am arguing) is fundamental to the *Groundlaying*'s initiating orientation and its accompanying claim to "rational moral knowledge." Without a robust concept of desert (as implied by the judgment that one is "worthy of esteem" and with it "happiness"), we could form no *rational* idea of the good at all.

Ethical rational knowledge consists, then, at the most "common" level, in an awareness of good will as the sole thing that has value in itself. Whether such a thing as a good will is "anywhere to be encountered" is a matter still to be established. But that good will alone merits our unconditional valuation, or esteem, constitutes the elemental moral knowledge on the basis of which the remaining argument unfolds.[16] The concept of good will as solely and uniquely estimable (i.e., as choice-worthy in itself and as that on which the choice-worthiness of everything else ultimately depends) "already dwells," as Kant puts it, in "sound natural understanding" and need not be "taught" but merely "developed" [*entwickelt*].

He does so starting with the conceptually "richer" notion of "duty," or good will under certain "subjective limitations and hindrances" [4: 397]. These limitations do not limit the goodness of good will objectively (*per impossibile*), but they do permit us to form the *subjective* concept (immediately accessible to finite rational beings like ourselves) of a will whose goodness is limited by something that is still "owing," as the concept of duty, as a morally outstanding "debt" [*Schuld*], implies.[17] An important distinction is thus made on which Kant will later draw between the *idea* of a good will that we arrive at by canceling in thought any outstanding debt or limitation that would make it less good than it might be, and the *concept* of a will bound by duty, and to which this limitation subjectively applies (for I indeed recognize myself as a will subject to such moral "hindrances").

As Kant's subsequent examples show, the same common moral understanding (in which the reader is presumed to share) that acknowledges the unconditional goodness of good will also readily grants a difference between actions that merely conform to duty (and that, as in the case of the selfishly honest shopkeeper, it may be desirable to encourage), and those, done for *the sake* of duty, that alone possess a value that we esteem [4: 399]. To this "first" proposition recognized by ordinary moral understanding,[18] a "second" adds that action done out of duty "has its value not in the aim that it would bring about but in the maxim according to which it is resolved upon." Precisely because all such aims *might* be achieved through something *other* than a good will (as with the shopkeeper who is honest for merely selfish reasons, etc.), they cannot explain the unconditioned value that we, in our capacity as moral knowers, necessarily place upon action done from duty. Where, then, does the basis of moral value lie? Not in the end, which might in principle be brought about by something other than good will; rather, it can "lie nowhere else than in the [formal] principle of the will, without regard for the ends thereby effected" [4: 400].

Unlike animals, who respond directly to the promptings of instinct, human reason has assumed the task "of thinking out the project of reason for itself" [4: 395]. "Maxims" are general rules of action that enable us to interrupt the circuit of animal desire either by resisting inclination or acquiescing in it.[19] Unlike animals, we not only feel pain and pleasure; we also estimate the value of our condition as a whole. On the basis of that estimation, we either acquiesce in inclination's immediate promptings or resist them. Our will is moved by inclinations only to the extent that it "takes them up into its maxim." The rules of prudence are the maxims that we form in an effort to maximize the value of our condition as a whole—a goal that we call happiness. But on what basis can one rationally choose to act, if not its estimated contribution to the total satisfaction of one's desires? If every value that might attach to (actualizing) a particular end is now cancelled in thought, nothing is left, Kant says, but the will's sheer capacity to adopt a maxim or not—its freedom, that is to say, either to acquiesce in or resist the promptings of sensual desire according to some rule or principle of its own choosing. To act for the sake of duty, or without primary regard to the value of some end, is thus to grant overriding value to reason's free capacity to make some rule its "principle"—the "ground," that is to say, on which it acts.

Combining Kant's two propositions thus yields a third: "*Duty is the necessity of an action from respect for the law.*" For a principle that has overriding value in all cases is, as Kant puts it, objectively valid and hence a law [4: 400].

But "what kind of law can it be," he now asks, "whose representation, even without regard [*Rücksicht*] for the effect expected from it, must determine the will so that it might be called good absolutely and without limitation?" [4: 402]:

> Since I have robbed the will of every impulse that could have arisen from following any [particular] law, there is nothing left other than universal lawfulness [*Gesetzmässigkeit*] of actions in general, which should alone serve the will as principle: that is, I should never conduct myself other than in such a way *that I could also will that my maxim should also become a universal law.* Here mere lawfulness in general (without there lying at its basis [*Grunde*] any law determining some specific action) serves the will as principle and also must so serve it, if duty is not everywhere to be an empty delusion and

chimerical concept; with this ordinary human reason in its capacity as moral judge [*in ihrer practischen Beurtheilung*] is also in full agreement and has the aforesaid principle always before its eyes. [4: 402]

The good will takes its bearings from "lawfulness" in the sense implied by such necessity. It is "lawful" not only in the thin sense of adopting as its principle a rule that is directed universally (e.g., "everyone should always lie") but in the normatively binding sense of necessitating the will objectively.[20] But such a principle cannot be other than compatible with its adoption by all other rational beings. Adopting such a principle is thus equivalent to that of never conducting oneself other than in such a way *that one could also will that one's maxim should also become a universal law.*

That we unconditionally esteem the will that acts on such a principle is known. That such a will is "anywhere to be encountered" remains, for now, an open question. That there exist rational beings who act on such objectively necessary principles has not (yet) been established.[21] As in the case of "Socrates" to whom Kant here alludes, the purpose of moral philosophy is not to teach ordinary reason anything new but merely "to make it attentive to its own principle." Kant is not attempting to pull a moral rabbit out of an a-moral hat, but only to draw attention to the rational criterion that is implicit in ordinary moral understanding. Why then not leave matters here (i.e., with the *philosophically refined* ethical rational knowledge with which Section One concludes) rather than setting out, in Section Two, "on a new path of investigation and instruction?" [4: 404].

Kant's answer throws light on the dialectical problem to which the remainder of the work will be devoted (a problem with which his earlier *Lectures on Anthropology* themselves had struggled): So long as one lacks insight into the *ground* on which rests one's capacity to conceive of a value that outweighs all else (a ground it is the business of philosophy to investigate) [4: 403], ordinary knowledge is "easily seduced," for:

> The human being feels in himself a mighty counterweight against all commands of duty that reason represents to him as so highly worthy of respect, in his needs and inclinations whose entire satisfaction he comprehends [*zusammenfasst*] under the name of happiness. [4: 405]

The problem lies not with our inclinations *per se,* or even with human neediness, but in a quality of *human* reason that tempts us to give inclination an unwarranted preference.[22] Reason's limitless pursuit of grounds or reasons in other contexts gives us apparent reason to respond to the law's command with the reply: "Why should I?"—i.e., "What [other] reason have I to obey it?" There thus arises, for ordinary human reason, a "natural dialectic." On the one hand, reason commands "unremittingly" without "promising anything" to inclination,[23] whose claims seem, on the other hand, so "fair" [*billig*], and which no command of reason can "cancel" [*aufheben*]. This dialectic gives rise, in turn:

> "to a propensity to ratiocinate [*vernünfteln*] against the strict laws of duty" and "draw into doubt the validity of duty's laws, or, at the very least, their purity and strictness—that is to say, to corrupt them at their ground [*im Grunde*] and thus destroy their entire dignity, which even common practical reason cannot in the end call good." [4: 405]

"Vernünfteln," Kant's general term for an abuse of reason, is here attributed to rational judgment itself. Like reason in its speculative use, common practical reason, as soon as it is "cultivated," finds itself in a situation of "perplexity" [*Velegenheit*] arising from competing claims that all seem "fair" and that reason cannot "cancel." Common practical reason thus finds itself impelled "to take a step into the domain [*Feld*] of practical philosophy," not out of any speculative need, "but from practical grounds themselves." Wisdom, as Kant puts it, *"needs science . . . in order . . . not to learn but to procure entrance and durability for its precepts"* [4: 405; emphasis added]. The goal of science is not to teach common moral understanding something new, but to enhance the force and staying power of the knowledge it already possesses.

The aid of philosophy (and with it, a "complete critique of reason") is thus still required in order to extricate human reason from a state of "ambiguity" of its own making that threatens to destroy all grounding ethical principles [*Grundsätze*]. Indeed the problem here is if anything more radical than the challenge faced by reason in its theoretical use. In that case, reason fell into "perplexity through no fault [*Schuld*] of its own" (cf. *Critique of Pure Reason* A vii); here reason is no longer "innocent" [*Unschuld*] [4: 404]. There it was enough, finally, to appoint reason as overarching judge.[24] Here human reason must also vindicate its own capacity to judge "fairly" (i.e., to be both practical and pure).

b. Section Two: "From Popular Moral World-wisdom to the Metaphysics of Morals"

That full vindication, however, is still a section away. The aim of Section Two is merely preparatory: namely, to gain "information" and "clear direction" as to the "source" and "correct determination" of reason's principle in the face of the above-mentioned perplexity [4: 405]. It thus begins *not* where Section One officially leaves off—i.e, with "philosophic ethical rational knowledge"—but instead with *populären sittlichen Weltweisheit* and its misguided resolution of the tension between the demands of reason and a natural aversion on the people's part to dry abstraction.

In beginning Section Two as he does, Kant takes up the plight of common moral reason whose "cultivation" and subsequent state of ambiguity force it to seek further philosophic aid. These efforts initially expose it to a sham "popular philosophy" (a philosophy, that is, whose practitioners lack a "true calling" for the task [4: 389, 409]). The result not only fails clearly to distinguish elements of moral knowledge according to their respective rational and empirical sources (a failure that also applied to unaided ordinary moral understanding) but actively (and, as it were, deliberately) confounds them.[25]

To be sure, not all philosophy prior to Kant's own is thus morally compromised. [Genuine] philosophers, Kant says, "have always come forward" who have denied the actuality [*Wirklichkeit*] of the moral disposition in human nature, without doubting the correctness of the concept as a criterion of moral judgment [4: 406–407]. And, indeed, it is impossible to prove this actuality by observation, given that we can see "actions" but not the "inner principles" on which moral value rests. The result is either an honest but morally despairing misanthropy or a false philanthropy on the part of thinkers who wish to help humanity by lowering the standard to what can be met with in experience. The ensuing "mishmash" [4: 409], which flatters human laziness, also suits the "enemies of virtue," who, in turn, ridicule morality,[26] which necessarily overreaches the limits of experience, as sheer mental self-conceit: "one cannot better serve the wishes of those who ridicule all morality [*Sittlichkeit*] as a mere brain figment [*Hirngespinst*] of imagination that overreaches itself through self-obscurity [*Eigendünkel*], than to concede [*einzuräumen*] to them that the concepts of duty must be drawn solely from experience" (as one is inclined to do, in the case of all other concepts, out of a desire for comfort) [4: 407].

Philosophy is thus now needed, not only to make ordinary moral understanding attentive to its principle (as in Section One) but also to secure an attachment that is weakened by philosophic observation, by misguided efforts at philosophic popularity, and by virtue's active enemies, who use the above to their own malign advantage [4: 409]. In short, philosophy must try to shore up the moral weakness that arises from the discrepancy—exacerbated in an age "like our own"—between rational certitude that good will alone is worthy of esteem and doubt, seemingly well-founded in experience, that good will is anywhere to be met with. Under such conditions, one need not display active malice, but only enjoy shrewd powers of observation, Kant says, to come to question whether any genuine virtue has ever actually [*wirklich*] been encountered in the world. At such a moment, "*nothing can protect us*" from "falling away" from our "ideas of duty" and "grounded respect" for law other than "*the clear conviction*" that the moral law "commands unremittingly" [4: 408; emphasis added].

In a different era, in other words, Section Two might well not be called for. In Kant's own age of popular semi-enlightenment, on the other hand, the people are confronted by a seductive pseudo-philosophic hybrid, which they naturally prefer (due to their natural dislike of "dry abstraction") to genuine philosophy. Section Two counters this tendency, as we shall see, by showing that pure moral concepts, despite their non-experiential source, have "some relation" to a possible object. A metaphysics of morals of the sort here proposed takes on the genuinely popularizing task of making comprehensible, by virtue of analogy with the world of sense, the intelligible relations that would necessarily apply to moral objects of this sort [4: 388; see also *Metaphysics Vigilantius*, 29: 945].[27] In so doing, it can also be said to make philosophy (at long last) truly philanthropic [4: 408–409; cf. 406].

Genuine morality, could it be brought to popular attention, would affect the people's minds more powerfully than any mixed appeal. Instead, there prevails a kind of everyday chatter [*alltägliche Geschwätze*][28] that repels the thoughtful from all moral discourse [4: 409–410]. The metaphysics of morals here envisioned is thus of the "highest importance," as Kant puts it, not merely for purposes of "theoretical cognition of our duties" (the main purpose of the work later published under that title) but also because without it the mind, confronted with a "mixed doctrine of morals" and thus lacking a single unifying principle, will necessarily waver [*schwanken*] between "motives [of both reason and inclination]" [4: 411]. Determination of the "complete range" of "practical [and hence] pure rational knowledge" is "necessary" not just for "theoretical judgment," in other words, but also for purposes of "moral instruction"—that is to say, because otherwise "it would be impossible in a common and practical use" to "ground morality on its genuine principles" and thus "effectuate [*bewirken*] pure moral dispositions" and "engraft them for the highest good in the world" [4: 412].

In sum: Kant provides us with an incipient moral history of the human race at a moment of general pedagogic urgency. Ordinary moral understanding, internally driven as it is to seek rational clarification, is initially confronted by a philosophy that grasps moral ideas correctly (i.e., as necessary criteria of moral judgment) while despairing of their human application. The only genuine remedy is not *Popularphilosophie,* whose higgledy-piggledy confusion of the moral and the empirical further emboldens virtue's active enemies, but a coming to awareness on the part of moral consciousness of its own ground [cf. 4: 405]. In bringing the source of its principle to light, Section Two, as we shall see, helps counter a suspicion—in part well founded, in part based on intellectual conceit and/or indolence—of concepts whose reality cannot be exhibited experientially.[29]

Before a metaphysics of morals can be attempted, however, the reader must be weaned from a *Popularphilosophie* that "remains wedded to examples." Kant thus begins by making practical reason an example to itself—by exhibiting by "natural steps" reason's own practical "rules of determination," up to the point that "there arises from it the concept of duty" [4: 412].

The first step lies with recognition that whereas "everything in nature works according to laws," only a rational being is capable of acting in accordance with its representation of laws (here understood as rationally necessary principles of action)—i.e., of "handeln" as opposed to "wirken." Kant's implicit justification of this step would seem to be as follows: I arrive at the rational concept of a perfectly rational being by subtracting in thought the susceptibility to deviation that I recognize from my own practical experience: Whereas a perfectly rational being (according to my idea) invariably determines itself according to its representation of such necessary rules, an imperfectly rational being (such as I know myself to be in practice) encounters them as **"imperatives"** that "necessitate the will without invariably determining it."

Hypothetical imperatives (i.e., rules of skill and prudence) necessitate only where an additional condition holds. Kant calls necessitation of this kind "analytic," because it follows from the very concept of "willing an end" that one must also will the means (at least if one is fully rational) [4: 413–414]. A moral imperative, by way of contrast, is not "grounded in any other aim" but instead necessitates immediately and is thus **categorical** [4: 415].[30]

"A question now arises" (related to a soon-to-be-mentioned worry): How are such necessitating rules of reason possible? On the one hand, the "necessity" of the moral law is "undeniable"; on the other, our inability to understand how that necessity is possible abets moral wavering, given our ordinarily reasonable doubts concerning concepts for which no object exists that can be met with in experience. With hypothetical imperatives, which necessitate "analytically," the necessity is as manifest to human reason as in the conclusion of a logical syllogism, though imperatives of prudence, given the indeterminacy of happiness, pose some additional complications [4: 417–419]. (Though I may not turn down seconds on dessert, I have no difficulty seeing why, given my chosen end of losing weight, I should.) Categorical imperatives, on the other hand, involve a practical "necessitation" whose "ground" is somehow dark [4: 420–421n]. Here, all examples fail us. There thus arises a morally troubling "concern" [*besorgen*] that imperatives that *seem* categorical are merely hypothetical (as the enemies of virtue would indeed have us think) [4: 419].

1. PHILOSOPHY'S "PRECARIOUS STANDPOINT." So far, we have "insight" into this much: first, that the categorical imperative alone "sounds as" a practical **law** [*als practisches* **Getetz** *laute*], and second, that having insight into "how it sounds" [*wie es lautet*] does not in itself tell us how such an absolute command "is possible" (a problem that cannot be resolved without the "difficult effort" of Section Three) [4: 420].[31] This complication, as Kant now informs us, partly follows from the fact that the necessity conveyed by that commanding tone involves a "synthetic" rather than an "analytic" judgment. No mere analysis on our part of the concept of a good will furnishes insight into the possibility of a categorical *imperative*.[32] No matter how much we analyze the concept of an absolutely good will, the peculiarly *commanding* tone of its imperative "will not be found." (For indeed, in forming that idea we "subtracted in thought" everything that might give it such a character.) That the principle of a good will commands our esteem is clear; how it is possible for it to do so is not.

But there is yet a further complication: Unlike the synthetic *a priori* propositions taken up in the *Critique of Pure Reason*, whose reality had experiential confirmation, the possibility of a *categorical* imperative must be examined [*untersuchen*] entirely *a priori*.

Philosophy's "precarious standpoint" thus takes us to the brink of the position staked out in the *Critique of Pure Reason*, prior to Kant's breakthrough discovery of the principle of autonomy. The development, in what follows, of two further "formulas" of the categorical imperative is specifically aimed (as I will argue) at addressing the aforementioned "fear" that moral concepts are "empty" in the specific sense of lacking any possible determinate object.

The first formula is already contained in the thought of "how [the categorical imperative] sounds":

> When I think of a *hypothetical* imperative in general I do not know what it will contain beforehand but only when the condition is given. But when I think of a *categorical* imperative I know at once what it contains. For since besides the law the imperative contains only the necessity that the maxim conform to this law, which contains no further condition that might limit it, nothing remains over except the universality of a law in general as that to which the maxim of the action should conform, and which conformity alone the imperative properly represents. [4: 420–421]

The categorical imperative not only commands me unconditionally but also tells me, through the mere thought of it in general, what I must do in order to obey: namely, reject any maxim whose transformation into a universally binding rule I am not also willing to accept. But this is nothing other than the formula of the categorical imperative itself: *Act only according to that maxim through which you can at the same time will that it be a universal law.*[33]

On the basis of an analogy between the two lawful systems (or "worlds") with which we humans are acquainted (namely, that of natural effects [*wirken*] and that of free actions [*handeln*]), that principle becomes, in turn: *So act as if the maxim of your action were to become through your will a* **universal law of nature.** With the help of that analogy (which rests, in part, upon the analogously synthetic character of our experience of nature), the concept of a categorical imperative also yields a principle for the derivation and/or division of particular duties, as Kant goes on to illustrate [4: 421–424].

Nothing yet satisfactorily indicates [*anzeigen*], however, that the concept of duty thus invoked is not "empty"—i.e., lacking in effect within the world we know [4: 421]. We have not come so far as to be able to rout virtue's enemies by showing [*beweisen*] that such an imperative effectually exists [*wirklich stattfinde*].

If anything, however, can show *our* objective "*assignment*" [angeweisen][34] to law, Kant now counters, it is precisely the imperviousness of its claim before the opposition of our natural inclinations [4: 425]. It must accordingly not "even enter one's mind" to derive the law's reality [*Realität*] from the specific qualities of human nature. With this warning, philosophy itself reaches the crisis point toward which the argument has thus far been building:

> Here we now see philosophy placed in fact [*in der That*][35] in a precarious standpoint,[36] which should be firm [*fest*] in disregard [**unerachtet**] of there

being nothing in heaven or earth from which it hangs/depends or on which it is supported. Here it should show [*beweisen*] its purity [*Lauterkeit*] as autocratrix [*Selbsthalterin*][37] of its laws, not as herald of that which an implanted sense or who knows what tutelary nature whispers/insinuates [*einflüstert*], which taken together may always be better than nothing but which never yield fundamental principles [*Grundsätze*] that reason dictates and that must have their source, and herewith at the same time their commanding authority, thoroughly *a priori* throughout: expecting nothing from inclination but rather everything from the supremacy of law and the respect owed it [*der schuldigen **Achtung** für dasselbe*] or, in default thereof, condemning [*verurtheilen*] human beings to self-contempt [**Selbstverachtung**] and inner abhorrence. [4: 425–426; emphasis added]

Like Catherine the Great, the famous "Autocratrix of all of the Russians," philosophy must be the self-sustaining mistress of its own laws, expecting nothing from human inclination and everything from reason's supreme authority/control [*Obergewalt*]—a setting fast of grounds that is here itself presented as an "ought" [*sollen*].

It is important to be clear about what is here at stake: not the moral outlook as such but our unwavering commitment to its demand. To conclude that that demand cannot be met (i.e., that pure reason cannot be effective in the world) leads, according to the above passage, not to skepticism but to self-contempt.

The immediacy of the connection between moral despair and self-contempt is here expressed in a series of variations on the word "achten" [= attentio].[38] Here, as in Kant's earliest moral work, spiritual elevation lies in freely turning one's attention from a perversely attractive abyss.[39] Paying attention to the law is bound up with refusing, as it were, to look down—i.e., indulge in that "low way of thinking" [*niedrige Denkungsart*] that seeks a ground other than the law itself [4: 426].[40]

Kant's subsequent "analysis" of the *a priori* concept of a rational being is prompted by this crisis and the related need that it makes evident to disregard all empirical motives. But our attention remains a wavering one, so long as we are vulnerable to doubt as to the possibility of what's demanded of us.

The question at issue is thus, Kant says, the following: whether a necessary law for all rational beings (including us ourselves) effectively exists [4: 426]. If such a law does exist in this sense (which is here merely assumed), then there must be rational wills capable of determining themselves accordingly. The formulas of the categorical imperative that follow specify, in turn, the maxims of such wills as member of a "kingdom of ends." Our moral concepts, as we will then be able to conclude, are not altogether lacking in a determinate object (as the enemies of virtue urge); for reason can "completely determine" the maxim by virtue of which objects of this kind (i.e., rational beings possessing a good will) collectively make possible a moral world. To be sure, we will not yet be able to fully silence the worry (that inevitably arises in "thoughtful" people) that our moral concepts lack "reality" [*Wirklichkeit*]. The presumption—that beings capable of a good will exist—may not be true, for all that has thus far been shown. (To fully allay *that* concern, the critique of pure practical reason taken up in Section Three proves necessary [4: 429n]). Still, we will at least have insight into how an intelligible world might itself come into existence—namely, if the moral law prescribed to rational beings "were universally followed" [4: 438].

This analysis begins with a "step"—needful even for those whose natural aversion to "pure rational cognition" makes them "reluctant"—into a new field of metaphysics [4: 426; cf. 4: 409]. This step involves the "thought" of the will as "a faculty *determining itself to action in accord with the representation of certain laws.*"[41] Nothing is yet said as to whether such a will is in fact to be anywhere encountered; Kant merely elucidates what is contained in our ordinary concept of duty and the "canon" that, as he has shown, necessarily accompanies it. The argument then continues roughly as follows: Every will must have some end. Subjective ends are those whose realization is a means to the satisfaction of some subjective inclination on our part. What, then, can serve as the objective end, valid for all rational beings, of a will that determines itself absolutely, in accordance with some law? By a process of exclusion, Kant brings us to conclude that only rational being as an end in itself, or limiting condition on all our other ends, can serve in this capacity. Thus if a supreme practical principle is "to be anywhere encountered," rational nature must be an end in itself.[42] Since the self-determination of a will in accordance with the representation of a universally valid law will necessarily have as its objective ground man (or any other rational being) as end in itself, the categorical imperative can be stated in the form of a second formula):

> *Act so as to use humanity [or rational being], as much in your own person as in the person of every other, always at the same time as end and never merely as a means.*
> [4: 429]

An additional argument for the above formula proceeds as follows: Insofar as all human beings necessarily represent their own existence as ends in themselves, doing so constitutes a "subjective principle of human actions." "But if every other rational being represents its own existence according to the same rational ground [*Vernunftgrund*] that is also valid for me, it is at once an objective principle." That I am *objectively* an end in myself (along with every other rational being) is here presented as a mere postulate which is to find its "ground" only in Section Three [4: 429].[43] In sum, although everyone treats his own existence as an end in itself "subjectively," one can do so "objectively," or with awareness that it is rationally warranted, only on the basis of a principle that extends that status to all other rational beings. Combining the "objective" ground of practical legislation, which "lies in the rule," with the "subjective" ground,[44] which "lies in the end," yields the "idea" of a will that through its maxim gives itself a universal law.

II. THE "PARADOX OF AUTONOMY." We have finally arrived at the idea of autonomy, and with it, the long-sought "supreme principle of morality." But we will not grasp the full significance of Kant's discovery if we do not recognize the peculiar "paradox" surrounding it—at least for rational beings like ourselves.[45] It is "no wonder [*Wunder*]," as he puts it, that all previous efforts to uncover the principle of morality have failed. For no one—including, until only very recently, Kant himself—recognized determination by self-given law as the "specific sign" of an imperative that is not merely hypothetical [4: 431].

> One saw man bound through his duty to laws, but one did not let it occur to one [*man liess es sich aber nicht einfallen*] that man was subject *only to his own and yet universal legislation.* . . . For if one merely thought of him as subject to a law . . . this would have to bring with it some interest as a stimulus or compulsion, since it did not arise from *one's own* will, but rather this will was necessitated to act thus lawfully from something else. . . . [Hence] all labor [*Arbeit*] to find the ground of duty was irretrievably lost.   [4: 432–433]

The "paradoxical" idea of human reason furnishing its own unconditional ground constitutes, as we have seen, a moment of crisis for philosophy, to which even Kant's own earlier *Critique* was not yet fully adequate [4: 339]. Still, once brought fully to light, this paradoxical idea itself proves morally empowering: "the concept of every rational being having to consider itself as universally lawgiving through all its maxims in order to judge itself and its actions from this viewpoint" leads to "a very fruitful concept that depends on it": that of a "kingdom" or "whole of all ends" in "systematic connection"]

[4: 433]. In the kingdom or systematic whole made possible by the principle of autonomy, everything has either a "price" (i.e., a value that is merely relative) or a "dignity" (a value that is internal or independent of anything external). In the former case, the thing's value is "determined by the law"; in the latter it is itself the source of law and thus has a value that is unconditioned or "incomparable" [4: 436].

Although the concept of such a world is merely an "ideal," it can be called "practically intelligible," in as much as we have rational insight into the practical conditions of its possibility (i.e., universal obedience to the same self-imposed law). To be sure, we still lack insight into both whether and how such autonomous obedience itself is possible—i.e., how pure reason can be practical. And lacking that insight, we still remain vulnerable to the despairing thought that our moral concepts—though valid as criteria of moral estimation (for there can be no other criteria than these)[46]–are without effectual application.

A certain helpful analogy with the "universal connection of the existence of things in accordance with universal laws," or what is "formal in nature in general," now suggests itself [4: 437]. Accordingly, the three moral formulas can be represented as respectively expressing the "form," "matter," and "complete determination" of a world of rational beings—or, alternatively, as a progression from "unity," and "plurality" to "allness" or "totality" [4: 436], thus countering the thought that moral concepts lack all possible relation to a determinate object.

Representation, through all three formulas, of a morally possible world has a further advantage: By thus bringing the law "closer to intuition," it is more useful than the first formula alone in gaining "access" [*Eingang*][47] for the law for purposes of moral instruction. For purposes of moral judgment, on the other hand, it is better to proceed "according to the strict method" [*nach der strengen Methode*] and rely on formula number one (that of "the law of nature"). Kant is clear as to the primacy of the first formula for purposes of moral judgment over all three together, which have an advantage only with a view to moral training [4: 436–437]. And since evasion of the law's "strictness" is just what Section Two aims mainly to combat [4: 405], we have good reason to take Kant's express preference seriously.[48]

Section Two ends by returning to the ethical rational cognition with which the *Groundlaying* as a whole began: the concept of an absolutely good will—i.e., a will whose goodness is unlimited. The "developed" version of that concept now yields (through a formal analogy with the world of nature) the idea of an "intelligible world" (*mundus intelligibilis*) that is possible as a kingdom of ends—i.e., which would exist if the moral law were universally followed [4: 438]. That the force of morality's command in no way depends on this actually happening flows from autonomy's specific "paradox": namely, that "respect for a mere idea" without any other end or advantage to be attained by it, should serve as "an unremitting precept of the will" [4: 439].[49] According to that paradox, our own will, "acting only under the condition of a possible universal legislation through its maxims," is itself the "authentic object of respect" [4: 440] and is as such self-motivating.

The bearing of this paradox is made clearer by a consideration of Kant's use of the term more generally. What, then, does he mean here by "paradox"? In Kant's other writings the term generally signifies both something that is "outside of" or "beyond" ordinary opinion (the literal meaning of "paradox" [*para+doxa*]), and something that is intrinsically perplexing (the term's more common modern meaning).[50] A paradoxical assertion may be either false or true, as in Kant's reference, in the *Critique of Pure Reason*, to Priestley's "paradoxical" (and erroneous) adherence to materialism [A 746 = B 774] *and* to the "paradox" of inner sense that Kant himself asserts [B 152].[51]

Kant's *Anthropology* employs an additional usage that is particularly apt in the present context. The asserter of a paradox is to be distinguished, Kant there insists, from the "logical egoist" in the following manner:

> The logical egoist considers it unnecessary to test his judgment by the understanding of others too, as if he had no need of this testing stone [*Probirsteins*] (*criterium veritatis externum*). But it is so certain that we cannot dispense with this means of securing the truth of our judgment as to make this perhaps the most important reason why learned people cry so urgently for *freedom of the pen*.... Let no one say that *Mathematics*, at least, is privileged to speak out on its own sufficient authority [*Machtvollkommenheit*], for unless the surveyor's judgment were not first seen to be in complete agreement with that of others who devote their talent and effort to the field, even mathematics would not be relieved of the concern of sometimes falling into error.... There are also many cases where we do not even trust the judgment of our senses.... It is true that in philosophizing we need not [and should not] appeal to the judgment of others, as jurists appeal to legal experts [*Rechtserfahrenen*]; still, should a writer find that his publicly declared [*erklärt*] opinion, though it be of importance, find no adherents, he would come under suspicion of error.

It is therefore, Kant concludes:

> a wager [*Wagestück*]⁵²: to put in play a public claim that contradicts general/universal opinion, even that of people who possess understanding. This semblance [*Anschein*] of egoism is called *paradox*. This does not entail the audacity [*Kühnheit*] of risking something to the danger that it might be in error but rather only to the danger that it might find few adherents.—An advanced love [*Vorliebe*] of paradox is, to be sure, a *logical eccentricity:* the wish to appear to be a rare human being rather than an imitator of others often produces instead only *oddity*. But because every one must have his own opinion [*Sinne*] and maintain it [*si omnes patres sic, et ego non sic.*, Abelard], the allegation of paradox has no negative significance, unless the paradox is grounded in vanity. [7: 129]

Read in light of the above passage, Kant's own paradoxical assertion of the "paradox" of autonomy is itself a "venture," as the *Anthropology* later puts it, into uncertain public territory. The task undertaken in the *Groundlaying* is to this extent a kind of "gamble." Were Kant to fail in his attempt to turn the tide of *Popularphilosophie* and similar corruptions of the enlightenment spirit, he too would be taken for a mere eccentric, as he himself was once tempted to regard Rousseau.

At the end of Section Two, we know that if morality is "something" [*Etwas*], autonomy must "lie at its ground." But (firm assertion) that morality is no chimera or *Hirngespinst*—which follows only if the categorical imperative is "absolutely necessary as an *a priori* principle"—itself requires a "possible *synthetic use of pure practical reason*"—a use on which reason "cannot venture" [*nicht wagen dürfen*] without a prior critical survey of its powers [4: 445]. The self-contempt that would inevitably attend our giving up on the possibility of duty is, evidently, not yet enough to show that morality is in*deed* something [real].

This additional requirement might at first seem puzzling. According to Kant's *Lectures on Metaphysics*, "an *ideal* arises by a necessary use of reason; a *chimera* or *Hirngespinst*, on the other hand, is an arbitrary predicate of a straying reason" [*Metaphysik 2*, 28: 555]. Through *Hirngespinster* (e.g., ghosts, mind reading, "theurgy" [the so-called art of entering into community with spirits] and the like), reason renders itself useless [*Metaphysik Volckmann* 28: 448]. But if the kingdom of ends is, indeed, an ideal (as Section Two maintains), what concern remains to be addressed? Why is the thoughtful reader still open to the suspicion that the concept of duty is a mere "figment of the brain"?⁵³

In the case of speculative metaphysics, the transcendental (rather than transcendent) use of reason is distinguished by its ultimate purchase on experience—its capacity, that is to say, to do "useful work" as registered, at least in part, by sensibility. (To take one example, our rational concept of the soul is not a *Hirngespinst* so long as we regard it as a regulative archetype useful to certain sorts of empirical inquiry, rather than as furnishing knowledge of the subject as a simple substance.) Reason in its theoretical use cannot transcend the limits of experience, despite a certain necessary illusion to the contrary. As Kant puts it in the *Critique of Pure Reason:*

> The light dove, parting the air in free flight and feeling its resistance, might seize upon the representation that it would succeed still better in airless space. In just this way Plato left behind the sensible world because it sets understanding such narrow limits and ventured out [*wagte sich*] beyond it on the wings of the ideas into the empty space of pure understanding. He did not notice that through his exertions he made no headway because he had no resisting force [*Widerhalt*], as, so to speak, a support [*Unterlage*] on which he might tread and upon which he might expend his forces in order to bring understanding from the place [*den Verstand von der Stelle zu bringen*].
> [A 5 = B 9]

In the case of a metaphysics of *morals* (the entirely new field into which the *Groundlaying* enters), such empirically confirmable purchase on reality is unavailable. An additional critique of reason is therefore necessary to lend assurance that in affirming the reality of duty, reason does not similarly soar (with Plato) beyond its proper limits.[54] For speculative metaphysics the touchstone of reality necessarily lies within the limits of experience. A metaphysics of morals, on the other hand, is postulated on the assumption that pure practical reason is possible not just logically (as a concept that involves no internal contradiction) but in fact. That "postulate" must now be justified.

c. Section Three: "From the Metaphysics of Morals to the Critique of Pure Practical Reason"

Section Three takes up directly, and at long last, whether and how pure practical reason itself is possible. In so doing, it seeks to provide a "deduction" of the categorical imperative in the specific sense of justifying our "venture" of a synthetic use of pure practical reason in the face of a lingering suspicion (on the part of any thoughtful reader who has come this far) that the concept of duty rests on an illusion [4: 462]. Section Three is sometimes treated in the contemporary literature (especially that falling in the Anglo-American tradition) as if it aimed at offering a "reason" to obey the moral law. But Kant's actual purpose is, as we have already seen, more modest:

> Thus the question, how a categorical imperative may be possible, can indeed be answered just this far: [to the extent that] one can indicate the sole presupposition under which it is possible—namely the idea of freedom—and, in similar fashion, as one can have insight into the necessity of this presupposition; [all of] which is sufficient for the *practical use* of reason, i.e., for conviction as to the *validity of this imperative* . . . ; but how this presupposition may itself be possible is something about which no human reason can have insight. [4: 461]

The aim of Section Three, in other words, is to parry a lingering suspicion as to reason's "right" to venture a synthetic *a priori* practical proposition. Show me how such a proposition on reason's part is possible, the moral naysayer in us insists. The "deduction" and "critique" that follow are mainly a response to this demand. Success means gaining as much insight into the "how" in question as will suffice for "moral conviction." It does not involve demonstration (*per impossibile*) of the categorical imperative's truth on the basis of some non-moral premise.

The argument of Section Three unfolds dialectically through roughly the following stages:

1. Freedom of the will and autonomy reciprocally imply one another, as can be established through a conceptual analysis of each of them [4: 447–448].

2. Nonetheless, the principle of autonomy with which Section Two concluded—"An absolutely good will is one whose maxim can always contain itself considered as a universal law"—is for us a synthetic *a priori* proposition. For, as we have seen, no amount of analysis of the concept of an absolutely good will yields the specifically synthetic necessity attaching to a categorical imperative, i.e., the moral law as it sounds to *us*. (For a holy will the necessity in question would presumably be analytic; or, to speak more precisely, the human mind cannot think such necessity in any other way.)

3. The categorical imperative does, however, bear a striking similarity to synthetic *a priori* judgments that "make possible" our ordinary experience

The "Paradox" of Autonomy

of the sensible world. Theoretical synthetic *a priori* judgments combine conceptual and intuitive cognitions through a third thing ([cognition of] "the world of sense") in which "they are both encountered." Guided by this analogy, already opened up in Section Two, Kant now argues that in the case of a *practical* synthetic *a priori* proposition, this "third" thing cannot be "the nature of the world of sense" but must instead somehow be "procured" through the concept of freedom as autonomy [4: 447].

What that third thing must be, to which freedom as autonomy "points and of which we have an *a priori* idea," cannot yet usefully be stated but requires, by way of preparation, that the "possibility of a categorical imperative" first be made conceivable [*begreiflich*] [4: 447].

4. For that, too, however, "further preparation is required." It is first necessary to establish that every being that cannot act other than under the idea of freedom is as bound by the moral law "as it would be were it declared [*erklärt*][55] free in a way that is theoretically valid." This does *not* mean, as is sometimes held, that the mere fact that we cannot act otherwise than under the idea of freedom itself suffices to establish that the moral law is valid. (If that were Kant's meaning, it is difficult to see why Section Three would not end here.) He is rather claiming that we are no worse off, for purposes of the present argument, than we would be could freedom be proven theoretically [4: 447–448]. We thus need not here regret the absence of such proof.

5. Although we must attribute the "idea of freedom" to all rational beings (for reasons laid out in #4 above), we cannot yet prove freedom to be something actual [*etwas Wirkliches*]. Similarly, although we may well be able to connect the concept of a will that is absolutely good with the necessity of action on the basis of the moral law, we cannot yet grasp why it is valid (as ordinary moral understanding—i.e., "conscience"—insists) for beings like us (or any other rational beings *to be encountered in the world*) in whom *pure* reason, for all we know, may not be practical—i.e., capable of worldly effect. "We" (i.e., the decent and reflective who constitute Kant's specific audience) still find ourselves at something of a loss. On the one hand, we hold the value of moral action to be so great "that there can nowhere be any higher interest" and we "believe ourselves able to feel our personal value through it alone." On the other hand, should someone ask us "on what we ground the value that we attribute to this way of acting"—to "him we can give no satisfactory an-

swer" [4:449–450]. Although we cannot help attributing an overriding value to the moral law, our reason remains troubled by our inability to state *"from whence* [woher] [it] *obligates*"[56] [4: 450]. To say that *reason is itself* that "from whence" this obligation arises does not yet suffice: Human reason cannot give itself a reason (which would presuppose some independent object of value as a source of interest) why it is bound by its own law.

6. In the face of this perplexity, a "suspicion" [*Verdacht*] arises that we may have been moving in a circle—i.e., that we assumed ourselves free in the order of efficient [*wirkende*] causes in order to think ourselves under moral laws in the order of ends; and then we think ourselves as subject to these laws because we have presupposed freedom of the will [4: 450, 453].[57]

7. Kant's "way out" of that "apparent circle" lies in inviting us to notice the complex dualism that informs our awareness of our own activity (i.e., the different standpoints we take when we choose to throw a ball and subsequently see it sail through the air) [4: 450]. On the basis of this "felt" distinction between the inner and outer aspects of our *own* acts, we "easily" come to regard action *in general* as the passive effect of some active inner ground [4: 451]. The upshot is a "crude" but fruitful distinction "between *the world of sense* and a *world of understanding* lying at its basis [*Grund*]"—a distinction similar to that staked out in Kant's *Inaugural Dissertation* of 1770. But, as Kant now adds (in keeping with his own more recent critical discoveries), even we ourselves, insofar as our self-acquaintance is premised on inner sensation, cannot presume to know how we are "in ourselves." That we cannot act other than "under an idea" of freedom (e.g., when we throw a ball) does not prove that we are actually free (contrary to what Kant himself had held through most of the 1770s). Still, it does allow us to assume that behind one's self as it appears to one, there lies some "purely active" ground, by virtue of which one may "count" oneself as "in" the intelligible world but about which one knows nothing more [4:451]. (We might, for all we know, "belong" to such a world only in the weak sense that would apply to any ground of physical motion.)

8. This, then, is the position to which a "reflective" human being is readily drawn, and that tempts more common understandings to such su-

The "Paradox" of Autonomy

perstitious animistic excess as belief in ghosts. But "actuality" (of a sort reminiscent of Kant's own critical breakthrough) at this point intervenes:

> Now the human being actually [*wirklich*] finds in himself a capacity [*Vermögen*] by which he distinguishes himself from all other things, and even from himself insofar as he is affected by objects, and that is reason.... Reason proves its noblest occupation [*ihr vornehmstes Geschäfte . . . beweiset*] in distinguishing from one another the world of sense and world of understanding, under the name of the ideas . . . , and thereby drawing the limits of understanding itself. [4: 452]

Reason establishes the actuality of its "pure spontaneity" through what it does as a self-critical theoretical agent. In drawing the theoretical limits of understanding in a "critical" manner, reason uncovers a capacity in itself for the production of ideas that *cannot* be understood as subject to sensibility [4: 453]. We are thus permitted to assume that we are *members* (not just parts, a in #7 above) of an intelligible world on the basis of an argument that does not take the validity of the moral law as such for granted.

9. The question "How is a categorical imperative possible?" can finally be taken up directly. It is possible, Kant now answers, "as a synthetic proposition *a priori*" analogous to the synthetic *a priori* propositions that inform our fundamental judgments about nature. The great difference, for purposes of grasping how the categorical imperative is possible, is that the reality of freedom (unlike that of nature) cannot be proven by experiential example (and this despite what might be deemed reason's own critical experience, as presented in #8 above) [4: 455].

10. To be sure, philosophy too is a matter of "doing and omitting" carried out under the idea of freedom; hence "the subtlest philosophy" is no more able than is the "the most common human reason" to "ratiocinate freedom away [*die Freiheit wegzuvernünfteln*]" [4: 456].

11. The warrant to regard ourselves as members of an intelligible world does not, however, fully meet the challenge at hand. Even when activity on the part of theoretical reason "carried out under the idea of freedom" is granted, there lingers an apparent contradiction [*Scheinwiderspruch*] between man considered as a free agent and man considered as a determinate object of nature, a contradiction that must be uprooted "in a

convincing way [*auf überzeugende Art*]" lest fatalism presume to enter the "bonum vacans" [vacant land] that the critique of speculative reason leaves behind [4: 456].

12. One aspect of that dispute is readily settled—practical reason's absolute right to make practical use of the "vacant land" in question. So long as practical reason merely *thinks* its way into this land (the world of understanding) without wishing [*wollen*] to *intuit* itself or *sense* itself *into* it [*sie sich hineinschauen, hineinempfinden*], it doesn't overstep its proper boundaries [4: 458]. It treats the world of understanding only as a "*standpoint*" [*Standpunkt*] that it must adopt in order to regard itself as an effectual cause. But reason can *securely occupy* this "point" [*Punkt*], where the mechanism of nature negatively ceases and an altogether different order of causation positively begins, only to the extent that it refrains from seeking to retrieve an *object* from that world as motive [4: 458].

13. It is to such needful self-restraint on reason's part that Kant now turns. The principle of autonomy can be thought of as the formal condition of such a world of understanding, for reasons already laid out. But to undertake [*unterfangen*] to explain/declare [*erklären*] "*how freedom is possible*"—i.e., "how pure reason could be practical"—would itself, as Kant immediately adds, indeed overstep reason's boundaries. For we can "explain" only what we can reduce to laws whose object can be given in some possible experience. Thus: "where [*wo*] determination in accordance natural laws ceases, there also ceases all *explanation/declaration* [*Erklärung*]" [4: 459]. The "woher" of moral obligation is off-limits with respect to all explanatory attempts [cf. 4: 450].

14. What can, however, be rightly mustered is a "defense" against those fatalists who "brazenly explain/declare" [*dreust . . . erklären*] that freedom is impossible on the grounds that they have intuited [*geschauen*] more deeply into the essence of things. Here, nothing remains other than to draw attention to their own admission that essence differs from appearance—i.e., that experience does not necessarily exhaust the existential possibilities. That being granted, the contradiction that they allege to find in freedom vanishes (and in a way that they themselves must see as "fair" [*billig*]) [4: 459].

15. The question "How is a categorical imperative possible?" can thus be answered just this far [*so weit*] (to repeat the passage once more):

The "Paradox" of Autonomy 149

[to the extent] that one can point out the only presupposition under which it is possible—namely the idea of freedom—and, in similar fashion, that one can have insight into the necessity of this presupposition, which is sufficient for the *practical use* of reason, i.e., for conviction as to the *validity of this imperative*. [4: 461]

This presupposition is not only possible (i.e., not in contradiction with natural necessity in the realm of appearances) but, practically (though not yet morally) speaking, necessary. And autonomy, for its part, is the formal condition under which alone such a determination of the will is thinkable [4: 461].

16. What is more, the moral imputability of actions makes the presupposition of freedom "necessary" in a way that speculative reason alone could not assert:[58]

To presuppose this freedom of the will is also not only entirely possible (without falling into contradiction with the principle of natural necessity in connection with the appearances of the sensible world, as speculative philosophy can show) but also practically *necessary*—necessary, that is to say, in idea, without any further condition, for a rational being who is conscious of his causality through reason (which is distinguished from desires), to lay under his actions as a condition. [4: 461]

What this presupposition furnishes, it is important to repeat, is not some further reason, beyond the law itself, to acknowledge the law as binding on us. Its moral use here lies, rather, in helping to refute the "fatalist," who "unfairly" claims, despite his own admission that essence and appearance differ, that human freedom is impossible.[59]

At the same time, what "ground" might be laid under freedom—i.e., "how pure practical reason can be practical"—is a question whose pursuit would yield nothing but "lost labor and effort," given that any such ground would take away what makes moral actions, in the well-grounded view of ordinary human understanding, moral—namely their being undertaken without any further interest [4: 460–461]. In sum: "freedom" may be the "key to explaining autonomy of the will," as Kant states at the beginning of Section Three; but to try to vindicate morality by attempting to explain freedom would be to put reason to entirely wasteful use. Reason, in its capacity as judicious husbander of the soul's forces, is thus brought to bear against reason as incipient moral "enthusiast" about the "intelligible world" [4: 462].

17. Reason can hold onto its ideal of an "intelligible world" (not just the "world of understanding" that fatalism implicitly assumes),[60] albeit only with this moral end in view: namely that of "limiting" the "principle of moving causes [*Bewegursache*] from the field of sensibility" by "bounding" it and showing "that it does not embrace all in all but that beyond it I am still more" [4: 462]. The intelligible world, so understood, signifies "nothing more" than that when I have excluded everything that counts as a determining ground of my will that belongs to the world of sense, "something" [*Etwas*] remains. The point, posited by critical reason, that is in one way a limit (i.e., as that left over when we cancel in thought everything belonging to sensibility) is in another way a boundary indicating that "there is yet more."

18. We hereby reach the "highest boundary of all moral inquiry"—a boundary whose determination is of "great importance," if reason is not, on the one hand, to "do damage to morality" by seeking the highest moving cause [*Bewegursache*] in a source that is conceivable [*begrieflichen*]; or, on the other hand, "beat [*schwinge*] its wings without force," under "the name of the intelligible world" (or the empty space of transcendent concepts) and thus "lose itself in *Hirngespinsten*" [4: 462]. In sum: The standpoint in question (as with that earlier mentioned in connection with [Kant's own] philosophic crisis) is both a limit internally derived by reason and a boundary by which it stops itself from overstepping itself.

19. But *something* further can be done with the idea of an intelligible world. Understood as a "whole of intelligences," it becomes a permissible vehicle of "rational faith." To be sure, that idea cannot itself serve as a moral incentive (a proposition Kant himself had still flirted with in the first *Critique*). It can, however, effect [*bewerken*] a "lively interest" in the moral law, through the "splendid ideal" of a kingdom of ends in themselves to which we can "belong as members" only when we conduct ourselves "in accordance with maxims of freedom as if they were laws of nature" [4: 463]. Thus understood, faith becomes a branch of moral anthropology as earlier described [cf. 4: 489].

In ending thus, the *Groundlaying* not only vindicates Kant's earlier claim as to the advantage of the three formulas taken together (along with the related concept of a "kingdom of ends") for the specific purposes of moral instruction, given popular dislike of dry abstraction. It also fulfills the maxim that he had earlier specified as the distinguishing mark of a genuinely *moral* philosophy: namely, not putting the end to be achieved (i.e., gaining popular "access" for the law) before the law itself [cf. 4: 389].

The dialectic of practical reason can finally be resolved by allowing human reason to "excuse itself" on grounds of "fairness" for its own failure to make "unconditional practical necessity" conceivable in any positive way:

> Though we do not, to be sure grasp/conceive [that unconditional necessity] we do conceive its inconceivability, which is all that can fairly [*billigermassen*] be required of a philosophy that strives in principles up to the boundary of human reason. [4: 463]

Human reason "excuses itself" (and to this extent exonerates itself from "guilt") when it not only "lowers its tone" in its capacity as litigant (as in the first *Critique*) but also renounces, in its capacity as judge, any ratiocinating insistence on a ground beyond the principle of autonomy itself. Reason in its speculative use falls into perplexity "without guilt";[61] reason in its practical use, by way of contrast, falls into perplexity through a loss of "innocence" from which it can recover only by the willingness of reason *in its role as judge* to submit itself to the same rule of "fairness" that it imposed (in the *Critique of Pure Reason*) on reason's "warring" interests. That reason vindicate its own authority with "reasons" is more (as we, Kant's audience, must bring ourselves to grant) than human reason is entitled to demand.

2. Kant's "Paradox of Method": Autonomy in the *Critique of Practical Reason*

If the above interpretation is correct, the argument of the *Critique of Practical Reason* is less of a departure from that of the *Groundlaying* than is commonly assumed—and certainly nothing like the "radical reversal" that Henrich and others claim.[62] Both works take their fundamental bearings from rational moral knowledge that is self-evident, as Kant insists, to ordinary human understanding.[63] And neither attempts to establish the moral law's positive validity theoretically or on the basis of some non-moral premise (such as the freedom we necessarily attribute to ourselves when we act in non-moral contexts). The clearest difference lies in their respective claims as to what ordinary moral understanding knows with unwavering certitude: In the *Groundlaying*, that good will, or a will determined by the moral law, is the sole object to be held worthy of esteem; in the *Critique of Practical Reason,* that the moral law, in commanding us categorically and unremittingly, bears immediate witness to our freedom (i.e., our capacity to obey it). The doubts on the latter score to which the *Groundlaying* had principally responded are left behind in favor of a new set of worries that bear especially on the possibility and character of rational faith. It is no longer a matter of "discovering and setting fast" the supreme principle of morality—a principle, as Kant now assures us, that "stands fast [*stehe . . . fest*] in itself" [5: 47]. The difficulty to be addressed lies, rather, in the idea of a highest good, a concept that for rational beings like ourselves is necessarily ambiguous [cf. *Critique of Pure Reason* A 810 = B 838]. Reason can arrive at an idea of the highest good either by looking backward to the ground of willing or forward to the end. Securing the proper relation between these two ways of conceiving of a highest good is the second *Critique*'s central task. For that purpose, the *Groundlaying*'s wholly negative treatment of the concept of an end of reason (i.e., the formula of humanity as an end in itself)—a treatment that served Kant's then purpose of placing the lawgiving "ground" before us in the clearest and most unambiguous terms—will no longer do.

These differences no doubt partly reflect changes in Kant's own circumstances, both professional and political. In 1786 the "enlightened" despotism of Frederick the Great was replaced by a regime far less friendly to intellectual freedom, especially with respect to matters of religion.[64] At the same time, early responses to the first edition of the *Critique of Pure Reason* were sufficiently uncomprehending or otherwise unsatisfactory to prompt Kant to prepare an expanded second edition that anticipates some themes later discussed in the *Critique of Practical Reason,* including a new "refutation of idealism" and related insistence on the parity of inner and outer sense. Inner sense, as he now especially stresses, gives no privileged access to reality.

The new arguments of the B edition of the *Critique of Pure Reason* themselves bear significantly on a related public dispute that had broken out between two figures with whom Kant was himself personally connected—Moses Mendelssohn and Friedrich Heinrich Jacobi.[65] The immediate subject of that dispute was the alleged "Spinozism" of their late friend Lessing; the deeper issue raised was whether philosophic reasoning does or doesn't ultimately lead to a fatalistic atheism (= "nihilism") destructive of morality and civic order generally.[66] Given the new king's worrisome proclivities on matters of intellectual freedom, the controversy had an especially urgent practical bearing. In his essay *How to Orient Oneself in Thinking* [1786] Kant responded with a new argument for "rational faith" arising from a subjective and yet rational "need"—a position that placed him in neither Mendelssohn's nor Jacobi's camp but allowed him, as he hoped, to remain on reasonably friendly terms with each.

The concept of a moral faith consistent with autonomy (as the treatment of faith in the *Critique of Pure Reason* was not) is treated more fully in the *Critique of Practical Reason*.[67] H. A. Pistorius, who had leveled several pertinent objections to the argument of the *Groundlaying*, proved in this respect a useful foil. Pistorius had taken issue with Kant for both 1) the alleged obscurity of his treatment of the difference between the phenomenal and the noumenal self and 2) the alleged impossibility of determining a concept of good will without a prior determination of a concept of the good. In responding to the former objection, Kant presents a critically rational defense of faith in immortality that replaces the failed dogmatic argument that had been advanced in Mendelssohn's *Phaedo*. In responding to the latter objection, he sets out the sole basis for belief in God that is consistent, unlike Jacobi's skeptical appeal to "faith," with the autonomy of human reason.

a. Autonomy and the "Fact of Reason"

Kant's new approach in the *Critique of Practical Reason* is related to these changes. His main intellectual targets are no longer amoral skeptics who abet moral "wavering" (i.e., "virtue's enemies" as presented in the *Groundlaying*); instead, he must take on skeptical defenders of religious faith who attack philosophy on behalf of ordinary moral life. In calling freedom the "keystone" of his entire system [5: 3], Kant speaks directly to Jacobi's charge that philosophy, consistently and systematically pursued, leads inevitably to Spinozistic fatalism.

These objectives call, in turn, for a new description of the fundamental moral insight by which practical philosophy is to be guided. Kant's appeal to the so-called "factum of reason" is a reflection of this need and of his own fuller understanding of the "ambiguity" that moral philosophy is thereby called on to address.

In both the *Groundlaying* and the *Critique of Practical Reason*, moral necessitation forces itself unbidden upon our consciousness on the strength of our own reason and its law. Kant now makes explicit the commanding role of legislating reason. The term "factum" does not here designate a "fact" in the now ordinary meaning of something passively accepted as "given" on the basis of experiential knowledge; Kant intends it rather in the double sense implied by the Latin original (factum=facere) and that is retained in the English "deed." "Factum" refers both to the doing and to what is thereby accomplished. Pure practical reason "proves its reality by what it does" [5: 8].

This lexical richness helps explain Kant's otherwise perplexing identification of the fact of reason with conscience, the moral law, and the positing of the law by pure practical reason, each of which evokes a different but related meaning of the term "factum." Consciousness of the moral law "may be called a fact of reason" as Kant adds:

> because one cannot reason it out [*herausvernünfteln*] from antecedent data of reason, for example, from consciousness of freedom (since this is not antecedently given to us) and because it instead forces itself upon us on its own [*fuer sich*] as a synthetic *a priori* proposition that is not based on any intuition.... However, in order to regard this law—without misinterpretation [*Mißdeutung*]–as *given,* one notes carefully that it is not an empirical fact but the sole fact of pure reason which thereby announces itself as originally lawgiving (*sic volo, sic jubeo*). [5: 31n]

The moral law is an "act" of pure practical reason that "forces itself," as it were, upon ordinary consciousness with an "immediacy" that bears witness to its noumenal source, as born out by the accompanying phrase *sic volo sic jubeo* ["as I will so I command"].[68] The phrase—uttered, in its original context, by an imperious mistress to condemn a slave in utter disregard of whether he is innocent or guilty—throws the "strangeness" of reason's factum (or "done deed"), which collapses legislation, judgment, and execution into a single moment, into especially sharp relief.[69] Reason is indeed the *Selbsthalterin* of its own laws.[70]

To be sure, *how* it is possible for law to determine the will immediately, and without regard for any (further) good intended, still remains an "insoluble problem" [5: 72]. The sole feeling adequate to its effect can, however, be readily described. Although the action of pure practical reason is not "felt" directly, it is negatively registered by a feeling, designated by Kant as "respect," of the sacrifice of all sensible pleasure *in totum.* Respect is at once a feeling of humiliation (or of the "infringement" of inclination and the "striking down" of self-conceit) and of uplifting self-appropriation that is literally beyond calculation [5: 73, 80]. Like its aesthetically sublime counterpart, respect registers supreme value indirectly, i.e., as the "Aufhebung" or cancellation of every value that is measurable. Yet whereas the aesthetically sublime is merely "enlivening" (as

Kant will later put it), respect signals the active presence of the law as what he here calls the "supreme life principle" [5: 79–81, 86, 116–117].

The "reality" of freedom from a practical (i.e., moral) standpoint "warrants," in turn, an extension of the categories to the good will conceived as *causus noumenon* [5: 50, 56]. Such a *causus* acts outside the boundaries of time.[71] Its effect on consciousness is thus "immediate" [5: 46, 48, 62];[72] just as we see, "without hesitation," what, morally speaking, is to be done [5: 36, 30].[73] Conscience immediately testifies to the action of the self as noumenal source. What is to be done by *us* (as phenomenal selves), however, must be achieved in time, giving rise to complications that specifically involve the (temporal) order of precedence.[74]

b. Kant's "Paradox of Method"

Pistorius had criticized Kant for discussing good will without first defining a concept of the good. Kant's "paradox of method" responds directly to that objection. According to this method—one that, as he claims, no previous moral philosopher has followed [5: 64]—the concept of good and evil must not be determined "*before the moral law*" but only "*after and by means of it*" [5: 63; original emphasis].

Kant's method is "paradoxical" for the following reason: Ordinarily, to understand "x bearing the quality y," one must first know the meaning of "y." (To understand "purple cow," one must first know the meaning of "purple.") Kant's determination of the concept of good will prior to determining a concept of the good would seem to violate this rule.

The concept of the good, however, is peculiar, owing to the imprecision of the term "highest" (as in "highest good"). "Highest" can mean either first in order of grounds (*supremum*) or last in order of ends (*perfectum*). Owing to that imprecision, pure reason "in its practical use" is subject to a dialectic that leads it to put the end before the ground in order of time—i.e., to seek to define the complete good before defining the supreme good. A "critique" therefore proves necessary—not, to be sure, to provide assurance that pure reason *can* be *practical* (which is given with the "fact of reason")—but to overcome a conflict that arises (in temporal uses of pure practical reason) over determination of the concept of the good [5: 110].[75]

The rational criterion with which the *Groundlaying* began—the idea of a good will as the only unconditionally held good that it is possible to think—does not exhaust the *interest* of pure reason, which aims not only at the unconditioned good but also at completeness *vis-à-vis* the good, as the opening paragraph of that work had already tacitly allowed [4: 493]. A world of virtuous yet unhappy beings is less than a (fully) rational being, provided with the means, would necessarily seek to bring about [5: 110].

The ancient Stoic and Epicurean schools, in keeping with the "dialectical spirit"[76] of their times, wrongly sought to unite virtue and happiness "analytically." What both missed was the "synthetic" character of the highest good [5: 111–112]. The question "How is the highest good practically possible?" thus remained unanswered, giving rise to an "antinomy of practical reason" between two ways of uniting virtue and happiness, *each* of which *seems* to be impossible. To make virtue conditional on happiness in one's synthetic concept of a highest good is impossible, because it destroys morality, and hence virtue, altogether. But to make happiness conditional upon virtue also seems impossible because there is no evident connection between the "most punctilious observance" of the moral law and happiness, which depends, rather, on our "knowledge of the laws of nature and our physical capacity [*Vermögen*] to achieve our ends" [5: 113]. But if reason cannot see how the highest good is possible "according to practical rules," morality must itself be rejected:

> Since the promotion of the highest good . . . is a necessary *a priori* object of our will that hangs together inextricably with the moral law, the impossibility of the first must also prove the falsity of the second. Thus if the highest good is impossible according to practical rules, the moral law which commands us to promote it must be fantastic and directed to imaginary ends and therefore in itself be false. [5: 114]

There thus arises a complication that the *Groundlaying* had not considered. If we are to act as the moral law commands, we must be able to grasp some rule-governed link between our own causality in time and the end that a good will necessarily has in view. If the object that the moral law commands is impossible "according to practical rules," then we cannot rationally act (in time) at all, and the moral law, which directs us toward "fantastic" and "imaginary" ends, must itself be false. The this-worldly theater of *human* action (and hence pure reason "in its practical use") puts us in the position of requiring additional assurance as to the possibility of achieving what the moral law commands, assurance not necessarily required by all rational beings as such [5: 119].

Religion is thus "subjectively" necessary—not as an incentive to moral obedience, or to help effect a lively moral interest (as the *Critique of Pure Reason* and the *Groundlaying* had respectively argued or implied)—but to overcome the thought—morally disabling for a moral understanding like our own—that the *aim* of pure practical reason is itself fantastic. Without the "postulates" of pure practical reason and a related faith in immortality and God's existence, the all-important priority of ground to end is placed subjectively in question. However "immediate" the law's determination of the will may be, human consciousness also involves a timely sense of expectation [*Erwartung*] or awaiting what is yet to come.

In sum: The paradox associated with autonomy [4: 439] has been significantly recast. It is no longer specifically linked, as in the *Groundlaying*, with the good will's indifference to whether or not the kingdom of ends is in fact to be achieved.[77] The stated paradox is now one of "method"—i.e., of how, or in what order, to proceed in determining the concept of a highest good.

Kant's earlier formulation of the paradox had undercut the argument for rational faith offered in the *Critique of Pure Reason* without replacing it. As presented in the *Groundlaying*, the paradox of autonomy reduces religion to at best a vehicle of moral anthropology, at worst an empty shell. Newly compelled to meet the charge that critical philosophy is hostile to religion, the *Critique of Practical Reason* restates that paradox in a manner that gives religion a more robust role by including rather than excluding the concern of human reason for the success of its own projects. Out of that concern, which the "precarious standpoint" of the *Groundlaying* had all but cast aside, there emerges a new argument for rational faith consistent with autonomy (as that presented in the first *Critique* was not).

But religion's newly robust critical role is not without its difficulties. The determination of moral principles, as Kant now puts it, is a "delicate" case in which "the slightest misinterpretation [*kleinste Mißdeutung*] corrupts dispositions [*Gesinnungen*]" [5: 109–110; cf. 5: 31n]. If reason's religious need is held to be other than "subjective," the autonomy of reason is itself denied. One can avoid such misinterpretation, it seems, only by keeping the *subjectivity* of reason's needs and the *objectivity* of reason's lawgiving simultaneously in view.

This consideration, I believe, best explains Kant's reprisal of the term "moral life"—which appears in various forms throughout the *Critique of Practical Reason*.[78] As we saw in Chapter 3, notions of moral and spiritual life had figured prominently in his earlier lectures on ethics and on anthropology, only to be retired with his critical discovery that the noumenal self is not theoretically accessible. Its critical reprisal in the *Critique of Practical Reason* has the specific function of guarding against the aforesaid misinterpretation.

"Moral life" in its current application is associated with pure practical reason in its noumenal, as opposed to specifically human, state. Moral instruction accordingly occurs through cultivation of the capacity to "feel" the "lively" effect of pure moral principles at the same time that one makes due allowance for the heart's own "natural principles" of vital motion [5: 155–157]. The law is "foreign to the [life] element" with "which we are accustomed." Hence, the principle of moral life appears only in the "shape" of a "compulsion" to abandon that accustomed element for one in which we can sustain ourselves only with "effort" and "constant apprehension of relapsing" [5: 158, 151]. Principles built on foundations [*Grundlage*] other than concepts produce only *seizures* [Anwandelungen]. In sum: The moral life makes itself felt in the compulsion to ascend from a state of morally inert comfort to one in which we can preserve ourselves only with difficulty.

With a view to aiding us in that struggle, the "right method" of moral instruction proceeds as follows. First comes practice in employing one's faculty of moral judgment (yielding a feeling of extended cognitive power that itself constitutes, he says, a "form of beauty"). Second come exercises that aim at fixing one's attention on one's own freedom (yielding a sublime feeling of "release" that lends the law easier access) [5: 160–161]. The accompanying self-respect (negatively felt as an overriding dread of self-contempt) prevents "ignoble and corrupting impulses" from "breaking out" into the mind, making it possible (at last) for "every morally good disposition [*Gesinnung*]" to engraft itself [5: 161].[79]

The *Critique*'s final evocation of "the starry heavens above us" and the moral law within us" places both life-outlooks in sublime juxtaposition [5: 161]. (Animal and moral life [subjective need and objective law] remain side by side and mutually exclusive. Only with the *Critique of Judgment*, published three years later, will they merge in a morally sublime representation of human history.) The former outlook "annihilates, as it were, my importance as an animal *creature*," endowed "we know not how" with "vital force," and who must "give back the matter" from which [in its capacity as animal creature] "it arose." The latter raises my value to infinity by revealing the presence of a "life" independent of what must be "given back" [5: 161–162].[80]

Bereft of the right method, however, moral feeling can be dangerous. Although "admiration" and "respect" can incite to inquiry, they "cannot supply the want of it." Just as man's vision of the starry heavens once issued in astrology, so our awareness of our personality now threatens to produce mere "Schwärmerei" and superstition [5: 162]. In ethics as in physics, science, "critically sought and methodically directed," remains "the sole narrow gate" to wisdom—a gate that must in turn be "guarded" by philosophy. The temporal process by which that philosophic insight has come to light historically must now be reversed. The doctrine of wisdom consists not only in "what one ought *to do,* but also in what ought to serve teachers as a guide and "secure others from an erring path [*Irrweg*]" [5: 163].[81] In his own delicate way, Kant calls attention to a deteriorating political climate that will soon make this task newly urgent.

II

COMPLICATIONS ON ARRIVAL

Introduction to Part II: Late Kant, 1789–1798

Between 1784 and 1787 Kant's presentation of the principle of autonomy underwent a subtle but far-reaching change due in part to a new political climate brought on by the death of Frederick II. Attention turns from shoring up our precarious hold upon a principle whose ground we ourselves must lay, to establishing a secure link between morality so understood and rational faith. As we saw in Chapter 4, Kant's initial presentation of the principle of autonomy seemed to challenge the very need for religion, making the issue of faith, in a time of tightening political restrictions, all the more pressing. The year 1789 marks the beginning of a second important shift in Kant's treatment of autonomy, a shift partially prompted by political events in France. But it also reflects, as I will argue, theoretical and moral complexities (brought to the surface, as it were, by those new circumstances) that are endemic to an ethic of autonomy as such.

1. Late Kant: 1789–1798

After finishing the *Critique of Practical Reason,* Kant turned almost immediately to his long-contemplated critique of taste. Kant's renewed attention to the theme of taste included teleological considerations almost from the start. A letter to Carl Leonhard Reinhold dated December 1787 mentions that he is at work on a "critique of taste" based on his discovery of a "new sort of a priori principles" related both to the "faculty of feeling pleasure and displeasure" and to "teleology" [10: 514–515]. In January 1788 a brief essay on "The Use of Teleological Principles in Philosophy" appeared in the *Teutsche Merkur*. A second letter to Reinhold of March 1788 indicates Kant's intention to complete his "Critique of Taste" by late September [10: 532]. In fact, the *Critique of Judgment* (as it was finally called) was finished more than a year later, in the final months of 1789 and the first two months of 1790.

As John Zammito has argued, the content and structure of the *Critique of Judgment* seems to have undergone a final "ethical turn" beginning in late summer 1789. According to Zammito, that turn is manifest in three main places: the "Dialectic of Aesthetic Judgment," the "Analytic of the Sublime," and #49 (the analysis of genius). It also led to a substantial revision of the original Introduction, and a much expanded version of the "Methodology of Teleological Judgment" [264].[1] In sum: It is reasonable to assume that beginning sometime in late summer 1789, Kant added an "ethical" dimension to the work that had not previously been present, including new sections on "the sublime" and on "beauty as symbol of the morally good" and new treatments of human history and rational faith as "ethico-theology." If these textual speculations are correct, in the summer and fall of 1789 Kant's project underwent a revision of focus that both "moralized" his treatment of aesthetic judgment and gave new critical prominence to human history. I would suggest that the dating of these developments, assuming this account is accurate, is more than happenstance—i.e., that the storming of the Bastille on July 14 and related political events in France prompted insights on Kant's part that inform the *Critique of Judgment* as we now know it, a fact with important implications for a full understanding of Kant's political and religious writings of the 1790s.[2]

a. Jacobi and Count von Windisch-Graetz

A suggestive letter to Jacobi, dated August 30, 1789 [11: 74–77], sheds light on Kant's state of mind in late summer of that year. Two matters stand out: Kant's general effort to win Jacobi over to his side (after Kant's bruising attack in the *Orientation* essay); and Kant's singular expressions of enthusiasm for the writings of Count Joseph Nicholas von Windisch-Graetz, whose work on constitutional monarchy along representative republican lines Jacobi had passed along.

On the former point: Kant praises Jacobi in the evident hope of convincing him that "reason's bark," under critical sail, can slip through the "cliffs of atheism" where Mendelssohn's dogmatic rationalism had failed [11: 76]. Jacobi's and Kant's intellectual sophistication and common interest in defending ordinary morality should make them allies rather than enemies in a time of rising religious obscuritanism. Accordingly, Kant now extols Jacobi's *Spinoza* book on two separate accounts: first, for its "clear presentation" of the "difficulties" with teleologico-theology that "seem to have led Spinoza to his system"; second, for Jacobi's "thorough refutation" of Herder's "syncretistic" pantheism. Kant's earlier criticism of Jacobi (in the essay on *Orientation*), he now assures him, was only meant to "cleanse [Kant] of the suspicion of Spinozism" (not, as he had earlier written to Marcus Herz, to expose the "humbug" and "inspired fanaticism" of Jacobi himself [10: 442]). Jacobi is now on the correct (anti-Herderian) side of the "genius-epidemic"—and this not least by refuting Herder's attempted merger of Spinozism and Deism. All that is required for Kant and Jacobi's full-fledged alliance is an admission on the latter's part that the "indispensable supplement to reason" of which he speaks is "something that, although not a part of speculative knowledge," originates "in reason itself." Kant (for the first time) calls that namable but ungraspable "something"—consistent with reason's autonomy—a "supersensible power of causality within us." Kant is here on the verge of the *ethico-theology* with which the *Critique of Judgment* will later end: conscience regulatively reconstrued as the confluence between an autonomous human will and the inscrutable intention of God.

Kant's overture to Jacobi also includes the following appeal:

> Whether reason could be merely *awakened* to this concept of theism through something learned only from history or whether it would require a supernatural inner inspiration [*innere Einwirkung*] incomprehensible to us, is a question which pertains merely to incidentals, namely to the emergence and advent of this idea. For one can just as well admit that had the gospels not previously instructed us in moral laws in their entire purity our reason would not yet have such complete insight into them; still, *once such insight exists,* we can (at the present time) convince anyone of their correctness and validity through bare reason. [11: 76]

As in his later work on *Religion within the Boundaries of Bare Reason*, Kant attempts to win allies among men of faith by punting on the question of the original source of moral knowledge. The main issue is the self-sufficiency of reason once it has insight (insight that Jacobi is invited to join Kant in acknowledging), however that insight may originally have been acquired. Although Kant here chooses the example of the gospels, the conclusion would apply with equal force to other historically instructive moments, such as those occurring during Kant's own time. In sum: Kant not only anticipates the strategy he will employ in works like *Religion within the Boundaries of Bare Reason;* he also opens the door to morally "revelatory" moments at other points in history, including the present one.

On the second matter: Kant initiates his overture of friendship toward Jacobi with an expression of thanks for transmitting a gift volume from Count von Windisch-Graetz.[3] In so doing, Kant also expresses a "passionate longing" for the Count's forthcoming *Provisional Solution to a Problem; or Metaphysical History of Animal Organization.*[4]

Kant's remarks on the Count's writings are worth quoting at length:

> The gift from Count von Windisch-Graetz, containing his philosophical essays, has arrived (thanks to you and to Privy Commercial Councilor Fischer), and I have also received the first edition of his *Histoire métaphysique* . . . etc., from the book dealer Sixt. Please thank the Count for me and assure him of my respect for his philosophic talent, a talent that he combines with the noblest attitudes of a cosmopolite. In the last-mentioned work I observed with pleasure that the Count discusses, with the clarity and modesty of one who is at home in the great world, the same matters with which I in my scholastic fashion have also been concerned, viz., the clear definition and encouragement of human nature's nobler incentives, incentives that have so often been confused with (and even taken for) physical incentives that they have failed to produce the results that one rightfully expects of them. I long passionately to see him complete this work, for it obviously is systematically related to his other two books (the one on secret societies and the one on voluntary changes in the constitution of monarchies). . . . No statesman has heretofore inquired so deeply into the principles of the art of governing men or has even known how to go about such an inquiry. But that is why none of the proposals of such people has succeeded in convincing anyone, let alone producing results. [11: 75]

Taken together with the Count's related essays on "secret societies" and on "voluntary changes in the constitution of monarchies," Kant anticipates a "system" that would have "great influence in the current European crisis, partly as a wonderfully realized prophecy, partly as sage advice to despots" [11: 75].[5] Even if one discounts the ebullience of its tone as partly intended for Jacobi's benefit, the content of Kant's praise is remarkable for its unstintingness. Indeed, many of Windisch-Graetz's suggestions in these essays will appear, more or less unchanged, in Kant's later political writings. Whatever one ultimately makes of this little-noted fact, the Count's essays open an enlightening window on Kant's revolutionary and post-revolutionary views on civic order.

Windisch-Graetz was a forceful advocate for constitutional monarchy with strong parliamentary limits on the executive at a time when such an outcome in France still seemed possible. In his essay on constitutional reform, he urged monarchs throughout Europe to both "legalize" and "limit" their authority by convening representative assemblies with the power to make "fundamental law." Other arguments also call to mind Kant's own later claims, including an insistence on the "illegality" of revolution that resembles Kant's later argument to that effect in *Theory and Practice*. As in the latter essay, this account is accompanied by the assertion of an unlimited right of citizens to make their thoughts known publicly.[6]

Whatever the actual influence of these (largely neglected) essays on Kant's later political writings—and even a cursory consideration suggests that it may well have been considerable[7]—they shed useful light on Kant's thinking in the late months of 1789 and early weeks of 1790, when a legal transition to a constitutional monarchy supportive of republican liberties still seemed possible. Based on the information conveyed by Kant's letter, it would seem that he finds himself, in late summer of 1789, in the grip of a political "crisis" of no little moment.[8]

It is hardly surprising that a thinker for whom republicanism had been a central unifying theme from early on should find developments in France riveting. His old "idea of history" had assumed a gradual process of political reform "from the top down" and of educational reform "from the bottom up." The vision of an organized constitutional republic in the making (along the lines urged by Windisch-Graetz) promised a more immediate and immanent route of historical deliverance. An emerging republican France not only furnishes Kant with a visible instance of civic "organization" in the making; it also, as we shall see, links two treatments of history (in Parts One and Two, respectively, of the third *Critique*) that together put the education of the human race in a clearer light than Kant had previously found possible.[9]

b. "Organization" and the French Revolution

In Section 65 of Part Two of the *Critique of Judgment* (a section entitled "things as natural purposes are organized beings"), Kant argues that the causality that attends organized products of nature is, "strictly speaking," inexplicable to us: Neither hylozoism (or the attribution of life to matter) nor appealing to an extra-natural "soul," will fill the bill, if we wish to remain within the confines of theoretical knowledge. (Herderian pantheism thus either contradicts itself or explains nothing at all). The organization of nature [of a sort exemplified by living beings] has nothing strictly "analogous," as he puts it, "to any sort of causality we know [*kennen*]." Still, as he proceeds to add:

> One can give light to a certain association, that is encountered more in the idea than in reality, through the analogy with these immediate natural purposes: in speaking of the recent [*neuerlich*] complete transformation [*Umbildung*] of a great people into a state the word "Organization" frequently served very readily for the establishment of magistries, etc., and even for the entire body of the state. For each member of such a whole should indeed not be merely a means but also an end; and while each member cooperates in the possibility of the whole, the place and function of each is determined in turn through the idea of the whole. [5: 375, 375n]¹⁰

Although, as he insists, there is, strictly speaking, no analogy between the causality attending natural purposes and the causality we know, the former *does* cast "analogical" light upon a causality of which history itself furnishes recent example: the self-transformation of a "great people" into a living moral whole. This "enlightening" comparison (which both is and isn't "analogical") between natural and political organization calls to mind Kant's expectation, in the aforementioned letter to Jacobi, that the Count's political essays and his forthcoming work on animal organization might "together constitute a system" of no little interest.

At one level, to be sure, the nature of the comparison between political and animal organization is easy enough to grasp: in both cases (i.e., with both the formation of a people and the constitution of a natural product) the reciprocal relation of the parts (as each other's ends and means) is conceivable as possible only through the idea of a whole. Indeed, one might almost say (against Kant's explicit statement) that it is political organization that sheds light upon its natural counterpart. For whereas the possibility of the latter is, in the last analysis, mysterious to us (resting on a causality that is unintelligible to us in principle), the possibility of the latter is fully intelligible insofar as it involves the conscious action of human beings.

To better grasp what Kant means by "organization" in a civic sense, however, it is necessary to turn to his extended treatments of history elsewhere in the *Critique of Judgment*. Here, too, the shadow of the French *Umbildung* (in its early and still potentially lawful form) is not difficult to trace.

Introduction to Part II **169**

c. History in the Critique of Judgment

Kant takes up the subject of human history in two widely separated passages. It will prove useful, after examining them individually, to read them in conjunction as related commentaries—from the unique standpoint adopted by the *Critique of Judgment* as a whole [5: 176]—on the political and moral education of humanity at large.

The first passage occurs near the end of Part One, in a section called "the methodology of taste," which is in fact devoted to establishing that there can be no such thing. In matters of taste, where no rules apply, there is only a "manner" *(modus)*, not a "method," of teaching [5: 355]. The true "propaedeutic" to a perfected fine art does not consist in "precepts" but "seems rather to lie" in "cultivation [*Culture*] of the forces of the mind through that foreknowledge [*Vorkenntnisse*] called the humanities." The latter term has presumably been adopted because "humanity"[11] refers both to a feeling for what is universally communicable [*das allgemeine Theilnehmungsgefühl*] and to the capacity to sympathize [*mittheilen*] most intimately and universally—qualities that together constitute the sociability by which man distinguishes himself from the limitation that applies to beasts [5: 355]. Kant then adds, by way of illustration:

> The age and peoples whose strong drive toward lawful sociability through which a people constitutes an enduring commonwealth, wrestled with the great difficulties that surround the difficult task of uniting freedom (and hence also equality) with a compulsion (more respect and submission from duty than from fear): such a people had first to discover the art of reciprocal communication between the most educated [*ausgebildetesten*] part [*Theil*] with the crudest, discover, that is to say, the attuning [*Abstimmung*] of the enlargement and refinement of the former with the simplicity and originality of the latter, and in this way that mean, between the highest culture and a sufficient [*genugsam*] nature, that also constitutes the right standard, given by no universal rule, for taste as universal human sense.
>
> A later age will not easily make these models dispensable: for it will be ever further from nature so that finally without having any lingering examples of it, it will be in a position in which it can hardly form the concept of the happy union in one and the same people of the lawful compulsion of the highest culture with the force and correctness of a free nature that feels its own value. [5: 356]

Kant here traces the emergence of the ancient republics to an "intimate communication" that fortunately combined the lawful refinement of the nobility (on the one hand) with the originality and freedom of the popular classes (on the other). But what if a modern people like the French (a people that he elsewhere calls "rich in spirit" [7: 85]) should reenact this very model? Does the promise of the revolution not reunite "in one and the same people" both "the compulsion that accompanies the highest culture" with "the force and correctness of a free nature that feels its own value"? If this should prove to be so, than the "humanoria" would no longer entirely depend (as now "seems" to be the case) on ancient formulas that are ever more removed from the natural "originality" of peoples.[12] If this proved so, in other words, modern republics might emerge on a newly enlightened basis no longer susceptible to the decay of ancient formulas.

This consideration casts a retrospectively political light upon Kant's earlier discussion of artistic genius (according to Zammito, another post-revolutionary addition). Read in light of the later passage, the genius exemplified by individuals also reflects that of a people, even as it brings their national spirit to a heightened state of literary and poetic consciousness. (The subject of great nation-forming poets will, of course, be an important Romantic theme.) In his discussion of genius (also apparently added in the latter months of 1789) Kant quotes only one poet at length—the late (and warlike) Frederick the Great, whose poetic rendering of the setting sun (as simile for his own imminent death) "animates" *his* rational idea of world-republicanism [5: 315–316].[13] The anonymous verse that follows instead celebrates the sublimity of dawn, as the symbol of the "virtue that brings peace." Does the recent (French) *Umbildung* not presage such a dawn?[14]

Whatever one makes of these suggestions, Kant is clear as to the ultimate dispensability of ancient models. However "difficult" it may be to do without them, and however things may "seem," the "true [*wahre*] propaedeutic" to the grounding of taste is the "development of ethical ideas and the culture of moral feeling"—a development and culture belonging to the present:

> Since . . . taste is fundamentally a capacity for judging the sensualization of moral ideas (by means of a certain analogy of reflection over both); from which, along with the thus to be grounded greater susceptibility for feeling out of [*aus*] the latter (which is called moral), is derived the pleasure that taste declares valid for humanity [*Menschheit*] as such and not merely for the private feeling of each: [this being so] it is clear that the true propaedeutic for the grounding of taste is the development of ethical ideas and the culture of moral feeling; for only if/when sensibility is brought into

> harmony with this can genuine taste assume a determinate, unalterable form. [5: 355–356]

The "Proteus" of taste that Kant had once decried[15] is now definitively superseded. The development of ethical ideas and the culture of moral feeling are the true and lasting school of taste. But taste, in turn, makes an essential civic contribution (e.g., by helping to sustain in a deliberate way the "lawful sociability" that ancient peoples hit upon, so to speak, by chance). The perfection of taste not only depends on moral education; it, in turn, sustains the civic culture needed to support that education over time. Morals and aesthetics are reciprocally "reflective"—from the peculiar standpoint of the *Critique of Judgment*—each relying upon a "certain analogy" that is common to both.

To better grasp that analogy (which resembles the natural-civic "organizational" analogy already discussed), it proves helpful to turn to the work's second extended treatment of history, which, like the earlier passage, appears in a section bearing the name "methodology." Unlike Part One, Part Two *does* have a doctrine of method [*Methodenlehre*]. To be sure, that method is peculiar: Although teleology has its rules, it does not hold a position (like other methodical or rule-governed studies) within the system of scientific doctrines, either natural or theological, but serves, rather, as a critical moment of transition whose function lies in the "articulation" or "organization" of the whole [5: 416–417]. Teleology thus understood has a "negative" role to play, Kant tells us, *vis-à-vis* natural science and a "propaedeutic" role *vis-à-vis* theology [5: 417].

On the former point: Critical teleology establishes the necessary subordination of mechanical to teleological principles for purposes of explaining natural products (=living organisms). Where such explanation is concerned, one must always presuppose some original organization (however finally inexplicable) [5: 418–420]. Both Spinozism and (Herderian) pantheism may thus be rejected on the grounds that they fail to provide for the unity of purpose that we necessarily attribute to such products. Kant's preferred solution is to appeal to the "formative drive" described by Johann Friedrich Blumenbach—a drive that while "inscrutable" has the virtue of leaving an explanatory share to natural mechanism that is both "unmistakable" and "indefinite" [5: 424]. Such a resort, it is to be understood, does not constitute objective knowledge of the world, but merely reflects the peculiar constitution of our own cognitive faculties, which cannot conceive of natural products other than by attributing to them some causally effective final purpose.

But the concept of an organized being, so understood, leads almost inevitably to the question of what such a being is there for, and hence to that of the final end (if any) of nature as a whole [5: 426]. If nature is to be judged a whole, it can only be by thinking man the final purpose of nature through which all other purposive beings constitute a purposive system (for no other being we know is able to so serve) [5: 429]. The basis of this sort of purposiveness in man is either happiness (as Herder insists) or culture—i.e., "the production of an aptitude for purposes generally." But the nature of man, which will not be satisfied, precludes the former [5: 430]. Hence, if nature is to be regarded as a teleological system at all, history must serve culture. With this hypothesis in tow, Kant turns (at last) to a (possible) progressive history of culture as a way of judging nature as a systematic whole—a move, as we will see, that blocks the pantheistic claims of Herder while at the same time demonstrating the impossibility of any rationally based physico-theology.

Kant's own foray into the attempt to grasp human history, and with it nature, as a "whole" takes its initial bearings, then, from the concept of culture as the final purpose of nature. But as such a history reveals, the culture of skill (especially in science and art) is difficult to improve without oppressive inequality (in which the majority produce life's necessities almost "mechanically"), giving rise to the luxury that Kant calls a "shining misery." Men's natural dispositions can thus develop to the utmost only when such oppression is offset by the lawful authority characteristic of the "whole" called civil society [*bürgerliche Gesellschaft*] [5: 432]. But such society is in turn retarded by the bellicosity of rulers and a related opportunity for the development of culture whose warlike character makes such opportunity at best bittersweet [5: 433].

The negative culture of discipline, on the other hand, proceeds more directly, through development of our "humanity" and a related "universally communicated pleasure." The insatiability unleashed by luxury is thus accompanied by refinement that ultimately "makes room" for something better. The accompanying state of civility [*Gesittlichkeit*], though not yet ethical [*sittlich*], readies man for the "sovereignty of reason," even as related evils "summon, increase and steel" the soul's forces in a manner that permits us to feel a hidden aptitude within for higher purposes [5: 434]. In the meantime, war and passion (however counterproductive from the standpoint of the people's permanent happiness) will exercise their own further goad to the development of man's natural dispositions, *perhaps* preparing the way toward the eventual establishment of a cosmopolitan system on a genuinely moral basis [5: 433].

In short: The "culture" of moral feeling and "development of ethical ideas" that was called for in Part One is revisited in Part Two, with striking result. We can judge nature to be a purposive whole only if we are thereby led to "feel" our higher aptitude for purposes beyond the natural. Natural teleology so understood brings us to the brink of reason's sovereignty without delivering what man must freely do collectively and individually. In contrast to Kant's earlier *Idea for a Universal History*, history itself prompts a judgment that articulates between the natural and theological/moral.[16] The future "philosophic head" that Kant had called for in that essay [5: 30] is no longer needed.

Without denying the necessity of employing teleological principles to judge natural products—indeed by insisting on their necessity—Kant can show why all attempts at physico-theology are doomed to failure.[17] He can also present the genuinely rational alternative to atheism (in either its pure or pantheistic forms) he had promised in his letter to Jacobi. That alterative, which lies in showing the indispensable contribution of belief in God to the maintenance of our own moral attitude, is convincing enough to win over even a "Spinoza" [5: 445–446]:[18]

Kant had spoken earlier in the *Critique* of a "not unimportant" "anthropological—teleological problem": namely, the natural human tendency toward "fruitless expenditure of force" through vain and idle longings [5: 178n; compare 20: 231n]. That tendency, he concluded, can itself be understood as naturally purposive: If we had to assure ourselves beforehand of our ability to realize the object represented to our desire, then our forces would remain largely unused. In the present case, the object of desire—the highest good possible in the world through freedom—cannot be held in view concretely, at least not by us. Only a supreme intelligence could have such an aim directly in mind. Hence (as we shall see) Kant's new "ethico-teleological" argument for the subjective necessity (if our moral striving in the world "is not to flag") of moral faith [5: 143].[19]

To summarize thus far: The political events of mid-summer 1789, framed, in part, by Kant's reading of the essays of Count von Windisch-Graetz, seem to have prompted a new conception of reflective judgment *à propos* human history. Such judgment mediates, through a reflective back-and-forth among analogous concepts, between the natural and moral realms whose relation can thus be critically (though not doctrinally) articulated in a new, more intellectually and polemically satisfying way. By virtue of his own "organizing" critical judgment, Kant is able both to link these realms and guard against their irrational and chaotic coalescence.

Kant finds in the political events about which he is known to have eagerly sought word an unprecedented instance of moral life historically, and hence naturally, realized (at least potentially). They thus help him see his way clear to an alternative rational theology—different from the physico-teleology in which both Spinoza and Jacobi had correctly found "great difficulties." This new *ethical* theology, based on reason's *moral* purposes, enables Kant to slip reason's bark (under partial, non-dogmatic sail) between "the cliffs of atheism," just as he had promised in the letter to Jacobi of August 1789. That standpoint also opens a new vista on human history as a self-articulating conjunction of the natural and the moral—a vista with instructional potential of its own.

As a (potential) realization of the republican idea, the French *Umbildung* is the occasion for a new interpretation on Kant's part of history as organized product of the "supersensible substrate." Human history is not, finally, to be compared with the physical formation of the stars (as in Kant's earlier essay on *The Idea of History*). The analogy that relates civic and natural organization also sets between them an unbreachable wall. The purposive causality of nature is, strictly speaking, inexplicable; though it can "shed light" on the practical causality of reason. There is no (humanly accessible) "idea" of history, according to Kant's new account; there is only the "purpose" we impute to a morally conceived God and share in through our own autonomous actions—actions at work (it may be hoped) in the recent transformation of a people. Neither nature nor human history can be grasped as a systematic whole without appealing to an end beyond it, an end whose realization rests, finally, with us.[20]

That end, however, can be given sensual expression only negatively—through the register of an historical representation that constantly flirts with terror (as in Kant's challenge to a hypothetical Spinoza). In this sense as well, progress and the potential for human failure go hand in hand.

If these arguments are correct, the occasioning influence of the French Revolution on Kant's practical thought—an influence he will later highlight—is already evident as early as 1790. The immediate result includes a broad sense on Kant's part that history has reached a point of no little moment—a "crisis" state for Europe generally.[21] On the one side, there is the imminent promise of a great European republic legally arrived at (if only barely so); on the other, the imminent danger of revolutionary chaos and the reassertion of despotic absolutism under the banner of religious obscurantism. What is immediately needful in such circumstances is a critique establishing both the theoretical necessity of teleological principles and their theological and moral insufficiency.

Introduction to Part II **175**

Kant's reassertion of the basis of the true religion in the autonomy of reason thus takes the emphatic form of a concluding "ethico-theology." Only an autonomously based morality can deliver us from the "cliffs of atheism" without plunging us into an ocean of unreason.

Enlightenment prospects around 1790 are likely, then, to have looked both more promising and more precarious to Kant than previously. The French Revolution (or some similar "transformation of a people") appeared as the very model of human purposiveness. And yet new political developments in Prussia, developments both preceding and exacerbated by events in France, made human efforts to secure the proper relation between moral autonomy and moral faith seem all the more urgent. The French Revolution (or its reception) is a "morally inflowing cause," as Kant will later put it [7: 85], that makes history practically recognizable (for the first time) as the theater of a providential will in which we too, in our capacity as autonomous moral beings, rationally participate—albeit without being able to represent the end of history concretely.

Already in the *Critique of Judgment* Kant's revised interpretation of human history (an interpretation that is itself divided between aesthetic "mode" and teleological "method") opens a new front in the ongoing *Pantheismustreit*, inserting a new critically informed wedge between Spinoza and Jacobi on the one hand and Herder on the other: Herder's pantheistic "syncretism" (or effort to secure alliances between the opposing forces of dogmatic theism and dogmatic atheism) papers over the "great difficulties" involved in any teleological theology—difficulties that both Jacobi and Spinoza, in Kant's view, rightly recognize.

At the same time, Kant does not lose the opportunity to move beyond the sublime juxtaposition of "the starry heavens above" and "the moral law within" with which his second *Critique* had ended. The difficulties with teleological theology can themselves be interpreted in a morally and theologically constructive way. Critically understood, the prospect of human "purposelessness" moves the upright man to the rational faith that it at first seemingly denied him. Human history itself—both its promise of unforeseeable success and its threat of catastrophic failure—becomes the occasion for a morally sublime response that can win over even a "Spinoza." Mode and method, in this sense, finally go hand in hand.

This double use of history—both as a blueprint for the unforeseeable realization of future goals *and* as a prompt to moral resolution in the here and now—marks the last decade of Kant's productive life through all its subsequent vicissitudes. Those vicissitudes include the tightening grip of Wöllner's regime through the early 1790s, including a particularly alarming edict of 1790 that required pastors to declare their public allegiance to the tenets of orthodox Lutheranism. That requirement forced upon Kant's current and prospective students—including those to whom Kant primarily looked to "educate the people"—the cruel choice of either abandoning their ethical vocation, or (what would amount to the same thing) publicly perjuring themselves. Kant's extraordinary effort to elude that edict's grip involved publication, at some personal danger, of *Religion within the Boundaries of Bare Reason,* and later, when the danger had subsided, *The Conflict of the Faculties,* Part One, much of which was written while Kant was still under substantial threat from a hostile government. The Treaty of Basel, signed in 1795, establishing a temporary truce between France and Prussia, opened a brief window of opportunity to publish more freely, resulting in the publication of *Toward Perpetual Peace,* perhaps Kant's most famous political work. Here Kant uses the example of republican France to "solve" a problem that, on his earlier account, no philosopher had yet been able satisfactorily to address: namely, how to tip history's opposing tendencies, especially as expressed in relations among so-called civilized states, toward progress rather than catastrophe. The death of Frederick William II and ascension of a new, more favorably disposed king, allowed Kant, in the waning years of the decade and in the face of his own declining powers, to take up the question of progress anew with special emphasis upon the university, the institution in and through which he had labored for some forty years.

2. Brief Overview and Summary of Part II

a. Late Kant

In a 1794 letter to Reinhold, Kant mentions a "noticeable decline" in his mental powers [11: 494; cf. 12: 222]. A similar sense of increasing mental weakness and related rush to complete his metaphysical system "before it is too late" is mentioned in a letter to Tieftrunk in 1797 [12: 222] and is also taken up in *How to Overcome Morbid Feelings through Sheer Willpower* (Part Three of *The Conflict of the Faculties*), which traces Kant's mental decline to the same period as that mentioned in the letter (i.e., 1794, around the same time that he was threatened by the government with "unpleasant measures").[22]

The gravest manifestation of lateness, however, is bound up with human reason itself (= "radical evil"). Reason, inasmuch as it is subject to conditions of time, is constantly tempted to become mere "rationalization" [*vernünfteln*]. The idea of an objective good that an autonomous reason generates spontaneously is all too easily eclipsed by "rationalizing" regard for supplementary goods—goods of which reason in its "calculating" mode is merely the tool or vehicle, and for the sake of which we do not so much "refuse" obedience to the moral law as "postpone" it until our happiness is first assured [6: 42]. We are abetted in this by the tendency of a rationalizing reason to question the adequacy of our own moral "capital." Kant's primary response to radical evil thus consists in bolstering moral confidence.

The main intention of Kant's late works is less to change the world, though that too remains important, than fortify us against suspicion of our own moral sufficiency. The significance of human progress thus can and should also make itself fully felt in the present. Did individual improvement require prior collective progress (as some recent scholars have argued), there would be no "duty to act now." Kant's emphatic concern with present personal transformation helps explain his relative indifference, in Part Two of *The Conflict of the Faculties,* to a precipitous end to human progress through the natural destruction of the earth. The prospect of natural catastrophe is infinitely less significant, from a practical standpoint, than that of ongoing human despotism into the foreseeable future. The former prospect can be practically offset by moral faith in the existence of a benevolent God. The latter, on the other hand, directly challenges conviction in the moral capacity of man as such by suggesting that the cultivation of reason does more harm than good in the world. *Religion*'s doctrine of grace attempts the difficult task of bolstering our confidence in this regard by assuring us of a divine supplement where needed without dampening the vigor of our own spiritual "investment."

To maximize that investment, we must know where to apply our moral forces. Kant's "authentic" interpretation of the Fall story in Genesis supplies the necessary target by pinpointing the site in narrative time from which moral hesitation initially irrupts. That site proves to be a state of nature, as it were, in which human beings coexist in a condition of mutual distrust. This condition prompts the morally fatal transition from a permissable concern for one's own safety to an "unjust" willingness to attack the security of others "preventatively." Evil roots itself, in other words, in our very need to act in time. Civil society partially addresses this problem but leaves nations in a condition of mutual distrust for which *Religion* provides no immediate remedy. "No philosopher to date," as Kant puts it, has been able either to reconcile international principles with morality or replace those principles "with better ones" [6:34]. Instead, Kant turns his attention to domestic political reform—above all, through an attempted appropriation of established church institutions that are in a position to touch upon the people's *Denkungsart* or "way of thinking." Transformation of that way of thinking would enliven the body politic with the true "spirit of republicanism." But Kant's expectations in this regard remain guarded. In the end, he pins the desired "reattunement" of moral judgment less on hopes for a progressive redirection of a politically established church than on an awakening *now* of moral feeling, prompted by a morally sublime representation of the very obstacles such progress must confront.

Kant's deepening concern over domestic political conditions is registered in his sardonically titled *The End of All Things* [1794], a work whose tone, as Kant reports in a letter to his publisher, is "partly doleful, partly humorous." In the same letter he complains of a confusion of theory and practice that forbids expression of all contrary views and that "will soon be felt with full force" in both secondary schools and universities [11: 496–497]. The obvious reference to Kant's essay of the previous year on *Theory and Practice* [cf. 23: 127] underscores his increasing pessimism as to the possibility of reconciling the right to speak openly with the duty of political obedience to one's sovereign, a possibility that his earlier works had pointedly urged. He is now content, as he reports, to leave matters "to providence" as the only available remedy against hopelessness.

The 1795 Treaty of Basel and an accompanying thaw in relations between Prussia and France brings some political relief. Kant seizes on what he calls a "stroke of luck" to publish *Toward Perpetual Peace* under the very eyes of the censors. True to his earlier promise to the government, the work does not address itself directly to religious matters; instead, it concentrates on the international virtues of republics with a view to encouraging the growth of a free federation of enlightened states. Contrary to its general reputation as an exercise in "Venus-like" idealism, there is nothing Pollyannaish about the essay, which walks a sinuous line between hope and despair. Kant's claims as to a natural "guarantee" of peace are hedged in qualification, including the admission that war will always "threaten to break out." At the same time, Kant's heightened emphasis on Europe's abuse of the inhabitants of other continents registers his increasing unwillingness to rely upon racial taxonomy to bolster moral hope.

Europeans can no more count upon the adequacy of their moral predisposition than can the cannibals of America and Africa.

Toward Perpetual Peace does make at least one important advance by suggesting how the problem of international order to which *Religion* had called attention might be adequately addressed for the first time by "philosophers." Still, *Toward Perpetual Peace* is in many ways Kant's darkest work to date, balancing assurance as to the possibility of growing international trust with intimations of an end of human civilization precipitated by Europe itself.

A bigger stroke of luck comes with death of Frederick William II in 1797 and an almost immediate loosening of censorship and other vexatious state policies. Kant lost no time in bringing out his *Conflict of the Faculties,* prefaced with an explanation as to why his earlier promise to desist from voicing his opinion on religious matters was now null and void (since its addressee was now deceased).[23] Kant had completed a version of Part One sometime in 1794. Despite its title ("On the Conflict between the Theological and Philosophical Faculties"), that version's thrust, as he explained in a 1794 letter to Carl Friedrich Stäudlin, was as much political as theological.[24]

The title of Part Two ("On the Conflict between the Legal and Philosophical Faculties") is thus somewhat misleading: Both parts are concerned, above all, with vindicating reason's claims without challenging state authority directly. And each presents that task as a race against time—in Part One, with a view to freeing "true" Christianity from its burdensome "Jewish" remnants; in Part Two, through insistence on a "sign" of progress that leaves its achievement in the present moment up to each of us. (Part Three, "On the Conflict between the Medical and Philosophic Faculties," addresses the same point ironically and with a view to Kant's own waning intellectual powers.)

The Conflict of the Faculties also resurrects the Archimedean imagery of the unpublished *Remarks* composed forty years earlier. In Part Two, Kant claims to find a point of "influx" between the moral and the physical worlds in the enthusiastic reception by disinterested spectators of news concerning the French Revolution: The "image" of an old "warlike" honor "vanishing" before the weapons of the people (and the accompanying "affect of the good" that it provokes) constitutes an event "never more to be forgotten." The betrayal of enthusiasm on the part of such spectators (despite the danger to which it exposes them) provides decisive proof, as Kant now claims, as to the sufficiency of man's moral *Anlage*—our inborn power of receptivity to the law. Communication of that historic event by Kant (and others like him) thus makes it possible to anticipate a process of civil and moral improvement in which "all peoples of the earth" will eventually participate. This "top down" progress does not depend, as in Kant's earlier "bottom-up" model, upon "enlightened" rulers like Frederick the Great. Instead, it only counts upon the inability or unwillingness of rulers to make their contempt for rights a matter of public record.

Kant's new expression of hope looks especially to the university, poised to become a living "factory" whose engines are directed toward reversing the people's current "way of thinking." Intellectual domination of the "higher" faculties by philosophy (which remains nominally "lower") should gradually effect enlightened attitudes among the "local preachers" who instruct the people directly. The resulting "church establishment" combines the claims of reason with the force of state authority, resisting precisely that perversion of moral faith into an instrument of policy of which *Religion* had complained. Something like the philosophic kingship called for in his *Idea for a Universal History* is seemingly at hand.

In this new Archimedean moment, Kant no longer claims to hold the lever personally. He is himself merely a communicant, albeit an especially responsive one, of the republican idea as such. (Virtue is represented in its "complete perfection," as he puts it in *The Metaphysics of Morals*, "not as if a human being possesses virtue but as if virtue possesses him" [6: 406].) Any effort on the part of "free professors of law" to wield power directly would merely reinforce the "dead weight" of legal mechanism that burdens the formation of the body politic into a living civic organism. Instead, Kant takes up the mantel of a "seer" whose prediction is "maintainable for the most strenuous theory."

b. Toward a Critical "Economy of Reason"

"Critical philosophy," as Kant puts it in a late reflection, is an "economy of reason":

> Critical philosophy is that [which] economy of reason [*Vernunftwirthschaft*], which first investigates its state of means [*Vermögenszustand*], in order to know how far it can go by way of outlay, and looks like a *Pinsel* [one who is moved by the hand of someone else] in comparison with the spirit-rich head [*geistreichen Kopf*] who brags, like a certain minister of state: the more debts I incur the richer I become. [Reflexion #6341; 18: 666–667]

Unlike the critical economizer who investigates his capital before expending it, he who philosophizes in the manner of genius [*geniemäßig*] "economizes" on the

Introduction to Part II **181**

basis of a store that "permits one to prophecy immanent [*naher*] bankruptcy" (in ironic contrast with Kant's other philosophic prophecy of an immanent [*naher*] conclusion of peace). In thus praising the thoroughness of the scholar over the false brilliance of the would-be genius, Kant also echoes the roughly contemporaneous *On a Recently Uplifted Noble Tone in Philosophy* (1796). There, Kant pointedly opposes philosophy understood as productive work with a false mysticism that wants to avoid all honest labor [*Arbeit*]. The discursive human understanding must "expend much labor" and mount many steps "with great effort" in order to make progress [8: 389]. And yet such effort continues to be resisted, not only out of natural inertia [*Trägheit*] but also "from the idlenss/vanity [*Eitelkeit*] of men, who when they have enough to live hold themselves as *noble,* be they rich or poor, in comparison with those who must work to live" ([8: 390]; cf. [A 5 = B 8–9]). In contrast to Plato, who at least did not stint in his own intellectual efforts, however misguided, and whose "idea of justice" remains exemplary,[25] latter-day Platonists like Schlosser are closer to savage tribes in their "misunderstanding" of freedom itself [8: 390].

Contempt for honest labor is as much a problem for philosophic as it is for legal progress. But Kant takes his economic analogy further even than this. Virtue, too, is helpfully conceived (i.e., for purposes of resisting evil) as an expenditure of resources undertaken with a view to maximizing the interest on one's (moral) capital. Kant thus puts a peculiarly modern economic spin on a famous New Testament parable.

According to that parable, a master entrusted money to his servants, rewarding those who invested it profitably. But he punishes the servant who buries his talents instead of investing them [Luke 19:20–27]. The bad servant's wickedness, on Kant's account, consists in a counter-purposive rejection of the system of spiritual interest in which the master and his household are invested. Thus, the servant is upbraided by the master for his failure to put the master's money on interest-bearing loan. (In Luther's words, "*warum hast du denn mein Geld nicht in die Wechselbank gegeben?*") If he feared that the master would demand more back from him than he was given, he had only, if he genuinely wished to please his master, make his deposit grow through profitable investment of the capital. But that would take a spiritual/economic revolution—an overturning of that moral arithmetic in which we can only passively return what we receive. The evil servant's unwillingness to expend his means without the guarantee of an immediate further return is an expression of the same Adamic "hesitation" that subjectively impedes our recognition of the objective sufficiency of the law's incentive. Worthiness—as that which alone gives worth to everything that makes life worth wishing for—trumps anything whose value must be measured in the currency of happiness. Religion, in its evil form, plays on our reluctance to expend the moral forces that have been deposited in us.

Cultivation of our *Anlagen* to the good means expending our forces, not for an immediate return in the medium of happiness, but at an interest that will accrue to us in the higher currency of dignity (i.e., moral worthiness). For this, however, one's inner scale of judgment must be "rightly adjusted" or "in tune"—so that what is objectively of infinite worth (i.e., gives value to one's very existence) subjectively receives its proper weight. Religion in its evil (gloomily penitential) form exacerbates the mood that puts out of tune the scale by which objective value is properly weighed—so that one looks about, with Adam, for an incentive to obey beyond that which is objectively sufficient. False religion does this, as we will see in Chapters 5 and 7, by playing upon the very sense of debt, or something owed, by which moral obligation registers subjectively. The direct opposite of such a morally disabling, penitential attitude lies in the good mood of fortitude and cheer—i.e., in the presumption [*vermuthen*] of self-improvement in the future—such a good mood furnishing, indeed, the only available inner sign of moral genuineness [*Ächtheit*] [6: 24n]. For only the cheerful heart resists dissuasion from the expenditure that the moral law demands, on the "self-swindling" pretext that one lacks the capital [*Pfund*] to fund it.

In Kant's version of the parable of Jesus, the investor makes himself a "free laborer" rather than a "bond servant" by becoming a co-shareholder in God's investment (or "deposit" [*Anlage*] of the seed of goodness). The well-disposed human being combats the evil weed of vice by exchanging the life currency of nature (his "debt" to whom must be returned)[26] for one of infinite value, an "effort" of self-cultivation and self-transformation for which he may legitimately take credit. The New Testament image of "engraftment" is thus given new and striking moral meaning, consistent with Kant's reading of the Parable of the Talents.

Kant's extended use of economic imagery evinces his qualified endorsement of the Baconian/Hobbesian/Lockean view of reason as a power of calculation, bent on maximizing total satisfaction. "Power," according to these thinkers, is—like money—a "means in general" for the production of a range of possible effects, rather than a potency (potential) linked to a specific actuality or "telos"

Introduction to Part II

in the traditional sense. (Power, one could say, *is* possibility, in that peculiarly modern and un-Aristotelean sense that Kant himself presents as humanly defining.)[27] Force is desirable for the same reason that money is: as a general means of satisfaction.

Work, on this view, is an application of power—an effortful "expenditure" of one's (life) force—that is rationally justified only as a means to greater (future) pleasure. But this view is disquieting on a number of fronts—not least in its inability to account for the rank ordering of goods necessary, it seems, to any serious conception of the moral life. Calculative reason, as understood by Bacon and Hobbes, leaves no room for a rationally justifiable hierarchy of goods or for notions of virtue and nobility that depend on such a hierarchy. Kant's initial response to this difficulty relies heavily on "aesthetic" modes of representation. Thus, in the *Universal Natural History* he holds out the "higher" pleasures as possible—not through rationally communicable knowledge—but through the sublime feeling evoked by maximum speculative effort. The mind's unstinting sacrifice (by taking effort to its limit) of the palpable good of taking things easy is itself the route to a higher, if itself partially painful, pleasure. Preference for contemplation cannot be justified directly but only "poetically," and in the register of failure.

This equation of desert with the willingness to make an effort reappears in Kant's later critical thought as the conviction that the human mind can represent "the good" only negatively and indirectly—i.e., as the rational willing of an infinite sacrifice of pleasure.[28] To be sure, the later Kant is too much a student of Rousseau to hold that action must be painful. Pure activity, or life, is desirable for its own sake. But life so understood (i.e., life divorced from everything connected with "dependence") is beyond human experience, which is temporal and hence always also passive. Man's situation as an embodied rational being renders him dependent, willy-nilly. Pure life is conceivable, according to Kant's late understanding, only in "moral" terms, as the harmonious subordination of all forces and faculties to freedom itself.[29]

In sum: Kant's critical turn ultimately involves a kind of trans-valuation of values, lifting us from nature's economy (in which we hardly count) to one in which we count absolutely. In the idea of such a timeless kingdom of ends, or moral world, community with other substances is thinkable (at last) without canceling the (subjective) conditions of our own personal existence. Though such considerations cannot constitute a Kantian reason for the moral "way of thinking," they surely explain some of its attraction.

The moral human being has this in common with the miser: both give up pleasure (or the good as sensibly ascertainable) for the sake of reason. But whereas the miser is finally irrational (inasmuch as he achieves nothing in return for the pleasure he gives up), the morally rational human being transcends calculative reasoning itself through a subordination of sensual pleasure to the law of freedom. In doing so, one not only gains "self-esteem"; one also achieves practical insight into the possibility of a noumenal existence in real community with others. The accompanying "moral revolution" resembles, in this respect, the conversion-dream of Carazan the merchant.

Kierkegaard, Nietzsche, and Heidegger will all take issue with Kant's understanding of the moral "way of thinking" as the sublime inversion of calculative reasoning, or as reason in this sense taken to its limit. And in calling for a "politics of pure means," Walter Benjamin puts the matter even more plainly. All four thinkers take Kant to task for failing truly to transcend the limits of a calculative, homogenizing reason. In our own era, their radical attack on "universal reason" has mostly degenerated into a bland ethics of "difference" and "inclusion." At the same time many of Kant's best-known current advocates associate reason with a proceduralism (and a related appeal to "reasonableness") that ignores the morally and anthropologically richest veins of his own investigations.

Kant's specific understanding of autonomy takes for granted a hedonistic empirical psychology that many today would discount.[30] But it also draws on a deeper and more primary awareness that not everything is permitted—i.e., that something is demanded of us that goes against the grain of common pleasure-seeking. In linking that awareness to the freedom to which moral imputation practically testifies, Kant provides liberal democratic practice with a peculiarly powerful moral tonic and foundation.

By Kant's own account, this foundation has its limitations. That the authority that commands us morally lies nowhere but in ourselves is an insight that human reason tends, naturally, to resist. It is "easier" to fall back on the traditional religious view that links such commands to the authority of an alien God.

Kant's response involved the adoption, for "regulative" practical purposes, of a progressive-catastrophic presentation of history and "organic" understanding of politics whose unhappy effects—especially in Germany—Kant did not foresee. Whatever the merits of "reflective judgment" in practical political matters, it lacks both the determinate certitude of *a priori* principle that is the hallmark of Kantian ethics and the openness to political phenomena as they immediately (or "naturally") present themselves that is the hallmark of Aristotelean prudence.[31] Given those demands, it is not altogether surprising that Kant's search for "meaning" sometimes interfered with his commitment to the "truth." This tension is perhaps nowhere clearer, as we will see in Chapter 9, than in his treatment of Judaism and the Jews.

5

Moral Hesitation in *Religion within the Boundaries of Bare Reason*

Religion within the Boundaries of Bare Reason has been the object of new and growing interest in recent years. Henry Allison, for example, finds in it Kant's fullest and most detailed treatment of the executive power, or "autocracy," of the will whereby we determine ourselves decisively for good or evil.[1] Felicitas Munzel has mined it for Kant's understanding of moral "character" as a crucial link between his critical philosophy and his anthropology.[2] And a number of scholars, including Allen W. Wood,[3] Philip J. Rossi,[4] and Sharon Anderson-Gold,[5] have used it as a springboard in their respective efforts to uncover a less "individualistic," more attractively "communitarian" Kant than he is generally taken to be. Mark Lilla, on the other hand, sees in these same communitarian tendencies ominous anticipations of the anti-liberal, quasi-religious German nationalism that was to have such tragic consequences for the twentieth century.[6] Each of these broadly conceived approaches to Kant's work draws valuable attention to neglected aspects of Kant's thought. At the same time, each, taken in itself, risks simplifying a text that is complicated, even by Kantian standards. Interpreting a text in which interpretation is itself a major theme is no simple task; and I will be happy if the following remarks go some way toward clarifying Kant's central argument.

That *Religion* is a particularly difficult work in which to gain one's footing is evident from the variety of responses it has provoked among serious readers from its inception. Is it an unworthy concession to religious orthodoxy (as Goethe accused) or merely a prudent restatement of his thought in Christian guise (as Herman Cohen, among others, have urged)? Or, finally, does it represent a new insight into the character of authentic (and authentically German) religious faith (as Schleiermacher and other romantics claimed)?

The dove-like yet serpentine elusiveness[7] of *Religion* partly results from the new political circumstances that both called it forth and famously threatened its arrival. The ascension to the throne of the Frederick William II, in 1786, and the subsequent installment of Wöllner as minister of education and religious affairs, had placed new obstacles in the way of public enlightenment of the sort that Frederick the Great had tolerated and even encouraged. In *What Is Enlightenment?* and other works of the early 1780s, Kant had, it seems, made his peace with a monarchy that allowed "public" discourse to flourish in return for "private" obedience. Hope of juridical and moral progress, through the gradual transformation of "enlightened" despotism, was not, for him, unthinkable, as is borne out by Kant's 1784 *Idea for a Universal History*. As we have seen, the French Revolution transformed those hopes, even as German reaction threatened to upend them. For Wöllner and his conservative allies, continuing political stability demanded a strengthening of popular belief in divine punishment for civil disobedience.[8] Wöllner's consequent policies threatened Kant's critical project of enlightenment on *four* distinct, yet related, fronts. *First*, by requiring of candidates in theology a formal profession of faith, it threatened to make the principle teachers (and potential enlighteners) of the people into tools of spiritual and moral despotism. *Second*, by reactivating the previously dead letter of the religious censorship laws, Wöllner threatened Kant himself (and his immediate followers) with public silence. The difficulties, culminating in formal censorship, that dogged Kant's effort to publish *Religion*, without violating his own principles of civic obedience and (outward) honesty, are well known and constitute one of the work's more obvious rhetorical challenges. *Third*, the threat faced by Kant was not only to *immediate* prospects for enlightenment—though that was serious enough; beyond the clumsy maneuverings of the new government lay a deeper challenge to Kant's fundamental conception of the rational life. Behind Wöllner's edicts lies a real question (raised by Rehberg and others) as to the adequacy of the moral law alone as an incentive to right action. That question raises doubts, in turn, as to the sufficiency of conscience, as Kant understands it, to govern the human soul.[9] As we shall see, such doubts, and a related "hesitation" [*Bedenklichkeit*] in human beings ("even the best") to obey the moral law, guide Kant's discussion of the source of human evil and the conditions that must be met if man is ever to improve. *Fourth*, and finally, by menacing prospects for "progress" on this triple front (among the masses, among the educated, and philosophically), Wöllner's edicts call into question the sufficiency of man's moral aptitude more generally; they thus pose a potentially disabling obstacle, both theoretical and practical, to moral resoluteness as Kant conceives it. Indeed, Kant's later "historical" essays are taken up with meeting precisely this challenge. A similar resort to "history," is, as I hope to show, at once the most urgent and the deepest goal of *Religion within the Boundaries of Bare Reason*.

I

Before turning directly to Kant's text, two preliminary remarks will prove helpful:

1) Kant's understanding of "true religion" follows in the revolutionary path, blazed by Rousseau, which subordinates religious faith to sincerity before the voice of human conscience.[10] Like Rousseau, Kant treats religion as a mere means, albeit an "exalted" one, to the fulfillment of demands "written on the human heart." Such demands, in this view, are known directly, by all normal human beings, without reliance on the authority of others. In this, Kant departs both from the classical philosophic tradition and from traditional Christian theology, for each of which such authority serves as an essential human remedy.

According to this new understanding, man's conscience, taken in itself, is unambiguous and incorruptible. Conscience represents what we cannot help believing (or, in Kantian terms, "holding to be true"). The foundation of virtue, on this view, is neither theoretical wisdom nor loving obedience to God (and his chosen representatives), but a kind of inner candor or "sincerity" in acknowledging what we actually hold to be true—a conscientiousness that is always in our power and for which we can therefore be held accountable.

Kant also follows Rousseau (or his Savoyard Vicar) in seeing in the primacy of conscience so understood a resolution to the conflict, in which human reason otherwise entangles itself, between dogmatic assurance and skeptical despair.[11] For both Rousseau's Vicar and Kant the primacy of conscience follows upon recognition of the limits of human reason insofar as it lays claim to ultimate metaphysical knowledge. Kant and Rousseau seem to draw different conclusions, however, from these limits. Whereas conscience competes in the Rousseauian corpus with other (non-moral) expressions of longing for an irrecoverable, prerational state, Kant makes conscience the ultimate basis for what Richard Velkley has described as the self-rectifying "unity of reason." Conscience, for Kant, becomes the court in which reason lays down for itself its own inner law. Finally, and perhaps most importantly, Kant goes further than Rousseau in insisting on the *sufficiency* of conscience, or the moral law, to motivate the human heart. Where otherworldly reward and punishment remains, for Rousseau, a necessary *ressort* of virtue, Kant urges the sufficiency of practical reason, or the moral law, as its own incentive. Reconciling that demand with our subjective *experience* of duty as an unremitting debt constitutes, as we shall see, the crucial task of his *Religion*.

2) In locating the foundation of morality in the certitude of conscience, Kant practices what has been called a sort of ethical Cartesianism. Although one's judgments as to what is right in a given instance can be wrong, "I absolutely cannot be mistaken as to whether or not I believe something to be right." (I may be wrong in saying that the earth is flat; I cannot be wrong about whether or not I genuinely believe it.) Such a foundation agrees with Kant's identification of personality with a capacity for imputable agency.[12]

And yet, if inner candor is always possible (and hence imputable to us), it is also, for Kant, strangely difficult: As he puts it in his essay on *Theodicy* (which appeared two years before *Religion*): Though "I absolutely cannot be mistaken" as to whether or not I believe something to be right, I can lack conscientiousness [*Gewissenhaftigkeit*] about becoming conscious of this belief. "Man knows how to distort even inner declarations before his own conscience" [8: 270]. Where the Savoyard Vicar had only to consult his interest "in the silence of the prejudices" [*Emile*, 269], Kant confronts a wilier enemy.[13] Something in the human soul *resists* becoming aware of that which we cannot help "holding to be true." For Kant, the highest human virtue is thus not perfect candor (or "openheartedness" [*Offenherzigkeit*]) but only sincerity [*Aufrichtigkeit*], understood as "[constant] care [*Sorghaft*]" in "becoming conscious" of our belief (or lack thereof) "and asserting no holding-to-be-true [*Fürwahrhalten*] of which one is not conscious" [8: 268].[14] Perfect knowledge of one's belief would be equivalent to perfect knowledge [*per impossibile*] of the inward motive of one's action.

Kant's late essay on *Theodicy* speaks not only to the peculiar perversity of the new state requirement but also to dangers inherent in all efforts to present a morally uplifting account of human history. Henceforth, Kant will stress inward sincerity (or "refraining from subtle inner self-deception") as the *sina qua non* of all effective efforts at moral self-improvement. Even more than laziness and cowardice (the inner vices he had previously emphasized) man is beset by an inner tendency toward mendacity (a "foul stain" intrinsic to the human species) which edicts like the present one only serve to encourage. Job was right. The effort to find moral purpose in the course of history with all its evils degenerates all too easily into an exercise in self-deceiving flattery (as with Job's comforters). Such histories are morally useful only when accompanied by a frank admission of our inability to comprehend God's purpose or transcend the limits of our own personal sincerity. Indeed, even this standard may be too high if taken to mean self-transparency. All we can do is strive to become conscious of what we genuinely "hold as true." This "formal conscientiousness" Kant calls "the ground of truthfulness":

> which consists precisely in becoming conscious of what we believe (or do not believe) and not pretending to something held to be true of which one is not conscious. Thus, one who says to himself (or—what is one and the same in religious professions—before God): *he believes,* without perhaps casting a single glimpse into himself as to whether he is in *deed* conscious of such a thing held to be true at least to some degree—then such a person *lies* not only the most absurd of lies (before a reader of hearts) but also the most heinous, because it undermines sincerity, the ground of every virtuous intention. [8: 268–269]

The intricate structure of the essay on *Theodicy,* and its not entirely satisfactory result, suggest that Kant was still searching for the proper form in which to convey what he calls in both works an "authentic interpretation." By "authentic," Kant has primarily in mind a quality associated with an interpretation of a legislator's will when that interpretation is that "made by the lawgiver himself." (An authentic interpretation of the American Constitution, for example, would be that provided by its framers.) Such authenticity is to be contrasted with an interpretation that is merely "doctrinal" or, alternatively, "reasoned out" [*herausvernünftelt*] on the basis of "expressions" [*Ausdrücken*] of which the lawgiver has made use [*sich . . . bedient hat*], in conjunction with his "otherwise known [*sonst bekannten*] intentions" [8: 263; see also 825]. "Authentic" theodicy will thus involve a justification of God true to the intention of the will of God as lawgiver.

How, then, is God's will made manifest to us? Here, according to the essay on *Theodicy,* we have only two reliable guides: the moral law itself, whose commands are unconditional and irrefutable, and the idea of a "highest good," which we are enjoined by that law to strive to realize. And yet it is the apparent impossibility of such realization—the manifest lack of harmony between the moral order and the laws of nature (including human nature, as accurately portrayed by "Count Verri" [8: 260])—that raises a legitimate challenge to God's wisdom in the first place. True or authentic theodicy, Kant concludes, can only be a "negative" one. Authentic theodicy is that interpretation of creation made possible by our own good conduct (or earnest effort to achieve it). The result of that effort, Kant suggests, is a wise "glimpse"—like that through which God enlightened Job—of both the beautiful and horrible sides of nature.

Authentic theodicy, then, will consist in "reading" nature as if it were God's book. Specifically, authentic theodicy will be "an *interpretation* of nature, insofar as God announces through it the moral intention of his will [*die Absicht seines Willens Kund macht*]":

> God himself, through our reason, becomes the interpreter of his will, announced through creation [*durch die Schöpfung verkündigten*]; and we can call this interpretation an authentic theodicy. But this is not the interpretation of a ratiocinating [*vernünfteln*] (speculative) reason but rather of a *might-having/efficacious* practical reason [machthabenden *practischen Vernunft*], which, just as in lawgiving it commands absolutely, without further grounds, can be regarded [*angesehen*] as the immediate clarification and voice of God through which he gives a meaning to the letter/bookstaff [*Buchstabe*] of his creation. [8: 264]

Authentic theodicy is drawn, not from consecutively ratiocinated insight (as per Job's hypocritical comforters), but "immediately," and out of the mood of the religious sublime to which Job himself is spiritually awakened. Whereas he had previously associated reliance on "expression" [*Ausdrück*] with interpretation that is merely doctrinal rather than authentic, Kant now strikingly joins "authenticity" and "expression" through the medium of "allegory."

"Allegory," means, literally, "to speak otherwise than one [literally] means before a public crowd"—"allo agoria"—as with the parables of Jesus. And like those parables, allegory is literally false without (necessarily) being untruthful. In *The Conflict of the Faculties,* Kant explicitly defends himself against the charge of being "allegorical and mystical" and therefore neither "biblical nor rational." Such a charge, he counters, mistakes "the mantle [*Hülle*] of religion for religion itself." His own, authentic reading of the Bible, by way of contrast, is both biblical and rational, i.e., allegory without mysticism [7: 45].

Frederick William II's recently imposed "profession of faith" on candidates in theology—the immediate impetus for Kant's essay in theodicy—thus poses a peculiarly acute threat to public enlightenment. A people accustomed to using external professions of faith "as a *means of gain* [Erwerbmittel]"— acquires a kind of falsehood in its "communal way of thinking [*Falschheit in die Denkungsart selbst des gemeinen Wesens*]." And yet, given current policy, Kant says, all efforts to purify the public way of thinking must be deferred to the indefinite future, when they can be undertaken under the "protection of free thinking [*unter dem Schutze der Denkfreiheit*]."

Allegory, so conceived, is, I would suggest, at once a subject and the vehicle of Kant's suggestively entitled "Religion within the Boundaries of Bare [or naked] Reason." Where the essay on *Theodicy* leaves us with a question—how to hold off [*abzuhalten*] the bad propensity to "subtle deceptiveness" [*feinen Betrügerei*] in which the human species as a whole is implicated (how, in other words, to acquire a character)—*Religion* will answer it in the medium of a more fully developed allegory: a mantle which, *as* mantle, publicly expresses the truth within.

In the meantime, Kant expends [*verwenden*] "a few lines" on consideration of the fact that "sincerity" is at once the "least that can possibly be required of a good character" and "the property farthest removed from human nature" [8: 267–269]. We need good character to become sincere; and we need sincerity to acquire good character. How, then, are we to avoid becoming (like Rousseau himself) a "contemplative" (and morally dispirited) "misanthrope"?[15]

II

This puzzle, along with the increasingly hostile political circumstances in which Kant finds himself, sets up the question to which *Religion within the Boundaries of Bare Reason*[16] initially addresses itself. Why should we need religion at all? For:

> So far as morality is grounded on the concept of man as a free being, who thus binds himself through his reason to unconditioned laws, it needs neither the idea of a being above man for him to recognize his duties, nor an incentive [*Triebfeder*] other than the law itself in order for him to observe it. At least it is man's own fault [*Schuld*] if such a need is found in him, though in this case too the need could not be relieved by anything else; for what does not originate from himself and his freedom provides no substitute [*Ersatz*] for a lack in his morality. [6: 3]

Man does not require religion to provide morality with an incentive (as Kant's current enemies insisted);[17] we require religion, instead, to satisfy a "natural need" that would otherwise constitute a "hindrance"[*Hinderniß*] to morality [6: 5].

Kant's argument seems at first perplexing. The difference between claiming (with Rehberg and his allies) that man needs religion because the incentives of the law are "not enough" [*Nitto gene*] and claiming that we need religion to overcome a natural hindrance to morality seems fine indeed. And yet its importance to Kant can hardly be overstated, given that "a profession of reverence for the moral law" that does not grant its self-sufficiency as an incentive, amounts to "hypocrisy" and "inner falsity" [6: 42n].

There is a further difficulty: If our religious need arises from a limitation intrinsic to our nature, how can it be our fault, as Kant newly insists?

Kant's answer to the second question is relatively clear. If we were, morally speaking, what we ought to be—if our virtue were unshakable—nothing could interfere with our adherence to the moral law, whose incentives are per se "enough." Our religious need is thus our fault in the same way that moral imperfection is our fault. Were we morally resolved, our religious need would cease. *Religion*, in short, is a moral exercise that aims to cultivate our "capacity and will to virtue" [compare 6: 412].

An answer to the first question is harder to work out, though it will prove essential to Kant's argument. As embodied rational—i.e., human—beings, we cannot act without entertaining some purpose: Without an end, "no determination of the will can take place in human beings at all." Hence, although the law suffices [*genug ist*] for morality, a will intent on acting in obedience to the moral law still needs to know the "whither" without which the will itself wouldn't "do enough" [*Gnüge*] [6: 4].[18] Thus, if we are to be adequate to the law's incentives, we need an end "determined by the law." Accordingly, morality itself gives rise to the idea—the highest good possible in the world—of what a will with principles would aim at. This idea is said to "meet our natural need, which would otherwise be a hindrance to moral resolve [*Entschließung*]," to "think [*denken*] for all our doings and omissions as a whole some sort of ultimate end that reason can justify." Such an end gives practical reality to the—for us—indispensable combination of the purposiveness of nature with one arising out of freedom [6: 5]. But this idea requires, in turn, that of a divine author, without whom the possibility of realizing that end remains unthinkable.

The idea of the highest good possible in the world is, as idea, not a possible object of experience, and yet, as "possible in the world," not experientially vacant either, at least insofar as we actively *make* it our end. The *Endzweck* is at once within our power (for otherwise it could not overcome impediments to our resolve) and beyond our power (for only the idea of a divine highest cause of such an end allows us to think of it as possible). Kant's "authentic" interpretation of biblical religion (as a "reading" of the intention of God made manifest in history) will join these opposing claims in a single allegorizing narrative. This narrative, in turn, gives temporal shape to the inner obstacle that limits our moral fortitude. In short: The authentic history (or nature read in accordance with the intentions of the Creator) that is called for in the *Critique of Judgment* becomes a history of religion itself.

"Radical evil" is Kant's name for that inner obstacle: "the thesis of innate evil," he says, "is useless in moral *dogmatics*" (it doesn't affect our knowledge of what the law demands); it is of use only in moral "ascetics" or "discipline" ([6: 50–51]; *The Metaphysics of Morals* [6: 484, 485]). Discipline, according to the *Critique of Pure Reason*, is the "compulsion through which the constant propensity [*beständige Hang*] to stray from certain rules is limited and finally eradicated [*vertilgt*]."[19] The *Critique of Judgment* calls discipline a "negative liberation [*Befreiung*] of the will from a despotism through which "we become made incapable of choosing for ourselves" [5: 432]. Discipline, then, constitutes a kind of negative culture that counters the propensities (or *Hangen*) that would otherwise obstruct development of our natural dispositions (or *Anlagen*).

Wherein, then, lies that obstruction to the (natural) development of our moral dispositions (or "active opposition to the good" [6: 23n]) which *moral* discipline (as distinguished from the discipline of taste that Kant dealt with in the *Critique of Judgment*) must counter? The original disposition, or *Anlage* to the good, according to Kant, is threefold, consisting in:

1. the *Anlage* to animality (insofar as we are living beings);
2. the *Anlagen* to humanity (insofar as we are living and also rational beings); and
3. the *Anlage* to personality (insofar as we are rational and also responsible beings). [6: 26]

Kant here insists upon the difference between embodied rationality as such, and embodied rationality endowed with personality. To be human in the sense of having personality is more than to be both animal and rational. "So far as we can see," he says, "the most rational being in the world" might not be able to determine [*bestimmen*] his *Willkür* without incentives coming from the objects of inclination. He might apply to them the most rationalizing [*vernünftigste*] reflection, concerning both the greatest sum of incentives, and the means of achieving the end thereby determined, without suspecting even the possibility of moral, absolutely binding law. The *announcement* of that law—what Kant elsewhere calls the "sole *factum* of reason"—on the other hand, is no mere ratiocination.[20] "If the law, which makes us conscious both of our freedom, and the accountability of our actions, were not given to us from *within*, no amount of reasoning would cleverly reveal it [*durch keine Vernunft herausklügeln*] nor persuade our power of choice" [6: 26n].

Whereas the animal drives associated with the *Anlage* to animality are concerned with immediate enjoyment, the inclinations associated with humanity (i.e., with reason with or without personality) exhibit themselves in a concern for "happiness" in general. These inclinations presuppose a timely rational capacity to defer present enjoyment with a view to maximizing the future total.

Reason so understood implies not only an ability to compare relative goods, but also a concern with what Kant calls "external freedom" as "the highest formal good of our natural condition."[21] As Kant puts it in the *Anthropology*, a man whose happiness depends on *another* man's choice (no matter how benevolent the other may be) "rightly considers himself unhappy," because he lacks a guarantee that his and his powerful neighbor's judgment concerning his well-being will agree now and in the future.[22]

As an embodied rational being, who seeks to maximize the satisfaction of my desires, I cannot help placing a supreme formal value on my external freedom from dependence on another's arbitrary will. And yet I cannot *feel* this freedom, Kant says, other than by measuring my freedom against the external freedom (and hence happiness) of others. I abhor others' contempt, in other words, because I thereby *feel* myself diminished in a good that I necessarily cherish.

Such considerations best explain, I think, Kant's striking claim at [6: 27] that "one judges oneself happy or unhappy only in comparison with others." Accordingly, *rational* self-love (which seeks satisfaction in one's total life condition, rather than mere animal pleasures of the moment) necessarily gives rise to "the inclination *to gain value in the opinion of others*" as a way of feeling provided for against a loss of external freedom, a loss one cannot help but find painful. Originally, this inclination will take the form of an insistence on *equal worth,* or not allowing anyone superiority over oneself. And yet "constant anxiety" that others might be striving for superiority over us gradually gives rise to an "unjust desire" for preemptive domination [6: 27]. What Kant calls the "vices of civilization" "do not [then] ... issue from nature as their root." As expressions of our desire for external freedom, "jealousy" and "rivalry" "make room for" vice without themselves requiring it. Moral evil arises not out of rational self-love per se, nor the ensuing competition (which ought to be a spur to culture),[23] but only (as we shall see) by an elevation of external freedom, or the "highest formal good of our natural condition," to the highest value simply. In short, it is only because we are both *human beings* and *persons* that we are capable of moral evil.

Against what target, then, is moral discipline to direct its forces? The propensity to evil must be rooted in the will (for otherwise we would not be responsible for extirpating it), yet without touching on personality (for otherwise we would not be capable of doing so). It must thus involve the will's fundamental choice, without implying the insufficiency of law as an incentive to obey it. There are, Kant finds, three ways in which that condition can be met. We can "take up" the incentive of the law into our fundamental maxim and yet neglect to apply it (fragility); or we can "take up" that incentive without taking care to distinguish it from others (impurity); or, finally, we can actively invert the order of incentives, so that we make our obedience to the law conditional on *first* satisfying incentives of happiness (perversity). Evil, so conceived, does not involve a repudiation of the law (which would be inconsistent with man's incorruptible *Anlage* to personality), but only its deferral, so that instead of morality trumping happiness, here and now, happiness trumps morality.

How, then, are we to account for this inversion (as we must try to do if we are to adequately counter it)?[24] That inversion must be both inextirpable (for it involves a corruption of the ground of maxims) and overcomable (for it is culpable—the result of human beings acting freely). Kant associates it with the same "competitiveness" that, for good and ill, marks the *Anlagen* to humanity. Evil, he says, springs from frailty and dishonesty in not screening one's intentions "even in the case of well-intentioned actions"—in short, a certain perfidy [*Tücke*] and "self deceit" in which one fails to trouble oneself [*zu beunruhigen*] about one's own way of thinking, and instead holds oneself justified to the extent that one compares favorably with others [6: 38]. (He ran the light. I stopped; hence, I'm justified.)

Our lazy failure to inquire, as we should, into our own inner way of thinking—an inquiry that might put us on the road to self-improvement—is ultimately rooted in a self-satisfaction we take in our own outward conformity to law (in comparison with others). That false self-satisfaction, or lack of inner conscientiousness, as Kant insists, "puts out of tune [*verstimmt*] moral judgment as to what one should take a person [*einen Menschen*] for," by making "imputation [or moral accounting] [*Zurechnung*] entirely uncertain [*ungewiß*]" [6: 38].[25] And it thus prevents the inner disposition to goodness from developing as it should. Moral judgment is thus like a moneychanger's scale, that—if sound—instantaneously registers the infinite superiority of the law's incentive to anything (else) that makes life worth choosing.

Elucidation of the source of evil (the *Verstimmung* of the scale) is complicated, however, by the fact that the origin of evil, as an act of freedom, cannot be located in some past moment of time. Nothing can obviate my duty *now* to better myself, which, therefore, must always still be possible. One can, however, inquire into the "inner possibility" of falling into evil—i.e., "the subjective universal ground of the taking up of a transgression into our maxim" [6: 41]. Kant pursues that inquiry through an allegorical interpretation of Genesis that expresses the origin of evil in temporal terms without implying its literal inheritability.

Accordingly, the origin of evil arises from an act, in which the human being (Adam), does not follow the law immediately as a sufficient incentive ("which alone is unconditionally good, and about which there can be no hesitation [*Bedenken*]").[26] Instead he:

> looked around [*umsehen*] for other incentives, that could only be conditionally good (i.e., insofar as they do not infringe upon the law). And he made it his maxim—if one thinks of the action as originating consciously from freedom—to follow the law of duty not out of duty but—just in case/in all events [*allenfalls*]—with a view to other aims. With this, he began to doubt [*bezweifeln*] the strength/rigor [*Strenge*] of the command, which excludes the influence of any other incentive, and thereupon to rationalize [*zu vernünfteln*] obedience to that of a bare, conditioned means (under the principle of self-love); so that finally the preponderance of sensible impulses over the incentive of the law was taken up into the maxim of action, and thus he became sinful/unsound [*gesündigt*]. [6: 42]

The human being hedges his bets, looking—just in case the law should not itself suffice (as if the law could fail to suffice!)—for another reason to obey it.

He thus begins to doubt the strength/rigor of the law, "which excludes all other incentives," and, in so doing, gradually "takes up" into his maxim incentives foreign to the law.[27] In his unwillingness to wager everything upon the law, he undermines its force, giving sensual impulses [*Antrieben*] preponderant weight [*Übergewicht*] against its *Triebfeder*. The radical corruption of the human will lies in its pursuit of incentives to obey beyond the law, its failure to incorporate the moral law into its maxims literally "without bethinking itself" (*unbedenklich*) [6: 42–43, 58n].[28]

But the human being, in this regard, confronts a difficulty he cannot get round: our need to see, in any practically contemplated action, what is it good for. Religion, indeed, is (as earlier noted) the concession that morality in general makes to the human "limitation" that leads us to seek, in every action, something that might serve us as an end, if only that of proving our own inner purity [6: 7n]. (It is this very limitation, intrinsic to our experience of ourselves as worldly actors, that makes possible the synthetic "extension" of the moral law, as a "duty" to make "the highest good possible in the world our ultimate end"—a duty beyond "the concept of all duties in the world" and arising "sui generis" in the human species.) Religion thus answers to the weakness that gets the procrastinating Adam in all of us in trouble—our dissatisfaction with a law whose unconditional goodness does not immediately attract us. Beyond the respect that motivates obedience to the law, we "seek something [we] can love" [6: 7n]. True religion will thus have the character of love, or unforced veneration—a veneration that can be "truthful" only if (contrary to Wöllner's edicts) it is given freely.[29]

To be sure, the formation [*Bildung*] of a character must begin with a transformation [*Umwandlung*] in the way of thinking [*Denkungsart*], a transformation that lies outside of time. Still, in no human being is moral judgment entirely uncorrupted: In "even the most limited [*eingeschränkteste*] human beings," including children, the slightest admixture of impure incentive destroys, "in a twinkling of an eye [*augenblicklich*]" all the moral value of an action. The *Anlage* to the good is thus initially cultivated "in no better way," Kant says, than by inviting students to ferret out the impurity in the apparently good deeds of others.[30] The engrafted vices of civilization can be combated, at least initially, through the same inclination to competitiveness that invites them.

Kant here takes explicit issue with classical ethical view according to which admiration of noble deeds is the appropriate starting point for moral education.

To teach pupils to admire [*bewundern*] virtuous activity, however great the sacrifice that it may cost, does not produce the "correct balance/attunement" [*rechte Stimmung*] that sustains the disposition to the good. On the contrary, such admiration [*bewundern*] puts "out of tune"/unbalances [as in *Abstimmung*] our feeling for duty, for it suggests that obedience to duty deserves "special merit" [6: 49]. What truly arouses wonder [*Bewunderung*] is not any particular human actor—who never, after all, can do more than what he owes—nor even duty as such, which does not lie outside "the common moral order," but rather, reason's inexplicable capacity to override "*vernünfteln*," i.e., its own calculus of finite value.

> What is it in us (one can ask oneself) through which we, as beings ever dependent on nature through so many needs, are at the same time lifted up so far above it in the idea of an original predisposition (in us) that we would hold the whole of nature to be nothing [*nichts*], and ourselves to be unworthy of existence, were we to pursue [*nachhängen*] an *enjoyment of nature that can alone make life worth wishing for* [*wünchenswerth*], against a moral law that reason commands without promising or threatening anything.
>
> [6: 49; emphasis added]

In the sublime unanswerability of this question—which Kant repeatedly puts to his readers—"worthiness" immediately trumps the collective value of *everything* that might make life worth wishing for. Hence, its peculiarly attuning "weight," as Kant has it, "for every man of the least capacity who has been instructed in the holiness of the idea of duty." We can best counter the perversion of incentives that obstructs cultivation of our *Anlage* to the good only by bearing witness, over and over again, to reason's sublime failure to comprehend how its own self-determination [or *Selbstbestimmung*] is possible [6: 50].

In the sublime experience of that necessary failure, *pure* religion enters the picture: the incomprehensibility [*Unbegreiflichkeit*] of our predisposition "to overcome with firm resolve" every incentive contrary to the moral law—a predisposition to which no concept (of reason) can be adequate—"announces the divinity of its origin," and affects the mind [*Gemüth*] "to the point of exaltation" [*Begeisterung*]. Unable either to deny or to comprehend the possibility of human goodness, reason registers a divinity within itself (or "enthusiasm" in the true and literal sense, and as distinguished from mere *Schwärmerei*) that (almost) makes law lovable.

Still, the effort to better oneself morally cannot stop here. The transformation [*Umwandlung*] of an evil into a good human being, must be "posited" as an alteration of the will's "highest inner ground" in such a way that the new ground (or heart) is now unchangeable [*unwandelbar*] (i.e., as a kind of new creation). Of such a transformation man can have no "immediate consciousness," nor can he attain conviction [*Überzeugung*] of it by any natural means, including the evidence furnished by his past life-conduct/exchange [*Lebenswandel*].

Given the immeasurability, in subjectively rational terms, of moral worth, we are prone to find our own powers wanting when we compare them with the infinite expenditure of moral force that is required of us. To be sure, "practical conviction as to the fact that one is judged morally good only on the basis of what can be imputed [*zugerechnet*] to one," *ought* to suffice to support the hope that "by the expenditure of [our] own forces" [*Kraftanwendung*] we can set ourselves on the right road [*Weg*] [6: 51]. And yet reason "naturally finds moral labor vexing/disheartening" [*verdrossene*]; it thus "summons up," against the aforementioned moral "presumption" [*Zumuthung*], and under the pretext of incapacity/bankruptcy [*Unvermögens*], "all sorts of impure religious ideas." These impure ideas seem to absolve us, in one way or another, from the hard labor of attending to our own self-improvement.

On the one hand, our "self-incurred perversity" can be overcome only through the idea of the moral good "in its absolute purity," along with "consciousness that it belongs to our original [moral] *Anlage*." Hence the crucial role of moral/religious exaltation in overcoming that contemplative misanthropy which puts possession of this *Anlage* in doubt.

And yet, the very need that leads to pure moral religion bespeaks a fundamental human vulnerability. The people, especially, "seek a more vivid way of representing things" than pure moral religion can furnish. They are thus tempted to make good their lack of moral confidence, with superstition, faith in false expiations, and *Schwärmerei* (inner illuminations) [6: 83, 53].

From this weakness, particularly associated with "the people," arises the need for a church faith, which provides pure moral religion with greater allegorical vividness without thereby mystically corrupting it. Accordingly, Kant divides all religion between "that seeking to acquire [divine] favor (bare cult)" and religion of good life conduct. In the first case:

> the human being flatters himself [*schmeichelt sich*] either that God can make him eternally happy without his having to do anything to become a better human being (through the remission of his debts), or, if this does not seem possible . . . that God can make him a better human being without his hav-

ing to do more than ask for it, which, since to an all seeing being such asking is no more than *wishing*, amounts to doing nothing. [6: 51]

In the case of moral religion, on the other hand (a religion, according to Kant, of which Christianity is the only known public example):

> It is a fundamental principle [*Grundsatz*] that each must do as much as lies in his forces, and only then, if he has not buried his inborn capital/talent [*Pfund*] (Luke 19:12–16), [i.e.] if he has used the original deposit [*Anlage*] to the good in order to become a better human being, could he hope that what is not in his means [*Vermögen*] will be completed through higher cooperation [*Mitwirkung*].
> [6:52; One should keep in mind that "Anlage" in German also means capital, or "money put out at interest."]

Kant's allegorical interpretation of Jesus's Parable of the Talents points to the crucial difference that divides a cultic "bond-service" [*Lohndienst*] to God (i.e., spiritual serfdom) from a service under what Kant calls "the dominion of the good."

According to that parable, a master, after entrusting money to his servants, rewarded those who invested it profitably while punishing the one who "buried his talents rather than investing them" [Luke 19:20–27]. Faith is here identified with the investor's confidence. (As Luther's Bible puts it: "warum hast du denn mein Geld nicht in die Wechselbank gegeben?") If the servant had genuinely wished to please his master, he had only to make his deposit grow through spiritual usury. But that would take a spiritual/economic revolution—an overturning of that moral arithmetic in which one gets back only what one puts in. The evil servant's unwillingness to invest his talents is thus a version of the "hesitation" that subjectively impedes our recognition of the objective sufficiency of the law's incentive. Religion, in its evil form, plays on our reluctance to invest our moral capital through a maximum expenditure of spiritual effort. For that, our inner scale of judgment would have to be "rightly adjusted" or "in tune"—so that what is objectively of infinite worth (i.e., gives value to one's very existence) registers subjectively. Religion in its evil (or gloomily penitential) form aggravates the bad mood that puts out of tune the scale by which objective value is properly weighed—so that one looks about, like Adam, for an incentive beyond what is objectively sufficient. False religion trades on the very sense of debt, or something owed, by which moral obligation registers subjectively. For if what is morally owed always overrides the incentives of human happiness, should they conflict, it can only be (to one who does not think rightly) because that debt is unremitting—a conclusion that furnishes a pretext for holding that one altogether lacks the means to satisfy it. The cheerful heart, by way of contrast, resists the moral hesitation that is encourages by the "self-swindling" pretext that one lacks the capital [*Pfund*] to fund it. Accordingly, a good mood of fortitude and cheer furnishes the only available inner sign of moral genuineness [*Ächtheit*] [6: 24n].[31]

In *The Metaphysics of Morals*, Kant identifies the rules of moral self-improvement with the attainment of two "attunements of the soul/mood" [*Gemüthsstimmungen*]: cheerfulness and valor [*wacker*].[32] Valor, which follows from the Stoic maxim of renouncing and enduring, constitutes a kind of "mental health," which, like bodily soundness, can't, as such, be felt. To this merely negative well-being there must be added, then, that which, though only moral, *positively* contributes to the "agreeableness of life," namely the always [*jederzeit*] cheerful heart proposed by Epicurus.

According to *The Metaphysics of Morals*, no one has more cause to cheer than he for whom it is "no longer even a duty" to put himself in an habitually cheerful mood, i.e., one who is both "conscious of no resolved upon transgressions" *and* "secured against the occasion for such." In lieu of absolute security on this account (an absolute security of which, as we have seen, our status as embodied rational beings [or "humanity"] necessarily deprives us), our only resort is a morally ascetic "gymnastics" through which one "combats natural drives sufficiently so as to be able, should the moral need arise, to master them." This "formal" awareness of one's means, and the cheer to which that awareness gives rise, is the closest one can come to actual "consciousness of one's recovered freedom."

To such gymnastic exercise, and a related moral mental health (or as close as we can knowingly come to it), Kant contrasts (a falsely Christian) penance, as a self-inflicted pain that serves no moral purpose. Penance cannot be what it is usually taken for: i.e., self-punishment (for to will to contradict one's will [as punishment must do] is itself self-contradictory); hence, it can only be a "serfdom" [*Frohndeinst*], in which one seeks to please through an expenditure of bodily force that leaves one's own moral capital untouched. The "discipline" that a human being perpetrates [*verübt*] upon himself can become deserving [*verdienstlich*] and exemplary "only through the sense of cheer [*Frohsinn*] accompanying it" [6: 485].

In light of these considerations, "true" Christianity, in the Kantian sense, becomes Christianity without penance—that is to say, without an expenditure of one's own forces in whose end reason cannot share. A human being so enslaved to the dominion of the evil principle is, as we have seen, a spiritual bondsman, who serves God only with his body [*Frohn*], because he refuses to undertake that moral change of heart by which God's final purpose in creation would become his own. True service to God, by way of contrast, is an exercise in spiritual freedom, because any action whose end one immediately shares—however difficult and painful it may be—is un-coerced, and hence free by definition. The true servant of God is not a serf, passively dependent on his master, but (as in Kant's version of the Parable of the Talents) a fellow spiritual capitalist. The spiritual bondsman mistakes the dignity invested in his own moral *Anlagen* for an external fund on which he can infinitely draw, allowing him to postpone applying his own forces indefinitely. The true servant, on the other hand, earns interest on that deposit through an expenditure for which he can himself take credit, Kant here proposing what could be called a "labor" theory of spiritual value.[33]

True Christianity, so understood, becomes both a positive and a negative vehicle of cheer—a means, however "exalted," whose end (as Kant's Latin references make clear) resembles that of "virtuous" Epicurus. The difference between Epicurean and Christian approaches to cheer lies mainly in Christianity's complex relation to the Judaism with which it is historically and institutionally entangled.[34] Paganism, with its many gods—the faith with which Epicurus grappled—was ethically far superior, Kant says, to the monotheism of the Jews, which represented slavish service in the extreme, and whose only contribution to world history was the commission of its laws to scripture. Christianity as a vehicle of cheer (good news) is thus Christianity born by a scripture that has been liberated from its Mosaic-messianic Jewish remnants—from everything that encourages an attitude of passive "waiting," as if anything other than the goodness of one's own deed could ground hope in ultimate salvation.[35] The negative purpose of *true* Christianity is to aid recovery from the false one.

The recovery from false religion begins with the allowance that a human being need not know in what the "divine cooperation" (of which good conduct gives us hope) itself consists [6: 52]. In this morally admissible ignorance lies an opening for "religion within the boundaries of bare reason," i.e., for harmonizing true religion with religion as it had been "handed down" historically.[36]

Accordingly, the figure of Jesus is to be interpreted, not as an historical redeemer (or "vicarious substitute" in the traditional sense),[37] but only as "an unequalled moral example"; for human beings, who cannot experience the transcendental without sensible clothing, cannot conceive of the force of their own moral *Anlage*—infinite as it is—other than by representing it as surrounded by obstacles and yet—amidst the greatest temptations—victorious. In other words, the main positive role of Christianity lies in the historically unequalled pedagogic power of the story of Christ's passion. Jesus, so understood, is an "ideal" in the precise Kantian sense—a concrete exhibition of the "idea of humanity" as a moral maximum [6: 61].[38] Unlike the presumed supererogatory virtue of ordinary human beings (representation of which puts moral judgment out of tune), the holiness of Jesus (whether or not he actually lived or was sent by God) evokes true wonder. Christianity, rightly understood, might thus serve as an historically unequalled teacher of the people, even as, wrongly understood, it threatens to become (as Judaism scripturally universalized) an historically unequalled vehicle of popular corruption.

The remaining sections of the work will sketch out the schema of an evolving human organism (the "kingdom of God on earth") as the idea of humanity transposed over time, that is to say, as mankind itself, progressively victorious over the greatest inner obstacles. The vehicle of that schema is scriptural Christianity (and its public institutions), gradually freeing itself from its own "Jewish" remnants, i.e., its "tendency" (historically rooted in its birth among the Jews, and continuing as "Pfaffertum") to take the letter for the spirit (or the clothing for the man).[39]

The visible church as Kant newly conceives it, is the (mystic) "shell" or "mantle" [*Hülle*] out of which the species as a collective organism can develop.[40] From this point of view, the proper translation of Kant's title is "Religion within the limits of Bare Naked Reason," "bare-naked" rendering with a peculiar precision the meaning of the German "blöße." (To be sure, it is ultimately difficult to tell what is *Hülle* [or clothing] from what isn't.) Removing Judaism from Christianity (distinguishing the clothing from the man) proves in several ways defining (as a study of *The Conflict of the Faculties* will further show)[41] of the human problem simply. In any case, the historical appearance of Christianity is both genuinely "fortunate," as Kant puts it, and—to the extent that the Church does not desist from promising a "vicarious substitute" for man's own deed—human reason's "salto mortale."[42]

Religion within the Boundaries is a response, not only to Kant's immediate political difficulties, but also to a problem intrinsic to the moral life as Kant conceives it: how to reconcile the injunction to put duty first and the acknowledged human "limitation" that forces us to seek, in every action, some end that reason can justify. This limitation exposes us both to a perpetual temptation to insist upon a justifying reason, beyond the law itself, for our obeying it and the perpetual danger (so far as we can tell) of our succumbing. We ought, and hence can, act *now* to make the moral law our overriding incentive—and yet—since such an act of transcendental freedom is timeless—we cannot (in this life at least) ever be *aware* of doing so. What Rousseau called "the science of simple souls" is thus anything but easy. If sincerity, which is always in our power (and hence justly imputable to us), is that for which, in the last analysis, we can alone take credit, insincerity is an inner enemy—an insinuating temptation—that cannot be consciously vanquished. What gives insincerity its power over us is our resistance to the spiritual labor that the moral law imposes on us—an unhesitating choice that goes against the naturally crooked grain of human reason, which cannot help but think discursively and hence in a timely fashion. Man's moral disposition [*Gesinnung*] must make up for the deficiency "which is in principle inseparable from the existence of a temporal being"—namely, "never to be completely what one has it in concept [*im Begriffe*] to become" [6: 67n]. We cannot represent our moral capital concretely; to think is thus to be tempted to hesitate or to "bethink" ourselves. Investment of our talents[43] requires an immediate expenditure of moral capital that defies ordinary calculations of profit and loss. Hence, our positive incentive toward the "self-swindling" that prefers the lesser good.

In the face of our self-doubt (Kant's own version of original sin), we must strive to cultivate receptivity to the law's incentive, in ourselves and others—above all, by contemplating the idea of the moral good "in its absolute purity" and becoming "conscious that it belongs to our original *Anlage*." Wöllner's edicts (and the political and spiritual movement behind them) threatened Kant's central and nearly lifelong effort to promote such cultivation. A new task thus historically emerges: Moral cultivation cannot go forward until certain newly resurgent obstacles—Wöllner's school of insincerity—are dealt with. That task must proceed within the letter of the law—hence not by defying the statutory authority of the church directly, but through resistance to the *Afterdienst* (publicly authorized in what has been handed down to us) that mistakes the letter of religion for the spirit.

True religion will have the character of love, or unforced veneration—a veneration that can be "truthful" only if it is given freely. Meanwhile, human authority seeks to coercively impose such veneration, by means of state-sanctioned censorship directed against writings that fail, in the state's view, to profess it.

And yet morality must also give human authority its due—albeit by way of a respect that does justice to the need for state regulation. That qualification gives Kant a saving recourse, by which, without openly defying authority, he can preserve that freedom of inquiry. Only work that encroaches on the public doctrine in which the state takes an interest is properly censorable. And only those divines who are also scholars are qualified to recognize such encroachments. Hence, it is the prerogative of the theological faculty, and it alone, to judge what can be censored. By such a process of removal, Kant seeks to secure protection for the "free thinking" without which human honesty would stand in jeopardy. The theological faculty secures that free inquiry through its scholarly authority to distinguish its own "biblical" study—a subject matter that is censorable in principle—from the philosophic study of religion—a study that is uncensorable because it is "merely" rational. One intention of Kant's work is thus to inform the theological faculty (or sympathetic figures within it) as to this crucial boundary [6: 10].

At the same time, the work's evocation of the mood of the religious sublime furnishes a more immediate moral remedy. Kant's discussion of the sublime, in the *Critique of Judgment*, sheds further light on the specific courage of the virtuous.

> We can consider an object *fearful* without *being afraid* of it if we so judge it that we merely *think* of the case [*Fall*] where we would want to make some resistance to it, and, in that case, that all such resistance would be altogether futile. Thus does a virtuous person fear God without being afraid of him, for he thinks of wanting to resist God's command as a case of no concern to him. [*keinen von ihm besorglichen Fall*]. [5:260]

The "just in case case" [*allenfals*] that occupies the sinful heart is no case at all to the virtuous soul, who can be certain in advance that he will never set himself in opposition to God's will. Job is thus courageous [*ihm zu Muthe ist*] in the specific sense of fearing God in a general way without actually being afraid of him [*Theodicy*; 8: 265]. As Kant puts it in the *Critique of Judgment*, "reverence" for the sublime (for the voice of God within us), as distinguished from a dread that fears God without esteeming him, is what "alone inwardly distinguishes" religion from mere superstition [5: 264].

How, then, are we to think of human history? Is it a beautiful confirmation of the moral purposiveness of human nature (in which case it will not properly attune us to the sublime); or is it a sublime confirmation of its moral recalcitrance (in which case, it will dash moral hope)? Or, finally, is Kantian history somehow both (as the artful arousal of moral feeling must be)? Aesthetically speaking, the answer seems to be as follows:

> The object of a pure and unconditioned intellectual being well pleased [*Wohlgefallens*] is the moral law in its might, which it executes on us above each and every mental incentive *that precedes it*; and that this might makes recognizable aesthetically only via sacrifice (which is a deprivation—though one at the behest of inner freedom, in which account it uncovers in us an ungroundable depth . . . whose consequences extend beyond what we can foresee). . . . [From the intellectual side, this being well pleased] . . . is connected with an interest. It follows that if we judge aesthetically . . . the moral good we must present not so much as beautiful, but much rather as sublime. . . . For human nature does not of itself harmonize with that good. [5: 271]

Kant's subsequent discussion, in the *Critique of Judgment*, of a certain self-isolating attitude is here additionally instructive. As universally communicable, our liking for the sublime (as with our liking for the beautiful) takes an interest in society (where such communication can take place). And yet self-sufficient isolation [*Absonderung*] from society also "approaches the sublime," so long as it is not fearfully or hostilely misanthropic. There is, however, a misanthropy ("very improperly so called"):

> the *Anlage* to which is wont to arise in the minds of many well-thinking human beings with age, which, to be sure, is philanthropic enough as concerns *benevolence* [*Wohlwollen*], but has broken away from *being pleased* with men through long and sad experience: of this a human being's propensity toward seclusion, or also fantastic wishes for a far off estate, or also (among younger people) . . . Robinsonades . . . give witness. Falseness, ingratitude, injustice, whatever is childish in the purposes that we consider important . . . and in the pursuit of which we inflict all conceivable evils on one another, these so contradict the idea of what men could be if they wanted to, and so conflict with the lively wish that they be better, that in order not to hate what he cannot love, the renunciation of all social joys seems a small sacrifice. [5:276]

Unlike isolation that approaches sublimity by "setting need aside," such misanthropy (improperly so called) seeks isolation to fulfill a need arising out of moral sadness [*Traurigkeit*]. Kant here cites the Alpine traveler and scientific explorer, Horace Saussure, whose description of the "tasteless [*abgeschmackte*] sadness" prevailing on a mountain called "Bonhomme," calls to mind a contrasting *interesting* sadness. Such sadness, aroused by the view of a wasteland [*Einöde*] to which a person disposed to such moral sadness might withdraw, shows that even wastelands have their not inhospitable uses [5:276].

The cascading ironies of these remarks—whose Rousseauian provenance is unmistakable—call to mind another Rousseauizing Alpinist-turned-anthropologist, later cited in Kant's *Theodicy*: M. de Luc. After exploring the mountains for anthropological verification of original goodness of our species, he concluded that man would be "good enough" with respect to his benevolence, but for some doubt as to his sincerity [8:271]. As Kant would put it in the *Metaphysics of Morals*, no *Einöde* is more distant than our own heart, whose ungroundable depths and unbounded heights overpower the vistas of the most sublimely dedicated traveler. The good man (or *bonhomme*) is a mountain and a valley unto himself. Still, only this willingness to fathom our own heights and depths, to scrutinize the heart, can both dispel the fanatical contempt "for the whole human race" to which a certain misdirection of humility leads us, and counter a self-loving self-esteem that takes wishes for deeds [6:44]. In the meantime, *Religion* addresses that contempt by exhibiting human nature even at its worst as a sublimely artful prompt to moral receptivity.

Recent communitarian interpretations are thus right to stress the importance of community for Kant, but wrong to link it with a "progressive" agenda in the simple sense that it is usually taken. It is, for example, misleading to imply, as do some recent commentators, that "Kant does not think [one] can achieve [the] inner revolution toward goodness entirely on [one's] own," but only with the help of others.[44] It is true that the *thought* of our collective struggle (and its always endangered success) is, on Kant's account, morally empowering. It would be going too far, however, to suggest that our personal effort to improve depends, for him, upon the historical transformation of society, not only because we are obligated *now* to make ourselves better human beings, but also because the precariousness of human progress is itself—as Kant indicates again and again—a necessary condition of our freedom.

It is thus, I think, a mistake to overstate Kant's confidence in organized religion (however free of state compulsion) or to insist that individuals are ethically obliged to form or join one.[45] The only clear-cut "duty" *Religion* imposes upon individuals at large is one of interpretive resistance to a penitential (or "judaizing") understanding of the true end of Christianity.[46] Until that penitential understanding is completely rectified (the inner circumcision by which the true spirit of Christianity is separated from its skin), the injunction to "leave the ethical state of nature" can have no other definite meaning.[47] As for rulers and others in a position to influence the people's way of thinking—they must resist their own evil propensity to make hypocrisy pay (via false professions of faith), i.e., to use man's moral capital as a mere means.[48] In Catholics, such resistance will especially involve a rejection of "probabilism" (Pascal's "just in case," and its morally perverse calculus of safety) [6: 186]; in Protestants, it will especially involve a rejection of false pride [6: 188–189].

In thus resisting the evil propensity (at least in others), rulers would, in turn, make purposive the human tendency, otherwise *counter-purposive*, to make moral conscience into a mere tool of politics and policy. *Toward Perpetual Peace* will sketch out in greater detail this "higher" anthropological perspective, from which (false) honor, or the human inclination "to gain value in the opinion of others," can be turned, finally, to moral account.[49] It will do so, however, in an ironic register that acknowledges that war—and, indeed, total war—will remain an ever-present danger, "constantly threatening to break out."

In the meantime, and whatever his political success, Kant's representation of the deliverance of the true church out of and against its own historical integuments,[50] bears immediate, sublime witness to man's innate goodness and hence to our own moral adequacy. Human nature, as Kant elsewhere puts it, does not of itself harmonize with [the] good [5: 271]. Our very *in*ability to represent the idea of humanity as a completed organism purposefully exhibits (in the catastrophic exposure of human history represented in that very intellectual failure) the sublime *in*adequacy of consequential, or timely reasoning to reason's "done deed" or moral *factum*. In the ineluctable tension (itself defining of the "boundaries" of reason) between temporal reasoning (reason as contained in our *Anlage* to humanity) and the timeless ground of the idea (reason as contained in our *Anlage* to personality), human reason registers its own moral sublimity and thus wordlessly answers the misanthropic question that the essay on *Theodicy* left hanging.[51]

The sublime is "a presentation that determines [*bestimmt*] the mind to think [*denken*] of nature's inability to attain to an exhibition of ideas" [5: 268].

In so doing, the sublime calls to mind the archaic sense of *Stimmung* as an attunement of the scales by which votes (or sums of money) are tallied.[52] Where the historicized figure of humanity (man as "species being") itself evokes a feeling for the morally sublime, we are moved by the discrepancy between *human* purposelessness—the recalcitrance of *human* nature to moral purposes— and some higher purpose served, however perplexingly, by that very recalcitrance. The historical sublime determines us to think the *in*adequacy of human reason (i.e., of thought itself) to the idea of personality. The moral-aesthetic force of Kant's educational project depends as much upon our common exposure to despair as upon the reach of our collective hope.

If this reading is correct, *Religion* belongs, in part, to that peculiar Kantian genre, of which *Observations on the Feeling of the Beautiful and the Sublime* provides, perhaps, the earliest example: a (beautiful) exhibition of the sublimity of human nature.[53] Such a portrayal is neither a direct cause of moral self-improvement (which would contradict human freedom), nor simply its effect,[54] but (as Kant here presents it) an invitation to "make room" for the moral idea, thus allowing it to "penetrate the heart" more deeply.[55]

This reading, I could add, helps answer some of the charges of moral inconsistency (or "unfairness") with which Kant's treatment of history is sometimes taxed.[56] Kant's sketch of the realization of the kingdom of God on earth is aimed primarily at overcoming moral hesitation—first by providing a great, offsetting goal, and second by dissolving a "contemplative misanthropy" that raises doubts as to the adequacy of man's (and hence our own) moral capital.[57] History, as Kant conceives it, is no less fair than nature itself, which not only kills infants in the cradle, but may also doom whole races (and the entire female sex) to a perpetual moral childhood.[58] Only God knows the hidden disposition that lies beneath appearances and the obstacles it has or hasn't vanquished.[59] In any event, nothing prevents us from enjoying, here and now, the "good fortune" of those who may come after us. We have only to make the highest good possible in the world our own to *already* belong to the true church or ethical commonwealth. Indeed, if one trusts the *Anthropology*, we have only to make that goal our own to already attain all the happiness that lies within our (present) nature.[60]

Still, there is a dangerous tendency unleashed by such an understanding of the dignity of man, which men like Heinrich Steffens and Houston Stewart Chamberlain would later seize on. If what gives each of us dignity is, in the last analysis, the racial germ we bear (the role we play in the historical development of man as a species-being or a pan-human organism), then groups whose relation to history can be portrayed as nil, or even parasitic, may well come to seem subhuman.[61] It is thus especially important to insist upon the altogether secondary role, for Kant, of church history as a self-organizing human construct.

6

Kant's "True Politics": *Völkerrecht* in *Toward Perpetual Peace* and *The Metaphysics of Morals*

Kant is neither an "idealist" nor a "realist" in the usual sense. Despite his reputation as a champion of peace and cosmopolitanism, Kant, unlike most so-called idealists, has a robust conception of national sovereignty and of the duty, as well as right, of nations to defend themselves—if necessary, preemptively.[1] And unlike many so-called realists, who reduce human behavior to the calculation of advantage, Kant has a lively—and some would say more genuinely realistic—sense of the "irrationalities" that beset human action, especially in politics.

Kant lays out his understanding of *Völkerrecht* [the right of nations] in two main writings: *Toward Perpetual Peace* [1795],[2] and *The Metaphysics of Morals* [1797].[3] The first and more famous work (which is cast in the form of a fictional peace treaty) is "dared" on the "lucky" occasion of a cessation of hostilities between France and Prussia that was to prove all too temporary. Kant's misleading reputation as a naïve cosmopolite is due, in part, to an overreliance by critics on this essay read in isolation, without due attention to the less rhetorically freighted *Metaphysics of Morals*. Certain seeming contradictions between the two works (such as their differing claims as to the permissibility of preemptive warfare and coercive regime-change) should at least urge caution against drawing hasty conclusions based on a reading of *Toward Perpetual Peace* alone.

1. *Toward Perpetual Peace: Völkerrecht* within a Free Federation of States

Toward Perpetual Peace is a forceful yet perplexing work. Perhaps the most frequently read and influential of all Kant's political essays, its argument builds through a dialectical tension that is anticipated in Kant's equivocal title.[4] *Toward Perpetual Peace* presents itself (in imitation of the Dutch innkeeper's sign picturing a graveyard from which that title is borrowed) as a fictional device that speaks ironically but truly. Indeed, as Kant later insists, the state of perfect lawfulness, or right made actual through power [*Gewalt*], is almost indistinguishable from soulless anarchy, the death of every body politic. And yet perfected lawfulness remains the goal without whose ever presence human life (as Kant also insists) is not worth living.

The innkeeper's sign recalls another "inn," mentioned by Kant in a work published the previous year—the inn [*Karavenserai; Wirthshaus*] as emblem of the world, where "each man must be content at every turn-in in life's journey to be soon pushed out by a successor." Kant there suggests that such an image of this world (an image whose rivals are the house of discipline, the madhouse, and the outhouse) is what remains if one lacks hope that man in this world constantly progresses. If our world is to be better than a hostelry for nomads (whose wandering and temporary settlement Kant elsewhere likens to dogmatism and skepticism, respectively)[5] the idea of perpetual peace must somehow be our orienting sign. Philosophy (to pursue Kant's metaphor) may critically secure itself a permanent worldly home; but mankind generally finds itself, at best, perpetually moving in the right direction. Constant progress implies constant approach, and with it, a perpetually deferred arrival. Kant's title (it is tempting to surmise), like the ambiguous signpost it replaces, advertises a repose at once attractive and repellent, promising a rest that draws us on while also putting us on guard.

The title and theme of *Toward Perpetual Peace* calls to mind the problem, specifically associated with relations among states, that *Religion* had left hanging. As Kant had there complained, rulers abide by principles that "no philosopher has ever been able to make harmonize with morality or, what is more vexing, replace by throwing down [*vorschlagen*] better ones"; hence "*philosophic chiliasm*," which "hopes for eternal peace," is "universally derided" [6: 33–34]. As we shall see, Kant's "philosophic *Entwurf*," which "throws down" [8: 386] transcendental principles of public right, attempts to meet that challenge—albeit in a way also open to constant, if declining, risk of failure.[6]

In April 1795 Frederick William II withdrew from the First Coalition and concluded a separate peace with revolutionary France (the so-called Treaty of Basel). In August of that year, Kant sent the text of *Toward Perpetual Peace* to his German publisher. *Toward Perpetual Peace: A Philosophical Project* was published simultaneously in French—the only one of Kant's works to so appear—and was greeted in France with much approval. The German reception was decidedly more mixed. Still, the new alliance between France and Prussia seems to have protected Kant from any serious political trouble. In an October letter to Kiesewetter, his main source of court gossip, Kant refers to the work, ironically, as his "reveries" [*Träumerei*] on peace, the same term he had used to describe his *Dreams of a Spirit-Seer* some thirty years earlier [10: 68].[7]

The same sardonic tone pervades the opening of the work:

> Whether this satirical title on that Dutch innkeeper's sign [*Schild*] on which a graveyard [*Kirchhof*] was painted is valid for *human beings* in general, or especially for *heads of state,* who can never be sated with war, or merely for philosophers, who dream that sweet dream, may here be left aside. Still, the author of the present [title] lays this down as a condition: namely, that since the practical politician views the theoretical politician with disdain, looking down with great self-satisfaction on the latter as merely school-wise, as one whose empty ideas bring no danger to the state, which must be guided by empirical principles, and as one who may be allowed to toss his eleven pins without the *worldly-wise* needing to turn in his direction: this being the case, if a conflict with the former should arise, the worldy-wise statesman must proceed with enough consistency [*sofern consequent verfahren müsse*] so as not to scent out danger to the state in the publicly uttered opinions that the theoretical politician ventures on good luck;—through this *clausula salvatoria* the author of this considers himself to be expressly guarded in proper form against malicious interpretation.
> [8: 343]

The *clausula salvatoria,* or "little saving clause," was a customary legal device enabling an author to protect himself from charges of heresy by declaring himself beforehand to have no such aim, whatever meaning his words might unintentionally convey.[8] Kant, who had himself recently felt the unpleasant weight of religious censorship, uses the device ironically, against "malicious intention," be it his own or that of his accusers. He thereby seeks a shield [*Schild*] in the very arrogance of the powerful, should they but be willing to submit to reason, i.e., proceed "consistently" [8: 343; cf. 8: 376, 378].

"To toss ten pins" is proverbial (as Kant notes in an earlier draft of the essay) for "doing the impossible" [23: 155].[9] Kant, as we will see, accomplishes what in 1795 is indeed no easy task, namely, showing that philosophy is both innocent and clever (both dove and serpent), and that statesmen in fact—and not only on the basis of unwarranted arrogance—have no good reason to distrust it. Kant's saving clause is thus ironic in another sense; in its endorsement of the indifference of the "worldly-wise," it as good as says to them: "Pay heed to my stipulation that you must not heed me," a strategy of open hiding we will return to.

Of course, the most obvious referent for "doing the impossible" concerns peace itself, whose specific agent (whether philosophers, statesmen or mankind at large) Kant here declines to name. What follows thus looks like a peace treaty (literally, "conclusion of peace" [*Friedensschluß*] without signatories. No heads of state have publicly endorsed the articles put forward, let alone formally agreed to them. And war continues unabated in the world—for example, in the agreement of the parties to the Treaty of Basel to the dismemberment of Poland. What is the bearing, then, of this draft or image of a contract and the conclusion it invokes?

It is useful at this point to take up Kant's suggestion that the *Entwurf* in question is no idle dream but a plan capable of realizing its own aim (like the divine *Entwurf* his *Universal Natural History* had once invoked). The two parts that make up the main body of Kant's sketch comprise six "preliminary" articles (all negative) and three "definitive" articles (all positive). Of the preliminary articles, three (one, five, six) must be effected at once, three (two, three, four) as occasion permits.

The first article deserves special attention, signaling as it does the difference between real peace and its outward or public appearance: "No conclusion of peace shall be held valid as such, that is made with secret holding back of matter [*Stoffes*] for a future war." Kant's very language (which specifies the conditions under which a peace treaty is not a peace treaty, thus denying what it nominally affirms) anticipates his claim shortly thereafter that the phrase "perpetual peace" is itself "suspiciously near pleonasm." Taken in its ordinary sense, of course, article one is clear enough in its demands: No country shall misrepresent its own intentions with a hidden clause to which it later refers to justify returning to hostilities. Yet by the larger meaning Kant immediately gives it (and by his open admission later in the essay), *every* peace other than the final one is a mere cessation of hostilities. Read in this way, the first preliminary article cannot be positively acted on until the peace to which it is presumably preliminary is itself permanently concluded. Prior to that time, every cessation of hostilities retains, by definition, matter for a future war. Still (as a preliminary, as it were, to the preliminaries), one can at least prohibit *willing* deception among signatories to a treaty—the mental reservation, that, unlike the "secret article" that Kant later openly invokes, obstructs peace rather than promoting it. The gap between the public and the private—what parties openly admit and secretly reserve—is what makes possible the peace treaty only in name, the obverse, one might say, of Kant's own philosophic *Entwurf,* a "*schluß*" no less "actual," as it seems, for lack of validating signatories. At the same time, article one is not without immediate bite: by calling for a judging of things "as they are in themselves," it openly reveals, against the enlightened concepts of state cleverness [*Staatsklugheit*], the intrinsic indignity of all such pretenses to dignity. It is only in the eyes [*in den Augen*] of those who equate the "true honor" of a state with "increase in power [*Macht*] by whatever means" that such a judgment, Kant insists, will seem contemptible.

In his opening article, then, Kant denies those who despise philosophy in the name of power the honor their contempt invokes. Articles two through four spell out more fully the basis of that denial.

Articles two, three, and four, on the acquisition of states by purchase, inheritance, and gift, on the abolition of standing armies, and on the disallowance of war debts, respectively, are linked together by Kant's "permissive" allowance that (unlike articles one, five, and six) they need not be enacted all at once, but may be instituted gradually, as circumstances permit, "so long as their ultimate purpose ... is not lost sight of [*aus den Augen zu verlieren*]" [8: 347]. These three articles also join up thematically with the end of the discussion that follows each article pointing to the next. Thus article two, which prohibits acquisition of states in violation of their moral personality, ends in a discussion of the abuse of citizens as cannon fodder, which leads into article three, prohibiting standing armies. The latter ends with a discussion of the power of money in conducting war, which leads into article four, prohibiting war debts. Of Kant's three discussions, the first, concerning article two, is especially instructive:

> A state, unlike the ground on which it has its seat, is no possession [*Habe*] (*patrimonium*). It is a society of men, which no one other than itself possesses [*hat*] to command or dispose of. But to incorporate a state, which has its own roots as stem/lineage [*Stamm*], as a graftling into the body of another state means to cancel [*aufheben*] its existence as a moral person, and make a thing

out of it, and thus contradict the idea of the original contract [*Vertrags*], without which no right over a people may be thought. [8: 344]

Kant's likening of the state as moral person to an organism (which contains, somehow, its own lineage) is echoed in his criticism of the uniquely European practice of "marrying" [*heurathen*] states to one another as a way of increasing state power and size through the union of families rather than the expenditure of force. This "new sort of industry" not only violates the ordinary rules of gain and loss but also, and more importantly, treats citizens as things to be "used [*brauchen*] and consumed/used up [*verbrauchen*]." That Kant employs the latter term to refer both to the use of citizens as cannon fodder and (elsewhere) to the "cannibal-like" injury inflicted on parties who engage in sex outside of marriage[10] highlights the issue at stake, namely, the very possibility of embodied moral personality—the juncture, as it were, of matter and will—without which legitimate authority (or right over a people) "is not even thinkable."

A deeper thematic connection between misuse of people and of money in the conduct of war thus emerges. Employment of standing armies [*stehende Heere*] (*miles perpetuus*) means buying men to "kill and be killed," (i.e., using them as "mere machines and tools" [*bloßen Maschinen und Werkzeugen*]). As a fungible medium of consumption (e.g., when one state hires the soldiers of another state), such troops are in principle no different than monetary credit as a means of conducting war. Unlike permissible forms of credit linked to "*Landesökonomie*"—e.g., road improvements and new settlements—debt incurred for the purpose of expanding state power and size through the consumption of men is limited only by the fragility of the credit system itself, whose eventual collapse (following, presumably, from the fact that demand in this case is potentially limitless) brings down innocent states along with the guilty, and thus constitutes what Kant calls a "public injury":

> There is no cause for suspicion if national debt is incurred for the purpose of improving the domestic economy. . . . But as an antagonistic machine of opposing powers [*entgegenwirkende Maschine der Mächte gegen einander*] . . . a credit system [*Creditsystem*], which grows beyond sight and yet is a safe debt [*Schuld*] for present requirements (because not all creditors demand payment at one time) . . . is a dangerous power of money, that is, a treasure to conduct war that exceeds the treasures of all other states, and which cannot be exhausted except by the forthcoming default of taxes (which can, however, be long delayed by the enlivening of trade by means of the reaction [*Ruckwirkung*] on industry and acquisition). This case of making war, combined

with the inclination to do so by the powerful, an inclination that seems indigenous [*eingeartet*] to human nature, is thus a great obstacle to perpetual peace. [8: 345]

There must thus be a preliminary article to forbid such a credit system, all the more because the state bankruptcy that is finally unavoidable must entangle many other states that are innocent [as in "unverschuldet"] of the damage [8: 345–346]. What is at stake, in the case of Kant's three permissive articles, is less an immediate danger than a tendency, set in motion by the ordinary human passions of the powerful [*Machthabenen*], that threatens to transform the very instruments of human culture—man's increasing "general means"—into the tools whereby mankind perversely feeds upon and, ultimately, consumes itself. To overturn such policies in an instant (e.g., by questioning the legitimacy of states formed on the basis of past conjugal alliances, or by immediately canceling all war debts) would undermine a counter-system whose coalescence (in the manner, as we shall later see, of an organic being generating itself, as it were, spontaneously) represents the only evidence for hope that history is moving in the opposite direction.

Kant's two remaining non-permissive preliminary articles, on the other hand, both of which concern a misplaced authorization to judge, are immediately binding. The first (article five) prohibits violent [*gewaltthätig*] interference [*Einmischung*] of one state in the constitution and governance of another state. "*Einmischung*," according to Grimm, is based on the Latin "*immiscere*," which means to mix one thing with another, to merge, or, alternatively, to confuse. Although Kant's primary topical target is surely the Holy Alliance against France (along with France and Prussia's counteractive dismemberment of Poland), his language speaks to the larger theme of history conceived as a world-organizing process that does justice (as violent intermingling, or confusion, does not) to the individual states (each a moral personality in its own right) that comprise it. This sense of the term is enhanced by Kant's identification of the internal wrongs *(scandalum acceptum)* of a state as a "sickness" [*Krankheit*], interference with which by an independent people constitutes outright injury [*gegebene Skandal*]. Violent interference of one state into the internal affairs of another thus makes insecure "the autonomy of every state" [8: 346], much (we may surmise) as forcible medical treatment of a person whose self-induced ills are not contagious and, indeed, serve as a helpful warning to others, would render insecure the freedom of individual human beings.

Article six prohibits "allowing such hostilities [*Feindseligkeiten*]" (such as use of spies and assassins) that would make future mutual confidence [*Zutrauen*] in time of peace impossible. Although one can surely imagine situations (such as that of the Israelites who sent spies into Canaan) when the survival of a people might depend upon resorting to such measures, Kant reserves his strongest language for this prohibition, violation of which destroys the trust [*Vertrauen*] "that must remain even among enemies in war," without which "peace could not be concluded" and war would turn out to be (or alternatively, germinate) one of reciprocal "extermination" or "uprooting" [*Ausrottungskrieg*; {*bellum internecinum*}].

Whereas article five denied the state's authority to juridically condemn parties whose action poses no injury to others (an immunity that applies to individuals and states alike), article six denies authority to condemn other states who do commit such injuries—authority allowed in the dealings of a state with its own citizens:

> For war in the state of nature is only a sad means of necessity [*traurige Nothmittel*] for asserting one's rights by violence [*Gewalt*] (where no court of justice [*Gerichtshof*] is at hand to judge with force of right [*rechtskräftig*]). In such cases, neither party can be called an unjust enemy (which already presupposes a judge's utterance). Only the *outcome/eruption* [*Ausschlag*] (as in the so-called judgment of God) determines who is right; between states, however, no punitive war permits itself to be thought (because between them a relation of superior to inferior finds no place). From this it follows that a war of extermination, whereby the obliteration [*Vertilgung*] of both parties, and with them all right, can happen, would allow perpetual peace to find a place only in the vast graveyard [*Kirchhof*] of the human race. [8: 346–347]

Without a human judge combining force with right, no enemy can be "declared" unjust; instead, the *Ausschlag* must be left to the so-called judgment of God. (One *Ausschlag*—divine judgment so-called—here stands proxy for another—a vast grave figured as a churchyard.) Punitive aggression against another state, in other words, transforms violence from a regrettable means into a final end, destroying the very possibility of mutual agreement. Not human selfishness *per se*, but the (moral) impulse to *retribute* (irrespective of self-interest)—an impulse whose pretension here to false superiority renders it perverse—threatens the annulment not only of the human race but also right itself. (But what then shall we make of—how are we to judge and by what standard—the enemy who resorts to *dis*honorable means, especially if they threaten to defeat us?)

A war of the sort described, and the means that might lead thereto, must, Kant says, be absolutely forbidden [*unerlaubt*]. And that dishonorable stratagems are such means—indeed, ones leading "inevitably" to such a war—is, he claims, "made clear" [*erhellen*] by the fact that once they come into use:

> these diabolical [*hollischer*] arts . . . do not long remain confined to war . . . since they draw on a dishonorableness/dishonesty [*Ehrlosigkeit*] . . . that can never be completely uprooted [*ausgerottet*]; instead they transfer over to the state of peace, entirely nullifying the latter's intention [*Absicht*]. [8: 346–347]

Human honor itself—i.e., all justified pretense to be more than something fit to be used—depends on the renunciation of such arts. As Kant puts it elsewhere, dishonor is the constant companion (or "shadow") of dishonesty, by which man throws away [*wegwerfen*] and, as it were, annihilates [*vernichten*] his human dignity, becoming less, even, then a thing:

> For a thing, being something real and given, has usable properties that others can make use of. But communication [*Mittheilung*] to another through words of thoughts that yet (intentionally) contain the contrary of what the speaker thinks . . . is an end that is directly opposed to the natural purposiveness of the speaker's capacity to communicate his thoughts, and is thus a renunciation by the speaker of his personality, and such a speaker is a mere deceptive appearance of a man, not a man himself. . . . Man as a moral being . . . cannot use himself as a natural being (*homo phenomenon*) as a mere means (a speaking machine) [*Sprachmaschine*] as if his natural being were not bound to the inner end (of communicating his thoughts), but is bound to the condition of using himself as a natural being in agreement with the declaration [*Erklärung*] . . . of his moral being and is under obligation to himself to *truthfulness*.[11]

This obligation to self-declaration or inner truthfulness, despite the ultimate impossibility, according to Kant, of knowing one's own motives, may be the one exception to his general dictum that "ought implies can." As *Religion* already showed, without truthfulness, man's collective progress as a species collapses on itself, our increasing ability to make use of nature (including human nature) as a general means done in by this intrinsic deceptiveness (the one "foul spot" in man that cannot be eradicated). In his deceptiveness—genuinely diabolical in its ability to "cancel out" reality—man is less, even, than a part of nature's mechanism (i.e., the world of appearances), which, being real, constantly maintains itself.[12] Thus even against unjust enemies (here defined as enemies whose maxims, if universalized, would make future peace impossible), deceptive stratagems of the sort mentioned are prohibited.

What, however, does it mean to prohibit such activities other than to declare that they are contrary to right (in the peculiar sense, admittedly "difficult to conceive," in which war and justice are thinkable together)? Since no (human) judge can enforce such a prohibition, one can anticipate (it seems) that states, feeling "threatened" [*bedrohen*], will continue to resort to these activities, unless means arise that assure sufficient force, consistent with right, to make such resort not only wrong (in the terms that Kant's *Toward Perpetual Peace* defines) but also imprudent. Hence, Kant's later admission—startling in its implications—that without a federation of republics (or states akin to them) "morality and politics cannot be combined" [8: 385].

Section Two, which contains "the definitive articles to perpetual peace," speaks to this need, by affirming that a condition of perpetual peace "must be instituted [*gestiftet werden*]," and this because the state of nature is itself (almost) [*vielmier*] a state of war—i.e., constantly threatening [*bedrohen*] an outbreak [*Ausbruch*] of hostilities, a threat that entitles each to treat his neighbor as an enemy [8: 348–349].

The first definitive article, which announces that "the constitution of every state shall be republican," looks primarily to the self-interest of citizens who, in a republican state, themselves decide for war and thus risk calling down upon themselves the burden of an inextinguishable [*nie zu tilgende*] debt ([8: 351; compare [8: 347].) For present purposes, then, the salient element of republicanism is the power of the people to veto a decision to go to war. In non-republics, by way of contrast, heads of state, who can decide for war without fear of opposition, can also do so without "the slightest sacrifice" of "hunts and banquets," and indeed, regard it as a sort of pleasure party [*Lustpartie*], examples that recall earlier images of politics as a perverse engine of human self-consumption.

By "republicanism" Kant means the "state principle of separating the executive power [*Gewalt*] (the government) from the legislative power." It is thus a governmental "form" understood not in terms of who governs (as with Aristotle) but how—i.e., in what way [*Art*]—the state, "grounded in the constitution [*Constitution*] (the act of the general will whereby a mass becomes a people), makes use of its plenary power [*Machtvolkommenheit*]." Here what is crucial is not material but formal, not whether rule is in the interest of the rulers or the whole (again, as with Aristotle), but that a separation be maintained *within* the whole—i.e., that government represent, rather than merging with, the general will whose self-constituting act is also in this way, and necessarily, self-divisive.[13] Despotism (government that is not "representative") is not a "perverse" form of government (in the sense of Aristotle's "tyranny") but government that lacks any form at all [*rein Unform*].

What is most important here is that the general will establish a government that is genuinely separate from itself without the general will thereby ceasing to be sovereign, i.e., that the head of state "rule" while himself remaining a citizen.[14] For this reason, monarchies and even aristocracies can govern in a way that harmonizes with the republican spirit (i.e., by ruling the people as their "servant")[15] and thus gradually transform themselves into governments that take up [*erheben*] republicanism; whereas democracies can become republics only through violent revolution [*gewaltsame Revolution*]—i.e., only by the people, who cannot thus become their own servant, declaring war against themselves [8: 353].

Kant's discussion of the second definitive article ("the right of peoples/nations [*Völkerrecht*] shall be grounded in a federalism of free states"), builds on Kant's earlier likening of rulers to cannibals:

> We look with profound contempt [*Verachtung*] on the way savages cling to their lawless freedom.... We might thus expect that civilized peoples (each united for itself into a state), would prefer to abandon so degrading [*verworfenen*] a condition as soon as could be: instead, each state sets its majesty[16] ... in not being submitted to any external compulsion, and the luster of its ruler consists precisely in being able, without danger to himself, to order many thousands to offer themselves up as sacrifice.... And the difference between a European and an American savage consists in the fact that whereas many tribes [*Stämme*] of the latter [sort] have been eaten by their enemies, the former know how to make better use of those they overcome than to make a meal of them, preferring to use them to increase their number of subjects, and thus augment their stock of tools for conducting even more extensive wars. [8: 354–355]

It is not that rulers are worse than ordinary men, but rather that, lacking as they do all external constraint, they reveal human depravity in an undisguised [*unverhohlen*] way. Still, Kant here insists, the homage (in words at least) that states continue to pay to the concept of right (however little it affects their actions) shows that there may be found in man a (still slumbering) moral tendency to become master of the evil principle in oneself and hope others do likewise. Otherwise "right" would never "come into the mouths" of feuding states, other than in mockery [*Spott*].

This verbal homage, even if no state has ever been moved to act on it, suffices, it seems, to establish the possibility of an alternative to the extermination of the species, and with it all justice, in a collective graveyard. In other words, rulers' sheer utterance of "right," however insincere, uncovers a hidden truth—the human good potentially more powerful than the depravity that rulers even more than cannibals (and by a different sort of oral usage) openly reveal. So interpreted, rulers (who measure human dignity perversely, in the currency of human flesh), communicate [*mitheilen*] despite themselves— their words willy-nilly imparting truth—without, it seems, thereby becoming "speech machines."

On this note, Kant undertakes to find an international equivalent to the right of individuals in the state of nature to compel others to mutually abandon it. On the one hand, states resemble individuals in the state of nature: Rights among peoples cannot be decided by judicial process [*Proceß*], but only by outcome [*Ausschlag*] of war, which, though it can bring about a particular peace treaty [*Vertrag*], cannot end the condition of war as such. On the other hand, states, which have their own internally lawful constitution, have outgrown [*entwachsen sind*] the coercive right of others and therefore cannot be compelled to submit themselves to a higher authority.

Kant's solution is to replace the "peace treaty [*Friedensvertrag*]" (that seeks an end to a particular war) with a "treaty among nations [*Vertrag der Völker*]" that seeks an end to war in general. Eschewing the acquisition of power [*Macht*] pursued by states, such a treaty among nations seeks only to "preserve and secure *the freedom* of each state in itself, along with all the other confederated states." Thus unlike individual states, whose formal self-division is materially unstable, and which are therefore susceptible to degeneration into formless despotisms, a federation of peoples is objectively (and not just ideally) self-limiting. Such a federation can maintain its form without (like states) needing to empower a coercive executive, a head whose conformity to right, depending as it does upon sheer will, is always doubtful [8: 356].[17] Unlike individual states, in other words, which can seek peace only *indirectly*—i.e., by augmenting a power that yields matter for future wars—a federation maintains, and indeed, augments itself by seeking peace *directly*, through pursuit of reciprocal freedom.

Although the only "rational" way for states to leave the condition of war is unite in an international state [*Völkerstaat*], states, "following their idea of international right," refuse to will such a union. In other words, if all human beings were wholly rational (i.e., moral) from the outset, a federation of this kind would not be needed—but such is not the case. Hence (given the actual perversity of man), if by the concept of international right "anything is to remain over to be thought," there is only the negative surrogate [*Surrogat*][18] of the free federation just described. Such a federation repels war [*den Krieg abwehrenden*], endures, and gradually expands to check the current [*Strom*] of right-shunning [*rechtscheuenden*], hostile inclination, albeit with constant danger [*beständiger Gefahr*] of it breaking out [*Ausbruchs*]. "Impious furor . . . rages in the ghastliness/savageness [*horridus*] of bloodstained lips. (Virgil)" [8: 357; cf. 348–349].[19]

The rational way to peace is barred by the initial presupposition [*Vorausetzung*] that peoples make up separate states rather than being melted down [*zusammenschmelzen*] into a single civic entity [8: 354].[20] The remedy here proposed is a substitute congruent (as the concept of a world republic is not) with the idea of a right of nations (in the plural)—not union through an ideal civil compact (in which all wills unite to constitute a single state) but federation through alliance [*Vertrag der Völker*].

As we saw in Chapter 5, man's "radical evil" is visible in a particularly acute way in the relation among states. As Kant there put it:

> We shall have enough of the vices of culture and civilization (the most distressing of all) to make us rather turn away our eyes from human carryings on, lest we be drawn into another vice, namely, misanthropy. And if we are not satisfied yet, we need but consider the outer condition of nations, a condition wondrously compounded [of both savagery and civilization], where civilized peoples stand *vis-à-vis* one another in a condition of raw nature (a state of constantly warlike character [*Kriegsverfassung*]), and have set themselves firmly in their heads [*sich . . . fest in den Kopf gesetzt haben*] never to get out of it; and we shall become aware of fundamental principles in the great societies we call *states* that directly contradict official policy and yet are never abandoned, and that no philosopher has been able to bring into harmony with morality nor (what is vexing [*arg*]) throw down [*vorschlagen*] better ones that could be united with human nature: so *philosophic chiliasm*, which hopes for a state of eternal peace, grounded on a union of nations [*Völkerbund*] as a world republic [*Weltrepublik*], is universally derided [*verlacht*] as *Schwärmerei*, as much so as theological chiliasm, which awaits the complete moral improvement of the entire human race. [6: 33–34]

International relations bring to a head the problem that permits the "vices of civilization," as Kant called them in *Religion*, to insinuate themselves. The transition from a permissible concern for one's own external freedom to an unjust desire for superiority over others proceeds via a "reasonable" worry, in the absence of assurance to the contrary, that others will do likewise. That in such conditions, this desire is enhanced, rather than muted, by an awareness of human equality (what I anticipate doing to others they must anticipate doing to me) invokes Rousseau's "prisoner's dilemma" in its classic Hobbesian form. The "unjust" (yet not altogether unreasonable) desire for superiority over others becomes "evil" [*Böse*], as we have seen, when it is no longer seen as a merely preventive measure, for security, but as having positive value in itself, a value that reaches its theoretical maximum in the devilish capacity to enjoy superiority altogether for its own sake.[21]

Kant's depiction of the dilemma out of which the "vices of culture and civilization" arise helps explain his repeated insistence that improvement of a people's way of thinking is to be expected from a good state constitution, rather than the reverse. (See [8: 366, 372, 377] and *The Conflict of the Faculties* [7: 92–93].)[22] In the case of individual citizens, Kant tells us, the sheer experience of lawful government has a morally beneficial effect, even on the ill-disposed. For even the malevolent flatter themselves that they would faithfully do right, if only they could expect others to do likewise [8: 375–377n]. But it is precisely this expectation that a good civil constitution secures.[23] By thus checking (albeit under a "moral veneer") the "outbreak" of unlawful inclinations "the development of the moral predisposition [*Anlage*] to immediate respect for right is greatly facilitated," and a "great step is taken *toward* [*zur*] morality (though it is not yet a moral step)" [8: 376n].[24]

Kant's "philosophic project" (which "throws down [*schlagt . . . vor*]" transcendental principles of public right two years later [8: 386]) offers a partial solution to the above dilemma posed in its most acute form.[25] "Devils" can be accommodated at the level of the individual state, where a good "state organization" suffices to offset their malevolence [*Bösartigkeit*] [8: 366].[26] International relations, however, brings out the worst in human beings by uniting the lawlessness of savages (whose propensity for war at least evinces a noble capacity to put honor before life [8: 365]) with the prudent calculation of civilized heads of state (who prefer to buy their honor with the lives of others) [6: 33–34; 8: 355, 358–359].[27]

But whence the power capable of actualizing a solution, absent a sovereign competent to judge with rightful force? Kant's "idea" of a "growing" free federation of republics (or their like) is here the answer ("if all isn't to be lost") to this practically crucial question.[28] This is so not only from a pragmatic or prudential point of view (in order to prevent political catastrophe); it also is required to solve a crucial conceptual difficulty. Absent such an ideal "surrogate" for a world republic, the concept of lawful relations among states has "no meaning at all" [8: 357].

Unlike individual states, who are inclined to seek "perpetual peace" by maximizing their power [*Gewalt*] over others,[29] a free federation of republics (or their approximate like) "does not look to acquiring any might of a state" but only at maintaining and securing the *freedom* of its members [8: 356].[30] By not aiming at such might, a federation of the sort Kant has in mind mirrors the command to "put the form before the end" by which alone morality and politics proves reconcilable [8: 376–377]. Kant's league does not seek perpetual peace in the manner of an ordinary head of state—i.e., by attempting to dominate every other state—but by maintaining the reciprocal security of its members according to a "principle of outer freedom." In short: It takes its immediate bearings from the principle of outer freedom and aims in only a secondary way at global security as such.

Such a federation would promote that end not by seeking world domination (in the manner of individual states) but, above all, by counteracting the destructive dynamic of mutual distrust that allows the vices of civilization to initially "take root." In place of the overarching power by which individuals are domestically assured that their respect for right will be reciprocated, Kant's federation substitutes an "unwritten code" of rightful (rather than "political") honor among states that are constitutionally inclined toward peace.

Such a counter-system of reciprocal trust works to reverse the diabolical machinery of war (the system of credit that, as we have seen, allows war debt to accumulate indefinitely) Kant describes as an "ingenious" invention of the commercial (literally, "commerce-driving" [*handeltreibenden*]) British:

> As a counter-effecting machine of opposing powers, a credit system of debts growing into the unforeseeable [future] and yet always secured against present demand (because this doesn't happen with all creditors/believers [*Gläubigern*] at once)—is . . . a dangerous money power [*Geldmacht*], that is, a treasury [*Schatz*] for the pursuit of war that exceeds the treasuries of all other states taken together, a treasury that can only be exhausted by the shortfall in taxes that is inevitable sometime (but which can yet be long postponed through the enlivening of exchange by means of its counter-effect on industry and acquisition). [8: 345]

This dangerous money-power, combined with the natural inclination of the powerful toward war, turns human credit (or belief) into an engine of universal, "undeserved harm." Kant's federation, by way of contrast, both relies on and encourages a growing sense of honor (in the sense of trustworthiness or integrity) as an independent source of credit.

The executability (and hence "objective reality") of the idea of such a federation, which "should gradually extend over every state," thus "permits itself to be exhibited [*lasst sich darstellen*]":

> For should luck [*Glück*] so fit things together that a powerful [*machtiges*] and enlightened people can form themselves into a republic (which must by its nature be inclined to perpetual peace), this would deliver [*abgeben*] a focus [*Mittelpunkt*] of federative union for other states, so that they join up with [*anschleissen*] the first, thus securing the freedom condition of each in conformity with the idea of international right [*Völkerrechts*], and through additional connections of this sort propagate [*ausbreiten*] bit by bit ever more widely. [8: 356]

The third definitive article (article nine) limits cosmopolitan justice [*Weltburgerrecht*]—the rights that human beings can claim as citizens of the world—to conditions "of universal hospitality [*Hospitalität*]" [8: 357]. As such, it sets boundaries (and, in lieu of a world state, gives objective meaning) to the concept of world citizenship, by defining it against the previously described ways of rulers whose "hunts and banquets" are anything but host-like to mankind generally, let alone their fellow citizens. "Hospitality," from "hospital," which historically denotes a place set up for the reception of pilgrims,[31] also calls to mind the figure of the Dutch inn, under whose ambiguous sign Kant's *Entwurf* as a whole proceeds. Indeed, as we shall see, Kant's discussion of this final article—which culminates with a "litany of evils" (delivered as a satire whose bitterness verges on sarcasm) to which the civilized, and in particular, commercial states of Europe, have, in the guise of travelers, brought upon the world—also deepens that ambiguity by reflecting back upon the civilized themselves the danger this sign warns us to anticipate. With the right to hospitality, moreover, the distinction between right and benevolence—a distinction on which Kant's later grounding of the possibility of moral politics depends [8: 385–386]—already comes explicitly to the fore. Here, as in the preceding articles, the issue [*Rede*] is not *philanthropy* but *right*; and in this context:

> *hospitality* (*Wirtbarkeit*) means the *right* of a stranger not to be treated as an enemy when he arrives on foreign land. He can indeed be turned away, if this

> can happen without his perishing, but he cannot be treated with hostility so long as he occupies his place peacefully. This is not the right of a *guest*, on the basis of which one can make a claim (which would require a particular friendly agreement [*wohltätiger Vertrag*] to be made a member of the household for a certain time) but a right of *visitation* [Besuchsrecht], to which all men are entitled, to offer themselves in society [*Gesellschaft*] by virtue of the right of communal possession of the surface of the earth, on which, since it is a spherical surface, they cannot disperse over infinitely [*ins Unendliche*] but must finally [*endlich*] put up with one another beside one another.
> [8: 357–358]

The subordination of benevolence to right, on which the affirmative version of the "transcendental principle of public right" will later turn, marks the difference between the claims of guests and those of "visitors." In the former case (i.e., that of "philanthropic hospitality"), a specific contract or agreement is required; visitors, on the other hand, have rights stemming from our common occupancy of the earth.

The earth affects prospects for hospitality however, in two opposing ways. Global intercourse also furnishes means for the enslavement and plundering of travelers [*Besucher*], in opposition to men's natural right (described above) to attempt [*versuchen*] intercourse with the older inhabitants of a place. Still, Kant claims, such intercourse at least makes it possible for peoples of the various continents to enter into peaceful relations "that eventually become publicly lawful," bringing the human species "ever closer to a cosmopolitan constitution"—or would, but for the inhospitable behavior [*inhospitale Betragen*] of the civilized, and, especially, the commercial [*handeltreibenden*] states of Europe [*unsere Welttheil*] toward the inhabitants of other continents. Comparison of such behavior to the mutual accommodation just described "stretches" the injustice perpetrated by our continent "to the point of horror" [*bis zum Erschrecken*]. This culminating breakdown of healthy communication [*mittheilen*] lies in treating entire continents [*Welttheilen*], and not just the inhabitable passages through and between them, as "belonging to no one," so that their inhabitants "count as nothing" [*rechnen sie fur nichts*] [8: 358–359]. (Kant is thus perhaps the first to both exemplify and criticize a standpoint for its "Eurocentrism.") The shift in the preponderance of power (from visited to visitors) brought about by "commerce-driving" states, in other words—a shift that brings down a whole litany [*Litanie*] of ills—also derails the hopeful sort of intercourse described immediately before.

In the face of this eventuality, Kant cites the resistance of newly wise non-European states, and (what is at once "most vexing" and "best from the view point of a moral judge") the fact that the worst abuses of the powerful (who "drink injustice like water") yield [*abwerfen*] no real profit [*Ertrag*], but only serve the "indirect and not very laudable purpose [*Absicht*]" of providing new human instruments for the expansion of wars in Europe [8: 359]. In its (partial) execution of the judgment of a higher (moral) court—a court that right, absent a world state, cannot supply—such futility of purpose must, it seems, substitute for Providence.

As such, however, we are also brought face to face with the ambiguity of an "opening" that is both "awful" and, potentially, the source of everything morally uplifting. For the *Ausschlag* by which evil eliminates itself in the long run—be the outcome happy or unhappy—is, from the perspective of the only viable court we can conceive of, entirely deserved. And yet, if man is born only to destroy himself (as hinted by the image of a *Kirchhof*—literally, a "church court"—in the absence of a court of justice or [*Gerichtshof*]), it "seems impossible to justify [*rechtfertigen*] by any kind of theodicy creation itself, namely, that such a corrupted race [*Schlag*] of being [as man] should ever have been created on earth." All that stands between us and such "inferences of despair" [*verzweifelten Folgerungen*]—inferences that both call upon and overturn the concept of an all-wise and all powerful judge, is, as he will later put it, the assumption that "principles of right are objectively real," i.e., "allow themselves to be executed [*sie lassen sich ausführen*]" [8: 380; cf. 356, 368, 386]. (The problem of juridical authority, which must combine legislation and execution without conflating them, repeats itself, and at the highest level.)

Article nine ends, however, on a more hopeful note: Community [*Gemeinschaft*] (narrow or wide [*engeren oder weiteren*]) among the peoples of the world has now come so far [*so weit gekommen ist*] that "a violation of right in one place on earth is in all places felt," i.e., to a condition in which all human beings and nations are virtually contiguous (in the manner of an organic body). What no international power exists to guarantee is now capable of being secured by individual states, whose own interest, for the first time, is immediately and palpably affected. On this basis Kant concludes:

> that the idea of cosmopolitan right [*Weltbürgerrechts*] is no fantastic and overstrained [*überspannte*] juridical way of representing [*Vorstellungsart des Rechts*], but a necessary supplementary addition [*Ergänzung*] to the unwritten codex of state, as much as international, right—right [leading] toward

public human rights in general and hence toward perpetual peace, to which, only on this condition, one may [*darf*] flatter oneself that one finds oneself drawing continually nearer. [8: 360]

The idea of *Weltbürgerrecht* justifies itself only as a necessary condition of hope (or "self-flattery," as hope is here unflatteringly [but honestly?] portrayed). At the same time, Kant prepares for the emergence, in the First Supplement "On the Guarantee of Perpetual Peace," of commerce (heretofore remarkable as the preeminent instrument of war) as the spiritual agency, or *Handelsgeist*, that "cannot stand together with war" [*mit dem Krieg nicht zusammen bestehen kann*] [8: 368]. Lest the idea's "executability" seem dependent on mere luck (of the sort Kant has just invoked and himself currently enjoys [8: 343]), this supplement aims to show that even absent such a formal league, nature "guarantees" a similar result by operation of men's inclinations. Kant's subsequent appeal, against the force of "commerce driving states," to a pacifying "commercial spirit" by which all peoples are eventually seized upon [*sich bemächtigen*], replaces "trieb" with "Geist." In other words, even nature's "guarantee" preserves *human* history in its irreducibility to a mere "mechanism" (cf. [8: 378]).[32]

Nature's "guarantee" contrasts with the *perpetuum mobile* described two years earlier as a "machine" that produces more evil human beings than it takes away.[33] Thanks to that guarantee, the propensity toward federation for the sake of war [cf. 7: 34n and note 18 above] is sufficiently outweighed, for all necessary practical purposes, by a countervailing substitute linked to the "spirit of commerce." Even if present fortune does not last:

> The *spirit of commerce* [Handelsgeist], which cannot stand together with war, sooner or later overpowers [*bemächtigt*] every people. Because, namely, of all the kinds of might [*Mächtigen*] (means [*Mitteln*]) that are ordered under the might of a state, the might of money may well be the most reliable, states see themselves compelled (albeit not by driving springs of morality) to further noble peace, and, whenever war threatens to break out anywhere in the world, to avoid war through mediation [*Vermittelungen*], just as if they stood in constant league for this; for great alliances for war can, in the nature of things, only very seldom be formed and even more seldom succeed [*glücken*]. In this way nature guarantees eternal peace through the mechanism of human inclination itself: albeit, not with sufficient security [*Sicherheit*] for theoretical prediction [*weissagen*], but enough to succeed from a practical point of view, making it a duty to work toward this (not chimerical) end. [8: 368]

This guarantee—a kind of "virtual" league of states that achieves the same effect by alternate political means—is insufficient, as Kant admits, for theoretical prediction. But it is enough for "practical purposes" and even in the absence of "good luck," to "make it a duty to work toward this (not chimerical) end" [8: 343, 368].

Kant, however, does not leave matters here. In Appendix One he points to the dilemma, even given nature's "guarantee," that is faced by a well-intentioned politician, who is caught between his duty to his fellow citizens and his duty to promote the general peace [8: 378].[34] Under such conditions, urges the "political moralist," rules of state prudence must prevail.

Kant's provisional solution is to put the "principle" before the "end," thus "leaving off" where the political moralist begins [8: 375]. The moral politician (as distinguished from the political moralist) will accordingly "make it his principle":

> that once defects are encountered in a state constitution or in international relations . . . a duty obtains, especially for heads of state, to be concerned with them [*dahin bedacht zu sein*], improving them as soon as possible so as to bring them into greater harmony with natural right . . . whatever the cost to their self-seeking. . . . [a duty] to take to heart [*innigste beiwohne*] the maxim of the necessity of such alteration so as to remain in a state of constant nearing to the end (of the best constitution according to laws of right). A state can already govern itself in a republican manner even though, by its present constitution, it possesses a despotic ruling might [*Herrschermacht*], until the people gradually becomes susceptible to influence of the mere idea of the authority [*Autorität*] of law (just as if it encompassed physical power [*Gewalt*]) and is thus found fit for its own lawgiving (which is originally grounded in right). [8: 372]

The problem as it is presents itself in a domestic context is easy enough to solve (as Windisch-Graetz had arguably already shown to Kant's satisfaction). A graver challenge, however, is posed by the relations among states. A state cannot be morally required to give up a despotic constitution, which is "stronger with respect to outer enemies," so long as it thereby risks being "immediately devoured [*verschlungen*] by others" [8: 373].

In addressing this challenge, Kant relies, once again, on the formal primacy of principle over end [8: 376–377]. Perpetual peace can be wished for either merely as a physical good (in which case the end is made primary) or as a state arising from the recognition of duty (in which case principle predominates).

To wish for peace in the former sense is to set oneself a "technical" problem whose solution is beset by uncertainty; to wish for it in the latter sense is to know "straight away" what one must do, with the additional, prudential "reminder" not to pursue it precipitously and with "violence" [*Gewalt*] but rather only as "favorable circumstances permit" [8: 378]. But precisely here lies the difficulty: how is one to judge in such matters without either (on the one hand) giving surreptitious primacy to the end or (on the other hand) doing less than "circumstances permit"? Kant's so-called "permissive laws of reason" that allow injustice to continue "either until everything has of itself become ripe" or almost so by peaceful means here offer no determinate guidance [8: 374n],[35] which would seemly require another principle to determine how such laws should be applied.[36]

The "transcendental principle of public right" that Kant "throws down" in Appendix Two speaks directly to this issue.[37] It is, he says, arrived at (as a "formula") by subtracting the entire "*matter*" of public right—e.g., from all empirically given relations, or the actual malevolence of human beings, which makes "coercion" necessary[38]—leaving behind the sheer "*form* of publicity" itself, which belongs to every claim to right, which can only be thought of as "publicly known" [8: 381].

The ensuing formula—"all actions relating to the rights of others are wrong if their maxim is incompatible with publicity"—furnishes a negative criterion by which political maxims may be "easily" assessed for their compatibility with a universal state of justice. For the divulgence of an unjust criterion would give rise to general resistance that is foreseeable *a priori* [8: 381].[39] A ruler who publicly announced his intention to rule despotically might well face insurmountable obstacles to carrying out his aim.

That criterion, however, is not foolproof: should a party be "sufficiently powerful" it could achieve its ends in any case. Only within a federation of states of the sort earlier described does the criterion hold universally [8: 383]. Accordingly, as Kant strikingly concludes, it is *only* within such a federation that the harmony of politics and morals is possible. It follows that "all state prudence" has for a "rightful basis" the "establishment [of such a federation] in its greatest possible circumference," lacking which end "all its cleverness is un-wisdom and disguised injustice" [8: 386]. The moral politician should thus make it his or her rule to promote such a federation to the extent that he or she is able.

Even *that* rule, however, does not suffice to formally describe the transcendental conditions of public (international) right. Political moralism in its "forked-tonguedness" [*Zweizüngigheit*] has a final ruse: namely, to deny right in the name of an alleged benevolence (as with those who govern "paternalistically.") Such rulers use the appearance of duty to put the end of government (i.e., the public happiness) before principle (i.e., upholding the rights of citizens). Philosophers could easily thwart that trick, did rulers "dare" [*wagen*] to let them publicize, a wager however that—as Kant now knows only too well—cannot always be counted on.

Seizing upon an opportunity, then, Kant "throws down" [*schlage . . . vor*] another "transcendental principle of public right"—this one affirmative: "all maxims that *need* publicity in order not to fail in their end harmonize with right and politics combined" [8: 386]. Such a maxim makes "removal of all distrust toward maxims of politics" a formal condition of any other goal that may be sought politically. If I need to let you know what I am thinking to achieve my goal, you have no reason to distrust me, for I must be honest out of prudence.

At just this moment, however, Kant breaks off, leaving the further "execution" [*Ausführung*] and "discussion" [*Erörterung*] of that principle to "another occasion" (and thus practices the permissive wisdom of "deferral" that, as we might be led to think, he has been preaching) [8: 386; compare 378]. His answer to the challenge he had posed in *Religion* proves, to this extent, abortive.

To summarize the difficulty that, as I see it, prompts this postponement: Kant seeks a rule that can serve as the formal basis for an "establishment" [*Stiftung*] that can be pursued without putting end before principle (that is to say, without proceeding "heteronomously"). This rule proves to be equivalent to the duty to promote a free federation of states. But Kant cannot (yet) show by what rule or principle that duty can be carried out effectively. Despite his earlier appeal to the *Grenzgott*[40] of morality [8: 370], he does not here establish in a manner sufficient, as Kant will later put it, "for the most strenuous theory," that the cleverness of the serpent and the innocence of the dove can in fact be combined. For this reason perhaps, the conclusion of *Toward Perpetual Peace* is surprisingly tentative:

> If there is a duty, and also a well-grounded hope, to make a condition of public right actual, even if only by an endlessly progressing growing closer, then *Perpetual Peace*, that follows upon what has up to now falsely been called "peace treaties" [*Friedenschlüsse*] (which are properly cessations of war [*Wassenstillstände*]), is no empty idea but a task that, gradually solved, constantly nears its goal (because the time in which similar progress occurs hopefully becomes ever shorter). [8: 386]

In sum: Both the argument of Kant's essay and its tone—from the gallows-humor of its title to its ironic comparison to their advantage of cannibals to falsely "enlightened" European statesmen—conveys the urgency of a race against time. Nothing is guaranteed except the sheer executability of the idea—and a related duty to make peace real, and even this is left in question at the essay's closing, which states that duty only conditionally [8: 386].[41] Kant's assertion of the barest preponderance of hope over despair [8: 380] seems calculated for maximum rhetorical effect; catastrophe, by implication, is to be averted only if we, his readers (and especially heads of state), do everything we can, i.e., act *now*.[42]

Kant's remedy for the "vices of civilization" works, however, only by extending the "step" out of a state of nature over an indefinite, and perhaps infinite, expanse of time (as is already suggested by the word "zur" in the work's title).[43] A state of peace cannot be conclusively established, but only, at best, continually approached as "occasion" may permit, and with "outbreak of war" an ever-present (if receding) threat [8: 357; cf. 8: 349]. Kant's projected "federation (either actual or virtual) checks the abysmal machinery of war debt that *Toward Perpetual Peace* earlier warns of.[44] Like a (Ponzi) scheme of international credit, international right rests upon hope that remains "well-grounded" only by deferring to the indefinite future (though not *ad calendas graecus*)[45] an ultimate day of (moral) reckoning.[46] The preliminary and definitive articles of a perpetual peace set out (or "publicize" from a "higher" anthropological standpoint [8: 374]) formal conditions of such a state of growing trust. (Hence, the mental reservation that is ruled out in article one is brought back for a final swipe against all trust-destroying casuistry [8: 385; compare 8: 344, 378].) Only within the framework thus established (i.e., only within the boundaries of federation of republics [or states that are at least governed "in a republican manner"]) can the "transcendental principle of right" be acted on consistently. Only thus can justice and the nature of man be brought into effective harmony, allowing for "the true politics" [*Die wahre Politik*], whose "proper task" is "making the public [*Publicums*] satisfied with its condition" [8: 380, 386].[47] The true politics conforms to "the public's universal end (happiness)" precisely by not aiming at it directly. Kant's parenthetical eclipse of "happiness" reminds us, however, that the decisive matter (whether or not there will come about a [moral] transformation of a people's way of thinking) remains undetermined. The international public exists in the fragile space in which philosophers are secretly allowed to "publicize" their maxims, i.e., via an authority to which those "having might" cannot honorably admit, as *Toward Perpetual Peace* also insists. What that work does *not* show is by what rule a "moral politician" is to act in the meantime. Between the articles of a peace treaty and the "transcendental principle of public right" those articles aim to actualize lies a gap that no (known) principle can bridge. Given this gap, prospects for human progress still remain unsettled.

2. From "Transcendental Principles of Public Right" to a "Metaphysics of Morals"

In postponing further treatment of his transcendental principle of public right, Kant may have had in mind an essay already completed in draft form. A letter to Carl Friedrich Stäudlin dated December 1794, looking forward to better days ahead politically, specifically mentions such a work. After suggesting George III as a potential "shield," Kant claims an essay called "the Conflict of the Faculties," which has been "ready for some time." The essay interests Kant:

> not only because it sheds light on the right of the learned professions to submit all matters of state religion to the *theological* faculty, arguing that the state has an interest in granting this permission;.... it also argues for the right of the *philosophical* faculty to sit in opposition.... Even though this essay is properly concerned merely with *publicity* and not theology [*bloss publicistisch und nicht theologisch ist*] (principles of right concerning religion and the church)... I have had to give some examples... to make clear why a sect is by its nature unfit to become an established religion [*Landesreligion*].... But I am afraid... that the censor—who is now very powerful in this locale—may... denounce these things. Therefore I have decided to refrain from publishing this work for now in the hope that the approaching peace [of Basel] may also bring with it greater freedom for innocent [*unschuldiger*] judgments. [11: 533–534]

Given the stress *Toward Perpetual Peace* had placed on religious sects as a natural cause of division among nations [8: 367], the connection with "publicity" leaps out: Was Kant's temporarily withheld essay on the conflict of the faculties the hoped-for vehicle for an extended commentary on the execution of the aforementioned transcendental principle?

In fact, the published version of *The Conflict of the Faculties* (which did not appear until 1797, a year after the death of Frederick William II) contained an additional section devoted to the subject of public law. As we will see in Chapter 8, that section, which takes up the question of human progress "anew," places Kant's anthropologically based hope on a more theoretically "stringent" foundation than he saw fit to offer in 1795. For related reasons, perhaps, transcendental principles of public right receive no explicit mention in either *The Conflict of the Faculties* or *The Metaphysics of Morals* (which appeared the same year) or any of his other published writings.

For its part, *The Metaphysics of Morals* treats "international right" from the standpoint of the "state of nature" in which states actually reside, albeit in a way that now includes a modified version of what he earlier called the sixth preliminary article of perpetual peace.[48] It also breaks with *Perpetual Peace* in basing the need for juridical coercion on grounds that entirely abstract from the fact of human malevolence [cf 8: 381]. Attentiveness to these and related changes, as I hope to show, not only helps one better understand Kant's own "impure ethics" by observing them in action;[49] it also sheds light on whether and in what way autonomy (which looks to the form of willing) and prudence (which looks to the end) can finally be reconciled.

3. *The Metaphysics of Morals: Völkerrecht* and the State of Nature

The state of nature from which *The Metaphysics of Morals* takes its initial bearings is discussed most fully in section #44 (on the "idea of a [not-rightful] state"). Kant's primary intention in section #44 is to show that in such a state of nature the concept of right cannot be actualized, because any attempt to do so would itself be contrary to right—a consideration that makes entrance into civil society morally, and not merely prudentially, necessary.[50]

In thus insisting that we are impelled by duty—not just by self-interested prudence—to enter civil society, Kant breaks with an earlier liberal tradition, which tended to ground entrance into the civil compact (though not subsequent allegiance to it) on rational self-interest alone. This change has important consequences for Kant's political theory—above all, an ennobling moralization of liberal conceptions of right.[51] Hereafter, securing rights to life and property becomes a cause for which one might reasonably be called upon to sacrifice one's life and property—e.g., to fight a war (like the U.S. Civil War) devoted, in part, to rescuing other human beings from slavery. A secondary implication for liberal theory of Kant's argument as to the duty to enter civil society is what might be called the "collectivization" of the individual right to life and property—i.e., an admission that all rights ultimately rest, conceptually and practically, on the idea of a communal, or collective "general will" formed by reciprocal recognition of the rights of each. The related admission that we are "all in it together" qualifies, for the political tradition stemming from Kant, the insistent individualism to which liberal politics in its more Whiggish forms often succumbs.

Kant's treatment of individual right introduces into the liberal tradition stemming from Hobbes and Locke (along with Hume) a distinctly Rousseauian element that elevates freedom from the largely instrumental status to which earlier contributors to that tradition tend to confine it. Already in early notes that reflect his reading of Rousseau, Kant, as we have seen, claims that (external) freedom is a greater good than life itself [20: 73]. This insistence on the intrinsic value of independence from the arbitrary will of others helps shape Kant's argument for the moral necessity of civil society.[52]

How, then, does Kant justify the claim that we are obliged to enter civil society? That obligation, along with a related authorization to compel others also to do so, is predicated on a prior contingent condition: the unavoidability of social contact. The first duty of right is to flee others if one can [6: 236–237].

This prior duty is an anomaly to be explained for anyone who tries to rest Kant's theory of right primarily upon teleological considerations, such as the development of men's natural and spiritual talents. The radical dispersal of the species for which the duty of right first calls would obviously pose an almost insuperable obstacle to such development. On what, then, does that prior duty rest?

Kant's full argument emerges most clearly in the opening sections of *The Metaphysics of Morals*, Part Two, devoted to the establishment of "public right" (section 44). To state the argument simply: Prior to the establishment of civil society, any attempt to defend one's property coercively—however well grounded one's claim may be in a "provisional" sense—constitutes an implicit injury to the fundamental right of others to do "what seems right and just to them" and not be dependent in this on the arbitrary will of someone else.[53] As a result, any attempt to realize private right is, as it were, self-canceling: I cannot defend my property—even property that is duly mine in a "provisional" sense[54]—without doing violence to the right of others to act as seems just and good to them. But desisting from defending my property is also morally impermissible: I cannot choose *not* to defend my property (even that acquired only provisionally) without violating another duty—that toward the right of humanity in my own person [6: 240].⁵⁵ Hence, in a state of nature in which people necessarily come into contact with one another, the concept of right is "unexecutable." And yet, as Kant repeatedly insists, the concept of right "cannot be given up" [8: 376n; 7: 87n].

There are only two ways out of this aporetic situation—a sort of juridical paralysis in which every possible deed (including doing nothing) necessarily fails to conform to the concept of right, a concept I cannot renounce. Either I can flee contact with others (the non-coercive, and hence juridically preferable option), or I can join with others, if necessary by force, in establishing a civil society in which the violence of the state of nature is replaced by a judge authorized to impute with "rightful force" [cf. 6: 226–227]. Formation of a state can thus be understood as a kind of "sublimation" of *Gewalt* (to use Kant's own expression [as in "sublimiren" {6: 355}]),⁵⁶ through which violence [*Gewalt*] becomes legitimate authority [*Gewalt*]. That Kant uses the same term for both states is itself significant, for it shows that the very meaning of the word turns on the presence or absence of a power competent, owing to the (ideal) consent of all, to combine right and force, i.e., to render right "executable."

To grasp the details of Kant's argument, it will be helpful to examine the relevant passage in full:

> It is not something *experiential* [*etwa die Erfahrung*], through which we are taught human beings' maxim of violent activity [*Gewaltthätigkeit*] and their malevolence [*Bösartigkeit*] in feuding with one another [*einander zu befehden*] before there appears an external lawgiving that has might [*eine äußere machthabende Gesetzgebung*];⁵⁷ hence, it is not something *factual/pertaining to a deed* [*etwa ein* Factum]⁵⁸ that makes public lawful compulsion necessary. On the contrary, one may think human beings to be as good-natured [*gutartig*] and right-loving as one likes; it still lies *a priori* in the rational idea of such a (not-rightful) state [*der Vernunftidee eines solchen (nicht-rechtlichen) Zustandes*] that, before a publicly lawful state is erected [*errichtet*] individual human beings, peoples and states can never be secure against violent activity from one another, and this, indeed, from each individual's own right to do *what strikes him* [*dünkt*] *as right and good* without his depending in this on the opinion of another; so that unless one wishes to renounce [*entsagen*] all concepts of right, the first principle upon which one is obliged to resolve is: one must leave the state of nature, in which each follows his own judgment [*Kopfe*], and unite oneself with all others (with whom one cannot avoid interacting), subject oneself to a public, lawful external compulsion, and hence enter a state in which what is to be recognized as *one's own* is *lawfully*

determined and *distributed* to one by a sufficient *might* (which is not one's own but external)—that is to say, one should before all *things* enter into a civil state/condition.

It is true that the state of nature need not perforce be a *state of injustice*:

> [*Ungerechtigkeit*] (*iniustus*), dealing with one another only in terms of the sheer amount of one's violent force [*Gewalt*], but it is a *state lacking in justice/ right* [*Rechtlosigkeit*] *(status iustitia vacuus)*, where, when *right is conflictual (ius controversum)*, there is no competent *judge* [*Richter*] to render a verdict/ speak out with rightful force [*rechtskräftig den Ausspruch zu thun*]. Hence, each may drive the others with violence/force [*Gewalt*] to enter into a rightful condition. For although each can acquire something external *according to his own concepts of right*, either through power [*Bemächtigung*] or contract, this acquisition is only *provisional* so long as it still lacks the sanction of a public law, because it is not determined through any public (distributive) justice [*Gerechtigkeit*], nor secured through an authority [*Gewalt*] executing [*ausübende*] this right. [6: 312]

Be human beings ever so "benign and right-loving," the right of each to do what "*seems right and good to him*"[59] conflicts—should one attempt to actualize this right—with that of all the rest.[60] Prior to the existence of a tribunal that can judge with "force of right," no one can attempt to actualize a right without doing violence to right itself; prior to such a union of force and right no one can assert a right without—performatively, as it were—denying it.[61]

The main point is this: civil society is instituted not only to protect men's life and property but also (and primarily) our freedom from subjection to the arbitrary will of our juridical (and moral) equals.[62] The primary right is the right to be recognized by others as "one's own master" [6: 237–238; 8: 295].[63] As we have seen, however, there is an exception to this right not to be subject to the coercive authority of other individual wills. Each individual in the state of nature, if he or she wishes to act consistently (and hence reasonably)[64] on the concept of right that he or she "cannot give up [*entschlagen*]" [8: 376n],[65] is presented with a choice: He or she must flee others if he or she can—or, if not, induce others, if necessary by force, to enter into a civil arrangement in which one overarching party is collectively authorized to judge and enforce the rights of all. Only where there is some sort of "law and order" does the concept of right cease to be self-canceling in practice.[66]

Kant draws explicit attention to that self-canceling feature of the state of nature by referring to it as a state "lacking in" or "empty" of right or justice

("[*Rechtlosigkeit*] [*status iustitia vacuus*]"). The state of nature is "empty" of right because it lacks a public judge (uniquely) "competent" (by virtue of the [ideal] consent of all) to lend right external (potentially punitive) force and thereby make it "actual" or effective in the external world.[67] Kant draws similar attention to the juridically aporetic character of the state of nature (in which we can neither do right nor give up on it) by insisting that we must enter civil society "before all *things*." [6:313]

At its most consistent and complete, execution of the concept of right requires a republican constitution that gives citizens control, through their elected representatives, over the laws that bind them. And, even more, it requires a civic culture that encourages individual independence, both intellectual and economic, without which the external forms of civic freedom and equality are, according to Kant, illusory at best.[68] It is only from the habit of living under such laws that one is entitled to anticipate a "transformation in the people's way of thinking" (a transformation, that is to say, from fidelity to the laws out of self-interest, to fidelity out of respect for law as such).[69] Rights as *lived* thus span a gamut between the minimum—the barest and most primitive sorts of "law and order"—and a "sublime" maximum that Kant favorably compares to Plato's ideal republic.[70] The point of decent politics is to approach that maximum as best we can without doing violence to the civic condition itself.[71]

The analogy between the individual and international state of nature is imperfect, however, in a decisive sense: The latter condition is not, strictly speaking, a "status justicia vacuus," i.e., "empty of right" [8: 355]. Each state is the realization, however imperfect, of the right of its own members, whose claims it at least partially "executes"—i.e., gives outward, reciprocally determinate force. The obligation to leave the international state of nature is thus qualified by the prior obligation of states to uphold the rights of their own citizens. States, as Kant puts it in *Toward Perpetual Peace*, have "outgrown" the status that makes individuals in a state of nature liable to outer compulsion. States are nothing (so far as permitting their members to actualize their rights is concerned) if they are not sovereign. Hence, they cannot be externally forced to submit themselves to a higher sovereign power [*Gewalt*] [8: 356].[72] In *Toward Perpetual Peace*, as we have seen, Kant holds out a tentative hope that the peoples of the world may one day voluntarily consent to join a world republic (or state of nations)—i.e., give up "their idea of international right" (or "right among states") entirely [8: 357];[73] but this goal is as far removed from everyday reality as is the full instantiation of an "ethical commonwealth" (or spiritual union of humanity) that would be needed to accomplish such a feat.[74] Such a "state of nations" could not be a "state of states," given Kant's understanding of states as exercising sovereign authority over their members, and would hence be predicated on the disappearance of international right, strictly speaking.

But if a sovereign juridical community of nations precludes the existence of individual sovereign states, how is a rightful relation among states (or "international right," strictly speaking) even to be thought?[75] In the case of the individual state of nature, right, though unrealizable in practice, at least remained conceptually coherent. In the case of the international relations, the very concept of a rightful (i.e., reciprocally lawful) condition verges on "unthinkability" [8: 357] given the conceptual connection between the right of a state and permission to go to war:

> In the state of nature among states the right to war (to hostilities) is the permitted way [*Art*] in which a state pursues its right, through its own force [*Gewalt*] against another state, when it believes itself injured; for this cannot happen through [judicial] process (the only way conflicts are settled in a rightful condition). [6: 346]

Still, despite the right of each state to be judge in its own case, the judicial framework implicit in the concept of a "right" allows a line to be drawn between an international state of nature and outright anarchy (a line that *Toward Perpetual Peace* had not yet clearly articulated). The right of war that follows, in a state of nature, from the very concept of a nation-state (formed to preserve the rights of citizens from internal and external injury) has predetermined limits. A state that claims permission to go to war must at least think itself actually or potentially injured by another. The state's right of war does not imply a freestanding right of conquest. No state is entitled to claim more for itself (the right to protect itself from perceived injury) than it allows to others. It may violently dispute another's claim to goods or territory, but it may not seek to punish, or, by the same token, fail to renounce a state of peace (that is, by openly declaring war) as a prelude (or at least accompaniment) to hostility [6: 346]. In short, in place of the juridical *aporia* that made immediate exit from the individual state of nature (i.e., "before all things") morally mandatory in an state of nature among *individuals*, Kant substitutes a permissive "right of war" that turns on the distinction between "active" hostility, which is contrary to the concept of right, and what one might call "neutral" or "reactive" hostility, which is in harmony with it, at least potentially.

Concerning the so-called "right to war" (*ius ad bellum*), for example, the difference between a permitted and a forbidden decision to go to war principally depends on whether or not one acknowledges the right of one's adversary to defend itself—i.e., whether or not one wrongly assumes the juridical prerogatives of sovereignty (as distinguished from brute force [*Gewalt*]). In a similar vein, right *after* war (*ius post bellum*) stipulates that terms be dictated solely on the basis of superior force [*Gewalt*] rather than right arising from pretended moral injury. The victor, for example, "cannot demand compensation for the costs of war, for he would then have to accuse his opponent of conducting an unjust war" (which would itself be contrary to right). [6: 348]. In short: Right *to* and *after* war mainly derives from the absence of authority, on the part of states, to judge each other punitively and with "rightful force"[76] as rulers are authorized to judge and punish their own citizens.[77] This stricture against coercive moral condemnation secures the conceptual distinction between active hostility, which is contrary to right, and the neutral or passive hostility that permissibly anticipates and/or responds to it.

Right *in* war, according to Kant, poses the gravest difficulty for "making a concept of international right," or "thinking it without self-contradiction," precisely because this distinction between active and neutral hostility does not suffice to determine the limits of what a state may and may not do while striving to defend itself by force.[78] The "concept of the right of a state"—even one that claims no wrongful moral privilege (e.g., that acknowledges the right of others to attempt to defend themselves)—is in itself consistent, for example, with an effort to obtain security by subjecting or exterminating others. Such "means of necessity [*Nothmittel*] [as subjugation or annihilation of a people as a people] for the sake of achieving a condition of peace does not in itself contradict the right of a state" [6: 347]. The permissible goal of self-protection—apart from any wrongful claim to act as moral judge—gives states a (rational) incentive to wish to destroy or dominate the rest. The right of a state to defend itself against an "unjust enemy" is, as Kant insists, "limitless" in both quantity and degree [6: 349]. Thus, if international right is even to be thinkable, what is permissible in war must be further explicated. It must include a duty to recognize, not only the right of others to *attempt* to defend themselves, but also their right to coexist by keeping what is theirs: "the idea of the right of nations" necessarily involves "the concept of antagonism according to principles of outer freedom," permitting "preservation of what belongs to one but not acquisition of what belongs to others" [6: 347].

But how is such a distinction meaningfully expressed in time of war, when each side is properly the judge in its own case? The problem calls to mind, once again, Kant's treatment, in *Religion,* of the competitive dilemma that allows the "vices of culture and civilization" to take root [6: 27].[79] In *Toward Perpetual Peace* Kant ultimately relied upon the "spirit of commerce" to sustain the fragile "thinkability" of international right [8: 368]. In *The Metaphysics of Morals,* by way of contrast, Kant's solution to the above dilemma turns on the distinction between "honorable" stratagems that are consistent, if universalized, with the possibility of future mutual trust, and "dishonorable" stratagems that if universalized would destroy it. The distinction between "honorable" and "dishonorable" means of war reconciles the savage's warlike, yet noble, preference for freedom with the ignoble, yet in its own way more reasonable, calculation of the "civilized," who prefer to fight their duels by proxy. On the basis of this distinction, Kant can finally assert, as we shall see, that the national right of self-defense, though "limitless" in quantity and degree, is reciprocally "limited" in *quality* [6: 349].[80]

This new tack, I would suggest, best explains the apparent disagreement between the two works as to the permissibility of preemptive war and interference in the internal workings of another state.

Concerning the first: The *Metaphysics of Morals,* as we just have seen, permits attacks against merely threatened harm. The relevant passage is worth quoting here in full:

> In the natural condition of states the *right to war* (to hostilities) is the permitted way by which a state pursues its right against another state: namely, by its own *force* [Gewalt], when it believes itself injured by it; for this cannot happen in a state of nature by legal process [*Proceß*] (through which alone disputes are settled in a rightful condition). In addition to active violations (first aggression, which is distinguished from first hostility), there is the *threat* of it. This includes another state's being the first to undertake *preparations,* upon which is based the right of prevention (*ius preventionis*), or even merely another's state's fearful increase in *might* [Macht] (through acquisition of territory) (*potentia tremenda*). This is a wrong to the less mighty merely by the *condition,* before any deed, of the mightier, and in a state of nature an attack by the former is indeed [*allerdings*] rightful. Upon this is also based the right to a balance of power [*Gleichgewicht*] among all actively contiguous states. [6: 346]

By way of contrast, *Toward Perpetual Peace* identified a maxim of preventive war with the notorious "political moralist," who uses morality for political ends [8: 379, 384]:

> If a neighboring power [*Macht*] that has grown to fearful size [*potentia tremenda*] arouses anxiety, may one assume that because it *can* subjugate others it *will* to do so, and does this give the lesser powers the right to attack it (in unison) even without prior injury? A state that was willing to have such an affirmative maxim *made out loud* [verlautbaren] would thereby only make the anticipated evil quicker and more certain. Hence this maxim of state prudence, publicly declared, necessarily makes idle its own purpose, and is therefore unjust.

In *Toward Perpetual Peace* Kant had urged that the transcendental formula of public right (which forbids preemptive war) applies *only* among members of an "enduring free federalism" where *alone* "international right can be spoken of." In *The Metaphysics of Morals* he takes a more capacious view of the law of nations, which, as he now claims, permits preemptive action of the sort just described. Thanks, in part, to Kant's new use of the distinction between "honorable and dishonorable stratagems," the "right of nations" can now be "spoken of" beyond the boundaries of the federation of republics (and their like) to which his earlier essay had explicitly confined it (as per preliminary article six).[81]

What other obligatory limits, if any, also apply outside the boundaries of a (virtual) free and enduring federation of republics (or their like)?[82] As we have seen, the right of states to defend themselves is limited in terms of quality. Specifically, states must not unjustly arrogate to themselves the status of an imputing judge *vis-à-vis* other states or otherwise engage in dishonorable stratagems that threaten the possibility of future mutual trust.

Have states no honorable special recourse, then, against those that themselves violate such strictures? Has "unjust enemy," in short, any effectual meaning, or is it, as he first suggests, altogether "pleonistic," given that each state is judge in its own case? [8: 349]. His definitive answer is as follows:

> What is an *unjust enemy* in terms of the concepts of the right of nations, in which—as is the case in a state of nature generally—each state is judge in its own case? It is an enemy whose publicly expressed will (by word or deed) reveals a maxim that, were it made into a universal rule, would make a peaceful condition among nations impossible, and instead eternalize a state of nature. *Violation of public contracts is an expression of this sort, which can be assumed to touch upon the matters of all nations, whose freedom is thereby threatened, and who are thereby called upon to unite against such mischief and take away the state's power to commit it.* To be sure, they cannot do so by *dividing up its territory,* so as to make the state disappear, so to speak, from the earth. That would constitute an injustice against the people, which cannot lose its

> original right to bind itself into a commonwealth. *But they can do so by requiring a people to accept a new constitution which is naturally less favorable to war.* [6: 349; emphasis added]

We may here leave aside the interesting implications of the above for the potential justice (if not prudence) of attempts at coercive regime-change (such as that undertaken in Iraq by the U.S.-led "coalition of the willing"), given a flagrant abuse, on the part of the offending party, of the conditions of international trust. The important point, for present purposes, is the implied solution to the political problem of uniting dove and serpent [8: 380]. Feuding parties do no injury to one another "given their mutual intention [*Vorsatz*] to be and remain in a condition of lawless freedom"; for "what is valid for one is valid for the other, as if by mutual agreement." In general, however, "they do injustice to the highest degree in wishing [*wollen*] to be and remain in such a condition" [6: 307–308; cf. 8: 380].

It is this wish and this intention, then—an internal disposition made manifest in external acts—that distinguishes active hostility (which is not juridically permitted) from a merely regrettable resort to force [6: 307–308n]. An honorable state will thus not indicate, by word or deed, an underlying maxim of contempt for promise-keeping. Nor will it resort to other measures (such as assassination, or direct and treacherous attacks upon civilians) that threaten the fragile bond of trust absent which no release from such a state is possible in principle. Resort to such measures exceeds the means that, *in extremis,* states are conceptually and morally permitted; for their use reveals that a state does not merely resort to war as a regrettable necessity but that it prefers domination to reciprocal security.

Hence, the sole named exception to the general rule against coercive action to bring states into federative union involves coercion of a state that breaks "public" faith.[83] "Violation of public contracts is an expression" (to return to the passage earlier quoted):

> which can be assumed to touch upon the matters of all nations, whose freedom is thereby threatened, and who are thereby called upon to unite against such mischief and take away the state's power to commit it. . . . They can do so by requiring a people to accept a new [republican] constitution which is naturally less favorable to war.

Coercive regime change of this sort would be unnecessary within a federation of republics (of the sort envisioned in *Toward Perpetual Peace*), and both impermissible and inadvisable against non-republics open to reform. But it is evidently allowed against rulers and governments who show by their own deeds that they would not leave the state of nature even if they could—i.e., whose "malevolence," which "can be seen," as Kant earlier put it, "at its most unconcealed in the free relation of nations" [8: 355], verges on incurable. Presumably, in such a case a people has no reasonable hope of lawfully realizing its rights through internal reform, and the general immunity of states from interference in their internal affairs (on grounds that they have "outgrown" susceptibility to being coerced by others) no longer holds. Still, it is a testament to hope that violations of the "public" trust can be spoken of at all.

4. Conclusion

Kant's thinking on international right opens up a space, on which recent U.S. administrations have seized, allowing for a (new) distinction between states that do and those that don't count as full-fledged members of the community of nations. The latter ("failed" and "rogue") states do not deserve and need not receive the normal prerogatives of sovereignty to which members "in good standing" of the community of nations (as we are accustomed to saying) are generally entitled. In making indirect, and perhaps unwitting, use of Kant's construction, the current U.S. administration might have profitably noted its intrinsically precarious character, as dependent upon nations' sense of honor as upon their narrow apprehension of self-interest.

In failing to provide the moral politician with a determinate rule of action, *Toward Perpetual Peace* falls short of showing how prudence and morality can indeed be united. Early drafts of Part Two of *The Conflict of the Faculties* ("A newly Renewed Question: Whether the Human Race Is Constantly Progressing Toward the Better") suggest that Kant may have at one point been contemplating a "constitutive" *a priori* principle of judgment to help remedy that defect. The *published* version of Part Two, which appeared two years later, eschews any such principle. What it *does* offer is a new argument for the moral sufficiency of human nature, based on a new appraisal of the French Revolution and its significance for human prospects generally. When Kant's long-awaited "metaphysics of morals" finally appears (in 1797), the "transcendental principle of public right" has been replaced by a newly formulated account of international "honor." Was that formula consistently adopted—as Kant's revised philosophic anthropology gives us new reason to hope—the progress that *Toward Perpetual Peace* had sought would indeed occur. To better understand the ground and implications of that hope, we turn, finally, to the *Conflict of the Faculties,* Parts One and Two.

7

Kant as Educator:
The Conflict of the Faculties, Part One

Lewis White Beck states the problem of Kantian education in its clearest and starkest form when he says that Kant's "strict moral philosophy has, and can have, no place for moral education."[1] This is so, not only owing to difficulties with which moral philosophy has struggled ever since Socrates famously asked whether virtue can be taught. It is also and especially the case because the foundation of virtue for Kant is based uncompromisingly on freedom understood as accountability [*Zurechtnungsfähigkeit*], or the responsibility of a moral person for deeds that are, as such, "imputable" to him. Our knowledge that we are free comes to us via "conscience"—that fundamental "factum" or "deed" of reason that commands obedience to the moral law, and in so doing "announces" to us that we *can* do what we *ought* to do.[2] Two difficulties for moral education here arise: On the one hand, the very possibility of external helps or hindrances to moral goodness seems to diminish the individual's own responsibility for his or her state of character. On the other hand, and on the assumption that we take full responsibility for our own moral improvement (or lack thereof), it is hard to see how such improvements can come about, given that in order to do so, as it seems, we would already have to be the improved beings we aspire to become. Difficulties of this sort led Kant to suggest that such improvement must ultimately be conceived as kind of noumenal or "intelligible" conversion, involving something like a "new creation."[3]

There is yet another problem, suggested by the reflection on Rousseau cited above: namely, how—assuming that moral education is possible—one can sacrifice oneself to it (as does the tutor in *Emile*) without committing an injustice to oneself. Kant's tentative early answer, as we have seen, relies on sheer numbers to offset the otherwise disturbing consideration to which *Emile* itself gives rise and which presumably explains the fact that Rousseau himself refused to conduct his own life as does his tutor—the consideration, in other words, that makes *Emile* less a prescription for universal reform than a testament to its impossibility.[4]

Despite these difficulties, Kant devoted his life to education—to which instruction in morality was central—first as a house tutor, and then, for more than forty years, as a private docent and professor at the University of Königsberg, where he eventually rose to the position of Rector. It is therefore likely that Kant's treatment of the university may contain important clues, not only to his understanding of education (and its limits) but also to the meaning and importance that he placed upon his own activity as educator.

Kant takes up the university explicitly in *The Conflict of the Faculties*, Part One (On the Conflict between the Faculties of Theology and Philosophy). Although an early draft was evidently ready as early as 1792, publication was delayed for reasons that have already been touched on. When circumstances improved with the death of Frederick William II in 1797, Kant rushed a revised version into print, despite his earlier promise to the king that he would henceforth desist from publishing on religious matters. (Kant excused himself by arguing that the agreement had applied only to Frederick himself, whose death absolved Kant from his former promise.) Two additional Parts (nominally devoted, at least, to the two other "higher" faculties of law and medicine, respectively) were also added.

1. The "Idea" of the University

Kant's only extended discussion of the university begins, strikingly enough, with the image of a factory geared toward mass production: "it was no bad whim [*Einfall*] of him who first seized [*faßte*] the thought and proposed its public carrying out, to handle the entire notion/content of learning . . . so to speak by *mass production* [fabrikmäßig]" [7: 17]. Organized, in the manner of factories, by a "division of labor" corresponding to the various branches of the sciences, the university is a "kind of commonwealth" made up of "public teachers" or "trustees." That "only scholars can judge scholars as such" confers upon the university its autonomy [*ihre Autonomie*] to perform, through its faculties [*Vermögen*], certain (still unnamed) tasks, to admit new students, and to confer by its own power [*Macht*] the rank of doctor as a status "universally recognized." The university may thus be thought of as a workshop whose main business is the production of new workers: a body of doctors for the appointment/ begetting of doctors [*"(doctoren) zu creiren"*]. The university, so understood is a self-replicating (or living) body, albeit one that also creates "unincorporated" scholars, who either labor [*arbeiten*] in workplaces [*Werkstätten*] (called academies) or busy themselves as amateurs [7: 18].

That the public standing of the scholar continues to express itself in terms of the Latin "doctor" (which literally means "teacher") signals both the (hidden) wisdom harbored within traditional institutions and their potential for abuse: The title of "dean" [*Decan*] descends (as Kant, with a pedantic flourish, notes) from astrology by way of warfare. We should be especially wary, in the university as elsewhere, of the ever-present desire of human beings (not least in Germany) to adorn themselves with titles [7: 18n].

But Latin usage also points to the university's ecclesiastical roots, which elevates (in descending order) theology, jurisprudence, and medicine above the "lower" faculty of philosophy. The conflict between theology and philosophy, as we are soon to learn, is the "exemplar" of the conflict of the faculties as such. Here, Kant only roughly sketches out his central strategy: to play upon the government's desire to rule, in order to bolster the independence of the scholarly community from religious censorship. The status of the people (whom the government wishes to influence) as "incompetent"[5] dictates the subservience of practicing priests (along with the lawyers and physicians) to the publicly authorized faculties. Precisely as the producer of such university graduates, whom Kant refers to as governmental "instruments" and "tools," the university can appeal directly, and on its own behalf, to the government's preponderant interest in achieving the strongest and most enduring (legal) influence upon the people [7: 18, 19]. If the government, as user of these tools, retains the right to sanction the higher faculties, it does so only by renouncing any authority of its own to teach, which would impugn the dignity of government by opening it, of necessity, to legitimate scholarly criticism. The lower faculty, on the other hand, which "has no commands to give," must be left "free to judge everything," both because reason admits no "order to believe"[6] and because otherwise truth (in which government also takes an interest) will not emerge. Government's need to influence the people "by the most powerful and enduring means" itself dictates (as Kant hopes convincingly to show) that philosophy remain at liberty [7: 20].

To be sure, that liberty confines itself within a scholarly commonwealth that is itself, at least in part, an established tool (or toolmaker) of government. If Kant had once counted on greater latitude for public criticism ("argue as much as you like, only obey!"), more recent events evidently convinced him of the utility (or need) of excluding from the relevant discussion those "men of affairs" (i.e., priests, lawyers, and physicians) whose "public" utterances his earlier essay *What Is Enlightenment?* had famously included. By Kant's current lights, such "technicians" [*Werkkundige*] may not publicly object (whatever their private thoughts) to the official doctrines they have contracted to uphold. Either the excesses of the French Revolution, or his unhappy experiences with King Frederick William II (whose "peculiarities" of temperament are noted in the Preface [7: 5]), or both, seems to have convinced Kant of the need to draw back from any attempt to influence the people directly on religious questions. The (relative) benevolence and competence of Frederick the Great had led Kant, in that earlier essay, to declare his age one of "enlightenment." In the current work he refers instead, and perhaps somewhat hopefully, to the new regime of Frederick William III as an "enlightened government." That government, which, through the freedom of thought that it presently allows, is "releasing the human spirit from its chains," now permits to be published a work on a subject for which Kant was earlier censured and, more importantly, censored. To Kant's great and evident relief, the palpable threat of public silence on the crucial matter of the relation between ethics and religion has now been lifted.

Preventive censorship had been established fact, even under the reign of Frederick the Great, with an exception made for work executed in and published by the universities, which were submitted to the relevant faculties. What was at stake in the affair—both in the writing that led to Kant's promise to desist from further public utterance on religion, and in the promise itself—was nothing less than prospects for human enlightenment as such. Under Frederick the Great the members of the Berlin Censorship Commission were themselves men of learning who could be counted on to exercise their authority with prudence and discretion. Frederick William II's peculiar susceptibility to the wiles of his ministers and mistresses threatened to replace such men with crude schemers and half-educated *Schwärmer*, drawn (in many cases) from the ranks of local pastors. Under these new circumstances the university seems to have assumed special importance for Kant as a bulwark against the twin dangers of despotism and popular fanaticism.

Under Frederick the Great (and, more ambiguously, even under Frederick William II), those whose work was executed and published in the universities could avoid the Commission by submitting it to the relevant faculty for approval. Kant seizes here upon the relative autonomy of the university in this respect as the key to its peculiar civic role: joining knowledge with state power.[7] He makes no effort to hide the fact that historically the university is a creature of the state: "Without attributing premature wisdom and learning to the government, [we can say] that by its own *felt need* (to "affect" [*wirken*] the people by certain teachings), the division that appears to have a merely empirical origin could have come from a principle, *a priori*" [7: 21]. Like the state itself, the university is (or may be thought of as) a kind of man-made organism, an historically embodied idea, however crudely it may initially have been grasped and articulated. The drive propelling this historical development (in the biological sense) is the state's "felt need" to exercise control over the populace—control which, precisely because man is free, cannot be accomplished by brute force alone. The division of the higher faculties corresponds, accordingly, to the fundamental incentives by which the government can achieve its end of "influencing" the people: appeal to their eternal well-being, their civil well-being (as holders of property) and their physical well-being[8] (as embodied rational agents) [7: 22].

Kant takes advantage here of the peculiar history of the German universities and their primary association with state, rather than ecclesiastical, authority. The apparent "primacy" of theology is itself based, as Kant here insists, on the state's wish to uncover and "steer" the "inmost thoughts" and "most secret directives" [*Willensmeisungen*] of its subjects. (That natural instinct here reverses their true order of importance allows Kant a wry jab at clergymen, whose hypocrisy, in this respect, is especially damning.) All three higher faculties base their teachings on statutory books (of which the Bible is preeminent), which derive their authority wholly from government's ability to command (absolute) obedience without regard to whether or not its statutes are reasonable [7: 22–23]. A written Bible is needed (as in the case of other statutory books) to supply a constant and accessible norm for the direction of the people. (As for claims as to its peculiar character as the language of *God*, Kant appropriates to himself the uttering of the Word [*das Worte reden*] [7: 21]). If the higher faculties (and Biblical theology especially) presume to any authority of their own, they place themselves under the command of the lower faculty, where the free play of reason prevails over the former's merely borrowed dignity; hence the importance, says Kant, for the sake of theology itself, of avoiding a mis-marriage with philosophy.

2. The Difference between the Theological and Philosophic Faculties

What, then, is the distinctive characteristic of the theological faculty? Biblical theology, Kant says, demonstrates the existence of God on the grounds that he spoke [*geredet hat*] in the Bible [7: 23]. A further showing that the latter actually happened not only is unnecessary to religion rightly understood (as Kant will later prove at length), but also an encroachment on the faculty of philosophy, to which the study of history properly belongs [7: 23, 28]. The theological scholar as such (Kant plays here on the Latin *puras*, and *putas*—terms connoting both chastity and immaturity) grounds himself, rather, on "a certain (indemonstrable and unclarifiable) *feeling*," on a "supernatural opening of his understanding," and on "grace," abjuring all independent appeals to morality, to reason, or to virtue. The theologian's adherence to pure faith, linked to an indemonstrable and unclarifiable feeling, dictates (if he is wise) a circumspective public silence as to the question of the Bible's origin, lest he raise doubts among the people that he cannot answer [7: 24]. Dogmatism, unchastened by criticism, is here, as elsewhere in Kant's thought, an open invitation to skepticism. Kant harbors few illusions that theologians in practice will remain so "[un]contaminated"; his point is, rather, to indicate what a theological faculty that was thoroughly consistent with itself could claim on its own behalf. The answer is a special feeling for the miraculous [*Wunder*], which Kant will later relegate to the realm of the "aesthetic."[9] Yet (as we shall see) this feeling is not as far as one might first suspect from the "wonder" [*Bewunderung*] from which pure reason draws its own [subjective] strength.

The mark of the lower faculty of philosophy, on the other hand, is freedom, or the power [*Vermögen*] to judge autonomously [*nach der Autonomie*], on the basis of reason alone—power that cannot, by its nature, be externally commanded [7: 27]. Such a faculty is necessary to the others (whom it aids by controlling), because truth is the first and necessary condition of learning as such. In addition, since philosophy, by its nature, seeks not to dominate but only to be heard, this faculty is, like a trustworthy minister of state, above suspicion.

The university so understood gives working effect to the truth through several levels of engagement: The faculty of philosophy's free criticism gradually corrects the historically established teachings of the higher faculties, which, in turn, produce increasingly enlightened popular practitioners who are prohibited from injecting, in their dealings with the people, their own (less enlightened) opinions and objections. And, in any case, such objections are likely to decrease, inasmuch as such officials, "becoming more enlightened about their duty, are not repelled by altering their discourse [*Vortrag*]" [7: 29]. Change can thus come about "without polemics or attacks that only stir up unrest." Precisely because people at large are uninterested in intellectual subtleties, and "feel themselves bound" [*sich . . . verbunden fühlt*] to keep with what state officials announce to them, learned discussion can be carried on without the people being thereby incited to disorder and rebellion. Thus insinuated, as the trainer of state officials, into the engine of government, philosophy puts the people's very tractability (which might otherwise seem to constitute an absolute stumbling block to popular enlightenment) to pedagogic use.

3. Philosophic Instruction in the *Critique of Pure Reason*

In what, then, does the education offered by the lower faculty consist? One cannot be taught to be a philosopher, according to the *Critique of Pure Reason*, but only "to philosophize":

> *Philosophy* is the system of all philosophical knowledge. It must be taken objectively, if by it one understands the archetype [*Urbild*] for the estimation of all attempts to philosophize, an archetype that ought to serve for the estimation of each subjective philosophy, whose structures are frequently so manifold and alterable. In this way, philosophy is a mere idea of a possible science, that nowhere is given *in concreto*, but which one seeks by many paths to approach, until the one footpath, very overgrown through sensibility, is discovered, and the till now so abortive image arrives at being like the archetype so far as this is granted to man. Until then . . . man can only learn to philosophize, i.e., to exercise the talent of reason, in accordance with its universal principles. [A 838 = B 866][10]

Prior to the emergence of Kant's own critical system, the concept of philosophy was merely scholastic, devoted to the systematic unity of science for its own sake. Now, however, there "is given" a "cosmic concept" that has always implicitly grounded the term "philosophy" (or lover of wisdom), especially as personified in the figure of the philosopher as legislator of "the essential ends of human reason"—an ideal in which the scientific knowledge is subordinated to the moral goal, or "entire vocation of man" [A 841 = B 869].

Kant makes no claims to be a philosopher in this morally exalted sense. As a teacher of philosophy his task is, rather (and with a view to that entire vocation), to elicit in the student a living confrontation with the dialectic of human reason:

> However [a] knowledge may originally be given . . . it is still, for him who possesses it, merely historical, if he knows it only at the level and as much as has been given to him from outside [*anderwärts*] . . . whether through immediate experience or narration, or even instruction ([of] general knowledge). He who has in the strict sense learned [*gelernt*] a system of philosophy. . . . knows and judges only what has been given to him. . . . He has formed himself [*bildet sich*] according to a foreign reason, but the imitative faculty is not the productive one; that is, knowledge has not arisen in him out of reason, and although objectively it may be rational knowledge, subjectively it is merely historical. He has grasped and retained, i.e., learned [in the sense of "learned by heart"], and is a plaster cast on which the shape of a living man has been imposed. [A 836 = B 864]

Knowledge that is rational objectively is so subjectively only when derived from "sources from which there can also arise the criticism and rejection" of what is learned, and hence only when at home with and able to withstand conflict [*Streit*]. The student must reflectively reenact that philosophic state of nature out of which arises criticism, understood as "reason's true tribunal." As Kant put it in a well-known passage:

> In the absence of . . . critique reason is in a state of nature, so to speak, and can make its assertions and claims valid only through war. The critique, on the other hand, which derives all decisions from the ground rules of its own installation, whose authority [*Ansehen*] no one can doubt, procures for us the rest/ peace [*Ruhe*] of a legal condition, in which our controversy [*Streitigkeit*] can be carried in no way other than by *juridical process* [Proceß]. What ends the quarrels of the former state is victory to which both parties lay claim, and which is generally followed by an uncertain peace, established by a magistrate who places himself in the middle; in the latter, however, the *Sentence* must secure eternal peace, because it touches the source of controversy itself. The endless controversies of a merely dogmatic reason thus finally necessitate a seeking of rest in some critique of this reason itself, and on the lawgiving on which it grounds itself. As Hobbes says: the state of nature is a state of injustice and violence, and one must necessarily forsake it in order to submit oneself to lawful compulsion that limits our freedom only to the extent that allows it to coexist with that of others and with the general good. [A 751–752 = B 779–780]

The freedom guaranteed by this state of peace entails, above all, the right "to submit openly for estimation[11] the thoughts and doubts that one cannot oneself resolve, without being decried/shouted down [*verschreit*] as a warlike and dangerous citizen," a freedom implied by the "original right of human reason, which recognizes no other judge than that of universal human reason, in which each one has a voice" [*Stimme*] [A 752 = B 780]. Such peace requires a "lowering of tone" from apodiectic certainty, in moral matters that concern the very foundations of the public welfare, to one of merely practical conviction [A 749 = B 777], and hence a (perpetual) willingness to give skepticism a hearing. The primary purpose of free discussion for Kant is therefore not, as some contemporary defenders of "public reason" would have it, to further the advancement of knowledge on a democratic basis, but a more immediately pedagogical one: to recreate, in each (would be) rational citizen, that struggle between dogmatic assertion and skeptical doubt which "necessitates" the critical solution. To enter the fray and attempt to shout down one's skeptical opponents with countervailing proofs (as dogmatic moralists are wont to do) is to keep "youthful reason" in a state of morally dangerous tutelage, a danger that speaks especially for the political and moral importance of the academy:

> Must not at least the young, who are entrusted to academic instruction . . . be preserved from a premature knowledge of such dangerous [skeptical] propositions, . . . until the teaching one would ground in them is so rooted as to . . . withstand all opposition?. . . . Nothing would be emptier or more fruitless than thus to keep youthful reason for a time under tutelage [*Vormundschaft*].

This, would indeed, guard against corruption [*Verführung*] for a while. And yet:

> Whoever, in order to withstand the attacks of his opponent, brings only dogmatic weapons, and doesn't know how to develop the hidden dialectic that lies no less in his own breast than in that of his opponent, sees apparent reasons with the advantage of novelty advance against apparent reasons which no longer have that advantage, but rather arouse all the more suspicion of abusing the credulity [*Leichtgläubigkeit*] of youth. He believes he can in no way better show that he has outgrown childish discipline than by throwing aside . . . well-meant warnings and, accustomed to dogmatism, drinks deeply from the draught of poison that dogmatically destroys his principles.
> [A 754–755 = B 782–783]

Dogma, like poison, has its use, but only as a counter-poison.[12] In describing the thoughts of an imagined student, Kant also portrays the contours of man's generic adolescence—the "adventurous and self-reliant reason" [A 850 = B 878] that in mistaking discipline for servitude jeopardizes its own self grounded development.

Kant's own approach to academic teaching is the opposite one of exposing the student to the most powerful skeptical arguments available:

> For in order to bring its principles as early as possible into application, and to show their sufficiency even when dialectical illusion is at its height, it is absolutely necessary that the attacks which seem so fearful to the dogmatist be allowed to direct themselves against the student's reason, which is still weak but critically enlightened, and that the latter be allowed to make the experiment of testing the groundless assertions of his opponent, one by one, with reference to those [critically established] principles. [A 755 = B 783]

Suspicion—corrupting in the ill-taught student—is saving when youthful reason turns it inward. Properly exposed to skepticism, the student "soon begins to feel [*fühlt*] his own power [*Kraft*] fully to secure himself against harmful deceptions" so that at last "all illusion for him must vanish" [A 755 = B 783].

Free discussion is thus crucial, less as a means of arriving at the truth (for the most important theoretical and practical truths are already known)[13] than as a means of fortifying reason at a moment of developmental crisis. The student may not neutrally stand aside while dogmatists and skeptics trade blow for blow but must recognize that struggle in his own breast, i.e., as intrinsic to reason itself. The struggle is thus best described, not as a true polemic, but as a tension or conflict (as in conflict of interest), which (as in the case of the Hobbesian civil contract) is reconcilable with peace to the extent that each party lays down its claim to absolute possession. In the case at hand, each party must recognize the right of the other party to a voice[14] and thus lay down its claim to unrestricted knowledge. This "lowering of tone" (which allows the other to be heard)[15] coincides with the maturing student's own ability to register the conflict that betrays reason's competing interests.[16] Only by exposing, and bringing to a climax, this "natural dialectic" does he come to *feel* within himself the force that actualizes philosophy's tribunal. It is not enough, in other words, to grasp critical philosophy conceptually; (here, as elsewhere) the juridical condition obtains only when force puts the juridical concept into action by enforcing the law against the conflicting interests of opposing parties.

The struggle against philosophic death—and, especially, against the skeptical hopelessness that threatens pure reason mortally[17]—must be conducted allopathically. Put otherwise, skepticism must be unleashed in order to be vanquished:

> Speculative reason in its transcendental use is dialectical *in itself.* The objections that are to be feared lie in ourselves. We must search them out like old but never superannuated claims in order to ground eternal peace on their annihilation. External quiet is merely apparent. The seed of these troubles, which lies in the nature of human reason, must be uprooted; *but how can we uproot it, if we do not give it freedom, and even nourishment, to send out shoots, so that we can thereby discover it and subsequently eradicate it with the root?* Devise, therefore, objections yourself, that have not yet occurred to any opponent, and even lend him the weapons or concede him the most favorable position that he could wish! There is nothing in this fear, but rather *much to hope,* namely, that you will come into a possession that in all the future will never more be disturbed. [A 777–778 = B 805–806; emphasis added] [18]

This digression sheds light on what was essentially at stake for Kant in the conflict between theological and philosophic faculties. The development of reason as a talent requires not only the positive instruction of "culture and doctrine," but, equally importantly, the negative instruction of a protracted and ongoing "discipline," by which alone reason's "habitual tendency to disobey" can be extirpated [A 709 = B 737]. Reason's "natural antithetic" wakes it up but also tempts it either to abandon itself to skeptical hopelessness or to fall back into dogmatic obstinacy. The primary justification for free and open discussion is not the discovery of new knowledge but preservation of moral truth from skeptical despair. Without the "felt" experience of self-correction, right reasoning falls on deaf ears.

4. The "Legal" vs. the "Illegal" Conflict of the Faculties

Equipped with some understanding of what philosophic education means for Kant, and assured that conflict is not only consistent with but also necessary to philosophic peace, we turn to Kant's distinction between an illegal and a legal conflict of the faculties.

A conflict of opinion is formally *il*legal, he says, if either party tries to prevail, not by objective argument, but by subjective appeals to inclination, i.e., through threats or flattery. Faculties engage in conflict in order [*ex hypothesi*] to influence the people by appealing (as all civil engines must do) to the interest that the people necessarily take in their own welfare [*Heil*]. But the people left to themselves (owing to the natural aversion to "self-exertion" in which their tractability essentially consists) recognize that welfare, not in freedom, as the faculty of philosophy would urge, but in natural ends (perpetual happiness, secure possession, and a long and healthy life). In keeping with their "preference for enjoyment and their unwillingness to work for it," they invite the higher faculties to provide them with easy, if immoral, shortcuts (such as the view that one may be saved by faith alone) [7: 30, 31].

Practitioners will always be such trimming and accommodating "miracle workers," Kant maintains, unless the faculty of philosophy is allowed to publicly work against them [*entgegen zu arbeiten*]—not, to be sure, by overthrowing them, but instead by "contradicting/countering [*widersprechen*] the magic force" that the people, owing to their laziness, superstitiously attributes to them, "as if by passively giving themselves over to such artful leaders [*Führer*]" the people would be "led with great convenience" to achieve their desired ends, and "excused from any self activity" [7: 31]. The original sin, so to speak, of the people is their desire "to be led"—a deliberate inertness consistent with Kant's comparison of primitive men to sheep and which goes together with a natural disinclination to "exert oneself," (above all, by exercising autonomy).[19] The infantile in man naturally craves a return to the womb-like Paradise where wishes are deeds and work (even that required to breath) unnecessary.

If the higher faculties themselves adopt such principles of leadership, they contest the lower faculty *illegally*, by virtue of the fact that the higher faculties themselves treat heteronomy not as hindrances (as they can and should), but as wished-for opportunities. Not only would a government that sanctioned such principles authorize anarchy (and be, in this respect self-canceling); it would also destroy the lower faculty, ending the conflict in a medically heroic sense, i.e., by killing the university (as with the "euthanasia of pure reason" described above) in order to save it [5: 32; 34n].

The *legal* conflict of the faculties, on the other hand, arises from the necessary gap, given human imperfection, between what reason dictates and what governments choose, through the higher faculties, to sanction [7: 32]. Government's own interest in the truth (if only to secure its aim of influencing the people) necessitates a faculty of philosophy as potential—and uniquely trustworthy—opposition. (For the lower faculty, unlike its higher counterparts, has no intrinsic wish to rule.) As such, the philosophy faculty has the right and duty to criticize teachings that are officially sanctioned, be their source reason, history (e.g., biblical testimony), or "aesthetics" (e.g., "pious feeling of supernatural influence") [7: 33]. Although the legal conflict of the faculties is "unending," it could happen that government one day comes to see philosophic freedom, rather than its own absolute authority, as the better way of securing its own ends, so that the "lower" faculty would become the "higher" [7: 35]. For the conflict of the faculties is not a war, that is, "a dispute arising from opposing final aims" (for all parties aim at influencing the people) but a reflection of the university's inherent combination of freedom and obedience, reason, and statutory authority. The university, one could say, institutionalizes the tension between knowledge and power, in a manner calculated to bring them into ever-closer alignment without ever (short of a moral conversion of the human race) collapsing them entirely. It thus replaces—at least to the extent that it succeeds—the merger, at once necessary and impossible, of philosophy and kingship.[20]

5. The Conflict between the Philosophic and Theological Faculties

The heart of the conflict between the two faculties (a conflict, as Kant notes, that may serve as model for the other two [7: 36]) lies in the competing claims of "biblical" and "rational" theology. The *biblical theologian* is learned in Scriptures with a view to church faith [*Kirchenglauben*], which depends for its authority on statutes—that is to say, on the *Wilkür* of another. The *rational theologian*, by way of contrast, is learned in the faith of reason, which is "based on inner laws that allow themselves to be developed out of every man's own reason" [7: 36]. The latter faith alone may properly be called one of *religion*, which is not (as generally thought) the sum of all teachings understood as divine revelations, but "the sum of all our duties . . . understood as divine commands." Whereas there can be many kinds of faith, which are ways of representing divine will in sensible form [*sinnlichen Vorstellungsart*] so as to exercise "influence" upon the mind [*Gemüth*], there can be only one religion, which consists in use of the Idea of God, which is "engendered [*erzeugte*] by reason itself," to give morality "influence on man's will toward the fulfillment of all his duties." Religion, then, differs from morality "only formally," each having the same goal (fulfillment of all man's duties) but differing inasmuch as morality through religion exercises particular "influence" upon the will [7: 36].

Among church faiths, Kant crucially adds, Christianity is "so far as we know" the most suitable [*schicklichste*] in form for "influencing the mind." Hedged by the uncertainty ("so far as we know") of a merely historical assertion, the (alleged) superiority of Christianity as a means of exercising mental "influence," marks the common ground on which moral and church faith meet and over which the two faculties stake their competing claims. The specific competence of the theological faculty is the study and transmission of those aspects of historical Christianity that best promote the influence of true moral religion. The theological faculty's "very human" tendency to inflate its own importance (in this case, by taking its own secondary status for primary) ensures, however, that it will always be in need of philosophic criticism.

Christianity thus consists of two "heterogeneous pieces [*ungleichartigen Stücken*]": a "canon," or pure religious faith, and its "vehicle" or "organon"—which "can be called" church faith. The organon of "church faith" rests entirely on statutes that "must be taken for divine revelation if they are to count as holy teachings and prescriptions for living" [7: 37]. But the moral duty to "use" church faith, provided that it can be adapted as a "guiding tool" [*Leitzeug*] to moral ends, suggests that the true "organon" [literally, tool] of Christianity may reside elsewhere than "church faith." It is on precisely this question—in what way and in what sense Scripture is to be regarded as a tool to salvation [*Heil*] or "eternal life"—that the conflict between the theological and philosophical faculties will prove to turn.

Although that which matters most—"concepts and principles of eternal life"—cannot, strictly speaking, be taught, i.e., learned from others, their development out of one's own reason can be "prompted" [*veranlasssen*], Kant says, by discourse [i.e., *Vortrag*, literally "something said/carried forward"]. Scripture contains this much (a pure doctrine of moral religion) but also something more: i.e., a historical faith that can be useful, in certain times and places, to pure faith as a "merely sensible vehicle" but is not essential. The theology faculty's *mingling* of the two is just what the faculty of philosophy contests [*widerstreitet*].

To this inessential vehicle belongs a method of teaching that is *not* a matter of revelation and that is valid according to the thinking of the times. Certain apostolic doctrines, for example, are to be understood as prudent temporary concessions, which do not essentially oppose true religion, to then prevalent illusions (such as demonic "possession") or to Jewish partiality to the old faith (concessions such as "interpreting the history of the old covenant as a fore-image [*Vorbild*] of the new"). As we shall see, Kant is at special pains to destroy this Jewish "piece" [*Stück*] (which concerns the entire story of the Jewish covenant, from Abraham's idol-shattering, to the circumcision and sacrifice of Isaac, to the Mosaic Decalogue ["thou shall have before thee no graven image . . ."] as a "wearisome" and "agonizing" remnant [*reliquia*] that has outlived its morally useful purpose [7: 38].[21]

From the ensuing difficulties, arises an interpretive conflict in which the faculty of theology favors dogma and letter, while the faculty of philosophy defends religion and the (moral) spirit. The exegetical principles by which the conflict can be settled, however, must themselves, *as* principles, be rationally (hence, morally) grounded.

According to those principles:

1. Morally indifferent scriptural doctrines that transcend (i.e., cannot be grasped by) reason *may* be interpreted morally. Doctrines that conflict with moral concepts *must* be interpreted morally.
2. Faith in Scripture that depends on revelation is not meritorious, nor is the lack of such faith blameworthy.
3. Action must be represented [*vorgestellt*] as "springing from man's own use of his moral forces" and not as the "effect" of "higher influence."
4. If man cannot justify himself by deeds (which follows from the nature of conscience itself), reason is permitted to assume (lest effort flag) a supernatural supplement [*Ergänzung*].

These principles are calculated to promote a single end—to bring moral exertion to the highest possible pitch. They do this both by insisting on the responsibility of the individual for his own action and, as importantly, by denying traditional church teachings that tend to diminish moral effort. To wit:

1. The claim that Christ is God incarnate (a claim that is both transcendent and morally indifferent) *may* be morally interpreted (so as to render it "practically effective") as a representation of the rational idea of "humanity in its full moral perfection" [7: 39], i.e., as the portrayal, in a sensibly represented form, of the supreme goal of rational human striving.[22] Paul's teaching concerning predestination, on the other hand, which directly contradicts concepts of freedom and the imputability of action (and so of the "whole of morality"), *must* be interpreted away, as a vestige of the "Mosaic-messianic scriptures" [cf. 7: 66].
2. The claim that faith in revealed doctrine is not only meritorious in itself but also lifted up [*erhöben*] over morally good works must be taken to apply to *moral* faith, i.e., "that which improves through reason and elevates

> [*erhebende*] the soul." (Should the doctrine as to the primacy of belief in revelation be regarded as essential to a church faith in which the state, as defender of the public peace, takes legitimate interest, the teacher should not attack this doctrine directly, but instead warn against treating it as intrinsically holy,[23] with a view to its gradual disappearance. [7: 42])

3. The doctrine of grace, which, according to the letter of the Bible, claims that man is passively sanctified, must be interpreted to refer to nothing other than "the nature of man, insofar as he is determined to action through his own inner, but supersensible, principle (the representation of duty)"—an original disposition [*Anlage*] to the good which we did not ourselves establish:

> Grace . . . (i.e., hope in the development of the good—hope enlivened [*lebendig werden*] through faith in the original disposition in us to the good and through the example of humanity well pleasing to God in his Son—can and should become yet more powerful in us (as free) if only we let it affect/work on [*wirken*] us, i.e., let the disposition to conduct resembling that holy example become active. [7: 43]

It must, in other words, be made clear "that *we ourselves must work*" to develop the original disposition to the good, a disposition that points to a divine source and is not itself meritorious [original emphasis].

4. Human reason may additionally assume, in order to avoid a morally enervating despair, that God will supplement what man cannot do to justify himself by his own acts. However (seemingly) at odds with principle #3, this assumption is warranted by the fact that without it, we may not be able (subjectively) to grasp [*fassen*] the courage and firm disposition [*Gesinnung*] to live rightly—given the limitless nature of our task (i.e., our subjective awareness, intrinsic to human frailty, of our guilt as unremitting) [7: 44, 47].

Even the principle of imputation—that one may be credited (or blamed) only for one's own actions—on which Kant's moral system seems otherwise to turn—bends (at least subjectively) to human reason's "need" to prompt itself to labor. This need arises from the necessarily ambiguous voice with which the moral law speaks to finite creatures like ourselves. Conscience is informed by a tension, intrinsic to human consciousness, between idea (the final end that conscience tells us we can arrive at, as in "ought implies can"), and its limitless approximation in space and time (the only way we can conceive of carrying out our duty). The idea by which reason sets itself a task is accompanied by the impossibility of conceiving its completion. The idea is thus shadowed by despair—a "wearying" feature that is itself linked to the unreasonable basis of reason's dogmatic employment.[24]

6. *A priori* Division of Sects

Owing to that wearying remnant, the church faith associated with Christianity is subject to sectarian division. "The idea of religion" is one, necessary and universal [7: 44]. Church faith, by way of contrast, readily breaks down into sects that mistake religion's vehicle for religion itself. Still, to the extent that sects *are in fact* true religion's vehicle, they are divisible (in ways to be considered below) according to an *a priori* plan [7: 48–49].

To be sure, if Christianity is understood as an historical faith in a Messiah, such enumeration would be a "Herculean and thankless labor," inasmuch as Christianity would then merely be one national messianic faith among others—e.g., Judaism in the final period of its "complete domination over the Jewish people." Christianity, so construed, would only be the (statutory) faith of a particular people and could not claim to be the final, universally valid revelation [7: 49]. A rational enumeration of all possible sects that can serve as vehicles of the true religion (and concomitant avoidance of a work as futile as it is heroic) goes hand in hand with an understanding of Christianity as other than a Mosaic-messianic faith linked to the history of a particular people.

Sects in general, according to Kant, are "admixtures" of religion and paganism, the latter of which he defines as a "passing off" of the "external"[25] as religiously essential. Empirically speaking, sects are as innumerable as settled nations (themselves a combination of rational and merely statutory authority), with which sects are historically connected.[26] The relation of religion and paganism is thus one of (more or less) living interconnection rather than of simple opposition. Paganism in a sect, however, can come to loom so large that the "entire religion" is transformed (literally, "goes over") into something wholly pagan, which "passes off usages [*Gebräuche*] for laws" and in which nothing (morally alive) remains [7: 50–51].

There arises in sects (not completely pagan) an effectual tension, then, between the "influence" upon the soul of "pure, religious faith"—influence which, since it is "bound up with consciousness of freedom," cannot be lost—and the "force/violence" [*Gewalt*] exercised on conscience by what is merely church faith [7: 51]. Accordingly, a plurality of sects is morally benign only where there is universal agreement about the essential maxims of religion and disagreement only as to the "greater or lesser appropriateness [*Schicklichkeit*] or inappropriateness of the vehicle" [7: 52].[27] Prussian Catholics and Protestants could, in this way, benignly coexist as "brothers in faith" (leaving it to time, and government forbearance in allowing freedom of belief, to adjust the "formalities"). Jews, on the other hand, can, as it seems, join that brotherhood (or "invisible church") only by publicly becoming Christians—Christians, that is, in the peculiarly Kantian sense. (We may gather, then, that Judaism, as Kant sees it, is [now] "wholly pagan"—i.e., morally speaking, a dead letter.):

> Without dreaming [*die Träumerei*] of a general Jewish conversion (to Christianity as a messianic faith), this [invisible church] is possible even in regard to Jews, if among them, as is now happening, purified [*geläuterte*] religious concepts awaken, and the clothing [*Kleid*] of the old cult that no longer serves for anything, and, what is more, represses [*verdrängen*] all true religious disposition, is thrown off. Since they have now for so long had *a garment without a man* [Mann] (church without religion), and since, moreover, a *man without a garment* (religion without a church) is not well preserved [*verwahrt*], they need certain formalities of a church that is most suitable to lead them in their present place/situation: so we can consider [*halten*] the proposal of Ben David, a very good mind [*Kopf*] of that nation, to publicly accept the religion of Jesus (presumably with its vehicle, the Gospel), not only very fortunate but also the only proposal [*Vorschlag*] whose carrying out would soon make this people noticeable [*bemerklich machen*] as one that is learned, well-civilized and ready for all civil rights, whose faith could also be sanctioned by the government, without their having to amalgamate with others in things of faith; [in keeping with this proposal] they would surely have to be left free to interpret the Bible [Torah and Gospels] so as to distinguish the way that Jesus spoke as a Jew to Jews from the way he spoke as a moral teacher of men in general.—The euthanasia of Judaism is pure moral religion with the leaving behind [*Veranlassung*] of all ancient regulatory teachings [*Satzungslehre*], some of which had to remain retained/held back [*zurück behalten bleiben müssen*] in Christianity (as messianic faith): this division of sects must, yet, also finally disappear, and so the conclusion of what is called the great religious drama of religious change on earth (the restoration of all things) leads hereby, at least in spirit, to there being only one shepherd and one herd/flock [*Heerde*]. [7: 52–53]

This extraordinary passage, so retrospectively ominous,[28] sheds remarkable light, not only on Kant's own complex attitude toward Judaism and Jews,[29] but also on the nature, as he sees it, of religion as such. For present purposes, two features of his discussion are especially important: the highlighted connection between sectarian division, governmental sanction, and religious progress (the "great drama of religious change on earth"); and the peculiar status of Judaism and the Jews.

On the first point: the statutory sanction (not just toleration) of religion is here not just an evil to be put up with—i.e., a temporary concession to historical conditions which would make opposition to established religion dangerous or politically destructive—but a positive good—the means by which enlightenment as such (in the terms laid out earlier in the essay) can be stably and lawfully advanced. Through its sanction of religious sects (for its own non-religious ends), government can regulate, through the faculties it authorizes, those religious practitioners who deal with the people in a direct way and who can therefore do most to help or hinder instruction at the most popular level. That Kant's most immediate political foes, in his own struggles with government repression, were often from precisely that group (as earlier defined) underscores the importance of this consideration to Kant's overall idea of a workable solution to the problem of education. By this mechanism Kant is able to reconcile, as he believes, religious freedom (from such "coercive" measures as would, by playing on "fear and hope," destroy the "true religious disposition" of the people), with the steady pressure necessary to regularize (not to say, routinize) moral and religious progress.[30] The government's non-moral interest in effective rule (i.e., in public order) is here harnessed to a moral purpose, through the intermediation of the faculties, whose interests (truth and ruling) are at once united and divided. The university can thus be thought of as a kind of coupling by which force tending one way is redirected in another—a spiritual mechanism, powered by "conflicting" human interests, that "providentially" addresses the problem of educating the human species—a problem that is otherwise, as Kant elsewhere states, "insoluble."

Kant's preference for an established church (along liberal lines) over the separation of church and state may or may not apply to states other than Prussia. Arguing in favor of flexibility on this point is the strong link he draws between national difference and distinctiveness of one's religious practice—not only in the case of the Jews but for all (European) nations.[31] The debate within liberalism between liberal "tolerationists" (who would leave religion almost entirely to the private sphere) and liberal proponents of a sort of positive civic religious "establishment" is ongoing, even in the United States. (Witness the constitutional amendment that added "under God" to the "pledge of allegiance" or, on a higher rhetorical plane, Abraham Lincoln's appeals to an American "political religion.")

The second point—Kant's attitude toward the Jews—is best considered in light of his "a priori" treatment of how Christian sects set about making men morally better (so that Christianity is "really encountered in their hearts") [7: 53]. Whereas all true Christians agree as to the end, there can be disagreement over means, from which arises an *a priori* "inward" division of religion (despite its essential unity) into two *religious* (not just historical, or nationally distinctive) sects. (Here, at last, is that *a priori* plan of which Kant earlier spoke [7: 49].)

The task of Christian [viz. moral] education—to work toward [*hinwirken . . . auf*] a [moral] disposition [*Gesinnung*]—must be supersensible, rather than empirical. What is more, because conscience, inasmuch as it "imposes" itself on us, is witness to the fact that we are not [now] good, this "working" must (i.e., is best thought of practically as) bring[ing] about a complete revolution, or transformation, as expressed by the question: "how can we be, not just better men, but other men?"

For those who take everything *supersensible* for *supernatural*, that question becomes: "How is rebirth [*Wiedergeburt*] (whereby one becomes another, new man) possible through the immediate divine influence of God?" [7: 54]. This version of the question—historically associated with Philip Jacob Spener, who founded the Pietist movement and indirectly prompted formation of the Moravian Brotherhood[32]—is "rationally grounded," as Kant insists, owing to its fundamental opposition to orthodoxy, i.e., the view that one can please God by merely carrying out prescribed observances. For those who pose the question in this manner, and who thus consider it a "trivial matter [*Kleinigkeit*][33] to ascribe natural effects to supernatural causes," the answer is necessarily mystical. That mysticism takes the form of calling man's *natural* predisposition to the good (a predisposition to which conscience *also* bears witness) "mere *flesh*" [Fleisch]. People make this error (i.e., identifying nature with flesh) because they lack a clear conception of the supersensible (which is distinct from flesh without necessarily ceasing to be natural), and therefore think that a true moral revolution is possible only through a super*natural* effect.[34]

For such people, for whom man's *nature* is hopelessly corrupt, and a person therefore "cannot hope to improve by his own powers," there are two ways of "feeling" such conversion understood as the result of supernatural influence: for the first group, man's heart is crushed with remorse; for the second, it dissolves in blessed community [*Gemeinschaft*] with God [7: 55]. According to the first hypothesis, good in human nature separates from evil through a supernatural "operation" felt as a penitential "breaking and crushing" of the heart. That is to say, conversion begins with a miracle and ends with rational (i.e., morally good) conduct. Yet "even in the highest flights of mystical imagination," moral reasoning asserts itself. Unwilling or unable to regard themselves as mere machines, believers take a kind of credit for the very penitence that they also attribute wholly to grace, *and thus contradict in practice their professed despair concerning the power of unassisted human nature* [7: 56].

On the second hypothesis, man makes the first step to moral improvement on his own, through rational awareness of his guilt in relation to the moral law; carrying out his resolution to make the law his maxim, however, is considered to be a miracle, requiring "awareness of continual intercourse with a heavenly spirit," which can be maintained only by "continuous cultivation through prayer" [7: 56].

In sum: Either one attributes conversion to divine influence and then takes credit for its implementation, or one takes credit for conversion and then attributes its implementation to divine influence. These opposing representations of the feeling by which divine influence communicates itself (one anguished, the other so "sanctified" as to mark one as a holy fool)[35] find their historical counterparts in the German Pietism and Moravianism that directly or indirectly informed Kant's own youthful upbringing[36] [7: 55, 57, 57n].

In each case, conscience, which is essentially bound up with consciousness of freedom, is "repressed," Kant says, by a kind of violence, itself associated with lack of hope concerning the power of human reason to bring about the goal it aims at.[37] That violent repression is facilitated, in turn, by a mistaken belief in the possibility of bearing witness through one's feelings to supernatural influence. Because "the idea of God lies merely in reason," "the claim to *feel* the immediate influence as God" *as* such an influence is "self-contradictory." (The chasm between reason and sense, in other words, cannot be breached by mere assertion.) Each side exemplifies, from opposite poles of sorrow and joy, the historic struggle of pure reason's "force" against the "drag" of that spiritual inertia which takes it to be "no small thing" to take what is supersensible for supernatural. Neither side can answer Spener's question adequately because each (out of a kind of intellectual lassitude)[38] relaxes, rather than striving to resolve, the tension between idea (by which human reason sets itself a task) and feeling.

There is, however, a "biblical" principle that *dissolves* Spener's problem. "In deed" [*In der That*], it not only falls upon the eye [*in die Augen fallend*] that such a principle is encountered in the Bible. It is also "convincingly certain," Kant insists, that only by virtue of such a principle could Christianity have acquired so extensive an influence and enduring an effect upon the world. This effect no other teaching of "revelation (as such)"—neither faith in miracles nor "united penitential voices"—could ever have brought about "because they would not have been drawn from the soul of man as such" and thus "would always have remained foreign to him" [7: 58].

Kant's "proof" of his solution is thus a moral proof, based on the nature of the human soul as revealed by conscience, by way of "sound common understanding":

> There is, namely, something in us we can never cease to wonder [*bewundern*] at once we have seen it [*ins Auge gefaßt habe*], the same thing that lifts up *humanity* in the idea to a dignity that one would never have suspected in *man* as an object of experience. That we are subject to the moral laws and determined/destined through reason . . . to sacrifice [to them] all conflicting pleasures of life one doesn't wonder at, for [this] . . . lies objectively in the natural order of things as an object of pure reason, . . . so that it would never occur [*einfällt*] to sound common understanding to ask [with a view to evading them] whence [*woher*][39] such laws might come to us or even to doubt their truth.—But that we also have the *ability* [Vermögen] to offer to morality, with our sensible nature, so great a sacrifice, that we *can* do what we easily and clearly grasp that we *ought* to do—this ascendancy/overlying [*Überlegenheit*] of the *supersensible* man in us over the *sensible,* an ascendancy against which (if it comes to a conflict) the latter is *nothing,* though in its own eyes [*seinen eigenen Augen*] it is *everything*—this morality, from a disposition inseparable from our humanity, is an object of the highest *wonder,* which only rises higher the longer one regards [*ansehen*] this true (not fabricated) ideal. [7: 58–59]

The object of this constant and ever-mounting wonder, once it is "seized upon in our eyes," is the ability or faculty [*Vermögen*] of one's soul to sacrifice as nothing [*nichts*], "with one's sensible nature," that which to it (to me?) is everything [*alles*]; i.e., to entirely negate, with my sensible nature, the value of what my sensible nature (I?) most esteem(s). That this negation is possible the moral imperative assures us; how it is possible is a question that is both dizzyingly unanswerable[40] and ever-increasingly uplifting once the vision/regard [*Ansehen*] for that capacity is seized on. Wonder is the morally sublime, or something like a rational affect, however difficult it may be to unite the two conceptually.[41]

The "inconceivability/ungraspability" [*unbegrieflichkeit*] of the "supersensible in us" which is yet "practical," must and can, as practical, be "seized on" [*gefasst*].[42] Nevertheless, this inconceivability "excuses" [*entschuldigen*] those seduced into taking [*halten*] the supersensible *in* us for the supernatural *beyond* us. And yet they remain "very lacking" [*sehr fehlen*] in this, because were the source of the effect external, "the effect of this faculty would not be our own deed, and could not be imputed to us" [7: 59].

The people err due to a lack of intellectual stamina that philosophic education must directly or indirectly reinforce. Unlike the "sophistry" of ordinary moral understanding addressed in the *Groundlaying*, the seduction now at issue arises without guilt on the people's part. The issue here is not one of insisting upon knowing "from whence the moral law arises" (as in the *Groundlaying*)— a question that "would never occur," as Kant here puts it, to a common understanding that was sound. The issue is rather one of making the specific mode of access to the supersensible that the *Critique of Judgment*, as we have seen, had opened up more popularly available. The ordinary mind balks before the labor that is required to grasp the supersensible "critically," preferring to lapse into contradiction on the crucial issue of how one may be saved.

The remedy lies in providing ordinary understanding with a version of the supersensible that is within its grasp. Accordingly, Kant reduces the problem of the "new man" to the question: How can we be the source of the effect by which we are made better without already being what we are thereby to become? Kant responds with an "idea" of a higher faculty (of reason) that "cohabits" with us, albeit "inconceivably." The "genuine solution" [*echte Auflösung*] of the problem of the new man consists in:

> The putting into use of the idea of this faculty that cohabits [*beiwohnen*] in us in an inconceivable manner, and its inculcation [*Ansherzlegung*; literally, "laying into the heart"][43] beginning in earliest youth and continuing on in public discourse. And even the Bible seems to have nothing else in view [*vor Augen*], that is to say, it seems to point, not to supernatural experiences and fanatical feelings which should effect [*bewirken*] this revolution in reason's place; but rather, to the spirit of Christ, which he demonstrated in teachings

and examples that we might make it our own, or more exactly, since it already lies within us with the original moral disposition, that we only procure it room. And so between soulless orthodoxy and reason-killing mysticism there is the faith teaching of the Bible, which can, by means of reason, be developed out of ourselves, which, working [*hinwerken*] with divine force upon all human hearts toward fundamental betterment, and uniting them in a universal (although invisible) church, is the true religious teaching, grounded in the critique of practical reason. [7: 59][44]

The effort to conceive the indwelling of the principle of autonomy within us prompts the same feeling for the sublimity of our moral destiny that the *Critique of Practical Reason* and the *Critique of Judgment* had aroused by a different and less popular route. The Bible, rightly interpreted, meets the instructional needs of those who themselves lack the intellectual stamina for critical philosophy.

Given the excusable susceptibility, on the part of ordinary decent folk (such as Kant's own parents), to "seductive" shortcuts—a failure that left to itself would bring about the "death of reason"—the chief vehicle of popular moral education is, then, the Bible (albeit, properly, or "scientifically," interpreted). And government, for its part, owing to its own interest in "tractable and morally good [i.e., externally faithful]) subjects," will refuse to sanction "merely natural" religion (or church faith without the Bible); instead, it will use its influence on the theological faculty to bind "public teachers of the people" to an "orthodoxy" (i.e., faith in the Bible as interpreted by philosophically trained and statutorily sanctioned teachers) that (for once) isn't "soulless" [7: 60]. In thus turning against itself the main obstacle to popular enlightenment (an obstacle manifested in the people's willingness to be "led," and which essentially consists in a lack of intellectual stamina), Kant's "idea" of the university negotiates (heroically?) the narrow path between a religious tolerance that places no breaks on popular fanaticism (and thus brings about the death of reason) and a soul-destroying religious establishment.

7. Toward a "Settlement" of the Conflict

The conflict of the faculties, accordingly, looks forward to a peace (one shepherd and one herd) without arriving at it "in the foreseeable future." Kant's solution to the crisis of reason avoids "heroism" (in the medical sense) by prolonging the remedy indefinitely.[45]

There is, however, one additional hurdle: the Bible's claim to authority on the basis of a *Mosaic-messianic* faith, which reads the Bible as God's literal covenant with Abraham and Moses. Mosaic-messianism (outside of its original Jewish context) leaves the difficult matter of interpretation not to sharp-witted experts, where it belongs, but rather to the "natural reason" of the laity, who are tempted by irrational credulity [7: 62, 61].[46] That this tendency flourishes especially in the Protestant sects just qualifiedly praised, and under the banner of "freedom of belief," makes the danger all the more pressingly acute.

Kant's strategy against such faith is fairly simple: to trace its presence within historical Christianity to a Judaism that has outlived its spiritual usefulness—the "wearying remnant" of which reason (and Kant himself) earlier complained.[47] The interpretive subtlety of that nation[48]—whose art might still be enlisted in the moral cause were they to publicly accept "the religion of Jesus"—instead involves them in prophetic complications[49] at once extravagant and morally empty (i.e., clothing without the man)[50] [7: 63].

Both acclaimed for its sublimity[51] and condemned to "euthanasia," Judaism assumes a special—indeed, crucial—place, of favor and disfavor, in Kant's great drama of religious change on earth. The very sublimity of the Jewish law against idol worship (or sensible representation of the idea) aimed, it seems, too high; unsupported by the protective mediation (or what he elsewhere calls "scaffolding")[52] of representation, the idea of religion, for them, simply collapsed, leaving behind a "wearying remnant" about which reason may rightly complain. Judaism, one could go so far as to say, is for Kant the very embodiment of the human problem of despair, if not the human problem simply. Both figuratively and literally, Kantian religion is the circumcision (or "cutting off") from humanity of Judaism as Judaism. The true Christianity, as Kant presents it here, is Christianity de-Judaized.

At the same time, unlike the Jew's messianic covenant with God ("marked" by the sacrifice or cutting off of Isaac), Christianity, as Kant understands it, abjures direct verbal communication between God and man (Judaism's own principle of divine-human mediation). Trust in the Mosaic-messianic covenant—i.e., in the promise of a voice in which one's own reason does not share—is the example, par excellence, of that "contagion" of sound common understanding of which Kant elsewhere warns.[53]

If one could *document* the authenticity of a divine statutory code that *also* harmonized perfectly in its end with morally practical reason, it would constitute, as Kant here admits, "the most forceful tool" [*das kräftigste Organ*] for human guidance. But given the impossibility of sensually apprehending the infinite, and thus of knowing that God is actually speaking to one, such "authentication" can happen only "negatively," through comparison with what is rationally known to be morally certain [7: 63].[54]

The only positive certification [*Beglaubigung*] of the Bible is neither the immediate voice of God, nor the allegedly divine learning of its author (who being human, could err), but the "most forceful influence" it exercises upon the people; such an influence, given that their preachers are as scientifically "incompetent" as they are, can only stem from the pure source of universal rational religion [7: 63]. But that this source dwells in "every common man" is not something that every man acknowledges. Hence the instructional need, for the foreseeable future, of the Bible as a statutory form, which, so far as its "spirit" or moral content—as distinguished from its "letter"—is concerned, is "self-accrediting" [7: 64].

By understanding the Bible's "work" [*Werk*] as "providential" in this specific Kantian sense—i.e., as the "effect of nature" in conjunction with the "result" [*Erfolg*] of a "progressing moral culture"—one can, moreover, avoid the twin threats of religious skepticism (which reduces the Bible wholly to nature) and superstition (which raises the Bible wholly above it). The problem of popular education is soluble, in other words, insofar as history is grasped, not according to the [superstitiously worshipped] letter of the Bible, but as what Kant calls the "great religious drama of religious change on earth" ([7: 64]; compare [7:52–53]). Of such providential (but not Mosaic-messianic) history, he presents the following striking example:

> The disciples of the Mosaic-messianic faith saw their hope in God's covenant [*Bund*] with Abraham completely sink with the death of Jesus (we had hoped that he would deliver [*erlösen*] Israel); for salvation was in their Bible promised only to the children of Abraham. Now it happened that when the disciples were gathered at Pentecost, one of them fell upon the happy notion [*Einfall*],[55] in keeping with the subtle Jewish art of exegesis [*Auslegungskunst*], that pagans (Greeks and Romans) too could be considered as accepted in this covenant, if they believed in the sacrifice of his only son that Abraham was willing to offer God (as the sensible image [*Sinnbild*] of the sacrifice of the world-savior [*des Weltheilendes*]); for then they would be children of Abraham in faith (first with, but afterwards without circumcision [*Beschneidung*]). It is no miracle/wonder [*Wunder*] that this discovery, which, in a great gathering of people, opened up so immeasurable a prospect, was accepted with the greatest jubilation and as if it were the immediate

effect of the Holy Spirit, and was held to be a miracle [*Wunder*] and came into biblical (Apostolic) history as such; by this, however, it belongs in no way to religion to believe [in these events] as a fact [*Factum*] and to press it upon [*aufdringen*][56] natural human reason. Obedience necessitated through fear in esteem [*Ansehung*] for such church faith as required for salvation is thus superstition. [7: 65n–66n]

In Kant's "great drama of religious change on earth" (which substitutes, explicitly, for the "book containing the entire history of Jewish covenant"), the letter of Christianity (i.e., the New Testament as distinguished from the Old) is the remnant [*Vermächtung*] worth preserving/holding onto [*aufbehalten*]: Like "old parchment/skin," that remnant may be illegible in places and yet serves humanity as a guiding band/ligament,[57] *"just as if it were a divine revelation"* [7: 65]. Against the Mosaic-messianic faith in God's promise as literally written, a belief that stands behind the traditionally Christian view that "historical faith is necessary to salvation," Kant proposes an "Evangelical-messianic faith" that is consistent with and preparatory to the moral transfiguration of the Gospel[58] [7: 66].

Historical Christianity, with its "dream" of Jewish conversion, is, rightly understood, the *Vorbild* of the true religion. (Historical Christianity, one could say, is the new Old Testament.) Like the cutting off of Isaac (and/or his flesh) by/from his father, which marked the Jewish covenant with God,[59] religion must eventually cut itself off from its protective clothing; the "scaffolding" must one day "fall away."[60] But the cut is not an easy or a clean one, inasmuch as religion needs such vehicles "for the foreseeable (but not perpetual?) future." Given that need, moral progress will continue to depend upon arbitrary statutes and, hence, continue to court misadventure.[61]

8. Conclusion

In *The Conflict of the Faculties*, Kant works out in its clearest and most explicit form his answer to the question: How is (moral) education possible "wholesale" [*in die Grösse*], i.e., with a view to the moral improvement of the people generally? His solution looks both backward, to traditional notions of Christian rebirth, and forward, to the modern organization of the factory. It also takes not only as given but also as providential a certain historical development of Christianity that finds its clearest expression in German religious sectarianism of the seventeenth and eighteenth centuries. His solution is thus, in an important sense, a national solution, as befits a conception of the university as, essentially, a state institution.[62] To be sure, sectarian warfare, so tragically intertwined with the German past toward which *Toward Perpetual Peace* sardonically alludes, is part of what Prussian Germany and Europe must put behind them, if theirs is ever to be an enlightened age. And yet, as Kant here labors to make clear, German sectarian division, rightly deployed and organized through the conflict of the faculties, provides a singular occasion [or *Veranlassung*] to effect the heart *en masse*.

The key to that deployment is the peculiar indirection with which the university manages popular education, without quite leading it. Readers familiar with Kant's famous paeans to equal dignity may be surprised at his emphatic insistence on intellectual *in*equality, not only, and notoriously, between men and women, but also, and more crucially, between scholarly or scientific heads and ordinary human understanding. The peculiar weaknesses of common understanding require (despite the latter's practical strengths) considerable and ongoing concessions for the indefinite future to historical modes of clothing the morally ideal in "sensible" garb. The university as indirect alliance between philosophy (or reason) and state power is more than a marriage of necessity or convenience but the only way pragmatically conceivable of lifting on a sufficiently massive scale the drag upon enlightenment that is exerted by popular credulity and/or servility. Indirectly at first, then more directly, the university becomes the true visible church dedicated both immediately, and through the disciplining of the professions, to the promotion of a national ethical culture. (Popular opinion is thereby not so much led as liberated [or delivered] from excusable but very wrong seductions.) So understood, the university is the providential engine which, in the words of the first *Critique*, "guides" and "influences" humanity collectively, and without prejudice to human freedom.

At the same time, the inability of human reason to represent worldly fulfillment of the aim it sets itself renders it prone, always, to a deflating apprehension of its own insufficiency. Kant's own apprehensions on this score are reflected in his peculiar antagonism toward (contemporary) Judaism, which not only passively awaits an external deliverer, but also absolutely rejects the representation of holiness, in the person of Jesus, by which the true law makes itself more lovable and hence less burdensome. If there is, for Kant, a likely place for Jews in an enlightened Prussian national culture, it is only as a peculiar Christian sect made up of (former) Jews. And yet (ancient) Judaism is in its way the very model of a people stirred (like the revolutionary spectators to be discussed in the next chapter) to ideal enthusiasm.

In thus "solving" the educational riddle with which, on Kant's account, Rousseau leaves us, Kant helped initiate a new kind of transformative pedagogy, which, for better and for worse, has deeply marked the nineteenth and twentieth centuries. He also gave liberalism newfound soul—and liberal education a new lease on life—for it is also accurate to say that Kant's "idea" indirectly inspired, through Humboldt and those who followed, the modern nation-building university—devoted at once to research and to "citizenship"—that America, especially, has embraced as model. But Kantian education also harbors darker currents, absent from Rousseau, who never sought such universal civic transformation. Religious and national identities continue to coexist uneasily in modern liberal democracies—not least within the university. The contemporary "crisis" in university education—one that we have thus far been unable to resolve—may well reflect a theological-political dilemma inherent in its founding.

8

Archimedes Revisited: Honor and History in *The Conflict of the Faculties,* Part Two

Honor figures importantly in Kant's mature practical writings—from the first moment of "release" from nature's womb, as sketched out in the *Conjectural Beginnings of Human History,* a moment Kant characterizes as both "dangerous [*gefahrvoll*]" and "honorable [*ehrend*]" [8: 114], to Kant's designation of "the political ambition [*Ehrbegierde*] of rulers," at the end of *The Idea for a Universal History with a Cosmopolitan Intention,* as one reason for attempting such a history in the first place [8: 31].[1]

But perhaps Kant's most striking treatment of honor arises in his famous, and famously puzzling, association in *The Conflict of the Faculties* of the defeat of ancient notions of honor with an event that signals, in a way sufficient (for the first time) "for the most rigorous theory"—that the human race is constantly progressing.

The subtitle of Kant's work, *An Old Question Newly Raised: Whether the Human Race Is in Constant Progress toward the Better?* [Erneuerte Frage: Ob das menschliche Geschlecht im beständigen Fortschreiten zum Besseren sei] points to the newness of its own departure. In *Toward Perpetual Peace,* which two years earlier had raised and affirmatively answered the question of human progress, Kant had specifically disavowed any claim to theoretical certitude. As he put it at the end of the first supplement ("On the Guarantee of Perpetual Peace"):

> Nature guarantees perpetual peace through the mechanism of human inclination itself, with an assurance that is admittedly not adequate for predicting [*weissagen*] the future (theoretically) but that is still enough for practical

purposes and makes it a duty to work toward this (not merely chimerical) end. [8: 368]

By way of contrast, in *The Conflict of the Faculties,* Part Two, Kant maintains the *truth* of progress—not just as a "well-meant" saying, "to be recommended for practical intentions," but as a proposition "tenable for the most rigorous theory" [7: 88].

In *Religion within the Boundaries of Bare Reason,* Kant delineated the narrow grounds of contestation between religion rightly and wrongly used, with a view to what we need to overcome the sophistry of moral unbelief, without succumbing, on the other side, to spiritual passivity. In *The Conflict of the Faculties,* Part One, that contest was given institutional weight in the state-supported struggle—which can, again, be well or badly used—between the theological and philosophic faculties of the university. Now, Kant turns to a different though related site of conflict, between the faculties of philosophy and law. Badly educated lawyers do to the *Regierungsart* of princes what badly educated clergy do to the *Denkungsart* of peoples [8: 353].

Religion had left its own "anthropological" problem hanging, namely, how to bring about an internationally lawful condition, given the natural propensity of states to "seek to subjugate all others to itself," by becoming a universal monarchy, only to split up before succeeding [6: 123n; cf. 8: 367]. Kant's proposal, in *Toward Perpetual Peace,* of a federation of republics (or their approximate like) did not so much resolve that problem as transpose it to another level. Establishing a single, well-governed state may, indeed, be possible "for a nation of devils," given a sufficiently enlightened founder [8: 366]. But, as *Religion* showed, the premature establishment of states by *unwise* leaders tends to lock in place a despotic misuse of men's religious need, all but destroying prospects for mass enlightenment. Where *The Conflict of the Faculties,* Part One, aims to counter that misuse directly, Part Two looks, instead, to the international system, with a view to countering the tendency of rulers to uselessly consume a spiritual profit (or *Ertrag*) that should instead (in ways shown below) be reinvested.

In *Toward Perpetual Peace* Kant left the establishing of such a system (or its near approximation) to a "lucky" strike (i.e., the fortuitous appearance of a powerful republic), combined with the "power of money" and the "spirit of commerce," which "cannot coexist with war" and which "sooner or later overpowers/takes hold of every nation" [8: 368]. Such a "mechanism" of the human inclinations at least guaranteed that the goal of perpetual peace was not simply an idle "dream" (as political moralists claim). Kant did so by showing that a phenomenon corresponding to that goal was not impossible on the basis of motivating forces that even skeptics would grant. What the resort to mechanism could not do, as he there admitted, was "to *predict* the future theoretically," prediction that would require proof that man's *moral endowment* is sufficient ([8: 368]; compare [7: 88–89]).

How might such a proof be had? According to *Toward Perpetual Peace*, that states speak of honor at all is enough to "prove" that "there is to be found in the human being a still greater, though presently dormant, moral *Anlage* to eventually become master of the evil principle within him . . . and also hope for this from others." Or, rather, it *would* constitute such proof, as Kant immediately adds, were it not possible to construe such talk of honor as mere mockery [8: 355]. Kant's ironic withdrawal,[2] in almost the same breath, of his proffered proof of the sufficiency of mankind's moral disposition underscores the ongoing challenge posed to Kant's practical project as a whole by skeptical "mockery," especially that of certain worldly lawyers.[3]

To show that an historical event is "really possible" is to establish that real human forces suffice to bring it about. The "guarantee" provided by *Toward Perpetual Peace* ensured, at least, that the cosmopolitan idea is not an altogether idle one (like that of spirit-seeing). What it did not do is show that perpetual peace, or a perpetual approach thereto, is also "really possible" (or certain to occur eventually, given the necessary external conditions), for it depended, finally, on the hypothesis that human fortune is actually favorable [8: 356].[4]

But what if fortune does *not*, in fact, come to our aid—what if the French Revolution aborts along with every future such experiment (like Cromwell's before it)? Here, *Toward Perpetual Peace*, as we have seen, falls short. Could the honor-talk of states be taken at face value, the real possibility of peace might still be established. And yet, without stringent proof that cosmopolitan peace is possible, there is no way to silence—as Kant grants we must—the mocking tone that undermines that purpose.

The partial failure of *Toward Perpetual Peace* frames Kant's effort, in Part Two of *The Conflict of the Faculties*, to raise the question of progress anew. *A Renewed Question* begins, however, with a demand [*verlangen*] that raises its own set of difficulties.

What is wanted, Kant says, is a predictive [*vorhersagende*] history that is guided neither by natural laws nor by supernatural insight. It is not a natural history of man (inquiring into the possibility of new human races) but an ethical one [*Sittengeschichte*], concerned with man not *singularum* (as bearer of a species concept [*Gattungsbegriff*]) but *universorum* (as the whole of men socially united on earth and divided into peoples). It is, then, concerned with man, not as *Gattung*-concept (which remains problematic)[5] but as *Geschlecht* (whose articulated unity is, *im Großen,* manifest in the geological and anthropological division of the globe) [7: 79].

But how can a history guided neither by natural laws nor by supernatural insight in fact be predictive? Prediction is called "prophecy" [*weissagen*], Kant says (by way of implicit answer), when it exceeds, *with* supernatural communication [*Mittheilung*], what can be known on the basis of natural laws. When it does so *without* such communication, it is usually referred to, derisively, as "soothsaying" [*wahrsagen*].[6] It is thus *wahrsagen* (literally, "truth-saying") and not *weissagen* that is here demanded: If a fragment of future history is to be known at all, it will be as a "soothsaying [*wahrsagende*] historical narrative [*Geschichtserzählung*]" and "exhibition [*Darstellung*], possible *a priori*, of events that are to come [*da kommen sollen*]" [7: 79].

Soothsaying history is possible, then, "if the foreteller of the future himself makes and arranges the events [*Begebenheiten*] that he announces in advance" [7: 80]. The kind of history Kant has in mind trades, in other words, on man's freedom to influence events to come. The Jewish prophets [*Propheten*] of old, for example, could easily prophecy [*weissagen*] the destruction of their state, since they themselves as national leaders [*Volksleiten*], by stubbornly clinging to an untenable [*unhaltbar*] constitution [*Verfassung*] of their own making, burdened [*beschwert*] it with so much ecclesiastical and civil freight as to render it unfit [*untauglich*]. In a similar way, "our politicians," who urge that men be taken as they are rather than as well-intentioned visionaries think they should be, are lucky [*glücklich*] in their soothsaying [*wahrsagen*], because they produce, through their previous oppression of the people, the lawless stubbornness that appears whenever the reigns of unjust constraint are lifted. Finally, [*Christian*] ecclesiastics sometimes prophecy [*weissagen*] the complete destruction of religion and imminent appearance of the Antichrist, and in so doing help to bring about the catastrophic end they warn of. For instead of attending to the moral improvement of the people directly, they fabricate duties that are supposed to work indirectly and thus employ the mechanical constraints appropriate to secure civil, but not moral, unanimity [7: 80]. The ancient prophets (and their peculiarly Jewish burden) are thus the model for modern politicians and pious enthusiasts alike, Machiavellian contrivance [*wahrsagen*] and religious divination [*weissagen*] amounting, in the end, to the same *untauglich* burden.

But more is evidently demanded by Kant's title than self-made history with a better outcome, as we learn from Kant's division of the "concept" of "what is wanted." There are, according to that division, three possible cases that between them seem mutually exhaustive: either the human race constantly regresses, or it constantly progresses, or it eternally stagnates at its present stage of ethical value [*sittlichen Werths*]. To these three cases there correspond three ways of representing history: the terroristic, the eudaimonistic (chiliastic), and the Abderitic.

The case of decline is equivalent to terrorism, because decline cannot be foreseen as going on forever. A human race getting ethically worse must at a certain point destroy itself or "wear itself out."[7] Exhaustion cannot be represented as an infinitely extended process (like that posited in Kant's refutation of Mendelssohn's immortality proof). Thus, this "way of representing history" looks forward to a cataclysmic end. But a final and absolute end is also unimaginable: hence the temptation to regard it as a (moral) day of judgment [*jüngste Tag*]), followed (in the dreams of pious *Schwärmer*) by a return of all things and renewal of the world.[8] Terrorism (which sees, e.g., "atrocities" [*Greuelthaten*] "heaping up [*sich aufthürmenden*] like mountains") would verge on the sublime, did its contradictory moral visions not subvert sublimity's (unseeing) moment of elation.

As with decline, improvement, too, it seems, cannot be foreseen continuing forever. We can imagine moral betterment only as the development and exercise of a pregiven moral *Anlage*. (No one is responsible for his/her *capacity* for goodness, i.e., for having a personality.) And since we are not holy beings, our capacity for goodness is (or must be thought of as) limited by a real capacity for evil. Hence improvement must reach a point when the individual will have achieved all that the original proportion of good and evil deposited in him allows. The "eudaimonistic way representing history [*Vorstellungsart*]" thus seems to "promise [*verheissen*] little," as Kant puts it, to a prophetic [*weissagen*] history of ever-enduring moral progress. (He thereby silently leaves open the possibility that eudaimonistic *wahrsagen* (or a "chiliasm" that is "philosophic" rather than merely "theological") might, in this regard, be more successful [7: 81–82].

Neither the "terroristic" nor the "eudaimonstic" way of representing history seems able to exhibit constant change, be it regress or progress. Each is forced to call a halt, in terror or in hope, without supplying what also "demanded" by Kant's initial question: an exhibition of historical infinity.

Case three—or perpetual oscillation between improvement and decline—delivers historical infinity of a kind. Here (in contrast to the previous cases), constancy is thinkable, but without real, representable result, be it positive or negative. Abderitism is totality conceived (as in the physical formula: For every action there is an equal and opposite reaction.), but not presented as a possible experience. Accordingly, Kant does not refer to Abderitism as a way of *representing* human history at all, but as its *predetermination*.[9] According to this "Abderitic" hypothesis:

> Busy folly is the character of our species; people hastily set off [*einzutretten*] on the path of the good but do not persevere [*beharren*]. Instead, if only for the sake of not being bound to a single end, indeed, if only so that there may happen diversion/alternation [*wenn es auch nur der Abwechselung wegen geschähe*], they reverse the plan of progress . . . and lay upon themselves hopeless exertion [*hoffnungslose Bemühung*]. . . . The principle of evil in the natural disposition of the human race and that of the good seem here to be not so much amalgamated (melted down together) as to be mutually neutralizing, which would result in inactivity [or "deedlessness" = *Thatlosigkeit*][10] (which is here called stasis [*Stillstand*]): an empty business [*Geschäftigkeit*], to so alternate/exchange [*abwechseln*] the good with the bad through going forwards and backwards, that the entire game of commerce [*Spiel des Verkehrs*] of our species [*Gattung*] with itself on this globe would have to be regarded [*angesehen*] as a mere farce [*Possenspiel*], which can endow our species with no greater value [*Werth*], in the eyes of reason, than other animal species [*Thiergeschlechter*] have, who drive [*treiben*] this game with fewer costs [*Kosten*] and without expenditure of understanding [*Verstandesaufwand*]. [7: 82]

Abderites alter their conditions, constantly, but accomplish nothing. The Abderites, in this respect, lead a wholly natural existence, in which (as in the physical world) positive and negative forces stand in perfect balance. In the economy of nature, reciprocating action and reaction cancel to zero. In the economy of reason, by way of contrast, every action (hence, every expenditure of force) must necessarily be seen as an investment in a greater good. The Abderitic hypothesis portrays all such investment, and especially the "expenditure of understanding," as pointless, inasmuch as no good that we pursue can be greater than the good we thereby sacrifice. It thus encourages the "hesitation" in self-expenditure that *Religion* located at the root of human evil. Its broad appeal

(Kant says it would most likely garner "the most voices/votes") is thus no surprise, for it gives false comfort to the evil principle in each of us.

Abderitism has another claim to our misguided support: its link with our intolerance for boredom. It is the peculiar weakness of the civilized mind to seek diversion (literally, alteration or exchange), even, as we see here, at the price of exertion that is pointless and hence hopeless. Abderitism (the "busyness" of which stands in marked contrast with the inertia of the savage) is a condition peculiar to the developed understanding. Unlike savages, we civilized human beings are less fearful of effort than of boredom, less reluctant to expend our forces without promise of greater return, than to anticipate a future in which "nothing happens."

It is no surprise, then, that Kant associates the Abderitic hypothesis especially with the worldly politicians who are Kant's main opponents in the present essay. Abderitism, as Kant puts it in an early draft, is the "wisdom of states," by which "all means by which progress to the better might be secured are expressly neglected" [23: 459].

The problem of progress, as we learn in Section Four, is one that experience cannot immediately resolve. No upward trend (e.g., the growing might of the French republic to date) can guarantee that the human species is not about to reach the point of its decline, owing to some limitation in the natural *Anlage* of the species (as, Kant elsewhere suggests, may have already occurred with the non-white races). And any downward trend (e.g., the increasing crimes of an imperialist Europe) might prompt a freely chosen reversal [7: 83].

Still, Copernican success in bringing order to the confusion of the Ptolemaic heavens suggests that a similar change of standpoint might bring order to the apparent confusion of human affairs (which also seem to move backward, forward, or both together [hence not at all]). Kant signals the essential difficulty: the "unfortunate" fact that we are both free and timely, both receptive to noumenal causation and active in a phenomenal world whose spatial and temporal extension we cannot fully encompass. To God's "eye" but not to ours, there is no difference between "seeing" and "foreseeing" [7: 84].[11] Man "sees" free action, and foresees, with the help of natural laws, the un-free movement of the heavens. What we cannot do, it seems, is "foresee" free actions, and hence predict his future.

Yet Kant finds a potential opening in the possibility of positing a character one cannot directly know: Could one credit [*beilage*] man with an unvarying, albeit limited, good will, the progress of the human race could be predicted with certainty, because prediction would "meet an event [*Begebenheit*] that man himself can make" [7: 84].

How, then, find the necessary point (like that of Archimedes and his lever)[12] from which we could see human history as a whole without ceasing to be part of it? A soothsaying history must (as Kant insists in Section Five) be "connected [*angeknüpt*] to experience" in some way:

> An experience must come forward [*vorkommen*] that as an event [*Begebenheit*] points out [*hinweiset*] a human endowment and capacity to be the cause [*Ursache*] and (since this is the deed [*That*] of a being endowed with freedom [*eines mit Freiheit begabten Wesen*]) author [*Urheber*] of its own progress toward the better. [7: 84]

Given this event, all that would additionally be required is assurance of the "cooperating" circumstances necessary to turn that noumenal, free causation into future phenomenal happenings:

> From a given cause [*Ursache*] an event as effect [*Wirkung*] can be predicted [*vorhersagen*] ... if cooperating circumstances [*mitwirkend Umstände*] come about/before the eye [*eräugnen*]. That these latter must sometime come about/before the eye can well be generally predicted, as with calculations of probability in a game [*Spiel*] ... without my knowing whether I will have the experience of it in my own lifetime. [7: 84]

What is sought, then, is an event [*Begebenhiet*] from which progress would follow as an inevitable consequence—an event that points out [*hinweisen*] the future of the human race (as natural laws point out the future of the heavens), but without failing to do justice to human freedom. Such an event would have to do for human history what the Keplerian/Copernican transposition from earth to sun did for the movements of the stars [see 7: 83–84].

Could such an event be found, it would reach backward, to the cooperating circumstances of the past, as well as forward to those of the future.[13] It would thus point out a tendency of the human race at large in its own dealings with itself. Accordingly, the human race would be regarded, not just as an aggregate of individuals (which would, indeed, call forth enumerable, Ptolemaic calculations), but as an historical community—an anthropological "whole divided into nations and states that we encounter on the earth" [7: 84].

Still, Kant's use here of the word "Spiel" (which means both dramatic spectacle and game [as in games of chance]) highlights mankind's disturbing resemblance to the fabled citizens of Abdera, whose madness lay in a conflation of play and audience. (All the world, as Shakespeare might say, is but a stage, and we are but players.) We too—all of us—cannot avoid being actors in a drama of which we are, just as inevitably, the viewers. What Kant seeks, then, is a place to stand *within* experience from which one can regard mankind's doings as intelligible—a vantage point that (like the Copernican hypothesis) substitutes order for absurd entanglement, without reducing history to a pointless spectacle.[14]

The sought-for event "in our time" which proves [*beweiset*] "the moral tendency of the human race" is described in Section Six. It consists:

> neither in important deeds or misdeeds directed by men, whereby what was great among men is made small or what is small among men made great, nor in ancient splendid [*glänzende*] state structures that vanish as if by magic as others come forth in their place as if from the depths of the earth.... It is merely the way of thinking [*Denkungsart*] of the spectators which, by this game [*Spiele*] of these great transformations [*Umwandlungen*], publicly/openly betrays itself [*sich ... öffentlich verräth*], and manifests/allows to become loud [*laut werden lässt*], such a universal and yet unselfish [*uneigennützige*] sympathy [*Theilnehmung*] for players [*Spielenden*] of one side over those of the other, despite the danger [*Gefahr*] that such partiality could be very disadvantageous [*nachtheilig*] for them if it should become known. [7: 85]

Such communicating sympathy testifies (like a resonating instrument) to the "inflowing" of a moral cause into the natural world—evidence, otherwise unavailable, of a decisive superiority of man's spiritual over his natural self:

> so [there] is demonstrated a character (owing to its universality) of the human race as a whole and at the same time a moral character (owing to its unselfishness), at least in disposition, a character that not only permits hope in progress toward the better, but is already itself such progress, in so far as the capacity for progress succeeds/suffices for now.... The revolution of a people rich in spirit [*geistreichen*], which we have seen going forth in our day, may succeed or fail.... this revolution, I maintain, still finds in the minds [*Gemüthern*] of all spectators (who are not themselves entangled [*verwickelt*] in the game/play [*Spiel*]) a wishful participation [*eine Theilnehmung dem Wunsche nach*], bordering on enthusiasm, and whose utterance/externalization [*Äusserung*] is itself bound up with danger, [and] which thus can have no cause other than a moral disposition [*Anlage*] in the human race. [7: 85–86]

The spectators "betray" their *Denkungsart*, which makes itself loud by thus making itself public. The spectators do not "entangle" themselves in the *Spiel*.

Indeed, they do not *act* at all, and hence cannot act deceptively, as actors. The event thereby evades the *faul Fleck* of duplicity that defeated Kant's earlier efforts to mount decisive evidence of human goodness. And yet the spectators are also traitors [*Verräter*] of a kind—betrayers, through their courting of real danger, of a secret that resisted all earlier efforts at disclosure. The veil that conceals the causality of the moral world within the natural world (and that made its troubling presence felt as early as Kant's *Observations*) is finally on the verge of lifting. The standpoint of such spectators, on the basis of whose way of thinking [*Denkungsart*] one can predict free actions without presuming supernatural guidance, is the sought-for equivalent, within the realm of human affairs, of the position of Copernicus.

That the "morally inflowing cause" to which they testify is the republican "idea" should be no surprise. As early as Kant's *Rermarks*, he claimed to find in "freedom" (*vis-à-vis* the arbitrary will of others) the Archimedean *Stetzungspunkt* from which to move the human affects [20: 56]. As idea, its influence cannot be directly seen but only indirectly registered, e.g., in a "warm desire," on the spectators' part, for newspapers [*Zeitungen*].[15] That cause involves first, that of the right of a people not to be hindered in setting up a constitution that seems good to them, and, second, that of the end (which also is a duty) of entering [*einzutretten*] that republican condition, i.e., that constitution which, alone, is disposed to avoid aggressive war in principle, a disposition that assures (for reasons to be taken up below) that this cooperating circumstance persists in perpetuity [7: 85–86].

But how can the (near) enthusiasm provoked by revolution (or its image) prove mankind's moral tendency, if revolution is, as such, contrary to duty (as Kant elsewhere claims) and enthusiasm (as he here insists) not altogether praiseworthy [7: 86]? The answer comes, partly, in a remark "weighty [*wichtig*] (as Kant puts it) for anthropology":

> True enthusiasm always goes toward what is ideal, and, indeed, purely moral, as is the concept of right, and it cannot be grafted onto self-interest [*Eignennutz*]. Monetary rewards could not pitch the adversaries of the revolutionaries to the zeal and greatness of soul which the sheer concept of right produced in them, and *even the concept of honor [Ehrbegriffe] of the old martial nobility [kriegerischen Adels] (an analogue of enthusiasm) vanished [verschwand] before the weapons of those who kept before their eyes the right of the people to whom they belonged and of which they thought themselves the guardians*. With what exaltation [*Exaltation*] the external, onlooking public [*Publicum*] then

sympathized [*sympathisirte*] without the least intention [*Absicht*] of cooperating [*Mitwirkung*]. [7: 86–87, 155–157; emphasis added]

Kant's public onlookers, who "take part" without meaning to cooperate, are exalted by the disappearance of one concept of honor before the weapons of another. Like the shimmering political structures that also vanish [*verschwinden*], warlike pride (which is not, as Kant elsewhere puts it, "nothing" [6: 336]) gives way before the even more fearless, but ultimately peace-loving, zeal that animates the guardians of and for the people. What the spectators "see" in the martially fore-grounded disappearance of the old, martial concept of honor is the signal task of history—to transform a desire for honor into love of honor—instantaneously, as it were, accomplished.[16]

Enthusiasm "always goes toward the ideal," because of all affects, it alone directly furthers reason's end, however blindly. According to Kant's *Anthropology* an affect is a feeling that overwhelms the mind's capacity to compare it with the totality of feelings of pleasure and displeasure that accompany our state, now and in the future. Affect cancels the mind's ability to undertake the sort of calculation implied by the rational pursuit of happiness. In this, affect (in contrast to passion "which takes time") bears a certain resemblance to moral decision, which also overrides our ordinary reckoning of goods.

But not all affects are, for reason's purposes, simply disabling. Sympathy [*Mitleid*], for example, is at least *naturally* purposive—a disposition "wisely implanted" to serve as a temporary social surrogate, until reason is strong enough to take the reins [7: 253].[17] There is also a kind of affect whose source is reason itself. Reason, says Kant:

> can bring about an enlivening of the will, by representing the morally good through connection of its ideas with intuitions (examples) set [*untergelegt*] to them [like words set to a tune] (in spiritual, or political addresses to the people,[18] or even simply to oneself). . . . [Such] soul enlivening is not the effect [*Wirkung*] but instead the cause of an affect [*Affekt*] regarding the good, so that reason always leads the reins, effecting [*bewirkt*] an enthusiasm of good resolution [*Vorsatz*]. [7: 253–254]

Unlike sympathy, such enthusiasm "of good resolution" is not to be "attributed [*gerechnet*] to *Affekt*, as to the stronger sensuous feeling," but to reason itself. Kant's parenthetical remark here is peculiarly pertinent, given *The Conflict of the Faculties*' special concern with spiritual and political "addresses to the people/nation." *The Conflict of the Faculties* can itself be read (and nowhere more than in the present section) as itself a "soul-enlivening" exercise for both audience and author. Kant's depiction of the "event" in question aims to rise beyond sympathy [*Mitleid*], reckonable to "affect," to an enthusiasm "of good resolution"; it aims to rise from nature's tutelary guidance, in other words, to that of reason proper.

That theme becomes explicit in what follows. There "must in principle [*im Grundsatze*]," according to Section Seven:

> be something *moral* that reason, which reason places before the eyes [*vor Augen stellt*] as pure but also, because of its great and epoch-making influence, as the recognized [*anerkannte*] duty thereto of the soul of human beings, and which pertains to the human race as a whole . . . , something the hoped for and attempted [*Versuchen*] success of which . . . [the human soul] jubilates over [*jujauchzt*] with so much universal and selfless participation [*uneigennütziger Theilnehmung*]. [7: 87]

That "something" is the appearance of an evolving institution of a right "exalted above all price (of utility [*Nützlichkeit*])" [7: 87n]; it thus represents [*vorstellen*], or, literally, "sets before the eye [*vor Augen stellt*]" [7: 87], man's "elevation," and hence removal from the zero-sum economy earlier mentioned.

But what the jubilating onlookers of Kant's time had in view, as we earlier learned, was the overpowering of an undeveloped and barbaric code of honor by the weapons of a modern citizen army—i.e., the "vanishing" of a "concept," flawed but real, before a popularly embodied and empowered "idea" [cf. 7: 86]. That jubilant onlooking is the event Kant here describes as the "phenomenon" [*Phenomenon*] of the "evolution" of a constitution according to natural right (or, alternatively, of a constitution that is both natural and just [*einer naturrechtlichen Verfassung*]) [7: 87].[19]

Kant's event testifies to the reality of human progress because it marks the inflowing of a moral cause that sets up conditions sufficient to gradually put an end to war, "the source of all evil and the corruption of all peoples" [7: 86]. That war (or warlike pride) is also, according to Kant, the source of man's advance from a state of natural peace, in which we lived contented, like cattle suggests its critical importance to the national/civic "rebirth" Kant here describes. Honor, even of the old martial and aristocratic sort, is not "nothing,"[20] for it indicates man's inability and unwillingness to remain satisfied with mere animal contentment. The difficulty is that honor that does not take its bearings from the equal dignity of man threatens to precipitate, as *Toward Perpetual Peace* made abundantly clear, a violent struggle for world power that puts the value of man's historical existence (and hence creation itself) in question.

The felt appearance, so to speak, to an international audience, of the idea of right (figured in the *disappearance* of honor aristocratically and martially conceived) is the sought-for connection between experience and a rationally self-authored cause from which a progressive history of the human race can be deduced. The spectacle of revolution in France is evidently to do for others what Rousseau's egalitarian transformation of honor once did for Kant.[21] (There is a nice symmetry, then, in the famous story of Kant interrupting his regular afternoon walk on only two occasions—once to read Rousseau's *Emile*, the other time to read late-breaking news concerning revolution in France.)

Even war, according to the *Critique of Judgment:*

> has something sublime about it, when it is conducted with order [*Ordnung*] and holy respect for civil rights, and it makes the *Denkungsart* of a people who conduct it all the more sublime, the greater the dangers before which it bravely . . . maintained itself. A prolonged peace, on the other hand, tends to make dominant the mere spirit of commerce [*Handelsgeist*], and with it, low selfishness, cowardice and softness, and to bring low the people's *Denkungsart*.
> [5: 263]

Toward Perpetual Peace falls short by pegging nature's guarantee upon the "dominance" of a *Handelsgeist* that undermines, as we here see, the very possibility of peace with honor; that work thereby withdraws with one hand the hedge against "despair" it offers with another. Kant's "event" answers to that difficulty by combining the courage of the soldier with the disengagement of the aesthetic spectator. The result is a "wishful participation" that, unlike other forms of "wishing" [5: 177n], seems to vindicate, at last, the "natural" propensity toward vain desires that the *Critique of Judgment* had deemed problematic.[22]

If my argument is correct, it is this consideration, above all, that lies behind the power Kant now claims to predict, "even without a seer's spirit," human attainment of the republican goal:

> I now maintain [*behaupte*] to be able to predict, even without a seer's spirit [*Sehergeist*], . . . the achievement of this end, and of a related progress toward the good that never more goes entirely backward. For such a phenomenon in the human race *is nevermore to be forgotten*; because it has uncovered an *Anlage* and a capacity [*Vermögen*] towards the better in human nature, which no politician could have cleverly ferreted out on the basis of the mere course of things, and which only nature and freedom, united in the human race according to inner principles of right . . . could have promised. [7: 88]

In questioning the promise of *supernatural* eudaimonistic prophecy, Kant, as we recall, left hanging the possibility of eudaimonistic prediction *within the limits of human experience*)—a "soothsaying" [*wahrsagende*] history of humanity [7: 87] that he now "opens up" (or "makes public") [*eröffnet*] [7: 89]. "Supernatural communication [*Mittheilung*]," which is knowably beyond the limits of human experience, gives way to "spiritual participation [*Theilnehmung*]." Kant's full statement reads as follows:

> Here, thus, is a proposition that is not just well-meaning and sufficiently valuable from a practical standpoint, but also maintainable [*haltbarer*] despite all unbelievers, and for the strictest theory: namely, that the human race has always been in progress toward the better and will be so henceforth, [a consideration which], if one has regard not only to what happens to one people, but also to the spreading among all peoples of the earth that gradually come to take part/participate [*Theil nehmen*] in it, opens up the outlook/ prospect of an unpredictable/immeasurable/unforeseeable [*unabsehliche*] time. [7: 88-89]

Kant's resort here to apodeictic utterance ["there *must* be"; "I now maintain"] calls to mind his effort, in an unpublished draft, to find a "constitutive principle of theoretical/judging reason" on which the necessity in question might be based.[23] In the published version, Kant stops short of thus granting principles of *a priori* judgment a constitutive, rather than only "regulative," status. The historical unification of nature and freedom remains merely a "promise," albeit one "*nevermore to be forgotten*" [7: 88]. Even if the French Revolution should founder, the enthusiasm felt by its audience "is too great [*gross*], too interwoven with the interests of mankind, and its influence too widely disseminated" not to be "brought to memory by peoples on the occasion [*Veranlassung*] of any favoring circumstance," thus arousing "a repetition of new efforts of this kind [*Art*]" [7: 88]. Accordingly, "the intended constitution [*beasichtige Verfassung*] must [eventually] attain the constancy [*Festigkeit*] that the instruction [*Belehrung*] of repeated experience cannot fail to effect [*bewirken*] in the minds [*Gemüthen*] of all" [7: 88].

Kant's prediction, in short, derives its own undiminishable force [7: 88] less from politics in the usual sense (which may succeed or fail, and, as an exercise of power over others, is, in any case, always suspect)[24] than from a kind of renewable instruction to which Kant's own essay (through the interpretation there provided) "gives occasion."

But what sort of instruction or teaching can this be? A clue is to be found in a remarkable footnote, appended to the passage, previously cited, on the "disappearance" of the old warlike concept of honor. "Why," Kant there asks:

> has no ruler ever dared to freely proclaim that he recognizes no right on the people's part against him; that the people owe their happiness entirely to the beneficence of a government that confers it on them, and that all presumption on the subjects' part to a right against the government . . . is absurd and even punishable?—The answer is: because such a public declaration would rouse all of his subjects against him; although, as docile sheep, led by a benevolent and sensible master, well-fed and forcefully guarded, their well-being would lack nothing of which to complain.—For a being endowed with freedom is not satisfied with enjoyment of life's comforts that falls to his lot [*Theil*] through someone else; what matters is rather the principle according to which he provides it for himself. [7: 87n][25]

The perverse result of this refusal on the part of unjust rulers to publicize their maxims is the real danger that the people's sense of honor will continue to lie dormant. So long as rulers do not publicly declare a right to govern autocratically *on principle,* their subjects need never face up to the stark choice of either (passively) resisting (at whatever danger to themselves) or utterly renouncing their claim to be valued as other than mere means. Absent this public declaration, ordinary men (not schooled as knights of old) need never face a choice that brings them to "betray" and thereby come to recognize their own preference, at once natural and in keeping with the moral law, for freedom over mere enjoyment. Absent such a proclamation [*aussagen*]—which, according to Kant, no ruler has ever made or ever will—ordinary men might never become conscious of what is for Kant a kind of *naturrechtlich* fact, namely, that "a being endowed with freedom is not satisfied" with a happiness for which he is dependent on someone else; what matters is rather the "principle" according to which he gains it for himself. But:

> a being endowed with freedom, in the consciousness of his privilege [*Vorzug*] over the reasonless animal, *can and should demand* [*verlangen*], according to the formal principle of his will, no other government for the people to whom he belongs than one in which they are co-legislative. [7: 87n; emphasis added]

Prior to Kant's epoch-making "event," which arouses, in all who call it to mind, an exaltation that bears witness to their own preference for freedom over mere enjoyment,[26] nothing would have permitted an observer to maintain "despite all unbelievers" and "for the most rigorous theory" that the human race was genuinely advancing. Unlike the religious prophecy [*weissagen*] based on supernatural communication [*übernatürliche Mittheilung*] that Kant earlier rejected, the prophecy at hand rests on a sympathetic participation [*Theilnehmung*] within the limits of human experience. Such communicable enthusiasm (which though not entirely estimable, participates [*theilnehmen*] in the good [7: 86]), bears witness to the human preference for freedom over mere enjoyment, recognition of which (preference) itself gives value to existence.[27]

Interpreted in this way, the spectacular occasion of the French Revolution turns the "play" of human affairs (a play that wise viewers would otherwise judge a mere farce) into the comedy, or "eudaimonistic way of representing human history [*Vorstellungsart der Menschengeschichte*]," that Kant had seemingly despaired of. The demand [*Verlangen*] for government that is republican in principle—like the demand [*Verlangen*] for a progressive history of the human race that drives Kant's essay [7: 79]—itself bears witness to the unity of nature and freedom on whose "promise" Kant pegs his newly confident claim. Against the terrorism of pietistic *Schwärmer*, and the "unbelief" of Abderitic skeptics, Kant asserts a "eudaimonism" that reason can, at last, accept.

Kant's vindication here of eudaimonistic soothsaying had been anticipated in an essay of the previous year (*On a Recently Uplifted Noble Tone in Philosophy*), which explicitly invokes the image of Archimedes' lever. The "tone" mentioned in the title referred to the recent translation of Plato's Seventh Letter by Johann Georg Schlosser.[28] Schlosser, an amateur classicist and would-be Christian mystic who was also friendly with members of the King's circle, had attacked critical philosophy for its allegedly "castrating" dryness. In the course of his sarcastically laced reply, Kant insisted that exhibition of freedom's "mystery"—i.e., our unaccountable ability to sacrifice all wishes that derive from nature to the moral law—would induce a feeling that would bring about the moral improvement of the human race if only it were often repeated:

> Now I put to man what he asks himself: what is it in me that brings it about [*macht*] that I [can make this sacrifice] . . . ? This question, through astonishment over the magnitude of the sublimity of the inward *Anlage* in humanity [*Menscheit*] and at the same time the impenetrability of the mystery [*Geheimnisses*] that veils it [*sie verhült*] (for the answer: it is *freedom*, would be tautological, since it is just this that constitutes the mystery), arouses the entire soul. One can never become sated of directing one's attention towards it

> and admiring in it a might that yields to no might of nature; and this admiration is just the feeling produced by ideas. And if, beyond the teaching of morality in school and pulpit, exhibition of this mystery constituted a special, oft-repeated business of instruction, this feeling would penetrate deep into the soul and would not fail to make men morally *better*. [8: 402–403]

Thus understood, the idea of freedom furnishes the long-sought ground of support for Archimedes' lever:

> Here and now is what Archimedes needed but did not find: a firm [*fester*] point upon which reason can apply [*ansetzen*] its lever; and this without resting it either upon the present or a future world, but merely on its own inner idea of freedom, that lies as a secure foundation [*Grunglage*] through the unshakable moral law—reason doing this in order to move, by its principle, the human will even in the face of the resistance of the entirety of nature.... *The tone* of one who fancies himself possessor of this true secret [*Geheimniß*] can never be superior/noble [*vornehm*] for only dogmatic or historical knowledge inflates [*bläht auf*]. [8: 403][29]

To be sure, to "feel" this "mystery/secret" requires "labor" [*Arbeit*], leading some (like Schlosser) to dismiss the mind's form-giving activity (as allegedly portrayed by Kant) as a mere *Formgebungsmanufaktur* (or production through the use of molds).[30] Kant responds to this attack with a "police"-like vigilance: the transition to the supersensible (to which Schlosser and his ilk pretend) can only succeed through practical laws that "make their principle" not the "matter of free actions (their end) but only their *form*" [emphasis added]. Hence:

> It is not an arbitrary *form-giving*, directed *by a plan or in a factory-like manner* [fabrikenmäßig] (at the behest of the state),[31] but above all a *manufacture*[32] [that deals with the given object by hand], and this indeed without thought of the forgoing laborious and careful work of the subject to receive and evaluate his own capacity (of reason). [8: 404]

The philosopher worthy of the trademark [8: 401] is a master whose craft transcends the efficiencies of mass production.[33] It is Kant's adversaries, by way of contrast, who put matter first and thus cannot deny their own dependence on "mechanical contrivance." Kant's prime example of such perverse contrivance is, in turn, Schlosser's "fanatical" figuration of morality as a goddess (Isis) whose veil is "thin" enough to allow one to guess what lies beneath—a nakedness that, as Kant adds, one should (for theoretical and practical reasons alike) avoid imagining [8: 405].[34]

In sum: The "secret" [*Geheimniss*] of education does not lie in a self-mystifying sublimation of sexual desire (as Schlosser clumsily implies [8: 400] and a much younger Kant had once suspected); it is, rather, freedom itself, exhibition of whose mystery [*Geheimniß*] "arouses the entire soul" and thus could not fail to make us better human beings if only that exhibition were "frequently repeated."

The "event" that Kant announces in *The Conflict of the Faculties* (under more permissive political circumstances) answers to just this challenge. Ever repeating for the reasons Kant has already suggested [7: 88], that event "opens" an outlook [*Aussicht*] onto a "*unabsehliche Zeit*" [7: 89]. Such a time—which cannot be foreseen because its end, literally, cannot be seen, and hence is not subject to calculative prediction—replaces both the Abdertic hypothesis and the "end of time" prophesied [*weissagen*] in the Book of Revelation [*Offenbarung*], in which the heavens departed and every mountain and island were moved out of their places.[35]

Kant continues, however, with the following qualifying disclaimer:

> The prospect of an immeasurable time opens up—unless, that is, there does not, after the first epoch of a natural revolution, which (according to Camper and Blumenbach) buried the plant and animal kingdoms, before there were yet men, follow a second, which plays with/mistreats [*mitspielt*][36] the human race in the same way, in order to let other creatures strut[37] upon the stage, etc. For before [*vor*] the omnipotence of nature, or, even more, its highest cause, which for us cannot be arrived at, the human being is, in turn, but a trifle [*eine Kleinigkeit*]. But for rulers [*Herrscher*] of his own species to take a human being for such—that is no trifle but the overturning [*Umkehrung*] of the final purpose of creation itself. [7: 89]

The proposition that man always has been and always will be progressing toward the good,[38] a proposition "tenable" (as the ancient constitution of the Jews was not), despite all unbelievers[39] and for "the strictest theory," opens up (and opens up upon) the prospect of an incalculable time—except that allowance must be made for nature's power to bury us.[40]

For Kant, no less than for the pious terrorists and theological eudaimonists he earlier criticized [7: 81–82], the prospect of an *unabsehlich* future is brought up short. The exhibition of ever-enduring progress lies not in that prospect, but in its failure—and the feeling that arises from the accompanying contrast between man's infinite smallness and his more than infinite greatness. That contrast juxtaposes to nature's revolutionary epoch an "epoch-making" event that is definingly human—the former making "the small great and the great small," the latter weighty [*wichtig*] in a way literally beyond calculation (cf.]7: 85, 87]).[41]

There is a "difficulty," however, with "publicity." According to Section Eight:

> *Enlightenment of the people* [Volksaufklärung] is the public/open [*öffentliche*] instruction of the people on their duties and their rights concerning the state . . . Since this concerns only rights that are natural, and derived from common human understanding, their natural announcers[42] and interpreters among the people are not state appointed officials, but rather free professors of law, i.e., philosophers. And yet the freedom the latter permit themselves is repulsive to the state, which always wants only to rule. They are thus decried, under the name "enlighteners," as people dangerous to the state. And yet their voice[43] is not directed *insinuatingly* to the people (who take no or hardly any notice of them and their writings), but with all honor [*ehrerbietig*][44] to the state whom they implore to take to heart the people's rightful need [*rechtliche Bedürfniß*], which, if a whole people wishes to bring forward its grievance [*Beschwerde*] . . . , can happen only through publicity [*Publicität*]. [7: 89]

The natural educators of the people concerning their natural rights do not speak to them directly, then, but rather to and through the state, whose human tools (lawyers and other ministerial officials) the state sets up universities to train [7: 18]. Universities, it seems reasonable to conclude, are the special home of civil pedagogy of the sort Kant has in mind.[45] Rightly instructed, those invested with the offices of government would not treat popular grievances paternalistically, in the manner of "political moralists," but as *demands* for what is just.

As current circumstances show, the criterion of "publicizability" that Kant had earlier proposed (in *Toward Perpetual Peace*) as the basis of a "transcendental principle of public right" is insufficient. Rulers, it now appears, can use "lying publicity" [*lügenhafte Publicität*] to promote unjust ends, as with the British constitution, which conceals despotism behind a show of public freedom. Whereas in France, honor martially conceived gave way to the republican enthusiasm of the people's guardians, in England those "who take the people's place" have a desire for "offices and dignities [*Ämter und Würden*]" that "wins [these representatives] over" to the king's unrestricted warlike bidding [7: 90n]. The letter of republicanism thus counts for nothing without the spirit—that true sense of honor that (invested in the rulers and their advisors) prevents wars other than defensive, and whose absence is exemplified, above all, by the British "trade in Negroes" [7: 90, 90n].[46]

If the human race is to progress without "hindrance," philosophers must be free to address the state through their own public writings. And yet the state, which "wishes only to rule," is not altogether wrong (as the example of Great Britain shows) in finding it imprudent to allow philosophers the freedom on which the second edition of *Toward Perpetual Peace* explicitly insisted and the new Prussian king is now willing to silently permit.[47]

The profit [*Ertrag*] to be anticipated, according to Section Nine, is not an ever-increasing quantity in the morality of attitude [*Gesinnung*] (as theological eudaimonists might claim), but only an increase in the products of its legality, i.e., in actions that conform to duty [7: 91]. But what moral good can be expected from actions that merely conform to duty? The question is all the more acute, given Kant's identification, elsewhere, of the human "stain" with a confusion of mere legality (or external conformity to duty) for genuine morality.[48] What makes a progressive history of the Kantian sort anything other than an ever-expanding expression of that ineradicable moral blemish?

That violence will gradually lessen and obedience to laws increase, leading, gradually, to the establishment of a cosmopolitan society, does not require, Kant says by way of answer, an increase in man's moral *Grundlage*, which would require a new creation, but only the working out (in indeterminate proportion) of two phenomenally accessible motives—"love of honor"[49] and "well-understood self-interest." Nothing in his prophetic representation [*Vorstellung*] of history [*Geschichte*] depends, in other words, on more than is available on the basis of "the empirically given," or "experience"—that is to say, the physical causes of our actions, "insofar as they happen [*geschehe*]," and which are themselves appearances [*Erscheinungen*], rather than the moral cause, establishable [*aufstellen*] *a priori* on the basis of the concept of duty, or what "ought to happen [*geschehen sollte*]." (Nothing in the evolutionary growth or increase here described requires what Kant elsewhere calls "engraftment on a new, morally good *Gesinnung*.")[50]

More than a combination, in unknown proportion, of well-understood self-interest and true love of honor one shouldn't claim lest one merit well-grounded scorn [*Spott . . . mit Grunde*]. But in dodging that scorn, does Kant promise enough? How, exactly, does an increase in legality produce a positive result [*Ertrag*]—a yield beyond the Abderitic "nothing"? Is there room, between terrorism and fantastic hope, for what he elsewhere calls philosophic chiliasm?[51]

Archimedes Revisited 297

Kant's discussion, in *Religion,* of human evil, suggests an answer. If confusing the merely legal with the moral is the essential human stain, its external occasion is the lawless state that allows one to take pride in a mere conformity to law which exceeds the law-conformity of others. Moral evil, as we recall, consists in frailty and dishonesty in "not screening one's incentives" even "in the case of well-intentioned actions." Deliberate guilt (*dolus*), the third and gravest stage of evil, is characterized by:

> a certain perfidy [*Tücke*] of the human heart (*dolus malus*), in deceiving itself about its own good or bad disposition and, so long as the actions of a bad *Gesinnung* do not have the results they might have according to their maxim, to not trouble itself on account of its *Gesinnung,* but instead to hold itself justified before the law. From this springs the quiet conscience [*Gewissenruhe*] of so many human beings (conscientious according to their own opinion), when, in the course of actions in which the law was not consulted, or at least did not count the most, they only luckily avoid the evil results; and [from thus springs] even the fancy [*Einbildung*] of their deserving to feel guilty of none of the transgressions with which they see others burdened, without inquiring whether the credit is owing perhaps to their own good luck. [7: 38]

A condition of outer lawfulness (in which one sees law-conforming actions all around) destroys the outer possibility, at least, of thinking oneself superior in this to others. It thus cancels one occasioning source of the "blue smoke" [*blaue Dunst*] by which we wickedly deceive ourselves concerning our true motives.

Here, "good luck" (a luck which, as Kant immediately reminds us, cannot itself "be imputed to us") is not an occasioning source of self-approval relative to others—not a prompt to honor of the false, self-deceiving kind. Members of the true juridical community are not necessarily genuinely virtuous; but they are afforded an unequalled opportunity to cultivate their *Anlagen* to the good:

> A human being's moral cultivation [*Bildung*] begins, not with an improvement of mores [*Sitten*], but from a transformation [*Umwandlung*] of the way of thinking [*Denkungsart*], and a grounding [*Gründung*] of a character. . . . But now, even the most limited human being is capable of expressing the greater respect for an action according to duty, the more he removes from it, in thought, other incentives that might influence its maxim from self-love. . . . This *Anlage* to the good is, accordingly, incomparably cultivated [*unvergleichlich cultivirt*] by adducing [*anfürt*] the *example* of good human beings (as touches their conformity to law), and by allowing apprentices in morality to judge the impurity of many maxims on the basis of actual

incentives of their actions. The *Anlage* thus gradually devolves [*geht... über*] upon the *Denkungsart*, so that *duty* for its own sake is boosted [*anhebt*] to receive in their heart a marked weight [*Gewicht*]. [6: 48]

The moral student who sees nothing but law-conforming actions around him (even without a teacher's "leading" [*anführen*]) will have opportunity "beyond comparison" to cultivate his *Anlage* to the good. This maximum is to be measured against the admiration for virtuous actions, which, as a way of teaching, "is not yet the right *Stimmung*" to support the student's mind/mood [*Gemüth*] for the good, since all we can do, by way of duty, is never more than what is owed [6: 48]. To this "mis-tuning" [*Abstimmung*] of our feeling for duty [cf. 6: 38], Kant contrasts the image of a world in which, externally speaking, all do exactly as they ought. Members of that world would not only be spared the sight of what Kant calls the "most offensive" vices of *culture* and civilization—and with it, a mind/mood-lowering temptation to "misanthropy" [6: 33–34]; more simply and crucially, given Kant's account of moral evil, an externally lawful condition emerges as necessarily the most favorable situation for true moral improvement. There is no other way that a maximum here can be conceived.

By dispelling anxiety about the future, a lawful and effective constitution loosens the graft of vice.[52] It also encourages a general culture of civility. In such circumstances, where all do, externally speaking, what they should, I could not think myself superior to others on the basis of my own conformity to law. The natural human tendency to jealousy and rivalry, in such a state, would cease to pose a direct temptation to depravity, but instead supply occasion for *self*-scrutiny (along the lines of the fledgling moral exercises that Kant praises). In ways both negative and positive, then, an externally lawful community maximizes the occasioning circumstances of moral self-scrutiny—just what is demanded, above all, to combat the "evil root." We are thus brought to the outer limits of what human history can contribute to a transformation that can be accomplished, in the final analysis, only in and by the individual.

An explanation is now in hand for Kant's characterization, in the *Idea for a Universal History*, of the "perfectly just civil constitution" as the "womb" within which "all the original *Anlage* of the human *Gattung* will develop"—even absent the "morally-good *Gesinnung*," without which, according to that earlier work, all "goods" are "empty *Schein* and shimmering *Elend*" [8: 28]. The subsequent fact (and [morally] sublime reception) of the French Revolution offers experiential proof of the inflowing of the moral idea of justice, making possible (at last) a chiliasm that need not lay claim to supernatural insight (cf. *Religion* [6: 33–34]).

Granting the ethical "profit" to mankind of a progressive increase in conformity to law (even without a change in inner disposition), Kant turns, finally, to the temporal order [*Ordnung*] in which "progress to the better" is to be expected. Since the people (still themselves uneducated) refuse the burden of educating their children, the task falls upon the state. But states, who spend "everything on war," have nothing left for honor-loving teachers, who take "devoted pleasure in their office [*Amte*]" (as distinguished from those popular representatives whose "desire for offices and dignities" has turned them into the tools of a warlike monarch (cf. [7: 90]). Instead:

> the entire mechanism [*Maschinenwesen*] of this education [*Bildung*] lacks coherence, for it is not designed/projected [*entworfen*] according an overlaying/superior [*überlegten*] plan of the highest state power and, put into play [*Spiel*] according to that intention, uniformly maintained thereafter.
> [7: 93]

(The false *Überlegenheit* [6: 27] associated with the vices of culture would thus be answered by a true one, transforming fragmentary tools into a self-organizing mechanism.)

Kant here throws us back upon Rousseau's "misanthropic" paradox: Who is to educate the educators?[53] Given that education must be effected [*bewirken*] by men themselves in need of education, progress can be "hoped for" only if contingent circumstances produce a "favoring effect [*Effect*]," i.e., only by an appeal to "providence [*Vorsehung*]" (or "wisdom from above that is invisible to us"). There remains, then (if we wish to depend only on what is to be expected of men as men [i.e., on human nature]), only the "negative wisdom" of rulers who "see themselves compelled [*sich genöthigt sehen werden*]," from "their own motives," gradually to put an end to war. Rulers, to whose "honor" Kant continues to appeal, can be counted on to further progress toward the better, whether by positive intention or (more likely) by allowing "free professors of law" to direct themselves (as in Kant's own essay) against the state's *mis*-education of its own future officers. If that freedom should at sometime in the future be refused, there will still remain the force of its historical representation, which, given human nature as here revealed, can be counted on to be remembered [7: 88].

We thus return to the cosmological question with which Kant's essay starts—how to assume a viewpoint [*Ansicht*] for predicting "the course of human things" equivalent to the self-displacement of Copernicus from earth to sun for purposes of predicting the movement of the stars. Kant makes or finds it in the "outlook" [*Absicht*] that his interpretation of a certain event opens up within the realm of human experience—an event resembling the moment, in which, thanks to Rousseau, Kant was himself "set upright." (That Kant describes this event in almost the same terms he employed forty years earlier to depict that personally transformative moment—each involving the "disappearance" [*verschwinden*] of an illusory concept of honor before its republican rival—gives further emphasis to the resemblance (cf. [20: 44]). Thanks to this event [*Begebenheit*], to which Kant's own (fortunate) education would seem to give privileged access, man is brought face to face with his own nature as a being given to be free [*ein mit Freiheit begabtes Wesen*], forestalling rulers' ongoing abuse of others of their kind. Foremost among *Volkserklären* is thus Kant himself, who publishes a history in which men see themselves, before the fact, freely compelled to peace—an "announcement in advance" that for once makes soothsaying honorable.[54]

For a prophecy that proclaims its own "undiminishable force," it is a remarkably downbeat ending—made more so by the "conclusion" [*Beschluß*], with its humorous "promise" of medical "improvement," that proves fatal [7: 93–94]. Only a negative wisdom can be counted on to finally put an end to war, and this only given the proclaimed inevitability of a republic that finally provides the necessary center for a growing federative order. And even the abolition of war (however distant) is itself but the necessary propaedeutic to establishing an educational "mechanism" absent which the enlightenment of humanity is not "to be expected."

What, then, is one finally to make of Kant's prophecy and the "event" on which it's premised? One needn't be as harsh a critic as Nietzsche (who called Kant an "idiot" for claiming the French Revolution as "proof" of the sufficiency of man's *Anlage* to the good)[55] to harbor doubts as to their reliability. Even Kant wonders, in an early draft, whether the event in question might not amount to nothing more than "a warm desire for newspapers." All one can say with certitude is that authentically interpreted, the *Factum* of such desire, for reasons that the published text spells out, furnishes new grounds for moral confidence (cf. [19: 604–607]).

Readers of Kant's historical and political works often themselves succumb to the mere "wishfulness" that he meant those works to counter, because they miss the "anthropological-teleological" problem that *any* testimony to the "purposiveness" of nature "within us" poses, given the stark demands of an autonomy-based ethic. This problem is nowhere clearer than in Kant's last attempted public portrait of the human race ("Schilderung des Characters der Menschengattung" [7: 330]) in the final, published version of the *Anthropology* [1798]. The difficulty with characterizing the human species is, as Kant there puzzlingly states, our inability to "experience" a way of being rational other than our own terrestrial sort, and hence the absence of a "middle term of comparison": "let the highest specific term be that of a *terrestrial* rational being: we cannot name its character because we have no knowledge of *non-terrestrial* beings that would allow us to state their characteristic property and so characterize terrestrial rational beings among rational beings in general." All we can do to assign man his place in the "system of living nature" is to attribute to him the character of having that which "he himself creates, in that he is endowed with the capacity [*vermögend ist*] to perfect himself according to the ends that he himself takes on" [7: 321].[56] Man is distinguished from other living inhabitants of the earth by a technical *Anlage* for manipulating things (a mechanical *Anlage*, as Kant puts it, combined with consciousness); a pragmatic *Anlage* (for using other men skillfully for his own purposes); and a moral *Anlage* (to act toward self and others according to the principle of freedom under law, i.e., a capacity for "intelligible character") [7: 322].

As for the third: man's consciousness of his own freedom through his awareness of the moral law establishes that he has an intelligible character and is thus good by nature. "Experience," on the other hand, shows that there is in him "a propensity [*Hang*] toward active [*thätigen*] seeking [*Begehrung*] of the unpermitted, even though he knows it to be unpermitted," and which stirs as soon as man starts [*anhebt*] making use of his own freedom [7: 324]. Our consequent judgment of the sensible character of man as a species avoids "self-contradiction," then, only "because we can assume that its natural determination/destiny consists in constant progress toward the better" [7: 324].

But *can* we make this assumption, and on what basis? When we reflect on its historical elaboration, the results are decidedly ambiguous:

> In a civil constitution, which is the highest level of artificial improvement [*Steigerung*][57] of the good *Anlage* in the human species to the final end of its determination, still, *animality* manifests itself earlier, and, fundamentally, more mightily, than does pure *humanity* [Menschheit], and the tame cow is more useful than the wild only through *weakening* by man. Man's self-will is always prepared [*in Bereitschaft*] to break out in counter-will against his neighbors, and always presses [*strebt*] its claim to unconditioned freedom

to be not only independent over others who are by nature his equals, but instead to be superior to them, as is noticable even in the youngest child. This is because nature in him strives to lead him from culture to morality, not (as reason prescribes) from a lifting up/commencing [*anhebend*] of morality and its laws to an accordingly directed [*angelegten*], law-conforming culture. This unavoidably [*unvermeidlich*] produces [*abgiebt*] a perverted, counter-purposive tendency [*verkehrte, zweckwidrige Tendenz*]: for example, when religious instruction, which necessarily ought to be a *moral* culture, begins with historical culture and vainly seeks to deduce from it morality.

[7: 327–328]

The fullest artificial enhancement of our *Anlage* to the good only increases the proportionate advantage of our animality over our pure humanity. The very purposiveness of nature, in striving to move culture toward morality, is counter-purposive and "perverted" at its root. On what grounds, then, is one to avoid Rousseau's conclusion that man was closer to realizing his end in the raw state of nature, i.e., that the development of human culture is worse than futile? The very progress that we prize for hints of nature's purposiveness is itself an exhibition of the necessarily more fundamental *counter*-purposiveness of nature within us. Every exhibitable step forward in time is an enhanced repetition of the first, inevitable collapse into evil. Only an immediate "seizing of the reins" on reason's part—a beginning outside of time—can stem a process in which evil seems to have the upper hand. History as presented in Kant's late works is thus a race against time. For every ground of hope (e.g., the "ennoblement" of men through the discipline of civil law, a discipline that will make them conscious of the resemblance of actuality to the ideal [7: 329]), there is an accompanying reason for despair (e.g., the contempt for the human race evoked by the sheer need of less-than-perfect human beings—even, and especially, those living under conditions of civil discipline—to hide their thoughts) [7: 332]. Even Frederick the Great, who ruled "publicly" in a "republican manner," could not help ruling in "private" fact by trickery [*Betrug*], leading to an unavoidable *Verstimmung* of character (be it his own or others'). As Kant states in a final note:

Friedrich II once asked the excellent Sulzer, whom he deservedly esteemed, and whom he had appointed director of the Silesian schools, how it was going. Sulzer answered: "since building forward from the fundamental principle (of Rousseau) that man is by nature good, it begins to go better." Ah (said the king [in French]): *My dear Sulzer, you do not know what an evil race*

> *you are dealing with.*—It thus also belongs to the character of the species: that in striving toward a civil constitution, it also needs discipline through religion, so that what outer compulsion cannot accomplish can be effected through inner compulsion (conscience). For that the moral *Anlage* of human beings is made use of politically by lawgivers is a tendency that belongs to the character of the species. But if morality does not go before religion in this disciplining of the people, religion becomes master of morality, and statutory religion becomes an instrument of state force [*Gewalt*] (Politik) under *despots of faith* [Glaubensdespoten]: an ill that inevitably disorders [*verstimmt*] character and leads to government by trickery (called state cleverness); whereupon even that great monarch who *publicly* claimed to be merely the highest servant of the state, in sighing [*seufzend*] could not hide his private confession to the contrary, excusing his own person by reckoning this depravity to the account of the poor *race* called the human species.   [7: 332–333n]

Even the vaunted Frederick, whose *public* claim to be the people's servant Kant had once famously cited as a basis of moral hope,[58] is here privately betrayed by his own sighing tone. It is not, then, merely a matter of countering obscurantist religious despots, like Frederick William II, his successor. *No* despot, however "enlightened," can be counted on to give evidence in favor of the moral adequacy of the human race. The only reasonable image of our species would therefore seem to be a "caricature" that provokes not "well-meaning *laughter*" but "*contempt* [Verachtung]," as the enemies of virtue have claimed all along [7: 332; cf. 4: 407].

Kant manages, however, once again to parry their thrust: such a conclusion would be correct:

> did this condemning judgment [*verwerfende Urtheil*] not betray in us a moral *Anlage*, an inborn invitation [*Aufforderung*] of reason to work against even this tendency; thus presenting the human species not as evil, but as a species of rational being upwardly striving against obstacles in constant progress from evil toward the good.   [7: 332–333]

In being thus turned against *oneself,* the judgment of contempt by which Frederick hypocritically sought self-exculpation is morally reversed:

> [Thus presented] the human species' will is generally good, but the fulfillment burdened in that the achievement of the end cannot be expected through the free accord [*Zusammenstimmung*] of *individuals* but only through the progressive organization of citizens of the earth [*Erdbürger*] in and towards the species as a system that is cosmopolitically [*kosmopolitisch*] united.   [7: 333][59]

With this tonal shift from sarcasm to hope, Kant utters (almost) his last public word.

His last published word, as it happens, was a brief "postscript written as a friend" appended to Christian Gottlieb Mielcke's *Lithuanian-German and German-Lithuanian Dictionary*. Kant there praises scholarly efforts to preserve old languages (and Lithuanian in particular) both for their theoretical value as evidence of early human migrations and for their practical importance for the formation [*Bildung*] of "every small people [*Völkleins*] in a country (for example, the Prussian Poles)." Accordingly Kant urges instruction of such peoples both "in the schools and from their pulpits" according to "the model of their purest language, even if it is only spoken outside the country," and at the same time "to make it ever more current" with a view to such peoples' own national enlightenment [8: 445].[60] Kant's only public comment on the issue of multinational statehood is remarkable both in its promotion of minority languages (even in cases where they are no longer commonly used in the country of residence) and in its stress on the importance of language to the cultivation of national-civic character, which in the Lithuanian case would seem to be exceptionally promising:

> The Lithuanian speaks to his superiors in a tone of equality and trusting candor [*Offenherzigkeit*]; while his superiors [for their part] do not take this amiss or refuse to offer him their hand, for they find him compliant [*willig*] in all that is fair [*allem Billigen*]. This is a pride altogether different from all arrogance [*Hochmuth*] of a certain neighboring nation when anyone among them is more noble [*vornehmer*]; or rather it is a *feeling of one's value*, a feeling that indicates courage and at the same time ensures one's loyalty.
> [8: 445; emphasis added]

Kant's strikingly positive characterization of the Lithuanians calls to mind his earlier description, in the *Critique of Judgment*, of the ancient Greeks and Romans, as peoples who solved the "difficult task of uniting freedom (and hence also equality) with a compulsion (more respect and submission from duty than from fear)," and as peoples who combined "the lawful compulsion of the highest culture" with "the force and correctness of a free nature that *feels its own value*" (emphasis added).[61] Like the Greeks and Romans before them, in other words, the Lithuanians seem to be a people especially apt for communication between the most educated portion and the crudest, that is to say, for what Kant calls "taste as universal human sense" [5: 356]. So viewed, the Lithuanian language opens a precious window on an era of national "originality" that (but for the models of the classics) have otherwise all but vanished from living memory [5: 355–356].

Read with both *The Critique of Judgment* and the *Anthropology* in mind, Kant's "postscript" suggests the following conclusion: Unlike the status-conscious Germans (who, as Kant tells us in the *Anthropology*, are overly concerned with titles [7: 319]) and unlike the "neighboring" Poles (who all want to be masters) [7: 313n], Lithuanians are an unmitigated civic boon to Prussia. As for the Jews—the *Völklein* that may well have posed the greatest civic opportunities and challenges, and whose own efforts at linguistic-civic revival could not have escaped Kant's notice—on this topic Kant here chooses to remain silent.[62]

9

Kant's Jewish Problem

Kant has been famously attractive to enlightened German Jews, from Marcus Herz to Hermann Cohen; and enlightened Jews, for their part, were among the most important early disseminators of his work. At the same time, it was partly on the basis of its own Kantian premises that German nationalism emerged as a specifically anti-Jewish movement.[1] These opposing legacies are less surprising than they may at first appear, once Kant's own complex attitude toward Judaism, along with the Jewish responses it provoked, are taken fully into account.

The chapter that follows traces four general stages in the emergence of Kant's views on Jews and Judaism: 1) An early stage in which Marcus Herz (and, to a lesser extent, Moses Mendelssohn) figure as major champions of Kant's pre-critical thought. 2) A second, critical stage, culminating in Kant's publication of the *Critique of Judgment* (in 1789). Judaism in its "ethical" or Hebraic form is here singled out and lauded for its "sublime" law against the making of graven images. Kant's early Jewish friends and followers (who fail to make the critical breakthrough) are now left behind, even as a new, critically inspired generation—including Lazurus Bendavid and Saul Ascher—arises in their wake. 3) A third stage following on the French Revolution in which Kant finds himself under the mounting pressures of political reaction. Where he had previously counted on political and moral progress "from below," he now seeks to subvert the orthodox establishment from within. Disappointed with his own early Jewish followers, Kant at this point presents Judaism as the morally empty shell that the true moral religion must entirely discard. Two negative aspects of Judaism that Kant especially stresses are its adherence to a purely ceremonial law (which encourages moral hypocrisy) and its "Mosaic-messianism" (which encourages passivity and pious "waiting"). 4) A late, forth stage, in which Kant comes to regard his *later* Jewish students and followers as useful vehicles of an impending civil and moral revolution.[2] His specific invitation to enlightened Jews to become apostles of the new moral faith (i.e., Jews for a Kantian Jesus) is, I suggest, what prompts David Friedländer's infamous letter to Probst Teller—a futile gesture of German Jewish hope whose Kantian provenance has heretofore largely been missed.

1. Kant, Herz, and Mendelssohn: The Early Years

Among Kant's several early Jewish students, none was more important than Marcus Herz. The son of a Torah scribe, Herz went on to found the first of the famous Jewish salons that served as cauldrons of enlightened and post-enlightened German thought. That Kant chose Herz as his academic respondent in 1770 is itself a singular mark of Kant's respect for him during this period.[3] Herz was Kant's personal physician and closest intellectual correspondent during the crucial decade of the 1770s, during which Kant composed the *Critique of Pure Reason*. Although his later relations with Herz were more distant, both geographically and intellectually, there is no gainsaying their early intimacy. Herz, who, in Kant's words, "delighted him as a student by grasping his ideas . . . more quickly than any of the others" [Letter to Herz, May 11, 1781 {X: 269}] and "penetrated [them] more deeply than anyone else" [Letter to Herz, May 1, 1781 {X: 266–267}] was also Kant's main early conduit to the most important figures of the Berlin enlightenment.

Herz's early efforts on Kant's behalf were helped along by Moses Mendelssohn, who was himself an important figure of the German enlightenment well before Kant became famous. Through the intermediary offices of Marcus Herz, Mendelssohn helped introduce Kant's thought to Berlin—a city to which Kant himself never personally traveled.[4] Their relations were thus cordial and friendly, if not overly warm. A poignant letter describes Mendelssohn's unheralded appearance in Kant's class—Mendelssohn was on a mission of mercy to the Jews of Königsberg, who had been forbidden to recite the *Alenu* prayer. On a personal level, Kant and Mendelssohn had much in common: Each subscribed to a rigidly ascetic diet. They were, at least in matters of regimen and physical hygiene, kindred souls.

Kant and Mendelssohn were also intellectual allies in their common defense of intellectual freedom and attack on moral skepticism. On other important intellectual matters, however, they parted company. As a follower of Wolff, and in his sanguine claim that the basic moral truths could be proven theoretically, Mendelssohn represented the old guard—well intentioned, perhaps, but out of step with the critical intellectual and moral revolution Kant was intent on carrying out.

Indeed, in several respects Kant and Mendelssohn served as each other's negative amanuenses: Kant's *Dreams of a Spirit-Seer* provoking Mendelssohn's *Phaedo*, which is answered in the "Paralogism" section of the first *Critique*. One could give a similar account of *Religion within the Boundaries of Bare Reason* as a reaction, in part, to Mendelssohn's *Jerusalem*. And Kant's late "How to Overcome Morbid Feelings Through Sheer Resolution" (Part Three of *The Conflict of the Faculties*) is a response to the "work" of Mendelssohn's own death, which Kant seems to have regarded as an unwitting suicide.[5]

The latter judgment was partly self-exculpatory on Kant's part. Mendelssohn died in 1786—following a bitter dispute with Jacobi over the alleged "Spinozism" (read: atheism) of Mendelssohn's friend Lessing. At the height of that dispute, Herz called upon his old teacher to help Mendelssohn in his defense of "reason." Kant belatedly responded with an essay, *How to Orient Oneself in Thinking*. His defense of Mendelssohn in that essay was at best lukewarm; Jacobi, in Kant's view, was indeed right to insist that God's existence (along with other moral truths) could not be proven theoretically. Herz must have been deeply disappointed; and Kant's failure to come immediately to Mendelssohn's aid was rumored in some circles to have been partially responsible for his sudden death.[6] When Kant insisted (ten years later) that Mendelssohn had in fact been done in by his irrationally restrictive diet, he may have had those old accusations partly in mind.

But self-starvation was only part of a general complaint that Kant would launch against Mendelssohn in the mid-1790s. The issue was not Mendelssohn's excessive attachment to worldly well-being—how could it be, when Mendelssohn's personal habits were, if anything, more abstemious and restrictive than Kant's own It was rather Mendelssohn's pointless self-denial that displayed the heteronomy of his basic posture and, hence, his bad faith. Pointlessness, rather than material selfishness, is the charge that Kant levels against Mendelssohn and, by implication, against Judaism as the latter understands it.

Kant was not always so publicly critical of Mendelssohn. Indeed, his initial response to Mendelssohn's *Jerusalem* [1783] gave Mendelssohn considerable delight.

Mendelssohn, an observant Jew, argues in *Jerusalem* that there is no conflict between observation of the ceremonial law and philosophic rationality. For one purpose of the law (as he surmises) is to engender the sort of (morally informed) critical inquiry that is likewise fostered by modern science and philosophy. Yet another purpose is to shore up the moral knowledge that is accessible to rational inquiry and "sound common sense" alike.[7] There is thus no reason to regard the special obligations of the Jews as inimical to their participation in the larger civil society. Judaism differs from Christianity in just this: that Judaism knows "no revealed religion in the sense in which Christians understand the term." The Jews possess a "divine legislation" but not a "supernatural revelation of religion" understood as creedal doctrines necessary for salvation [90].[8]

Mendelssohn, however, also argues that since the destruction of the Temple, Mosaic law is binding in conscience only. He thus urges that the Jewish community be stripped of its traditional "autonomy" and the civil monopoly that it conveyed in matters such as burial rites. Judaism, so construed, is at least as open to reason and hence maintainable with true sincerity as Christianity. In the name of their shared understanding of the importance of such sincerity, Mendelssohn challenges Christians to forego imposing their own ecclesiastical doctrines as a matter of coercive law.

The truly radical character, from the standpoint of traditional Judaism itself, of Mendelssohn's proposed settlement with the larger civil society is often ignored.[9] Mendelssohn argues in *Jerusalem* that Jews be permitted to retain their ceremonial laws, while being stripped of their juridical autonomy as a community. Judaism, thus construed, becomes a matter of individual conscience, rather than being subject to the coercive power of the community at large.

But there is a price to be paid for thus relinquishing communal autonomy. The obligations of the sacred law are now modulated by a question that it is up to each (Jewish) individual to pose for himself: Does obedience help me become a better (or more enlightened) human being? The unchangeable ceremonial law, in Mendelssohn's hands, becomes (whatever his intention) merely a means to a higher rational and moral end. But questions as to means are, by Mendelssohn's own account, historical rather than rational truths, and subject, as such, to honest civil disagreement.

It is no wonder, then, that an anonymous critic charged that Mendelssohn, in denying the coercive authority of ecclesiastical law, had "removed a cornerstone"[10] of Judaism. Why not then, the critic asked, become a Christian? To this Mendelssohn responds in a famous passage of *Jerusalem* that will in turn be taken up by Kant. If it be true, Mendelssohn says:

> that the cornerstones of my house are dislodged, and the structure threatens to collapse, do I act wisely if I remove my belongings from the lower to the upper floor for safety? . . . Now Christianity, as you know, is built upon Judaism, and if the latter falls, it must necessarily collapse into one heap of ruins. . . . Surely, the Christian who is in earnest about light and truth [the title of the critic's pamphlet] will not challenge the Jew to a fight when there seems to be a contradiction between truth and truth, between Scripture and reason. He will rather join him in an effort to discover the groundlessness of the contradiction. For this is their common concern. Whatever else they have to settle between themselves may be postponed for a later time. For the present they must join forces to avert the danger, and either discover the paralogism[11] or show that it is only a seeming contradiction. [87]

The ironies of the passage are, of course, multiple. In challenging Jews to a fight, Christians implicitly extend the civic honor they outwardly deny them. Only a gentleman could receive, or be expected to accept, such a challenge.[12] And yet among fellow citizens, subject to a common civic law, all such challenges would be inappropriate. At the same time, Mendelssohn's own challenge would force his Christian interlocutor to live by the standard of universal truth that he allegedly professes. Either the Christian must admit that his doctrines are indeed contrary to reason, or he must be willing to join forces with whomever claims to be able to prove the compatibility of Scripture with the demands of reason.

Finally, according to the biblical passage to which the image of a "cornerstone" alludes, the rock in question originates in Israel. By the standards of the *New Testament* itself, then, Jesus is the common "rock" of both Judaism and Christianity. The objection that "cuts [Mendelssohn] to the heart" (and might thus appear to circumcise him inwardly) is not the "good news" of the Apostles (which, as Mendelssohn implies, contains nothing that is not already essentially contained in Judaism) but the persistent insistence of so many Jews on communal autonomy and an accompanying submission to coercive religious law. A second Paul, Mendelssohn holds out common reason as a means uniting mankind without dispensing with Jewish difference. Jews can remain a separate sect, united by a shared historical opinion as to the usefulness of the ceremonial law, without ceasing to be members of the larger civic commonwealth. Coexistence is to be secured by Jewish relinquishment of the coercive character of their religious law and by the joint granting by Jews and Christians alike that although necessary truth is eternal and immutable, historical truths (including those of revelation) are ones over which men may reasonably part company.

Kant's immediate response to *Jerusalem* was apparently positive (at a time when he still hoped for Mendelssohn's support in the reception of his own *Critique of Pure Reason*). As he wrote to the author, after first inveighing his help with the *Critique*, "I regard [*Jerusalem*] as the announcement of a reform that is slowly impending, a reform that concerns only for your own nation but others as well. You have managed to unite your religion with a degree of freedom of conscience that one would hardly have thought possible and of which no other can boast" [10: 347]. Mendelssohn had showed, moreover, that every religion must have such unrestricted freedom of conscience, "so that even the Church will have to consider how to rid itself of everything that burdens . . . it," a burden that lies "in making salvation contingent on belief in the truth of [certain] historical propositions." Kant joins Mendelssohn not in the latter's way of reconciling the truths of reason with those of Scripture (for here Kant had taken up a very different path that Mendelssohn had shown himself reluctant to investigate) but a common rejection of belief in contingent truth as the necessary path to salvation. Kant does not so much misread Mendelssohn (as is sometimes charged) as stake out a position they still share. For Mendelssohn's own reconciliation of scripture and reason depended on his conviction that the fundamental moral and religious truths are indeed provable by theoretical reason [94]—a claim that Kant's *Critique* [1781], which Mendelssohn had confessed himself unable to understand,[13] directly contradicts.

There is more at stake, however, then Kant's measured praise of *Jerusalem* lets on. Mendelssohn's provision for diversity in unity (and hence for the ongoing existence of the Jews within a larger civic community) compels him to deny the thesis of Christian supersession either in its traditional religious form or as put forward by Spinoza and other enlightenment figures. History is not a progressive movement from Judaism to Christianity and beyond. Enlightenment is not the apotheosis of Christianity but the shared portion of a variety of peoples and religions spread out over time. Human history, then, does not progress, but only repeats [96].

Kant implicitly contests this point by making Mendelssohn's own successful argument a basis for hope in a better human world to come: the latter has "so thoroughly and clearly shown" the "necessity of freedom" as to enable one to conclude that "mankind must eventually be united on the essential point of religion" [10: 347]. But if freedom, and the enlightenment that flows from it, makes such unity inevitable, what role will then remain for Judaism as a separate creed?

Both Mendelssohn and Kant hold that certain fundamental moral principles (such as the existence of a benign and all-powerful God) are universally accessible to reason. But whereas Mendelssohn holds them to be provable theoretically, Kant counters that they are known only practically. For Kant, the necessity of belief in God rests not on theoretical knowledge, but on our *moral* need to view history as progressive. Under the relatively benign reign of Frederick the Great, during which Kant counted on progress "from below" (as he puts it in *What is Enlightenment?*) this crucial disagreement could remain largely submerged. Enlightenment, in the age of Frederick, could be expected to make its way without the direct intervention of the state—i.e., through the sheer freedom to publicize.[14] However theoretically flawed Mendelssohn's defense of Judaism may have been from Kant's own point of view, it tended to support the cause of freedom generally. Thus, for all their important differences, he and Mendelssohn could remain political allies.

2. Mosaic "Sublimity" in the *Critique of Judgment*

The religious and political restrictions that followed on the death of Frederick the Great gravely complicated the alliance between Kant and Mendelssohn. No longer able to count on freedom to publicize his views directly, Kant would turn increasingly to the church establishment itself as the most efficacious vehicle of popular enlightenment. Hereafter, progress would have to come "from above," i.e., through a cooption of the organs and agencies of the state—and, indeed, of organized Christianity itself. With that change of tactic comes increasing emphasis on what distinguishes Kant from Mendelssohn.

In the initial years of the new French Republic, such drastic measures did not yet seem necessary. In his *Critique of Judgment* [1790] Kant insists upon the primacy of ethics over religion with an unembarrassed vigor and directness that would prove impossible two years later. He also presents early Judaism in a favorable light that strikingly contrasts with his treatment of Judaism and the Jews elsewhere:

> There is perhaps no more sublime place in the lawbook of the Jews than the command: "thou shalt not make to thyself any graven image, nor the likeness of anything which is in heaven or in the earth or under the earth," etc. This command can alone explain the enthusiasm [*Enthusiasm*] that the Jewish people in their civilized [*sittlich*] epoch felt for their religion, when they compared themselves with other peoples, or explain the pride that Mahommedanism inspires. [5: 274]

It is the same, Kant says, with the moral law and of the tendency to morality in us. "When the senses see nothing more before them," and only the idea of morality remains, its power is strengthened rather than weakened. It is for this very reason, he adds, that governments willingly allow religion to be adorned with childish images; for they thereby discourage subjects from extending their spiritual powers and thus render them more tractable.

The Jewish nation (in its civilized epoch) is here the forerunner of the revolutionary enthusiasm that Kant will subsequently praise as the sublime sign that mankind is constantly progressing. And historical Christianity—in its resort to childish images and rituals—is here the preferred tool of despotism.

In sum, the *Critique of Judgment* seems to lift Judaism, at least in its "ancient," radically iconoclastic form, above Christianity as historically practiced. This elevation, as we shall see, contrasts sharply with Kant's treatment of Judaism only two years later, when he presents it as unique among historic faiths in having no moral content at all. In Kant's later work Judaism's radical rejection of all sensual mediation of the transcendent becomes a fatal defect rather than a strength. It is understandable that Jewish figures like Saul Ascher (and later, Ernst Cassirer), in their own efforts to construct an "enlightened" Kantian religion, will be drawn especially to the *Critique of Judgment*.

3. Kant's Treatment of Judaism and the Jews in the Early to Middle 1790s.

a. Religion within the Boundaries of Bare Reason

In *Religion within the Boundaries of Bare Reason* [1792] Judaism represents all that Christianity must shed in order to become the true, moral religion of Jesus. This new, radically negative public attitude toward Judaism can be partially explained by Kant's own worsening personal circumstances. As we have seen, *Religion* was written at a time when Kant and his critical project were under intense political and religious pressure, following upon the ascension of the Frederick William II and his reactionary responses to the French Revolution.

Kant's critical teaching on religion up to this time had stressed two things: the strict priority of morality to religion both as to the content and as to incentive. Neither religious faith nor a specific revelation is needed either to know what we ought to do or to motivate obedience to the moral law. The content of morality is universally accessible through reason alone; and acting morally means doing what we ought without regard for earthly or divine reward and punishment. The purpose of religion is, rather, to support morality by providing assurance that the good we strive to realize morally is in fact attainable. That assurance, Kant argues in the *Critique of Practical Reason* [1787], requires us to believe both in a just and omnipotent God and in our own immortality. These postulates of pure practical reason cannot be known in a theoretical sense either to be true or false; instead, they are practically necessary assumptions we must make if we are to overcome the dialectical challenges to which practical reason is otherwise prone. Kant already notes the importance of establishing the right relation between morality and religion, a relation whose perversion damages moral attitudes [5: 109–110].

By the early 1790s the government's abridgments of religious freedom had reached what were from Kant's point of view crisis proportions.[15] A new state edict imposed a confession of orthodox faith on all clerics, who were, perforce, also officials of the state. Under such conditions, no one who ascribed to Kantian principles could ascend to the pulpit without dishonestly dissembling his true opinion in violation of those very principles. *What Is Enlightenment?* had proposed the following compromise: Ministers who were privately required, in their capacity as state officials, to promulgate official religious teachings contrary to reason were still free, as members of the "public," to call things as they saw them. The new king's edicts closed that loophole, and with it prospects for reform "from below." Kant could no longer count on the eventual transformation in the "people's way of thinking" that had seemed possible, and even likely, under previous conditions of relative intellectual freedom. *Religion*—whose publication entailed some personal risk to Kant himself—was intended, at least in part, to address this new and alarming situation.

Religion counterattacks on two parallel fronts. On the one hand, it seeks to reassert a morally empowering progressive view of history, despite evident contemporary obstacles. On the other hand, it seeks to isolate the precise point within the human soul that gives rise to threats of an historical reversal, the better to oppose them: thus the famous doctrine of "radical evil" that so dismayed Goethe and others. As we saw in Chapter 5, that doctrine is most accurately understood, not as a dogmatic assertion about human nature, but as an exercise in what Kant calls "moral ascetics" [6:51], i.e., identification of the practical target against which to apply our effort to become "better human beings." Radical evil—another name for that target—lies in our "hesitation" to act as we ought. Every normal human being knows right from wrong. And yet, instead of immediately doing as we ought, we look about for a *further* reason to obey the moral law. Something in us resists doing right just because it's right, i.e., acting autonomously. Kant identifies this moral "hesitation" with a perversion of the correct relation between morality and religion. Every assertion of the priority of religion over morality is an endorsement of the inner hesitation in which radical evil essentially consists. Recapture of the religious establishment is thus crucial to Kant's purpose. With this end in view, *Religion* lays out a threefold designation: those aspects of Christianity as historically practiced that are contained within the boundaries of unaided human reason, those aspects that are outside those boundaries but abut them in a decorative though not supportive capacity (the "parerga"), and those aspects that must be entirely discarded if the relation between religion and morality is not to be irrevocably perverted.

Kant grants in *Religion* that the spiritual message of Christianity—pure moral religion—must first be sensualized, especially for purposes of popular education.[16] Christianity is superior to all other known historical faiths in maximizing the effect of such sensualization at minimum spiritual cost. The key to Christianity's superiority, for Kant, lies not only in the moral teaching of the Gospels (which on a strict Kantian understanding must be accessible at all times and places); it lies even more in the figure of Jesus himself as an "ideal" that makes concrete the idea of moral holiness.[17] Kant explicitly rejects, on moral grounds, the divinity of Christ along with the doctrine of redemption. Morality itself precludes both the orthodox notion of original sin and that of Christ as vicarious substitute. The importance of the figure of Jesus lies, rather, in its sensualization, as a limit case of undeserved suffering, of the sublime ideal of moral holiness itself—hence, as Kant sees matters, its manifest historical power. Jesus not only presents a pure moral teaching; his suffering and death bring that teaching home to the popular mind in a uniquely compelling way.

How, then, to account for the very different teaching of the church as generally understood? The history of Christianity is itself a story of emergence of its pure moral germ, as exemplified in the life and message of Jesus, from its inessential shell [see 6: 121]. At every stage, a "counter-service" of "spiritual bondsmanship" has had to be contested for this process to go forward. What is now required is recognition of everything morally extraneous, i.e., that cannot be justified on strictly moral grounds, as in the service of an eventual emancipation of the human will from all authority external to itself. Only if their subsidiary and temporary status is thus admitted can such extraneous acts as public prayers and other ceremonial rites be performed in a truly Christian spirit. Seen in this light, Mendelssohn's attempted reconciliation of Judaism and universal reason could not be more counter-purposive, for what Mendelssohn stresses is, precisely, Jewish acceptance of the ceremonial law in perpetuity. To carry out ceremonial rites forever on the basis of an authority that cannot in principle be shared by man is to put heteronomy, as Kant conceives it, at the core of one's faith.

To be sure, Mendelssohn is here following in the footsteps of Maimonides, who also argues that the revealed law is given for the sake of reason. They start, however, in different places: Maimonides does not deny the right of the community to exclude those who deny the sanctity of the law. An obedience that is, for Maimonides, a condition of free rational inquiry as well as of remaining a Jew becomes, in Mendelssohn, a matter of free choice. Observance of the ceremonial law is no longer a necessary prerequisite either of engaging in philosophy or of remaining a Jew. Mendelssohn's argument makes more sense as an apology for his own observance of the law before non-Jewish rationalists than as a plea to fellow Jews to remain observant. It is hardly surprising that his enlightened co-religionists (including his own children) generally did not follow his observant example.[18]

But Kant has additional reasons for making Judaism a symbol for heteronomy. Kant's Jewish students and associates, who had their own reasons for disparaging their unenlightened co-religionists, may have (unwittingly) confirmed Kant in his prejudices concerning the moral insufficiency of ordinary Jews. An early letter from his student Marcus Herz is here telling; Herz writes (in the same year that he served as correspondent for Kant's dissertation):

Eternally unforgettable teacher,
    Highly esteemed Herr Professor,
    Forgive me, dearest Herr Professor, for paying my respects to you only now even I have been here since last Thursday. . . . [After the discomforts of

the journey back to Berlin] I was unfit for any other important business, and how much more unfit for conversation with you! The mere thought of you sets my soul in reverential astonishment . . . . It is you alone that I have to thank for my change in condition, you to whom I owe everything I am; *without you I would still be like so many of my kinsmen, pursuing a life chained to the wagon of prejudices, a life to be set beside that of a beast. I would have a soul without forces, an understanding without activity, in short, without you I would be that which I was four years ago, in other words I would be nothing* . . . . Let it ever remain the consolation of the ignorant that with all our science we have not progressed beyond them; it is always the complaint of hypochondriacal savants that our knowledge only increases our unhappiness. I scorn the former and pity the latter; I shall never cease to regard the day that I gave myself over to the sciences as the happiest and the day you became my teacher as the first day of my life. [10: 99–100; emphasis added][19]

Even discounting the excesses of an intellectually besotted young student, Herz's statement is remarkable. Rousseauist fantasies as to the moral superiority of simple men do not excuse the animal-like prejudices of his religious brethren, from which Kant has single-handedly delivered him. (Solomon Maimon's *Autobiography* will later give a similar account of Talmudic "backwardness.") Mendelssohn himself was forced to concede that his enlightened view of Judaism was fiercely opposed by a majority of his co-religionists. Given these internal struggles within the Jewish community at large, Kant's very friendship with enlightened Jews may have further reinforced his prejudices as to the moral bankruptcy of traditional Judaism as such. Adapting Spinoza's views as to the wholly political character of biblical legislation, Kant concluded that the "ethical" aspect of Judaism had also vanished with the destruction of the Temple.[20] As with Hobbes, the Jewish state is the prototype of a "merely" juridical condition, without ethical content or motivation. The Jewish notion that one can obey the law without improving morally makes it a "pure" cult, without intrinsic moral content. The sublimity of Judaism in its ethical period subsisted wholly in its iconoclasm—rather than any alleged moral universalism. Indeed, as the above quoted passage from the *Critique of Judgment* goes on to make clear, the sublimity of the Mosaic law only served to support an arrogant pride with respect to other nations. And, in any case, the Jewish state was intrinsically aristocratic and hence inimical to the essentially republican structure of authority that is prefigured in the Christian Trinity [6: 142]. In sum: Kant's qualified admiration for the sublimity of Judaism and his no doubt genuine affection for individuals like Herz did not interfere with the general view, expressed in his last extensive published work, that the "Palestinians" of Europe were "a nation of cheaters" [7: 205n]. Indeed, the Jews would not have lasted historically as a nation, in Kant's view, without the Muslims, and, even more, the Christians, whose adoption of the Old Testament preserved an exhausted—and even perverse—way of life that left to its own devices would have faded away (as it had in India and China) [6: 136–137n].

These divergent strands of thought support a governing argument in *Religion* as to the relation between Judaism and Christianity: Judaism is only the occasion for a Christian revolution that is continuous in spirit with the freedom of ancient Greece and Rome. Reduced to a metaphor: The Jewish people are the passive maternal womb or husk; freedom is the active paternal germ [6: 80n; 6: 121]. The spiritual "rebirth" of the human species out of nature can now take on the sensualized form of a progressive separation of the church from its initially supportive Jewish "integuments." Paul's circumcision of the heart is recast as the literal "cutting off" of the burdensome remnant that weighs down the newly resurgent spirit of humanity that is even now in a state of emergence from its Jewish matrix [6: 121].

In this account, historical Judaism merely furnished the "occasion" for a "moral revolution" without itself actively causing it. On the one hand, its theocratic constitution—devoted, at least in name, to the principle of good—kept in Scriptural "remembrance" the original idea of right [6: 79]. On the other hand, its burdens, and a related discontent, readied its people for the influences of Greek wisdom:

> Now there suddenly appeared among these same people, at a time in which they felt in full measure all the ills of a hierarchical constitution, and also felt it, perhaps, through the Greek philosophers' moral teaching concerning freedom, teaching that shook the sense of slavery and had gradually gained influence over them, inducing most to reflection so that they were ripe for revolution—a person whose wisdom, even purer than that of the previous philosophers, was as though descended from heaven; and he announced himself indeed as a true human being, so far as his doctrines and example were concerned, yet also as an envoy of such heavenly origin. [6: 80]

Christianity thus does not stem from Judaism (as Mendelssohn had rhetorically assumed in calling Judaism Christianity's "first floor") but arises out of an "entirely new principle." If elements of Judaism were retained "as a connected strand," it was only as a temporary concession to an initiating people that was habituated to its uses. The "total revolution" effected by Christianity is a "total abandonment" of the Judaism in which it originated, a Judaism with which much Greek thought was already "intermingled" [6: 127].

> Thus from a Judaism—but from a Judaism no longer patriarchal and unmixed, no longer standing solely on a political constitution (which had already been much shattered); but from a Judaism, rather, already mingled with a religious faith because of the moral doctrines which had gradually become public; in a condition in which much foreign (Greek) wisdom had already become available to this people otherwise still ignorant, wisdom that presumably further enlightened it through concepts of virtue despite the oppressive burden of its doctrinal faith, readying it for revolutions as occasioned by a diminution of the priests' power, owing to their subjugation the rule of a people who regarded every foreign popular faith with indifference—it was from a Judaism such as this that Christianity suddenly arose albeit not unprepared. [6: 127–128]

Thus far from being essential to religion, the doctrine that *every Christian must be a Jew whose Messiah has come* is merely the "apt" procedure of Christianity's first propagators who sought thus to introduce its teaching among their people. Indeed, Christianity owes its own dark history solely to the fact that "what should have served at the beginning" to "win over to the new faith" a people full of prejudices was "later made" (owing to man's perversity) into the basis "of a universal world-religion." Thus Kant can now say "without hesitation" that of all periods in the entire history of the church, the present one is "the best" [6: 131].

Mendelssohn, exhibiting the same national "cleverness" [*Kluglichkeit*] as those first propagators [6: 166], seized on the weakness in their procedure to "preempt any suggestion of religious conversion made to a son of Israel." Any such suggestion, according to Mendelssohn, would amount to asking someone to "demolish the ground floor in order to feel secure on the second." His true opinion, however, shines forth, Kant says, in a manner agreeable to Kant's own teaching. What Mendelssohn "meant" to tell Christians was that they should first remove the Judaism in their own teaching (in which case nothing would be left but "pure moral religion") after which enlightened Jews would be "able to take [conversion] under advisement." Understood in light of Kant's own interpretive principles, Mendelssohn becomes an unlikely ally in the effort to disencumber Christianity of its Jewish husk (though the latter might remain as an "antiquity") [6: 166n]. The charge of being an all-destroyer of traditional religious faith—a charge that Mendelssohn's image of the two-storied house was intended to combat—is truer than he was willing openly to admit.

It is hard to escape a certain uncomfortable and uncanny parallelism: Kant's Jewish associates are his witting and unwitting disciples: raised from ignorance, like their Hellenized forbearers, by their exposure to a foreign philosophic culture, they have now been primed to spread a *new* revolution "in thinking" beyond their narrow circle into the educated public world beyond. The Jewish gift for priestly propaganda, formerly in the service of an aristocratic "oral law," can finally be enlisted on behalf of human freedom.[21]

b. The History Writings of the 1790s

For that effort to succeed, however, Mendelssohn's continuing hold on proponents of enlightened progress must be firmly laid to rest. In both *Theory and Practice* [1792] and in *An Old Question Newly Raised: Whether the Human Race Is in Constant Progress Toward the Better?* [1798], Kant singles out the "pointlessness" of history as Mendelssohn conceives it. In *Theory and Practice* he writes (in a section subtitled "against Moses Mendelssohn"):

> Is the human race as a whole lovable, or is it an object to be regarded reluctantly, an object we must wish well (to avoid becoming misanthropists) and yet without expecting it . . . ? The answer to these questions depends on the answer one gives to another one: is there in human nature dispositions indicating that the race will always progress and improve . . . ? If this were the case, we could at least love the human species for its constant approach to the good; otherwise we should have to hate or despise it, notwithstanding the protests of universal philanthropy. . . .
>
> Moses Mendelssohn was of the latter opinion . . . which he opposed to his friend Lessing's hypothesis of a divine education of mankind. To Mendelssohn "that the whole of mankind . . . must constantly progress" is a mere phantom of the brain. "We see," he says, "the human race as a whole making small swings back and forth . . . Man as an individual progresses; but mankind constantly fluctuates back and forth between fixed limits, and considered as a whole . . . [and thus] maintains at all times roughly the same level of morality, the same amount of religion and irreligion, of virtue and vice, of happiness (?) and misery." [8: 307–308]

Kant counters that such a sight is unfit "not so much for a god" as for an ordinary decent human being, for whom the drama thus unfolded eventually becomes a "farce." An otherwise decent and upright man (Spinoza, perhaps), as Kant had argued in the *Critique of Judgment,* cannot adopt such an unbelieving view without damaging his own moral attitude by sapping his own eagerness to act to make the world a better place [5: 452]. In *Theory and Practice* Kant adds that one has an "inborn duty to affect posterity in such a way that they will become ever better" and "that this duty can be rightly passed down from one member of the species to the next." The "worthy [*gute*] Mendelssohn" must in fact have reckoned upon "hope in better times" given his "exertions [*bemühen*] on behalf of the enlightenment and wellbeing of his own nation" [8: 309]. (Mendelssohn, then, is not quite a lover of humanity at large, whatever his attachment to "enlightenment.") Kant had earlier held, in his gloss on Spinoza, that we must believe in God in order to be able to understand moral acts as disinterested and yet not pointless. Kant now adds that history itself must have a point. Confronted by the "sorry spectacle" of the evils men inflict on one another, our spirits can be raised only by the assumption of moral progress in and by the species.

Kant's own ultimate purpose, in Part Three of *Theory and Practice*, is to proclaim the moral necessity of hope in an eventual world state—that is to say, a condition of international right based upon enforceable public laws [8: 312–313]. Three years later, in his famous essay *Toward Perpetual Peace*, he will replace that expectation with more modest hopes for a voluntary federation of states—hopes, he says, that do not constitute theoretical "prophecy" [*weisssagen*] but suffice for purposes of practice [8: 368]. In *The Conflict of the Faculties*, published three years thereafter, he will advance his claims as to the constant progress of mankind even more emphatically than in *Theory and Practice*. Progress is no longer merely a "well-meaning and commendable" moral assumption but a "soothsaying" [*wahrsagen*] valid "for the most rigorous theory and despite all skeptics" [7: 88].

In the same work Kant takes up again the "Sisyphusian" views of Mendelssohn (though he does not mention him by name),[22] which he now links to what he calls "the Abderitic hypothesis of the human race for the predetermination of its history":

> Busy folly is the character of our species; people hastily set off on the path of the good but do not persevere. Instead, if only for the sake of not being bound to a single end, indeed, if only so that there may happen diversion/ alternation, they reverse the plan of progress ... and lay upon themselves hopeless exertion. [7: 82]

"Abderitism" is here explicitly associated with "the many" who adopt an incorrect (or unjust) [*unrecht*] standpoint on the course of human affairs. The *correct* standpoint would take the disinterested enthusiasm of revolutionary spectators as the sign of mankind's preponderant goodness, and hence of the inevitability of progress over time. But why does Kant call the opposing view that mankind neither advances nor recedes the Abderitic Hypothesis?

The ancient Greek city of Abdera was the home of the materialist philosopher Democritus. Its citizens were also legion for a certain sort of folly pertaining to dramatic spectacles.[23] Christopher Martin Wieland's *Geschichte der Abderiten* had recently brought the term into popular currency. In *The Conflict of the Faculties,* Part Two, Kant conflates the position of the ancient prophets of Israel with contemporary "politicians" whose denial of the possibility of moral progress similarly becomes a self-fulfilling prophecy:

> Jewish prophets could well prophecy [*weissagen*] that sooner or later not merely decay but also complete dissolution would befall their state; for they were themselves the authors of its fate. As leaders of the *Volk* they burdened its constitution with so much ecclesiastical and accompanying civil burdens that their state became totally inept at subsisting for itself and even more next to neighboring peoples. Hence the jeremiads of its priests were naturally enough thrown away into the air as something dispensable; for they stiff-neckedly persisted in their resolve for an untenable constitution of their own making, and thus could infallibly foresee the outcome. [7: 80]

"Our politicians," Kant adds—and even some ecclesiastics—do exactly the same thing, so far as their influence extends, by way of self-fulfilling prophecy: that is to say, they make civic and moral improvement impossible. In each case, what is properly required, according to Kant, is a willingness to reform the letter of the (positive) law according to its "spirit" as understood by his own critical philosophy. Mendelssohn's position in *Jerusalem*—namely, that the ceremonial laws of the Jews were given by God "as a remembrance" to be followed in perpetuity[24]—here becomes an emblem for all that is or might go wrong in contemporary Europe. Reception of the French Revolution, replaces the Mosaic Law, as the "sign" ever more to be remembered on which Kant pegs the certainty of mankind's constant progress toward the better.

We are now in a better position to discern why Mendelssohn is, from Kant's late point of view, an Abderite. Indeed, Mendelssohn's appeal in *Jerusalem* to a certain "Athenian philosopher" already seems to makes Kant's point [75]: in rejecting progress,[25] Mendelssohn turns Judaism into something that is essentially pagan.[26]

It would have been logically open to Mendelssohn to reject both horns of Kant's dilemma in one of two ways: First, he might have insisted on the rational and moral superiority of Judaism as such. This would have meant falling into the apologetic trap in which Lavater had earlier laid: convert or prove that Bonnet (who had allegedly demonstrated the superiority of Christianity) is wrong. Mendelssohn refused to attempt such a proof—an attempt that would only have played into the hands of the Jews' civil and religious enemies. But Mendelssohn also had a second option, which would be taken up by some of Kant's Jewish followers: Accept progress without conceding Christian supersession. The price of that alternative, however, was the abandonment of ceremonial law as inessential to the spirit of Judaism. What was retained as the essential core, as we shall see, proved even less tolerable to the Christian majority than Jewish orthodoxy.

The one path that was not open to Prussian Jews at this time was the liberal one, so beautifully captured in the exchange between George Washington and the Jewish congregants of Newport, Rhode Island, which granted the irrelevance of confessional faith to the requirements of citizenship once certain minimal civil and moral conditions were met. Thus Locke argued that Jews (but not public atheists or Catholics who refused to foreswear allegiance to the Pope) should be granted full civil rights. Judaism as traditionally practiced was presumed by many Prussians otherwise sympathetic with the enlightenment to fall short of meeting such requirements. Given these circumstances, some enlightened Jews turned eagerly to Kant's own hopeful promise as to the possibility of a Jewish-Christian Kantian vanguard.

4. *The Conflict of the Faculties* and Kant's Jewish Reception in the late 1790s

Whatever his earlier successes and disappointments, Kant was not yet finished with the Jews. A new easing in his own political circumstances, following the death in 1797 of King Frederick William II, permitted him to bring out another major work on the subject of religion: *The Conflict of the Faculties*. Given that the work also included a sardonic essay on his own declining powers, one can assume that it constituted a kind of final statement on matters religious.

The Conflict of the Faculties adds two new elements to the position Kant had previously staked out: a final, "dramatic" presentation of human history and a concrete proposal for emancipating the Jews. As we shall see, the two are not unrelated.

Beginning with the second: In 1793, the same year in which *Religion* was published, Lazarus Bendavid had written an extraordinary essay, *Notes Regarding the Characteristics of the Jews*. Bendavid, a German-Jewish mathematician and educator, was a devoted follower of the philosophy of Kant. Indeed, he brought out many volumes in the 1790s seeking to explicate Kant's thought for a wider audience—volumes that cannot have escaped Kant's attention at a time when he was confronted with a deepening polemical crisis involving former advocates like Johann Gottlieb Fichte. That Fichte's own brand of Kantianism had taken a decidedly anti-Jewish turn was also widely known.[27]

Bendavid does not so much defend Judaism (he is as far from Judaism, he says, as he is from [Kant's hated] *indifferentism*) as the small class of enlightened Jews who are ready to abandon it for "the pure teaching of Moses," that is to say, "pure moral religion" in the Kantian sense. As for the rest, Bendavid distinguishes a first class, still the largest, that is sunk in superstition; a second, dissolute class that has abandoned the ceremonial law for wholly venal reasons; and a third class of "worthy Jews" who remain tied to the ceremonial law owing to an inferior education. Among the first class, he insists, there are many who, despite their superstition, are exceedingly worthy men, at least with respect to their sincerity and unstinting zeal to help their fellow Jews. It would therefore be wrong to conclude (with Michaelis) that the ordinary run of Jew is by nature morally and civilly inadequate. The third class is more promising: Though their intellects have not been cultivated by proper education, their "hearts are without blemish" and they remain tied to the ceremonial law only out of "fear of immorality." Given these conditions, men of the smallest, highly educated class (such as himself) face an intolerable civic situation, both personally and as "disciples of the genuine natural religion." On the one hand, they are prevented by their own moral integrity from making the even formal confession of faith that would allow them to become Prussian citizens. On the other hand, Jews of the other classes take them for wicked men who have abandoned Judaism owing to its obligations. In light of this situation, their exceptional mental faculties and acquaintance with "men of the better sort" are in fact "misfortunes."

It is important to note what Bendavid, in leaving Judaism behind, is unwilling to concede: its moral inferiority, as an historical faith, to Christianity. The "genuine moral religion" is nothing other than "the pure teaching of Moses." Kant's 1798 response ignores or mutes this crucial qualification. From his own point of view, Christianity as an historical faith is indeed decisively superior to Judaism. It is thus acceptable for Catholics and Protestants to retain their old dogmas, for this need amount, in principle, to nothing more than a difference of opinion as to the most efficacious means to bring about a final moral end [7: 52]. Jews, on the other hand, need to exchange their old garment for a new one. As Kant, as we have seen, observes:

> Without dreaming [*die Träumerei*] of a general Jewish conversion (to Christianity as a messianic faith), this [invisible church] is possible even in regard to Jews, if among them, as is now happening, purified [*geläuterte*] religious concepts awaken, and the clothing [*Kleid*] of the old cult that no longer serves for anything, and, what is more, represses [*verdrängen*] all true religious disposition, is thrown off. Since they have now for so long had *a garment without a man* [Mann] (church without religion), and since, moreover, a *man without a garment* (religion without a church) is not well preserved [*verwahrt*], they need certain formalities of a church that is most suitable to lead them in their present place/situation: so we can consider [*halten*] the proposal of Bendavid, a very good mind [*Kopf*] of that nation, to publicly accept the religion of Jesus (presumably with its vehicle, the Gospel), not only very fortunate but also the only proposal [*Vorschlag*] whose carrying out would soon make this people noticeable [*bemerklich machen*] as one that is learned, well-civilized and ready for all civil rights, whose faith could also be sanctioned by the government, without their having to amalgamate with others in things of faith; [in keeping with this proposal] they would surely have to be left free to interpret the Bible [Torah and Gospels] so as to distinguish the way that Jesus spoke as a Jew to Jews from the way he spoke as a moral teacher of men in general.—The euthanasia of Judaism is pure moral religion with the leaving behind [*Veranlassung*] of all ancient regulatory teachings [*Satzungslehre*], some of which had to remain retained/held back [*zurück behalten bleiben müssen*] in Christianity (as messianic faith): this division of sects must, yet, also finally disappear, and so the conclusion of what is called the great religious drama of religious change on earth (the restoration of all things) leads hereby, at least in spirit, to there being only one shepherd and one herd/flock [*Heerde*]. [7: 52–53]

Kant does not strip away *all* vestiges of Jewish difference: his Jews for Jesus will still have their Torah, in addition to the Gospel, to interpret "in their own way." The essential point lies in their acceptance of Jesus, rather than Moses, as the exemplary moral figure par excellence.[28] Once that is granted, the Jews will have marked themselves as ready for all rights of citizenship in a manner that the government can readily sanction. Kant does not quite say that this is the *only* way that Jews can make themselves fit for citizenship.[29] It is, however, the only way that they can make their readiness immediately obvious to the larger community without ceasing to remain in some way "distinctive."

Kant's modification of Bendavid's plan is thus a most ingenious attempt to preserve the uniqueness of the Jews while absorbing them into the "great drama of religious change on earth." Judaism, thus transformed, becomes one Christian sect among others. Unlike Michaelis, who excluded the Jews from citizenship on the grounds that they constitute an alien Oriental race, Kant invites them to join the civil community through a "common brotherhood of faith" [7: 52].

Mendelssohn's own *cleverness*, which Kant had formerly touted, now does no "credit" to his "good will." Implicitly weighing in Bendavid's side, Kant amends his earlier appropriation of Mendelssohn in *Religion:* although the latter "apparently" meant to say that Christians should give up the Judaism in their faith before Jews would give up theirs, "it is up to his co-religionists to decide" whether he was indeed justified in thus cutting them off from any hope of relief. Mendelssohn's own stiff-necked willingness to wait in perpetuity for an improvement on the part of Christians that (in his own view) would never come marks him as less than kind even toward his fellow Jews [7: 52n]. Mendelssohn, so understood, does not measure up to those "worthy" benefactors that Bendavid commonly found among Jews of the least educated class. Mendelssohn's former honorific sobriquet (as in "the worthy Mendelssohn")[30] has silently been dropped.

As to the second point—it now proves essential, if the sacred narrative of Christianity is to be "authentically" interpreted, to ascribe its "messianic" elements not only to "clever" policy, given the popular conditions in which the first propagators found themselves (as Kant had maintained in *Religion*) but also to a "happy thought" that enabled them (psychologically, as it were) to regard pagans as admitted to the Jewish covenant. Thus (to cite this passage once again):

> The disciples of the Mosaic-messianic faith saw their hope in God's covenant [*Bund*] with Abraham completely sink with the death of Jesus (we had hoped that he would deliver [*erlösen*] Israel); for salvation was in their Bible promised only to the children of Abraham. Now it happened that when the disciples were gathered at Pentecost, one of them fell upon the happy notion [*Einfall*],[31] in keeping with the subtle Jewish art of exegesis [*Auslegungskunst*], that pagans (Greeks and Romans) too could be considered as

> accepted in this covenant, if they believed in the sacrifice of his only son that Abraham was willing to offer God (as the sensible image [*Sinnbild*] of the sacrifice of the world-savior [*des Weltheilendes*]); for then they would be children of Abraham in faith (first with, but afterwards without circumcision [*Beschneidung*]). It is no miracle/wonder [*Wunder*] that this discovery, which, in a great gathering of people, opened up so immeasurable a prospect, was accepted with the greatest jubilation and as if it were the immediate effect of the Holy Spirit, and was held to be a miracle [*Wunder*] and came into biblical (Apostolic) history as such; by this, however, it belongs in no way to religion to believe [in these events] as a fact [*Factum*] and to press it upon [*aufdringen*][32] natural human reason. Obedience necessitated through fear in esteem [*Ansehung*] for such church faith as required for salvation is thus superstition. [7: 65n–66n]

It is no "miracle" that the apostles of a "Mosaic-messianic faith" thus succumbed to a sublime enthusiasm, but entirely consistent with the laws of nature, given their continuing acceptance of the Abrahamic covenant. Contemporary disciples of the "pure teaching of Moses" are more morally enlightened, in this respect, than Christianity's earliest Jewish apostles. The old Jewish national pride had been sublated, in that earlier moment of enthusiasm, by the "immense prospect" opened up by the idea of a *universal* Abrahamic covenant. But it was still marred by the acceptance of that messianic covenant in principle. Mosaic-messianism is the consequence of a *quid pro quo* whose "quid" is the willingness to butcher innocents in exchange for some future good. The new "brotherhood in faith" entirely avoids such messianic haggling and the morally disabling passivity that it encourages.

Kant's identification, in Part Two of *The Conflict of the Faculties*, of contemporary Machiavellian politicians with the ancient Hebrew prophets is now easier to understand: Both predetermine human history and thus turn what ought to be the "great drama" of religious change on earth into a mere *Poppenspiel* (or puppet show). Freedom and nature can only be aesthetically united if the self-fulfilling prophecy of Mendelssohn and his ilk is cancelled by a new "sign of remembrance" that testifies definitively to the ultimate accomplishment of that true revolution—a sign that Kant locates in the (near) enthusiasm of Prussia's own French sympathizers [7: 85]. Revolutionary sympathy supplants the Pentecost as the true moment in which spirit enters human history.

One is here reminded of Rousseau's suggestion that the great religious founders be regarded not as imposters (as Voltaire had insisted) but as figures of "genius" whose minds have been disturbed by "continual meditation on divinity and enthusiasm for virtue."³³ Kant projects Rousseau's insight across a progressive series of religious moments: the original Mosaic command to make no graven image; the "lucky thought" at Pentecost that opened the sacrifice of Abraham to humanity at large, and the reception among revolutionary spectators of the Republican Idea.³⁴ Only the third moment, which "borders on enthusiasm" without succumbing to it [7: 85], counts as the "sign," nevermore to be forgotten, that mankind is continually progressing toward the better [7: 88]. Only with this moment can the end of the "great drama" of the human race finally be brought in view.³⁵

Kant's three religious/revolutionary moments thus suggest a thought that Fichte and other members of the Christlich-Deutschen Tischgesellschaft will run with: de-judaization as the negative image of the republican idea. To be sure, Kant's own intentions toward Judaism and the Jews remain decidedly more friendly. In thus rewriting Christian Scripture ("Now it happened . . ."), Kant marks out a new religious path for his newfound Jewish disciples.³⁶ By eschewing all vestiges of Mosaic-*messianism* they can be followers of Jesus and the Gospel without ceasing to be loyal to the purely moral teachings of Moses. Educated Jews can adopt Bendavid's plan without sacrificing either their intellect or their moral integrity.

There is one point, however, that Kant leaves disturbingly unclear. If the church, he says, commands belief in the dogma (of an infusion of the Holy Spirit, speaking in tongues, etc.) as necessary to salvation, it commands superstition—if one "obeys out of fear." But what if one obeys for reasons more honorable? Precisely which historically based dogmas, if any, might Kant's Jewish disciples reasonably be required to formally accept in order to "mark" themselves as "educated" and "civilized"? This remains unsettled.

The largely ignored fact of Kant's remarks and their uncertain meaning helps explain, I would suggest, the infamous public letter that David Friedländer, himself a semi-Kantian,³⁷ sent anonymously the following year to Wilhelm Abraham Teller, a liberal theologian and local church official. In that letter, Friedländer requested clarification of what dogmas he and other Jewish subscribers to a "pure moral religion" would be required to publicly accept in order to gain admission to the Church.³⁸ The spirit of that letter was no doubt misunderstood. Even liberal Christians found it arrogant; and posterity has for the most part treated it as a dishonorable act of communal abandonment and betrayal. I think it is more likely that Friedländer was merely putting to the test Kantian hopefulness as to the minimal conditions of Jewish civic improvement.[39] It was, after all, Kant himself who confidently claimed that Bendavid's plan "would quickly call attention to the Jews" as an enlightened people "who are ready for all the rights of citizenship" [7: 53].[40] In the event, those hopes proved wanting. Or perhaps it would be more accurate to say that Friedländer could not bring himself to concede the moral inferiority of Judaism to Christianity understood as strictly historical faiths, a concession that Kant had himself taken for granted.[41] Instead, Friedländer spends a good deal of the letter defending the moral character of Judaism in its "essence," which had nothing to do with messianism as such. The pathway tentatively opened up by Kant through his suggestion that Jews could become like Christians in all essential respects by giving up their messianism thus proved to be an unwitting trap. Far from receiving the promised encouragement of morally enlightened Christians, Friedländer's letter mainly provoked anger on all sides.

If one genuinely believed that Judaism (minus the messianism) was morally on par with Christianity, Teller replied, why seek to become a Christian? Why not remain a Jew and endeavor to reform Jewish practice from within? To make his point with utter clarity, Teller held out, as a condition of entering the Church, a specific profession, unique to converting Jews, that *"Christ is the founder, chosen and sent by God, of a better religion than your entire previous ceremonial practice was and could be"* [132]. For his part, Friedländer, who remained an active figure in the enlightened Jewish community, seems never again to have seriously broached the subject of conversion.

In the complex image of human history as "drama"—so important, given Kant's late and urgent fears as to his own philosophic legacy—Jews play the highly ambiguous role as a "remnant" that must both be saved and cast aside. The old Lutheran "dream" of Jewish conversion is here refigured in a new, politicized form. Even for Kant, the price of civic acceptance of the Jews is the explicit sacrifice of Jewish national pride.

Was there an acceptable alternative consistent with basic Kantian principles? Might Prussian Christians and Jews have been incorporated conceptually, on coherent Kantian grounds, into a common civic order?

The unusual career of Saul Ascher, a Jewish book dealer and prolific writer, suggests such a possibility. Ascher, himself a student of Kant's critical philosophy, published his own response to Mendelssohn's *Jerusalem* in 1792, a year before *Religion within the Boundaries of Bare Reason* appeared.[42] Ascher reacts, in short, to the work of Kant prior to the latter's elaboration of a theory of religion that takes "anti-messianism" as a central theme. Instead, his *Leviathan*[43] takes its bearings from "ethico-theology" as presented in Kant's *Critique of Judgment* [1790], applying them to the problem of Jewish law and its compatibility with civic emancipation of the Jews. Unlike Mendelssohn, he urges Jews to free themselves from the ceremonial law as incompatible with the moral autonomy in which the true spirit of Judaism consists: "Judaism posits the true autonomy of the will." "Hope for redemption through the agency of His Messiah" is not inconsistent, in Ascher's view, with Kantian autonomy.

Leviathan, which appeared the same year as Fichte's *Critique of Revelation* (which was published with Kant's help) was, as Hess points out, one of the first extended attempts to apply Kant's critical principles to religion as such. There is no sign that Kant ever read it, though Ascher's subsequent career as a critic of Fichte's peculiar brand of anti-Semitism may have come to his attention. In 1793 Fichte published his *Contribution to the Correction of the Judgments of the Public on the French Revolution*—a defense of the Revolution that went much further than Kant would ever go. It also contained a particularly radical declaration as to the absolute unsuitability of Jews for European citizenship of any kind. Jewry, according to Fichte, not only constituted a "state within a state"; it also grounded itself "in hatred of the entire human race." Jewry and the principles of the French Revolution were thus fundamentally at odds. "I would see no other way to give the Jews civil rights," he declared, "than to cut off their heads in one night and put others on them in which there would not be a single Jewish idea." Ascher answered Fichte in a book called *Eisenmenger the Second* [1794], and continued to oppose, in his later *Germanomania*, the rising anti-Jewish sentiments that followed the Napoleonic invasions. (*Germanomania* was burned by German nationalists at the Wartburg Festival of 1817.)

Despite his ambitions, Ascher's program for a reformed Judaism consistent with emancipation does not seem to have gotten much positive response from his contemporaries.[44] Bendavid, referring perhaps to Ascher's qualified retention of certain Jewish traditions, called his early book "dried cod" rather than a "Leviathan." Something of a social outsider, Ascher did not even enlist the sympathy of Heinrich Heine, who later mocked him for his "special malice" against Christianity.[45]

Specifically advanced as an application of Kantian principles, *Leviathan* makes Judaism, rather than Christianity, the true basis for a genuinely universal moral religion. In thus privileging Judaism *over* Christianity, Ascher no doubt went further than could have been acceptable to a Christian majority, however well-wishing toward the Jews. In the face of an increasingly respectable philosophic anti-Judaism, it can only have seemed inflammatory. Still, Ascher's presentation of the early history of the church has this in common with that of Kant himself: Jews (as Jewish Christians) play a crucial role in the early dissemination of Christianity.[46]

In his critique of the alternative account of that dissemination presented in Kant's *Religion,* Ascher specifically takes issue with Kant's treatment of the early history of the church, which Ascher finds contrary to true Kantian principles of critical historiography.[47] To treat Jesus's message as something "altogether new" is to do violence to the actual evidence, which reveals clear precedents among Jewish writings. To this charge, however, Kant would no doubt reply (as he almost does in so many words) that the early period of the church, like all other events recounted in Scripture, predates a learned public that could validate any testimony in a critically reliable fashion. The early years of the church, like all (other) stories of the Bible, falls outside of "history" proper.[48] Thus the methodology that rightly applies to the period beginning with the Greek historians must yield, where biblical matters are concerned, to other, less direct approaches. With a nod to Johann David Michaelis, the Orientalist historian [see *The Conflict of the Faculties* 7: 8], Kant dismisses the entire Rabbinic tradition as an authority on Judaism's past [6: 129–130]. Jews, it seems, have nothing trustworthy to report concerning their own history. Given the essential doubtfulness of all evidence that falls outside documented public (=Gentile) history, historical reconstructions of such periods will inevitably be fragmentary and hypothetical. In light of that eventuality, they can be rationally conducted only on the basis of reflective principles that themselves ultimately serve a moral end. Among narratives consistent with whatever facts can tentatively be gleaned from ancient relics, one should choose the one that is most morally edifying. This, in a nutshell, would seem to sum up Kant's reason for adopting an account of the early church (as in his version of the illumination of the Pentecost) that itself lacks clear documentary support. Ascher's objection—that Kant's denial of the essential contribution of Judaism to Christianity is contrary to the facts—carries no weight for Kant (even assuming that his Jewish sources could be trusted), given the decided advantage that such an account offers from the standpoint of Kant's own "moral aesthetics."

In sum: It is hardly shocking that Ascher's efforts to recast Judaism in the light of Kantian principles mainly fell on deaf ears. Kant himself may have had the intellectual resources, but he lacked either the confidence or the human sympathy that might have lead him to conceive of Jewish civic integration on terms other than their conversion to some version of Christianity. Jews could become Kant's saving remnant only by giving up their Jewish burden. At the same time, enlightened Jews such as Ascher and Bendavid failed to make Judaism sufficiently attractive to their non-Jewish contemporaries to overcome traditional Christian attitudes of suspicion and contempt. In short: They did not find a way to defend Judaism without attacking Christianity. If an important opportunity was thereby lost, it is much to be regretted; but it cannot be a matter of much surprise.

There is further, regrettable irony in Kant's complex attitude toward Judaism. If the argument laid out in this chapter is correct, Kant initially saw in Marcus Herz both an avid student and a pathway to the enlightened German circle that he hoped to influence. Jews like Herz and Mendelssohn were pivotal in the dissemination of his thought in the 1770s. The inability of Herz and Mendelssohn to grasp the meaning of his final critical breakthrough must have been a severe disappointment.[49] When the hoped-for favorable reviews by Mendelssohn did not appear, Kant turned elsewhere for support. Even the qualified approval of Solomon Maimon, who wrote Kant many admiring letters in the early 1790s, did not allay that disappointment; Maimon may have been the opponent who best understood his thought, as Kant wrote to Herz in May of 1789 [11: 49], but he was also, as he later confided to Reinholdt, one who "like all Jews," always "seek[s] to gain an air of importance for themselves at another's expense" [11: 494–495]. The emergence of a second generation of enlightened Jews such as Bendavid—men who were both devoted to his critical teaching and critics of Mendelssohn—seems to have awakened new hopes on Kant's part for an enlightened Jewish vanguard.[50] Like the Jewish disciples of yore, contemporary Jews might yet play an important role in propagating the new moral faith. To do so, they would have to become Jewish Christians— civilly acceptable in their profession of a "religion of Jesus and the *Gospels*," yet separate in their exegetical attentiveness to what "Jesus said to Jews as Jews." Kant's Jewish Christians were to influence the larger society from within, as an alien elite. The problem of the Jews as described by Michaelis was to be solved not by colonization (as the latter proposed) but by putting "aristocratic" Jewish national traits in the service of Kant's own moral revolution. In short, Kant's new Jewish disciples were to swing both ways, exercising a benign effect through their own priestly talents both on their fellow Jews and on the emerging German nation. That, however, would require Jews to admit the radical inferiority of Judaism to Christianity as historical faiths. What Kant failed to do was to show how Jews could become German citizens without giving up what they and others could not help but understand to be their own dignity as Jews.

In the event, by encouraging men like David Friedländer and Lazarus Bendavid in the manner that he did, Kant helped make them a stalking horse for his own critical philosophy, a stalking horse that absorbed the first shock of romantic opposition. Thus Schleiermacher, himself a regular among the Jewish salons of the period, saw in Friedländer's letter the ominous sign of a "judaizing" Christianity on the march. Jews should be granted citizenship as Jews, responded Schleiermacher, precisely on the grounds that it would discourage them from infiltrating, and thereby corrupting, the pure spirit of the church.[51] The spectacular rise to wealth and influence on the part of a select group of Jews—a rise that attracted Kant (who had himself risen from very modest circumstances)—struck others as a threat, even before the Napoleonic invasions apparently confirmed such fears.[52] Jews were thus damned any way they turned: If they failed to convert, they remained an internal colony of Prussia. If they attempted to convert in the ordinary way, the ensuing betrayal of their own people cast a dishonorable pall upon their motives. And if they converted under something like Kantian terms (to become a special Jewish-Christian vanguard of enlightened religious ideas), they raised the specter of foreign infiltration and corruption from within.

By absorbing Christianity into a spiritualized religion of reason, the German Enlightenment that culminated in the thought of Kant posed both a special opportunity for Prussian Jews seeking integration into the larger society and what proved to be an especially acute danger. On the one hand, it held out the prospect of tandem reform of Jews and Christians as joint (if asymmetrical) participants in a common ethical and civil project. This was clearly the opportunity on which Kant's Jewish admirers hoped to seize. And yet, as would unfold, in holding out to the Jews a special (if secondary) role in his own project of civic renewal, Kant exacerbated the precariousness of their position *vis-à-vis* the Christian majority. Unwittingly, perhaps, Kant used his Jewish friends for his own purposes and at what would prove to be their own considerable civic expense. At the same time, Kantian successors like Fichte and Schleiermacher felt no compunction in specifically excluding Jews from the project of German spiritual renewal, precisely on the grounds that they would at best dilute and at worst corrupt it. In encouraging the path to Jewish emancipation that he did, Kant invited the rejoinder that the Jews' specialness, as he saw it, testified to their essentially alien character.

It is hard to avoid the following conclusion: Kant not only used Judaism for his own ends, and without full regard for the available factual evidence; he also made use of his own Jewish acquaintances and followers without full regard for the dangers to which he thereby exposed them. Jews might help lead others to Kant's new promised land; they could not enter it without admitting the radical inferiority of Judaism to Christianity. Far from furthering the integration of Jews into German civil society, the self-abasement that was required as a "ticket of admission," to borrow Heine's words, only encouraged growing anti-Semitic claims that Jews were a people without honor.[53] There is nothing in Kant, in this respect, that can match the simple eloquence of George Washington, responding in 1790 to a letter of blessing and thanksgiving from the Hebrew Congregation of Newport: "May the children of the stock of Abraham who dwell in this land continue to merit and enjoy the good will of the other inhabitants, while every one shall sit in safety under his own vine and fig tree, and there shall be none to make him afraid."

Concluding Remarks: The Limits of Autonomy

The idea of autonomy is particularly well suited to inspiring the public dedication without which no free community can flourish. Indeed, it is doubtful that liberalism could have survived the stresses of the nineteen and twentieth centuries without its help. From Lincoln to the Progressives, the New Deal, and, most recently, the War on Terrorism, Kantian idealism has furnished both a language and a moral blueprint around which liberal democrats could rally. But if Kant's liberal legacy is to be adequately judged, its claims must be taken at full strength. Kant's understanding of autonomy involves two propositions to which the contemporary scholarship often gives short shrift: *first*, that the categorical imperative—act only on that maxim that you could at the same time will to be a universal law—is genuinely binding on the will (albeit in a way that meets our resistance) and *second*, that common notions of desert—notions of a sort that ordinary human beings routinely employ—have an irreducible moral primacy that cannot be "reasoned" away.

As the above study has aimed to show, attention to the history of Kant's thinking on these matters alerts one with particular force to the importance of those claims. Kant's moral philosophy begins in recognition of good will as the one thing unconditionally good that it is possible to think. Kant's normative model is not the zetetic Socrates, ascending from opinion to knowledge, including the knowledge that the theoretical way of life is best. Nor is it the patient saint, attending to God's will in humble supplication and submission. It is instead a pure abstraction: the concept that remains when we "cancel in thought" every obstacle that limits the value of a thing in our own estimation. Since the value of any object of our will is conditional on our desire for it, unconditional value cannot lie with the will's end but only in a law that it imposes on itself. Autonomy is Kant's name for our paradoxical capacity to act out of respect for such a law and nothing else. Kant takes his primary philosophic bearings from the awareness of any ordinary decent human being that something is demanded of us morally, that happiness is not enough. At the same time, Kant denies the possibility of theoretical knowledge of the highest good and with it philosophic wisdom in the ancient sense. The result is a new understanding of reason as fundamentally a faculty of law-giving rather than of theoretical knowledge. Without susceptibility to the ordinary claims of moral duty, it would be impossible for us even to think of something good without limitation. Pursuit of theoretical knowledge of a highest good—knowledge, that is to say, independent of our practical awareness of the moral law—is, for Kant, necessarily misguided. But this awareness is inseparable, in turn, from certain ordinary notions of desert that inform the moral understanding that constitutes Kant's starting point. For Kant's moral philosophy, as we have seen, is not primarily philosophy *about* morality but philosophy directed by the moral rational knowledge that is available to everyone to whom deeds can be imputed.[1] This knowledge holds action for the sake of duty to be choice-worthy in itself and at whatever cost. In thus upholding ordinary moral understanding, Kant meets the challenge of Glaucon in the only way it can rationally be met without transcending the limits of that outlook.

An alternative, "juridical"[2] conception of rational autonomy has recently been taken up by several schools of criticism.[3] What makes that conception especially attractive in the present academic and political climate is its suggestion of a path between the Scylla of a naïve "foundationalism" and the Charybdis of an anarchic postmodernism. By tracing the law-giving "authority" of reason to the "agreement of free citizens" [A 738=B 766], Kant seems to validate the self-understanding of contemporary liberalism as a matter of freestanding consensus. However initially attractive, however, such approaches tend to slight the obligatory or practically "necessitating" force of autonomy as Kant conceives it. They thus do little to help shore up the moral authority that liberalism today would seem to be especially in need of.

To be sure, Kant sometimes seems to flirt with such a view—most famously, an analogy drawn in the *Critique of Pure Reason* between critical philosophy and the workings of a civil court. Critical philosophy so understood is "directed [*gesetzt*]⁴ toward determining and judging the rights [*Rechtsame*]⁵ of reason generally, according to the principles of its first institution [*Institution*]."

Lacking such criticism, he says:

> reason is, as it were, in the state of nature, and it cannot make its assertions and claims valid or secure other than through war. Critique, by way of contrast, which derives all decisions from the ground-rules of its own constitution [*Einsetzung*], whose authority none can doubt, procures for us the peace of a lawful condition in which we ought not conduct our controversy other than through *court proceedings* [Process]. What ends the quarrel in the first condition is a *victory* of which both sides boast, a victory from which there mostly follows only an uncertain peace, established by a magistry [*Obrigkeit*] that inserts itself into the middle; in the latter condition, on the other hand, the quarrel ends in a *sentence* [Sentenz],⁶ which, since it goes to the source of the controversies themselves, must secure an eternal peace.   [A 751–752 = B 779–780]

The "endless controversies" of dogmatic reason "make it necessary" to seek peace in a "critique of reason" and "a law-giving that is derived from it"; indeed, it is just as Hobbes maintained:

> The state of nature is a state of injustice [*Unrecht*] and active violence [*Gewaltthätigkeit*],⁷ and one must necessarily abandon it in order to submit oneself to lawful compulsion that only limits our freedom so that it may stand together with the freedom of everyone else, and thus [*eben dadurch*] with the general highest good [*gemeinen Beste*].   [A 752 = B 780]

But Kant, as we have seen, did not rest satisfied with the characterization of reason's authority as it is here presented. To be sure, prior to the *Groundlaying*, in which the principle of autonomy appears for the first time, Kant may well have been unsettled in his own mind as to what way and to what extent reason's legislation, both theoretical and practical, is binding on the will. Passages like the one quoted above still leave the source and meaning of rational "necessitation" tantalizingly obscure. What, exactly, makes it needful for reason to leave the philosophic "state of nature?" Is critique directed or commanded (i.e., "*gesetzt*") by first principles, as Kant first states, or is it driven by self-interest, as the analogy with Hobbes suggests? Or are the two (principle and interest) somehow the same?

In invoking the juridical analogy as presented in the *Critique of Pure Reason*, contemporary scholars have largely failed to note this potentially vitiating ambiguity, which leaves in doubt the ultimate incentive of philosophic self-critique and, in the last analysis, moral action as well.⁸ Kant's "principle of autonomy," first enunciated in the *Groundlaying*, meets this concern. The highest lawgiving authority of reason no longer rests on a seemingly circular appeal to the "free consent of citizens" (who are citizens, after all, only by virtue of reason's first "institution") but is immediately conveyed by "how it sounds" [*wie es laute*]. In short, the "critique of pure practical reason" presented in the *Groundlaying* takes autonomy into account in a way his earlier critique did not. With Kant's discovery of the concept of autonomy comes an insistence on the executive power of (human) reason—a power that he had previously specifically denied:[9] reason now combines legislation and execution in a single act. Reason, beginning with the *Groundlaying*, speaks not only as a civil judge (who allows all litigants to be heard) but first and foremost with the commanding tenor of a *Selbshalternin*, i.e., dictatorially.[10]

At the same time, autonomy so understood is "paradoxical" (as a comparison of the *Groundlaying* with the earlier first edition of the *Critique of Pure Reason* helps bring home). Moral resolution wavers before a skeptical denial that reason can be both pure and practical, i.e., that it is possible to act for the sake of duty alone and without regard for any (further) end. Kant's ensuing "critique of pure practical reason" (Part Three of the *Groundlaying*) aims to demonstrate that the demanded proof is neither possible nor necessary.

Kant's relocation of that paradox in subsequent works is, as earlier chapters have argued, partly a reflection of his own changing political fortunes and related shifts in target from skeptically armed "enemies of virtue" (his main adversaries in the *Groundlaying*) to a skepticism that presents itself as the religiously and morally engaged enemy of philosophic reason. Kant's new challenge is to "make room for faith" (as the *Critique of Pure Reason* had earlier claimed to do) without undermining an autonomy that his earlier critical theology had not fully taken into account. He responds by returning to the concept of a highest good, a topic that the *Critique of Pure Reason* had already addressed, but with this difference. In contrast to that earlier presentation, Kant now draws a distinction between reason's *subjective* need for religious faith (as a condition of our holding the necessary end of reason—i.e., the highest good—to be a realizable goal) and its *objective* ability to execute the law without it. This subtle but crucial difference is echoed in the related distinction, to which he now brings newly emphatic attention, between reason as a timeless noumenal agent and reason as we subjectively encounter it—reason that must execute the law in time. Hence the peculiar "ambiguity," as he puts it, inherent in *our* concept of the "highest" (as in "highest good"), which can refer either to good will ("highest" understood as the first and ultimate ground) or to maximum virtue accompanied by proportional happiness ("highest" understood as the most perfect or complete). Everything turns, in Kant's new formulation, on the (temporal) order in which one proceeds—i.e., on what Kant calls his "paradox of method." If one determines reason's end in light of the concept of a good will, all goes well; if one attempts to reverse that process, all is lost.

Following on the events of 1789 and with the help of the new insights that inform *The Critique of Judgment* and *Religion within the Boundaries of Bare Reason*, autocracy itself becomes an explicit practical goal. Thanks to Kant's new concept of a "super-sensible substrate," the choosing self can now be regulatively conceived in noumenal terms.[11] Such regulative principles are "reflective," rather than constitutive (like the determinate judgments that characterize theoretical knowledge proper). They also differ from the regulative principles that are directly bound up with the ideas of reason. At the same time, the peculiarly human status of those principles makes them especially apt for guiding the action of embodied moral agents. One suspects that it was this new factor, above all, that enabled Kant to complete his long-promised *Metaphysics of Morals*, whose myriad appeals to man's natural and moral perfection take such principles for granted. Guided by this new discovery, Kant's understanding of autonomy undergoes another subtle redirection. Already with the *Critique of Judgment*, "autonomy" ventures beyond the moral realm to help inform a theory of both taste [5: 282][12] and reflective judgment generally [5: 389]. For related reasons, vanquishing the "inner lie" (rather than overcoming sensual temptation) becomes the primary goal of moral discipline. The intellectual distance Kant has traveled since publication of the *Critique of Pure Reason* can be measured by the fact that when reason, in a late work, revisits the philosophic "battlefield" that the first *Critique* had seemingly pacified, it comes not as a judge, or even a "*Selbsthalterin*," but as a would-be (self) "conqueror" [8: 416]. In sum: There is no final peace in time. Although the *Grenzgott*[13] of morality need not yield to Jupiter (the *Grenzgott* of power) [8: 370], philosophy, as Kant now puts it, must be ever-armed, if only against the ratiocinating deception that equates paradox with contradiction.

Faced with these and similar perplexities, it can be tempting to equate autonomy with transgression pure and simple, in the manner of Michael Foucault and other students of Nietzsche. Freedom, on such a view, lies in shattering the limits of the law.

No one, perhaps, has shown more clearly what freedom without the *Grenzgott* of morality might mean than Martin Heidegger. In 1930, midway between *Being and Time* (1927) and the Rectoral Address that he delivered as a newly minted member of the Nazi Party (1933), Heidegger devoted a series of lectures to the topic of autonomy.[14] For Kant, as Heidegger sees it, autonomy mainly means "self-responsibility," which is "the essence of the personality of the human person, the authentic essence, the humanity of man" [202–203]. Freedom demonstrates its own reality for Kant in our "actual willing of the pure ought" [202]. Kant goes astray, however, in failing to recognize that freedom is prior to causality. Far from being merely a kind of causality (namely a "practical" one), freedom, as Heidegger insists, is *"the condition of the possibility of the manifestness of the being of beings, of the understanding of being."*

And yet causality, as Heidegger also insists, is only "*one* ontological determination" of such comportment among others. Freedom understood as causality lets things be only in the manner of objects, i.e., things standing against one another. Beings "can only show themselves as *objects*" if the appearance of beings, and "that which at bottom makes this possible"—i.e., "the understanding of being"—"has the character of letting-stand-over-against." But "letting something stand-over-against as something given" basically allows for "the manifestness of beings in the binding character of their so- and that-being." "Objectivity" is thus possible, according to Heidegger, only where the comportment to beings already acknowledges this binding character. Both theoretical and practical knowledge, then, presupposes an original self-binding, or, "in Kantian terms," a "giving of the law unto oneself." Autonomy, one could say, is the original "self-binding" that allows beings to manifest themselves as "objects," or (in Kantian terms) the condition of the possibility of all causality theoretical and practical. Autonomy, in short, is the original self-binding that makes possible the comportment toward beings that allows them to appear as causally determined. Far from constituting our "authentic essence," autonomy confines or limits our freedom to will authentically [207]. Accordingly, autonomy must be "questioned." Philosophy is neither a "theoretical science" nor a handmaiden of morality but "actual being free" in the questioning of freedom's essence. If we are to take on that all-important task, we must, it seems, give up on (or at the very least suspend) ordinary (moral) notions of "responsibility."

Heidegger helps us see where autonomy without desert or binding moral law—autonomy, as it were, "beyond good and evil"—might lead if thought through to the end. And yet autonomy as Kant himself conceived it—autonomy, that is to say, with both desert and binding moral law intact—poses its own difficulties, as we have seen, for political and moral action—one powerful reason, one suspects, for the current popularity of less metaphysically and morally encumbered versions. Kant never found a way to formulate "universal law" as called for by "the wise and astute" Count Windisch-Graetz, a law, in other words, that would hold not merely "generally" but "universally." Without such a formula, which would make exceptions to the law inconceivable in principle, "the so-called *ius certum* will always remain," as Kant admitted in a rueful note, merely a "pious wish" [8: 348n].

> For the possibility of such a (mathematically-similar) formula is the only authentic proof stone of a lawgiving that remains consistent [*einer consequent bleibenden Gesetzgebung*], without which the so-called *ius certum* will always remain a pious wish.—Otherwise one would have merely general laws (that are valid *in general* [im allgemeinen]) but no universal laws (that are valid *universally* [allgemein]), as the concept of a law yet appears to demand. [8: 348n]

Kant's admission arises in the course of a discussion of so-called "permissive law," which he calls upon to handle the problem of transition from a state of nature to one that is (entirely) civil. Such a transitional condition gives rise to the distinction between "strict laws," which must be applied immediately, and "broad laws" which do not. The latter:

> subjectively widen one's authorization—not, to be sure, as an exception to the rule—but in regard to the circumstances in which they are to be applied, and contain permission to *postpone* fulfillment so long as one does not lose sight of the end, so that this deferral does not mean, for example, abandoning the *restoration* of the freedom of certain states[15] . . . until doomsday [*Nimmertag*] (*ad calendas graecas*, as Augustus used to promise) . . . but rather permits delay only so that fulfillment does not over-rush and thus happen [*geschehe*] contrary to intention. [8: 347]

The distinction here drawn between deferral and exception underscores the more general problem that confronts the "moral politician." In the ongoing absence of a principle to guide the political actor that is both determinate and comprehensive, Kant seeks intermediary rules that distinguish between what has happened in the past and what may be allowed to happen henceforth. The freedom of a people that has been illegitimately deprived of it need not be immediately restored. But such "transitional" rules (which allows un-rightful conditions to persist indefinitely) only puts off the day of reckoning rather than evading it (like the merchant who when asked for payment always cheerfully responds "please come back later").[16] Eventually, we will require another rule to tell us when and how such holdings are to terminate, and so on, seemingly *ad infinitum*.

Kant's responded to this problem, first, with the so-called "transcendental principles of public right," which were intended to fill the gap between pure ideas and action on the part of moral politicians in the here and now; and second, with history philosophically co-opted to serve moral ends. History, in Kant's late works, becomes a second nature to be read for "signs" of human progress. But anticipated progress and possible catastrophe go hand in hand, furnishing the moral politician with a reflective schema for action that is ambiguous at best. Faced with that indeterminacy, Kant, too, stumbled. Kant's efforts to make history morally edifying led him, as we have seen, into political byways that were not always either necessary or wise. To cite one example, nothing intrinsic to his philosophic system required him to make his Jewish friends and followers the shock troops of his attempt to politically co-opt an established Church for moral ends. These were judgment calls on his part, aided and abetted by his late discovery of *a priori* principles of judgment but not determined by them. Those principles also gave new impetus to an organic metaphor that he had earlier toyed with, investing the body politic with living spirit of a sort and in a manner that proved dangerous beyond Kant's reckoning. In sum: Kant's perceived need to interpret history as morally "meaningful" sometimes tempted him to slight the facts as they presented themselves—a difficulty that his (brief) flirtation with an *a priori* "constitutive principle of theoretical/judging reason" did nothing to allay.

Still, Kant's "true politics" continues to merit our attention for its promise of a liberalism that draws necessitating strength from ordinary concepts of moral freedom and responsibility—concepts that even self-professed skeptics are wont to honor in their daily conduct. This is not the place to offer a lengthy catalog of what a liberalism guided by the principle of autonomy in the full Kantian sense might mean today. Still, the following suggestions may be useful.

On the domestic front: A genuinely Kantian liberalism would take its primary bearings from the civic dignity that accrues to individuals with the wherewithal to live productive, self-directed lives. It would honor effort, not just "success." And it would place a premium on self-reliance as the *sina qua non* of civil and moral maturity. It would make room for religion, not just grudgingly but in recognition of its inescapable connection, for both good and ill, with our moral interest. It would defend market rights but limit market outcomes. It would support the poor, not as an entitlement on their part but for the sake of general civic health. It would frown on treating sex as a commodity like any other. It would promote monogamous marriage as an institution that is both particularly favorable to the dignity of adults and particularly well suited to the nurturance of future liberal citizens. A genuinely Kantian liberalism would temper a concern with domestic security with the primary insight that crimes must be punished in a manner that does justice. Above all, it would understand civil liberty not merely as the (Millsian) right to do as one pleases so long as one harms no one else, but as a badge of honor with accompanying civic duties.

On the international front, a foreign policy that is genuinely Kantian in spirit would have due regard for the primary claims of individual states to defend the rights of their own citizens. And it would pay attention to motives—including, above all, the desire for domination—not fully captured by the bland term "self-interest." A genuinely Kantian politics would understand that prosperity and security go hand in hand and that credit is always a two-edged sword. It would recognize the combination of morality and politics as an always troubled union this side of earthly paradise. Finally and not least: A truly Kantian liberalism would leaven its political and moral hopes with an appreciation of the dangers, both external and internal, to which human freedom is continually exposed. Ever precarious, the authority of reason rests (as Kant would say) upon a "hair-tip."

Notes

Introduction

1. On Kant and Stoicism, see Stephen Engstrom and Jennifer Whiting, eds., *Aristotle, Kant, and the Stoics: Rethinking Happiness and Duty* (Cambridge: Cambridge University Press, 1996).
2. On this point, see, for example, J. B. Schneewind, "Kant and Stoic Ethics," in *Aristotle, Kant, and the Stoics.*
3. See *Groundlaying of the Metaphysics of Morals* [4: 439]; and *Critique of Practical Reason* [5: 62–63].
4. On this point, see Devin Stauffer, *Plato's Introduction to the Question of Justice* (Albany: State University of New York Press, 2001).
5. Karl Ameriks mounts an instructive defense in *Kant and the Fate of Autonomy: Problems in the Appropriation of the Critical Philosophy* (Cambridge: Cambridge University Press, 2000).
6. Although there are a number of recent studies of Kantian autonomy, to my knowledge none focuses on its peculiarly paradoxical character and its implications for his practical thought more generally. On autonomy as a kind of "sovereignty" of the will, see Andrews Reath, *Agency and Autonomy in Kant's Moral Theory: Selected Essays* (Oxford: Oxford University Press, 2006). Henry E. Allison's *Kant's Theory of Freedom* (New York: Cambridge University Press, 1990) has been especially influential. The "incorporation thesis" laid out there is particularly helpful in clarifying (though not fully explaining) how freedom and autonomy can be identified without calling into question the possibility of morally imputable wrongdoing. Gerald Dworkin's *The Theory and Practice of Autonomy* (New York: Cambridge University Press, 1988) presents an alternative to Kantian autonomy, as does Thomas Hill's *Autonomy and Self-Respect* (New York: Cambridge University Press, 1991).

7. See John Rawls, *Political Liberalism*, 2nd ed. (New York: Columbia University Press, 1996), 28, 77, and *Lectures on the History of Moral Philosophy*, ed. Barbara Herman (Cambridge, Mass.: Harvard University Press, 2000), 226–230. For a valuable discussion of the implications of Rawls's basic position for notions of moral freedom, see Ameriks, *Kant and the Fate of Autonomy*, 70–77.
8. On this point, see especially Michael J. Sandel, *Liberalism and the Limits of Justice*, 2nd ed. (Cambridge: Cambridge University Press, 1998); for a forceful criticism of Rawls on related grounds, see William A. Galston, *Justice and the Human Good* (Chicago: University of Chicago Press, 1980), 170–172. As Sandel argues, a self not responsible for its own willingness to make an effort is not a self we can in any way intelligibly conceive.
9. Rawls, *A Theory of Justice* (Cambridge, Mass.: Harvard University Press, 1971), 15, 74.
10. See, for example, Rawls, *Political Liberalism*, 319: "our sense of our own value, as well as our self-confidence, depends on the respect and mutuality shown us by others."
11. See also Rawls, *A Theory of Justice*, 310: "there is a tendency for common sense to suppose that income and wealth, and the good things in life generally, should be distributed according to moral desert. Justice is happiness according to virtue. . . . Justice as fairness rejects this conception."
12. Rawls, *Lectures on the History of Moral Philosophy*, 220, 224, 313–316, 318, 322.
13. Rawls, *Political Liberalism*, 25n, 48n.
14. To be sure, Rawls resists the charge of "skepticism" on the grounds "that political liberalism" allows one to remain agnostic on the question of whether or not any comprehensive theory of the good is "true"; he continues to insist, however, that no such truth (if truth there be) could be "fully established by reason" [*Political Liberalism*, 150–153].
15. See Rawls, *A Theory of Justice*, 252: "Kant held, I believe, that a person is acting autonomously when the principles of his action are chosen by him as the most adequate possible expression of his nature as a free and equal rational being." The moral law is binding—for those who so acknowledge it [*Lectures on the History of Moral Philosophy*, 267]; "Kant's doctrine . . . is not one of a legitimate authority that enacts principles for us to obey," or that primarily involves feelings of "obligation"; instead it is "one of mutuality and self-respect" [*Lectures on the History of Moral Philosophy*, 298]. Rawls adds, "those who think of Kant's moral doctrine as one of law and guilt badly misunderstand him" [*A Theory of Justice*, 256].
16. I am claiming that Rawls's discomfort with notions of both obligation and desert arises from a profound, if not fully acknowledged, skepticism in moral matters that is foreign to the letter and spirit of Kant. Whether the primacy of the concept of moral deservingness can be successfully detached (as Rawls insists) from Kant's moral theory overall without intruding on its normative character will be taken up again in Chapter 4. In Rawls's view, they reflect the

unexpunged remnants of an alien Leibnizian perfectionism. (See *Lectures on the History of Moral Philosophy,* 316–317.)

17. On the latter, see especially Richard L. Velkley, *Freedom and the End of Reason* (Chicago: University of Chicago Press, 1989).

18. For a singular exception, see Brandt's helpful editorial introduction to the Akademie edition of the *Lectures on Anthropology* (Immanuel Kant, *Gesammelte Schriften,* vol. 25, ed. Reinhard Brandt and Werner Stark, *Akademie* edition [Berlin: Walter de Gruyter, 1997]).

19. For an incisive overview, see Paul Guyer, *Kant's System of Nature and Freedom* (Oxford: Clarendon Press, 2005), 126–132.

20. See, for example, the letter from Johann Cristoph Berens, December 5, 1787 [10: 507].

21. Early intimations of trouble are already evident in correspondence with Friedrich Victor Leberecht Plessing in February and March of 1784 [10: 363–364, 371–372], and the letter from Johann Erich Beister of June 11, 1786 [10: 57].

22. Manfred Kuehn, *Kant: A Biography* (Cambridge: Cambridge University Press, 2001), 338.

23. In the early years of the Revolution, however, Kant seems to have been an unflagging defender—at least with a view to its aims. As his friend Johann Metzger reported, Kant upheld the goals of the Revolution "with great frankness and fearlessness," and at some personal risk, at noble tables and among men of the highest offices of state. (See Kuehn, *Kant,* 342.)

24. See Allen W. Wood, *Kant's Ethical Thought* (Cambridge: Cambridge University Press, 1999), 314, 332. In *Unnecessary Evil: History and Moral Progress in the Philosophy of Immanuel Kant* (Albany: State University of New York Press, 2001), Sharon Anderson-Gold asserts the dependence of individual moral self-transformation on a prior transformation of society at large even more strikingly: "Kant implies that our hope to effect a revolution 'within' rests upon the transformation of the social conditions of our existence" [46].

25. Helpful recent studies of this context include Frederick C. Beiser, *The Fate of Reason: German Philosophy from Kant to Fichte* (Cambridge, Mass.: Harvard University Press, 1987); Kuehn, *Kant: A Biography;* John H. Zammito, *Kant, Herder, and the Birth of Anthropology* (Chicago: University of Chicago Press, 2002); Schneewind, *The Invention of Autonomy* (Cambridge: Cambridge University Press, 1998); and Ian Hunter, *Rival Enlightenments: Civil and Metaphysical Philosophy in Early Modern Germany* (Cambridge: Cambridge University Press, 2001).

26. For an explicitly "historicist" approach to issues treated in Part I, see Jerome B. Schneewind's informative and learned *The Invention of Autonomy.* Schneewind attributes Kant's "invention" of autonomy largely to his effort to reconcile two competing theological movements of the seventeenth and early eighteenth centuries: a "voluntarism" that traces morality to the free and unimpeded will of

God, and a "rationalism" that rebels against this notion on the moral (and religious) grounds that such a God is impossible to love. In Schneewind's view, the desire for a morality based on universal reason arises from a historically contingent moral and religious need (of which "voluntarism" is the main pre-Kantian expression) to establish a shared community between God and man. This is so much the driving thrust of his argument as to lead him to misstate Kant's position on just this point, in an otherwise careful and erudite summary of Kant's thought. (Compare Schneewind, *The Invention of Autonomy*, 512 and 521, and Kant, *Groundlaying of the Metaphysics of Morals* [4: 414]; contrary to Schneewind's claim, it is by no means clear that the divine will, on Kant's account, involves a synthetic *a priori* use of reason.) Now that "voluntarism" as a potent historical force has waned, the demand for necessary and universal moral knowledge, in Schneewind's view, has lost its main *raison d'être*. As he suggestively concludes, "those of us who hope to see the development of a fully secular understanding of morality need not have any interest in some of the problems that Kant tried to solve . . . if, for instance, we do not think that a prime task for moral philosophy is to show that God and we belong to a single moral community, then we will not have Kant's reason for insisting that our theory show how there can be moral principles necessarily binding on all rational beings. There may be other reasons [for so holding] but we will not think the requirement self-evident. Principles for humans may be enough." If parts of Kant's thought remain useful, it is due, in Schneewind's view, to a shared "passionate conviction" as to the equality moral capacity and dignity of all "normal human beings" [554]. The underlying purpose of Schneewind's study would seem to be to show that "principles for humans" need not, indeed, be rationally or universally binding (as Kant, for historically contingent reasons wrongly assumed)—i.e., that our "passionate conviction" concerning equality may well be, if not "enough," all that an historically informed person should expect. This presumption makes it difficult for him to see the problem of autonomy as Kant himself saw it, i.e., from the "inside" and in a manner that still can and should disturb us.
27. On peculiar stylistic challenges involved, see also Willi Goetschel, *Constituting Critique: Kant's Writing as Critical Praxis,* trans. Eric Schwab (Durham and London: Duke University Press, 1994).
28. On the peculiar felicities, as Kant saw it, of his own geographic situation, see *Anthropology from a Pragmatic Point of View* [7: 120–121].

1. "Carazan's Dream"

1. For recent exceptions, see Peter D. Fenves, *A Peculiar Fate: Kant and the Problem of World History* (Ithaca, N.Y.: Cornell University Press, 1990), and Martin Schönfeld, *The Philosophy of the Young Kant: The Precritical Project* (Oxford: Oxford University Press, 2000).

Notes to Pages 17–25 349

2. This was the second of two dissertations that enabled Kant to qualify for appointment as a university lecturer [*Privatdozent*]; the first was the Latin treatise *On Fire*.
3. For a fuller account of these controversies, see Eric Watkins, *Kant and the Metaphysics of Causality* (Cambridge: Cambridge University Press, 2005), 23–100; Susan Meld Shell, *The Embodiment of Reason: Kant on Spirit, Generation and Community* (Chicago: University of Chicago Press, 1996), 31–80; and Thomas Friedman, *Kant and the Exact Sciences* (Cambridge, Mass.: Harvard University Press, 1992), 1–14.
4. On these events, see Lewis White Beck, *Early German Philosophy: Kant and his Predecessors* (Cambridge, Mass.: Harvard University Press, 1969).
5. *New Elucidation* [1: 412]: "if the human soul were free from real connection with external things, the internal state of the soul would be completely devoid of changes." Kant concludes as to the strong likelihood that "some kind of organic body must be attributed to all spirits whatever."
6. On this topic, see also Alison Laywine, *Kant's Early Metaphysics and the Origins of the Critical Philosophy*, vol. 3 of North American Kant Society Studies in Philosophy (Atascadero, Calif.: Ridgeway Publishing, 1993); and Rae Langton, *Kantian Humility* (New York: Oxford University Press, 1998), 97–108.
7. Consider, for example, Kant's early insistence that a substance could have existed in another world (with its own spatial-temporal configuration) without this altering its essential character. (See Watkins, *Kant and the Metaphysics of Causality*, 146.)
8. This is substantially Crusius's objection to the Leibnizian principle of sufficient reason.
9. Cf. Martin Schönfeld, *The Philosophy of the Young Kant*, 108–127. Schönfeld confuses the organized perfection of material nature with the perfection of creation as such, which lies in its contemplation by rational beings.
10. Except where noted, all translations from the Latin are from Immanuel Kant, *Theoretical Philosophy, 1755–1770*, ed. and trans. David Walford and Ralf Meerbote, The Cambridge Edition of the Works of Immanuel Kant (Cambridge: Cambridge University Press, 1992). The translation here has been slightly altered.
11. The *Universal Natural History* was probably completed sometime shortly before Kant wrote the *New Elucidation*. Among its genuine astronomical insights is a novel theory of galactic formation resembling one that Laplace was developing around the same time.
12. These views, which appear both in the *Universal Natural History* and the nearly contemporary treatise *On Fire* suggest the following general account of the relation between matter and spirit: The soul stands in a relation of worldly interconnection with other substances, including certain bodily substances (or substance) that establish the soul's physical location. The soul is both passive—susceptible, through its faculty of sensation, to "determination" by external

physical forces—and active—able to combine its representations into ideas of ever greater generality. How easily it can do so is a function of its position in the universe. Those positions vary both in the density of their matter and (in inverse proportion) their quantity of heat. The density of matter varies with its closeness to certain gravitational centers, such as the sun and other, similarly attractive bodies. Fire, for its part, is an "imponderable," ether-like element that permeates the interstices of matter, thereby facilitating the communication of motion between substances. Where matter is relatively dense, its repulsive forces become sluggish, and more heat is necessary to achieve the same communicative effect. In the case of living beings, Kant postulates the following: Where matter is densest (e.g., on planets nearest the sun), life can sustain itself only with much heat, which facilitates the movement of the "animal spirits." Where matter is rarer and more elastic (e.g., on planets further from the sun), animal spirits require less heat to have the same effect. Accordingly, the inhabitants of Saturn and Jupiter combine sensations readily and quickly. The inhabitants of Mercury, on the other hand, combine sensations slowly and with great difficulty.

13. Kant flags that difference by restricting his use of paternal imagery to descriptions of the spiritual "center" of the universe, while reserving to the material centers descriptions whose register is unmistakably feminine.
14. Indeed, it was probably composed while he was serving as a house tutor for the Von Keyserling family. Kant remained on very warm terms with the family—and, in particular, with Countess von Keyserling—through the remainder of his life.
15. Cf. *Job* [16:2]; The phrase reappears in *On the Failure of All Philosophical Attempts at Theodicy* [8: 265–266] and *Toward Perpetual Peace* [8: 355].
16. Cf. [1: 356–357]; the "monstrous cloud" to which Kant here refers would seem to be philosophic materialism.
17. Further evidence of Kant's dissatisfaction can be found in an unpublished draft "On Leibniz's Optimism" written around this time. Kant there looks to Alexander Pope (another poet favored in the *Universal Natural History*) to correct Leibniz's view that in choosing to create the best world possible, God was constrained by "necessity" or "fate" to admit the bad. As these reflections reveal, Kant finds it difficult to banish from his own preferred theodicy the error he attributes to the "optimism" of Leibniz: namely, treating God's choice both as free and as constrained by an independent necessity. Whereas Leibniz's theodicy, according to these reflections, turns on an abstruse argument for the existence of God, Pope appeals to the visible harmonies of nature in a manner that is popularly accessible. (See *Reflections* #3703–3707 [17: 229–239].) Although the practical advantages of Pope's approach are clear enough to Kant, the above theoretical difficulty remains unresolved—one reason, perhaps, that Kant did not complete the prize essay on optimism that he was evidently contemplating. His preferred solution at this time to the

problem of evil seems to have involved associating freedom (both human and divine) with intellectual rather than "blind" determination. A later essay "On Optimism," appended to a course announcement of 1759, takes an even firmer stance against Crusius, partly on the Leibnizian grounds that evil is indeed "nothing." Kant would decisively reject Leibniz's position four years later in his *Essay on Negative Quantities*. The 1759 essay "On Optimism" also refers to the "general will" of God to promote the greatest good (as opposed to his "permission" of "particular" evils necessary to that end). It is instructive to compare this theological employment of the term "general will" with the radically modified Rousseauian usage that Kant would soon come to adopt. (On the early history of "general will" as a theological term, see Patrick Riley, *The General Will Before Rousseau: The Transformation of the Divine into the Civic* [Princeton: Princeton University Press, 1986].)

18. See especially Richard L. Velkley, *Freedom and the End of Reason: On the Moral Foundation of Kant's Critical Philosophy* (Chicago: University of Chicago Press, 1989); Dieter Henrich, "Über Kants früheste Ethik: Versuch einer Rekonstruktion," *Kant-Studien* 54 (1963): 404–431; and Josef Schmucker, *Die Ursprünge der Ethik Kants in seinen vorkritischen Schriften und Reflektionen* (Meisenheim am Glan: Anton Hain, 1961). John H. Zammito makes a convincing case for the decisive influence of Rousseau from 1762 onward. See his *Kant, Herder, and the Birth of Anthropology* (Chicago, University of Chicago Press, 2002), 91–113.

19. For an illuminating discussion of the portrait, see Zammito, *Kant, Herder, and the Birth of Anthropology*, 292.

20. For a fuller treatment, see Watkins, *Kant and the Metaphysics of Causality*, 160–180.

21. On this point, see Alison Laywine, *Kant's Early Metaphysics*, 52–54.

22. Kant claims to have taken the story from the Bremen Magazin [Band 1V, 539ff.], of which I have been unable to find an extant copy. (An almost identical story entitled "Carazan, the Merchant of Bagdad" appeared in John Hawksworth's *Adventurer* (#132), a popular periodical published in London between 1752 and 1754; the latter version is reproduced in *A Compendium of English Literature*, ed. Charles D. Cleveland [Philadelphia: E. C. & J. Biddle, 1858], 617–619.) The unusual name "Carazan" sounds vaguely Persian; the name also occurs in the "Persian Tales" (albeit without the accompanying story) adapted and made famous by the Italian writer Gozzi and later drawn upon by Tennyson and Schiller, among many others. Persian or not, modern readers will recognize in "Carazan's Dream" the basic elements of a German "ghost story" that Dickens would later transform into his famous *A Christmas Carol*.

23. Ian Hunter has recently drawn very helpful attention to the significance of Samuel Pufendorf and Christian Thomasius as competing sources of enlightened thought in Germany. (See his *Rival Enlightenments: Civil and Metaphysical Philosophy in Early Modern Germany* [Cambridge: Cambridge

University Press, 2001].) Hunter is surely right to stress the importance of the school metaphysics of the past as an ongoing reference point for Kant. In seeking to recover a "lost" enlightenment, however, he risks substituting one simplification for another. Indeed, his accompanying reduction of Kant to a mere "extension" [xii] of metaphysical *Schulphilosophie* verges on caricature. (See, for example, the author's description of Kant's alleged cultivation of the "elitist" discipline of university metaphysics" as both "life-long" and "unwavering" [280].) Given his generally careful attention to sources, Hunter's neglect of Kant's regard for such important thinkers as Hobbes, Locke, Hume, and Rousseau (who are barely mentioned, if at all) is here especially striking. (One might say the same for Hunter's almost complete neglect of Kant's extended personal flirtation with their thought throughout most of the 1760s.) *Pace* Hunter, Kant *does* seriously grapple with the "civil natural law" alternative in question, albeit mainly as represented by the thought of Hobbes, Locke, Shaftsbury, and Hume, rather than by their (arguably less intellectually weighty) German counterparts. Hunter's omission of Locke, given his well-known and influential rivalry with Leibniz, is thus especially odd. More crucially, Hunter's effort to turn Kant into an unregenerate champion of "contemplative autarky" [287] in the "Christian-Platonic" mold [289] flies in the face of Kant's critical assault upon the traditional claims of contemplation; it ignores, in other words, the Rousseau-inspired revolution that Kant himself describes as all important, and his ensuing personal dedication, following upon that revolution, to this-worldly republican goals. Partly as a result, Hunter fails to appreciate Kant's critical appropriation of the university for the Trojan horse it (mostly) is. On Kant's own not-insignificant appropriations of Hobbes's thought, see Chapters 5 and 6 below.

2. Kant's Archimedean Moment

1. Compare Rousseau, *Emile*, Book Three.
2. See, for example, *Dreams of a Spirit-Seer* [2: 327, 327n]. Kant there attributes his inclination to assert the existence of immaterial natures in the world (including his own soul) to a certain principle of life—a reason that he admits is "very obscure." "The principle *of life*," he says, "is to be found in something in the world that seems to be of an immaterial nature. For all *life* is based upon the inner capacity to determine itself *voluntarily* [nach Willkür]."
3. Significant exceptions include the works by Schmucker and Velkley cited in chapter 1, note 18 above; on the historical and biographical context, see Zammito, *Kant, Herder, and the Birth of Anthropology*, 113–135.
4. See Marie Rischmüller's excellent and extensive notes on Kant's sources (Immanuel Kant, *Bemerkungen in den "Beobachtungen über das Gefühl des Schönen und Urhabenen,"* ed. Marie Rischmüller [Hamburg: Felix Meiner Verlag, 1991]).

5. All page references are to the *Akademie* edition, vol. 20 (Immanuel Kant, *Gesammelte Schriften*, ed. Reinhard Brandt and Werner Stark, *Akademie* edition [Berlin: Walter de Gruyter, 1997]); quoted passages follow the newer Rischmüller edition (Immanuel Kant, *Bemerkungen in den "Beobachtungen über das Gefühl des Schönen und Urhabenen,"* ed. Marie Rischmüller [Hamburg: Felix Meiner Verlag, 1991]).
6. Schmucker, *Die Ursprünge die Ethik Kants*, 12–13.
7. For contrasting views on this point, see Richard L. Velkley, *Being after Rousseau: Philosophy and Culture in Question* (Chicago: Chicago University Press, 2002), 34–48; and Christopher Kelly, "Rousseau's "Peut-etre": Reflections on the Status of the State of Nature," *Modern Intellectual History* 3, no. 1 (April 2006): 75–83.
8. But cf. [2: 214]: "boldly undertaking danger for our own rights, for those of the fatherland, or for those of our friends is sublime [in a proper, rather than adventurous sense]"; and [2: 11n] (on "Carazan").
9. On Kant's own physical deformity, see, for example, Reinhold Jachmann, *Immanuel Kant geschildert in Briefen an einen Freund*; reprinted in *Immanuel Kant: sein Leben in Darstellungen von Zeitgenossen* (Berlin: Reprografischer Nachdruck der von Felix Gross herausgegebenen Ausgabe, 1912), 184–186.
10. She would also disdain as "trifling" what Kant here and elsewhere associates with bad philosophizing.
11. The latter claim is historically associated with Montesquieu, whom Kant mentions in passing [2: 247].
12. On the healthy "stomach" of Germans and Englishmen in matters of love, see [2: 250].
13. On Kant's allusion to King Alphonso and the Manichean doctrine, see Rischmüller's helpful note in Kant, *Bemerkungen in den "Beobachtungen über das Gefühl des Schönen und Urhabenen,"* 200–203.
14. Cf. Addison, *Spectator* No. 128—Friday, July 27, 1711: "When I survey this new-fashioned Rotonda in all its Parts, I cannot but think of the old Philosopher, who after having entered into an Egyptian Temple, and looked about for the Idol of the Place, at length discovered a little Black Monkey Enshrined in the midst of it, upon which he could not forebear crying out (to the great Scandal of the Worshippers), 'What a magnificent Palace is here for such a Ridiculous Inhabitant!'"

3. Rousseau, Count Verri, and the "True Economy of Human Nature"

1. Most of these lectures were published for the first time in Immanuel Kant, *Gesammelte Schriften*, vol. 25, ed. Reinhard Brandt and Werner Stark, *Akademie* edition (Berlin: Walter de Gruyter, 1997). See especially the editors' valuable comments on Verri, pp. XLII–XLVI. The lectures on anthropology have not yet been the subject of much extended scholarly commentary. One exception is

Essays on Kant's Anthropology, ed. Brian Jacobs and Patrick Kain (Cambridge: Cambridge University Press, 2003).

2. *Recension von Moscatis Schrift: Von dem körperlichen wesentlichen Unterschiede zwischen der Struktur der Thiere und Menschen.*

3. Unless otherwise noted, all translations of Kant's Latin works are from Immanuel Kant, *Theoretical Philosophy, 1755–1770*, ed. and trans. David Walford and Ralf Meerbote, The Cambridge Edition of the Works of Immanuel Kant (Cambridge: Cambridge University Press, 1992). Occasionally I have made very slight emendations with a view to consistency of style.

4. For a fuller discussion, see Richard L. Velkley, *Freedom and the End of Reason*, (Chicago: University of Chicago Press, 1989), 124–135; and Manfred Kuehn, "The Moral Dimension of Kant's Inaugural Dissertation," in *Proceedings of the Eighth International Kant Congress*, vol. 1, part 2, ed. Hoke Robinson, 373–389 (Milwaukee: Marquette University Press, 1995).

5. See also his letter to Marcus Herz (February 21, 1772), in which Kant admits to having "silently passed over" in the *Dissertation* the question of "how a representation that refers to an object without being in any way affected by it can be possible" [10: 130]. This question, as he here reports, is the major stumbling block to his completion of a planned book on *The Limits of Sensibility and Reason*.

6. As he elaborates: "I know . . . that thinking and willing move my body, but I can never reduce this phenomenon by means of analysis; hence, I can recognize this phenomenon but I cannot understand it. That my will moves my arm is no more intelligible to me than someone's claiming that my will could halt the moon. . . . The only difference is this: I experience the former, whereas my senses have never encountered the latter. I am acquainted with the alterations that take place within me as within a living subject; . . . and since these, taken together, constitute my concept of body, I naturally think of myself as an incorporeal and permanent being. Whether this incorporeal and permanent being will also think independently of the body can never be established by appealing to the nature of that being, which is known only by experience. I am connected with beings of my own kind through the mediation of corporeal laws, but I can in no wise establish from what is given to me whether . . . I am not also connected with such beings in according with other laws which I shall call pneumatic." [*Dreams of a Spirit-Seer* {2: 370}]

Similar views are expressed by Rousseau's Savoyard Vicar.

7. See Immanuel Kant, *Gesammelte Schriften*, vol. 15, ed. Reinhard Brandt and Werner Stark, *Akademie* edition (Berlin: Walter de Gruyter, 1997): 717n]. Volume 15 of the *Akademie* edition of Kant's work contains generous excerpts of the German translation by Christoph Meiners [15: 717n–722n].

8. See Pietro Verri, *Del piacere e del dolore ed altri scritti* (Milan: Feltrinelli, 1964), 16, 37; and John Locke, *Essay on Human Understanding*, Book Two, Chapter 21 ("Of Power"); Chapter 20, §6: "the chief if not only spur to human industry and action, is uneasiness."

9. For an early description of the task, see *Dreams of a Spirit-Seer* [2: 368]. "Metaphysics is a science of the *limits of human reason*. . . . Although I have not precisely determined this limit, I have indicated it sufficiently . . . to spare the reader the trouble of all futile research into a question whose answer demands *data* that are to be found in a world other than the one in which he exists as a conscious being." The insight of 1769 promises to open a new path to the world in which such data might be found. See also *Remarks* [20: 145].
10. On this threefold division, see also the letter to Marcus Herz dated February 21, 1772 [10: 129]. Kant's identification of feeling as a fundamental faculty in its own right represents a marked departure from Baumgarten's text (from which he lectured); Baumgarten identifies only knowledge and desire as "fundamental faculties," and addresses pain and pleasure almost in passing. Although the proximate source of Kant's treatment of feeling as a basic faculty seems to be Moses Mendelssohn (and not Johannes Nikolaus Tetens, as is often assumed), its deeper inspiration, I would suggest, can be traced to the novel role of "sentiment" in establishing an organic theory of life as sketched out in Rousseau's *Emile* and *Second Discourse*.
11. Cf. *The Metaphysics of Morals* [6: 211].
12. See, for example, Rousseau, *Emile*, trans. Allan Bloom (New York: Basic Books, 1979): 61, 270, 42: He "has lived the most . . . who has most felt life."
13. Dated "toward the end of 1773" [10: 145].
14. Cf. *Dreams of a Spirit-Seer* [2: 370].
15. Readers familiar with Kant's later work will recognize here a rough anticipation of his critical distinction between the physical, the moral, and the aesthetic.
16. See, for example, [15: 367]: Pleasure is the "feeling" through which "the value of the human condition is determined."
17. Kant at this stage emphasizes the ultimate dependence of such character on nature: "one who has a bad character, will never achieve the opposing good one, because the true *seed* is lacking, a seed which must be deposited [*gelegt*] in our nature as its end." All we can do is encourage or hinder the development of this seed [25: 438].
18. Cf. *Metaphysik 1:* "the general character of the object of inner sense [i.e., the general determination of action] is thinking and the general character of the object of outer sense is motion." "Motion" (or action in space and time) only applies to objects of outer sense, i.e., bodies [28: 222]. "Spiritual motion," unlike "thinking without a body," is indeed a contradictory concept, from this point of view, for reasons already anticipated in *Dreams of a Spirit-Seer*.
19. See, for example, his reference to wisdom (i.e., the understanding necessary to estimate the "universal or relational value of things") as involving a "palingenesis" or "rebirth" [25: 150, 159]. See, too, his assertion that the "transition between bodily and spiritual movement cannot be further clarified"; "it follows that Bonnet and various others very much err when they believe they can securely draw conclusions from the brain to the soul" [25: 9].

Nevertheless, a prime purpose of anthropology, according to *Collins*, is observation of the "mind in isolation from the body" with a view to discovering the question of whether "the influence of the body is necessary for thinking" [25: 9].
20. See especially *Emile*, 357–364, 373–377, 384–387.
21. Without the falsely high regard paid to them by civilized men, women would be slaves, according to Kant—as they remain among the savage nations.
22. Cf. the parallel section of Kant's roughly contemporaneous lecture on metaphysics (*Metaphysik 1*): The feeling of one's own existence testifies to the presence in the human soul of an independent principle of life: "the consciousness of the mere I proves that life does not lie in the body, but rather in a separate principle . . . ; consequently that this principle can also survive without the body, and that its life is not thereby diminished but increased. This is the only proof [as to the status of the soul after death] that can be given *a priori* . . ." [28: 287]. As Kant goes on to admit, however, what "feeling" is "hard to determine" [28: 246]. Kant also leaves open the question of whether the human soul without the body can think: "my intuition of myself does not include my thinking and willing," since thinking and willing "*cannot be intuited*" [28: 226]. The possibility of "thinking spirit" unconnected to a body can neither be confirmed nor denied on the basis of rational psychology [28: 278]. In sum, the spiritual character of the human soul to which the *feeling* of self testifies is enough to establish that we remain alive after death but not necessarily as thinking beings. In his later thought Kant will explicitly link thought with *Gemüth* rather than spirit [cf., e.g., *Metaphysics Dohna*, 28: 680].
23. Not unrelatedly, Kant calls in *Metaphysik 1* for the further development of "empirical psychology" as an academic field devoted to studying "the first principles of the human soul" and which would ultimately involve "*trips to cognize human beings, such as have been undertaken to become acquainted with plants and animals*" [28: 224]—i.e., "anthropology" as it is now generally understood.
24. In *Metaphysik 1*, Kant continues to insist that our ability to think "I" constitutes "the one case in which we can immediately intuit substance" whose concept we borrow for our thought of all other substances. Without the body, however, "one cannot locate oneself within the world" [28: 225]. Kant now keeps a guarded silence on the question of whether and how thinking without the influence of the body (and the worldly connection it implies) is possible.
25. Cf. Kant's descriptions of juridical community in *The Metaphysics of Morals* [7: 231]: Punishment, on this account, is literally a life enhancing remedy for the body politic.
26. See also *Metaphysik 1:* Life is threefold: "animal, human, and spiritual" [28: 248]. Kant also proposes the following hypothetical progression: "I . . . find a transition from the mineral kingdom to the plant kingdom, which is already a beginning of life; then from the plant kingdom to the animal kingdom, where

there are also various small degrees of life; but the highest life is freedom, which I find with human beings. If I go even further, then I am already among thinking beings in an ideal world" [28: 205]. I have an immediate feeling of my own existence. "But *if I maintain [that there are] thinking beings of which I have an intellectual intuition, then that is mystical.*" As Kant is here at pains to insist, God maintains the series without merging with it. To hold otherwise is "Spinozism" or "Platonic idealism" [28: 207].

27. See, for example, *Reflexion* #938 [15: 416]: "Because spirit goes forth from the universal it is, so to speak, a particular divine aura [*divina particula aurae*], drawn from the universal spirit. Thus spirit has no particular properties; rather according to the various talents and sensibilities [*Empfindsamkeiten*] that it precipitates, it variously enlivens, and because this is so multifarious, each spirit has something that is peculiar. One must not say: the genius's. It is the unity of the world soul."

Other notes from around the same period identify spirit's capacity to "enliven" with its status as an originating source of unity: "Spirit is aroused and cultivated, if we set a talent from one standpoint in relation to all others. Then the entire force of the soul is aroused and the universal life is moved" [*Reflexion* #937; 15: 416]. Spirit is thus called the "production ground" of the ideas (which "determine whole[s] through concept[s]"): "The 'moving force' by which the mind is first moved lies in the products that obtain unity through relation to their idea. . . . Spirit is the enlivening of sensibility through the idea." Such enlivening must proceed from understanding to sensibility; otherwise it is merely feverish heating. The power of spirit to "enliven" "sensibility" thus bears an obvious relation to the male's "active" role in generation. "Man [*Der Mann*] has not only suitability [*Geschicklichkeit*] but also spirit. Spirit is . . . not a particular talent, but an enlivening principium of all talents" [*Reflexion* #933, 935; 15: 414–415]. Similarly, "spirit is the inner . . . principium of the enlivening of (the forces of the mind) thoughts. Soul is that which is enlivened. A new series of thoughts originates out of itself. From this, ideas. Spirit is the original enlivening, that comes from itself and is not derived. (Aptitude [*Naturell*] is the receptivity of the forces of the mind, talent their spontaneity.)" [*Reflexion* #934; 15: 415]. Moral freedom, or spontaneity as an individuating source of moral agency, has yet to separate as decisively as it later will from aesthetic freedom, or spontaneity as an individuating source of original production. Freedom in the latter sense eludes the power of our free will [*Reflexion* #932; 15: 413]. See also *Reflexion* #1033 [15: 463]: "The life spirit seems to be a particular principium of the union of the soul with the body . . . on which the will has no influence. The heart is seized, and this is the basis of [their] commerce." For further analysis, see Georgio Tonelli, "Kant's Early Theory of Genius, 1770–1779," *Journal of the History of Philosophy* 4 (1966): 109–131, 209–224.

28. See *Metaphysik 1* [28: 153–156].
29. Compare *Conjectural Beginning of Human History* [8: 116n].

30. Cf. Kant's characterization of his later *Toward Perpetual Peace* as a "philosophische Entwurf."
31. Kant apparently equates consciousness during this period with "inner sense." (See [28: 277].)
32. Kant, as is well known, was an avid reader of travel literature.
33. To good character, so described, Kant now contrasts the weak [*schlecht*] character who is "bound" to the "discipline" of "rules" as to a "go-cart" [*Gängelwagen*]. Some human beings have a *naturell* that accepts no discipline, which is equivalent to having a bad character [25: 650–651]. Much follows on the national and racial implications of the variety of *naturell*, talents and temperaments. The specific superiority of the Greeks, for example, lies in their balancing a northern European talent for concepts with an Asiatic talent for images [25: 655]. And Kant writes still more on the complex interplay on bodily and metal formation as reflected in physiognomy (discussion of which is much reduced in later versions of the lectures) [25: 661–664]. Honesty and dishonesty, for example, can be read in men's faces [25: 672]; and physiognomy furnishes similar indications as to which nations are susceptible to "respect for law" and hence capable of "freedom" and which can be disciplined "only through compulsion" [25: 674].
34. In *Metaphysik 1* Kant experiments with various ways of reconciling such natural incapacity with larger issues of moral fairness; thus he speculates that savages "who have no knowledge of the moral law" and young children "who die early" might find themselves in more favorable circumstances in the future (i.e., when liberated from the "sheath" of this bodily life) [28: 290].
35. An alternate meaning of "tropische" is "figurative or metaphorical." Compare Kant's historical prediction, at the end of *Friedländer,* that the earth is gradually becoming a more perfect sphere, making the tropics and antipodes more and more alike [25: 696–697].
36. Cf. Kant's similar complaints about world monarchy in *Toward Perpetual Peace* [8: 367].
37. This emphasis on the greater life force reproductively required of the male is an addition on Kant's part to an account of the relation between the sexes that otherwise follows Book Five of *Emile* very closely. Kant consistently maintained that sexual intercourse as such (and not just, as with Rousseau, when indulged in excessively) brings about in men a depletion of vital force comparable in danger to that of childbirth for women.
38. Similarly, unlike Rousseau, who encourages honesty in the child as a means of controlling him, Kant stresses only its moral aspect.
39. Cf. *Emile*, 257.
40. *Emile*, 314.
41. See, for example, the following statement: "In nature there rules the greatest harmony with nature's ends, *philosophizing about the ends of nature is very agreeable*" [25: 614; original emphasis].

42. Not surprisingly, this is also the period during which Kant's active support for Basedow's institution reaches its peak. (See especially his letters to Basedow and to Christian Heinrich Wolke, headmaster of the school, of March and June 1776 [10: 156–159]. During the same year, Kant used Basedow's *Methodenbuch* for his own lectures on pedagogy.)
43. See *Friedländer* [25: 599–612]; cf. *Pillau*, according to which anthropology has "little to say" about the community of soul and body [25: 813].
44. Concerning the feeling of pleasure and displeasure, Kant now writes: "this is very important and indispensable material," which "contains the principles of the human passions" and on which an Italian has written [25: 784–785]. "It is easy to understand something [of this matter], but not so easy to have insight." As Verri says, enjoyment cannot be determined [conceptually]. Enjoyment is the feeling of the promotion of life; not life itself, since pain conveys the feeling of being alive even more than pleasure does [25: 786]. Enjoyment of life cannot exceed the pain of life, but the reverse can easily occur. That which "lets us feel our existence is not *easy* for us." It "makes time long for us," and "pains us" [25: 787]. (Verri also distinguishes between physical and moral pains and pleasures.) See Verri, *Del piacere e del dolore*, 9–15. Not least of the advantages of Verri's argument is its immunity to Kant's early objection, on the grounds that all pleasures and pains are not homogeneous, to similar claims earlier advanced by Maupertuis. (See *Negative Magnitudes* [2: 181–182].)
45. See [25: 734, 804–807].
46. See [25: 814–816, 831–847]. This characterization of "peoples" (which *Friedländer* had disposed of in a few [relatively early] pages [25: 654–661]) is now called "a necessary condition of world-knowledge," and the "final end" of both histories and travel [25: 831]. Kant's earlier worries as to the intrinsic inferiority of the non-European races here hardens into doctrine: whereas he had once allowed that Greenlanders contain the same "germs," ripe for development, as do Parisians, he now insists that future progress will come only from the peoples of Europe. Peoples of the other continents are at a "standstill" [25: 846], owing to their lack of "spirit." (Americans, he speculates, will die out completely [25: 839–840].) Kant's treatment of the "character of the female sex," by way of contrast, is now meager to the point of being perfunctory [25: 835–838].
47. Where Kant had once identified "intelligence" and "spirit," reason now stands out clearly as a distinct faculty of "laws" (as distinguished from mere rules), a faculty whose "supreme value" lies in providing "the highest ground of unity." Thus "understanding gives the unity of appearances"; whereas reason gives the rules of understanding their unity. Rules relate themselves to a given end. Law, on the other hand, "determines the end." And "because the end is the highest ground of unity, reason is the lawgiver" [25: 777]. Spirit, for its part, is what gives all capacities unity—i.e., the "general unity or harmony of the human mind," or the "enlivening of sensibility through the idea" [25: 782]. Spirit is in

turn bound up with newness and discovery, since progress requires, in knowledge as well as art, making new use of our talents [25: 783].

48. See [25: 841]; progress of non-European races, however, has come to an end.

49. *Negative Magnitudes* [2: 181–182]. Kant there characterizes displeasure [*Unlust*] as not merely a lack of pleasure [*Lust*], but, rather, as "the ground of the latter's deprivation [*Beraubung*]" [2: 180]. By this he means not only that displeasure is a positive feeling in its own right, but that it is opposed to pleasure in a way that "subtracts from" the latter (just as a debt subtracts from a credit). His example of the latter is the Spartan mother (also described at the beginning of *Emile*) whose joy on hearing that her son has fought heroically for his country is diminished by the news that he has died in battle. Estimating the total value of one's whole [*gesammten*] pleasure is like calculating the total yield of an estate, i.e., a function of income (pleasure) minus expenses (displeasure). Pleasure and displeasure, to the extent that they really oppose each other, stem from opposing grounds. When both grounds are lacking, the result is indifference. When both grounds are present and equal, the result is equilibrium. On the basis of such concepts, Kant says, Maupertuis argued that the sum of human happiness is negative—a calculation that is humanly impossible, according to Kant, owing to the "diversity" of our feelings. Only if our feelings were, like money, homogeneous [*gleichartig*] could such a calculation succeed. See Pierre Louis Maupertuis, *Essai de philosophie morale* (London: chez Jacques Brakstone, 1750), 4–10; cf. Verri, *Del piacere e del dolore*, 31.

50. Cf. *Critique of Judgment*; see also *Anthropology* [IX: 239].

51. But cf. Kant's later claim that "activity" [*handeln*] makes life both more pleasant and more "real" to us and hence retrospectively more satisfying [25: 1081].

52. Cf. *Parow*, [25: 414]: "the mind full of feeling and at rest is the greatest enjoyment."

53. Cf. *Groundlaying of the Metaphysics of Morals* [4: 418–419].

54. Locke makes a similar argument in the *Essay Concerning Human Understanding:* Man is naturally driven to act, not by contemplation of some good but by feelings of "uneasiness": "'It is better to marry than to burn,' says St. Paul, where we may see, what it is, that chiefly drives men into the enjoyments of a conjugal life. A little burning felt pushes us more powerfully, than greater pleasures in prospect draw or allure" [II: XXI, §34].

55. For Zeno and the Stoics, sufficiency is achieved through self-mastery; for Diogenes and the Cynics (of whom Rousseau, according to Kant, is a latter-day example), by relinquishing unnecessary desires. Kant's persistent objection to Stoicism, is not its principle of *animus sui compos*—a principle he basically shares—but its inability to show how such a rule can be effectual. See, for example, [25: 39]; cf. *The Conflict of the Faculties* [7: 100].

56. On real opposition in Kant's metaphysics, see Peter König, *Autonomie und Autokratie: über Kants Metaphysik der Sitten* (Berlin: Walter de Gruyter, 1994).

57. Kant notes, in this regard, that "human beings may well call themselves satisfied with their condition" so long as they think they have "means to free themselves from any pain." Hence the attraction of liquor, opium, and other intoxicants to the rude and uncultivated, despite the fact that such remedies are also immediately painful [25: 1072].
58. In his roughly contemporary lectures on ethics Kant adds Plato's understanding of the highest good as spiritual community with God—an idea we are also incapable of representing to ourselves as a real possibility [27: 250].
59. *Idea for a Universal History* [8: 19–20].
60. Kant notes that nations to whom nature "gives all" have fewer "true enjoyments" than those (e.g., in Northern Europe) where nature's harshness prompts activity [25: 1078].
61. Cf. *Dreams of a Spirit-Seer,* where "Organ" (problematically) designates the "soul's sensorium"—i.e., that part of the brain whose movements usually accompany the images and representations of the thinking soul, "as the philosophers maintain" [2: 339n].
62. The word *verwandeln* can mean "to change," "convert," "transmute" (as in alchemy), and "transubstantiate" (as in the Christian Mass); Kant's usage here suggests "convert" as in the realization of an investment through its conversion into money or other immediately useful wealth.
63. Kant plays here on the Parable of the Talents [Matthew 25:14–30], with which the term "talent" (meaning, allegorically, a deposit from God) is etymologically associated. See also *Anthropology* [7: 234–239]. Happiness understood as perfect satisfaction is thinkable only as a kind of living death. Relative satisfaction, on the other hand, consists in pursuing a "great end," through "planfully progressive occupation." As one who has devoted himself in singular fashion to "philosophy" so defined, Kant has himself followed what he here designates as the only course of wisdom, securing him a "capital [*Capital*] of satisfaction" to draw on that does not depend upon "contingencies or the law of nature" [7: 237]. Kant will later make extended use of that parable in *Religion within the Boundaries of Bare Reason.*
64. According to the *Akademie* editors, this passage is found in the Petersburg manuscript but not in *Menschenkunde.*
65. The *Akademie* editors give "Hume" as an alternate reading.
66. Not least of these advantages is the ability of social intercourse to counter a dangerous tendency in some to self-preoccupation. Like pragmatic anthropology itself, social intercourse is a powerful remedy against hypochondria and related illnesses [25: 862–863]. On the latter point, see also Shell, *The Embodiment of Reason,* 283–285.
67. The first edition of the *Critique of Pure Reason* appeared in 1781.
68. See *Critique of Pure Reason* [A 416–417 = B 443–455].
69. See, for example, *Metaphysik 2* [28: 593]; *Metaphysik Volckmann* [28: 446]: "here on earth happiness is nothing but a progress, each sensation drives us to go

from one to another; accordingly we cannot think at all of an *enduring* state after this which would be happy in a constant way, for we think of happiness only in progress."
70. See also *Critique of Pure Reason* [A 839 = B 867].
71. Compare, for example, *Critique of Pure Reason* [A 807 = B 835] and [A 812–813 = B 840–841]; on the one hand, Kant assumes "that there really are pure moral laws that determine completely *a priori*," and "without regard to empirical motives, i.e., happiness"; on the other hand, as "commands" they necessarily carry with them "*promises* and *threats*" absent which they would lose their motivating force. Kant here distinguishes our *judgment* of the law, which takes place in accordance with ideas, from our *observance* of the law, which is a matter of "subjective maxims." To be sure, happiness cannot be the incentive of moral action. And yet for moral maxims to govern our entire course of life, reason must be able to connect the moral law, which is merely an idea, with an efficient cause linking such conduct with an "outcome corresponding to our highest ends." Hence, without God and an afterlife "the lordly [*herrlichen*] ideas of morality" are "objects of approval and admiration" but not "incentives for resolve and execution" [A 811 = B 839]. The difference between Kant's position here and that later adopted in the *Critique of Practical Reason* is taken up in Chapter 4.

4. The "Paradox" of Autonomy

1. Both Robert Pippin and Terry Pinkard treat Kantian autonomy as "paradoxical" in the sense of being self-contradictory. The contradiction arises, in Pinkard's words, "from Kant's demand that, if we are to impose a principle . . . on ourselves, then presumably we must have a reason to do so; but if there was an antecedent reason to do so, then that reason would not be self-imposed [as here assumed]" (59). A major virtue of Hegel's practical thought, on both of their accounts, is its ability to overcome the difficulty that is contained in the original Kantian formulation. See Pippin, "Hegel's Practical Philosophy," in *The Cambridge Companion to German Idealism*, ed. Karl Ameriks (Cambridge: Cambridge University Press, 2000), 194; and Pinkard, *German Philosophy 1760—1860: The Legacy of Idealism* (Cambridge: Cambridge University Press, 2002), 58–65, 230, 259–60, 220. Pinkard treats the Idealist legacy as largely a response to the problem of autonomy as described above. On Kant's own, more positive understanding of the term "paradox," see page 286–288 and note 51 below. Kant's treatment of the larger issue raised by Pippin and Pinkard is the subject of the present chapter.
2. For three at least partial exceptions, see Jens Timmermann, *Kant's* Groundwork of the Metaphysics of Morals (Cambridge: Cambridge University Press, 2007), especially xii–xiv; Paul Guyer, *Kant on Freedom, Law, and Happiness* (Cambridge: Cambridge University Press, 2000), 207–231; and Dieter

Henrich, *The Unity of Reason: Essays on Kant's Philosophy*, ed. Richard Velkley (Cambridge, Mass.: Harvard University Press, 1994), 55–87, originally published as "Der Begriff der sittlichen Einsicht und Kants Lehre vom Faktum der Vernunft," in Dieter Henrich, Walter Schulz, and Karl Heinz Vollkmann Schluck, eds., *Die Gegenwart der Griechen im neueren Denken: Festschrift für Hans-Georg Gadamer* (Tübingen: J. C. B. Mohr, 1960), 77–115. As Guyer observes, ordinary moral understanding on Kant's account is mainly threatened from "within" [211, 214–215]. My interpretation differs from theirs in locating the essential problem not only in the ineluctability of our desire for happiness or in the undeniable necessity that governs nature, but also and primarily in the ground-seeking character of human reason itself.

3. Immanuel Kant, *Practical Philosophy*, ed. and trans. Mary J. Gregor and Allen Wood (Cambridge: Cambridge University Press, 1996), 82. Translations, unless otherwise stated, are my own.

4. Cf., e.g., Guyer, *Kant on Freedom, Law, and Happiness*, 230; Christine M. Korsgaard, *Creating the Kingdom of Ends* (Cambridge: Cambridge University Press, 1996), 161.

5. See also Guyer, *Kant on Freedom, Law, and Happiness*, 217.

6. Eckart Förster has made a strong case for the importance of an unpublished review by Christian Garve, himself a well-known *Popularphilosopher*, in prompting Kant to take this final step. Garve had objected to Kant's claim that God and an afterlife are necessary to the truth, or at least the efficacy, of the moral law, given Kant's earlier destruction of people's conviction as to these very matters. See Förster, *Kant's Final Synthesis: an Essay on the Opus Postumum* (Cambridge, Mass.: Harvard University Press, 2000), 122–127.

7. "Übergang von der gemeinen sittlichen Vernunfterkenntniss zur philosophen." In rendering this phrase as "common rational ethical knowledge," or even as just "ethical knowledge," many standard translations give insufficient emphasis to the link that is verbally implied in the original text between "knowledge" and "reason." On the meaning of *Vernunfterkenntiss*, see *The Critique of Pure Reason* [A 320 = B 377], where it is said to involve knowledge of ideas understood as necessary criteria or standards of judgment. Such ideas are "framed from notions" (i.e., pure concepts of the understanding) but not to be confused with them. Speaking more loosely, Kant explains theoretical knowledge [*theoretische Erkenntniss*] as "one whereby one knows *what exists* [was da ist]" and practical knowledge [*practical Erkenntniss*] as "one whereby one knows *what ought to exist* [was dasein soll]" [A 633 = B 661]. "Erkenntniss" differs from "wissen" (or "science"): To know in a scientific sense (as in *wissen*) is also to know *that* one knows [A 7n]. I generally translate *Erkenntiss* by "knowledge" rather than "cognition," which has a technical ring missing in the German original.

8. See also Guyer, *Kant on Freedom, Law, and Happiness*, 216–217. For a discussion of some of the issues pressing on Kant, see Frederick C. Beiser, *The Fate of Reason: German Philosophy from Kant to Fichte* (Cambridge, Mass.:

Harvard University Press, 1987), 165–169; and John H. Zammito, *Kant, Herder and the Birth of Anthropology* (Chicago: University of Chicago Press, 2002), 8–11.

9. As *Vigilantius* puts it: "that negation on whose account a quantum is not the greatest = *maximum* =, can be called either *limitation* or *boundedness*, according to whether it is an object of mere reason or of the senses." Limits thus differ from boundaries. According to *Vigilantius*, limit is a negation "thought merely according to the understanding"; hence "a being of the understanding (noumenon) has only limits." Kant also calls limitation a "noumenal quantum," or "magnitude thought through the understanding, and limited insofar as it is not the greatest," as when one speaks of limits of the (human) will. Boundaries, by way of contrast, arise through a "positive" negation through which something is limited in intuition and thus belong to experience [29: 994]. On the difference between limits and boundaries, see also *Critique of Pure Reason* [A 761 = B 790; A 767 = B 795]. "Without limitation" means "in any reference" or "absolutely" [A 324 = B 381]. For helpful discussions of idea-formation in Kant, see Peter König, *Autonomie und Autokratie: über Kants Metaphysik der Sitten* (Berlin: Walter de Gruyter, 1994); and Klaus Steigleder, "The Analytic Relationship of Freedom and Morality (GMS III, 1)," in Christoph Horn and Dieter Schönecker, eds., *Groundwork for the Metaphysics of Morals* (Berlin: Walter de Gruyter, 2006), 225–230.

10. On practical ideas, see Kant's nearly contemporaneous *Lectures on Philosophical Theology* [28.2.2: 993–996]: "Human reason has need of an idea of highest perfection, to serve it as a standard according to which it can make determinations. . . . A person can render friendly service . . . but still take his own welfare into consideration, or he can offer up everything to his friend. . . . The latter comes closest to the idea of perfect friendship." Similarly, to form an idea of vice, "we leave out anything that might limit the degree of vice" (such as extenuating circumstances). Ideas of this kind require three elements: completeness of the subject with respect to predicates, completeness with respect to derivation, and completeness with respect to community or relation to the whole. As an example of an idea, Kant cites Rousseau's *Emile* (which Kant here contrasts with Xenophon's *Cyropaedia*).

11. Kant uses the same term elsewhere to describe God's own approval of morally good actions.

12. Cf. Samuel J. Kerstein, *Kant's Search for the Supreme Principle of Morality* (Cambridge, Cambridge University Press, 2002), 67. For Kerstein, who finds Kant's claim here "dubious," a "scenario" in which both the virtuous and wicked are happy is good, albeit less good than one in which everyone is both happy and virtuous. Kerstein ignores the essential interdependence of the "ethical rational knowledge" Kant invokes and the conditionality of the goodness of happiness on one being worthy of it. To deem the good will the sole thing that it is possible to think good without limitation is to be unable to approve (in the

intended sense) a state in which the wicked flourish. Were the flourishing of those lacking good will necessary to the happiness of those possessing it, it might perhaps elicit qualified approval (of the sort here intended) but only in the manner of a "necessary evil," and owing solely to the desert claims of the morally good.

13. For an alternative view, see Allen Wood, "The Good without Limitation," in *Groundwork for the Metaphysics of Morals* (note 9), 28–32. According to Wood, Kant does not present "the goodness of the good will" as a "value-claim that is fundamental to his ethical system as a whole." If one wishes to extract from the *Groundlaying* such a "value-claim," Wood prefers the claim (in keeping with his general interpretation of Kant's ethical thought) that rational nature is "an end in itself" or, alternatively, that it is "universally legislative" [31]. I am contending, to the contrary, that the unconditional goodness of good will is fundamental to Kant's mature moral thinking as a whole—indeed, that it is a grounding premise and/or insight.

14. See *Lectures on Philosophical Theology* [29.2.2: 995–996]. A being possessed of a calculating or prudential reason but lacking in the ability to estimate moral value (i.e., to adopt the standpoint of an "impartial rational spectator") would necessarily lack a rational concept of perfect goodness. Such a being would be incapable of holding *anything* "good without limitation." The prosperity of a good will may well be preferable to its misfortune (a matter to which Kant's *Critique of Practical Reason* will later return). And yet a good man thus favored is not himself more worthy of existence than a good man who is not.

15. Thus the famous debate over the alleged consistency of Kant's moral theory with "compatibilism." Henry E. Allison is one of the few contemporary critics who emphasize the importance of imputation to Kant's concept of freedom. (See his *Kant's Theory of Freedom* [Cambridge: Cambridge University Press, 1990], 41–51.) His "two-aspect" theory tends, however, to subvert the robust understanding of freedom that a serious commitment to related notions of moral responsibility would seem to demand. If belief in my authorship of my own acts is only one, not necessarily privileged way of looking at things, I have no good reason to take it to heart. For an illuminating discussion of this difficulty, see Karl Ameriks, *Kant and the Fate of Autonomy* (Cambridge: Cambridge University Press, 2000), 17–23. My own position here is closer to that of Allen Wood in "Kant's Compatibilism," *Self and Nature in Kant's Philosophy*, ed. Allen Wood (Ithaca: Cornell University Press, 1984), than to the view Wood expounds in *Kant's Ethical Thought* (Cambridge: Cambridge University Press, 1989), 178–182.

16. This fact helps explain Kant's later insistence that to conclude that duty is impossible leads to moral self-contempt rather than to the a-morality one might expect on the basis of the reading common among analytic philosophers, who often seek (in opposition to Kant's own express intentions) a justification of morality capable of "answering" the a-moral skeptic in a *theoretically*

convincing way. [See 4: 426 and pp. 291–302 below.] That a rational being might lack such knowledge is born out a page later, when Kant imagines beings who are rational in merely a contemplative sense, but in whom nature has not allowed practical reason to "break out" and are thus incapable of willing that things be other than they are [4: 395]. Indeed, as Kant will argue in a later work, beings might have a capacity to reason practically, i.e., to "think out for themselves the project of happiness and the means of attaining it," without being able to assume the standpoint here described (i.e., without possessing what Kant calls "personality"). Rational beings of this sort would presumably not be troubled by the unbroken flourishing of scoundrels, so long as they were not personally harmed by it. (See *Religion within the Boundaries of Bare Reason* [6: 26].) See also Dieter Henrich, "The Concept of Moral Insight," in *The Unity of Reason* (note 2), 55–88. In my view, Henrich does not dwell sufficiently on the central difficulty such (alleged) moral insight poses, namely: reconciling morality's obligatory force with the claim that it is true "only" from a practical standpoint.

17. See, for example, Kant, *Metaphysics of Morals* [6: 227]; for an explication and singular criticism, see Martin Heidegger, *Being and Time*, tr. John Macquarrie and Edward Robinson (New York: Harper and Row, 1962), 2:2.58.

18. Kant does not identify the first principle explicitly.

19. John Locke gives a similar analysis of human desire in the *Essay Concerning Human Understanding*.

20. Compare Bruce Aune (*Kant's Theory of Morals* [Princeton: Princeton University Press, 1979]). Contrary to Aune's suggestion, Kant's conception here of a general "lawfulness of actions" already has the "directive" normative content implicit in the concept of a good will. Aune, by way of contrast, understands "lawfulness" here so broadly as to include the maxims of a pure egoist as when, proverbially, the King of France and the King of Spain both wanted the same thing. On the complex meaning of *Gesetzmäßigkeit* and the related inadequacy of Aune's argument, see Harald Köhl, "The Derivation of the Moral Law," in *Groundwork for the Metaphysics of Morals* (note 9), 99–104. None of this is to deny that Kant's argument may face other difficulties.

21. Critics often misunderstand Kant's insistence that, for all we know, the concept of duty and related moral ideas might be a "phantom of the brain." What is here in question, on Kant's account, is not the unique ability of such ideas to command our esteem (which follows from the "ethical rational knowledge" that constitutes his starting point); what is at stake is, rather, whether we or anyone else can *act* solely on the basis of such ideas, i.e., whether pure reason can be practical—a question that must be satisfactorily answered lest our attachment to the law be put unnecessarily at risk.

22. Cf. Guyer, *Kant on Freedom, Law, and Happiness*, 211–212.

23. Cf. *Critique of Pure Reason* [A 811 = B 839].

24. See *Critique of Pure Reason* [A 744 = B 772]. With the critique of reason in its speculative use, "the dispute is not about the *matter*," as Kant puts it, "but the *tone*."
25. Kant's allusions here combine appeals to Plato, Luther, and Adam Smith in a single striking metaphor: The true calling of philosophy is to ensure that the gain yielded by the modern division of labor is not squandered in an effort to flatter public taste but that each producer in the fields of reason and experience attend to his "own business" [4: 388].
26. Cf. Leo Strauss, *Spinoza's Critique of Religion*, trans. E. M. Sinclair (New York: Schocken Books, 1965), 28–29. Here Kant may have especially in mind figures like Voltaire, whose contempt for ordinary morality Rousseau famously criticized. On ridicule as the last refuge of scoundrels, see also *Toward Perpetual Peace* [8: 355].
27. As Allen Wood observes, "form, matter, and complete determination" refer, in the context of Kant's ontology, "to the conditions for the possibility of an individual thing." The progression of these formulas corresponds, in turn, to the so-called categories of quantity in the *Critique of Pure Reason*—i.e., "unity, plurality, and totality" [A 70 = B 106; Wood, *Kant's Ethical Thought*, 184–185]. Wood invokes the analogy to argue (mistakenly, in my view) for the normative primacy of the formula of humanity as an end in itself.
28. Kant's argument here anticipates in some respects Heidegger's treatment of *Gerede* ["idle chatter"] in *Being and Time;* on related themes in Kierkegaard and the German Romantics, see Peter D. Fenves, *"Chatter": Language and History in Kierkegaard* (Stanford: Stanford University Press, 1993).
29. It is striking that in the *Groundlaying*, unlike the first *Critique*, metaphysics *precedes* the critique of reason. But Kant has good cause, as we shall see, to work out the conceptual conditions of a system of *a priori* moral knowledge before addressing directly the more difficult issue of whether objects that are conceptually determinable by pure reason are to be encountered in the world—the issue, that is to say, of whether pure reason can indeed be practical, which will be taken up in Section Three.
30. Of course, human beings often aren't fully rational in this sense—e.g., when one breaks a diet out of weakness or otherwise fails to act in the manner that reason dictates as necessary given one's chosen end. On the two kinds of rational "necessitation" at issue, see Klaus Steigleder, "The Analytic Relationship of Freedom and Morality (GMS III, 1)," in *Groundwork for the Metaphysics of Morals* (note 9), 225–230. For a helpful discussion of Kant's "hedonism," see Barbara Herman, *Moral Literacy* (Cambridge, Mass.: Harvard University Press, 2007), 178–202.
31. On our inability to silence the voice [*Stimme*] of conscience, see also *The Metaphysics of Morals* [6: 438]: "Every man has a conscience . . . And this power [*Gewalt*] watching over the law in him is not something that he himself

(voluntarily) *makes.* . . . He cannot avoid *hearing* it." The importance of the "inner judge" to moral consciousness is already thematic in Rousseau. See, for example, *Emile,* "Profession of Faith of a Savoyard Vicar."

32. Cf. Nietzsche's insistence that the "hollowness" of (Kantian) ideals must become audible [*"laut werden muss . . ."*] through philosophy's special "tuning fork" which "sounds out idols" (Foreword, *Twilight of the Idols*). The theme of "sound" and "sounding" is taken up in Chapter 8 below.

33. To be sure, much more would need to be said to establish the adequacy of this derivation. Wood's objection—namely, that conformity to a universal law cannot be tested without knowing in advance the *content* of that law—does not, however, hold. Kant's point is that we can indeed test conformity to universal law without independent knowledge of the law's content. The test is a formal one. If I am unwilling for my maxim to hold as a universal rule, I can rightly conclude that to adopt it would be to act upon a principle that does not apply with unconditional necessity. Cf. Wood, *Kant's Ethical Thought,* 79–80. For a persuasive elaboration of Kant's argument, see Köhl, "The Derivation of the Moral Law (GMS 402, 420–421)," in *Groundwork of the Metaphysics of Morals* (see note 9), 92–114.

34. In its reflexive form, *angeweisen* means "to be thrown back on one's own resources"—a secondary meaning Kant may here also have in mind, given the paragraph that immediately follows.

35. Cf. Kant, *Groundlaying* [4: 420n].

36. Cf. Kant, *Groundlaying* [4: 390]: Where a moral ground is lacking, conformity to law is only "precarious" [*mißlich*]. Ordinary and philosophic moral understanding are, in this respect, in the same slippery position.

37. According to Grimm and Grimm, *Selbsthalter* means "autocrat." In the parlance of the time, Catherine the Great was commonly referred to as "Kaiserin und Selbsthalterin" of all of Russia. (Königsberg was from 1755 until 1762 under Russian military occupation.) On "autocratrix," see also Timmermann, *Kant's* Groundwork of the Metaphysics of Morals, 89n.

38. As Henrich notes, it is only with Kant that "Achtung" acquires its current morally charged meaning of "reverence" or "respect." See Henrich, *The Unity of Reason,* 109; and Kant, *The Metaphysics of Morals* [6: 468].

39. Hence the accompanying image of virtue as a "naked" woman whose sublime shape is linked to an absence of sensual "charm" [4: 427n]—an image that is also repeatedly invoked in Kant's earlier work, as discussed in Chapters 2 and 3. Here, as elsewhere, the abyss of reason is metaphorically likened to the canceling of the conditions of inner sense experienced during moments of sensual rapture.

40. See also [4: 405], where reason is said to "command unremittingly [*unnachlasslich*]" and "without promising anything to the inclinations," but rather with "disregard" [*Zurücksetzung*] and contempt [*Nichtachtung*] for their claims.

41. This thought goes beyond Kant's earlier definition of a rational being (at [4: 412]), which spoke merely of the capacity *to act* in accordance with the representation of laws rather than, as here, of the capacity of the will *to determine itself* in accordance with its representation of certain laws.
42. See also Paul Guyer, *Kant's System of Nature and Freedom* (Oxford: Oxford University Press, 2005), 149–150. The notion of humanity as a "limiting condition" on our ends permits one to characterize negatively, as it were, the necessary "matter" of a good will.
43. We are still operating merely on the assumption that there exist beings capable of good will, a capacity that alone makes one an end in oneself, objectively speaking. Christine Korsgaard's generally careful treatment of Kant's argument passes over his crucial qualifying footnote here. (Cf. Korsgaard, *Creating the Kingdom of Ends*, 123.) On Kant's general argument, see also Samuel J. Kerstein, "Deriving the Formula of Humanity," in *Groundwork for the Metaphysics of Morals* (note 9), 206–208.
44. "Subjectively" here refers not to what is true merely for the "subject," but to the fact that a rational will (at least any will that acts within nature as we know it) "sets itself" an end. Since the objective ground of the will must lie in the law, the end can only be conceived as a limiting condition on whatever other ends one might (also) will [4: 436–437].
45. Henrich's discussion of what he calls "moral insight" addresses some of these issues (Henrich, *The Unity of Reason*, 95–113).
46. Cf. *Critique of Pure Reason* [A 570 = B 598]: Ideals provide us "with an indispensable standard of reason."
47. Cf. Kant, *Groundlaying* [4: 389].
48. Cf. Wood, *Kant's Ethical Thought*, 189–190.
49. Here Kant goes beyond the corresponding discussion in *The Critique of Pure Reason*, where moral concepts are still assumed to be partly empirical (i.e., as concerns motivation) [A 568 = B 597].
50. Compare, however, *Remarks* [20: 34–35]; As we saw in Chapter 2, Kant had once worried that Rousseau's "paradoxes" might be nothing more than expressions of inflated *amour propre*.
51. On other uses of "paradox" in the first *Critique*, see also B 230 (an apparent paradox concerning permanence and change); B 392 (an apparent paradox concerning reason's ability to "hit upon" the concept of an absolute); and A 374n (a paradox concerning the fact that nothing is space except what is represented in it).
52. On the natural effects of venturing stakes, see *Anthropology* [7: 275]: Boys play, men gamble, and citizens try their luck in public societies. In all these cases, "a wiser nature goads them, without their knowing it, to a venturing of stakes [*Wagestücken*] and thereby tests their forces in conflict with that of others, but really [*eigentlich*] to protect the life force generally from lassitude and maintain it in alertness." The opponents "believe that they play with one another; but in

fact nature plays with both." However counter-purposive gambling may seem, it serves nature's purpose by maintaining the life force and hence inspires a peculiarly intense sort of passion out of affinity with what Kant calls "ideas of illusion" [7: 275]. On the healthful effects of gambling, see also *The Conflict of the Faculties*, Part Three. In his early years, Kant partly supported himself by gambling at billiards.

53. According to Grimm and Grimm, *Hirngespinst* is largely a coinage of the early eighteenth century. Its literal meaning suggests "something spun by the brain." "Gespinst" is obviously derived from the verb *spinnen* = to spin (as in spinning wool); *spinnen* also means, colloquially, to talk nonsense, or to be daft (as in one who spins around). Kant's employment of the term in a number of key passages suggests that a more complicated set of verbal associations may also be intended (in keeping with his earlier reference to "taking clouds for Juno" [4: 426]). Grimm and Gimm give as alternative meanings for "Gespinst" both "betrothed" (from the Latin "sponsa") and "mother's milk" (also spelled "gespünst"). To take a mere figment of the brain for a real object of rational devotion is equivalent to feeding on one's own ideas.

54. Cf. *Critique of Pure Reason* [A 568–571 = B 596–599].

55. Compare the initial subheading of Section Three, which can be translated as "the Concept of Freedom is the Key to the Declaration/Explanation [*Erklärung*] of the Autonomy of the Will" [4: 446].

56. Timmermann makes a similar point at 129 and xxiii: "Kant's problem is the worry of someone who is well disposed toward morality but can't understand it."

57. The accusation thus resembles the charge Kant earlier leveled against ontological perfectionism, to which he attributed an "ineluctable propensity to turn in a circle" associated with "presupposing the [very] morality it would explain [*erklären*]" [4: 443].

58. "Thus does it come about," as Kant here puts it: "That man arrogates to himself a will that lets nothing be put to its account that belongs merely to his desires and inclinations, and indeed thinks of actions through itself as possible, or even necessary, that can happen only by setting aside all desires and sensible stimuli. . . . so that whereforesoever [*wozu*] inclinations and impulses (thus the entire nature of the world of sense) stimulate him, they cannot damage him, and this in such a manner [*so gar*] that he does not answer for the former and does not ascribe it to his authentic self, i.e., his will, although he does ascribe it to the indulgence [*Nachsicht*] his will might bear [*tragen*] toward them to the disadvantage of its own rational laws" [4: 457–458].

What the "authentic self" is ultimately responsible for, on this account, is indulgence, on its part, as a moral judge—a capacity that the *Groundlaying* as a whole aims to rectify.

59. As we saw in subsections 7–8 earlier, presuming freedom on a practical but not-yet moral basis allows one to conceive of man as essence and man as

appearance as synthetically united in a single subject—a unity that the fatalist is unable even to think.
60. In other words, it is a world without intelligent constituents or "members."
61. *Critique of Pure Reason* [A vii].
62. See especially Dieter Henrich, "Die Deduction des Sittengesetzes: über die Gründe der Dunkelheit des letzen Abschnittes von Kant's Grundlegung der Metaphysik der Sitten," in *Denken im Schatten des Nihilismus* ed. Alexander Schwan(Darmstadt: Wissenschaftliche Buchgesellschaft 1975), 55–112; see also, for example, Henry E. Allison, "Justification and Freedom in the *Critique of Practical Reason*," in *Kant's Transcendental Deductions*, ed. Eckart Förster (Stanford: Stanford University Press, 1989), 115–116; and Karl Ameriks, *Interpreting Kant's* Critiques (Oxford: Oxford University Press, 2003), 256. Concerning the relation between the two works, Kant says the following: "[the *Critique of Practical Reason*] . . . presupposes the *Groundlaying* . . . , albeit only insofar as this constitutes preliminary acquaintance with the principle of duty and provides and justifies [*rechtfertigt*] a determinate formula of it" [5: 8]. I take "justification" here to include his own limited "deduction" of the categorical imperative in Section Three of the *Groundlaying of the Metaphysics of Morals* [4: 463]. Unlike Henrich, I do not read the passage as implying a wholesale rejection on Kant's part of the argument he had employed in Section Three.
63. See, for example, [5: 91; original emphasis]: "that pure reason is . . . practical for itself alone . . . : one [has] to be able to show this from the *most common practical use of reason*, by certifying [*beglaubigen*] the supreme practical principle as one that every natural human reason knows [*erkennt*] for the supreme law of its will. . . . One [has] first to establish [*bewahren*] and justify the purity of its origin even *in the judgment of this common reason* before science might take it in hand in order to make use of it as, so to speak, a fact [*Factum*] that precedes all subtle reasoning [*Vernünfteln*] as to its possibility and all the consequences that may be drawn from it." Paul Franks has made the striking suggestion that the famous example of the bordello and the gallows in the "Analytic" section of the *Critique of Practical Reason* is intended to bear witness to reason's factum by eliciting the reader's own moral feeling (Paul W. Franks, *All or Nothing: Systematicity, Transcendental Arguments, and Skepticism in German Idealism* [Cambridge, Mass.: Harvard University Press, 2005], 280–290). Without going this far, I share his view that Kant's readers must themselves bear practical witness to reason's factum.
64. Note the special plea, in the B edition Preface to the *Critique of Pure Reason*, for *scholarly* freedom [B xxxv].
65. For allusions to the controversy, see, for example, [B xxviii–xxxi, xxxlx–lxii], which speak to the opposing claims of Mendelssohn and Jacobi respectively. Contra Mendelssohn, knowledge of the existence of God and the immortality of the soul is strictly practical. Contra Jacobi, knowledge of the existence of things outside me is not a matter of faith but verified by "experience of my

existence in time"—experience that "immediately" includes knowledge of external objects. That Jacobi's early intellectual formation owed much to his own reading of Rousseau's *Emile* is an irony that is unlikely to have been lost on Kant.

66. For instructive treatments of this dispute, see Beiser, *The Fate of Reason*; John H. Zammito, *The Genesis of Kant's "Critique of Judgment"* (Chicago: University of Chicago Press, 1992); Franks, *All or Nothing*; and George di Giovanni, *Freedom and Religion in Kant and His Immediate Successors* (Cambridge: Cambridge University Press, 2005).

67. On this point see also Ameriks, *Kant and the Fate of Autonomy*, 318.

68. The phrase appears in the following passage from Juvenal's sixth *Satire* (On Women): "Crucify that slave!" says the wife. "But what crime worthy of death has he committed?" asks the husband; "where are the witnesses? who informed against him? Give him a hearing at least; no delay can be too long when a man's life is at stake!" "What, you numskull? you call a slave a man, do you? He has done no wrong, you say? Be it so; *this is my will and my command: let my will be the voucher for the deed*" [Loeb edition]. As Walter Pluhar notes, the full Latin text here reads: "*Hoc volo, sic iubeo, sit pro ratione voluntas*," which literally translates as "that [is what] I will, this I command, instead of reasoning let there be the will." See Immanuel Kant, *Critique of Practical Reason*, trans. Werner S. Pluhar (Indianapolis: Hackett Publishers, 2002), 46n.

69. According to Kant, our idea of the moral law contains the thought that transgression of the law *deserves punishment* [5: 37; original emphasis].

70. Cf. *Groundlaying of the Metaphysics of Morals* [4: 425–426] and note 37 above.

71. It is to this "timelessness" (and a related lack of *pre*determination) to which Kant here appeals both to refute "Spinozism" and to reconcile divine omnipotence with human responsibility for moral evil [5: 101–102]. (If, as he here says, "the ideality of time and space is not accepted, nothing remains but Spinozism, in which space and time are essential determinations of the original being itself, while things dependent on it (hence, including ourselves) are not substances but merely accidents adhering in it.") What Kant specifically fails to show here is how we can be held accountable for actions that while not "predetermined" appear ultimately to depend on something over which we have no control. Even he admits that the argument here is "less than lucid" [5: 103]. *On the Failure of All Philosophic Attempts at Theodicy* [1791] will later criticize all philosophic efforts to reconcile divine omnipotence, etc. with human culpability for evil.

72. In the B edition of the *Critique of Pure Reason*, Kant uses the same term to describe our general awareness of the existence of outer things [B 276n]. On the bearing of the Paralogisms section of the B edition on the "Faktum" argument, see also Ameriks, *Interpreting Kant's* Critiques, 259.

73. This new emphasis on lack of temporal duration as the distinguishing mark of noumenal activity is anticipated in the B edition of the first *Critique*. (See the

Preface to the Second Edition [B xxxix–xli n], "Refutation of Idealism" [B 274–279], and "Refutation of Mendelssohn's proof of the persistence of the soul" [B 414–415].) In the Preface to the Second Edition and in the "Refutation of Idealism," Kant argues against the false assumption that temporal as distinguished from spatial awareness gives privileged access to the noumenal. In the refutation of Mendelssohn, Kant shows that given temporal duration, the sheer inwardness of consciousness furnishes no guarantee against possible cessation through "vanishing"—i.e., by a gradual remission of all one's forces.

74. The factum (=done deed of reason) is not to be understood as carried out by the phenomenal self, but by the "moral person" to whose presence conscience testifies. (Allison, by way of contrast, associates the fact of reason with a performative act of *submission;* as discussed in Barbara Herman, "Justification and Objectivity," *Kant's Transcendental Deductions,* ed. Eckhart Förster, 132.) As Werner Hammacher observes, "Conscience [for Kant] is . . . never the consciousness of the self but consciousness of the difference that splits the self of the "moral person" off from the empirical self. This consciousness of the difference—Kant speaks of a "doubled self" and the "two-fold personality, which is how the man who accuses and judges himself in conscience must conceive of himself—can . . . only appear as the consciousness that someone else has of me, and this "someone else" cannot be reduced to another egological consciousness." (Hammacher, *Premises,* trans. Peter Fenves [Cambridge, Mass.: Harvard University Press, 1996], 105.)

75. "Pure reason always has its dialectic," because "it seeks for the given conditioned an absolute totality of conditions." Although pure practical reason, once it is shown to exist, "needs no critique" [cf. 5: 3, 15], the same cannot be said for pure practical reason when put to (this-worldly) "use" [5: 107].

76. Kant calls this ancient dialectic "the most beneficial error in which human reason could ever have fallen," leading, as it does, to what "we did not seek and yet need" [5: 107–108]. The implicit foil here would seem to be the "syncretistic spirit" of Kant's own age. Ancient philosophic disputes arose from conflicts internal to reason itself, not (as in the modern case) from external efforts to lower reason's own intrinsic standard.

77. Cf. *Groundlaying of the Metaphysics of Morals* [4: 439]: "And just here lies the paradox: that the mere dignity of humanity as rational nature, without any other end or advantage thereby to be achieved . . . should serve as an unremitting prescript for the will."

78. Hence, too, the importance of the new definition of "life," consistent with autonomy, that Kant inserts in an early note [5: 510n]. Life is no longer defined in terms of action "determined" by the representation of an end (as in his earlier anthropology lectures).

79. For a helpful discussion of the notion of "engraftment," see G. Felicitas Munzel, *Kant's Conception of Moral Character: The "Critical" Link between*

Morality, Anthropology, and Reflective Judgment (Chicago: University of Chicago Press, 1999), 335–345. The ultimate source of the analogy would seem to be Paul's Letter to the Romans.

80. Cf. the similar use of juxtaposition at [5: 78–79] (to evoke the feeling of respect).

81. "Methodos" is Greek for "way" or "path"; on method in this sense, see *Critique of Pure Reason* [B xv–xx; A 855 = B 883].

Introduction to Part II: Late Kant, 1789–1798

1. John H. Zammito, *The Genesis of Kant's Critique of Judgment* (Chicago: University of Chicago Press, 1992), 264.

2. On this matter, see also Yirmiahu Yovel, *Kant and the Philosophy of History* (Princeton: Princeton University Press, 1980), 167n. Strangely, few scholars have explored that possibility in any detail. Zammito, for his part, attributes the "ethical turn" mainly to Kant's "bitter rivalry with Herder" over the related Pantheism controversy [Zammito, *Genesis*, 9–10].

3. Windisch-Graetz, *Discours dans lequel on examine les deux questions suivantes, un monarque a-t-il le droit de changer de son chef une constitution évidemment vicieuse? Est-il prudent à lui, est-il de son intérêt de l'entreprendre? Suivi de réflexions pratiques*, and *Objections aus sociétés secrètes*. London, 1788–1789. A German edition of the latter appeared under the title *Über die geheimen Gesellschaften* (Leipzig, Frankfurt am Main [i.e., Nürnberg]: Felsecker, 1788).

4. That work, which had in fact already appeared, combines elements of the psychologies of Locke and Condillac with a strong insistence on the possibility of free will. It also contains the proposal of a "prize question" (concerning the possibility of an all-embracing *lex permissiva*) to which Kant later approvingly refers in *Toward Perpetual Peace* [8: 348n]. (See Windisch-Graetz, *Solution provisoire d'un problème, ou histoire métaphysique de l'organization animale; pour servir d'introduction a un essai sur la possibilité d'une méthode générale de démontrer & de découvrir la vérité dans toutes les Sciences. Précédée d'un avertissement relatif à un autre problème qu'il a proposé en 1784* [Nuremberg: chez George Frédéric Six, Imprimeur du Sénat, Avril 1789].) On Kant's peculiar approach to the question of "permissive law," see Reinhard Brandt, "Das Erlaubnisgesetz, oder: Vernunft und Geschichte in Kants Rechtslehre," in *Rechtsphilosophie der Aufklärung*, ed. Reinhard Brandt (Berlin: Walter de Gruyter, 1982), 233–275; and Katrin Flikschuh, *Kant and Modern Political Philosophy* (Cambridge: Cambridge University Press, 2000), 134–143.

5. In early August the National Assembly, whose validity the king had recognized, abolished feudalism, and on August 26 the Assembly published the "Declaration of the Rights of Man and of the Citizen," loosely modeled on the U.S. Declaration of Independence. In *The Metaphysics of Morals* Kant treats Louis XVI's laying of the burden of the nation's war debt on "the people" (just

prior to this time) as the beginning of a "natural" process that constitutes a voluntary (if unwitting) transfer of sovereignty [6: 341–342]—Kant's own working out, it seems, of the systematic principles concerning the "voluntary changes in the constitution of monarchies" to which he here alludes. See also Kant's favorable reference to the Count in *Toward Perpetual Peace* [8: 348n]. As the Cambridge Edition editors note, Kant sent the Count a copy of the *Critique of Judgment* (Immanuel Kant, *Practical Philosophy*, tr. and ed. Mary J. Gregor [Cambridge: Cambridge University Press, 1996], 320).

6. Cf. Kant, *Theory and Practice* [8: 303–305], and Windisch-Graetz, *Discours*; like the Count, Kant finds lack of such freedom to be the occasioning cause of "all secret societies." On freedom to speak publicly and secret societies, see also *Toward Perpetual Peace* [8: 368–369]. Windisch-Graetz's essay on constitutional reform anticipates other themes later stressed by Kant, including the relative unimportance of governmental "forms" and the crucial distinction between despotic government and one that is legally restrained by a representative assembly [52; cf. Kant, *Theory and Practice* {8: 290–304}; *Toward Perpetual Peace* {8: 352}]. Additionally, the Count's distinction between perfect duties of right and imperfect duties of benevolence not only jibes with that of Kant on a number of important points [20–21, 23, 75; cf. Kant, *The Metaphysics of Morals*, Introduction]; it also leads the author to conclude both that duties (as Kant will himself later put it) cannot contradict one another [76] and that the legitimating end of the use of the state's coercive force is not the people's happiness but protection of their rights [76; cf. Kant, *Toward Perpetual Peace* {8: 385}]. The essay also insists upon the right to publish [6: 110–111] on grounds similar to those that Kant himself will later invoke in Part Two of *Theory and Practice*. And it stresses the peculiar "horror" involved in executing a monarch, an act called far graver than the involuntary amputation of a limb [18n; cf. *The Metaphysics of Morals* {6: 322n}]. Finally, there is something recognizably "Kantian" in Windisch-Graetz's entire formulation of the current problem as he sees it—namely, how, without breach of standing law, to replace the prevailing despotisms of Europe with the "new social order" that reason demands and that "*tout le monde* has made its cause." (For other similarities, see also *Discours*, 99, 110–111). In *Toward Perpetual Peace*, Kant notes as "regrettably" abandoned the "ingenious" but "still unsolved" competition question proposed by the "wise and astute" Count von Windisch-Graetz (concerning the possibility of unambiguously formulated contracts) [8: 348n]. To my knowledge, the connection between Windisch-Graetz's work and Kant's later political writings has not previously been explored.

7. Windisch-Graetz also speaks in his essay on constitutional reform of a current European "crisis." An Austrian nobleman, his own views seem to have been partly shaped by the unfortunate example of Joseph II of Austria, whose unrestrained zeal for "rational" reform (in roughly the sense intended by the

French *philosophes*)—i.e., reform carried out without respect for constitutional restraints or other historically recognized limits—provoked the famous Revolt of Brabant in 1789. Windisch-Graetz's later writings mainly address themselves to the situation of Belgium, where he ultimately settled.

8. That impression is further strengthened by Kant's own late reference to these events (or, to speak more precisely, their disinterested *reception* by observers like himself) as the sign, "nevermore to be forgotten," that mankind is "constantly progressing toward the better." See *The Conflict of the Faculties* [7: 85–86], discussed in Chapter 8 below.

9. See Chapter 2 above.

10. Although scholars (e.g., the editors of the two most recent English translations) have disagreed over whether Kant is here referring to America or France the preponderance of evidence points to France. In addition to Kant's heightened interest in France at this time, there is the matter of the term *organization*. That term, still unusual in Germany or England (especially when used in a political sense), is employed matter-of-factly in a famous contemporary French essay by the Abbé Sieyès (*What is the Third Estate?*) with which Kant is almost certain to have been familiar. Sieyes's usage of the term could well be taken to apply to the transformation of the Estates-General into a governing National Assembly. ("It is not sufficient," Sieyès says, "to show that privileged persons, far from being useful to the nation, cannot but enfeeble and injure it; it is necessary to prove further that the noble order does not enter at all into the social organization; that it may indeed be a burden upon the nation, but that it cannot of itself constitute a nation.") That Kant was rumored to be planning to visit France on Sieyès's invitation makes Kant's acquaintance with his work all the more likely. On the existence of such rumors, see J. P. Gooch, *Germany and the French Revolution* (London: Longmans, Green and Company, 1920), cited in Lewis White Beck, "Kant and the Right of Revolution," *Journal of the History of Ideas* (1971), 411–422. As Paul Guyer points out in his edition of the *Critique of the Power of Judgment*, Kant later uses the term *organization* with France clearly in mind. See *Theory and Practice* (1792) [8: 302n], and Kant, *Critique of the Power of Judgment*, ed. Paul Guyer (Cambridge: Cambridge University Press, 2000), 389n; compare Kant, *The Critique of Judgment*, ed. and trans. Werner S. Pluhar (Indianapolis: Hackett, 1987). Commenting on events in France at this later point in time, Kant writes: "Even if the actual [*wirkliche*] contract of the people with the ruler has been destroyed: still, this cannot be immediately counteracted [*entgegenwirken*] as a *commonwealth* but only as a mob. For the people have torn up their previously standing constitution; but their organization into a new commonwealth has not yet happened."

11. On "humanity" as a kind of "humanizatio" or humanization, see also marginal handwritten notes to the *Anthropology* in Kant, *Anthropology, History and Education*, ed. Günter Zöller and Robert B. Louden (Cambridge: Cambridge University Press, 2007), 377n (7: 276).

12. Cf. Rousseau, *Emile*, tr. Allan Bloom (New York: Basic Books, 1979), 468–469.
13. Compare the darker appraisal of Frederick's cosmopolitanism at the end of the *Anthropology* [7: 332n]. See also Georg Cavallar, "Kant's Judgment of Frederick's Enlightened Absolutism," *History of Political Theory* 14, no. 1 (1993): 103–132.
14. Kant is reported to have exclaimed, on hearing of the declaration of the Republic, "Now let your servant go in peace to his grave, for I have seen the glory of the world." (cited in Kuehn, 343–344) Unlike the later execution of Louis XVI, that declaration, by Kantian lights, was entirely legitimate, since the king, in Kant's view, had already implicitly ceded sovereignty when he transferred the debts incurred by the crown to the Estates-General (*The Metaphysics of Morals* [6: 341–342]).
15. Kant, *Observations* [2: 255]. For the larger context, see Chapter 2 above.
16. Compare Yovel, *Kant and the Philosophy of History*, 154–157. In dismissing the *Idea for a Universal History* as "a vestige of [Kant's] "dogmatic" thinking," Yovel misses its emphatically inconclusive and ironic character.
17. This partially explains Kant's relative silence on the question of immortality, to which the rational theology of the *Critique of Practical Reason* had, as we have seen, devoted much attention.
18. The righteous man ("Spinoza, for example") who "remains firmly persuaded that there is no God," confronts an abyss of purposelessness that not only "limits" his effort but also "damages his moral attitude" [5: 452–453]. Whatever hope a progressive history supports is obliterated, absent the right sort of moral faith, by the "one vast tomb" that "embraces all."
19. In a final, roughly contemporaneous statement on human race, Kant singles out lack of "perseverance" [*Emsigkeit*], rather than of conceptual intelligence or of temperamental balance (as in his earlier treatment of the moral implications of racial difference) as the primary source of the (likely) inferiority of the non-white races. Beyond the capacity to work, he says, there is "an immediate drive to activity"—a drive that is "interwoven with certain natural predispositions" that facilitate active moral endurance [8: 174n]. Though he admits that the empirical evidence remains inconclusive on this score, he makes no secret of his own suspicion (shared with Hume and others) that reports that non-Europeans lack the (natural and/or moral) quality of perseverance are essentially correct.
20. Cf. Yovel, *Kant and the Philosophy of History*, 273. Yovel finds in the duty to promote the highest good a "new concept of moral will" and a gap between Kant's earlier "personal morality" and later "vision of a moralized nature." Even for the later Kant, however, the idea of the highest good remains merely a regulative rather than constitutive principle—resisting the Hegelian/Marxian push that Yovel wants give it.
21. Cf. Windisch-Graetz, *Discours*, 99.

22. For other aspects of "lateness" in Kant, see Peter Fenves, *Late Kant* (New York: Routledge, 2003).
23. Kant's title calls to mind his earlier treatment of a "harmony of the faculties" in the *Critique of Judgment* [5: 190], with specific reference to aesthetic judgment.
24. In declining Stäudlin's offer to publish Kant's essay outside of Prussia, Kant wrote: "Even though this essay is really not theological but concerned with *public law* (the legal principles concerning religious and ecclesiastical matters), I have had to give some examples . . . [to] make clear why a sectarian religion . . . is unfit to become an established religion and why certain articles of faith cannot be enforced by public authorities . . . but only be the credo of a sect" [11: 533].
25. See [A 5 = B 8–9].
26. See *Critique of Practical Reason* [5: 86, 162].
27. *Critique of Judgment* [5: 401–404]; see also Richard L. Velkley, "Kant on the Primacy and the Limits of Logic," *Graduate Faculty Philosophy Journal* 11, no. 2 (1986): 147–162.
28. See *Critique of Practical Reason* [5: 72–75].
29. *Critique of Practical Reason* [5: 86]; cf. *Remarks* [20: 116].
30. Nevertheless, the core of that psychology—a reductively "genetic" explanation of human behavior in terms of efficient causes—continues to inform those branches of the field that are today deemed most "scientific" or that otherwise enjoy the highest reputation (e.g., "cognitive psychology" and "artificial intelligence").
31. Hannah Arendt is perhaps the most famous expositor and promoter of the political use of "reflective judgment" in a (roughly) Kantian sense (with practical consequences, in her own case, that readers may judge for themselves). Arendt draws a sharper line between "action" and "judgment" than Kant, in my view, would allow. On the general problem of regulative and reflective judgment in Kant, with particular attention to whether and in what sense it is objectively "guided," see Richard N. Manning, "The Necessity of Receptivity," in *Aesthetics and Cognition in Kant's Critical Philosophy*, ed. Rebecca Kukla (Cambridge: Cambridge University Press, 2006), 61–84. For a recent exploration of the political use of regulative and reflective judgment, see Elizabeth Ellis, *Kant's Politics* (New Haven: Yale University Press, 2005). Other problems with Kant's approach are helpfully discussed by Ronald Beiner in Hannah Arendt, *Lectures on Kant's Political Philosophy*, ed. and with interpretive essay by Ronald Beiner (Chicago: University of Chicago Press, 1982), 142–156.

5. Moral Hesitation in *Religion within the Boundaries of Bare Reason*

1. Henry E. Allison, *Idealism and Freedom* (Cambridge: Cambridge University Press, 1996).

2. G. Felicitas Munzel, *Kant's Conception of Moral Character* (Chicago: University of Chicago Press, 1999).
3. Allen W. Wood, *Kant's Ethical Thought* (Cambridge: Cambridge University Press, 1999).
4. Philip J. Rossi, S.J., "Public Argument and Social Responsibility: The Moral Dimensions of Citizenship in Kant's Ethical Commonwealth," in *Autonomy and Community*, ed. Jane Kneller and Sidney Axinn (Albany: State University of New York Press, 1998); and Rossi, "The Social Authority of Reason: The 'True Church' as the Locus for Moral Progress," in *Proceedings of the Eighth International Kant Congress*, vol. 2, ed. Hoke Robinson (Milwaukee: Marquette University Press, 1995).
5. Sharon Anderson-Gold, *Unnecessary Evil: History and Moral Progress in the Philosophy of Immanuel Kant* (Albany: State University of New York Press, 2001).
6. Mark Lilla, "Kant's Theological-Political Revolution," *Review of Metaphysics* 52 (December 1998).
7. Cf. *Toward Perpetual Peace* [8: 370].
8. For a somewhat different appreciation of Wöllner's role, see Ursula Goldenbaum, *Appell an das Publikum: Die öffentliche Debatte in der deutschen Aufklärung, 1687–1796*, 2 vols. (Berlin: Akademie Verlag, 2004). See also Ian Hunter, "Kant and the Prussian Religious Edict: Metaphysics within the Bounds of Political Reason Alone" (unpublished paper, 2003), and Michael Sauter, "Visions of the Enlightenment: The Edict on Religion of 1788 and Political Reaction in Eighteenth-century Prussia" (PhD diss., University of California at Los Angeles, 2002). Sauter argues for a more nuanced understanding of Wöllner's role and motives, which Sauter sees as more "enlightened" than the common wisdom has it. Wöllner's policies, which called for state oversight of public orthodoxy while allowing private freedom of belief, might have suited an enlightener like Hobbes but would have denied Kant's sincere students and followers any public religious role. Ian Hunter makes a strong case for Wöllner's sharing in the goals of an alternate German enlightenment that valued public peace above either moral sincerity or republican self-government. Hunter's claim notwithstanding (12), "political liberals" could support the Edicts only if they were willing to lie publicly, something that the policies of the previous government had not made necessary (at least as Kant interprets them in *What Is Enlightenment?*).
9. See the Editor's Introduction in Immanuel Kant, *Religion and Rational Theology*, ed. Allen Wood and George di Giovanni (Cambridge: Cambridge University Press, 1996), xiii.
10. Sincerity is already a potent vehicle for Hobbes and Locke, each of whom appeals to it (in different ways) as a means to the preservation of civil peace. The view that we should not be held to account for the doctrine in which we were raised (which, for Rousseau, vindicates decent women, who quite properly

assume the religion of their parents and then their husbands) is, for Kant, itself a snare that justifies moral "passivity" [6: 132n]. On Rousseau and sincerity, see also Arthur Melzer, "Rousseau and the Modern Cult of Sincerity," in *The Legacy of Rousseau*, ed. Clifford Orwin and Nathan Tarcov (Chicago: University of Chicago Press, 1997). For a brief and lucid account of the views of Rousseau's Savoyard Vicar, see also Mark Lilla, *The Stillborn God: Religion, Politics, and the Modern West* (New York: Random House, 2007), 118–132.

11. See *Critique of Pure Reason* [A 710 = B 738].
12. *The Metaphysics of Morals* [6: 223].
13. Cf. *Emile*, 267–269.
14. Cf. Kant's own declaration of "full conscientiousness" in his letter of response to the Royal edict of censorship; Kant published both the edict and his letter of response in the Preface to *The Conflict of the Faculties* [7: 10].
15. On Rousseau's "gloomy hypochondria" concerning the human species, see *Anthropology* [7: 326–332].
16. The history of the work's composition and publication bears noting. Professors in Prussia were entitled to have their books censored by a dean of their own faculty. For transient political reasons, Kant sent an early version of the work to the philosophy faculty at Jena, where it passed although (as Kuehn notes) part had already been banned by the Berlin censors (See Manfred Kuehn, *Kant: A Biography* [Cambridge: Cambridge University Press, 2001], 365). Minister von Zedlitz, Kant's friend, had once used Kant's own distinction between public and private speech to defend a Lutheran preacher who endorsed determinism in his role as public author. In 1791 the preacher was removed from office through the direct intervention of the king, who punished his defenders with a substantial loss of salary. It was under such conditions that Kant ventured to publish Part Two of his *Religion*, insisting throughout, and against the perplexed protests of his editor, to submit his manuscripts to the censors in Berlin—a route not strictly necessary as a matter of law. Following its rejection, Kant repaired once again to his legal right as a faculty member, relying on his colleagues in the faculty of theology to declare the work to be within the disciplinary boundaries of philosophy (and thus, one could say, putting the "conflict of the faculties" to his own goodly use). On the historical background, see Kuehn, *Kant*, 363–366; see also Allen Wood's comments in the Cambridge edition of Kant's *Religion and Rational Theology* (Cambridge: Cambridge University Press, 1996), 46–47, and Kant's letters to Beister of April and May 1794 [11: 496–47, 501]. Wood suggests that it was Kant's *The End of All Things* [1794], rather than *Religion within the Boundaries of Bare Reason*, that finally provoked the king's formal rebuke.
17. And Kant himself, as we have seen, had once allowed.
18. "Although on its own behalf morality needs no representation of an end . . . it may well be that it has a necessary reference to such an end . . . For without any relation to an end no determination of the will can take place in a human

being ... who must [at least] be able to represent and end as the consequence [*Folge*] of the determination of his will. Without this, a power of choice [*Willkür*], unable to add in thought [*hin zu denkt*] ... a determinate object to an action before it, is instructed, to be sure, as to how but not *whither* [*wohin*] it is to have an effect [*zu wirken habe*], [and thus] cannot satisfy/do enough [*nicht Gnüge thun kann*]" [6: 4].

19. As such, it differs from culture, which produces one readiness [*Fertigkeit*] without canceling [*aufzuheben*] another [A 709 = B 737]. The *Critique of Judgment* calls discipline a branch of culture, whose other branch is skill [5: 42]. In *The Metaphysics of Morals*, Kant defines "moral ascetics" as "that part of the doctrine of method [of a metaphysics of morals] in which is taught ... how to put into practice and cultivate the *capacity for virtue* [Tugendvermögen] as well as the will thereto" [6: 412].

20. "*Vernünftelei*" is elsewhere defined as "a use of reason that ignores its final end." "Vain *Vernünfteleien*," though not "untrue," constitute "an unprofitable expenditure of understanding." *Vernünftelei* in its proper form is called *Scharfsinnigkeit* or "acumen," and consists in the "talent of noticing even the slightest similarities and dissimilarities" [7: 200–201].

21. See Kant's anthropology lectures of 1788–1789: "Freedom is fundamentally a *negative* condition of the satisfaction of our desires and consists in the distancing of all opposition to determining oneself according to one's own inclination. It is the greatest formal inclination and is held by everyone to be the greatest good. It permits itself to be felt [*empfinden*] only through comparison with the condition of others or through diminishment [*Beraubung*] of the latter. Crude nations therefore have great contempt for *subalterns*. They cannot think as having any value [*Werth*] a human being who is *at the behest* [*befehligt*] of another" [25: 1520].

22. *Anthropology* [7: 68].

23. Competition [*Wetteifers*] is literally a kind of bet or wager, in which we risk failure in an attempt to prove ourselves. In the *Anthropology*, Kant highlights "competition" as the site of passion "of the most intense and enduring kind"—a passion attached to what Kant calls "the inclination to illusion." (On gambling and illusion, see also Chapter 4, note 52.)

24. Since man is in a morally dangerous state through his own fault, he is obliged to expend as much force as he can to work himself out of it. But how? "That is the question" [6: 93].

25. Kant goes on to cite Walpole (and, indirectly, Hobbes) to the effect that "every man has his price, for which he sells himself," If this is so—and here each may "add things up [*ausmachen*]" for himself—if no virtue is to be found that has the wealth/means [*Vermögen*] to cast down [*stürzen*] every vitiation/contamination [*Versuchung*] (*stürzen* also means "count the cash"), if the victory of the good or evil principle depends only on "which bids the most and pays off most quickly,"—then, "as the Apostle says," we are all under sin [6: 38–39].

Kant's refutation of original sin in the traditional sense rests on "finding" in man a moral capital sufficient to offset the values by which calculative reason necessarily reckons.

26. Compare Kant's insistence that we are "certainly and immediately conscious" of a capacity [*Vermögens*] of being able to overcome, by firm resolve [*Vorsatz*], every possible incentive to transgression, and that, nevertheless, we are all uncertain whether we might not, in a given situation, waver in our resolve [6: 49n–50n]. Certitude as to our capacity and incertitude as to our performance are intrinsic aspects of the human conscience.

27. Moral faith, on the other hand, is registered in one's willingness to stake everything upon it. Cf. *Critique of Pure Reason* [A 824 = B 852ff.].

28. I am indebted to Peter Fenves for calling my attention to the importance of this term in Kant's late writings.

29. This requirement will be the main theme of Kant's *The End of All Things*.

30. In this way, duty for its own sake begins to acquire, in the novice's heart, a "noticeable weight [*Gewicht*]" [6:48].

31. In Kant's spelling, *Achtung* and *Echtheit* appear related.

32. According to Grimm and Grimm, "wacker" derives from an old root (related to the English word "awake") meaning "to stand watch"; "wacker" conveys a sense, not just of general courage, but of aroused and militant alertness against an enemy.

33. *Religion*'s supplementary "side-works," or *parerga*, on the other hand, specifically address reason's consciousness of its own lack of means (i.e., its impotence or bankruptcy) to "do enough for," [*ein Genüge zu thun*] or satisfy, its moral needs and its consequent resort to extravagant [*überschwenglichen*] ideas that it cannot take up into its maxims of "thought and action," and hence can make no proper moral use of. And yet, since such ideas "make up for" that bankruptcy, however unknowably, reason "reckons them available to its good will." Reason thus supplements its lack, without self-swindling, by consciously drawing against the same *unerforschlich* ground in which its own inner disposition lies hidden. (For who is to say how, in this inscrutable region, good will might or might not be aided?) Such a mode of dealing with reason's "difficulties" with respect to that which in itself "stands fast" (namely, reason's ultimate moral sufficiency) can remain "sincere" only by expelling itself beyond the boundaries of reason's proper work, as a merely secondary occupation [*Nebengeschäfte*] or *parergon*. (Without that acknowledgment, such moral borrowing is just another way of slipping off the hook—another version of the human propensity to "subtle self-deception." See [6: 52].)

34. Judaism in its purity "entails absolutely no religious faith." Thus the sublimity of the Jewish law against idolatry (as famously celebrated in *The Critique of Judgment*) must be radically discounted: "we should not place too much weight on the fact that [the Jews] set up . . . a God that could not be represented by any visible image. For we find in most other peoples that their doctrine of faith

equally tended in that direction" [6: 127]. Kant also plays with the notion of a non-epigenetic (re)birth of the human species. (See [6: 79–82, 102] and Chapter 9 below.) Judaism is the womb from whose fetters humanity (or the true church) must completely free itself and/or to which it remains attached only by a common written word or Scripture—i.e., the "Leitband" of holy tradition [6: 121]. On the other hand, Scripture, which "hinders the church's unity and universality," is pure religion's "still indispensable *Hülle.*" And yet, a people with a sacred text "never assimilates" with a people [like the Roman Empire] that has "nothing of the kind" [6: 135n]. The most potent sensible exhibition of true religion is wordless or ineffable: The "letter . . . should finally fall away" [6: 197–198]. Judaism is the letter or shell from which humanity absolutely must free itself and yet which it still, it seems, cannot do without.

35. To be sure, the superiority of Christianity over all other known public religions is itself merely historical, and thus might itself be superseded. [6: 52].

36. For who can be certain, as Kant adds, that the moral truths taught by Jesus, which are fully available to human reason, were not also delivered as a timely revelation, aimed at hastening human improvement? See also *The Metaphysics of Morals* [6: 488]: Religion within the boundaries of bare reason is not derived from reason alone, but "is also based on the teachings of history and revelation" and "considers only the *harmony* [Übereinstimmung] of pure practical reason with these (shows that there is no conflict between them). [Hence in this case] . . . religion is not *pure*" but rather "*religion applied* to a handed down [*vorliegende*] history."

37. Accordingly, the figure of a "vicarious substitute" becomes a personification of the death of the old man "that each of us ought to endure," so that what, from the point of view of the "old man" would be punishment, becomes, from the new point of view, "self-discipline." Such a personification specifically addresses the assault on moral confidence [*Vertrauen*] that arises from our awareness of the impossibility, in temporal terms, of wiping out the debt incurred by our previous moral inadequacy [6: 75–76].

38. Cf. *Critique of Pure Reason* [A 568–569 = B 596–597]. Christianity, rightly understood, seems to accomplish what would be "preposterous" [*unthunlich*] in a novel: realization of "the ideal in an example, i.e., in appearance."

39. See also Kant's *Reflexionen zur Religionsphilosophie* [19: 652]. Among the few handwritten notations in Kant's personal Bible, the editors of the *Akademie* edition note the following: "old clothing" [*alt Kleid*] [cf. Matthew 9:16] is underlined in black, over which is written "Judenthum." (Luther's text reads: "Niemand flickt ein altes Kleid mit einem Lappen von neuem Tuch; denn der Lappen reißt doch wieder vom Kleid, und der Riß wird ärger." [No one puts a patch of new cloth on an old garment for the patch tears away from the garment and the tear is more vexing.].)

40. See [6: 121].

41. For an anticipation of that task, cf. [6: 41n]; see also Chapter 8 below.

42. [6: 121]; The phrase is an allusion, of course, to his ongoing conflict with Jacobi.
43. On "talents" as moral capital (or *Anlage*), see also *Critique of Practical Reason* [5: 160].
44. See Wood, *Kant's Ethical Thought*, 314; the dependence of moral self-transformation on a prior transformation of society at large is asserted even more emphatically by Sharon Anderson-Gold: "Kant implies that our hope to effect a revolution 'within' rests upon the transformation of the social conditions of our existence" [*Unnecessary Evil*, 46].
45. The true church is "an idea of reason, whose representation in an adequate intuition is impossible for us, but which has objective reality as a practical regulative principle in working toward this end of unity of the pure religion of reason." Human nature, on the other hand, furnishes little hope of bringing about such unity "in a visible church" [6: 123n]. Still, a personal duty to partake of rituals, church going, and so on, follows only if one finds it "morally enlivening" [6: 196] and only if the church in question "does not contain formalities that might lead to idolatry" [6: 199]—a proviso that excludes all churches other than the (invisibly) true one. Lilla's suggestion that Kant *requires* an established church (or that Christianity is the only possible moral-religious vehicle) is, however, overdrawn. (Compare Lilla, *The Stillborn God* [New York: Alfred A. Knopf, 2007], 153, 160–162.)
46. See, for example, [6: 43n–44n]. With the exception of the duty not to hold any merely historical faith for salvational, *Religion* does not add (to the duties sketched out in *The Metaphysics of Morals*) a single injunction on which individuals are necessarily obliged to act. Thus, it is left entirely to the individual to judge for himself how much of the historical faith, rightly interpreted, "he finds beneficial" to the vitality of his religious [i.e., moral] disposition [6: 182]. And any moral duty of churchgoing only applies if and when it does not involve formalities that *could* lead to idolatry [emphasis added]—a proviso that, given the human proclivities Kant has just laid out, furnishes what amounts to a general escape clause [6: 199]. Even the "duty" to find the right meaning in Scripture—a duty that seems to inform Kant's own effort—is conditional on the judgment that lack of moral confidence would otherwise give rise to belief in superstition, miracles, false expiation, and enthusiasm [*Schwärmerei*] to make up for what is missing [6: 83, 53]. From Kant's own point of view, publishing *Religion* is an exercise in what he elsewhere calls moral prudence in attending to the "call of nature." (See *Toward Perpetual Peace* [8: 373n]. I am indebted to Corey Dyck for calling my attention to this phrase.)
47. To be sure, Kant also speaks of historical Christianity as a "fact," without which the "special duty" of humanity to form a visible church (whose specific purpose is to counter historical Christianity's morally harmful effects) would remain inoperative [6: 158].

48. See here especially Kant's preference for the "pure doctrine of virtue," which is "already contained in the human soul in full, though undeveloped," along with what he calls a religious "doctrine of divine blessedness." The immediacy of moral resolve contrasts with the "Bedenklichkeit" he urges in *Religion* upon hypocritical authorities [6: 187].
49. Cf. [6: 35n]. The distinction between false religion and true turns on the "immediate pleasure" "human beings take in attestations of honor"—an immediate pleasure that leads them to believe that God, too, is vainglorious [6: 104]. Religious education is thus inseparable from an education in the true meaning of (human) honor, an argument he will develop further in *Toward Perpetual Peace* and in *The Conflict of the Faculties*, Part Two.
50. Cf. [6: 64n–65n]: "it is plainly a limitation of human reason, not any time separable from it, that we cannot think of any significant moral worth in the actions of a person without at the same time portraying this person or his expression in a human way.... for we always need a certain analogy with natural being in order to make supersensible characteristics comprehensible to us." To transform such a "schematism of analogy," to one of "object determination" has, however, "most injurious consequences." Compare, too, his elusive definition of the "true (visible) church" as "that which exhibits the kingdom of God on earth to the extent that it can be realized by human beings" [6: 101].
51. Compare the apostrophe at [6: 190n] to "Astraea [*Aufrichtigkeit*]" brought down to earth as *Wahrhaftigkeit* (not saying anything that isn't true) with *Theodicy* [8: 270] and the "veiled goddess" mentioned in *On a Recently Uplifted Noble Tone in Philosophy* [8: 405]. Honesty is reconcilable with humanity only as a resistance to lying (as distinguished from full candor or "openheartedness"). Kant's history of the church is meant to overcome doubts as to the existence of a capacity for truth telling (in this sense) without which "the human race would have to be in its own eyes the most contemptible." It thus overcomes misanthropy—provided, as Kant immediately adds, that one can count upon reversal of our "way of education," in which "one attributes one's own moral condemnation to an all-powerful God" [6: 190]. Overcoming one's own morally counter-purposive misanthropy and facilitation of Kant's critical pedagogy more generally, are thus interdependent.
52. See Jacob Grimm and Wilhelm Grimm, *Deutsches Wörterbuch* (Leipzig: Verlag von S. Hirzel, 1854), vol. 18, 3091: "stimmen" in this sense is synonymous with "bestimmen."
53. Cf. Kant's reply to Schiller at [6: 23n]: the "glorious picture of humanity, as portrayed in the figure of virtue, permits attendance of the graces," but only "at a respectful distance."
54. See [6: 170n]: the mutual influence of the sensuous and intellectual principles "must never be thought as *direct*." It is only in "deed" [*in der That*], i.e., "in the determination of our physical forces through free *Willkür* as relates to actions,"

that cause and effect are represented as "of like kind." It is thus, precisely, in the resolve to expend those forces that the effect of the intelligible upon the sensible, and vice versa, become homogenous, or are necessarily so represented.

55. *Critique of Judgment* [5: 267]: If the beautiful "prepares us" to love something without interest, as Kant says elsewhere, the sublime "prepares us to esteem it against our interest."
56. See, for example, Paul Stern, "The Problem of History and Temporality in Kantian Ethics," *Review of Metaphysics* 39 (March 1986): 505–545.
57. "The ethical communion of [true] believers" constitutes "the essence of the true church" [6: 133n].
58. Cf. [6: 121n]: thus man can at least be comparatively deserving, i.e., in relation to another.
59. Those who lack the opportunity to acquire a character (e.g., children who die in infancy) might (or can for moral purposes be presumed to) have personality (i.e., intelligible character), albeit of a sort that does not express itself in timely (worldly) terms. Why some (but not other) intelligible beings might be in a position to "acquire a character for themselves" seems to be, for Kant, an unfathomable mystery to us. A central purpose of his moral philosophy is to make of that unfathomability an aid rather than an obstacle to moral effort.
60. See *Anthropology* [7: 234–235].
61. Cf., in this regard, Kant's restriction of religious "history" to "that portion of the human race in which the *Anlage* to the unity of the universal church has been brought close to development. . . . We can, for this purpose [*Absicht*] deal only with the history of that church that from its beginning bore the germ [*Keim*] and principles of the objective unity of the true and *universal* religious faith to which it is gradually being brought nearer—and this shows, first of all, that the *Jewish* faith stands entirely in no essential connection [*Verbindung*] with that church faith, i.e., in no unity from concepts, through the latter immediately arose from it, which gave physical occasion [*Veranlassung*] for its grounding" [6: 125]. The problem of human development, out of and against nature, is reenacted in the relation between Christianity and Judaism. Judaism is, at best, the historical occasion for a human development in which it does not participate and, at worst, the historical expression of the propensity of *human* reason toward self-subversion.

6. Kant's "True Politics"

1. Brian Orend makes this point forcefully in *War and International Justice: A Kantian Perspective* (Waterloo, Ontario: Wilfred Laurier Press, 2000), 51–55. For an alternative viewpoint, see Georg Cavallar, *Kant and the Theory and Practice of International Right* (Cardiff: University of Wales Press, 1999), 113–131, and "Commentary on Susan Meld Shell's 'Kant on Just War and Unjust Enemies: Reflections on a Pleonasm,'" *Kantian Review* 11 (2006):

117–124. Cavallar ignores Kant's more pessimistic pronouncements and, in particular, his repeated insistence that cosmopolitan justice, strictly understood, is unachievable. (Cf., for example, Cavallar, "Commentary," 118, and Kant, *Toward Perpetual Peace* [8: 386] and *The Metaphysics of Morals* [6: 350, 355].)

2. Persuasive arguments can be made for either "perpetual" or "eternal" as the best translation of Kant's "ewig." For a helpful discussion of the alternatives, see Peter Fenves, "Under the Sign of Failure," *Idealistic Studies* 26, no. 2 (1996): 146n.

3. See also *Theory and Practice*, Part Three [1792], which anticipates elements of *Toward Perpetual Peace* and in which Kant's "philanthropic" purpose is especially clear.

4. Critics often dismiss these tensions as outright contradictions. When the essay is read with due attention to its peculiar political aims, a more consistent argument emerges than has generally been recognized.

5. *Critique of Pure Reason* [A 761–762 = B 789–690].

6. In a juridical context, "*Entwurf*" can mean "draft" or "bill," as in the drafting of a law or treaty. Grimm and Grimm's *Wörterbuch* defines "*Entwurf*" as a sketch or plan [*Anschlag*]; "*entwerfen*" can also have the meaning of "throw back" (as in the "throwing back" of an echo) and "abort" [*verwerfen*].

7. Kant's letter to Kiesewetter continues as follows: "With all the conflict among intellectuals it doesn't mean much if only they refrain from intrigues and make common cause with the politician's trade, and like Horace's 'atrum desinit in piscem' conceal their ugly fishtails with their courtly manners" [12: 45]. In taking Kant to mean here that philosophers should not engage in politics of any kind, Otfried Höffe misses an important layer of Kant's irony. That "the possession of authority [*Gewalt*]" always "corrupts the free judgment of reason" [8: 369] is no bar to political activity as such, which does not necessarily involve authority or the right of command. On this point see also *The Conflict of the Faculties* [7: 19] and Chapter 8 below. Nothing could be more "truly" political (or less capable of "command") than striving to elicit a revolution in a people's "way of thinking." (Cf. Höffe, *Kant's Cosmopolitan Theory of Law and Peace*, trans. Alexandra Newton [Cambridge: Cambridge University Press, 2006], 145.)

8. On the earlier history of the phrase, see Volker Gerhardt, *Immanuel Kants Entwurf "Zum Ewigen Frieden": eine Theorie der Politik* (Darmstadt: Wissenschaftliche Buchgesellschaft, 1995), 33–40.

9. Presumably, it is impossible because the game in question restricts players to fewer than ten tosses. An early draft, which mentions "ten means toward eternal peace," omits the sixth preliminary article (prohibiting means of war that preclude future trust). The "eleven pins" mentioned in *Toward Perpetual Peace* as published might refer to the nine articles plus the two appendices, or, alternatively, to the nine articles, the supplement, and the appendices. (The second supplement appears only with the second edition.) According to

Grimm and Grimm, the expression "throwing ten pins [*Kegeln*]" means something like "putting snow through a sieve"—i.e., doing (or attempting) the impossible. Grimm's long entry under "Kegel" also links it with the game of bones, associated mythologically with "wild, bloodthirsty men," or gods (like Wotan) who go bowling with bones left over from human sacrifices. Kant may have such associations in mind when, on the following page, he explicitly likens heads of state to cannibals. "Kegel" can also mean "illegitimate offspring" and "bullet" (in which case Kant's throws are less innocuous than the colloquial meaning of the phrase in question would suggest). The last meaning is evidently the one Nisbett had in mind in translating the phrase of Kant in question as "fire off his whole broadside." (Hans Reiss, *Kant: Political Writings*, 2nd enlarged ed. [Cambridge: Cambridge University Press, 1991], 93.)
10. *The Metaphysics of Morals* [6: 283].
11. *The Metaphysics of Morals* [6: 429–430]; and this despite the fact that in the state of nature lying does not constitute a violation of right (compare [6: 225–226]).
12. Man's potential political reduction to a mere "mechanism" is already a thematic worry in *What Is Enlightenment?* [8: 36–37, 42].
13. cf. Aristotle, *Politics*, 1278a 40–1279a 24.
14. Kant compares the relation between legislative and executive powers to that between a major and a minor premise in a logical syllogism [*Vernunftschluß*], a term that calls to mind the rationally guided *Friedensschluß* that Kant's sketch is itself meant to promote.
15. As Frederick the Great famously declared; cf. *What Is Enlightenment?* [8: 41].
16. Literally, "largeness"; as Kant notes, popular majesty [*Volksmagistät*] is an "absurd expression" [8: 354].
17. On the intrinsic stability of republics, compare [8: 366] and [8: 377]. Although Kant at first adopts the argument that republics are "most difficult to establish and preserve," he later seems to except a "genuinely republican" [*ächtrepublicanische*] "way of governing," a way requiring a moral-political mind [*Sinn*]—hence the ultimately crucial importance of morally good intentions, as well as prudence, at the top. Although (as Kant puts it in a famous phrase) the problem of organizing a state can be solved "for" [*für*] a nation of devils, it cannot, it seems, be solved "by" them alone (as several common translations suggest).
18. From a Latin term meaning "to elect or appoint a substitute or successor." According to Grimm and Grimm, the word "*surrogat*" was uncommon in Germany until the early nineteenth century. Although the German term generally denotes an inferior substitute, this is not true of earlier usage elsewhere. According to the *Oxford English Dictionary*, for example, "surrogate" could also mean a (superior) replacement (as in Christianity as the "surrogate" Israel).
19. *Aeneid* I, 294ff. The highly ironic Virgilian context is a retroactive (and, as it happens, inaccurate) foretelling of the reign of Augustus Caesar when "wars

shall cease": Then "the gates of war, grim with iron and close-fitting bars, shall be closed," within which "impious furor, sitting on savage arms, his hands fast bound behind with a hundred brazen knots, shall roar in the ghastliness of bloodstained lips." "Impius" has the primary meaning in Latin of failing in regard to one's obligations. Cf. Kant's denigration elsewhere of the so-called Pax Romana [8: 359n] and later reference to *Aeneid* VI, 95–96 [8: 379], where, in the face of wars in which "rivers stream with blood," the Cumaean Sybil advises a boldness that can accomplish even what the Goddess Fortune disallows. On Kant's own boldness, see [8: 343]. Like the philosophic poet Virgil, Kant is forced to make rhetorical concessions to an autocratic government. See also note 46 below.

20. As long as there are separate nations (with their own ideas of international right, supported by differing historical faiths as described in *Religion*) there can be no perfectly just cosmopolitan condition.
21. See *Religion* [6: 27–29].
22. Compare his description, in *Idea for a Universal History from a Cosmopolitan Intention* [1784], of a cosmopolitan [*weltbürgerlicher*] condition as the "womb" in which the original "Anlagen" of the human race can develop [8: 28].
23. On the general inclination of human beings to lord it over others when they feel superior in might, see the discussion of *Religion* [6: 27] above, and *The Metaphysics of Morals* [6: 307]: "everyone can quite well perceive within himself the inclination of human beings generally to play the master over others (not to respect the rights of others when one feels superior in strength or cunning)." As Kant puts it in *Toward Perpetual Peace*, "possession of power [*Gewalt*] unavoidably corrupts the free judgment of reason" [8: 369].
24. Cf. the work's title: *Toward* [zur] *Perpetual Peace*.
25. Compare *Toward Perpetual Peace* [8: 366–368, 385–386] and *Religion* [6: 34n]: "If one looks at the history of these [so-called states] as phenomena of for the most part hidden predispositions of humanity, one becomes aware of a certain machine-like course [*machinenmäßigen Gang*] of nature toward ends that are not the ends of nations but of nature itself. Each state strives, as long as there is another next to it that it may hope to compel, to enlarge itself by subduing its neighbor, and thus strives toward universal monarchy—a constitution that must extinguish all freedom and with it (as its consequence) virtue, taste and science. Yet after this monster (in which laws gradually lose their force) has swallowed up all its neighbors, it ultimately dissolves of itself, and divides through rebellion and factionalism into many smaller states, that, instead of striving after a union of states (a republic of free united peoples [*freier verbündeter Völker*]), begin the same game again in turn, so that war (this spur [*Geisel*] of the human race) will never cease. War, though not so incurably evil as the grave of universal despotism (or even a union of peoples [*Völkerbund*] pitted against despotism coming into disuse in any state), nonetheless, as an

ancient said, produces more evil men than it takes away." Kant makes use of the same saying in *Toward Perpetual Peace* in reference to the relative nobility of savage, as distinguished from civilized, warfare [8: 365].

26. "The problem of establishing a state . . . is soluble for a nation of devils if only they have understanding" [8: 366].

27. Hence *Toward Perpetual Peace*'s extended comparison, to their disadvantage, of the rulers of Europe to savage cannibals: "thus a Bulgarian prince gave the following reply to the Greek emperor's goodhearted offer to settle their conflict through a duel: a smith who has tongs will not pull the glowing tongs out of the coals with his bare hands" [8: 355n]. For further discussion of the comparison, see Susan Meld Shell, "Cannibals All: The Grave Wit of Kant's *Toward Perpetual Peace*," in *Violence, Identity, and Self-Determination*, ed. Hent de Vries and Samuel Weber (Stanford: Stanford University Press, 1997). The comparison invokes themes first raised in Montaigne's famous essay "On Cannibals."

28. Cf. Georg Cavallar, "Kantian Perspectives on Democratic Peace: Alternatives to Doyle," *Review of International Studies* 27 (2001): 229–248. Cavallar's unusual claim that the federation urged in *Toward Perpetual Peace* includes *all* states, whatever their character, overlooks the bearing of Kant's "first definitive article," which declares that all states admitted to the treaty-like arrangement there envisioned are to be republics (or, at the very least, if one allows that requirement a looser meaning, must make becoming one their public goal). (Cf. Cavallar, "Kantian Perspectives on Democratic Peace," 243–247.) His claim would have more merit, as we will see below, if limited to *The Metaphysics of Morals*.

29. "The craving of every state (or of its head) is to attain a lasting condition of peace by ruling the whole world if possible" [8: 367].

30. A republican constitution checks the warlike tendencies of rulers, whose sheer possession of power (otherwise) "inevitably corrupts" the "free judgment of reason" [8: 350, 369]. There is, of course, a large and growing literature, stimulated by the work of Michael Doyle, on the alleged reluctance of liberal democracies (republics in a roughly Kantian sense) to go to war against one another.

31. Originally from the Latin "*hospes*," which means both "guest" and "host." According to the nineteenth-century edition of the Grimms' *Wörterbuch* (which does not include a listing for "*Hospitalität*"), "hospital" had already acquired in German (as in English) a specific association with places set aside for aiding the sick.

32. Were this not the case, Kant's prediction would be like that of the "political moralists," who throw "man into one class with other living machines" [8: 878]. As the Second Supplement (added in 1796) makes emphatically clear, nature's "guarantee" leaves well-intentioned human guidance—if only on the part of philosophers who are permitted to speak openly—a crucial role to play [8:

368–369]. Indeed, a human being need only be conscious that he isn't a free being to become "in his own judgment the most miserable [*elendesten*] of earthly beings" [8: 878]. On this issue, see also Paul Guyer, *Kant on Freedom, Law, and Happiness* (Cambridge: Cambridge University Press, 2000), 408–434; and Reinhard Brandt, "Zum 'Streit der Facultäten'," in *Neue Autographen und Dokumenten zu Kants Leben, Schriften und Vorlesungen, Kant Forschungen*, vol. 1, ed. Reinhard Brandt and Werner Stark (Hamburg: Felix Meiner, 1987), 31–78. As Guyer notes, to put forward the contrary view (that natural mechanism suffices to ensure progress) would likely be to bring about a relaxation of moral effort [429].

33. Cf. Kant's claim (*à propos* of the slogan "let justice prevail though [all the rogues in] the world perish") that "the world will by no means perish by there coming to be fewer evil human beings" [8: 379].
34. This dilemma had served as a basis for Christian Garve's claim that rulers are not bound by ordinary moral constraints.
35. The only determinate guidance they offer is negative—e.g., that positive public law must not be violated.
36. Thus the "regrettable" early abandonment of the competition problem proposed by Count Windisch-Graetz—a problem whose solution would make permissive law determinate [8: 348n].
37. For a helpful discussion of some difficulties with Kant's transcendental principles, see Elizabeth Ellis, *Kant's Politics: Provisional Theory for an Uncertain World* (New Haven: Yale University Press, 2005), 104–109.
38. *Toward Perpetual Peace* [8: 381]; for Kant's contrasting later view, see *The Metaphysics of Morals* [6: 312].
39. Kant assumes that such incompatibility could only arise from the "universal resistance" prompted by divulgence of an unjust maxim. He does not here consider the fact that incompatibility with publicity might arise from other factors, such as the need for secrecy in time of war.
40. According to Grimm and Grimm, "Grenzgott" translates the Latin "terminus." Termini were Roman gods who presided over boundaries and other territorial markers and to whom it was said even Jupiter must give way. ("Terminus" is also the Latin word for "end, boundary, or limit.") Kant's appeal at [8: 370] to the "terminus" of morality (which is said here to provide sufficient "brightness" [as in "*hell*"]) flags the problem at issue ("the disagreement [*Mißhelligkeit*] of morality and politics") rather than resolving it.
41. In the final analysis, the "objective reality," or "executability" of "pure principles of right" is described as an "assumption" we must make to avoid "conclusions of despair" [8: 380].
42. See *Religion* [6: 41].
43. To treat that delay as holding "merely for the time being" in the sense of representing only a short-term concession, as Cavallar does, is seriously to misunderstand Kant's essay. (Cf. Cavallar, "Commentary," 118.)

44. For a helpful account of other aspects of such trust-building, see Sharon Anderson-Gold, *Unnecessary Evil: History and Moral Progress in the Philosophy of Immanuel Kant* (Albany: State University of New York Press, 2001), 85–100.
45. See [8: 347]; Kant warns specifically against deferring implementation to a "non-existent date (*ad calendas graecas*, as Augustus used to promise)." The term "calendas" is from a Latin word meaning "accounts." The first day of the month was so designated because it was the day on which Roman tax payments typically were due. (The Greek cities famously lacked any uniform calendar, each state abiding by its own rules. In Athens, the first day of the lunar month was called by a term meaning "new moon"; but Athens also had other, non-lunar ways of mapping the year, each with its own differing purpose.) The phrase "according to the Greek calendar" thus suggests a day of reckoning that never arrives. Kant's comment here can be usefully compared with his later reference to Virgil's ironic praise of the Augustan peace from a seat of exile [8: 357; cf. *Aeneid* I 294–296]. (I am grateful to Judith Swanson for drawing my attention to the general importance of Virgil for an understanding of *Toward Perpetual Peace*.)
46. Cf. Antonio Franceschet, "Sovereignty and Freedom: Immanuel Kant's Liberal Internationalist 'Legacy'," *Review of International Studies* 27 (2001): 209–228.
47. As distinguished, presumably, from a politics that is "fork-tongued" (a term that calls to mind the "serpentine twistings" [*Schlangenwendungen*] of the political moralist [8: 375]). The moral politician must be *both* serpentine and innocent [8: 370].
48. That article six was not included in an earlier draft [23: 155] suggests that even in *Toward Perpetual Peace* its specific role may have remained somewhat tentative in Kant's mind.
49. On Kant's applied ethics and its relation to politics, see Robert B. Louden, *Kant's Impure Ethics: From Rational Beings to Human Beings* (New York: Oxford University Press, 2000), and Scott M. Roulier, *Kantian Virtue at the Intersection of Politics and Nature*, vol. 7 of North American Kant Society Studies (Rochester, N.Y.: University of Rochester Press, 2004).
50. Antonio Franceschet gets this half right in insisting on the *a priori* rather than experiential basis of the duty to leave the state of nature. But the reason he gives—the malevolent tendency of men to exempt themselves from laws they would apply to others—ignores Kant's stipulation that the duty in question applies regardless of how "justice-loving" and "benevolent" we may be. See Franceschet, "Sovereignty and Freedom," 219. Campare, on this point, Bernd Ludwig, "Whence Public Right," in *Kant's Metaphysics of Morals: Interpretative Essays*, ed. Mark Timmons (Oxford: Oxford University Press, 2002), 180-183.
51. On Kant's general relation to Hobbes and the tradition stemming from him, see Howard Williams, *Kant's Critique of Hobbes* (Cardiff: University of Wales Press, 2003).
52. While these factors make Kant attractive to many left-leaning liberals, his detachment of the obligation to respect the rights of others from any

necessary link with the desire for happiness also makes him a potent ally of the libertarian right. The poor are bound to respect the property rights of the rich—even in the face of the "greatest inequality in quantity and degree of possession" [8: 291]—and not even in part (as with Locke) because they, too, benefit. From a strict Kantian viewpoint, the complaint of the poor that they do not materially benefit from the unequal distribution of property falls on deaf ears (though there are other Kantian arguments for a redistribution of wealth favoring the poor). In short, Kant's argument as to the obligation to enter civil society, like his treatment of rights more generally, has had a complicated political and philosophic legacy about which one should not be in a rush to draw definitive conclusions.

53. On this point see Wolfgang Kersting, "Politics, Freedom, and Order: Kant's Political Philosophy" in *The Cambridge Companion to Kant*, ed. Paul Guyer (Cambridge: Cambridge University Press, 1992), 351–355. See also in this regard what Kant calls the only "innate right" of a human being, namely, "independence from being constrained by another's choice" consistent with independence of everyone else "according to a universal law" [6: 237]. See also note 63 below.

54. Rights "provisionally" acquired in the state of nature are discussed in the section of *The Metaphysics of Morals* entitled "On Private Right." For helpful treatments, see Richard Brandt, "Das Problem der Erlaubnisgesetze im Spätwerk Kants," in *Zum ewigen Frieden*, ed. Otfried Höffe (Berlin: Akademie Verlag, 1995), 69–86; Katrin Flikschuh, *Kant and Modern Political Philosophy* (Cambridge: Cambridge University Press, 2000), 117–134; and Ellis, *Kant's Politics*, 120–126.

55. That is, the primary (juridical) duty to be "an honorable human being (*honeste vive*)," which consists in "asserting one's value as a human being in relation to others" [6: 236]. For an insightful treatment of the juridical (as distinguished from merely ethical) status of this duty, see Höffe, *Kant's Cosmopolitan Theory*, 122–123, 125–126.

56. On the "sublime" character of the republican constitution, see [6: 320–622]; see also *Toward Perpetual Peace* [8: 366, 350n], and Susan Meld Shell, "Organizing the State: Transformations of the Body Politic in Rousseau, Kant, and Fichte," *International Yearbook of German Idealism*, vol. 2 (Berlin and New York: Walter de Gruyter, 2004), 49–75.

57. In other words, it is not human malevolence that makes removal from the state of nature juridically necessary, as the paragraph goes on to make clear. (Compare, in this regard, *Toward Perpetual Peace* [8: 381].) Terry Pinkard's puzzlement on this point would thus seem to be misplaced. See Pinkard, "Kant, Citizenship and Freedom [#41–52]," in *Metaphysische Andfangsgründe der Rechtslehre*, ed. Otfried Höffe (Berlin: Akademie Verlag, 1999), 156–157.

58. An alternative translation would be "something based on a deed."

59. Cf. Kant's comments in *Toward Perpetual Peace* on putative "possession in good faith." Such possession in the state of nature is prohibited only "after it is recognized as such" [8: 348n].
60. See *Toward Perpetual Peace* [8: 381].
61. And this despite the comparative juridical advantage of those with a "provisional" right (e.g., who refrain from taking the property of others without their consent) [6: 256–257]. Presumably, the right to be one's own master here trumps any such "provisional" claim.
62. Cf. Hobbes, *Leviathan*, Chapter 13; Locke, *Second Treatise of Government*, Chapter 2; and Rousseau, *Discourse on the Origin of Inequality*, trans. Donald Cress (Indianapolis: Hackett, 1987), 58.
63. Unlike "private right," there is nothing "provisional" about this right.
64. Compare Kant's stipulation, at the beginning of *Toward Perpetual Peace*, that his opponents (the political moralist) be "consistent [*consequent*]" [8: 343].
65. Why this might be so Kant does not here make fully clear; in the *Anthropology*, however, he calls the "inclination to freedom" (or, alternatively, the "passion to freedom") the "most vehement [*heftigste*] of all in the natural human being who *cannot* avoid [a situation of] reciprocal claims toward others." He "whose happiness depends upon another's choice," however "benevolent," "rightfully feels himself to be unhappy" [7: 268].
66. [6: 230]; see also section #42 (on the "transition" from what is "mine or yours in a state of nature to what is mine or yours in a rightful state in general"): "From private right in the state of nature there now proceeds the postulate of public right: you should—in relations of an unavoidable living side by side—pass over with the others to a rightful condition, i.e., one of distributive justice.—The ground of this allows itself to be developed analytically from the concept of right in outer relations in opposition to violence [*Gewalt*] (*violentia*). No one is bound to refrain from encroaching on the possession of another if the other gives him no symmetrical assurance that he will observe the same restraint toward him. He therefore need not wait until he learns from sad experience of the latter's opposing frame of mind [*Gesinnung*]" [6: 305–308]. Given the unavoidability of mutual contact, one is both *authorized*, in a state of nature, to force others to enter into a civil condition *and obliged* to do so, given the impossibility of otherwise carrying out one's juridical duty to oneself. (This consideration meets the objection raised by Robert Pippin in "Dividing and Deriving in Kant's *Rechtslehre*," in *Metaphysische Anfangsgründe der Rechtslehre* (note 57), 63–85.)
67. It is not only a question of making right "determinate" (the issue Ludwig stresses), but also of constituting an agency juridically competent to *punish*. (Compare [6: 331] and [6:346].) On the relation of "provisional" right to "permissive law," see also Brandt, "Das Problem."
68. Cf. Kant's later treatment of the British constitution as a nominal example of republican separation of powers that is actually a disguised despotism [7: 90n].

On related aspects of the Kantian *Rechtstaat,* see Patrick Riley, *Kant's Political Philosophy* (Totawa, N.J.: Roman and Littlefield, 1983), 103–113.
69. On this point, see also Roulier, *Kantian Virtue,* 46–50.
70. "The **Platonic Republic** has become proverbial as a striking example of visionary [*erträumter*] perfection, which has a seat only in the brain of an idle thinker; and [Plato has been ridiculed] . . . for maintaining that a prince can govern [*regieren*] well only insofar as he participates in the ideas. We would do better, however, to follow up this thought, and (where the great man leaves us without help) to place it, through new exertions, in the light. . . . *A constitution of the greatest human freedom according to laws, which makes it so that the freedom of each can stand together with that of all the rest* (not of the greatest happiness, for this will follow of itself), is yet at least a necessary idea, which one must lay as foundational [*zum Grunde legen*] not only in the first plan/projection [*Entwurfe*] of a state constitution, but also in all laws. . . . Indeed, nothing can be more harmful or less worthy of a philosopher than the vulgar [*pöbelhafte*] appeal to supposedly adverse experience. . . . For what the highest grade may be at which humanity must remain, and hence how large may be the gap necessarily remaining over between the idea and its execution [*Ausführung*]—that no one can and should determine, because the issue on which it hinges is freedom, which can overcome every specified [*angegebene*] limit" [*Critique of Pure Reason,* A 317 = B 373–374]. On the comparison with Plato, see also Höffe, *Kant's Cosmopolitan Theory,* 144–149; and Volker Gerhardt, "Der Thronverzicht der Philosophie. Über das moderne Verhältnis von Philosophie und Politik bei Kant," in *Zum Ewigen Frieden* (note 54), 171–193.
71. Cf. *Critique of Pure Reason* [A 569 = B 597–598]. On reason's practical authorization to regard ideas as immanent and constitutive insofar as they "are grounds of the possibility of *making real* the necessary object," see *Critique of Practical Reason* [5: 135]; cf. *The Metaphysics of Morals* [6: 221].
72. Cf. Kant's claim at [8: 354] that states "can and ought to ask [*fordern*]" others to enter with them into a constitution similar to a civic constitution. In light of Kant's repeated insistence elsewhere on the free or voluntary character of the federation in question, "ask" seems a more accurate rendition of "fordern" than "demand" or "require" (as it is sometimes translated).
73. Hans Reiss misleadingly translates this as "their *present* conception of international right" [emphasis added], as if the idea of justice among *states* didn't need to be somehow overcome if perpetual peace is to be fully realized. From a Hegelian point of view, a state of nations would be the *Aufhebung* of the idea of international right—an arrival that, for Kant, cannot be conceived in ordinary temporal terms, as is conveyed by the phrase "the idea of a [not rightful] condition."
74. Cf. *Religion* [6: 33–34]. As Paul Guyer observes, the goals of *Toward Perpetual Peace* cannot be fully achieved without a radical moral transformation. (Guyer, *Kant on Freedom, Law, and Happiness,* 408–433.)

75. On the conceptual "impossibility" of international right, see also Leslie Mulholland, "Kant on War and International Justice," *Kant-Studien* (1987): 32.
76. Thus "no one can be *declared* an unjust enemy" and a punitive war isn't even "thinkable" [8: 346–347; emphasis added]. This stipulation against punitive war places Kant firmly outside the just war tradition as formulated by Augustine and Aquinas, for whom "punitive" (and hence retributive) intent is not only permitted but itself a *sine qua non*. (See *Summa Theologica* 2: 2, question 40.) Even Grotius, who is in other respects a less than faithful follower of scholastic teaching, considers punitive war legitimate. (See *On the Law of War and Peace*, Book 2, Chapter 1.) It might be more accurate, then, to call Kant a "modern" (or post-Hobbesian) just war theorist. That earlier punitive element is rarely stressed in contemporary descriptions of "traditional" just war theory. Matthias Lutz-Bachman, for example, in an otherwise careful analysis of *Toward Perpetual Peace* in its historical context, treats Kant's rejection of punitive war as altogether in line with "classical international law," rather than as the significant departure (and remarkable concession to Hobbes) that it actually is. (Lutz-Bachman, "Kant's Idea of Peace and a World-Republic," in *Toward Perpetual Peace: Essays on Kant's Cosmopolitan Ideal* [Cambridge: MIT Press, 1997], 63.) For Kant, the stipulation against punitive war is not primarily addressed, as with Pufendorf, against belligerent action undertaken by third parties (on the grounds that third parties may rightly deem themselves at risk in doing so), but at belligerent action undertaken with retributive intention. Right in war against an "unjust enemy," for Kant, is "unlimited in quantity and degree," precisely because its rightful purpose is *not* "punishment" (where retributive proportionality comes into play) but rightful self-preservation, the limits of which each state may determine for itself, subject to the qualifications noted. These qualifications have nothing directly to do with "proportionality" in either a retributive or a prudential sense, but hinge, instead, on the possibility of future mutual trust. Kant's understanding of international law is fundamentally at odds with the sort of coercive "international tribunal" with which his name today is frequently associated.
77. Cf. *The Metaphysics of Morals* [6: 331–337].
78. On further difficulties in conceiving a Kantian "right in war," see Orend, *War and International Justice*, 56–57.
79. Cf. Kant's reference to healthy competition in the First Supplement of *Toward Perpetual Peace* [8: 357–358]. Competition [*Wetteifers*] is literally a kind of bet or wager, in which we risk failure in an attempt to prove ourselves. In the *Anthropology*, Kant highlights "competition" as the site of passion "of the most intense and enduring kind"—a passion attached to what Kant calls "the inclination to illusion." This inclination has the natural purpose of "stimulating the vital force" to "make us more active" and "prevent our losing the feeling of life completely in mere enjoyment." This tendency to take objects of imagination for real ends is a ploy on nature's part to arouse the lazy to healthy

exertion [7: 274–275]. The ensuing sense of bodily well-being, as Kant notes, makes illusional passions (such as that for gambling, an activity that he himself is reputed to have enjoyed as a younger man) especially intractable. On the politics of wagering, see Chapter 4 above.

80. Perplexingly, Cavallar claims to be unable "to see where Kant makes this distinction." See his "Commentary," 119.

81. For related reasons, the "federation" of which Kant speaks in *The Metaphysics of Morals* is not limited to "republics" and their ilk, but a federation of states is also no longer the sole context in which "international right" can seriously be spoken of (as Kant had held in *Toward Perpetual Peace*).

82. The very existence of such a federation should encourage political reforms even among non-members by removing one excuse for despotism—namely its more effective conduct of war (see [8: 373]).

83. In his earlier *Lectures on Ethics*, Kant observes that in a mutually acknowledged "state of nature," knowingly telling a falsehood (or "lying") under duress is not true deception [27: 448–449]. The highwayman who demands to know the location of one's purse can't reasonably expect an honest answer. As for the dishonorable activities that make one unfit to be a citizen: Kant allows, both in *The Metaphysics of Morals* and within the narrower constraints sketched by the articles of *Toward Perpetual Peace*, for the employment of spies *other than* one's own fellow citizens—a fact rarely noted. This moral limit on the use of one's own citizens (and the likelihood that an immoral politician or despotic ruler will ignore it) may help explain Kant's conviction that in a war between republic and a despotism, the latter, all things being equal, has the advantage—i.e., that despotic governments are more effective in the conduct of war [see 7: 86n]. Although even the despotic ruler loses in the long run from the corruption of his people's way of thinking [*Denkungsart*] [8: 346], he may not have the long run in mind.

7. Kant as Educator

1. Lewis White Beck, *Essays on Kant and Hume* (New Haven: Yale University Press, 1978), 210.
2. Kant's most famous statement to this effect is in the *Critique of Practical Reason* [5: 55–56].
3. For a discussion of this problem, see *The Conflict of the Faculties*, Part Two [7: 81–84].
4. See, for example, Rousseau, *Emile*, trans. Allan Bloom (New York: Basic Books, 1979), 49–50.
5. "idiotes"
6. Compare *Critique of Pure Reason* [A 821 = B 849–850]. Kant there defines belief or faith [*Glaube*] as a subjectively sufficient "holding to be true" [*Fürwahrhalten*] that is the same time taken as objectively insufficient, i.e., not

necessarily held for true by every rational being, and hence not "commanded" by reason as such [A 821–822 = B 849–850]. All transcendental use of reason, to the extent that it holds something to be true, does so "as a matter of faith" and from the standpoint of practice, be it that of skill or of morality. The term "faith" specifically refers here "to the guidance [*Leitung*] that the idea gives me and the subjective influence [*Einfluß*] on the advancement of the actions of my reason [*meiner Vernunfthandlungen*], which holds me fast [*festhält*] to them even though I am not in a position to give an account/justification [*Rechenschaft*] of it from a speculative standpoint" [A 827 = B 855]. There is, Kant admits, a kind of faith—e.g., in the existence of God, insofar as we are led to it by our investigation of nature—which is not, strictly speaking, practical. There is in such belief, however, "something unstable" [*etwas Wankendes*], given the susceptibility of such belief to "speculative difficulties" which "put one off," at least for a time. With moral faith (e.g., in God's existence), on the other hand, the end, to which faith is known to be a necessary means, is itself fixed and absolutely necessary; here one is sure "that nothing could make this belief unstable, because thereby my ethical grounding principles would also be overturned, principles that I cannot renounce [*entsagen*] without being worthy of abhorrence in my own eyes" [A 828 = B 856]. According to *The Critique of Practical Reason*, the "end" in question is realization of the highest good. Faith arises from reason's inability otherwise to satisfy its need to make the object of the law "intelligible" to itself [5: 126].

7. The explicit task of Kant's *Religion within the Boundaries of Bare Reason* was to "mark" the relation between religion and the good and evil dispositions [*Anlagen*] of human nature and, in so doing, "define" [*bestimmen*] the concept of religion. Kant was there so bold as to suggest his essay as matter for a "final course" for students of the theological faculty, which possessed, as Kant acknowledged, the right to censor philosophic examinations of religion. Kant's attempt at a direct intrusion into the faculty of theology came to immediate grief, to be replaced, in *The Conflict of the Faculties*, by an external appeal hardly more likely to appease (cf. his stated intention "to control [the faculty of theology] in order to be useful to it"). The larger question concerning the role of representation (or "marking") as an analog of that marking (by circumcision) which accompanied God's original promise to Abraham, will be taken up below. (See also Genesis 17:11; Romans 2:25–29.)

8. The word used for "well-being" is in each case *Heil*, the same term Kant will later use to mean "salvation."

9. Cf. *On a Recently Uplifted Noble Tone in Philosophy* [8: 405].

10. Education *(Bildung)*, on this account, is not imitative [*nachbildende*] "self-formation," but the rationally generated (rather than abortive) image of philosophy itself.

11. Cf. Kant's earlier definition of philosophy as the *Urbild* for the estimation of all attempts to philosophize.

12. Cf. Rousseau, *Discourse on the Origin of Inequality*, trans. Donald Cress (Indianapolis: Hackett, 1987); and *Critique of Pure Reason* [A 743 = B 771]: "Even poisons have their use: they serve to counteract other poisons generated in our bodily humors, and must have a place in every complete pharmacopoeia."
13. That is, the moral law and, thanks to Kant's own teaching, the limits of theoretical reason.
14. See also [A 407 = B 434]: "[Reason's natural antithetic] certainly guards reason . . . from the slumber of an imaginary conviction [*Überzeugung*], but at the same time tempts [*Versuchung*] it either to abandon itself to skeptical hopelessness [*Hoffnungslosigkeit*], or to assume a dogmatic obstinacy, setting its head stiffly on certain assertions without allowing the grounds of the opposing party a hearing and to be done justice. Both are the death of a healthy [*gesund*] philosophy, though the former might also be called the *euthanasia* of pure reason." Kant's notion of "critique" links judgment, in a juridical sense, with the related medical notion of a "crisis" as the moment of truth in which the body either prevails over or succumbs to its own unbalanced humors. Hence the aptness of "counter poison" as an ingredient in Kant's own critical arsenal. On the "self-preservation" of reason, see also *Critique of Judgment* [5: 261]. In contrast with the more optimistic account of human development proposed by Herder, mental and physical puberty, for Kant, are fraught with danger in which the self-preservation of pure reason is itself at stake. For a different but related treatment of "engrafting" as a potentially life-threatening procedure, see Kant's discussion of vaccination in *The Metaphysics of Morals* [6: 424].
15. Compare Kant's later reference to "united penitential voices," in which, presumably, the individual (with his own particular moral history) is no longer heard as such.
16. See *Critique of Pure Reason* [A 466–468 = B 494–496].
17. See *Critique of Pure Reason* [A 743 = B 771].
18. Kant's example of such an objection, against which "weapons of war" are permitted, is the apparent proof by experience that the exaltation/elevation [*Erhebung*] or derangement [*Zerrüttung*] of our spiritual forces are merely different modifications of our organs. The "force" of that proof can be weakened by the hypothesis that the body is nothing more than a "fundamental appearance." Though it exceeds the conditions of real knowledge, this speculative hypothesis is "polemically" permitted as a weapon against the moral "hopelessness" that such a view of the relation between body and soul would otherwise effect. Without such an excuse, that hypothesis, on Kant's own account, would be "visionary" if not deranged [A 769–772 = B 797–810]. Kant's strategy here is anticipated in *Dreams of a Spirit-Seer*, which juxtaposes to materialism a "kabbalistic" hypothesis that would be similarly "deranged" if it were not intended for a solely moral purpose.

19. In a similar vein, Kant elsewhere voices the suspicion that certain non-white races may well lack the vital stamina required to fully cultivate the rational *Anlage* that all humans share. (See *On the Use of Teleological Principles in Philosophy* [8: 174n.].)
20. Cf. *Idea for a Universal History* [8: 23].
21. Kant here quotes Cicero [*Ad familiam* 12: 4], the original of which reads: *Nunc me reliquiae vestrae exercent* ("Now your vestral remains weary me."). Kant changes the singular to plural and omits "vestrae" (clothing). It seems plausible that he does so because on his account, Judaism is nothing but the garment. Kant also plays here on the Protestant aversion for "relics" in a Catholic sense. It is hard to say what pertaining to the Jews is a "saved remnant" in the proper Lutheran sense and what is merely a relic to be discarded at the earliest possible moment. Kant's dismissal here of the Mosaic Decalogue sharply contrasts with his earlier praise, in the *Critique of Judgment*, of the "sublime" Jewish law against graven images [5: 274]. For more on this and related issues, see Chapter 9 below.
22. Viewing Christ as the human incarnation of God, who by his existence redeems us (without any effort on our part), resembles, on Kant's account, the ravings of one "Postellus," who thought that he had found the special redeemer of women in one young and pious maiden of Venice. If the idea of humanity is taken to be a "real human being," we are confronted with the difficulty that human beings come in two sexes, whose "weaknesses and transgressions" are "specifically different" from each other [7: 39n].
23. Such doctrines, in other words, must not be finessed [literally, "gone over with dry feet {*mit Trockenem Fuß übergangen werden*}"], and yet should be gone over/surpassed [*überzugehen*] [as one may urge] without delay [7: 42]. "Dry feet" may be an allusion to the biblical crossing of the Jordan "dry footed."
24. See *Critique of Pure Reason* [A 467 = B 495]: In addition to the "practical interest" that every well-disposed human being takes in the dogmatic determination of the cosmological ideas, an interest that is in some sense justified, Kant lists a "speculative interest" on reason's part in gaining "unconditioned footing and support" in an unconditioned being; and, not least, a "popular advantage," deriving from the "comfort" it affords the common understanding, which is disinclined to undertake that "restless ascent from the conditioned to the condition," an ascent in which "there can be no satisfaction." Given that reason's speculative interest in empiricism far outweighs its speculative interest in dogmatism, the endemic appeal of the latter finds its principle non-moral source in intellectual inertia (or lack of "perplexity") on the part of ordinary understanding. Kant carefully avoids identifying this "popular advantage" with a true "interest" of reason.
25. That is, "das Äußerliche" (or, alternatively, "that outside the essence" [*das Außerwsentliche*])
26. See *The Conflict of the Faculties* [7: 50n].

27. Otherwise, the existence in a state of many sects is good, according to Kant, only as a "sign that government allows the people freedom of belief," i.e., that the people are not, in matters of faith, externally coerced.
28. On this point see Mark Lilla, "Kant's Theological-Political Revolution," *Review of Metaphysics* 52 (December 1998).
29. Kant counted a number of Jews among his closest students and admirers, including Lazarus Ben David, David Friedländer, and Marcus Herz, who served as Kant's second during his Inaugural Dissertation Defense. Kant once told Herz that of all Kant's students, he was the one "who penetrated [Kant's thought] [most] deeply" [10: 266-267].
30. On the political and theological effect in Germany of this transformation of liberal thought, see Lilla, "Kant's Theological-Political Revolution."
31. *Anthropology* [7: 327-328].
32. See Introduction to Philip Jacob Spener, *Pia Desideria*, ed. and trans. Theodore G. Tappert (Philadelphia: Fortress Press, 1964).
33. Cf. *The Conflict of the Faculties* [7: 89].
34. Defense of an *a priori* concept of the supersensible (as specifically distinguished from the supernatural) was, as we have seen, a guiding aim of Kant's *Critique of Judgment*.
35. See Kant's claim that a whole people educated [*erzogen*] in one of these sects would reflect it in their "national physiognomy." "Repeated impressions, especially contrary to nature, upon the mind [*Gemüth*], externalize themselves in gesture and tone of speech, and expressions [*Mien*] finally become permanent facial features." As he notes, such "*sanctified*" faces would "distinguish such a people from other civilized [*gesitteten*] and developed peoples," in a way not to its advantage, for "this is a brand/sketch [*Zeichnung*] of piety in caricature" [7: 58n]. Kant here suggests a mechanism by which sectarian differences (at least among the "civilized") influence the formation of national character. On the connection between national and sectarian difference, see also *Toward Perpetual Peace* [8: 367]; and Kant's "Postscript" to Christian Gottlieb Mielcke's Lithuanian-German dictionary [8: 443-445].
36. Although Kant's parents were "Pietists," his praise of their serenity also links them with the Moravian Brotherhood as here described. On the generally "cheerful" and moderate character of Pietism in Königsberg, see Michel Desplant, *Kant on History and Religion* (Montreal: McGill Queens University Press, 1973), 101-102.
37. See *The Conflict of the Faculties* [7: 51].
38. Compare *Critique of Pure Reason* [A 473 = B 501], which also ascribes this tendency of ordinary human understanding to a certain vanity, inasmuch as both the more and the less intelligent are equally at a loss, once the limits of human reason are exceeded. For an earlier version of Kant's antagonism toward intellectual lassitude, see his early *Universal Natural History and Theory of the Heavens*, Part Three [1: 349ff.] and Chapter 1 above.

39. Compare *Groundlaying of the Metaphysics of Morals* [4: 450].
40. As indicated by the many "eyes" or viewpoints contained in the above passage; cf. Martin Luther, *Freedom*, Works, vol. 31, 357.
41. Compare *Critique of Judgment* [5: 272]; and *Critique of Practical Reason* [5: 161]. See also *Anthropology* on the related notion of "astonishment" [*Verwunderung*] (or perplexity [*Verlegenheit*] before the unexpected), an "affect," according to Kant, that is excited wholly by reason [7: 261]. It is precisely this perplexity that ordinary understanding (which "does not know what it means to conceive") is inclined to miss, but into which human reason is yet fated to fall (as Kant puts it in the opening lines of the *Critique of Pure Reason* [A vii]).
42. Here, beyond "conceivability," popular and scholarly intelligence are, at least potentially, on equal footing.
43. Cf. "Auslegung," meaning "interpretation."
44. A fuller account of how this good disposition cohabits with an evil one was taken up more fully in Kant's *Religion within the Limits of Reason Alone*, whose explicit aim was to make "notable" [*bemerklich*] the relation of religion to a human nature loaded with both good and evil *Anlagen*, through the representation [*Vorstellung*] of good and evil principles as "two self-subsistent, inflowingly-effectual [*einfließender wirkenden*] causes influencing men" [6: 11]. On the "idea" in us that gives us "force," but of which we are not ourselves the author, see [6: 61–62].
45. See *The Conflict of the Faculties* [7: 64].
46. The Jews, during their "ethical" or "civilized" period, would seem to have avoided this fate owing, in part, to the natural interpretive gifts of their nation and, in part, to the "theocratic" organization of their constitution.
47. The enlightened practice of attacking Christianity by attributing what one finds disagreeable in it to Judaism—a technique widely employed by figures ranging from Voltaire to Karl Marx—was originally perfected by Spinoza. (See Leo Strauss, "Preface," *Spinoza's Critique of Religion* [New York: Schocken, 1965], 16–17.)
48. See *The Conflict of the Faculties* [7: 66n].
49. As Kant makes clear [7: 62n–63n], this tendency is responsible for the "Pietist" interest in historical "signs"—a problem to which Part Two of *The Conflict of the Faculties* specifically addresses itself.
50. See also Kant's *Reflexionen zur Religionsphilosophie* [19: 652]. Among the few handwritten comments in Kant's personal Bible, the editors of the *Akademie* edition note the following: "old clothing" [*alt Kleid*] (at Matthew 9:16) is underlined in black, over which is written "Judenthum" [19: 652]. (Luther's text reads: "*Niemand flickt ein altes Kleid mit einem Lappen von neuem Tuch; denn der Lappen reißt doch wieder vom Kleid, und der Riß wird ärger.*" [No one puts a patch of new cloth on an old garment for the patch tears away from the garment and leaves a more vexing tear].)

51. See *Critique of Judgment* [5: 274]: "Perhaps there is no more sublime place in the law book of the Jews that the commandment: Thou shalt make no image [*Bildniß*], or any likeness either of what is in the heavens or on the earth nor under the earth, etc." This commandment alone can explain "the enthusiasm that the Jewish people during their ethical [*gesitteten*] epoch felt for their religion [*Religion*], when it compared itself to other people."

52. That is, "Bevestigung"; a similar formulation already appears in Kant's letters to Johann Caspar Lavater dated April 28 and following, 1775 [10: 175–179].

53. By the same token, lying (the "one rotten stain [*Fleck*] of our species") is morally intolerable because, over time, it puts "moral judgment out of tune" by damaging one's ability to credit one's own inner voice, rendering "imputability entirely uncertain." (See *Religion* [6: 38–39].)

54. Kant's example of such contrariety is the "myth" of the sacrifice of Isaac (the only appearance of the word "myth" in the work). Kant goes out of his way here to emphasize (in a manner that calls to mind both the traditional blood libel and traditional portrayals of the Christian Passion) both the brutality of Abraham's act, which Kant refers to as "the butchering [*Abschlachtung*] and burning [*Verbrennung*] of his only son," and the pathetic innocence of Isaac (who unknowingly carried the burden of his own wood); Abraham, Kant adds, "should have answered this supposedly divine voice [*Stimme*], even if it should ring down [*herabschallte*] from (visible heaven)": "that I should not kill my good son is entirely certain; but that thou who appearest to me to be God, of that I am not certain and also can never become certain." The story of the sacrifice of Isaac is the lightning rod of Kierkegaard's later criticism, in the name of "authentic" Christianity, of a moral "legalism" he associates (following Kant and Hegel) with philosophy as such.

55. Cf. *The Conflict of the Faculties* [7: 17].

56. Cf. the "verdringen" or pressing down by the Judaic remnant of all true religion [7: 52–53].

57. That is, "Leitband," a verbal compromise, it seems, between two other terms that Kant makes frequent use of: "Leitfaden" for the guiding thread that reason spontaneously projects, and "Gängelband" for the leading strings that hobble the unenlightened. For Kant's most famous treatment of the latter, see *What Is Enlightenment?*. (The related "Bandes" means "volume or book.")

58. Biblical faith [*biblische Glaube*] (as distinguished from Bible faith [*Bibelglaube*] of the kind Kant favors) is a "messianic historical faith, that has at its basis a book of God's covenant with Abraham, and consists in a Mosaic-messianic and an Evangelical-messianic church faith, and gives such a complete account of the origin and fate of God's people . . . [from the beginning to the Apocalypse] . . . that one might expect a divine author—but for the presence of questionable [*bedenkliche*] Kabalistic numbers. . . . which must somewhat weaken one's faith in its authenticity" [7: 62]. On the moral meaning for Kant of "Gospel" (literally, "good news" [*frühe Botschaft*]), the following late note [1799] may be

relevant: "it is impossible that a man without religion be joyful [*frühe*] in life." *Reflections on Philosophy of Religion* [19: 649].
59. See Genesis 17:11.
60. See Kant's letter to Lavater, April 28, 1775 [10: 176; compare 179]. The distinction between religion's dispensable "scaffolding" [*Gerüste*] and the indispensable "garment" [*Bevestigung*] is arguably one that Kant never made entirely clear. See also in this regard the morally ambiguous "parerga" in *Religion*, which touch upon without being part of religion within the boundaries of mere reason. "Parerga" (or "Nebenwerken": literally, "works beside the main work") were classically associated with the secondary labors of Hercules. Kant also uses the term to refer to the "drapery" covering statuary figures.
61. This theme is taken up at length in Part Two of *The Conflict of the Faculties*, which explicitly confronts the despair-inducing view of history that Kant here, as elsewhere, associates with Moses Mendelssohn.
62. Kant's own political reliance on the university faculties of states other than Prussia suggests the emerging outlines of an institutionalized, politically autonomous German cultural life. On Kant's early interest in a German national culture, see Chapter 1 above.

8. Archimedes Revisited

1. See also *Lectures on Anthropology* [25: 1202–1203]; the purpose of history "from a cosmopolitan standpoint," according to lectures dated immediately prior to the appearance of Kant's essay, is to motivate princes to pursue cosmopolitan ends by appealing to their "desire for honor."
2. See his immediate reference to a certain French prince, who defined "right" as the "the prerogative of the stronger over the weaker, that the latter should obey him" [8: 355].
3. See, e.g., *Toward Perpetual Peace* [8: 369].
4. For example, progress might be halted by a catastrophic change in geological conditions [7: 89]. As Kant there makes clear, the crucial issue is not whether the goal in question can be fully achieved (a question that he elsewhere clearly answers in the negative) but rather what the attitude of (current) rulers and their advisors toward the possibility of progress reveals about mankind's moral aptitude.
5. See *Idea for a Universal History* [8: 18].
6. As Kant's note makes clear, the usual sense of "wahrsagen" is pejorative (something like "fortune telling"): "From Pythia [the Delphic priestess of Apollo] to the gypsy girl, of one who meddles [*pfuschert*] in foretelling the future [*Wahrsagen*] (doing it without either knowledge or honesty [*Ehrlichkeit*]) it is said: he **engages in soothsaying** [er wahrsagert]" [7: 79n; 141n].

According to Deuteronomy [18:10–22], genuine prophets are known by the truth of their predictions; false prophets (i.e., those who engage in soothsaying ["Wahrsagerei" in Luther's translation]) should be put to death.

7. The theme of mutual "wearing out" [*sich aufreiben*] also figures in Kant's private speculations as to the likely future extinction [*Ausrottung*] of the non-European races. See *Reflexionen zur Anthropologie* [15: 878-879].
8. Cf. *The End of All Things* [1792].
9. His reason may be the following: Unlike terrorism and eudiamomism, Abderitism fails to tell a story [*Erzählung*]. Abderitism gets us immediately to the end, which is the very place we start. From a moral point of view, there is no real result because nothing is invested.
10. Kant elsewhere defines "deeds" as actions that are morally imputable. (See his "Introduction" to *The Metaphysics of Morals* [6: 223].)
11. The relevant passage reads as follows: "That the course of human things seems so senseless [*widersinnisch*] to us lies, perhaps, in the incorrect [*unrecht*] choice of standpoint from which we regard [*ansehen*] it. Viewed from the earth, the planets sometimes move backward, sometimes stand still, sometimes move forward. If the standpoint assumed is that of the sun, however, which only reason can do, the planets move, according to the Copernican hypothesis, with constant forward regularity. Some [people], however, who are otherwise not stupid, like to stubbornly persist in their way of interpreting appearances, and to maintain the standpoint they have once taken, even if they entangle themselves thereby in Tychonic cycles and epicycles to the point of absurdity.— But this is precisely the misfortune [*Unglück*]: we lack the ability [*Vermögen*] to place ourselves in this [true] standpoint when it is a matter of predicting free actions. For that would be the standpoint of providence, which lies outside of all human wisdom [*Weisheit*], and which stretches also to the free actions of man, which human beings can certainly *see* but not *foresee* with certainty (for the divine eye there is no difference here)" [7: 83–84]. (The "Tychonic" system [elaborated by Tycho Brahe] combined elements of both the Ptolemaic and the Copernican systems, the sun and moon revolving around the earth, and the planets [not including Earth] revolving around the sun.)

    The later sections of Kant's essay show how adopting the standpoint made possible by certain bystanders (including Kant himself) makes an otherwise senseless course of things intelligible and in a way that comes to terms with human freedom (something the Copernican transposition from earth to sun did not attempt).
12. See *Vorarbeiten zum Streit der Fakultäten* [23: 459].
13. Kant's reasoning seems to be as follows: Since a noumenal cause is always active, and since previous circumstances were sufficiently "cooperative" to bring us to the present moment (from which constant progress, *ex hypothesi*, extends), past history, too, is one of "constant progress."

14. Kant's comparison of human history to a *Possenspiel* anticipates the dark imagery of Georg Buchner's *Woczek,* which presents man as a puppet without a puppet master.

15. See the reference to spectators' "warm desire for newspapers [*heissen Begierde . . . nach Zeitungen*]" in an unpublished fragment [19: 604] (also discussed in Peter D. Fenves, *A Peculiar Fate: Metaphysics and World-History in Kant* [Ithaca, N.Y.: Cornell University Press, 1991], 253)—a description that calls to mind Kant's own legendary postponement of his daily walk to read the latest newspaper accounts of revolution in France.

16. See, for example, the portrayal of the storming of the Bastille, reproduced in *Immanuel Kant und die Berliner Aufklärung,* ed. Dina Emundts (Wiesbaden: Dr. Ludwig Reichert Verlag, 2000), 150. In the picture in question, the republican soldiers (and we "behind" them) literally have in view a building (the Bastille) in flames, whose smoke blends with that produced by their own musket fire. The picture thus portrays an attack, not against individual men, whose humanity might cry out to us, but against what Kant himself describes: an "ancient and splendid state structure" that vanishes "as if by magic," that is, in smoke (or what he elsewhere calls *Blauedunst*). This and very similar images appeared in newspapers that circulated widely in Germany during this period. Another famous episode that Kant may have had explicitly in mind is the Battle of Valmy (September 20, 1792). Kant's references to "the republic" and "the rebirth of the state" in an unpublished fragment [19: 604–612] speak especially for the latter possibility, as do his alleged words on learning of the proclamation of the French Republic: "Now I can say, like Simeon, let thy servant depart in peace, for I have seen the day of salvation." (The latter statement appears in Karl August Varnhagen von Ense, *Denkwürdigkeiten* [Leipzig: 1843–1859], quoted in Frederick C. Beiser, *Enlightenment, Revolution, and Romanticism: The Genesis of Modern German Political Thought, 1790–1800* [Cambridge, Mass.: Harvard University Press, 1992], 36. Varnhagen von Ense was the husband of the salonist Rahel Levin.) The battle, in which French regulars overcame the standing armies of the First Coalition (many of whom were Prussian regulars), was, above all, a moral victory. The commander of the republican forces is said to have inspired his troops (consisting of both regulars and recent conscripts) by parading on horseback on the front lines in sight of enemy artillery; he then ushered them into battle with the cry "Viva la Nation!" This cry, which was repeated by the entire army (with their hats on bayonets), was reputed to have cowed the opposing side. On the following day the monarchy was abolished and the French Republic officially proclaimed. Some sense of the battle's historical importance may be gauged from the famous comment of Goethe, who was present (fighting on the side of the First Coalition): "From this place and from this day forth commences a new era in the world's history, and you were present at its birth."

17. See also *The Metaphysics of Morals* [6: 455–456, 125], discussed by Fenves, *A Peculiar Fate*, 264–265.
18. Cf. Fichte's use of the phrase in his own *Addresses to the German Nation*.
19. The irony involved in characterizing this morally crucial, yet strangely apolitical event as a "betrayal" (cf. "Verträter" = traitor) should not go unnoticed. So long as it is unaccompanied by (further) practical intention, such public betrayal of feelings escapes the culpability that otherwise condemns all public expressions of political disloyalty. (That the event in question, and related courting of danger on the part of visibly aroused spectators, involves neither activity [*Täthen*] susceptible to imputation on their part nor action reducible to physical causality marks its status as moment in which morality "flows into" nature.)
20. Compare *The Metaphysics of Morals* [6: 336].
21. See *Remarks* [20: 35] and Chapter 2 above.
22. In *The Critique of Judgment* Kant speaks of a "not unimportant" "anthropological—teleological problem": namely, the natural human tendency toward "fruitless expenditure of force" through vain and idle longings [5: 178n]. That tendency, he concluded, can itself be understood as naturally purposive: If we had to assure ourselves beforehand of our ability to realize the object represented to our desire, then our forces would remain largely unused.
23. One early draft sheds suggestive light on what Kant intended here by "must": to conclude that "mankind constantly progresses" on the basis of a "regulative principle of moral-practical reason" is unobjectionable [*unbedenklich*], for the human race has a duty, in all times and for all peoples, to effect such progress, however "problematic" its success. And yet, Kant adds, "one demands [*velangt*] more": namely, "to be able to maintain [*behaupten*] assertorically, according to the constitutive principle of theoretical/judging reason, that the human race is in constant progress, and has been from the beginning." What is demanded, in short (according to this early draft), is a "constitutive principle" of "theoretical/judging reason" that overrides Kant's usual tightly drawn distinctions between the theoretical and practical use of reason, and between the regulative and the determinative use of judgment. As he here goes on to say: Since such progress cannot be "made out" on the basis of any experience, "it follows that a judgment *a priori*, thus with consciousness of the necessity of this progress," must be a ground that is pronounceable apodictically. For without this, "progress in the order of human events could not be predicted in a naturalistic manner, as required for knowledge of its necessity" [22: 621–622]. In the published version Kant seems to make just such an "apodictic" pronouncement, e.g., at [7: 88] ("I now maintain . . ."). (On principles of practical reason, as distinguished from theoretically judging reason, as "practically" or "subjectively" constitutive, see *Critique of Judgment* [5: 453, 458].) What is new, in short, is the amalgamation of "theoretically judging reason" (formerly limited to merely regulative principles) with an *a priori*

constitutive principle (a kind of rational principle formerly limited to the realm of practice). The demand that motivates the various versions of Kant's essay—a demand occasioned by "contempt" from lawyers [23: 623]—is, in any case, inter-worldly. (Cf. [23: 459].) (Hegel will later make his own professed overcoming of the distinction between regulative and constitutive principles of judgment a major point of difference with Kant.)

24. See *Toward Perpetual Peace* [8: 369]: Possession of power [*Gewalt*] "inevitably corrupts the free judgment of reason."
25. See also *Vorarbeiten zum Streit der Facultäten* [23: 459–460].
26. "To one accustomed [*gewohnt*] to freedom," as Kant once put it, "there can be no more horror-filled misfortune" than to find oneself subjected "to a creature of one's kind" [*Remarks* {2: 72}].
27. Cf. [7: 89]
28. Schlosser, who was partly influenced by Jacobi, was joined in his efforts by Count Friederich Leopold zu Stolzberg. (Concerning Jacobi, see [8: 398].) Sharing in the mystical proclivities and pseudo-aristocratic aspirations of the circle that surrounded the then-monarch, Schlosser was highly critical of Basedow's democratic educational reforms, claiming instead that most human beings were suited for steady menial labor and unfit for a refined education. (Schlosser was also, as it happens, Goethe's brother-in-law.) (see Manfred Kuehn, *Kant: A Biography* [Cambridge: Cambridge University Press, 2001], 394). Kant's insistence on the necessity of philosophic "labor"—labor, to be sure, that is anything but mechanical or plodding—is thus ironic on a number of levels. Philosophic laborers are to conduct themselves as "free and equal" members of a guild (like Kant's own father), not as leisured aristocrats whose thought "costs them nothing" and who pride themselves on living off the work of others [8: 390, 394].
29. Compare *Dreams of a Spirit-Seer* [2: 348].
30. "The contemptuous way of decrying the formal in our knowledge (even though it is the principle business of philosophy) as pedantry under the name of "a molding factory" confirms this suspicion, namely of a secret [*geheimen*] intention to ban all philosophy while proceeding under the banner [*Aushängschilde*] of philosophy, and as victor to act superior [*vornehm*] to it" [8: 404]. Hermann Cohen specifically links the comparison of Kantian reason to a "Formgebungsmanufaktur" with Jacobi. See Cohen, *Kants Theorie der Erfahrung* (Berlin: Ferd. Dümmlers Verlagsbuchhandlung, 1885), 154.
31. Compare *The Conflict of the Faculties* [7: 717] and Chapter 7 above; to the extent that the university is in the sole service of the state, it remains merely "factory-like"—i.e., mechanical.
32. This term is intended here in the literal (and still usual) sense of "making by hand" (e.g., in the manner of the traditional guild master).
33. Compare [8: 389].

34. As Kant puts it: "the Platonizing philosopher is inexhaustible in . . . pictorial expressions, which are supposed to make such intimations [*Ahnen*] understandable"—for example, "to approach so close to the goddess of wisdom that one can perceive [*vernehmen kann*] the rustle of her robes", and also in praising the art of *false Plato* [Afterplato] "which while not able to lift the veil of Isis, makes it so thin that one can *intimate* the goddess underneath." How thin is not here said, "although presumably not so thin that one cannot make of the apparition [*Gespenst*] what one will: for otherwise it would be a seeing/vision [*Sehen*], which certainly should be avoided" [8: 399].

35. See Rev. 6:13–14: *und schwur bei dem, der da lebt von Ewigkeit zu Ewigkeit, der den Himmel geschaffen hat und was darinnen ist, und die Erde und was darinnen ist, und das Meer und was darinnen ist, daß hinfort keine Zeit mehr sein soll.* (Luther translation) [and sware by him that liveth for ever and ever, who created heaven, and the things that are therein, and the earth, and the things that are therein, and the sea, and the things that are therein, that there should be time no longer.] The passage is thematically discussed in *The End of All Things*. On authentic (biblical) interpretation and history, see Rudolf A. Makreel, *Imagination and Interpretation in Kant: The Hermeneutical Import of the "Critique of Judgment"* (Chicago: University of Chicago Press, 1990), 141–153.

36. "mitspielen" means "to play with" as in a game or play (i.e., as actors) but also, figuratively, "to use" (in a pejorative sense) as in the phrase "das Schicksal spielte ihm hart mit" [fate used him very ill].

37. "treten": Kant's usage here contrasts ironically with his discussion of human progress [*Fortschritt*], which literally means a "stepping forward."

38. Cf. Rev. 22:11.

39. Cf. Rev. 21:8.

40. Cf. Rev. 20:1: "And I saw an angel come down from heaven, having the key of the bottomless pit" ("Abgrund" in Luther's translation).

41. That "epoch" literally denotes a fixed point in time (from the Greek *epochal*, meaning "stoppage, station, or position," as in the position of a planet) is worth pondering: The epoch-making event Kant claims to uncover marks a moment, or determinate point of transition, between temporal and moral revolutions.

42. Compare *The Conflict of the Faculties* [7: 80].

43. Compare *The Conflict of the Faculties* [7: 82].

44. See *The Conflict of the Faculties,* Part One [7: 19]: For the state to pursue scholarship directly would open it to legitimate criticism that would, in turn, undermine the respectful obedience the state is owed. Kant "honors" the state by warning it not to interfere with the freedom of the "lower" faculty (i.e., philosophy), whose public "role" [*spielen*] is to "examine everything" without commanding anything.

45. This is particularly so, given the new restrictions on publication that Kant was forced to contend with during this period of his life. On the special role of the

university, see the Preface to *The Conflict of the Faculties* [7: 5–11]. Among university graduates Kant distinguishes between scholars proper and "tools" of government (clergymen, magistrates, and physicians) who deal directly with the people (who are themselves incompetent [*Idiotes*]). Because possession of a civil office does not itself ensure that such graduates possess an understanding of the theoretical principles underlying their specialty, they are not "free to make public use of their reason as they see fit" but are subject to government control in the form of censorship by the faculties—a marked departure from Kant's earlier position in *What Is Enlightenment?*. In a properly functioning system of *Volkserklärung*, popular education is mediated by a class of government officials, themselves trained by and subject to scholars who aspire to philosophic wisdom in the precise Kantian sense.

46. During the intervening period, in which France and Prussia continued to remain formally at peace (as would continue to be the case until 1807, around the time of the Napoleonic invasion), Britain had emerged as France's most powerful military adversary. It is noteworthy that Kant now singles out British offenses against cosmopolitan right for special opprobrium. Compare [7: 90] and *Toward Perpetual Peace* [8: 358–359]; see also Kant's criticism of the British Constitution in an unpublished contemporary fragment [19: 607]: The constitution of Great Britain "is not that of a free people" but merely a "political machine" for carrying out the monarch's "absolute will."

47. Kant's "second Supplement" ("secret supplement for perpetual peace" according to which "the maxims of philosophers about the conditions under which public peace is possible shall be taken into consultation by states armed for war" [8: 368–369]) first appeared in the second edition [1796]. Frederick William II died in November, 1797; the *Conflict of the Faculties* was published in the fall of 1798.

48. See *Religion* [6: 38] and Chapter 5 above. See also Fenves, *A Peculiar Fate*, 235n; cf. Emil Fackenheim (quoted in Fenves), "Kant's Concept of History," *Kant-Studien* 48 (1957): 396: "How then can the freedom of discipline [legality] prepare for morality, which alone can be an end in itself? Astonishingly enough, to this decisive question Kant has no clear answer."

49. See *Idea for a Universal History*, which attributes the "happening" [*geschehen*] of the "first true steps from rudeness to culture"—steps that consist in what Kant calls "the social value [*gesellschaftlichen Werth*] of man"—to men's effort to be "more [than] human [*mehr als Mensch*]," a verbal ambiguity that neatly captures the dialectical character of honor in its undeveloped (i.e., non-egalitarian) state [7: 21]. Man initiates the process of his own cultivation, and thus becomes more fully human, by (wrongly) claiming superiority over other men. Kant designation of "social value" as the activator of historical progress anticipates in broad outline Alexandre Kojève's famous "dialectic of master and slave." (Readers familiar only with Kojève's earlier work may be surprised to find his

monumental, posthumously published *Phenomenologie du droit* more Kantian in flavor and substance than Hegelian.)

50. Cf. *Idea for a Universal History from/with a Cosmopolitan Standpoint/Intention:* "Everything good that is not engrafted onto a morally-good attitude [*Gesinnung*], is nothing other than empty appearance [*lauter Schein*] and glittering misery [*schimmerndes Elend*]" [8: 26]. The evolutionary "event" (which Kant's essay of 1784 does not and cannot take into account) evidently provides Kant with a new way to save the appearances.

51. *Religion* [6: 34].

52. See also *Anthropology* [7: 327]: "A civil constitution is the highest grade of the artificial enhancement [*Steigerung*] of the good *Anlage* of the human species to the final end of its *Bestimmung*." Yet a civil constitution also makes human animality "mightier" than it would be in raw nature. Man's self-will is always ready to "break forth against his neighbors," and to claim not only independence, but also "mastery of those who are by nature his equals." Kant's explanation for this fact is that nature within him strives to lead from culture to morality; whereas the order according to reason is from morality to culture. This course "unavoidably leads to a perversion" of nature's own purposive tendency [*Tendenz*], "as when, for example, Scriptural teaching, which ought to be a form of moral culture, begins with historical culture." All moral encouragement we take from signs of nature's purposiveness within us are also—insofar as they express that very purposiveness—an enhanced temptation toward evil. The problem of reconciling natural purposiveness and human freedom reduces, in the end, to whether one begins (with nature) in time (in which case perversion is inevitable) or outside it. See also *Critique of Practical Reason* (the "paradox of method" [5: 62ff.]) and Chapter 4 above.

53. See *Anthropology* [7: 325–326].

54. See Kant's reference to himself as a "teacher of the people" [*Volkslehrer*] at [7: 8]; see also [7: 80, 79n]. Kant's exhibition [*Darstellung*] of history calls to mind representations of the aesthetic sublime, which evoke analogous affects of "enthusiasm." According to the *Critique of Judgment:* "Even war has something sublime about it" if it is carried out with due respect for citizens' rights. "At the same time, it makes the way of thinking [*Denkungsart*] of a people that carries it on in this way [*Art*] all the more sublime in proportion to the number of dangers before which it was able to stand its ground." The same "way of thinking" is debased, however, by the merely "commercial spirit" that arises from a prolonged peace [5: 263]. These remarks, which contrast dramatically with the views later advanced in *Toward Perpetual Peace*, suggest Kant's ongoing ambivalence as to the ultimate possibility of peace with honor. As he puts it in his final published work: The idea of a cosmopolitan society is "in itself unattainable" and constitutes only a "regulative principle" to "pursue it diligently [*fleißig*]."

55. See Nietzsche, *The Anti-Christ*, #11 (*Werke* [Munich: Hanser Verlag, 1955], vol. 2, 1172): "Kant was an idiot. . . . Did [he] not see in the French Revolution

the transition from the inorganic form of the state to the *organic?* Did he not ask himself whether there was an event that could not otherwise be explained than through a moral *Anlage* of humanity, so that with it, once and for all, the "tendency of humanity toward the good" was *proven?* Kant's answer: it is the revolution." As we have seen, Kant's answer was rather more complicated than Nietzsche here allows. (On "idiotes" see note 45 above.)

56. Cf. Rousseau, *Discourse on the Origin of Inequality,* trans. Donald Cress (Indianapolis: Hackett, 1987), in Rousseau, *On the Social Contract,* ed. Donald A. Cress, (Indianapolis: Hackett, 1983), 125, 130.
57. The term suggests something like the "improvement" of land.
58. Cf. *Toward Perpetual Peace* [8: 352–353]: "Frederick II . . . at least *said* that he was merely the highest servant of the state, whereas a democratic constitution makes this impossible, for there everyone wants to be the master."
59. On the problem of how a species able to take credit for itself can be conceived, compare *Idea for a Universal History* [8: 18] and *Universal History and Theory of the Heavens* (discussed in Chapter 1 above).
60. Kant's interest in national minorities was no doubt partly prompted by significant expansion of Prussia's territorial boundaries following upon the Treaty of Basel, which partitioned Poland and destroyed largely Catholic "Greater Lithuania" (whose territories fell to Russia). In comparison with other recent and more ancient *Völklein* (i.e., Poles and Jews), the Prussian Lithuanians (who made up "Little Lithuania") were a well integrated minority. Unlike the Poles, whose presence in Prussia was of very recent (and unhappy) date, "Prussian Lithuanians" had been willing inhabitants since the Treaty of Melno in 1422, becaming Protestants in the next century along with their Teutonic neighbors. The Reformation precipitated a new influx of Lithuanian immigrants, many of these highly educated; indeed, some joined the faculty of the newly founded University of Königsberg. By the will of its founder (Albert, Duke of Prussia), church services continued to be offered in Kant's time in Lithuanian as well as German. A second preface to the *Dictionary* was contributed by Daniel Jenisch, who was a former student of Kant's who went on to publish on his moral philosophy. (On the latter point, see Editor's Introduction in Kant, *Anthropology, History, and Education,* ed. Robert B. Louden and Günter Zöller [Cambridge: Cambridge University Press, 2007], 430.)

Jews had an ancient, and not always happy, presence in Prussia arguably dating back to Roman times. During Kant's lifetime, a few "protected" (and mainly wealthy) Jews were permitted to live within the confines of cities such as Berlin and Königsberg, where small communities prospered. "Unprotected" Jews tended to be very poor and were much more heavily restricted as to occupation and place of residence. The many Polish Jews newly under Prussian jurisdiction were both less restricted, and more fully integrated economically in the territories they historically occupied, posing both new civic and economic opportunities and additional strains upon traditional communal relations.(See Stefi Jersch-Wenzel, "The Conditions of 'Protection' and Reforms of the Late Enlightenment," in *German-Jewish History in Modern Times*, ed. Michael A.Meyer [New York: Columbia University Press, 1997], vol. 1, 8-10.)

61. On this passage see also the Introduction to Part Two above.
62. Königsberg was home to a modernizing revival among educated Jews of the Hebrew language. *Hameassef*, the first Hebrew language journal of the Jewish Enlightenment, was started in 1784, in Königsberg. Kant's student, Isaac Abraham Euchel (whom Kant in his capacity as Rector considered but ultimately rejected for a professorship in Hebrew language at the University of Königsberg), was a founding editor. On the latter, see also Chapter 9, note 3 below.

9. Kant's Jewish Problem

1. That antipathy has not gone unnoticed. (For a recent treatment, see Michael Mack, *German Idealism and the Jew* [Chicago: University of Chicago Press, 2003].) In addition to the late-appearing *Anthropology*, his unpublished lectures on anthropology, as well as many private remarks, often betray highly negative feelings toward Jews, whom he routinely describes as cowards and cheaters. This antipathy may reflect relations between the burghers with whom Kant associated and the sometimes beleaguered Jewish community of Königsberg, which found itself compelled on at least one occasion to call upon the help of Moses Mendelssohn. At the same time, Königsberg was an important city for the enlightened Berlin Jewish elite. As Steven M. Lowenstein puts it, "the association of Königsberg with the Berlin Haskala was especially great, not only because such influential leaders of the Enlightenment as David Friedländer and Isaac Euchel had lived there, but also because Enlightenment institutions, especially the Hebrew periodical *Hameassef*, were founded there. The Berlin Jewish elite also had family ties to Königsberg (above all, through the Friedländers)." (See Lowenstein, *The Berlin Jewish Community: Enlightenment, Family, and Crisis, 1770–1830* [New York: Oxford University Press, 1994], 35.) On the general condition of the Jews of Königsberg, see also Steffen Dietzsch, *Immanuel Kant: Eine Biographie* (Leipzig: Reclam Verlag Leipzig, 2003), 171–195. Still, although one could hardly call Kant a friend of the Jews, his relations with individual Jewish students were cordial and, in at least one case, very close.
2. Kant's stance on Jewish emancipation was, given the political context, rather liberal. If Kant had wished to curry favor by "blaming the Jews," he could have gone much farther. (Johann David Michaelis, the famous Orientalist, was already calling Jews a foreign race that should be transplanted to the colonies.)

Michaelis, "Ueber die buergerliche Verbesserung der Juden," *Orientalische und Exegetische Bibliotek*, 19 (1782), translated and republished in *The Jew in the Modern World: A Documentary History*, ed. Paul R. Fendes-Flohr and Jehuda Reinharz (New York: Oxford University Press, 1980), 36–38; see also Michael Hess, *Germans, Jews and the Claims of Modernity* (New Haven: Yale University Press, 2002), 221. Michaelis cites Jewish "national pride," along with observation of religious laws that keep them from "intermingling" and a "messianic expectation" that casts doubt on their political loyalty and willingness to fight for their country as major impediments to Jewish emancipation. As for the latter, "a people which nurses these hopes will lack, at the very least, a patriotic love for the fields of their fathers." Although, as he adds, many Lutheran theologians, including Philip Jacob Spener, deny the biblical authority of such an expectation, this will hardly convince the Jews, whose greatest biblical commentators say otherwise.

3. For a compelling account, see Heinz Moshe Graupe, *The Rise of Modern Judaism: An Intellectual History of German Jewry, 1650–1942* (Malabar, Fla.: Krieger, 1978), 113–122. As Graupe observes, "the Jewish element among [Kant's] students must have been quite large. . . . When Kant first became Rector in 1786, among the nineteen signatories of his students, who presented him with a eulogistic poem, four were Jews. Letters of commendation which Kant gave to some of his Jewish students reveal an accurate personal knowledge of them. Among the younger members of the Mendelssohn circle was . . . a group from Königsberg which was influenced by Kant. . . . Of Kant's Jewish students two achieved particular prominence: *Isaac Euchel . . .* and *Marcus Herz. . . .* Kant had applied on [Euchel's] behalf for a lectureship in Hebrew in the philosophical faculty, just at the time he became Rector. He himself as Rector then had to sign the letter of rejection to his Jewish pupil" [118–119]. (See also Kant, *Correspondence,*[12: 406, 426ff., 429].) It was Herz, as Graupe notes, to whom Kant entrusted the job of printing and binding the first edition of the *Critique of Pure Reason* and of distributing copies as gifts to important scholars and dignitaries [120]. Among the attractions of Kant for enlightened Jewish students was his rejection of the divinity of Jesus and of the doctrine of original sin. On the relatively high number of Jewish students at the Albertina, Kant's university, see also Dietzsch, *Immanuel Kant*, 188–195. Abraham Moses Levin was the first Jewish student to matriculate at Albertina University (in 1731), despite resistance. The first Jewish student was admitted to a higher faculty (medicine) in 1766. Prior to 1781 Jewish students of medicine had to find another university from which to graduate (in Herz's case, the University of Halle). For a more detailed account see Steven Naragon, "Kant in the Classroom," www.manchester.edu/kant/, accessed October 11, 2008. Additional Jewish students of note who studied with Kant include Michael Friedländer (nephew of David Friedländer), who later became Madame de Staël's personal physician, and Aron Isaak Joel, whom Kant later employed in a similar capacity.

4. For some indication of the importance of this friendship to Kant's career, see especially his correspondence with Herz between 1777 and 1781 [10: 211–214, 230–232, 240–249, 265–270]. For a fuller treatment of their intellectual and personal relations, see Susan Meld Shell, *The Embodiment of Reason: Kant on Spirit, Generation and Community* (Chicago: University of Chicago Press, 1996), Chapter 10.
5. *Reflections on Anthropology* #950 [15: 235–236].
6. See Frederick C. Beiser, *The Fate of Reason* (Cambridge, Mass.: Harvard University Press, 1987), 92–108; and Lewis White Beck, *Early German Philosophy: Kant and his Predecessors* (Cambridge, Mass.: Harvard University Press, 1969), 353–360.
7. I am indebted to Allan Arkush for his helpful comments on an earlier version of this chapter.
8. Moses Mendelssohn, *Jerusalem*, trans. Allan Arkush with introduction and commentary by Alexander Altmann (Hanover, NH: University Press of New England, 1983), 90.
9. An exception is Allan Arkush, *Moses Mendelssohn and the Enlightenment* (Albany: State University of New York Press, 1994).
10. Cf. *Acts* 4:10–11. "[Jesus] is the stone which was rejected by [Israel's] builders, but which has become the head of the corner. And there is salvation in no one else."
11. One wonders whether in using this unusual term, Mendelssohn was not obliquely alluding to Kant's *Critique of Pure Reason* and its treatment of the Paralogisms of Pure Reason. If Mendelssohn was attempting to making "common cause" against the enemies of enlightenment, it was rebuffed in the B Edition of the "Paralogisms," which contains an explicit refutation of Mendelssohn's proof of the immortality of the soul in the *Phaedo*.
12. Moritz Itzig would later famously be denied the opportunity of responding "as a gentleman" to what he regarded as rudeness on the part of Achim von Arnim. Challenged by Itzig, Arnim replied that no Jew possessed the honor necessary to engage in a duel. (For a discussion of the incident, see Deborah Hertz, *Jewish High Society in Old Regime Berlin* [New Haven: Yale University Press, 1988], 258–259.) The theme is ironically reprised in the famous Mendelssohn-Jacobi exchange concerning Lessing's alleged "Spinozisim." For the relevant texts, see the Editor's Introduction by Leo Strauss to *Morning Hours* and *Lessing's Friends*, in Moses Mendelssohn, *Gesammelte Schriften Jubiläumausgabe* vol. 3.2 (Berlin: Friedrich Frommann Verlag, 1931), lix–xcv.
13. Letter to Kant, April 10, 1783. Mendelssohn attributes his inability to ill health [10: 308].
14. This is the main point of Kant's famous *What Is Enlightenment?* [1784]; Mendelssohn wrote an essay on that topic for the same prize competition.
15. For a detailed discussion of changes in government policy, see Klaus Epstein, *The Genesis of German Conservatism* (Princeton: Princeton University Press, 1966), Chapter 7.

16. See Yirmiahu Yovel, *Kant and the Philosophy of History* (Princeton: Princeton University Press, 1980), 202.
17. See, for example, *Religion* [6: 82–83]: "the representation of [Jesus's] death ought to have had, and could have had, the greatest influence on human hearts at that time—indeed, so it can at any time—for it most strikingly displays the contrast between the freedom of the children of heaven and the bondage of a mere son of earth." The true meaning of the redemption thus lies here: "It is easy to see, once we divest of its mystical cover this vivid mode of representing things, apparently also the only one at the time *suited to the common people,* why it (its spirit and rational meaning) has been valid and binding practically, for the whole world and at all times: because it lies near enough to every human being for each to recognize his duty in it. Its meaning is that there is absolutely no salvation for human beings except in the innermost adoption of genuine moral principles...." Christianity, rightly understood, answers with special force to the natural need of human beings to demand for even the highest concepts of reason and grounds "something that can be *sensually grasped [etwas Sinnlich-haltbares]*," a need that must especially be taken into account when the intention is "to *introduce* a faith universally" [6: 109]. It is for this reason, apparently, that Kant claims in the *Conflict of the Faculties,* that of all historic faiths, Christianity is, so far as we know, the most adequate" [7: 36]. Sacred narrative serves moral ends by making moral principle "vivid" [6: 132]; it is a tool, in other words, of what Kant elsewhere calls an aesthetic way of representing moral objects [8: 405].
18. None of his children remained observant and all but two eventually converted to Christianity.
19. The letter follows with a description of the first phase of what would prove to be tireless efforts on his part to introduce Kant's thought to the intellectual worthies of Berlin. His "first visit" is to Mendelssohn. And it closes with solicitous inquiries, on the part of the young physician, as to Kant's challenged health.
20. Hermann Cohen's later attempt to blame Kant's negative portrayal of Judaism almost entirely on Spinoza cannot, however, be supported. For an instructive discussion of Kant and Spinoza's divergent rhetorical uses of the Bible, see Yovel, *Kant and the Philosophy of History,* 214–215.
21. Compare *Religion* [6: 132] and Mendelssohn, *Jerusalem,* 127–128.
22. Mendelssohn's name appears, however, in earlier, unpublished versions of the essay. See the "Krakauer fragment" and the discussion by Peter Fenves, *A Peculiar Fate: Metaphysics and World-History in Kant* (Ithaca: Cornell University Press, 1991), 186n.
23. See also Chapter 8.
24. Mendelssohn, *Jerusalem,* 99, 129. On the subject of remembrance, see Fenves, *A Peculiar Fate,* 279ff.

25. As we saw in Chapter 2, Kant himself had once experimented with an oscillating, or non-progressive theory of history rooted in Rousseauian principles.
26. The charge of "paganism" had already appeared in Johann Georg Hamann's *Golgatha and Scheblimini*, which accuses Mendelssohn (with whom Hamann was personally on friendly terms) of "Attic" infidelity to the faith of his fathers.
27. As Deborah Hertz notes, this did not stop the *solonnière* Rachel Levin and her brother, Ludwig Robert, from happily attending his Berlin lectures of 1807–1808, which aimed at arousing a new Prussian patriotism in the face of the French occupation. (Hertz, *Jewish High Society in Old Regime Berlin* [New Haven: Yale University Press, 1988], 147.) Like several other major figures in the intellectual turn against Jews and Jewish converts, Fichte had himself been a frequent visitor of the Jewish salons.
28. Kant is also careful to exclude Abraham, who was willing to "butcher" his son at God's (alleged) command, from the list of biblical exemplars [7: 63]. Kant's insistence that Jesus was wholly human saves him from the orthodox Christian reply that God, too, sacrificed his only Son. Kierkegaard will famously take up the challenge on Abraham's (and Christianity's) behalf.
29. As Jonathan M. Hess mistakenly states (see his *Germans, Jews and the Claims of Modernity* [New Haven: Yale University Press, 2002], 157).
30. Cf. *What it Means to Orient Oneself in Thinking* [8: 138n]. (The term is here specifically applied to Mendelssohn as author of the *Phaedo.*); *Theory and Practice* [8: 309].
31. Cf. *The Conflict of the Faculties* [7: 17].
32. Cf. the "verdringen" or pressing down by the Judaic remnant of all true religion [7: 52–53].
33. Rousseau, *Letter to Beaumont* (Paris: Gallimard [Pléiade Edition], 1969), vol. 4, 796–797. I am indebted to Natalie Wills Culp for bringing this passage to my attention.
34. If one associates that third moment with the historical period surrounding the Battle of Valmy and proclamation of the Republic in 1792 (rather than the storming of the Bastille in 1789), the case for such a juxtaposition becomes even stronger. On such a view, the period in which Kant finished the *Critique of Judgment* (and was still praising the sublimity of the ancient Jews), precedes that crucial final moment by several years. It was evidently just after the Battle of Valmy (i.e., in "late August 1792") that Kant decided to set in motion the academic machinery that enabled him to publish the complete version of *Religion within the Boundaries of Bare Reason.* (See his letter "To the Theological Faculty in Königsberg" [draft] [11: 357–359].)
35. See *The Conflict of the Faculties*, Part Two [7: 87–89]. Nietzsche singles out this claim, which he calls "absolutely anti-historical," for special ridicule; cf. *Anti-Christ* #11; *Beyond Good and Evil* #38; *The Will to Power* #382. See also Kant, *Religion* [6: 129n].

36. *Acts* 2 recounts the story of those gathered at Pentecost and specifically concerns the Jewish remnant that is saved through "fear" of the Lord.
37. Although Friedländer, who was an early acquaintance of Kant's, is better known as a disciple of Mendelssohn, it seems fair to say that after the latter's death, Friedländer moved closer to the views of the younger members of the Berlin Haskala, who were deeply influenced by Kant. Even before Mendelssohn's death, Friedländer resisted the latter's identification of Judaism with ritual observance. Friedländer was for many years the senior member of a wealthy Königsberg family with particularly close connections to the Jewish enlightenment. David Friedländer supported both Marcus Herz and Isaac Euchel financially and was in possession of several prized sets of transcripts of Kant's course lectures, including the 1775–1776 *Lectures on Anthropology* that now bear his name. Friedländer later donated a number of such transcriptions to the Royal Prussian Library (see editor's note, [25: CXXXV]). On Friedländer's rejection of Mendelssohn's views on the ceremonial law, see Lowenstein, *The Berlin Jewish Community*, 99–101; see also Christophe Schulte, *Die jüdische Aufklärung: Philosophie, Religion, Geschichte* (Munich: C. H. Beck, 2002), 205. On his financial support of Herz and Euchel, see Schulte, *Die jüdische Aufklärung*, 94–95.
38. *Sendschreiben an seine Hochwuerdigen Herrn Oberconsistorialrat und Probst Teller zu Berlin, von einigen Husvaetrn juedischer Religion* (Berlin, 1799). Among the many Kantian concepts and phrases he invokes is the Kantian charge of Jewish slavishness and messianic passivity, a charge Friedländer grants *vis-à-vis* Rabbinic and Caballistic practices—practices that in Friedländer's view contradict Judaism's "essence" [*Sendschrieben*, 34–36].
39. Telling in this regard is the latter's adoption of certain Kantian formulations— e.g., war as the "goad of humanity"—a goad that is becoming milder "thanks to enlightenment" and increasing "conviction as to the dignity of human beings and their rights" [*Reden*, 76–77].
40. Also arguing in favor of this interpretation is Friedländer's energetic leadership in the struggle for Jewish emancipation throughout, both between 1786 and 1793 and between 1808 and 1812. For a sympathetic portrayal of Friedländer's role, see Lowenstein, *The Berlin Jewish Community*, 78–83.
41. Friedländer writes: "[Beyond the ceremonial laws Judaism contains at its core principles] which we deem to be the foundation of every religion. The principles upon which the religion of Moses is built have for us the highest certainty. We do not doubt that the creed of the Church corresponds to the principles of our faith in spirit, if not in wording, and we would [be ready to] embrace it. [Moreover,] we would [be ready to] make a public confession of that which the Christian teacher has taught, for we do not [merely] believe in his teaching as an aggregate of truths but are convinced of their correctness. From this direction, therefore, there is no obstacle facing us and we need not fear that we would be repulsed [by the Church]. These principles are not all

that we will bring with us from Judaism, however. In addition to them we shall bring other principles of the utmost significance, the truth of which is equally clear to us and which we are obligated to accept with equal conviction. Will these principles conform to the teachings of the religious society that we are choosing? Will the teachers of the Christian Church be prepared if not to accept these principles then at least to display tolerance toward them, allowing us to publicly acknowledge these other principles which for us are convincing and beyond all doubt? We do not venture to answer this question in the affirmative. At the very least we must not make a decision regarding this without the consent of a teacher of religion as respectable, learned and noble as you, worthy Sir" (*The Jew in the Modern World*, 97). Teller, from whom Friedländer might have reasonably expected a sympathetic reception, publicly replied that conversion to the Church would require both a confession of the superiority of Christianity to Judaism and an acceptance of baptism and other sacraments deemed to symbolize Christ's founding.

42. As Hess notes, Ascher, "like his friend Salomon Maimon (1754–1800) and contemporary Lazarus Bendavid (1762–1832), . . . enthusiastically supported the philosophic revolution unleashed by Kant's *Critique of Pure Reason* (1781), a work that Mendelssohn in his final years was not ashamed to admit he simply could not understand" [*Germans, Jews and the Claims of Modernity*, 139]. Ascher belonged to what Shmuel Feiner has called a second generation of Jewish intellectuals in Berlin, who departed both from Mendelssohn's commitment to philosophic rationalism and from his particular view of Judaism.

43. Saul Ascher, *Leviathan, oder ueber Religion in Ruecksicht des Judenthums* (Berlin, 1792).

44. It established, however, a tradition of which Hermann Cohen's *Religion of Reason out of the Sources of Judaism* was a late fruit.

45. For a more detailed discussion, see Hess, *Germans, Jews and the Claims of Modernity*, 165–166.

46. Hess, *Germans, Jews and the Claims of Modernity*, 163.

47. Yovel makes a similar point in *Kant and the Philosophy of History*, 221–223.

48. See also *Idea for a Universal History* [8: 29n]: "the first page of Thucydides (says Hume) is the proper beginning of true history."

49. See, for example, Kant's letter to Herz ("after May 11, 1781" [10: 270]): where he reports his great "discomfort" over Mendelssohn having put the *Critique* aside: "I hope," he adds, "that it will not be forever." "[Mendelssohn] is the most important of all the people who could explain this theory to the world; it was on him, on Herr Tetens, and on you, dearest man, that I counted most."

50. Bendavid echoes Kant in identifying the "main failing" of the Jews as "slavishiness." (Lazarus Bendavid, *Etwas zur Charakteristik der Juden* [Leipzig: 1793], cited in Schulte, *Die jüdische Aufklärung*, 108. Bendavid published appreciative works of introduction in the 1790s (when Kant's thought was

coming under increasing attack by former followers) to all three of Kant's *Critiques*.
51. Friedrich Schleiermacher (annon.), *Briefe bei Gelegenheit der politisch theologischen Aufgabe und des Sendschreibens juedischer Hausvaeter. Von einem Prediger ausserhalb* (Berlin, 1799).
52. On rising anti-Semitism in the early 1800s, see Hertz, *Jewish High Society in Old Regime Berlin*, 262–263.
53. The example and fate of the Jewish *salonnières* is here especially instructive.

Concluding Remarks

1. See *Groundlaying of the Metaphysics of Morals* [4: 390]; and *The Metaphysics of Morals:* A practical philosopher is one who "makes the *final end of reason* the principle *of his actions*" [6: 375n].
2. On the specifically "juridical" meaning of a philosophic "deduction" for Kant, see Dieter Henrich, "Kant's Notion of a Deduction and the Methodological Background of the First *Critique*," in *Kant's Transcendental Deductions*, ed. Eckart Förster (Stanford: Stanford University Press, 1989); and Susan Meld Shell, *The Rights of Reason: A Study of Kant's Philosophy and Politics* (Toronto: University of Toronto Press, 1980).
3. For variations on this theme, see Christine M. Korsgaard, *Creating the Kingdom of Ends* (Cambridge: Cambridge University Press, 1996); Onora O'Neill, *Constructions of Reason* (Cambridge: Cambridge University Press, 1989); John Rawls, *Political Liberalism*, 2nd ed. (New York: Columbia University Press, 1996), and *Lectures on the History of Moral Philosophy*, ed. Barbara Herman (Cambridge, Mass.: Harvard University Press, 2000). See also J. B. Schneewind, *The Invention of Autonomy: A History of Modern Moral Philosophy*, (Cambridge: Cambridge University Press, 1998); and Otfried Höffe, *Kant's Cosmopolitan Theory of Law and Peace*, trans. Alexandra Newton (Cambridge: Cambridge University Press, 2006; German edition: *Königliche Völker* [Frankfurt am Main: Suhrkamp, 2001]).
4. According to Grimm and Grimm, the verb "Gesetzen" is a strengthened version of "setzen"; its three basic means include 1) "to bring into a certain state of order," 2) "to order" or "direct" (as in *anordnen*), and 3) to "set fast" or "establish" (as in *festsetzen*). "Gesetzen" is, of course, directly related to the term for "law" (*Gesetz*).
5. According to Grimm and Grimm, *Rechtsame* is a version of *Gerechtsame*, a relatively rare term for "rights" especially in a sense connoting immunity from prosecution (as conveyed by the traditional expression "with benefit of clergy").
6. Presumably, as in the Latin "sentencia," meaning an authoritative judgment or decree.
7. Cf. *The Metaphysics of Morals* [6: 312].

8. Compare, for example, [A 807 = B 835] and [A 812–813 = B 840–841]; on the one hand, Kant assumes "that there really are pure moral laws that determine completely *a priori*," and "without regard to empirical motives, i.e., happiness"; on the other hand, as "commands," they necessarily carry with them "*promises* and *threats*" absent which they would lose their motivating force. Kant here distinguishes our *judgment* of the law, which takes place in accordance with ideas, from our *observance* of the law, which is a matter of subjective maxims. For moral maxims to govern our entire course of life (as they, indeed, should), however, reason must be able to connect the moral law, which is merely an idea, with an efficient cause linking such conduct with an "outcome corresponding to our highest ends." If moral conduct over a lifetime does not fulfill our highest ends, we lack sufficient reason to undertake it. Hence: Without God and an afterlife, "the lordly [*herrlichen*] ideas of morality" are "objects of approval and admiration" but not "incentives for resolve and execution" [A 813 = B 841]. Kant still conceives of moral motivation in terms of a reckoning of profit and loss: If reason's highest end is not guaranteed, it lacks sufficient reason to expend the effort necessary for a lifetime of good conduct.
9. Compare *Critique of Pure Reason* [A 813 = B 841].
10. Compare Kant's denial of reason's dictatorial authority at [A 738 = B 766].
11. I am grateful to Cyril O'Regan for this insight. The basis for conceiving human choice as itself a noumenal act is already laid in Kant's discussion of *naiveté* in the *Critique of Judgment* [5: 335]. *Naiveté* is there described as the unintended eruption [*Ausbruch*] of an original human sincerity and as something in which both animal and intellectual feeling are "posited together." On "naiveté" see also Peter D. Fenves, *A Peculiar Fate: Metaphysics and World-History in Kant* (Ithaca, N.Y.: Cornell University Press, 1991), 279.
12. Autonomy in this case involves what Kant calls "lawfulness [of imagination] without a law" [5: 241].
13. That is, "Terminus," the Roman "god of limits."
14. Martin Heidegger, *Vom Wesen der menschlichen Freiheit* (Frankfort am Main: Vittorio Klostermann, 1982); citations are to the English translation by Ted Sadler (Heidegger, *The Essence of Human Freedom: An Introduction to Philosophy* [London: Continuum, 2002]).
15. See Preliminary Article 2: "No state existing for itself (be it small or large) shall be able to become acquired by another state through acquisition, exchange, purchase or donation" [8: 344].
16. See *Dreams of a Spirit-Seer* [2: 358].

Index

Abderitism, 282–283, 321–322, 405n9
Action: as free, 2, 19–20; limits to free, 2; just, 2–3, 3; right, 4; as undetermined by antecedent causes, 18; exercise of free, 61, 63; moral, 86, 145; for duty's sake, 128–129; maxims as rules of, 129; lawfulness of, 366n20
Afterlife, 92, 113
Allegory, 191–192
Allison, Henry, 186, 345n6, 365n15, 371n62, 373n74, 378n1
Anderson-Gold, Sharon, 196, 392n44
Ameriks, Karl, 345n5, 346n7, 362n1, 365n15, 371n62, 372n67, 372n72
Arendt, Hannah, 378n31
Aristotle, 221–222, 183, 185
Arkush, Allan, 415n9
Aune, Bruce, 366n20
Animality, 95, 194–195
Anthropology: Kant's focus on, 34–36, 40; Kant's lectures on, 86, 88–114; nature's knowledge revealed in, 95; pragmatic, 95, 107; metaphysics' boundary with, 103
Anxiety, 294, 298
Archimedes, 82, 292–293

Archimedean, 42, 52, 55–56, 83–84, 179–180, 286
Ascher, Saul, 306; career of, 329–330
Attention, 36, 137, 158, 292–293; power to focus, 23–24
Attraction: social force of, 55, 66
Authority: of God, 4; of reason, 4, 336–338; morality and human, 206
Autocracy, 186, 339
Autonomy, 151–159; as defined, 1; right suggested by, 1; of self, 1–2; Stoicism and, 2; term, 2; full political, 5; rational, 5, 336; Kantian ideal of moral, 5–6; moral, 5–6; Rawls on, 5–8; limits of, 8–14, 335–343; morality and, 11, 142–143; resistance demanded by, 122; rational self-legislation as, 112; paradox of, 122–159, 338, 362n1; formula of, 123; as possible, 125; principle of, 144, 148, 271, 337–338; of will, 149; moral faith and, 153; ethic of, 163; idea of, 335; as paradoxical, 338; without desert, 340; Heidegger on, 340; as original self-binding, 340; difficulties posed by, 341; invention of, 347n26

Beauty: as maximized, 28; feminine, 49, 66–67; moral, 73; judgments of, 93

Beck, Lewis White, 248, 376n10

Beiser, Frederick, 347n25, 363n8, 372n66, 415n6

Belief: in God, 321; freedom of, 379n8; as defined, 397n6

Bendavid, Lazarus, 306; on Judaism, 324–325

Benevolence, 46; duties of, 63–65; rights v., 227–228; subordination to right of, 228

Benjamin, Walter, 184

Berlin Censorship Commission, 251

Body: soul's relationship with, 35; passive receptivity associated with possession of, 91

Brandt, Reinhard, 347n18, 393n54, 394n67

Causality, 111–112, 407n19; purposive, 167–168, 174; Heidegger on, 340

Cavallar, Georg, 377n13, 386n1, 390n28

Censorship, 179, 187, 205, 214, 420n45; edict of, 12, 380n14

Character, 49, 119; national, 50, 95, 304, 401n35; moral,,118–119, 186, 192, 386n59; human, 301, 321

Chastity, 69–70, 253

Christianity, 76–77, 260; true, 202–203; historical appearance of, 204, 384n47; pure religious and church faiths making up, 261; sects of, 264–271; spiritual message of, 315; history of, 315–316, 319; Judaism and, 318–319, 329; as historical faith, 325; narrative of, 326–327; as absorbed into spiritualized religion of reason, 333

Church, 384n45; established, 266–267

Cohen, Hermann, 186, 306, 408n30, 416n20, 419n44

Communication: intimate, 169–170; supernatural, 292

Community, 229; spiritual, 39; free, 335

Competition, 67, 104, 196, 381n23, 396n79

Conflict: faculties' legal v. illegal, 258–260; of philosophic/theological faculties, 260–264, 271–274; settlement of philosophic/theological faculties, 271–274

Conflict of the Faculties, The (Kant), 79, 179–180, 247, 294, 327; public law in, 235–236; university in, 249; moral education in, 274–275; history in, 277–305; honor in, 277–305; human history and, 323–324

Conjectural Beginnings of Human History (Kant), 277

Conscience, 2, 367n31; primacy of, 188; true religion and, 188–189; moral, 209; knowledge of freedom via, 248; force/violence exercised on, 265; as repressed, 268–269

Consciousness: of freedom, 301

Cosmology, 17,,19, 24, 35, 39

Cosmopolitanism, 172, 212, 279, 377n13

Credit, 217–218, 226–227, 234

Crisis, 399n14

Critique of Judgment (Kant), 207, 304, 339; content/structure of, 164; history in, 169–176; war in, 289; primacy of ethics in, 312; force in, 407n22

Critique of Pure Reason (Kant), 8, 85, 135, 143, 339; rational will in, 124; paradox in, 141; autonomy in, 151–159; responses to, 152; philosophic instruction in, 254–258; critical philosophy in, 336–337

Critique of Revelation (Fichte), 330

Crusius, Christian August, 17–20, 24, 76, 349n8, 351n17

Culture: aesthetic, 50; of moral feeling, 174; instruments of human, 218; vices of, 225; first steps to, 410n49

Del piacere e del dolore (Verri), 88

Democritus, 322

Dependence, 82; terror held by, 57–58

Desert, 183, 335, 364n12; as primary moral phenomenon, 6, 8; autonomy without, 340; Rawls on, 346n16

Desire, 53, 97; expansion of, 59; idealizing object of, 71; as primary faculty of soul, 89; will dominated by sensible, 109; laws of, 110–111; as arises, 117. *See also* Sexual desire

Despotism, 187, 222–223, 231, 233, 251, 289n25, 397n83

Dignity, 140, 182, 210–211; of human nature, 46–47

Discipline: of boys, 106; negative culture of, 172; moral, 196

Dishonor, 220

Disillusionment, 68–69

Disposition, 172, 245; moral, 194, 197–199, 225, 262–267, 384n46

Dogma, 256–257, 262, 328

Dreams of a Spirit Seer (Kant), 39–40, 214, 355n2

Duty: as primary moral phenomenon, 8; concept of, 125, 134, 136, 143–144; actions done from, 128–129; law and, 129–130; of nations to defend themselves, 212; inborn, 321; as impossible, 365n16; moral ideas related to, 366n21; moral, 384n46

Education, 78–79, 106–107, 401n35; Kant on, 51–52; moral, 113–114, 198–199, 248–249, 274–275; Kantian, 248; philosophic, 258–259, 270; secret of, 294; of educators, 299. *See also* Instruction

Effort, 5, 6, 10; strenuous, 21–25, 29; moral, 61; cost of, 101, 118, 181–183

Ellis, Elizabeth, 378n31, 391n37

Emancipation, Jewish, 413n2

Emile (Rousseau), 52, 58, 109, 189, 248–249, 289; and Jacobi, 371–372n65

Enjoyment, 359n44; after pain, 115; as conservative, 115–116. *See also* Pleasure

Enlightenment, 351n23; age of, 12

Enthusiasm, 286; toward ideal, 287; of good resolution, 287–288

Equality: as grounded in objective moral principle, 2; rule of, 56; drive for, 66

Essay on the Various Races of Man (Kant), 85

Eternity, 27, 104, 113

Ethics: modern, 122; as naturalized, 127, 365n15; autonomy and, 163; primacy of, 312

Evil, 32, 222, 350n17; as necessarily allowed by God, 21–22; Kant on, 36; science caused, 78–79; radical, 194, 224; source of, 197; transformation of, 199–200; form of religion, 201; as eliminated, 229; human, 297

Experience, limits of, 113

Fairness, moral, 358n34

Faith, 71, 192; religious, 4; natural/supernatural, 74–75; autonomy and moral, 153; moral, 153, 261, 382n27; rational, 153; church, 261, 264; grace through, 263; as defined, 397n6; biblical, 403n58

Fanaticism, 165, 251, 281

Fear, 117, 135, 169; of God, 206; obedience out of, 327–328

Feelings: virtue and, 46; moral v. aesthetic, 46–47; life and, 89; as primary faculty of soul, 89; taste and, 89; of pain, 95; culture of moral, 173; moral, 178. *See also* Moral feelings

Fenves, Peter, 348n1, 367n28, 378n22, 406n15, 416n22, 421n11

Fichte, Johann Gottlieb, 83, 324, 328, 330, 333

Flikschuh, Katrin, 374n4, 393n54

Force, 143, 183, 407n22; homogeneous, 35; moral, 39–40, 63, 200; active, 56, 65, 97; social, 66, 82; living, 90, 96, 118, 158; rightful, 238, 242

Foreign policy, 343

Förster, Eckart, 363n6, 420n2

Franks, Paul, 371n63, 372n66
Frederick the Great, 11–13, 152, 170, 251–252, 302–303; misanthropy of, 302–303; cosmopolitanism of, 377n13
Freedom, 218, 250–251, 293, 365n15; in sexual conduct, 1; as grounded in objective moral principle, 2; law as *ratio cognoscendi* of, 3; as *ratio essendi* of law, 3; universalized, 4; law's relationship with, 9; as internal determination, 10; in *New Elucidation*, 17–24; Kant's early theory of, 17–38; power over attention as vehicle of human, 23–24; in *Universal Natural History*, 24–33; ordered, 55, 58; state of nature and, 55–59; corruption and, 56–57; acceptance of necessity and, 58; as challenged, 58; as valued, 58; under primitive conditions, 58–59; love of, 66–67, 82–83; sexual desire and, 66–68, 82–83; state of, 86; motivation and, 89–90; as desirable, 92; awareness of, 92–93; lawless, 96; maximum, 96; reality of, 111, 155; experience of, 111–112; defining, 112; of will, 144; as proven, 145; autonomy of will and, 149; possibility of, 149; conditions to, 208, 281n21; external, 224–225; knowledge of, 248; as mark of philosophy, 253; peace and, 255–256; consciousness of, 301; intellectual, 308; religious, 314; limits of law and, 339; of soul, 349n5; of belief, 379n8; inclination toward, 394n65
French Revolution, 12, 167–168, 175, 187, 251, 279
Friedländer, David, 307, 333; letter by, 328; views of, 418n37; on foundations of religion, 418n41
Friendship, 126, 364n10; marriage and, 69–70
Future: knowledge of, 102; reason and, 114–115; concern about, 298

Galston, William, 346n8
Genius, 42, 180–181, 357n; originality associated with human, 5; artistic, 164, 170
God, 174; authority of, 4; command of, 4; as substances common source, 18–19; as ground of worldly connection, 19; time/space and, 19; goodness of, 20–21; justice of, 20–21; evil as necessarily allowed by, 21–22; creative, 24; universal harmony communicated by, 29; presence of, 31; will of, 75–76, 190–191; virtual presence of, 89–90; gratitude toward, 107; pleasing, 267; belief in, 321; moral law and, 363n6
Goetschel, Willi, 348n27
Good, 156; promotion of greatest, 63; will, 109, 124, 126–128, 130, 133, 140–141, 335, 364nn10, 12, 369n43; without limitation, 125; concept of, 155–156; highest, 194, 336, 338–339; original disposition to, 263; principle of, 318; knowledge of highest, 336
Good will, 62, 65, 109, 124–128, 156; absolutely, 135, 140
Grace, 83, 177, 253, 263, 268
Groundlaying of the Metaphysics of Morals (Kant), 8, 11, 120, 123–124; basic claims of, 122; as seminal work of modern ethics, 122; autonomy in, 337
Guilt, 151, 263, 268, 270, 297
Guyer, Paul, 347n19, 363n2, 363n5, 369n42, 376n10, 391n32, 395n74

Happiness, 361n69, 362n71; of spirit world, 32; obstacles to, 54–55; judgment implied by, 89; indeterminacy and, 94; pleasure and, 94; as determinate sum of pleasure, 116; defining, 116–118; as sufficiency, 117; through labor, 118; luxury and,

Index

120; goodness of, 126–127; limiting, 126–127; virtue and, 156; pure moral laws and, 421n8
Heidegger, Martin, 184, 340, 366, 367n28
Henrich, Dieter, 151, 351n18, 366n16, 368n38, 420n2
Heraclitus, 52
Herman, Barbara, 367n30
Herz, Marcus, 90, 306, 316–318, 332
Hesitation, 155, 282, 319; moral, 8, 186–211, 315
History, 168; end of, 105; idea of, 105–106; human, 164, 323–324; Kant on, 169–176, 210, 277–305, 320; grasping, 172; double use of, 175–176; presentation of, 184; Kantian, 206–207; thinking of human, 206–207; preserving human, 230; predictive, 279–280; representations of, 281–282; as repeating, 311–312; of Christianity, 315–316, 319; a drama, 329; as morally edifying, 342; religious, 386n61
Hobbes, Thomas, 7, 67, 182, 237, 255, 257, 317, 337
Höffe, Otfried, 387n7, 393n54, 393n57, 420n3
Honesty: inner, 13; as reconcilable with humanity, 385n51
Honor, 279, 296; inequality of, 67; drive for, 68; love of, 80; human, 220; Kant on, 277–305
Hope, 30, 48, 180, 266; in another life, 73, 121; in progress, 282–285; necessary condition of, 230
How to Orient Oneself in Thinking (Kant), 153
Humanity, 169, 194, 204; Rousseau on, 44; predispositions of, 389n25
Hume, David, 34–35, 237, 352, 419n48
Hunter, Ian, 347n25, 351n23, 379n8
Husbands, respect for, 67
Hylozoism, 167

Idea for a Universal History (Kant), 180, 298
Ideal(s): of righteousness, 4; of moral autonomy, 5–6; true v. false, 85–86; physical/moral necessity of, 86; mind as arriving at, 87; as arising, 142
Idealism: transcendental, 127; refutation of, 152; Kantian, 335
Ideas: primacy of law-giving over, 111; rational, 124; arriving at, 125–126; practical, 126, 127; moral, 366n21
Imagination, 26–27, 58–59, 421n12; male, 68; ideal of, 120
Imperatives: categorical, 6, 134–135, 144–145, 147, 335; hypothetical v. categorical, 6, 136; moral, 134
Infinity, 273; totality v., 120
Instruction: moral, 107, 140, 158; philosophic, 254–258; academic, 257
Intellect, 87; pleasures of speculative, 47; sensibility as separate source of knowledge from, 86
International relations, 13, 179, 223–229, 231–236, 240–247
Intoxicants, 361n57
Intuition, 6; of self, 91; intellectual, 104
Isolation, 207–208. *See also* Solitude

Jacobi, Friedrich Heinrich, 152–153, 164–166, 168, 173–175, 371n65, 408n28
Jerusalem (Mendelssohn), 309–312
Judaism, 264–265, 313; Kant's attitude toward, 266–267, 275, 306–334, 413n1; law in, 272; in ethical form, 306; ceremonial law and, 307, 316; Mosaic-messianism of, 307; negative public attitude toward, 313–314; as heteronomy symbol, 316; sublimity of, 317–318, 382n34; Christianity and, 318–319, 329; Bendavid on, 324–325; as base for universal moral religion, 330–331; as used by Kant, 334; in purity, 382n34

Judgment, 145, 195–196, 219; happiness, 89; of misery, 89; of beauty, 93; of taste, 93, 170–171; moral, 121, 140; rational, 131; aesthetic, 164; reflective, 184–185, 378n31; of contempt, 303–304; crisis and, 399n14

Justice, 56, 81–82; constructing system of, 7; God's, 20–21; feeling of, 63; cosmopolitan, 227; moral idea of, 298

Kant, Immanuel: on rule of reason, 2; on human morality, 3; paradox of method, 5, 151–159; liberalism of, 5, 342; on desert, 6; on self-esteem, 6; limits of autonomy and, 8–14; on freedom/law relationship, 9; on age of enlightenment, 12; on inner honesty, 13; political situation of, 13; historical context of thought of, 14; early theory of freedom by, 17–38; cosmology of, 19, 39; Leibniz v., 19; theodicy of, 22, 71, 350n17; theory of heavens, 24–33; interplanetary pneumotology of, 25; anthropological revolution of, 33–38; anthropological focus of, 34–36, 40; Rousseau's influence on, 34–36, 39–44, 85, 108–109; on evil, 36; on *Carazan's Dream*, 36–38; on women, 48–50; on education, 51–52; state of nature for, 55–59; good will as understood by, 62–63; religion and, 76; Archimedian moment of, 77–82; revolution in thought of, 85; anthropology lectures by, 86, 88–114; moral work of, 137; on taste, 163–164; on history, 169–176, 210, 320; mental decline of, 176–177; late work of, 176–180; economic imagery used by, 182–183; reputation of, 212; as educator, 249; on university, 249–252; Judaism and, 266–267, 275, 306–334, 413n1; in Berlin, 307; Herz as student of, 307–308; Jewish students of, 307–312, 414n3; liberal legacy of, 335; normative model of, 335; true politics of, 342; as war theorist, 396n76; national minorities interest of, 412n60; on Jewish emancipation, 413n2

Kennedy, Anthony, 1

Kerstein, Samuel, 364n12, 369n43

Knowledge: importance of, 77–78; sensibility as source of, 86; as primary faculty of soul, 89; of future, 102; ethical rational, 125–126, 128, 363n7; of freedom, 248; as rational objectively, 255; of highest good, 336

Knudsen, Martin, 10, 17–18

König, Peter, 360n56, 364n9

Korsgaard, Christine, 363n4, 369n43, 420n3

Kuehn, Manfred, 347n23, 347n25, 380n16, 408n28

Labor, 118, 367n25; contempt for honest, 181. *See also* Work

Law(s), 136; as binding, 3; freedom as *ratio essendi* of, 3; human beings' as co-legislators of, 3; as *ratio cognoscendi* of freedom, 3; recognition of, 3; goodness of, 4; majesty of, 4; freedom's relationship with, 9; of reason, 102–103, 146; by reason, 109; of desire, 110–111; moral, 111–112, 134–135, 138, 146, 154, 156, 190–191, 193, 421n8; duty and, 129–130; practical, 135; of philosophy, 137; moral instruction and, 140; value determined by, 140; obeying, 197–198, 296; public, 235–236; Jewish, 272, 330; ceremonial, 307, 309, 316; Mosaic, 309; as executed, 338–339; limits of, 339; permissive, 341; strict v. broad, 341. *See also* Laws of nature; Moral law

Laws of nature, 136; rule of reason and, 2; laws of freedom in tandem with, 55

Laywine, Allison, 349n6, 351n21

Index

Laziness, 59, 132, 190, 259
Leibniz, Gottfried: 86, 349n8; world understanding of, 18–19; Kant v., 19–21, 24; Kant on optimism of, 350–351n18
Liberalism, 276, 342. *See also* Kant, liberalism of; Political liberalism
Life, 96–98, 107, 115–116, 198, 352n2; feeling of, 85, 88–89; science of 90–95; defining, 373n78. *See also* Organization
Lilla, Mark, 186, 380n10, 384n45, 401n28, 401n30
Limits: of free action, 2; of autonomy, 8–14, 335–343; of reason, 26, 102–104, 113, 385n50; of experience, 113; good without, 125
Locke, John, 6, 9, 237, 323
Love, 48–49, 64–70, 104–107; of freedom, 66–67, 82–83; of honor, 79–80, 287, 296, 343; tender, 94, 99
Lucretius, 24–25, 116
Luxury, 172; as vice, 59; moral feelings and, 73–74; happiness and, 120
Lying, 196, 220, 388n11; under duress, 397n83

Marriage: 99, 106, 343; friendship and, 69–70. *See also* Husbands; Wife
Matter: spirit's relationship with, 25–29, 349n12; conservation of, 35
Maturity: 99, 101, 104, 342; lack of, 101, 253
Maxims: 129, of healthy reason, 103; as rules of action, 129; corruption of ground of, 196; political, 232; publicizing of, 234, 291, 297
Melzer, Arthur, 380n10
Mendelssohn, Moses, 152, 307, 316, 319, 415n11; death of, 308; intellectual freedom defended by, 308; on law, 309; on moral principles, 312; Sisyphusian views of, 321; as Abderite, 322; cleverness of, 326

Metaphysics, 77, 86–87; anthropology's boundary with, 103; of morals, 124–125, 133–134, 143; speculative, 143
Metaphysics of Morals, The (Kant), 236, 339, 243; moral self-improvement in, 202; *Völkerrecht* in, 212; public right in, 237–238
Method: paradox of, 5, 155–159; of Newton, 55; for arriving at truth, 78; teaching, 261
Minorities, national, 412n60
Misery, judgment implied by, 89. *See also* Pain
Modesty: of women, 48–49; sexual, 66–70
Monarchy, constitutional, 166–167
Money: power of, 216, 278; misuse of, 217
Moral feelings: understanding, 61–62; accounts of, 61–63; as defined, 62–63, 65; luxurious conditions and, 73–74; will of God and, 75–76; as dangerous, 158–159; culture of, 174. *See also* Good will
Morality, 152, 156, 380n18; Kant on human, 3; autonomy and, 11 142–143; sexuality and, 48; doctrine of wise simplicity grounding, 60–61; natural, 74; sacrifice and, 86; youth's positive instruction in, 107; principle of, 125; weakness of, 132–133; genuine, 133; supreme principle of, 139, 152; force of command of, 141; ordinary, 165; foundation of, 189; human authority and, 206; prudence united with, 246; of attitudes, 296; tendency toward, 313
Moral law, 111–112, 134–135, 138, 146, 154, 156, 190–191, 193, 421n8; Kant on, 3; as will's incentive, 122; God and, 363n6
Moral necessity, 63
Morals, metaphysics of, 124–125, 133–134, 143

Motion: of matter, 28; law of, 55; applied to outer senses, 355n18. *See also* Spiritual motion
Motivation, 126; of science, 80; freedom and, 89–90
Mulholland, Leslie, 396n75
Munzel, G. Felicitas, 186, 373n79, 379n2

Nation, 5; European, 50–51, 103–104, 179, 266; non-European, 358n33, 359n46, 360n48, 377n19, 405n7. *See also* Race
Nature: wastefulness of, 26–27; as fatality's source, 29; as site of progressive advance, 29; Rousseau on state of, 35; state of, 35, 43, 52, 55–59, 63, 81, 223, 234, 236–237; human, 46–47; appeal to, 52; standard of, 53; order of, 54, 168; collective human, 55; laws of, 55, 136; freedom and state of, 55–59; ills of, 57; regulated state of, 63; of soul, 91, 269; anthropology revealing knowledge of, 95; developmental process of organic, 99; true economy of human, 114–115, 120; economy of, 182–184; as God's book, 191; expanse of time v. state of, 234; self-canceling feature of state of, 239; as corrupt, 268; dependence on, 355n17; harshness of, 361n60; rights acquired in state of, 393n54. *See also* Laws of nature
New Elucidation of the First Principles of Metaphysical Cognition (Kant): as metaphysical cosmology exercise, 17; freedom in, 17–24
Newton, Isaac: constructive methods of, 55; law of motion, 55; laws of, 65–66; moral order and, 65–66

Obligation, 146; natural, 63; Rawls on, 346n16
Observations on the Feeling of the Beautiful and the Sublime (Kant), 10, 34, 36–37, 43, 45–52, 210; Kant's transition with, 45; appeal to nature in, 52; difficulties in, 52

On a Newly Uplifted Noble Tone in Philosophy (Kant), 181
On the True Estimation of Living Forces (Kant), 18
O'Neill, Onora, 420n3
Opposition, real vs. logical, 35–36, 360n56; active to the good, 194
Orend, Brian, 386n1, 396n78
Organization: of nature, 168; political v. animal, 168–169, 174; of beings, 172

Paganism, 264, 417n26
Pain, 9, 87; resisting, 58; as displeasure, 61, 163, 287; soul and, 92; feeling of, 95; pleasure as outweighing, 108; Verri on, 108–110; enjoyment following, 115; in human life, 115; power of, 116–117
Paradox, 141; of practical thought, 3; of method, 5, 151–159; of Rousseau, 42; of autonomy, 122–159, 338, 362n1
Peace, 106; forms of, 97–98; of mind, 118; perpetual, 213, 215–216, 221, 226, 231–232, 277–278; treaty, 223; rational way to, 224; wishing for, 232; state of, 234; freedom and, 255–256
Pedantry, 99–100, 408n30
Perfection: goal of human, 33; human, 33, 40, 82–84; moral, 63–65, 81–82, 87, 93; natural standards of, 64–65; as defined, 82; character of human, 94; moral/physical joint, 104; rest and, 112–113
Personality, 194, 386n59
Phaedo (Mendelssohn), 308
Philanthropy, 132–133, 227–228
Philosophy, 86, 131, 216; as lawgiver of human reason, 114; moral, 124–125, 151, 153; practical, 131; as morally compromised, 132; popular, 132; as philanthropic, 133; precarious standpoint of, 135–143; laws of, 137; doing/omitting of, 147; critical, 180–181, 336–337; as innocent/clever, 215; freedom as mark of, 253; faculties

Index

associated with, 253–254, 259; concept of, 254
Philosophical Theology (Kant), 126
Physical geography, 34, 103
Pistorius, H. A., 153, 155
Plato, 3–4; Kant on, 110, 143, 181, 395n70, 409n34
Pleasure, 9, 56, 87; unnecessary, 59, 68; from exercise in free activity, 61, 63; soul and, 92; aesthetic, 93; happiness and, 94, 116; intellectual, 96; inactivity as intrinsic, 97; moral, 97; physical, 97; in active rest, 98; pain as outweighed by, 108; Verri on, 108–110; giving up, 184; immediate, 385n49. *See also* Pain
Political liberalism, 7
Pope, Alexander, 54, 350n17
Power, 194;; work as application of, 183; of money, 216, 278; shifts in, 228; legislative v. executive, 388n14; of rulers, 390n30
Pride, 79–80, 304, 313; woman's, 94; false, 209; warlike, 287
Progress: precariousness of human, 13; constant, 213, 405n13; truthfulness needed for, 220; human, 236; truth of, 278; problem of, 283; moral, 322
Prophecy, 280–281, 290, 300, 404n6; supernatural communication and, 292. *See also* Soothsaying
Providence, 43, 65, 117, 178; justifying, 53–55; appeal to, 299
Psychology, 184, 378n30; metaphysical, 85–86
Ptolemy, 53–54, 284, 405n11

Race, 85, 95, 103–107, 280, 400n19. *See also* Nation
Rational beings, 137–138, 194–195, 369n41; embodied, 195
Rawls, John, 10, 11, 15, 346nn8; moral theory of, 5–6; autonomy and, 5–8; on personal qualities, 6; on primary moral phenomena, 6; on rational v. reasonable, 6; on self-esteem, 6; skepticism and, 346n14; on obligation/desert, 346n16
Reason: Kantian, 2; laws of nature and rule of, 2; rule of, 2; in ordinary/instrumental use, 3; authority of, 4, 336–338; sovereignty over itself of, 4, 9; victory of, 4–5; principles of sufficient, 17–18; principle of determining, 19; limits of, 26, 102–104, 113, 385n50; self-improvement and, 80; development of, 101; moral necessity of, 101; lover of, 102; laws of human, 102–103; maxim of healthy, 103; as tool, 103; as lawgiver, 109; theoretical use of, 110–111; law-giving of, 111, 114, 359n47; world-forming functions of, 112; philosophy as lawgiver of human, 114; future and, 114–115; pure practical, 121, 123, 253, 371n63, 373n75; standard for, 126; grounds as pursued by, 130–131; abuse of, 131; practical, 131, 134, 151; demands of, 132; transcendental use of, 143; law of, 146; intelligible world ideal of, 150; legislating, 153–154; aim of, 157; as rationalization, 177; moral sublimity of, 209; dogmatic, 337; lack of, 382n33; interest of, 400n24
Religion: faith and, 5; moral necessity of, 6; branches of, 71–72; moral interests as served by, 72; natural, 72, 74; primitive, 72; purpose of, 72–73; artificial, 74; Kant's treatment of, 76, 314; as necessary, 157; role of, 157–158; true, 188; need for, 192–195; weakness and, 198; moral, 200–201, 261–263; evil form of, 201; false, 203; character of true, 205–206; sublime and, 206; organized, 208–209; claims of, 262–263; statutory sanction of, 266; freedom of, 314; false v. true, 385n49; history of, 386n61; foundations of, 418n41. *See also* Christianity; Judaism

Religion within the Boundaries of Bare Reason (Kant), 165–166, 204–205; interest in, 186; moral hesitation in, 186–211; religion in, 192–195, 278; Judaism and, 313–320; publication of, 380n16; task of, 398n7

Remarks in "Observations on the Feeling of the Beautiful and the Sublime" (Kant), 39–40; state of nature in, 43; argument of, 52–82

Representation, failures of, 26

Republic (Plato), 4, 395n70

Republicanism, 221–222

Repulsion, social force of, 55, 66

Respect, 137, 154, 368n38; for husbands, 67

Rest: forms of, 97–98; active, 98; natural inclination for, 104; perfection and, 112–113

Revolution, 307, 327–328; Copernican, 53; moral, 318, 267; enthusiasm provoked by, 286. *See also* French Revolution

Rights: of nations to defend themselves, 212; benevolence v., 227–228; benevolence' subordination to, 228; transcendental principle of public, 232–232, 235, 342; individual, 236–237; public, 236–237, 244, 295–296, 342, 394n66; judicial framework implicit in concept of, 241; to war, 241–242; natural, 295; market, 342–343; acquired in state of nature, 393n54

Riley, Patrick, 351n17, 395n68

Rousseau, Jean-Jacques, 188, 327–328; Kant as influenced by, 34–36, 39–44, 85, 108–109; reading, 34–36; on state of nature, 35; paradoxes of, 42; anthropological insights of, 44; on humanity, 44; on general will, 76; suspicion and, 119–120

Sacrifice, 64, 73, 82, 86, 269–270; respect and, 154, 207; of Isaac, 261, 272, 403n54

Sadness, moral, 208

Sandel, Michael J., 346n8

Satisfaction: passive, 61; as ongoing task, 120

Sauter, Michael, 379n8

Science, 78; evil caused by, 78–79; inclination for, 79–80; motivation of, 80; role of, 81; goal of, 131

Schneewind, J. B., 345n2, 347n26, 420n3

Schönfeld, Martin, 348n1, 349n9

Secret societies, 166, 375n6

Self: autonomy of, 1–2; intuition of, 91; as most perfect singularity, 91; spiritual over natural, 285; authentic, 370n58; transformation, 384n44

Self-esteem, 6, 56, 70, 79, 184; self-loving, 208

Self-improvement, 80, 200; moral, 202

Self-interest, 11, 64, 126, 286, 296; crude, 47; and selfishness, 219; of citizens, 221; and criticism, 337

Senses: distractions of, 28–29; motion applied to outer, 355n18

Sexual desire: impulses derived from, 47–50; moral perfection's relationship with, 48; refinement of, 49; freedom sacrificed for, 65; love of freedom and, 66–68, 82–83; of women, 69. *See also* Love

Simplicity: natural, 59; doctrine of wise, 60–61

Sin, 30, 77, 315; as function of geography, 29; refutation of doctrine of, 381n25

Sincerity, 70–72, 77–78, 188–189, 205–208, 379n10; as least that can be required, 192; original human, 421n11

Skepticism, 256–258; vs. dogmatism, 213; moral, 308; Rawls and, 346n14

Social intercourse, special value of, 119

Solitude, 37

Soothsaying, 280, 284, 290–292, 300, 321, 404n6

Soul(s), 168; healthy, 2; as self-governing, 2; Crusius on, 18; forces of, 18; attention

Index **433**

and, 24; powers of, 24; in restfulness, 27; substance of, 32; noble, 33; body's relationship with, 35; of women, 50; civilized life's corrupting effect on powers of, 59; sensitive, 60; tranquility of, 60; faculties of, 89; nature of, 91, 269; pain and, 92; pleasure and, 92; strength of, 92; as affected, 95; immortality of, 95, 356n22; as governed, 187–188; influences on, 264; freedom of, 349n5

Space: existence of, 19; as phenomenal co-presence, 87

Spinoza, Baruch: 165, 173–175, 311, 317, 320; and Spinozism, 152, 372n71

Spirit: matter relationship with, 25, 349n12; happiness of world of, 32; thinking, 356n22; properties of, 357n27

Spiritual motion: inconceivability of, 93

Stäudlin, Carl Friedrich, 179, 235

Stauffer, Devin, 345n4

Steigleder, Klaus, 364n9, 367n30

Stoicism, 92; autonomy concept and, 2; self-rule and, 2

Strauss, Leo, 366n26, 402n47, 415n12

Sublime, 30, 49–51, 67, 113, 154–158, 164, 411n54; morally, 175, 178, 207–210, 270

Substances: interactions among, 17, 19–20; as windowless monads, 17; mutual dependence of, 18; God as source of, 18–19; source of, 18–19; worldly connection of, 19; of soul, 32; change in, 33; as defined, 35; essential character of, 349n7

Superstition, 159, 200, 206, 274, 324

Sympathy, 287; artificial, 61; duties of, 63–64

Taste: feelings and, 89; judgments of, 93, 170–171; importance of human, 94; society's promotion of, 94; Kant's theme of, 163–164; methodology of, 169

Teaching: methods of, 261. *See also* Instruction

Teleology, 40, 163, 171–175, 300

Teller, Probst, 307, 328–329

Terror, 37, 83; dependence held, 57–58

Theodicy: of Kant, 22, 71, 350n17; authentic, 191

Theology, 252; biblical, 253; faculties associated with, 253–254; dogma/letter favored by, 262

A Theory of Justice (Rawls), 6

Time: existence of, 19; need for, 29; as phenomenal eternity, 87; state of nature v. expanse of, 234

Timmerman, Jens, 362n2, 368n37, 370n56

Totality, infinity v., 120

Toward Perpetual Peace (Kant), 178–179, 288; *Völkerrecht* in, 212–235; argument of, 213; in French, 214; conclusion of, 233–234; religious sects in, 235; world republic idea in, 240–241; federation of republics as proposed in, 278

Treaty of Basel, 1795, 178, 215

Trust, 219, 226, 243–244

Truth: method for arriving at, 78; love of, 79; inner, 220; university giving working effect to, 253–254; of progress, 278

Understanding: as common, 100; without sensibility, 100; of women, 101; moral, 123, 127, 128; discursive human, 181; ordinary human, 401n38

Universal Natural History and Theory of the Heavens: New Elucidation (Kant), 10, 22, 37, 43, 183; freedom in, 24–33; goals in, 26, 43–44

Universe: material center of, 27; center of, 91; spiritual center of, 350n13

Universities: Kant's discussion of, 249–252; titles and, 250; as bulwark against despotism/fanaticism, 251; German, 252; publishing by, 252; working effect to truth given by, 253–254; role of, 409n45

Vanity, 27, 3–31, 42, 49, 69, 80, 401n38; and paradox, 142; as idleness, 181, 401n38

Velkley, Richard, 189, 347n17, 352n3, 354n4, 378n27

Verri, Pietro, 9, 88, 354n8, 359n44; on pain/pleasure, 108–110; and economy of human nature, 114

Vice(s): luxury as, 59; moral illusion as, 59; of culture, 225; of civilization, 234

Virtue: feeling accompanying, 46; true, 46; of women, 69–70; happiness and, 156; cultivating capacity/will to, 193

War, 288, 289; condition of, 223–224; right to, 241–242; time of, 243; preventative, 243–244; punitive, 396n76; weapons of, 399n18

Watkins, Eric, 35, 351n20

What Is Enlightenment? (Kant), 11–12, 187, 251

Wife, natural need for acquiring, 67–68

Will, 41; motives of, 20; indeterminacy of, 22–23; as moved, 23; dependence on, 57; moral standing guiding, 64; moral perfection of, 64–75; of God, 75–76, 190–191; general, 76; intellectual concepts moving, 99; good, 109, 124, 126–128, 130, 133, 140–141, 335, 364nn10, 12, 369n43; sensible desire dominating, 109; character and free, 118–119; free, 118–119; moral law as incentive of, 122; rational, 124; inclinations moving, 129; lawfulness and, 130; self-determination of, 138; freedom of, 144; autonomy of, 149; as esteem worthy, 151–152; as determined, 154–155; highest inner ground of, 200; absolutely good, 244; value of objects of, 336; on body, 354n6; moral, 377n20; absolute, 410n46. *See also* Good will

William II, Frederick, 179, 187, 192, 214

William III, Frederick, 251

Williams, Howard, 392n51

Windisch-Graetz, Joseph Nicholas von, 164–167, 173, 374n3, 375n6, 375n7, 377n21; question of, 341, 391n36

Wöllner, Johann Christoph, 12, 186–188, 205, 379n8

Women: special role of, 1–6; modesty of, 48–49; Kant on, 48–50; beauty of, 49, 66–67; soul of, 50; European v. non-European treatment of, 50–51; as property, 67; sexual capacity of, 67; as divinized by men, 68; needs of, 69; ordinary qualities of, 69; perfect, 69; sexual desire of, 69; virtue of, 69–70; understanding of, 101; gratitude to, 107

Wood, Allen, 186, 347n24, 365n13, 365n15, 367n27, 368n33, 380n16, 384n44

Work, 259, 108–110, 118, 120, 259; useful, 143; as application of power, 183; and acquisition of character, 263. *See also* Labor

Wright, Thomas, 27, 31

Yovel, Yirmiahu, 374n2, 377n16, 377n20, 416n16, 416n20, 419n47

Zammito, John, 164, 170, 351n18, 352n3, 364n8, 372n66, 374n1, 374n2